**PAUL WILSON** was born in Macclesfield and took to unusual journeys early in life when, aged two, he fell out of his third-floor bedroom window. He went to King's School, Macclesfield, before reading History and Ancient History at New College, Oxford.

Paul has lived in North, South and Central America and travelled extensively in Asia, Africa, Europe and Australasia, but he now lives Down Under. He has worked as a consultant to the WTO's Silk Road Project and, when not teaching in Sydney, writes novels that never get published.

On his trips to the Orient he has maintained his support for Macclesfield Town Football Club, making him a true 'Silkman' on the Silk Road. He is currently laying down the route for the first-ever Silk Road Cycle Rally (see box, p157).

**The Silk Roads – a route and planning guide**
First edition: 2003; this second edition: 2007

**Publisher**
Trailblazer Publications
The Old Manse, Tower Rd, Hindhead, Surrey, GU26 6SU, UK
Fax (+44) 01428-607571
info@trailblazer-guides.com
www.trailblazer-guides.com

**British Library Cataloguing in Publication Data**
A catalogue record for this book is available from the British Library

**ISBN 978-1-905864-00-3**
(ISBN-10: 1-905864-00-0)

**© Paul Wilson 2003, 2007**
Text, maps and photographs (unless otherwise credited)

The right of Paul Wilson to be identified as the author of this work has been asserted by him in accordance with the Copyright, Designs and Patents Act 1988

**Editor**: Henry Stedman
**Series editor**: Patricia Major
**Layout**: Henry Stedman
**Proof-reading**: Anna Jacomb-Hood
**Cartography**: Nick Hill
**Index**: Jane Thomas

All rights reserved. Other than brief extracts for the purposes of review no part of this publication may be reproduced in any form without the written consent of the publisher and copyright owner.

Every effort has been made by the author and publisher to ensure that the information contained herein is as accurate and up to date as possible. However, they are unable to accept responsibility for any inconvenience, loss or injury sustained by anyone as a result of the advice and information given in this guide.

Printed on chlorine-free paper from farmed forests by
D2print (☎ +65-6295 5598), Singapore

# THE
# SILK ROADS
## A ROUTE AND PLANNING GUIDE

PAUL WILSON

Developed and expanded from
*Silk Route by Rail* by Dominic Streatfeild-James
Original edition shortlisted for the
Thomas Cook Guidebook of the Year Awards

**TRAILBLAZER PUBLICATIONS**

## Acknowledgements

Thanks to: Arlene both for holding the fort while I was away and making China so fantastic; Bryn and Anna for making the book possible; Henry for a crash course in the English language; Frankie for putting Turkey together; Chris for doing it in style at both ends; Ezra for being the best guide in Istanbul; Lars, Kaili and Mike for their generous hospitality in Göreme; Parashtoo for opening up Iran; David for getting me to Kazakhstan; Oxana for letting me stay – perfick!; Zia for his unlimited generosity and knowledge of Central Asia; Alisher – the King of Tashkent; Tricky for still being my best mate.

## A request

The author and publisher have tried to ensure that this guide is as accurate and up to date as possible. Nevertheless things change. If you notice any changes or omissions that should be included in the next edition of this book, please write to Paul Wilson at Trailblazer (address on p2) or email him at 🖳 paul.wilson@trailblazer-guides.com. A free copy of the next edition will be sent to persons making a significant contribution.

Updated information will shortly be available on the Internet at
**www.trailblazer-guides.com**

**Cover photo**: Dome on the Shir Dor Madrassah in Samarkand's Registan (see p217).
(Photo © Paul Wilson)

# CONTENTS

**INTRODUCTION**

**PART 1: PLANNING YOUR TRIP**

### Routes, costs and making a booking
Route options 8 – Costs 11 – When to go 11 – Making a booking 13
Visas 15

### Before you leave
Who to go with 18 – What to take 19 – Vaccinations and health safeguards 22
Travel insurance 24 – Background reading 24 – Internet resources 30

**PART 2: THE SILK ROAD**

### History
The route 31 – Alexander the Great 37 – Zhang Qian 40 – The Parthian
Shot 41 – The Royal Purple 43 – No more secrets 44 – A New Golden
Age 45 – The Mongols 47 – Pax Mongolica 51 – The end 51

**PART 3: THE MIDDLE EAST**

### Facts about the region
Geographical background 53 – History 54 – The people and their
religion 65

### Practical information for the visitor
The route 69 – Documents 71 – Climate 71 – Accommodation 72
Transport 74 – Travel agencies and tourist information 75
Electricity 76 – Time 76 – Money 76 – Communications 77
National holidays 78 – Customs and attitudes 78 – Food 79 – Drink 80

**Istanbul** 81 – **Cappadocia (Göreme)** 95 – **Antakya** 100
**Aleppo** 105 – **Hama** 108 – **Krak des Chevaliers** 111 – **Palmyra** 114
**Damascus** 117 – **Malatya and Kahta** 124 – **Erzurum** 126
**Doğubeyazit** 128 – **Tabriz** 130 – **Ghazvin** 132 – **Tehran** 134
**Esfahan** 142 – **Shiraz** 149 – **Persepolis** 152 – **Mashad** 155

**PART 4: CENTRAL ASIA**

### Facts about the region
Geographical background 158 – History 159 (Turkmenistan 167,
Uzbekistan 169, Kyrgyzstan 170) – The people 172

## PART 4: CENTRAL ASIA (continued)

### Practical information for the visitor
The route 174 – Documents and formalities 174 – Climate 177 – Safety 178
Accommodation 179 – Travel agencies and tourist information 180
Transport 182 – Electricity 182 – Time 182 – Money 182
Communications 183 – National holidays 184 – Food 184 – Drink 185

**Mary and Merv** 186 – **Ashgabat** 190 – **Konye-Urgench** 194
**Nukus** 197 – **Khiva** 199 – **Bukhara** 205 – **Samarkand** 215
**Tashkent** 222 – **The Ferghana Valley** 230 – **Osh** 232 – **Bishkek** 234
**Issyk Kul** 238 – **Song Kul** 240

## PART 5: PAKISTAN AND THE KARAKORUM HIGHWAY

### Facts about the region
Geographical background 243 – History 243 – The people 252
The economy 253 – Religion 253

### Practical information for the visitor
The route 254 – Documents 256 – Climate 256 – Accommodation 257
Travel agencies and tourist information 257 – Transport 257
Electricity 258 – Time 258 – Money 258 – Communications 259
National holidays 259 – Customs and attitudes 259 – Food 260 – Drink 262

**Sost** 263 – **Passu** 263 (**Hiking around Passu** 264) – **The Hunza and Nagar valleys** 267 (**Karimabad** 268) – **Gilgit** 271 – **Rawalpindi and Islamabad** 274

## PART 6: CHINA

### Facts about the country
Geographical background 278 – History 278 – The people 287
Religion 288

### Practical information for the visitor
The route 289 – Documents 289 – Climate 291 – Accommodation 292
Travel agencies and tourist information 293 – Transport 293
Electricity 297 – Time 297 – Money 297 – Communications 298
National holidays 298 – Customs and attitudes 299 – Food 300 – Drink 301

**Xinjiang** Geographical background 302 – History 302 – **Kashgar** 205
**Kuqa** 309 – **Turfan** 312 – **Southern Taklamakan route** 320 – **Khotan** 321
**Charklik** 323 – **Dunhuang** 324 – **Jiayuguan** 329 – **Lanzhou** 334
**Xi'an** 340 – **Pingyao** 349 – **Datong** 351 – **Beijing** 354

**APPENDIX** Useful words and phrases (Arabic 375, Russian 376, Chinese 376)

**INDEX** 379

# INTRODUCTION

For many people the Silk Road conjures up images of caravans of baggage-laden camels ploughing a dusty path across Asia. As the title of this guide suggests, however, the route was never a single superhighway; rather a series of smaller trade paths* which, once united, formed an intricate network between the Mediterranean and the Orient. For over one thousand years it was the most important and best-known trade route in the world, transporting not just silk but all manner of exotic goods such as jade, gunpowder and rhubarb. Just as importantly, this increase in interaction brought about the spread of many ideas, beliefs and technological advances, from the invention of paper to the great religions of Buddhism, Islam and Christianity. Yet it was unusual for an individual traveller to make the entire journey himself; instead, merchants would trade back and forth across their 'patch' with goods often changing hands a dozen times before reaching their ultimate destination. Therefore anyone emulating Marco Polo and going the full distance will be creating his or her own little piece of history, joining an exclusive club packed with some of history's greatest adventurers.

The Silk Roads tie together some of the most fantastic and romantic attractions in Asia and nearly all the sights which made the routes famous have been preserved. From the mosques of Damascus and the archaeological wonders of Palmyra, the routes wound their way past the standing stones of Nemrut Daği, skirted Persia's extravagant palaces, trod the Golden Road to Samarkand and joined up with the Great Wall of China. The list goes on and on.

Following the collapse of the Mongol Empire, however, and advances in sea travel, the land routes slipped into neglect and obscurity, synonymous as much with danger as with mythical treasures. It was left to the minds of poets and dreamers to drift eastwards past the once glorious cities of Esfahan, Khiva, Xi'an and Xanadu, while real-life explorers ran into the innumerable obstacles presented when crossing so many modern, political boundaries. It was only in the early 1990s, following the collapse of the old USSR, that relatively unrestricted travel to Central Asia became viable. Similarly, Syria, Iran and China are once again welcoming independent visitors, while the opening of the Karakorum Highway revived another significant branch of the Silk Road, this time through Pakistan.

Thus, despite September 11 and the war in Iraq, all the countries included in this guide are accessible as never before. We have suggested a series of routes and itineraries in each region to take in as many of the old Silk Roads as possible, making it a unique opportunity to witness the marvels that Asia has to offer, before coachloads of the less adventurous arrive.

* **Note**: In order not to confuse readers by switching between the Silk Road (singular) and the Silk Roads (plural) when discussing sections of the route or the entire network we have opted for the singular – the Silk Road – throughout, that being the generally accepted form.

# PART 1: PLANNING YOUR TRIP

## Routes, costs and making a booking

### ROUTE OPTIONS

The fundamental choice, of course, is that of **direction**. Europeans will probably want to begin in the West and track Marco Polo eastwards. But for others it may be easier to follow John Keats's poem *The Eve of Agnes*: 'From silken Samarkand to cedar'd Lebanon' – after all, this was the way the silk came.

It doesn't, in fact, make much difference and we have tried to accommodate both options in the guide (though it is set out west to east). The real Marco Polo addict might want to emulate William Dalrymple and begin in Jerusalem, though the visa hassles this throws up make it a tricky option (see p17); others might side with Nick Danziger and judge the only true way to complete such a trip is entirely by land from your front door, in which case you can take the train from any European capital through Eastern Europe to Turkey and join this guide in Istanbul. Then again, you might not be able to complete this trip in one go, so we have chosen Istanbul, Damascus, Tashkent, Islamabad and Beijing as the five most practical (and cheapest) points to start and finish.

More significant in your choice of route should be the **time** you have available. There are numerous shortcuts which we point out and you may choose to miss out some of the excursions but we assume that most of you have chosen

---

### Silk Road by rail

Silk Roadsters might be surprised to learn that in theory you can now travel *almost* the entire way from Istanbul to Beijing by train. Indeed, if you so wanted you could take the weekly *Trans-Asia Express* from Istanbul to Tehran; then from there to Mashad, then to Sarakhs/Saraghs, then Turkmenabat, Tashkent, Almaty, Ürümqi, and finally from Ürümqi to Beijing. We say 'almost' because there are breaks. For one thing, the *Trans-Asia Express* is actually two trains connected by a bus journey around Lake Van. Secondly, you must walk from one train to the next at Sarakhs/Saraghs because Iranian and Turkmen trains run on different gauges. And finally, there are no longer any direct trains between Tashkent and Almaty, thereby forcing you to double back through Kazakhstan via the town of Turkistan.

In reality, few foreign visitors use trains outside of China as they are slow, unreliable and inefficient – the *Trans-Asia Express*, for example, takes 70 hours (on a good run!). They have largely been reduced to transporting cargo rather than passengers and few governments seem intent on reversing the trend. Train buffs eager to see old steam engines in action will also be disappointed as they have been withdrawn from general use everywhere, even rural China, and can be seen only in museums (see Datong, p351). *(cont'd opposite)*

this guide because you specifically want to complete the Silk Road from one end to another which means at least 8000km lie between you and your finishing point. We are also assuming that you wish to complete the trip 'overland' and have therefore largely ignored internal flight options.

As a rule of thumb we suggest you allow at least six weeks in the Middle East, a month in Central Asia, six weeks to loop through China and two weeks in Pakistan. The Polos, of course, took years and Danziger nearly as long but, if you are in a real hurry, three months gives you just about enough time to see everything on a straight line between Istanbul and Beijing – although it doesn't allow for much leeway should anything go wrong.

Because of the **political situation**, Iraq has been avoided despite its clear importance to the Silk Road. Afghanistan (see box p10) and Tajikistan (see box p176) have also been omitted, though they were accessible in one way or another at the time of writing so don't be too put off from visiting them. A similar problem faces anyone wishing to traverse the 18,000ft Karakorum Pass linking Khotan and Kashmir: for centuries this was used by Buddhist pilgrims but it has not been crossed since 1949 because of a dispute between China and India over the exact border position (plus, of course, there's the whole Kashmiri problem).

Even without such man-made obstacles it would still be almost impossible to follow the old routes: paths have evolved – most obviously the Karakorum Highway which runs up the opposite bank of the river to the old Silk Road path – and some cities on the modern Silk Road lie ten or twenty miles away from their original sites, whether for political or environmental reasons. Some, like Bactria/Balkh (once a 'Paradise on Earth') have been erased forever and, along with them, many passes through the mountains have been swallowed up – at the Road's peak such passes would have been kept free of snow by regular traffic but now they present the traveller with an immovable white wall.

---

That said, train travel in China is great fun; the train ride between Tehran and Sari is spectacular (see box p138) and if you are in Pakistan you shouldn't miss the opportunity of trundling up the Khyber Pass (see box p277).

Watch out for a new 'Iron Silk Road', too. Work has begun on a high-speed link between Almaty and Ürümqi and its designers are talking up plans to extend it into a 'Eurasian Land Bridge' to rival the Trans-Siberian Express. Critics, however, say it is just a pipe dream, pointing out that we are still waiting for the promised extension from Kashgar to Bishkek. Certainly, no one has as yet agreed to any new route between Kazakhstan and Europe, but Hu Jintao, China's president, has given the plan his personal backing along with US$750 million and Kazakh authorities are already talking of a 2010 completion date.

The *Thomas Cook Overseas Timetable* (🖳 www.thomascookpublishing.com), published every two months, includes most of the journeys you will use and is worth buying. In addition 🖳 www.seat61.com is a rail fanatics' website and is regularly updated, while Duncan Peattie (🖳 Chinatt@eudoramail.com) sells an English translation of the complete Chinese Railways timetable over the Internet; you can contact him by email through the address above.

The other difficulty with following the original Silk Road, or at least locating it (and you can find yourself drawn into arguments for hours over this if you're not careful) is that wherever you go locals will not stop telling you how important their part of the Silk Road is. For the Chinese all Silk Roads begin in Xi'an but whether they went to Central Asia, Afghanistan, India, Korea, Japan or Burma (which they all did at some time) is of little consequence to them because the road was built only for their prize export – nothing important, so they would have you believe, came back the other way. Speak to a Turk, however, and the destination of all the Silk Roads was Constantinople. Similarly, Pakistanis will tell you how important their section through the Karakorum Mountains, the Hunza Valley and the Khyber Pass was, whereas in fact from Xinjiang most caravans would have preferred to cut across the Pamirs through Tajikistan. Finally, to this day, you can meet people who refuse to admit the Silk Road ran through the Caucasus.

Much of the romance of the Silk Road, however, lies in its myth, so don't be hypercritical, or too pedantic, and enjoy what there is on offer.

### Afghanistan

After so many years of isolation, the treasures of Afghanistan – or what's left of them – are once again open to foreign visitors. After the war against the USSR and the internal battles against the Taliban, however, do not expect an easy trip. In fact, crossing from one side of the country to the other by land is still a hazardous affair and that is why we have not yet included it in this guide.

If you do go, remember that the great cities of the past are but shadows of their former selves. Similarly, the **Buddhist statues** at **Bamiyan** have been famously destroyed and, despite governmental claims to the contrary, it will be years before they are rebuilt/repaired. Yet the lakes at **Band-e Amir** and the **Jam Minaret** are still intact and the natural beauty of the mountains defiantly shines through everywhere.

**Practicalities** Obtaining a visa is straightforward for most nationals. The embassies/consulates in Pakistan and Iran are only too happy to issue a 30-day visa for US$30 (the process usually takes less than 48hrs). Buses run daily from most cities but between Kabul and Herat you need private transport (allow at least a week to see everything). The border crossing at Termiz is still closed to foreign visitors so any plans to circumvent Turkmenistan from Uzbekistan should be put on hold. The road between Herat and Mazar-i-Sharif has also been blown to smithereens over the years so can be completed only in a 4WD (allow three days!). The road between Kabul and Dushanbe is open and foreigners can use this crossing to enter/exit Tajikistan (see box p176).

From Iran your best bet is to apply for your visa in Mashad, take the daily bus to Herat and try to hook up with others there. From Pakistan several tours will take you to the Khyber Pass (see box p277) and drop you there; once through the nearby border checkpoint, there are plenty of buses into Kabul. If the road between Kabul and Herat is looking particularly dicey there are daily flights you can take instead. There are a couple of good agencies based in Kabul: Sitara Travel (see p14 and p270; ✉ kabul@sitara.com) and Great Game Travel (see box, p176; ✉ www.greatgametravel.co.uk). You are best off contacting at least one of them to find out the latest information.

## COSTS

*'Betwixt Aleppo and the Mogul's court, victuals being so cheap, that I often-time lived competentlie for a pennie sterling a day.'* **Thomas Coryate**, 16th-century English traveller.

The cost of your trip can vary wildly and is not helped by the fluctuating value of most of the currencies involved; because of this most major expenditures in this guide are in US dollars – see 'Money', p21.

Hidden costs also mount up and the most significant of these (after visas) are **entrance fees**. We cannot stress enough the importance of carrying, if at all possible, an **International Student Identity Card** (ISIC). To get one you are required to prove that you are in full-time education but this process is not always strictly adhered to and something that suggests you're a student, like a National Union of Students card, which is more easily obtained, might suffice. If you are not eligible for either of these, try to lay your hands on something because in certain Silk Road countries you will receive as much as 90 per cent off the tourist price. Indeed, we estimate a card could save you a few hundred dollars during the trip as it is also valid for some bus journeys and even hotels. If you cannot get any sort of proof, you may still want to ask for the student rate at every opportunity because you are not always asked for proof.

Most of the countries you will visit are still cheap – we met one backpacker in China who had never paid more than a dollar for a meal – but you must appreciate that the distances you are going to cover are enormous and this trip cannot be compared, financially at least, to beach-bumming around Thailand.

We have rejected the 'What can we eat/see/sleep on for less than a dollar?' approach and if something is worth doing, even if it is relatively expensive, we have recommended it. Having said that, we have avoided the other extreme as exemplified by one of Leo Tolstoy's descendants who hired her own personal camel, horse, guide and 4WD to complete an expedition from Merv to Xi'an (Ms Tolstoy's account of the journey, *The Last Secrets of the Silk Road*, is one to miss).

If money isn't a problem, you can pay other people to organize this trip for you; you can also stay in five-star hotels at over half the stops along the way. For those hoping for no more than to travel independently, stay in clean accommodation and have the occasional treat, however, **we would budget for US$25-US$35 a day** depending on whether you have a student card or not and how much you eat, drink and smoke. The longer you go for, of course, the cheaper it gets per day as the travel and entrance costs are more spread out; bottom-line **budget travellers can manage on around US$15 a day** but they should be prepared to lose weight.

## WHEN TO GO

Bear in mind that most of the routes that make up the Silk Road skirt around or plough straight through deserts, so that in mid-summer (June, July and August) the heat is fearsome. In Turkmenistan's Karakum Desert summer temperatures go up to 45°C, while in Turfan it is possible to cook an egg merely by placing

> **Islamic holidays**
> Islam follows its own **calendar**, dating from AD622 and Mohammed's fleeing to Medina from Mecca. As this is a lunar calendar, however, each Islamic year is 10 days (11 days in a lunar year) shorter than the Christian calendar, making it more difficult to convert dates (eg AD2007 = 1428, not 1385 as it would be if the Christian and Muslim years were the same length). Similarly, all the religious festivals change by 10 or 11 days each year.
>
> **Ramadan** is a month-long festival and could potentially disrupt your trip the most. Muslims are not supposed to eat, smoke or even drink water during daylight hours and non-Muslims are expected to conform, at least in public. In stricter countries (such as Iran) you have little choice because all the restaurants and cafés are closed. At the moment Ramadan falls during autumn: the next two Ramadans will start on 11 September 2007 and 31 August 2008. Though it's worth visiting a Muslim country during Ramadan at least once in your life, as it is a unique experience, we recommend you try to avoid it on this trip because you will have enough problems as it is. The end of Ramadan is marked by the **Eid al Fitr** festival that lasts for three days – and, as you can imagine, is usually a very happy time.
>
> In 2007 the **Prophet's Birthday** is on 31 March; the **Eid al Adha** festival, celebrating Abraham's near-sacrifice of his son Ishmael and marking the beginning of the pilgrimage season to Mecca, is on 20 December 2007; **Islamic New Year** is on 9 January 2008. **Ashura** (see box p68) takes place on 20 January 2008; Shi'ites also hold various processions to begin the forty days of mourning for Hussein's death at Karbala.

it in the sand (the highest recorded temperature here is 49.3°C/121°F). The good thing about the heat, though, is that it is a dry heat; while this means that you'll die faster if you aren't careful, at least you won't be feeling sticky and clammy as you go.

At the other extreme, winters in the mountains surrounding China can be deadly cold and two of the main routes – the Torugart Pass and the Karakorum Highway – can be closed by snow from October to March or April (they are officially closed between November and February) while Sir Aurel Stein was hit by a snowstorm in the Pamirs in July!

If you can, you want to avoid the heat as much as possible but this is easier said than done if you are travelling for four months or more. Our advice, especially if you are going west to east, is to begin in April and finish in July. This way the weather is already bright and sunny when you are in the Middle East (although you might see snow in the Turkish mountains), Central Asia and China won't be too hot and by the middle of summer you are in the relative cool of the Pakistani mountains. This plan beats the autumn alternative, as from September the weather deteriorates and while that's good for your body it can be disappointing for photos.

The final factor you really ought to consider is that in August the Chinese are on holiday. Few families can afford or are allowed to holiday abroad so China's 1.6 billion population tends to visit its home-grown attractions, turning most forms of travel, accommodation and sightseeing into an overcrowded nightmare.

## MAKING A BOOKING

### On your own
We have included contact details for the hotels listed in this guide, though most people we met preferred to book their hotels on arrival as they went along.

If you want help along the way but don't want to travel as part of a full-on tour you might want to contact a local operator at various stages in your trip and get them to put together an individual mini-tour. With the Internet this has become much easier than you might think and you can really haggle over the price when you go direct. Unfortunately, many of the operators in the countries covered are stuck in a time warp and won't understand the type of tour you may want but in most places we have managed to track down at least one reliable outfit and these are listed in the relevant 'Practical information' sections. You can also try the Silk Road Tour Operators Group, see p30.

### With a tour from the UK
Few companies cover the entire Silk Road and even fewer provide more than a quick glimpse but there are some who know what they are doing. The following guarantee you a virtually hassle-free holiday but this comes at a price.

● **Silk Steps Ltd** (☎ 0117-940 2800; 🖳 www.silksteps.co.uk) can put together a package for most countries on the Silk Road.
● **Silk Road and Beyond** (☎ 020-7371 3131; 🖳 www.silkroadandbeyond.co.uk) offer trips throughout the Middle East and Central Asia and cater for large and small groups.
● **The Oriental Caravan** (☎ 020-7582 0716; 🖳 www.theorientalcaravan.com) cover Kyrgyzstan and China only but they are one of the few companies to offer a guided trip around the whole of the Southern Taklamakan.
● **Steppes Travel** (☎ 01285-880980, 🖳 www.steppestravel.co.uk) focuses on tailor-made travel for individuals and covers most of the countries in this guide.

---

**Flight tickets**
The biggest task before you set off is to buy your airline ticket. Unfortunately, one-way tickets rarely carry the same reductions as returns and 'bucket' shops and discount centres tend not to cover our area. Direct flights into Silk Road countries tend to be expensive from Europe but if you are happy to make a stopover the price should fall dramatically; from Australasia the cheapest flights go via Bangkok but check flights with other stopovers, too; you're unlikely to find a direct flight from North America to the region but you shouldn't have to make more than one stopover.

Reliable travel agencies focusing on independent travellers and with offices in many cities/countries in Europe, North America and Australasia include: **Trailfinders** (🖳 www.trailfinders.com), **STA Travel** (🖳 www.statravel.com), **Council Travel** (🖳 www.ciee.org), **Flight Centre** (🖳 www.flightcentre.com) and **Travel CUTS** (Canada; 🖳 www.travelcuts.com).

The following websites are the most reputable for cheap flights: 🖳 www.cheaptickets.com; 🖳 www.priceline.com; 🖳 www.travelocity.com; 🖳 www.expedia.com; 🖳 www.lowestfare.com; and 🖳 www.skyauction.com.

## 14  Making a booking

- **Peregrine Tours** (☎ 0844-736 0170, 🖳 www.peregrinetours.co.uk) offer trips to both China and the Middle East. Is an Australian company (see below).
- **Intrepid Travel** (☎ 020-7354 6170, 🖳 www.intrepidtravel.com) run trips to all parts of the region.
- **Sundowners** (☎ 020-8877 7666, 🖳 www.sundownerstravel.com) is another Australian company which operates a number of trips throughout the region both in small groups and for independent travellers.
- **Explore Worldwide Ltd** (☎ 01252-319448; 🖳 www.exploreworldwide.com) have a good reputation amongst independent-minded travellers.
- **Exodus Expeditions** (☎ 020-8675 5550; 🖳 www.exodus.co.uk) are the best bet if you are looking to keep costs down. They do a trip from London to Beijing that you can join at various stages. You travel in huge live-in trucks, which you share with 20 or so fellow travellers.

### From Europe
Agencies worth trying include: **Voyagistes Orients sur les Routes de la Soie** (☎ 01 40 51 10 40; 🖳 www.orients.com), France; **Association Française des Amis de l'Orient** (☎ 01 47 23 64 85), France, and **Banoa** (☎ 93 318 9600; 🖳 www.banoa.com), Spain.

### From the USA
**Geographic Expeditions** (☎ 1-800-777-8183; 🖳 www.geoex.com) have an excellent selection of pre-planned tours. Other companies worth trying include **Adventure Center** (toll-free ☎ 800-227-8747; 🖳 www.adventurecenter.com); **GAP** (toll-free ☎ 1-800-676-4941; 🖳 www.gapadventures.com), and **World Expeditions** (toll-free ☎ 1-888-464-8735; 🖳 www.weadventures.com).

### From Canada
Both **Sitara** (☎ 604-264-8747, tollfree ☎ 1-800-888-7216, 🖳 www.sitara.com) and **Silk Road Tours** (☎ 1-888-881-7455, 🖳 www.silkroadtours.com) offer tours in the region. Sitara also has a branch in Rawalpindi (see p276).

Other companies worth trying include: **The Adventure Center** (☎ 416-922-7584; 🖳 www.theadventurecenter.com) and **GAP** (toll-free ☎ 1-800-708-7761; 🖳 www.gapadventures.com).

### From Australia
**Helen Wong's Tours** (🖳 www.helenwongstours.com), **Sundowners** (see above; ☎ 03-9672 5300, 🖳 www.sundownerstravel.com) and **Travel Indochina** (☎ 1-300-138755, 🖳 www.travelindochina.com.au) organize tours in the region. Other companies that cover at least part of the Silk Road route include: **Adventure World** (🖳 www.adventureworld.com.au); **Exodus Expeditions** (☎ 02-9251 5430), agents for Exodus (UK); and **Peregrine Travel Centre** (☎ 03-9663 8611; 🖳 www.peregrine.net.au); Peregrine has a branch in the UK.

### From New Zealand
Companies worth trying are: **Silk Road Adventures Ltd** (☎ 03-762 6673, toll-free ☎ 0800-349739; 🖳 www.silkroad.co.nz) and **World Expeditions** (toll-free ☎ 0800-350354; 🖳 www.worldexpeditions.co.nz).

## VISAS

The main reason we recommend going from west to east is that the many countries at the western end (Syria, Iran, Turkmenistan in particular) may grant you a visa **only** for specific dates and by the time you get there from the east some of your visas may no longer be valid.

Obtaining visas is going to be the most time consuming, costly and annoying part of your preparations so plan ahead and allow yourself at least two months before departure to arrange them. All the countries involved require you to have at least six months left on your passport at the time of application. You will also need to fill in many forms and provide lots of **passport-size photographs**; it's a good idea to take at least a dozen such photos with you on this trip, although you can have more done quite easily/cheaply in most big cities. In some cases you will need a **letter of invitation**/recommendation (LoI), which can be bought from a travel agent in the destination country or (if you are already on the road) from your own embassy in a neighbouring capital – they can cost as much as US$50 (on top of the US$30-50 for the visa). If you do need an LoI, we have recommended local agencies in each of the capital cities. You can also pay agencies in your own country to apply for you but they are usually more expensive.

Some visas dictate the exact dates when they may be used, others allow you three months before you have to start using them; either way, if you are going for more than three months you will have to apply for visas on the road. The countries below are listed in the order of perceived difficulty when applying for a visa, starting with Iran, the most difficult. Some nationalities (such as the Japanese and citizens of the Silk Road countries) will have fewer problems than others when it comes to securing visas. One tip: if questioned about your profession, avoid references to writing or journalism as these will lead at best to delays, at worst rejection.

We have not included costs as they vary from country to country, embassy to embassy and from applicant's nationality to applicant's nationality. But you can guarantee they will be around US$40-50 each (and on the road you will usually be required to pay in US dollars, not the local currency). We have included as many contact details as possible for those embassies you will need en route. When applying at home you will find most embassies in your capital city. Furthermore, most embassies usually accept applications by post (although this slows the process down).

**Note: If you carry an Israeli passport or have any evidence of a previous visit to Israel in your passport you will not be allowed a visa or entry into Syria, Iran, or the Lebanon.**

### Iran

You do not officially need a letter of introduction but you may well need to give **exact details of when and where you are going and where you are staying**. Whatever the case, your application will usually take at least **two weeks** to process and don't be surprised if you are rejected at the end of that time: **most**

**American passport-holders are rejected**. Decide exactly when you want to be in Iran and work the rest of the holiday around that. Help is at hand from Tehran agencies but they prefer (as the government does) that you fly in and out of the country rather than enter/exit overland. Iran has an embassy in most capitals but if it doesn't have one in yours try the Syrian or Jordanian embassy as these often act as representatives for Iran.

If you don't get one before you leave, you should be able to get a visa from the Iranian Embassy in **Istanbul** (allow two weeks) or, more unpredictably, from the Iranian Consulate in **Erzurum** (even if they won't give you a full visa they might still give you a **transit visa**). If you are really stuck, there is a travel agent in Doğubeyazit who might be able to help once you get there (see p128). Getting an Iranian visa (even a transit visa) in Turkmenistan is currently very difficult, so east–west travellers should apply in Tashkent, for which they should allow two weeks.

**Transit visas** last **five to seven days** but you should be able to extend them in Tabriz and Mashad (don't wait until you get to Tehran, as the office there is a nightmare). When you have completed the form you need to go to a nearby Bank Melli to pay the fee. Agencies inside Iran can easily get your transit visa extended for you, for a fee.

**Women** should not forget to wear a headscarf when visiting an Iranian embassy and in any photos submitted with their applications.

## Turkmenistan

Like much of the former Soviet Union everything is possible in Turkmenistan – but at a price. The root of the problem is that, in reality, the government doesn't actually want you there so has made obtaining a visa as expensive and as difficult as possible. In world terms Turkmenistan ranks alongside North Korea as a red-tape nightmare for independent travellers. To obtain a **full tourist visa** you must arrange, through a travel agency in Ashgabat, to be accompanied at all times by a state-approved tour guide. **This service costs US$90 a day** – on top of the visa fee of US$45. Allow at least **two weeks** for the agency to organize this and be prepared to state exactly when you want the visa to be valid for and where you will travel.

The only alternative is to apply for a **transit visa** (the government would prefer not to issue these but does so under pressure from its neighbours). These usually last for five days but can be as short as three or as long as nine (if you are cycling, see box p157, apply in your own country and you have a chance of being given nine days). However many days your transit visa is valid for, allow a full day for both entering and leaving the country; borders often close in the evening, in which case your visa will have expired by the time they reopen the next morning and you will be hauled off back to Ashgabat to pay a massive fine! (This really does happen, although a large bribe can sometimes prevent it.) You will still need a **letter of invitation** from an agency in Ashgabat or from your own embassy if you are applying on the road and it still takes at least **ten days** to process and costs US$40.

Turkmenistan has an embassy in most countries but if not try a fellow Central Asian embassy. You used to be able to apply at one embassy and pick up the visa at another further along your route but recently they have clamped down on this practice and it's now unlikely to be an option. The only good news is that if the present regime changes so, most probably, will its visa requirements.

### Syria
Syrian embassies usually take a week to process your application. A **30-day visa is no longer available** – instead you will receive **15 days**. Visas can be **extended** (usually for 30 days but sometimes more and for just US$1!) at one of the many immigration centres inside the country (Hama, see p108, is the best place while the offices in Aleppo and Damascus can be slow and tedious), but wait until your visa has almost expired before applying for an extension. To secure a visa, you need **a letter of support from your embassy** *only* if you are applying on the road. What's more, citizens of some countries have even been known to get a visa at the border, though Syria does enjoy refusing entry to any foreign visitors they suspect of having visited **Israel**. As such, deny having ever been to 'Occupied Palestine' – as they refer to Israel – on the application form.

### China
China can be a bit of a pain because many of its embassies open for a few mornings a week only. Nevertheless, unless you are travelling east to west you will probably want to pick this visa up en route. **Tashkent** is the best place to try because the embassy there can issue a visa on the same day (for an extra fee). The advantage of applying for your visa on the road is that it is unlikely to expire before you get there, as there is a three-month window from the date of issue.

You shouldn't need a **letter of invitation** but if you do it might take some time to organize. Ask your local Chinese embassy to recommend an agency, such as the CITS or the CTS, who provide this service. In Britain you can try:
- **China Travel Service** (☎ 020-7836 9911, 🖳 www.ctshorizons.com), 7 Upper Saint Martin's Lane, London WC2H 9DL.
- **China Travel Service and Information Centre** (☎ 020-7388 8838, 🖳 www.chinatravel.co.uk), 124 Euston Rd, London NW1 2AL.

If you are applying on the road you will need to contact an agency in China (see p369) and ask them to email/fax one to you. Standard Chinese visas are valid for **thirty days** and cost US$30-50 although **sixty-day** visas are increasingly available on request and often cost no extra (see p289 for **visa extensions**).

### Uzbekistan
Uzbekistan is no longer as user-friendly as it once was. Its embassy may require **letters of invitation or support** and is unlikely to issue a visa on the same day (if it does, it will charge more). Furthermore, it's best to apply for this visa at the relevant embassy in a neighbouring country's capital, as you often have to state the exact dates you want your visa to cover. Prices vary depending on which country you come from and how long you want to stay, with **one-month** visas standard.

### Kyrgyzstan, Kazakhstan

Neither of these countries requires a letter of support and both can issue a visa on the same day (although at a cost). Their standard visa is valid for **thirty days**. You can easily apply for these visas at the relevant embassy in a neighbouring country's capital. Prices vary depending on which country you come from. Kazakhstan has the added attraction of having a consulate in Ürümqi.

### Pakistan

Pakistan's visa policy has been in a state of flux since 9/11, so check with your local embassy before applying. Before this date you could get a visa on the same day as your application at any embassy and if you were crossing from China to Pakistan you could rely on being issued with at least a transit visa at the border which gave you seven days to get to Islamabad and apply for a full visa. Some Pakistan embassies do still issue a visa on the same day or the next day (US$45) and do not require a letter of invitation but some take two or three weeks. **Transit visas**, alas, seem to have died out.

Note that when applying for a Pakistan visa the usual duration of stay is **thirty days** but sometimes you get only what you ask for (whether this is four days, sixteen days or a month); the price doesn't change so it's worthwhile applying for the maximum possible.

### Turkey

Most European nationals (including French and Germans) don't need a visa for Turkey. Those that do (including British passport holders) can, like most other nationalities, simply buy a visa sticker (US$15) at the border or on arrival at a Turkish airport. These are usually valid for **three months** and allow **multiple entries**, so you can go into Syria and come back out again before heading for Iran. Check your local Turkish embassy to see which category you fall into.

# Before you leave

## WHO TO GO WITH

Before you decide what to take, you should decide *who* to take. Even if you have done some lengthy trips before, we wouldn't recommend this expedition for your first attempt at 'flying solo'. The route is still quite unexposed to the backpacking masses and, especially in those Islamic countries which do not allow alcohol, there is often little to do in the evenings, giving fewer opportunities than normal to meet fellow travellers. We would particularly advise women not to travel alone, at least not all the time, as, although some of the problems are blown out of all proportion, even the most hardened female travellers we met admitted that countries such as Iran and Pakistan do take their toll. What's more, accommodation works out much cheaper if you go with someone else as dorms are not always an option.

## WHAT TO TAKE

If you are travelling on an upmarket tour it doesn't really matter how much luggage you take because there will almost certainly be someone at the other end to help you carry it. If you are not, think carefully about what you will really need. Budget travellers' fashion standards aren't that high, so don't bother with all those spares or the fancy toiletries. Don't use the excuse that your bag isn't full yet to start poking in all those bits and pieces that 'might come in handy' because you will probably want some space for souvenirs.

For any documentation you have (eg tickets, passports, visas, letters of support, health certificates) make two photocopies, leave one set with a contact at home and keep the other separate from the originals, just in case you lose any on the road.

### Clothes

Be prepared for some frighteningly high temperatures but note that wearing shorts and short sleeves in many countries can be considered offensive, especially when visiting religious sites.

Lightweight trousers (preferably with zip-off legs so they convert into shorts) are the most versatile and two or three pairs of these, plus a pair of shorts which can double as swimming shorts, will be about right for your lower half. Some women might prefer long skirts (and throw in a swimsuit) but most find trousers more practical. For the top half, two or three T-shirts or short-sleeve shirts are ideal, along with a long-sleeve shirt (for the religious sites) and a good jumper or fleece. Try to take loose, light-coloured (ie sun-reflecting) clothes. Take as few items of underwear as you feel comfortable with, remembering that there are cheap laundry services in most towns. If you are taking hiking boots don't forget hiking socks. (For further details on trekking, see box p265.)

> **Dress codes for women**
> In addition to the above considerations regarding dress, women, of course, have the extra burden of Islam. The Koran demands women 'dress modestly' (see box p57). As such, everything needs to be loose fitting and opaque so as not to reveal any body shape. But it does not have to be black or even dark. In Iran the practice goes as far as wearing a headscarf (*hejab*) at all times in public – which is everywhere outside your hotel room. But you do not need to go for the full *chador* and you will probably be surprised by how fashionable some Iranian women manage to be. In other Islamic countries matters are not so strict (Pakistan is probably the next most rigid) although you may find it more comfortable to stick to a similar wardrobe throughout.
>
> A common solution is a pair of trousers, a T-shirt and a long-sleeved top or coat coming down to around the knees. Try not to expose your ankles, though showing your feet is fine. If you want to blend in a little more, buy a local *shalwar kameez*, which solves all your problems in one go and is said to be very comfortable. You will probably find it easier and certainly cheaper to buy one on the road: both Istanbul and Damascus have plenty in their shops and bazaars, as do Kashgar and Rawalpindi for those coming the other way.

A solid pair of trainers or lightweight boots is essential and you'll want to take a pair of sandals in which you can walk all day if necessary. You will need a sunhat or cap at some stage but the Silk Road is home to some of the most fantastic hats in the world so you might like to buy one out there. Don't forget your shades – and make sure they are as effective as they are fashionable.

If you are not travelling in the early or late parts of the year, a jacket is an optional extra. If you are going in winter, however, a thick jacket is recommended, though you can pick up a very cheap one in all of the countries you might need it.

## Luggage

For travellers carrying their own luggage, the basic choice is between a large or small **rucksack**. It is also important to bring a small **shoulder bag** or **daypack**, too, for day trips, as you will need something for carrying your camera, films, maps, guidebooks and so on (if you have gone for a big rucksack, try to allow space for this smaller bag to fit into it, for it's so much easier to move around in a station or on a bus with just one bag).

A **money belt** or similar safe document carrier such as a shoulder holster is essential. Remember that these should be worn underneath your clothing; if you have a pouch, carry it on your front rather than as a 'bum-bag'. Check that the pockets are big enough to take your passport, airline ticket and travellers' cheques without having to fold them up into postage-stamp-sized wads.

As camping (see box p73) isn't really an option, a sleeping bag is pretty pointless unless you are travelling in winter, although a **sheet sleeping bag** and a pillowcase are advisable if you are planning on budgeting hard because some beds can look a bit grim and bed bugs are not uncommon.

## Medical supplies

Come prepared, as you may have trouble getting hold of the simplest pharmaceuticals on this trip. As a guideline, essential items would be: aspirin/paracetamol; suntan lotion; lip cream (try to get the small pots of Blistex as they are better than the sticks); insect repellent; something for an upset stomach (eg Imodium); a tube of antiseptic cream, a few plasters and an anti-AIDS kit containing sterile syringes and swabs for emergency medical treatment (you can now buy a good compact first-aid kit with these in from any camping shop). Other items you might want to bring include multivitamins, moisturizing cream and water purification tablets. Don't forget to stock up on your favourite brand of tampon and contraceptive and bring adequate supplies of prescribed medications.

## General items

In no particular order: an alarm clock; earplugs and eye-mask (you should get these free on your flight); a Swiss army knife (essential for opening bottled drinks); pens and writing paper; a diary; a copy of your address book (don't bring the original as you may lose it); that epic novel you have always wanted to read; a strong torch or flashlight (really important for looking inside the many caves and castles you will come across); a universal bathplug; a couple of metres of string (useful as a washing line if nothing else); a padlock and length of chain (for securing your rucksack while you sleep; a bike lock would be OK, or you can buy mini combination locks with extendible steel cord in travel shops); a water bottle is a good idea for purifying your own water and drinking tea on trains in China; and a compass.

If you bring a personal stereo bear in mind that everyone will want a go, so have a suitably gargantuan supply of **batteries**; although they are available along the route, they are usually of poor quality.

Toilets are a very hit-and-miss phenomenon on this trip and range from absolutely disgusting holes in the floor, through squat/sit-down toilets as dirty as you would expect from a public convenience, to fully functional hotel toilets with an automatic bleach dispenser. Wherever you decide to go, however, you can guarantee they won't have any **toilet paper**! This isn't a major disaster as it is sold in every corner shop but make sure you always have some to hand and some spare in your daypack.

## Money

Times have changed considerably in recent years and the money situation is now much improved all along the route (see 'Costs', p11). **Credit/debit cards** are the easiest and safest form of money to carry and you can now use them to receive cash advances in more places than you can cash travellers' cheques. If you pick the right bank/card company you should also find that your money is exchanged at a competitive commission rate and many companies also give you insurance on any major purchases you might make with the card (some might even give you travel insurance if you buy your flight ticket with them).

**Visa** and **MasterCard** are by far the most accepted (for a comprehensive list of every participatory ATM on the route go to 🖳 www.visa.com/pd/atm and 🖳 www.mastercard.com/atmlocator/index.jsp). **NB Iran does not accept any Western-issued cards**. If you are worried about the interest charges on credit cards, remember that you can put money into your account(s) before you go which means that you don't have to pay a penny for using them as long, of course, as you don't spend any more than you've put in and go beyond your limit! It would be wise to have at least US$200 in **travellers' cheques**, just in case there is a problem with your cards. Make sure these are in US dollars.

Whatever you decide, however, you can't avoid carrying quite a lot of hard **cash**. Again this must be in US dollars. If you want a decent exchange rate, the actual notes must be in good condition and dated 1996 or later (pre-1996 notes are considered less valuable). You should have a good balance of fifties and twenties, with a few lower denominations for border charges and visas (which do not usually cost a round figure). Try and keep a reserve of about US$200 for emergencies – you will probably need it at some stage.

If you are relying on credit cards, you must have enough dollars to last you throughout your stay in **Syria** and **Iran** because cash advances on cards are impossible in those countries, although travellers' cheques are now accepted in Syria. Stock up on US dollars in Turkey (you might have to withdraw Turkish lira from a bank and then change it into dollars) or Uzbekistan and Turkmenistan, depending on which way you are heading.

> ❑ **Smiling on the Silk Road**
> Many travellers propagate the adage 'take only photographs, leave only footprints' but on closer inspection such a philosophy seems to revolve a little too much around us the traveller and not the people and places we meet. We, therefore, prefer the motto of Tim Padmore, a cyclist we met on the way: 'Everywhere you go, try to leave a smile.'

Finally, it's only common sense to keep most of your money in a **money belt** (or something similar) worn under your clothing, while keeping a small amount of spending money to hand. Emergency money should be kept separately from both of these (along with the numbers of any travellers' cheques, of course).

The **black market** in most of these countries is hardly worth the risk because it rarely offers a significantly higher exchange rate. See p77 (The Middle East), p182 (Central Asia), p258 (Pakistan) and p297 (China) for the relevant exchange rates for each country.

### Photography

Most people will want to travel with a camera. Digital cameras are great, especially for making friends with locals and showing them your pictures. **Film**, if you need it, is widely available but is often a cheap brand so you would be well advised to bring your own, especially if you take slides or use unusual film (ie high ASA). If you do buy it locally check that it's in date. Wait until you get home before having your film processed, although services in large Chinese cities are generally pretty safe.

Taking snaps of military installations or other 'sensitive' areas is not recommended; if you are unsure, don't. It's perfectly OK to shoot film from the train, but the windows are usually so grotty that you will have trouble, so look for a broken window or a door with a window that opens. Finally, when taking pictures of locals do ask your subject before you start clicking away.

## VACCINATIONS AND HEALTH SAFEGUARDS

No vaccinations are listed as official requirements for foreign visitors on this trip but you should give serious thought to some of the following. If you are unsure check with your doctor. Remember it's a good idea to know your blood group.

● **Diphtheria** There have been several outbreaks of diphtheria in the region over the past few years. Check with your doctor that you were given the initial vaccine as a child and a booster within the last ten years. The WHO recommends a combined booster dose of tetanus-diphtheria toxoid. If you've never had the diphtheria vaccine in any form you'll need two jabs one month apart, followed by a booster after six months.

● **Tetanus** Tetanus vaccine needs renewal every ten years. If you cut yourself and you haven't had one, you may have serious trouble trying to get the right treatment abroad, so check.

## Vaccinations and health safeguards

- **Hepatitis A** The serious ailment that's most commonly contracted by travellers, Hepatitis A is spread via food, water and infected eating utensils. Though it probably won't kill you, it can lay you out for anything up to a couple of months. Gamma globulin, given just before departure, affords protection for up to six months. Havrix Monodose lasts twice that time, and a second shot, given a year after the first, extends protection for up to ten years.
- **Polio** This vaccine lasts ten years; check whether you are up to date.
- **Typhoid** A new vaccine, Typhim VI, gives protection for three years.
- **Rabies** Probably not worth it unless you are the sort who actively hunts down and plays with stray animals. The vaccine consists of two (or in some cases three) shots a month apart and means that if you get bitten you won't have to go through the ordeal that others will be enduring. Medical treatment will be necessary but this vaccine buys you time.
- **Malaria** For nearly all this route anti-malarial treatment is not required but it *is* if you plan on going to Pakistan. Having said that, the medication they give you will not stop you contracting malaria and you will still need to go to hospital so an increasing number of travellers don't bother and use the more traditional prophylactic: clearing out of an area ASAP if malaria is reported.
- **SARS** and **Bird flu** could become major problems at any time (especially in China) but at the time of writing both seemed to be under control.

### Potential health problems
The potentially serious ailments with which you are most likely to come into contact are sunburn, dehydration, altitude sickness and diarrhoea. Prevention is the key to **sunburn** and **dehydration**. The desert sun is incredibly hot; always wear sunglasses and a hat and get into the shade long before you think you may be burning. If you are badly burned and feel nauseous or dizzy, consult a doctor immediately as you may have sunstroke. Drink plenty of fluids day and night.

Unless you are doing some serious trekking, **altitude sickness** shouldn't hit you too hard because you won't be at high altitude for long. But if it does, rest, drink fluids, eat something sugary for energy and try to drop down to a lower height as quickly as possible.

For **diarrhoea**, the best thing to do is simply to wait, as it is far better to let your body sort itself out than to mess around trying to 'cure' it. Most people will get an upset stomach at some point, if only as a reaction to the spicy food. Don't panic, drink plenty of purified water, rest and eat simple food such as boiled rice. If you have no choice but to keep on travelling, Imodium is usually effective at keeping you 'blocked up' over long journeys. Don't take too many tablets, however, or you will regret it later.

The best way to find **a reliable doctor** fast is through any of the large hotels used by foreigners. Simple treatment should be free.

### Drinking water
Water in many of the countries is not always safe, so you should stick to drinks made with boiled water (eg tea or coffee) or bottled drinks. Having said that, you don't have to go mad; most travellers use local water to wash their teeth, most

salads that look good and fresh are fine – just give the dubious-looking ones a miss. Do make sure, though, that those vegetables which can be peeled, like any fruit of the same category, *are* peeled. Ice cubes can be dodgy but judge them by the establishment in which they are served. Water may be purified by boiling or adding purification tablets. If you don't like the strong chemical taste, bring along fruit juice powders to disguise it. Note that chlorine-based purification tablets are ineffective against the bugs that cause amoebic dysentery and giardia.

In China, water which comes from one of the thermos flasks in a hotel will have been boiled. Don't worry if you are using someone else's mug at a tea-shop – just rinse it out with boiled water.

## TRAVEL INSURANCE

You would be foolish not to take out a combined medical and luggage travel insurance policy before you leave, but this is not as easy as it sounds. Most companies do not cover all the countries you will want to visit, especially not those cheap 'Worldwide Insurance' policies which are advertised so heavily. You may have to pay quite a bit (about US$250 for three months) to get the cover you want. Direct Line (in the UK) cover everywhere in Asia. Check what **existing cover** you have through your house insurance or private medical insurance before you start.

## BACKGROUND READING

Many books have been written about the Silk Road or travelling along it and most of them are very good, so you shouldn't run out of reading material.

### Travel writing
Some of the most famous travel writers past and present have won their spurs somewhere along our route so there is plenty of choice:
- ***Danziger's Travels*** – Nick Danziger. You may wish Danziger hadn't felt the need to flaunt his sexual conquests quite so often during this account of his land journey from England to China but in the end you let him off because he had the 'balls' to live an adventure which will continually surprise and excite you – the 20th-century's Marco Polo?
- ***In Xanadu*** – William Dalrymple. During a summer break from university, Dalrymple set out to retrace Marco Polo's journey from Jerusalem to the fabled palace of Kublai Khan. The account of his adventures en route and the constant comparisons with Marco Polo's original descriptions make this a fascinating and thoroughly enjoyable book.
- ***From The Holy Mountain*** – William Dalrymple. Another from Dalrymple, this tour of the Near East/Eastern Mediterranean is a fascinating attempt to explore the modern reality of some of the most famous place names in ancient and biblical times.
- ***The Travels*** – Marco Polo. This is, of course, the classic volume (translated by RE Latham in the Penguin Classics series). It's widely available and quite fun, although it's not the easiest read of the books here. If you have access to a

good library, try looking up the original translation by Sir Henry Yule as his early editions have some real treats, such as a copy of Marco Polo's will and a 19th-century plan of Beijing.

● ***The Marco Polo Expedition*** – Richard B Fisher. This book is not easy to find anymore but recounts a scientific/historical expedition in the 1980s which was the first to be allowed all the way through to Beijing, including going via the old USSR – thanks to a letter written in desperation to the attention of one 'Mr M Gorbachev (President)'.

● ***Journey To The West*** – Wu Cheng En (translated by Arthur Waley as part of the Penguin Classics series). You may be more familiar with these stories from the TV series *Monkey*, dubbed into English. Monkey (Sun Wu Kong) was the naughty hero/protector who, along with Pigsy and Sandy, was sent to protect Tripitaka (the Buddhist monk Xuan Zang, see box p345) on his journey to India from China in the 7th century, to collect the true Buddhist scriptures. Over the centuries hundreds of tales emerged involving this quartet and in the 16th century the poet Wu Cheng En brought them all together, along with some of his own interpretations, in a classic, if dauntingly massive, volume. Waley has also selected some of the best for his own volume, ***Monkey***. Videos of *Monkey* episodes are available from Channel 4 (in the UK).

● ***Shadow of the Silk Road*** – Colin Thubron. Thubron describes the eight-month trip he made to write this book as the most difficult he has made in his 40 years of travel. The result, however, is a particularly fine account of life along the whole length of our route, both now and through history. ***The Lost Heart of Asia*** and ***Behind the Wall*** are two other books by Thubron, in which he follows much of the Silk Route through Central Asia to China. While containing some depressing scenes, they are nevertheless beautifully written and the history is impeccable.

● ***Extremes Along the Silk Road*** – Nick Middleton. This book accompanied the TV series and each chapter goes into the subject matter in depth. It's particularly interesting as it shows just how much the route changes from season to season.

● ***A Book of Traveller's Tales*** – Eric Newby. This astounding compendium contains snippets from all the best travel writers, both modern and ancient. A pleasing number relate to the Silk Road, the rest will spur you on to new adventures.

● ***The Great Chinese Travellers*** – Edited by Jeanette Mirsky. This collection gives you the juicy highlights of Fa Hsien's Buddhist pilgrimage across Xinjiang and the Karakorum in the 5th century and also that of Xuan Zang's (see box p345) from both of the original accounts.

● ***An Adventure on the Old Silk Road, from Venice to the Yellow Sea*** – John Pilkington. Unfortunately, on this 1988 trip, Pilkington was turned back from Iran, Iraq and Syria so he had to fly over the middle section to Pakistan and carry on from there, but it's no less of a read for all that.

● ***Forbidden Journey*** – Ella Maillart; ***News from Tartary*** – Peter Fleming. This couple set out from Peking for Kashmir in 1935. Both books are amusing accounts of the same journey and are considered 'classics' by travel aficionados. They give a particularly good insight into the southern Taklamakan route and it is worth picking up one of the two. Both travellers would much rather have done the trip alone and this shows in their writing. James Bond buffs might side with Ian's brother but most will appreciate Maillart more. Look out for her ***Turkestan Solo*** as well.

- ***Alone on the Great Wall*** – William Lindesay. Lindesay was the first Westerner to walk (and run!) the length of the Great Wall of China. This is his account and it is as good as any book on the subject.
- ***East to Cathay: The Silk Road*** – Robert Collins. A 1970s' account that's particularly interesting for a snapshot of the Silk Road before it really opened up.
- ***On the Trail of Marco Polo: Along the Silk Road by Bicycle*** – Brady Fotheringham. Cycling along the Silk Road is no mean feat. This account details a ride from Beijing to Pakistan in the late '90s and is essential reading for anyone intending to set out on two wheels.
- ***Peking to Paris*** – Warren Brown. This book accompanies a four-part documentary from ABC Australia. In 1907 one of the first great car expeditions/races took place when five intrepid drivers answered the challenge to test their cars across Asia in the 'Peking To Paris Raid'. In 2005 Brown persuaded an equally eccentric group of motor enthusiasts to re-enact the race using almost identical vintage cars. Their route was to the north of ours but it's a great story nonetheless.
- ***East is West; Valleys of the Assassins; Beyond the Euphrates*** – Freya Stark. These are only a small selection of books by a woman synonymous with travel writing in the Middle East. Do check out at least one of them.
- ***Damascus, Hidden Treasures of the Old City*** – Brigid Keenan. During her time as the wife of the British Ambassador to Syria, Brigid fell in love with this city and its old buildings and was so upset at their gradual demise that she decided to do something about it. This involved not only buying a traditional merchant's house and restoring it to its original beauty but also beginning a crusade to highlight the Old City's plight. This is a unique collection of photographs and stories from inside the city's houses – where few get the opportunity to venture.
- ***Central Asia: A Traveller's Companion*** – Kathleen Hopkirk. Peter Hopkirk's obsession with Central Asia and the Great Game was obviously contagious: his wife caught it, too. She doesn't write quite as well as he does, though, and you may get a bit bogged down if you're not a history lover but she does relate many of those fascinating anecdotes that travel guides can't fit in.
- ***Eastern Approaches*** – Fitzroy Maclean. A brilliantly written account of pre-war travels in Central Asia and the Caucasus, as well as subsequent wartime special missions in Yugoslavia and Persia.
- ***Journey to Khiva*** – Philip Glazebrook. The best CIS book for this trip. Glazebrook visits Central Asia and ponders the Great Game, the Uzbeks, the Russians, life and other distractions.
- ***The Gobi Desert*** – Mildred Cable and Francesca French. These venerable female missionaries travelled throughout Xinjiang province in the early 20th century. Another book by them on the same subject is ***Through the Jade Gate***, though ***The Gobi Desert*** is better. Both books are overtly religious at times but give an excellent insight into the area. They are out of print but can be found quite easily if you look around secondhand bookstores.

- ***Carpet Wars*** – Christopher Kremmer. Kremmer arrived in Afghanistan in 1990 and spent the next ten years hooked on the country and its culture. This book uses the world of carpets as a backdrop to his fascinating tales.
- ***From Heaven Lake*** – Vikram Seth. In 1981, whilst a student at Nanjing University, Seth hitched home to Delhi via the Silk Road to Xinjiang, and then south through Tibet. By the much-lauded author of *A Suitable Boy*.
- ***Apples in the Snow*** – Geoffrey Moorehouse. Veteran travel journo Moorehouse explores Soviet Central Asia in the days when it was still Soviet Central Asia. A well-researched, thoughtful and thought-provoking book.
- ***Journey to Turkistan*** – Eric Teichman. The British Foreign Office sent this diplomat the length of China by car in 1935. Another classic.
- ***The Road to Oxiana*** – Robert Byron. This travel diary of a trip from England to Afghanistan rivals Teichman's work for its imperial tone but is nonetheless beautifully descriptive.
- ***Riding the Iron Rooster*** – Paul Theroux. These accounts of his various travels by train in China are a good read even if most of the action does take place off the Silk Road. ***The Great Railway Bazaar*** is a must for all train enthusiasts and anyone considering travelling the Silk Road by rail (see box pp8-9).
- ***Night Train to Turkestan*** – Stuart Stevens. The author sets out to retrace Maillart and Fleming's crossing of China using the southern Taklamakan route and doesn't make it – which sort of sums up the book – but once you've had a go you might be more sympathetic.

### History

The history of the Silk Road contains some of the world's best-known historical figures and most of the following books do them justice.

- ***The Silk Road*** – Frances Wood. As you'd expect from the head of the Chinese section of the British Library, this history is heavily centred on the eastern half of the route but it is no less informative or enjoyable for that. The illustrations are also superb. You might also enjoy her ***Did Marco Polo Go To China?***
- ***The Silk Road: A History*** – Francke and Brownestone. For a straightforward history of the Silk Route try to find a copy of this fully comprehensive, if a little over-simplified account. Unfortunately it is now out of print.
- ***The Silk Road: Art and History*** – Jonathan Tucker. This hardback is expensive but it contains a marvellous collection of archive photography and whilst the emphasis is on art, the 'History' section is thorough and a welcome addition now that *The Silk Road: A History* is no longer in print.
- ***Foreign Devils on the Silk Road*** – Peter Hopkirk. Essential reading for anyone interested in Chinese history, archaeology or just plain adventure, this is the story of the Western explorers (see box p304) who prised open the history of the 'Lost Cities' of the Taklamakan Desert, collecting crates of antiquities as they went, usually at immense personal risk. Hopkirk's ***The Great Game*** is a fascinating account of the Central Asian operations carried out by Russian and British spies during the 19th century; intrigue, espionage, massacre and more. Meanwhile, ***In Search of Kim*** is a must for fans of the novel, describing Hopkirk's attempt to track down the places and characters Kipling so masterfully brought to life.

- *Life along the Silk Road* – Susan Whitfield. Set around ten characters, this unusual story of the Silk Road (it's told in a similar style to *The Canterbury Tales*) is well managed by Whitfield and provides some impressive insights. The author is also one head of the joint British Library/National Library of China's International Dunhuang Project which has a very informative website at http://idp.bl.uk. The British Library held a Silk Road Exhibition in 2004 (www.bl.uk/silkroad) and the subsequent book and catalogue, **The Silk Road: Trade, Travel, War and Faith**, contains ten essays by Silk Road scholars and runs to over 400 splendid pages. *Aurel Stein on the Silk Road* is another of Ms Whitfield's offerings.
- *Alexander The Great* – Robin Lane Fox. Forget the terrible Hollywood film (to which Lane Fox was the historical advisor), this definitive account of Alex's life is a rare combination of academic excellence and enjoyable narrative.
- *Xuan Zang, a Buddhist pilgrim on the Silk Road* – Sally Hovey Wriggins. Like Lane Fox, Wriggins has spent years tracking her subject and this book is as much a study of the man as it is of his achievements.
- *Crusades* – Terry Jones and Alan Ereira. As you'd expect from an ex-Python, this is as entertaining as it's academic; as a popular history book, it can't be beat.
- *A Ride to Khiva* – Fred Burnaby. Our Fred, strongest man in the British army, speaker of numerous languages and all-round *bon-oeuf*, sets off for Central Asia. Along the way he encounters frostbite, Russian bureaucracy and 'insubordinate natives' before actually arriving in Khiva in 1877. Sadly now out of print.
- *Journey to Khiva* – Nikolai Muravyov. This Russian envoy very nearly lost his head, literally, whilst trying to nurture his country's foreign relations with Khiva in 1819. Contains reams of information about the city, including some particularly gruesome details concerning torture and execution. Now out of print.
- *An English Lady in Chinese Turkestan* – Lady Macartney. The wife of British diplomat Sir George describes life in their consulate at Kashgar at the end of the 19th century. Fascinating.
- *Buried Treasures of Chinese Turkestan* – Albert von Le Coq. German archaeologist and explorer von Le Coq, travelling across Xinjiang in the early 20th century, took along a case of Veuve Cliquot for special occasions. This account of his expeditions is wonderfully understated and makes excellent reading.
- *The Great Wall* – Julia Lovell. Lovell is a Cambridge historian and uses the history of the Great Wall as an elegant metaphor for the history of China as a nation. The level of detail describing the evolution of the Wall is fascinating.
- *Religions of the Silk Road* – Richard Foltz. The Silk Road is either home to, or helped spread, all the world's great religions. Foltz is an authority on Asia and its beliefs.
- *The Long March* – Harrison Salisbury. Salisbury retraced Mao's entire route before writing this in the 1980s and he seems to give you a genuine insider's view because of it. A photographic account, **China: The Long March**, was also compiled by Anthony Lawrence in the eighties to commemorate its 50th anniversary.
- *Wild Swans* – Jung Chang. This true account of the lives of three generations of women living in China during the 20th century is compulsive reading (it is

the biggest selling non-fiction paperback in publishing history) and throws more light on what real life was like in the Land of Mao than any history book. Chang has followed this success with *Mao: The Unknown Story*, a collaboration with her husband, the historian Jon Halliday.
● **The Good Earth** – Pearl S Buck. This is rightly heralded as a Chinese classic of the 20th century. It follows peasant Wang Lung on his long road to destiny amid China's various political upheavals.

### Fiction
These may not be so historically accurate but are real page-turners.
● *Flashman, Flashman and the Great Game, Flashman at the Charge* – George MacDonald Fraser. Whatever happened to Harry Flashman, the big bully from *Tom Brown's Schooldays*? Well, in 1966 Fraser decided to 'rediscover' Flashman's lost diaries and the result is a collection of rip-roaring tales through the major events of the 19th century – a cross between PG Wodehouse and James Bond (Fraser went on to write *Octopussy*). You might find yourself reading the whole series but start with these ones as they are the most relevant to your route.
● *Samarkand* – Amin Maalouf. This fictional account of the great Persian poet and mathematician, Omar Khayyam, is a must for romantics and scholars alike.
● *Kim* – Rudyard Kipling. This classic, set in India under the British Raj and during the Great Game, is a little off our track but those who are doing the Pakistan leg can comfort themselves with the knowledge that India at this time included Pakistan and much of the action takes place in the Northern Territories. Those not going to Pakistan can just enjoy catching up on a book they were supposed to have read years ago.
● *The Silk Road* – Jeanne Larsen. This tale about Greenpearl and her adventures in China during the Tang dynasty is a bit like *1001 Nights* in that it brings

> **Mapping the Silk Road**
> Maps of areas, regions and even whole countries become obsolete notoriously quickly in this part of the world, with many susceptible to what at times feels like almost daily changes. Their accuracy has been similarly unreliable with map-makers (under the instructions of their political masters) often deliberately setting out to confuse or mislead the map-reader. Satellite systems have done much to improve the situation in recent years but this is still one of the least mapped areas of the planet. If you are driving (see box p74) or cycling (see box p157) you should really try to stock up before you leave as better maps are often available outside the Silk Road countries. In the UK, contact **Stanfords** (🖳 www.stanfords.co.uk), London, or the **Map Shop** (🖳 www.themapshop.co.uk), Worcestershire; in Australia try **Mapland** (🖳 www.mapland.com.au), Melbourne, **Mapworld** (🖳 www.mapworld.com.au), with branches in Sydney, Canberra and Perth, or the **Travel Bookshop** (🖳 www.travelbooks.com.au) in Sydney; in North America contact **Maplink** (🖳 www.maplink.com), Santa Barbara, CA.
> The upside is that hundreds of fascinating old maps now exist portraying the Silk Road and its host countries in all manner of different guises. There are a few antique map/book shops along the route but you will probably find a better selection at home (many capitals are home to annual antique map fairs – in the UK contact 🖳 www.londonmapfairs.com, who hold quarterly fairs at the Rembrandt Hotel in London). Another good source of maps and geographical images is the Internet (see p30).

together all the local legends and poetry of the era. A good one to read to the children.
- ● ***Stories from the Silk Road*** – Cherry Gilchrist. This is another worthy addition to any small child's library. The stories are classics and the illustrations beautiful.

### Magazines
For cultural information on Central Asia have a look at the new ***Steppe Magazine*** (💻 www.steppemagazine.com).

### Phrasebooks
We set out for the first edition without knowing many words in any language of any country we were about to visit (something we are not proud of) and we aren't much better today, so don't panic if you are no linguist either (English is certainly much more prevalent than it was just a few years ago). Phrasebooks, however, come in very handy if you want to get to know the locals or are planning to spend a long time in one place. Lonely Planet produces as good a series as any. The ones for Arabic, Russian or Mandarin Chinese will prove the most useful to supplement the essentials given in the 'Appendix' (see pp375-8).

## INTERNET RESOURCES

A good place to start looking is the Silk Road Foundation (💻 www.silk-road.com); based in California, they have collected lots of good tips from previous travellers. Another is The Silk Road Project (💻 www.silkroad project.org), based in New York and part funded by The Aga Khan Trust For Culture. The Silk Road Tour Operators Group (💻 www.silkroadtog.com) is an umbrella organization representing lots of tour operators along the Silk Road. Silk Road Seattle (💻 http://depts.washington.edu/uwch/silkroad) has maps, historical and cultural information. There are also plenty of travellers' chatrooms and blogs; a quick search with any search engine will throw up the latest offerings.

### Country by country
The official sites tend to be pretty bland but they do list embassy details, the latest visa information, customs rules and regulations etc. A good site for **Turkey** is 💻 www.turkeytravelplanner.com. The **Syrian** Tourist Board's site (💻 www.syriatourism.org) isn't that good; try 💻 www.syria-net.com. Net **Iran** (💻 www.netiran.com) is again is very dry; a better site is Pars Times (💻 www.parstimes.com/travel/iran), which gives a myriad of useful links. The **Kyrgyz** Embassy in Washington hosts 💻 www.kyrgyzstan.org. For **Pakistan** try 💻 www.travel.web.pk or 💻 www.tourism.gov.pk. The **Chinese** government heavily monitors the Internet within its borders but 💻 www.confucius.org is interesting.

### Others
The World Tourism Organization has a Silk Road Project (💻 www.world-tourism.org/projects/silkroad/silkroad.html). UNESCO's World Heritage Committee (💻 www.whc.unesco.org/en/list/) has an in-depth website listing all its protected sites. The World Monuments Fund (💻 www.wmf.org.uk) is actively involved in restoring endangered sites and returning them for use in the community.

# PART 2: THE SILK ROAD

# History

When in the 19th century the geographer and explorer, Baron von Richtofen, first used the phrase 'die Silkenstrasse', it seemed that at last we had a term worthy of the immense network of trails that had linked East with West for centuries. Yet von Richtofen (as much a headline-seeker as his nephew, 'The Red Baron', it seems) had also succumbed to that era's desire for order in creating his new term, leaving us with a name that has often been as misleading as it has been enlightening. Not only was the network no *autobahn* from Europe to the Orient, it was just as integral to the diffusion of man's ideas and development as it was to the commerce of silk. Indeed, the history of the Silk Road in many ways mirrors the history of civilization prior to the discovery of the New World. Writing, horse riding, paper and gunpowder all spread from countries on the Silk Road, and not just China. Yet it was because the Chinese managed to keep the process of silk production so secret that for centuries silk remained the ultimate prize.

Unfortunately, there has been virtually no period during its history that some section of the Silk Road was not at war or in the midst of revolution, so no one route could ever be guaranteed and literally hundreds of alternatives were devised to ensure the supplies kept coming, making modern tracking of 'The Road' an endless task.

## THE ROUTE

To understand its history, we must first understand the Silk Road's geography. As you will appreciate when you travel across it, the broad band of Asia covered in this guide between the Mediterranean and the Japan and China seas contains the whole spectrum of terrain from flat steppe to towering mountains, yet it shares a similar climate throughout: it is very, very dry and, for most of the year, very, very hot. Geographers agree that it is much drier now than one thousand and two thousand years ago, with a massive increase in desertification in areas like the Taklamakan Desert, but even in ancient times it was no picnic.

Looking at the physical map of Asia it would seem far more sensible (outside of winter at least) for the Silk Road to have taken a more northerly route. Merchants could have left Europe via the Ukraine, travelled across the southern reaches of Siberia to Lake Baikal and descended the Mongolian steppes into China. Not only would they have escaped the worst of the heat, there would have been plenty of water and they would have avoided most of the various deserts and mountain ranges that make such a trip so hazardous. Furthermore, the hard, flat land would have been ideal for their carts, horses and camels (the terrain is so amenable, in fact, cars were driving this route long before the advent of roads – see 'Driving the Silk Road' p74). Unfortunately, this route was also inhabited by a variety of hostile peoples and tribes who often preferred attacking the merchants' caravans to trading with them.

One solution could have been to fight their way through, destroying any obstacles that dared cross their path, and throughout the Silk Road's history would-be world dominators regularly took this approach, especially from the East. More commonly, however, those in search of wealth and riches through less confrontational methods chose routes further south.

Early traders would have been brave but they were not stupid: they picked their way through the least inhabited areas to minimize the chance of bumping into and being attacked by bandits. This would have meant turning to the deserts and mountains, which in turn meant travelling along some of the most inhospitable routes on Earth. As such, the time needed to cover the near 8000km trip would have run into years, particularly as it wasn't just the animals that walked, for beasts of burden were far too precious to spare for carrying men; even a hundred years ago walking was the only option, as Sir Aurel Stein – see boxes p304 and p326 – lamented. Few could afford such a slow turnover and fewer still were prepared to gamble such high stakes. Indeed, it is not until the Mongol period that we have any evidence of an expedition carrying out the entire trip in one go. So for most of the Silk Road's life merchants tended to stick to their own patch, buying and selling goods only over a region of a few hundred or so square miles.

With the routes constantly deviating to avoid all the geographical obstacles and to keep out of the way of the bandits, over time there were just as many routes running north to south as east to west. Furthermore, goods frequently changed hands five or six times before they reached their final destination, and as many as fifty times on a bad run. The journey was slowed down even further as merchants waited to team up into big caravans before setting out to offer better protection against attack – caravans that would often travel only at night in the desert areas to avoid the heat, using the stars to navigate.

## In the beginning

Because of his unique travelogue and undeniable PR skills, the Silk Road has most regularly been associated with Marco Polo. Yet by the time he came along the route was already on its last legs and we need to go back to a time when his ancestors were still in togas to find its heyday; and still further to find its origins.

It is impossible to say when the first piece of silk made its way to the West but fragments have been found in Scythian and even European graves dating back to the sixth and seventh centuries BC. How they got there will remain another mystery because, just as the Silk Road was cultivated over the centuries, so other ancient trade routes developed as well. The most obvious alternative was to miss out land altogether and go by sea (see map opposite pp32-3. Ships would leave from the southern ports of Nanhai (Canton) or Cattigara

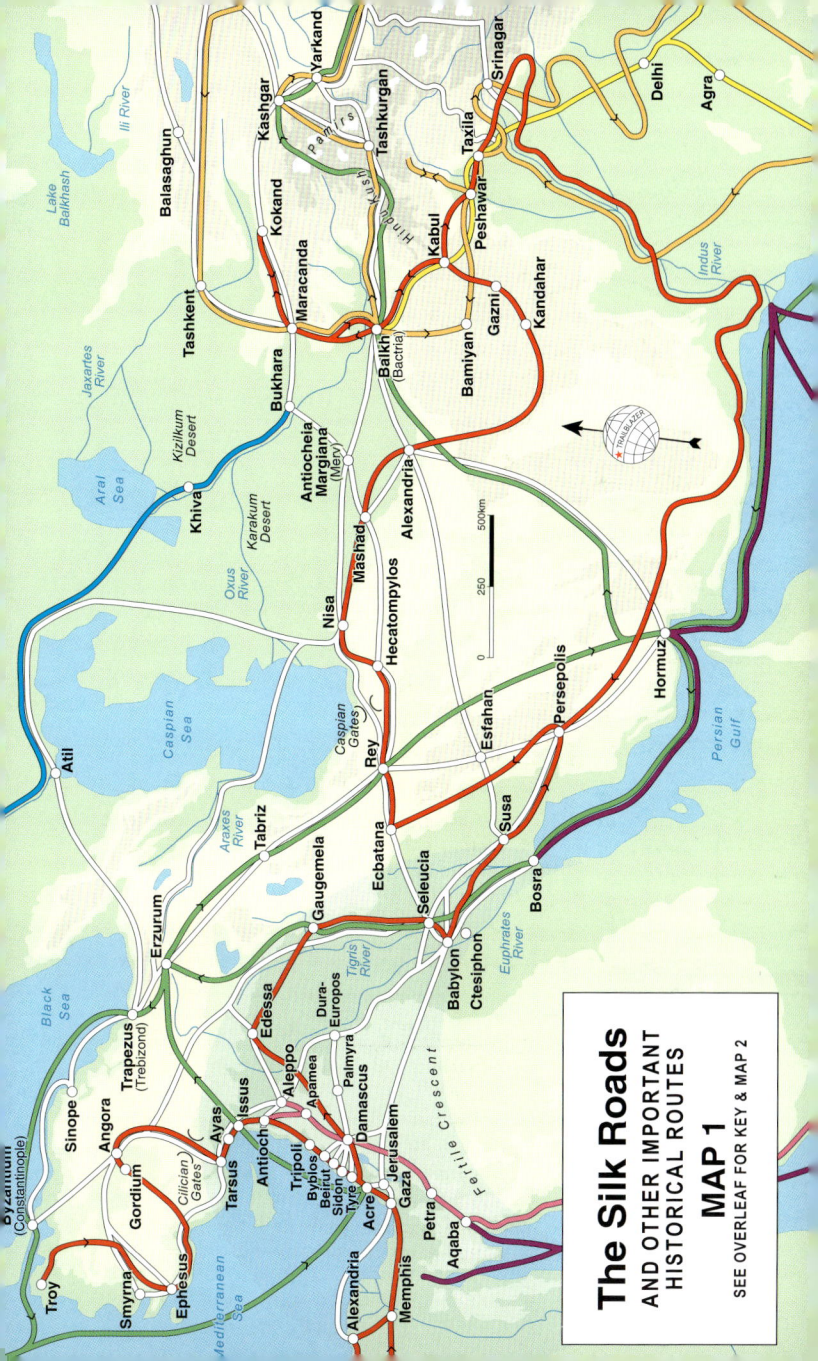

# The Silk Roads
AND OTHER IMPORTANT HISTORICAL ROUTES

## MAP 1

SEE OVERLEAF FOR KEY & MAP 2

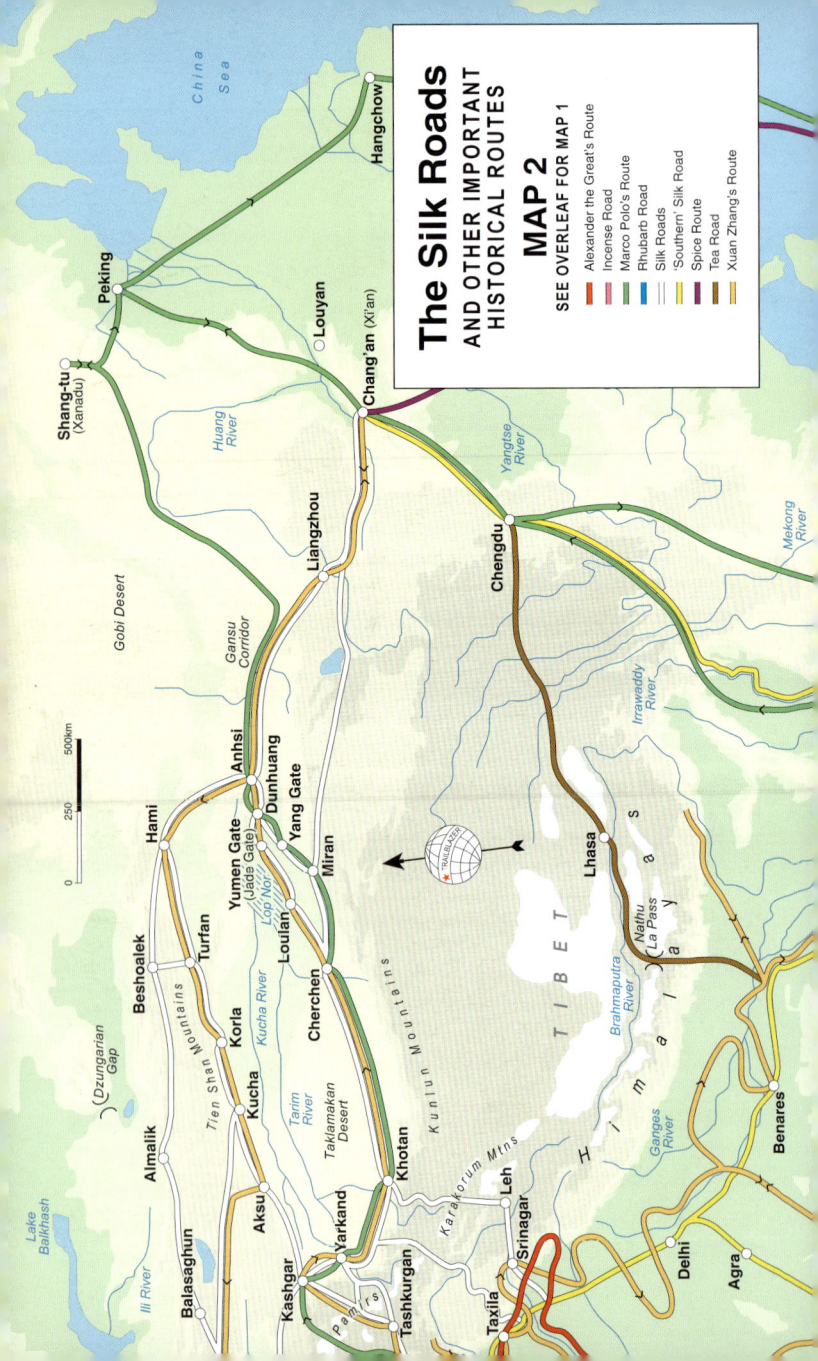

# The Silk Roads
## AND OTHER IMPORTANT HISTORICAL ROUTES

### MAP 2
SEE OVERLEAF FOR MAP 1

- Alexander the Great's Route
- Incense Road
- Marco Polo's Route
- Rhubarb Road
- Silk Roads
- 'Southern' Silk Road
- Spice Route
- Tea Road
- Xuan Zhang's Route

### The Stone Tower

The Stone Tower is the legendary meeting place where merchants from East and West were supposed to have traded the first bales of silk on the Silk Road. The location of this tower, however, has raised more unsolved questions than any other site on the route. Marinus of Tyre heard about the tower from the Macedonian trader Maes Tibianus in AD120, Ptolemy received vague instructions on how to get to it in AD150 and for centuries it seems to have been the agreed meeting place for hundreds of caravans from China and Central Asia. But by the 19th century it seemed to have disappeared.

That it was in the Pamirs seems sure enough though that doesn't narrow the search down much. The Pamirs were known as 'The Roof of the World' by the Persians and the 'Onion Mountains' by the Chinese (because of the altitude sickness it induced in them – they mistakenly blamed eating the local onions for their condition).

The word 'Pamir', however, means a wide pass and, unsurprisingly, this range has plenty such passes – unlike the Karakorum Mountains, for example, which have only a few viable crossing points. We can expect the traders to have stuck to the same passes every year but as we don't know which ones these were, the task of locating the tower is not easy.

We know, however, that the early Silk Road merchants would have predominantly used the Southern Taklamakan Route on their way out of China. We know, too, that they would have gone as far as Yarkand (rather than Kashgar) before heading into the mountains and that they would have been aiming for Bactria through present-day Tajikistan. As such, the most obvious initial route would have been to follow the Yarkand River.

Modern politics, however, prevents any search of this area. Certainly, if you applied logic, to have built the tower near a river would have made sense as this would have given travellers another landmark for reference and as you head up the Yarkand, there is a sharp turn to the east where it would be likely many caravans struck out west (see map p290): for many this seems the most likely position. On the other hand, Aurel Stein considered the tower's location to be in the Karateghin Valley which runs east to west, splitting the Pamirs in the south from the Alayskiy Khrebet Mountains to the north.

The biggest problem is that 'Tashkurgan' (the Turkic translation for 'Stone Tower') is the name of many sites in the region and, as the whole area is at such a high altitude, whatever remains there tends to be covered in snow for most of the year. The most accurate guess, therefore, would seem to be that the tower was in the vicinity of the modern-day Tashkurgan on the Karakorum Highway (KKH). But wherever it is, let's be honest – wouldn't it be boring if we knew all the answers?

---

(Hanoi) and hug the land down to Singapore. From here they would follow the coast around the Bay of Bengal, cut through the Palk Straits separating Ceylon (Sri Lanka) and India and cross the Arabian Sea. They would then find themselves at modern-day Oman and, depending on the captain, would either head up the Persian Gulf to Bosra (modern-day Basra) or round to Aden (from where goods would travel by land along the Incense Road, see box p45, or continue by sea to the Red Sea ports of Suez and Aela, modern-day Eilat). This whole route from East to West became known as the Spice Route and eventually, as ships grew larger and faster, it was this route that spelt the end of the Silk Road.

> **The Southern Silk Road**
> There is some evidence that silk was sold southwards from China into Burma where it was traded by land through modern-day Bangladesh. This was never a popular route because of the disease- and bandit-infested jungles along the way but once across the Ganges merchants could join up with India's Grand Road, later the famous Grand Trunk Road of the British Raj. This ran from Calcutta through Benares, Delhi, Lahore and Taxila to the Khyber Pass and Kabul. From here they would cross the Hindu Kush and on to Bactria or head for Herat. A spur also ran south from Agra to the coast at Bombay where the merchandise could then be carried by sea.

Yet it was the route described in this book that would dominate for over 1500 years and how it came about involved many of the greatest names in history.

Some of the world's oldest civilizations had developed in Egypt, Mesopotamia (the 'Land Between Two Rivers'), India and China and, following recent excavations in the Margiana Oasis, it seems we can add Turkestan to this group. It is therefore unsurprising that they provide the backdrop for the earliest trade routes. Copper, tin and turquoise found their way out of Iran, gold came from the Altai Mountains, lapis lazuli and rubies from Afghanistan and furs from Siberia. Loads were carried by donkeys (bred from the asses of Nubia on the Upper Nile), horses bred from the tiny Przewalski-type ponies of central Asia (named after the great 19th-century Russian explorer, Nicolai Przewalski, see box p238), and both the one-hump (dromedary) camel domesticated in North Africa and Arabia, and its two-humped cousin (Bactrian) from Afghanistan. Yet all this trading was done without the aid of a recognizable common currency or language. In fact, most early trade was conducted under the ancient '**dumb barter**' system: certain sites, usually in remote highland areas, became earmarked as trading posts. One party of traders would wait until another one turned up (how long they waited is anybody's guess but it is most likely that trade was carried out on a seasonal basis so to a certain extent opportune meeting times could be estimated). The first party would arrange the goods they wanted to trade in a clearing and retire to their camp. The next day, the second party would take a look at the goods on offer and lay down as many of their goods as they felt to be of equal worth beside those goods they desired. The original vendors would then return and adjust their pile depending on what they thought of the others' wares – and so on until one day the original vendors would arrive to find no adjustment, at which point they would gather their booty and return home.

And so the system continued across the continent, spreading the goods far and wide. Invading armies also helped to spread trade, uniting territories under one rule which simplified the commercial process. As the horse was turned into a fighting machine – ridden by cavalrymen dressed in the latest invention, 'trousers' – so these raiders and invaders were able to travel both further and faster. So it was that the Hittites, Slavs, Balts, Germans, Celts and Armenians began moving west from central Asia, while the Scythians, Iranians and Indians/Aryans rode east.

Nevertheless, it is easiest to consider the early development of the Silk Road as that of two 'roads', one in the east and one in the west, that joined in the middle, with the dividing line being the great walls of mountains (the Himalayas, the Karakorum, the Pamirs and the Tien Shan) that form present-day China's southern and western borders. Indeed, Ptolemy saw these ranges as the split between the known and unknown worlds, describing the Pamirs as the 'Imnos' which separated his 'Inner' and 'Outer' Scythia.

## The eastern routes

The discovery of silk (see box below) is anecdotally attributed to Lei-tzu, the wife of Huang Ti, the Yellow Emperor of China from about 2697 to 2597BC. She is revered as 'Si Ling-Chi' ('The Lady of the Silkworm') who is said to have been playing with a silkworm cocoon whilst sipping tea in her mulberry garden. The cocoon accidentally fell into the tea and on retrieving it, she found that she could now unravel the material into one long filament.

### Silk

Silk is produced by the *Bombyx* moth, usually *Bombyx mori*, commonly known as the 'silkworm' (not to be confused with the 'wild silk' moth, which has been prevalent in the Aegean since Roman times). The larvae of this moth gorge on the leaves of mulberry trees and then surround themselves with a cocoon made of one continuous thread, usually 600-900cm long, which they hatch out of once they have transformed into a moth. Unfortunately for the moth, if it breaks the cocoon the thread will break too, so silkworms are killed before they have a chance to do this, usually with blasts of steam or hot air. The cocoons are unwound in a process known as 'reeling', and a number of filaments are wound together to make yarn by another process called 'throwing'.

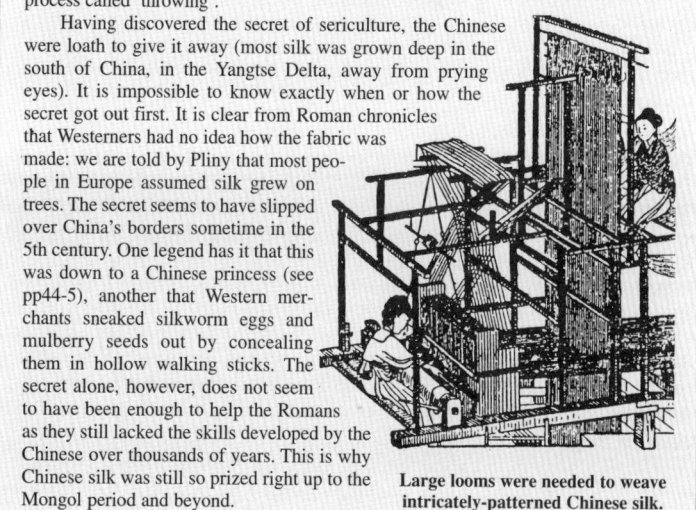

Having discovered the secret of sericulture, the Chinese were loath to give it away (most silk was grown deep in the south of China, in the Yangtse Delta, away from prying eyes). It is impossible to know exactly when or how the secret got out first. It is clear from Roman chronicles that Westerners had no idea how the fabric was made: we are told by Pliny that most people in Europe assumed silk grew on trees. The secret seems to have slipped over China's borders sometime in the 5th century. One legend has it that this was down to a Chinese princess (see pp44-5), another that Western merchants sneaked silkworm eggs and mulberry seeds out by concealing them in hollow walking sticks. The secret alone, however, does not seem to have been enough to help the Romans as they still lacked the skills developed by the Chinese over thousands of years. This is why Chinese silk was still so prized right up to the Mongol period and beyond.

**Large looms were needed to weave intricately-patterned Chinese silk.**

Even if this is not true, we know sericulture was definitely present in China by 2000BC and the Chinese half of the Silk Road is first talked about in the ancient Chinese legend, *The Travels of Emperor Mu*. This god-like ruler is said to have been part of the Chou dynasty in c1000BC. His legendary exploits, like those of the Ancient Greek Gods and Heroes, cover much of China's early development as human successes were attributed to divine intervention. He is said to have been the first to travel west from his capital at Xi'an into the Gansu Corridor, through the Yu Pass (later to become the Jade Gate near Dunhuang), across the Taklamakan (by the southern route) and on to the Kunlun Mountains (like Mount Olympus for the Greeks, this range was seen as the Home of the Gods). On his way he describes the region of Khotan as 'famous for its beautiful women and valuable jade'; he even had time to meet up with the 'Royal Mother of the West' (the identity of whom remains a mystery, although the Queen of Sheba is a likely contender as she is thought to have been alive at the same time).

There is also evidence of jade from Khotan and Yarkand (which at the time were outside her borders) reaching China as early as 2000BC. We must remember, however, that China in this period and for most of its history was small compared to its present size. Not only did it not include Tibet or Xinjiang, it was confined to its heartlands between the Yellow and the Yangtse rivers, thus excluding Inner Mongolia, Manchuria and much of its present southern territories. Each district had its own petty ruler and feudal disputes between them would last until the 3rd century BC – an environment that may have been conducive to the likes of Confucius (born 551BC) but which scuppered most plans for silk exportation, and indeed any other sort of exportation.

## The western routes

The ancient Assyrians, Medes and Babylonians were initially dominant in much of this part of the world but it was in the second half of the first millennium BC, when these powers were replaced by the Persian Achaemenids (founded by King Achemenes in the 7th century BC), that western routes really began to take shape.

The Persians originated in south-west Iran and Achemenes's great-grandson, Cyrus the Great, allied himself with the Babylonians to defeat the Medes. From the Mede capital of Ecbatana (Hamadan), he pushed into Asia Minor, taking the old Assyrian capital of Nineveh (Mosul) on the way, destroying the Lydian Empire of King Croesus (centred on Sardis) and pushing the Greeks back from Anatolia, before returning to double-cross his former allies, sack Babylon and famously release all its Jews. His successor Darius I (or Darius the Great) expanded even further – west into Egypt and North Africa, and east into Afghanistan and India – and although he was finally halted by the Greeks at Marathon (490BC), he developed with his son, Xerxes, a sophisticated road network to help him keep such a large empire together. New surfaces were built, maintenance and accommodation posts were established at regular intervals and bandits were given very short shrift.

The most famous of these highways was the Royal Road (constructed during the 5th century BC), which ran from the new Persian capital of Susa to Angora (Ankara) and Smyrna (Izmir), following the Tigris up to Anatolia and crossing, initially, northern Cappadocia (although within a short time a more southerly route through the Cilician gates and Tarsus was preferred). It was so efficient it could be covered by a relay of king's messengers in a matter of days and other routes were equally as impressive. One network linked Susa to the Phoenician ports of Tyre, Sidon, Byblos (famous for making books, hence our name for 'The Bible') and Tripoli. Between them, they handled all the trade in and out of the Mediterranean and new trading centres soon sprung up along the way, particularly in Haleb (Aleppo), Damascus, Hama and Homs. Another network linked the Persian capital with the East: the most obvious route was to cross the triangular-shaped desert (the remains of an ancient salty sea) which covers the plateau in the middle of modern-day Iran but few caravans were prepared to take this on. Instead, a northern detour to Rhagae (modern-day Rey) in the more fertile Elburz Mountains was incorporated into the plan. From here merchants could either cut through the narrow pass known as the Caspian Gates to the Caspian Sea and then go up around the north side of Kopet Dağ Mountains into Merv and across to the Ferghana Valley; or keep south of the Elburz and head for Herat and Bactria from where they could link up with the Southern Silk Road in Kabul or cross the Pamirs to Yarkand (see maps opposite pp32-3).

At the same time as the road-building projects, a similarly audacious canal network was carved out of (and sometimes under) the ground which massively increased crop production. This helped to further boost the region's wealth and, in turn, increase the desire for luxurious goods (particularly in the twin capitals of Susa and Persepolis) which again encouraged the merchants to keep on expanding their trading empires. Silk would have played a relatively small part in this; nevertheless, the basis for the western end of the Silk Road was now formed.

In later centuries, some merchants tried to avoid the region covering modern-day Iran and Iraq (and the excessive taxes its rulers frequently imposed on traders) and more northerly routes were developed for the western half of the Silk Road. However, usually the goods that originated from within the region itself (primarily horses and carpets but also minerals and gems from the desert) were too tempting to the caravan leaders, and they stuck to the old Persian routes in order to gain access to the local bazaars.

## ALEXANDER THE GREAT

Alexander may have bullied and cajoled his way to become leader of the Greeks, and he certainly wasn't one for the Athenian Democracy purist, but in terms of military skill and imperial leadership he was without parallel.

To the Greeks, anyone who would rid them of the Persians was a godsend whom they would willingly follow but the fact that Alexander did not stop in Anatolia and proceeded to devour the entire Persian Empire and much, much more is a tribute to his vision and ability. That he maintained and incorporated so much of what he inherited from the Persian Empire into his own army and administration is also an indication of his shrewdness.

After defeating Darius III he pushed south-west into Egypt, north into Central Asia and east into India where he is famously reported to have wept on the banks of the River Indus, 'because there was no more world to conquer'. Whether this is true or not is not important to our story; what is significant is that in Alexander's eyes, or at least in his official historian's eyes, the world stopped in India and that was the ultimate goal. Nevertheless, such an empire had never been seen before and Europe had never been closer to China. Another bonus was that though political gains were Alexander's priority, he was also keen to exploit the trade benefits which such gains offered: for example, after first defeating Darius at Issus in 333BC, Alexander refused to pursue him into Persia where he might well have been able to destroy him once and for all – and instead turned his attention to the Phoenician ports.

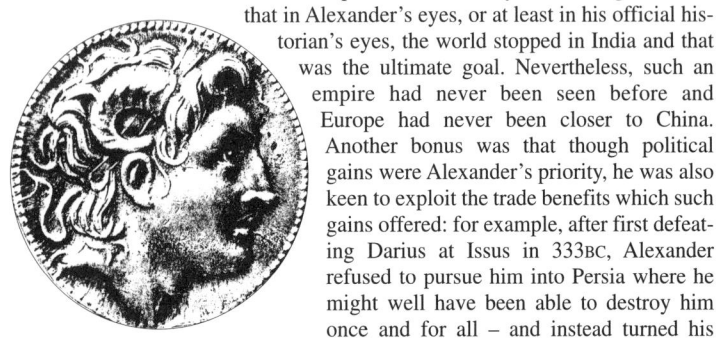

**Alexander the Great**
(From a silver coin minted by Lysimachus, his successor, in 290BC)

As bases for the Persian fleet it was necessary to neutralize such strategic targets but their economic worth was not lost on Alexander. Similarly, the massive programme to found and colonize cities throughout his newly won lands was designed not only to produce important

---

### BUDDHISM

**The Buddha** Everything you hear about the Buddha is unfortunately speculation as there is nothing concrete about his life; some points, however, are generally agreed upon. A prince, Siddhartha Gautama, was born sometime during the fifth or sixth centuries BC in northern India or Nepal, and after a period of experimentation with religion, notably self-mortification and yoga, he obtained a state of higher spiritual insight which he termed **Nirvana**, or 'The blowing out'. The crux of this state was the banishment of cravings and desires which otherwise bound him to the punishing cycle of transmigration, or reincarnation. Thus he became The Buddha: 'Buddha' is not a name, rather a term of recognition ('Enlightened One'). In fact, he is referred to by a number of names, another popular one being **Sakyamuni**, literally 'Sage of the clan Sakya'.

With Nirvana attained, he went out to teach the world what he'd discovered in the form of **The Four Noble Truths**: 'What is suffering'; 'What are the origins of suffering'; What is life without suffering'; and 'How to remove suffering'. Since his death, numerous stories about his life have been told, many of which are allegorical or refer to his supposed previous incarnations. Subsequent followers have therefore disagreed as to his message and many of the 'facts' about him are tenuous if not conflicting. His life is regularly depicted in the murals of the different cave complexes around China.

**Mahayana and Hinayana** These are the two most important schools of Buddhism. The **Mahayana**, 'The Greater Vehicle', believes that everyone can obtain Nirvana with help and that this help comes not just from Buddha but the Bodhisattvas and monks' prayers in monasteries. This school is most popular in Tibet, Mongolia, China, Korea and Japan. The **Hinayana**, 'The Lesser Vehicle', is considered the more

tools for the policing and government of the empire but also to provide centres where merchants could congregate and trade with the locals. Antiochia Margiana (Merv), Maracanda (Samarkand) and 'Alexandria the Farthest' (Kokand) were magnificent examples of this.

Even after Alexander's death in 323BC, his successors managed to continue many of his economic improvements despite being unable to hold his empire together: Antioch was built by the Seleucids (founded by one of Alexander's generals, Seleucus Nicator) as a true 'Greek' city superseding Aleppo as the western terminus for the Silk Road; Seleucia rose up on the Tigris, replacing Susa and Persepolis as Persia's capital and even outshining Babylon (though the glory days of Nebuchadnezzar and his Hanging Gardens, see p54, were now long gone). These cities were populated by a massive influx of new people, not just Greeks to run the governments but (as under the Persians) Armenians, Sogdians and Jews to conduct the trade. Despite Egypt and the Levant breaking off under the Ptolemies, India being lost to Chandragupta's Mauryan Empire (builders of The Grand Road) in 321BC and Bactria seceding to form its own empire (250BC), the trade routes continued to flourish. Nor did the transfer of power over to the Romans and the Parthians do anything to halt the merchants' successes. Indeed, during this period silk finally made its grand mark on the world stage and their services were in demand as never before.

---

pure form and was the only one before the Mahayana breakaway in the 1st century AD. In Hinayana, Nirvana can be achieved only by renouncing all worldly goods and rejecting worldly values (ie becoming a monk). This is the Buddhism practised in Sri Lanka, Thailand, Burma, Cambodia and Laos.

**Red Hats** These are worn by leaders of the three oldest schools of Buddhism: Nyingma, Kagyu and Sakya.

**Yellow Hats** These are worn by leaders of the reformist sect known as Geluk, founded by Tsongkhapa (1357-1419), a great Tibetan leader and philosopher. Following the Mahayana school, its founding monastery was built in Ganden in 1409. By the end of the 16th century it was the dominant school of Tibetan Buddhism and remains so today.

**Bodhisattva** These are followers who, as they are attaining Nirvana for themselves, help others to succeed with them; in Christian terms, the saints and angels of Buddhism.

**Amida (Amitabha)** Mahayan tradition dictates that Amida was a monk so good that he created a 'Western Paradise'. This paradise was so elevated that the step from here to enlightenment was fairly straightforward. Popular religion soon turned the paradise into a kind of Heaven and Amida himself became the centre of a devotional movement.

**Maitreya** It is generally held that Buddhism can never die – it simply fades away over the centuries until one person (the last one was Buddha Sakyamuni) stumbles upon its truths and advocates it again. Maitreya is the Buddha of the future who will rediscover the eternal truths when all around him have forgotten.

**Lamas** Believed to be the reincarnations of highly evolved beings; the Dalai Lama and Panchen Lama are the two most important leaders of the Yellow Hat Sect.

## ZHANG QIAN

In 261BC, a North Indian king, Asoka, converted to Buddhism and his biographers say that he encouraged Buddhist missionaries to cross the Himalayas into China. Herodotus tells us of a Greek traveller named Aristeas who claimed to have travelled with the Scythians to the gold mines of Siberia and the outskirts of China. Persian legend has it that their ancient King Jamshid married the daughter of the king of Machin (Great China). No matter how true these stories are, without serious support from the Chinese side nothing but a few fragments of silk would ever make its way out of China's domains.

Finally, in 221BC, a ruler emerged strong enough to unite his own lands and those around him. This first Emperor of China, Qin Shihuang (the 'Great Unifier'), pulled together the previous defences of the various states and built the earliest form of the Great Wall. He also began to build and standardize great roads for wagon travel across his lands (not to mention constructing his famous tomb guarded by the Terracotta Army). This continued under his Qin descendants and the following Han dynasty.

As the Han emperors grew stronger they began to look farther afield not just for new land but also for trading and political allies. Their greatest threat, however, was the northern barbarians of the Mongolian steppes known as the Hsiung Nu. In 138BC Emperor Wu (145-87BC) sent Zhang Qian, a young officer in the Imperial Household, to go in search of lands to the west where he had heard the 'Heavenly Horses' (see box p230) were bred and the people were equally hateful of the Hsiung Nu. The historian Suma Chi'en (known as 'China's Herodotus') tells us how Zhang Qian was captured by the barbarians, both on his outward and return journeys (delaying his eventual return by over ten years) but managed to struggle on across the Taklamakan (by the northern route), over the Tien Shan, into the Ferghana Valley, south into Bactria, back over the Pamirs and back home across the Taklamakan (by the southern route), thus earning him the epithet of 'Great Traveller' in Chinese annals ever since.

He returned west 20 years later and this time brought back not only 'Heavenly Horses' but also examples of Chinese silk and bamboo work. He was told, however, that these had come to Central Asia from India (they had probably arrived

---

### The Tea Road
Like the Silk Road, this was a network rather than a single path. Tea is thought to have been first cultivated in Pu-erh (in modern China's Simao Prefecture) in ancient times. The Tea Road linked central China with India via Sichuan and Tibet, and also via Yunnan and Burma. As well as tea, salt was carried and this network later formed part of the Southern Silk Road (see box p36).

Those of you wanting to travel the Tea Road are in luck. In 2006, after 44 years of blockades, the Indian and Chinese governments finally agreed to reopen their border crossing at the **Nathu La Pass**. The road between Sikkim and Tibet is now open, (although not to foreigners). It is still mostly used by traders and Indian pilgrims hoping to visit Mount Kailash in Tibet, revered by Hindus as the home of Lord Shiva.

there from China via the Tea Road, see box opposite). Zhang Qian appears to have been unaware of India but this might be explained by our earlier analysis of China's borders: any route from India northwards through the Himalayas or the Karakorum would bring one out in Tibet or Xinjiang, still over a thousand miles away from Zhang's 'China'; similarly, the north-east route into southern China passed through lands that had only recently been conquered by the Han.

Because of Zhang Qian, the date for the opening of the full Silk Road is traditionally given as 115BC. His success was quickly built upon as the Hsiung Nu were driven out of the Gansu Corridor and the province of Chui-Ch'an ('Fountain of Wine') was established in their place. The Great Wall was extended to reach Dunhuang and the Yuang Kuan and Yumen Kuan ('Jade Gate') were erected as entrances to the northern and southern routes through the Taklamakan. The route was open – but that was only the beginning. Because, now the chance of great riches was on offer, everyone wanted to get in on the act and the inevitable theatre of politics and counter politics began.

## THE PARTHIAN SHOT

Back in the west, the Parthians had gradually expanded from their role of underling tribe within the Seleucid Empire to build their own capitals at Nisa (in modern-day Turkmenistan) and Rey (Tehran). They took over much of their master's lands from the Euphrates to India and allegedly exchanged an ostrich egg for their first bolt of silk in the 2nd century BC. At the same time, the Romans expanded into Asia from Anatolia and it wouldn't be long before the two sides would meet face to face. It happened in 53BC at the Battle of Carrhae (near modern-day Harran).

The Parthians were already famous for their ability to control their horses using only their legs, thus allowing themselves enough movement in the upper body to turn and fire arrows even in retreat (the Parthian Shot) but here they unveiled a new weapon: 20ft-high silk banners. We will never know quite why they were so effective but they were enough to see off a Roman army led by Crassus; this was no mean feat, for he had been the commander who eventually defeated Spartacus and was part of Rome's First Triumvirate alongside Julius Caesar and Pompey. That Crassus paid for this loss with his life only confirms its significance.

Rome bounced back and went on to take Egypt from Cleopatra (30BC), which gave a tremendous boost to trade between Europe and the East. Rome also took Palestine and Syria, but Parthia was left alone and the merchants there began expanding their trade ventures into China; embassies were exchanged with China around this time. They increasingly bought up supplies of *seres* (the Latin word for 'silk', hence 'sericulture') and then sold them on to Rome. Just how significant this trade was has been spelt out to us by the 1st-century historian Isidore of Charax in his *Parthian Stations*, an early forerunner of Marco Polo's *Merchant Guide Book*. Yet it is important to note that Isidore still considered India to be the source of silk and therefore, along with its ivory stocks, the ultimate goal. (It is also interesting that Christian legend has one of the

Three Wise Men coming from India at this time, in the shape of King Gondophanes – that they also travelled by night supports the belief that many of the Silk Road caravans preferred to travel after dark – see p32.)

Ambassadors, however, still took eight or nine years to complete the trip from Parthia to China's new eastern capital at Luoyang (previously it had always been at Xi'an). This was despite the development of a new northern route around the Taklamakan which would leave the old route at Korla, head through Turfan, Hami and Anhsi (the 'Melon City'), and miss out Dunhuang and Loulan. Merchant caravans took even longer and there was little the Parthians could do to enhance the network between the two empires because the fear of attack from the Hsiung Nu remained immense and only the Chinese had the power to defeat that threat. Indeed, trade really flourished only following AD70 after China's General Pan Ch'ao lead his forces to a comprehensive victory over the northern marauders and established himself as 'Protector of the Western Territories' – by which time the Parthian merchants had been superseded. One of their subject tribes, the **Kushans** (descendants of the Yueh-Chih), had managed to carve out an independent state up in the mountains. They built their first capital at Bactria (which soon earned the title, 'Mother of all Cities') then, as they expanded into the Indian subcontinent after converting to Buddhism, a second one at Peshawar (it was at this period that Bactria lost its Greek name and became Balhika or Balkh – its Indian name). Their territory was known as the 'Land of One Thousand Cities' and the 'Babylonia of the East', because not only did the Oxus and Jaxartes flow here from the mountains but the Kushans (like the Persians) built a complex of underground canals which were as sophisticated as those still operating in places like Turfan. Politics held little interest for these quiet people: what they wanted was money and they made it through trade. Hundreds of their caravans began arriving in Xinjiang willing to do business and, with the Parthian and Roman nobles crying out for more silk (see Emperor Heliogabalus, above), they knew they would never run out of buyers at the other end; in AD14, the Roman Senate had to forbid the wearing of silk by men because it was becoming such a drain on the empire's resources.

**Emperor Heliogabalus, AD218-22**
'For him life was nothing except a search after pleasures.... He was the first of the Romans, it is said, who wore clothing wholly of silk, although garments partly of silk were in use before his time. (*The Life of Antoninus Heliogabalus*, Aelius Lampridius).

## THE ROYAL PURPLE

As if silk wasn't expensive enough in the Roman Empire, another trend had sprung up which was just as mysterious and just as exclusive. The **Phoenician cities** on the Levant coast had for many years been creating their famous royal purple in secret dye factories. The dyes were made from molluscs found on the Mediterranean shore and their shade depended on the length of their exposure to the sun (though for another three or four centuries even that was a secret). The combined price of the silk and the dye made such fabric so expensive that even the most wealthy senator had to settle for just a purple border on his tunic or a small purple trim. Nevertheless, the demand kept increasing. This led to another shift in the Silk Road: the caravans would still follow the north-westerly curve of the Euphrates but not all of them would carry on to Antioch. Many would split off at the Greek city of Dura-Europus (founded by Alexander's successors in 280BC) and head straight across the Syrian Desert to **Palmyra**, an ancient sulphur-spring oasis used only by local nomads until it was taken by Marc Antony in 41BC and developed into 'one of the wealthiest, most luxurious, and most elegant towns' in the empire (as Mikhail Rostovtzeff tells us in his *Caravan Cities*). From here, there was easy access to all the Phoenician ports. Roman soldiers also stamped out the robbers in the desert who had previously made the direct crossing from the Euphrates to the Mediterranean so hazardous. One negative impact of this new route was that it spelt the death of the route from the head of the Persian Gulf to Gaza or Alexandria via Petra, leading to that city's ultimate demise.

Everybody involved did their best to keep this new trans-Asian network open and see it flourish (Emperor Augustus even razed Aden to eliminate it as a rival) and despite Roman sailors successfully managing the first naval expedition from the Red Sea to China in AD166, the old Incense Road and Spice Route were thoroughly eclipsed for the next two hundred years. Nevertheless, such harmony could not last forever and eventually a series of disasters led to a near total collapse of the route.

The Han dynasty, already in a state of decline, collapsed in AD220 with the death of its last emperor. This led to the break up of China into small kingdoms that were prey to invasions from a new group of barbarians on the Mongolian Steppes, driven south by a lack of rain in their traditional homelands. The Parthians were also overthrown, this time by one of their subject tribes in southern Persia, the Sassanids, who subsequently went on to defeat the Kushans and their northern trading partners, the Sogdians.

Rome suffered its first **plague** in the reign of Marcus Aurelius (AD161-180) as new breeds of bacteria arrived in Europe (the irony is that these bacteria probably arrived from China with the very same caravans that were carrying the silk). Rome was also feeling the pressure from northern marauders because the nomads who had been driven off the Mongolian steppes pushed west as well as south and this had a 'domino effect' across Asia and into Europe. In AD330 Emperor Constantine took the dramatic step of moving much of his government to his new city Constantinople and in AD476, after a series of defeats against

> **The Nestorians**
> Nestorius, a Syrian bishop, was appointed Patriarch of Byzantium in AD428. He supported the view that Christ was both human and divine, as opposed to Rome which maintained that Christ was purely divine. In 431, at the Council of Ephesus, the Catholic Church decreed that Nestorius was a heretic and excommunicated him. His supporters were not intimidated, however, and the church split.
>
> A new Church of the East, centred on Ctesiphon (the old Parthian capital that was now under Sassanid control; see below), was established and its followers were known as Nestorians. Much of the Middle East and Central Asia, it seems, converted to Nestorianism en masse. By the 7th century there were over twenty Nestorian archbishops east of the Oxus, overseeing cathedrals as far apart as Kashgar, Lhasa, Kerala and Bahrain. Even Kublai Khan's mother was a Nestorian.

Goths, Visigoths (who took 4000 silk tunics as booty) and Attila's Huns, Rome finally fell to the Vandals.

As the demand for Eastern goods dried up, many routes along the Silk Road were abandoned by all but a few pilgrims. The most common of these on the western half of the routes were the **Nestorians** (see box above). Similarly, Buddhist monks used the Silk Road's infrastructure to go in search of more pure teaching – the most famous, perhaps, being **Fa Hsien**, who struck out from China to the Buddhist heartland of northern India in AD399. He was on the road for twelve years and helped to open up the arm of the Silk Road through the Karakorum Mountains.

## NO MORE SECRETS

The Sassanid dynasty, which overthrew the Parthians, was certainly a force to be reckoned with but it did little for the Silk Road. The founder, Shapur, preferred to trade by sea through the Persian Gulf and so keep all the profits for himself, a trend which was to last for 500 years. Sassanid merchants kept some trading relations with the Romans but more often than not the two empires were at war (Emperor Valerian was taken prisoner in AD260 at the siege of Edessa – modern-day Sanliurfa – and kept hostage in Ctesiphon) or, at best, an uneasy peace. Constantinople, as capital of Eastern Rome and, after AD476, the head of its own **Byzantine Empire**, still had the wealth to attract silk merchants (there were five guilds just for silk in the city) but their supply could no longer be guaranteed. The Phoenician ports lost their dye monopoly at this time as well when they were sacked by the Sassanids and forced to disclose the secret of their dying methods. Antioch was also sacked, in AD540, ending its dominance over Aleppo which, once again, became the major western terminus at the head of both the Silk Road and the Incense Road (see box opposite). Palmyra, incidentally, had been destroyed in AD273 after a succession of rulers ending with Queen Zenobia had challenged Roman authority once too often.

In around AD400, Xuan Zang tells us that a Chinese princess was sent to marry a prince of Khotan and, appalled by the prospect of being without new silk clothes, she hid some silkworm eggs and mulberry tree seeds in her hair and began to cultivate them in her new garden. Once out of China (Khotan was still considered a foreign country by the Chinese at this time) the secret seems to have spread more rapidly and although Chinese-produced silk remained the best and most desirable for centuries because of the country's superior techniques honed over generations, silk was soon being cultivated across Asia and even in Europe.

Up in the northern steppes the Avars had been overrun by the Turks (the word 'Turk' refers to their type of helmet) and they began expanding at a similar pace, creating their own empire of Turkestan by AD565, comprising most of modern-day Turkmenistan, Uzbekistan, Kyrgyzstan, Kazakhstan, Tajikistan and Xinjiang. They also challenged the Persian monopoly over the east–west trade network by allying themselves with Byzantium in AD568 and establishing their own direct trading route. This lasted only ten years but it opened up two new arms of the Silk Road permanently: goods travelling from China to Central Asia could now come around the north of the Tien Shan rather than through them; and once in Central Asia merchants could head north to Astrakhan on their way to the Black Sea or head across the Caspian Sea to Baku and through the Caucasus, following the Araxes River, rather than go south through Persia. Sea travel again became a factor as shipping goods across the Black Sea was quicker than crossing Anatolia. This led to the ports of Sinope (modern-day Sinop) and Trapezus (later Trebizond, modern-day Trabzon) becoming key stops on the Silk Road – as well as, of course, Constantinople's legendary harbour, the Golden Horn.

## A NEW GOLDEN AGE

Things were looking up again in China, too, as the country was united under the Sui dynasty in AD581. They built a fantastic new capital outside Xi'an and constructed the Grand Canal linking the Yellow and Yangtse rivers. The Sui lasted only one generation but they did much to lay the foundations for the Tang dynasty which followed, and which gave birth to some of China's most successful emperors. They subdued the Turks, absorbed the Tarim Basin kingdoms, pacified Tibet and encouraged the arts to blossom in the newly won peace. This

---

**The Incense Road**

Arabia Eudaemon ('Arabia the Blessed', modern-day Aden) was and still is one of the world's greatest ports. Ships from all over Asia and East Africa made a beeline for the city and its legendary markets and it quickly established itself as a terminus for many of the sea routes in the ancient world.

At Aden, some ships would carry on to Egypt and the Red Sea ports but most would transfer their goods onto camel caravans. These 'ships of the desert' would plough their way up the Arabian coast through the legendary city of Sheba to Aqaba. Here they would meet up with caravans from the even older King's Highway from Egypt, and head north again to Petra, the Levant, and Damascus.

Incense (particularly frankincense and myrrh) was obviously the prime commodity but all of antiquity's precious goods made their way along the route at one time or another.

> **Tibetans on the Silk Road**
> The inhabitants of the 'Roof of the World' were not always the peace-loving Buddhists we associate with Tibet today. In the Silk Road era they were fierce warriors who regularly came down from their mountain strongholds to raid caravans and cities, and in AD763 they took the Chinese capital, Xi'an, itself. In the seventh, eighth and ninth centuries they controlled huge parts of the Gansu Corridor but refused to participate in the Silk Road's trading network, preferring to maintain their raiding practices. The result was that for many years Chinese merchants were forced onto a more northerly route through the Mongolian Steppes.
>
> The Chinese invasion of Tibet in 1950 led to the establishment of the Tibetan Autonomous Region, a drastically reduced version of original Tibet. Around 130,000 Tibetans now live in exile with the Dalai Lama in Dharamsala, India. In centuries gone by Tibet also controlled large areas in what are now India and Pakistan and in many ways Baltistan ('Little Tibet') in Pakistan and Ladakh in northern India are said to be more Tibetan than Tibet, as they were spared the ravages of Chinese rule and the Cultural Revolution.

paved the way for such breakthroughs as block printing and Xuan Zang's translations of sacred Buddhist texts into Chinese. Traders were similarly encouraged (with a special bazaar and living quarters being built for foreign traders in Xi'an) and the extent of the wealth they made from the Silk Road can still be seen today in the statues they built at the Magao Caves. Korea and Japan also became part of the Silk Road as it was extended eastwards.

Back in western Asia, a caravan leader on the Incense Road (see box p47) began having some mightily impressive visions and Islam was born. Mohammed died in AD632 but the forces he had stirred swept through the Middle East under the Umayyads and finally defeated the Sassanids in AD651. Interestingly, the ousted Persian rulers fled to China which gives us some idea of how much the Silk Road had brought the two countries together; it was they, we think, who introduced the underground canal systems to the Tarim Basin. The new Umayyad capital at Damascus now rivalled Constantinople and caravans – still carrying silk but now laden with other goodies – began favouring this destination again. The Umayyads also made enormous strides in science and the arts, and it is their scholars we in the West should thank for preserving much of our earlier knowledge through the European Dark Ages. Meanwhile, the more northerly arms of the Silk Road were being kept open by the arrival of the enterprising Kazakhs between the Caucasus and the Volga; they were so prolific that the Caspian Sea became known as the Kazakh Sea (and many people living around its shores still know it by that name).

The Chinese and Islamic empires grew closer and closer together until they finally met in AD751 at Talas. But it wasn't to talk about the price of silk. The increasingly extravagant Umayyads had been overthrown and the Muslim world was now ruled by the more fundamentalist Abbassid Caliphate of Baghdad, who was joined in this offensive against the Chinese by the Turks. The battle led to a major defeat for the Chinese and the loss of another of their secrets: many of the captured men were paper makers (some were silk makers too) and they were forced to reveal their ability to turn old rags into paper, a much cheaper material than papyrus or parchment. More Chinese defeats followed against the Tibetans in the south and yet another steppe invader from the north – the Khitai (it was this tribe that would give us the term Cathay). The Uighurs make their first appearance around this time, too, taking control of much of the Tarim Basin.

With the fall of the Tang dynasty in AD907, chaos returned and China turned its back on much of the Western world. Buddhism, Christianity and Islam were all banned and Confucianism and Taoism, with their inherently pro-Chinese messages, were brought back to the fore. The Abbassids fared little better as a succession of splits occurred within their empire, most notably those of newly politicized Shi'ite sects (such as the Assassins), who were fed up with discrimination from their Sunni rulers. So the power base which had reached its peak during the glorious reign of Haroun al-Rashid (AD786-809) was gradually chipped away until a military revolution instigated by the Abbassids' **Seljuk-Turk** military commanders brought it crashing to the ground.

With China unwilling to trade outside its borders, the Seljuks turned their attention westwards to the **Crusaders**, who had journeyed from Europe to the Middle East in response to calls for help from the Byzantine rulers, following the latter's crushing defeat to the Seljuks at Manzikert in 1071. The First Crusade managed to overturn many of the Seljuk gains but this was only a temporary setback for the men known to the Crusaders as the Saracens. The Seljuks soon added Fatimid Egypt to their domains, along with most of the land previously under Byzantium's rule, thanks largely to great military leaders such as Zengi, Nur ed-Din and Saladin. Nevertheless, the European merchants, who had manipulated the Holy Wars to gain access to the Silk Road fortunes (the Venetians even persuaded the Fourth Crusade to attack Constantinople and reinforce their trading dominance), were never going to be fussy about who they traded with. Business boomed as it had never done before with goods and traders moving all over the western half of the Silk Road. Jews were in particularly high demand as their religion did not prevent them from making money out of money as Islam and Christianity did, which is one reason why they became the world's bankers. At the same time, however, one man from the banks of the River Orkhon in Mongolia was on a mission that would eclipse them all.

## THE MONGOLS

Because they spoke a Turkic language and came out of the steppes, the Mongols have often been conveniently banded with the Huns, Goths, Turks and Scythians who came before them. In fact, they were a completely different race with completely different looks. They came from the far north-east of the Mongolian steppe and had more of the look of Koreans and Chinese than any of the preceding invaders; they were also notorious for their body smell as they deemed water too precious to waste on washing.

Their most famous and, indeed, infamous leader, was **Genghis Khan**. Genghis initially adopted the steppe city of Karakorum as his capital, like the

> **Genghis Khan**
> Genghis Khan was born just to the south of Lake Baikal in 1162, fatherless and in fear of his life. By 1196, however, he had used his enormous political skill and courage to have himself proclaimed 'Supreme, All-Conquering Ruler of the Mongols'.
>
> In 1219 Genghis led an estimated 200,000 men west. From the Altai Mountains they descended into Central Asia and wrought havoc and devastation. He sacked cities for fun as his soldiers raped and pillaged, famously declaring to a stunned congregation in Bukhara's central mosque: 'I am God's punishment for your sins'.
>
> Following Genghis's death in 1227, his body was taken to Mount Burquan Qaldun, near his birthplace. After he was buried, a herd of horses was driven backwards and forwards across the site to disguise the burial plot and prevent looters.

Hsuing Nu and the Turks before him, and set about devising how to plunder as many riches as he could before his death. China, as so many times before, was the first to suffer and Peking was sacked in 1215. Next, Genghis turned west against the Khitai and the unlucky Khorezms (they had just carved out an empire for themselves from the Seljuks, were in control of much of Turkestan and even had designs on Baghdad, but within a decade they had been wiped out and their cities smashed to smithereens).

A particularly ferocious force at Genghis's disposal was the Tartars – a subject people of the Mongols who were defeated very early in Genghis's reign: the story goes that Genghis ordered the execution of the entire race except for the young boys, whom he adopted himself and trained into his front line fighting force.

Like their leader, the Mongol court and capital did not stop moving. Genghis's mobile force, reinforced by captured soldiers and artisans, in many ways resembled that of Alexander's 1500 years earlier. Like Alexander, Genghis was prepared to incorporate into his army any of his newly conquered subjects whom he felt could be of benefit. This was good news for the Chinese: intellectuals and philosophers such as Ch'ang Ch'un and Yeh-lu Ch'u-ts'ai were summoned around 1220 to create a more lasting infrastructure for the government of the empire. (Ch'ang Ch'un left us with an account of his 12-year trip through the Mongol Empire in which he explains that, for the Chinese at least, Indian cotton was at this time rarer and therefore more precious than silk. Furthermore, just as the West had been so off the mark in guessing the origins of silk, so the Chinese could not believe that cotton was grown on trees and in the 6th century had invented the myth of the 'Vegetable Lamb' which, although an animal, was planted in the ground and sheared for its cotton fleece each spring.)

While humans were *occasionally* spared, however, the cities that lay in the Mongol's path tended to fare less well. Bukhara was destroyed in 1219, Samarkand in 1220, Tblisi and Urgench in 1221. Urgench, the Khorezm capital, received particularly harsh treatment for daring to hold out for seven months. In the end, the Mongols (led by Genghis's most brutal son Tuluy) broke open the dams of the river Oxus and diverted the water straight through the city walls. This changed the course of the river for three hundred years as, following a prehistoric riverbed, it now flowed into the Caspian rather than the Aral Sea. Merv lost 700,000 citizens in its massacre and, like Balkh (another city destroyed at this time), the city never recovered. In the Caucasus, the Kazakhs fared little better, finding out the hard way that the impregnable Derbend Pass was no longer impregnable. The Kazakhs' new neighbours, the Rus (a people of Swedish Viking descent), also received a sound beating from the Mongols.

A halt was finally called to the Mongols' expansion on the announcement of Genghis's death, as all the commanders returned to Karakorum to elect a new leader. The peace was only temporary, however. Genghis's first son (Jochi) had died two years before him so his third son, Ogedei, immediately succeeded him as supreme khan and ordered the final conquests of southern China, Hungary and Poland – with the last only saved by Ogedei's own death in 1241. Genghis's second son, Chagatai, inherited East and West Turkestan, while two other sons, Orda and Batu, found further glory with their White and Golden Hordes. The term 'horde' actually comes through French from the Turkic word *orda*, meaning a large yurt, tent or pavilion where a khan held court; as the sight of such tents usu-

---

### Marco Polo

The most famous Silk Road traveller was by no means the first European to complete the journey to the Far East in one go; not only do we have records of early missionaries such as William of Rubrick making their way along the route, but Marco Polo went on his trip only because his father and uncle took him, two men who themselves had just returned from China. Brothers **Niccolo and Maffeo Polo** were Venetian traders and had first headed east in 1260 but ended up, thanks to a Tartar feud, stranded in Central Asia. Knowing that they could not get back, they kept going east until they arrived at Bukhara, where they stayed for three years. Here they were approached by one of Kublai Khan's emissaries who invited them back to Khanbalik (the Mongol name for Beijing) as guests and ambassadors. From Bukhara they travelled to Samarkand, the Pamirs, which they crossed, Kashgar, the northern Taklamakan route and finally the Chinese capital. This leg of the journey took over one year.

The khan was delighted to meet the two Italians and was particularly intrigued by their religion. He sent them back to Italy as his envoys, instructing them to seek out the Pope and demand he send 100 men 'learned in the Christian religion, well versed in the seven arts and skilled to argue and demonstrate plainly to idolaters and those of other persuasions that the Christian religion is better than theirs' along with some of the holy oil from the 'everlasting lamp' in Jerusalem's Church of the Holy Sepulchre.

Upon arriving home three years later (1269), they discovered that the Pope, like Niccolo's wife, was dead. They made arrangements to return to China and decided to take Niccolo's 15-year-old son, **Marco**, with them but they then had to wait for a new Pope to be elected. Their slice of luck was that they picked Acre as their waiting post: not only did this give them easy access to Jerusalem and the holy oil but it also brought them to the attention of **Theobold of Picenza**, an old friend of Thomas Aquinas and Papal legate for the Holy Lands. It was Theobold who won the Papal election and took the name Gregory X, though by this time the Polos had given up hope of the election ever reaching an outcome and had set sail for Ayas, their first port of call.

*Continued on p50*

> ### ❏ Marco Polo
> *(Continued from p49)* They turned back, however, to receive the Pope's blessing and two Dominican friars whom they were to escort to the khan, although these men later fled at the first sign of trouble. It has been suggested that if more friars had been sent, Kublai Khan, whose mother was a Nestorian Christian, might have been converted to Christianity, along with his court and country, thereby changing the face of history; it seems more likely, however, that the khan's request was spurred by the desire for knowledge rather than any religious yearning.
>
> After a number of detours the Polos arrived in the Hunza Valley and from there made their way over the Karakorum Mountains to Kashgar. They went east along the southern Taklamakan route and then, on learning that the khan was at his summer palace, straight up to Shang-Tu (Xanadu, see box p368).
>
> They stayed with him for 17 years, during which time Marco was given several diplomatic posts. Indeed, they were lucky to ever get away as Kublai wanted them to stay: As *The Travels* puts it: 'Time and time again they asked the khan to give them leave to depart, but he was so fond of them and so much enjoyed their company that nothing would induce him to give them leave'. The trio finally escaped by sea, as escorts for a princess who was to be married to Arghun, Khan of the Levant, and made it back to Venice in 1295.
>
> After that things didn't go so well for Marco. In 1298 he was captured by the Genoese at the Battle of Curzola when fighting for his home city-state, Venice, and thrown in jail in Genoa. Here he met Rustichello of Pisa, a famous romance writer of the time who had worked for the likes of Prince Edward of England (later Edward I), and the two embarked on their most famous work. Rustichello's creative input should not be underestimated (think of the work in terms of Shakespeare's *History* plays) and therefore we cannot expect all of Polo's tales to be true. Nevertheless, recent revisionist theories which claim Polo never went to China at all seem to be even more far-fetched. We'll leave the last word to Polo himself who, when asked on his deathbed if his stories had been exaggerated, replied: 'I have not told the half of what I saw'.

ally heralded a massive invasion of European lands it quickly came to denote the attacking soldiers themselves. Another of his sons, Gordan, led raiding parties into the mountains of Tibet.

Genghis's grandsons also prospered: Kublai (son of Gordan) and Mongke both became future supreme khans, while another grandson, Hulegu, took over western Asia and adopted Islam to appease his subjects (receiving the title *Il Khan* and founding his own *Il Khanate* dynasty). Even the Assassins (see p133) were flushed out and defeated in the 1250s, having been accused of murdering one of Hulegu's sons.

The Mongols suffered only one major defeat: it occurred in 1260 against the Mamelukes at Ain Jalut, north of Jerusalem. The Mamelukes were a strange collection of enslaved soldiers who had turned the tables on their masters, the Sultans of Egypt, quite dramatically in 1259 and went on to run those lands and much of the Near East for nearly three hundred years. It should be noted, however, that the Mongol army was seriously depleted before this battle as many officers and soldiers had returned east to elect a new khan, following the death of their leader.

## PAX MONGOLICA

Despite the mayhem they wreaked wherever they went, within the Mongols' territory peace and prosperity flourished for over one hundred years and, as virtually all of the Silk Road fell within the empire's boundaries, the route enjoyed a last 'Hurrah'. It was boasted at this time that the road was now so safe that a young virgin could walk alone from one end of Asia to the other carrying a bar of gold on her head and everything would still arrive intact!

If any young female virgins *had* walked the route at this time, she would have met an incredible array of fellow travellers. Because, for the first time in its existence, it was feasible to traverse the Silk Road in one go. Traders, of course, led the way and the Polos may not have been the only ones to complete the round trip, for merchants from all over Asia and Europe would have desired a share of the fortunes on offer. They were joined by missionaries such as John de Plano Carpini, who was sent from Europe to spread the Christian word, and artists of every description who were keen to show off their talents to potential Mongol paymasters. Nor was it all one way traffic: Kublai Khan sent his own envoys to Europe (Rabban Sauma made it as far as Paris) and hundreds of Muslim pilgrims used many parts of the Silk Road every year whilst on their Haj to Mecca.

## THE END

Nothing can last forever, however, and the end of the Mongols spelt the end of the Silk Road. It didn't happen overnight, but the early 14th century saw Marco Polo (see box pp49-50) languishing in jail and the Chinese overthrowing their Mongol masters in a revolt which heralded the Ming dynasty.

This dynasty has become famous throughout the world because of its vases and other artifacts, though the politics of the period remain unclear. What we do know is that they were taking no more chances with possible invaders from the north or east and much of the Great Wall which we see today was constructed at this time, bigger and stronger than ever.

Many foreigners (including all the Uighur traders) were expelled or driven out and trade through the Tarim Basin dried up. The Il Khanate in Persia also

---

### The Silk Road lives on
The true Silk Road buff, of course, will know that with the advent of the Industrial Revolution mass silk production, like the other textile industries, shifted to northern England – Macclesfield to be precise – and, even today, the Queen's silk buttons (amongst other prize items) are still made in Macclesfield's last remaining silk mill. This side of Macclesfield's history has earned its football team their 'Silkmen' nickname and to commemorate the borough's former glory, the town's new bypass built at the end of 1999 was named 'The Silk Road' with a plaque to prove it (see picture on p1). To join in, take the Manchester Piccadilly train from London Euston and get off two stops before it terminates; come out of Macclesfield station, turn right, go back under the railway bridge and there you are, on the only living Silk Road in the world!

## 52  History – The end

took a xenophobic stance after converting to Islam and even the all-conquering Tamerlane couldn't turn back the clock.

In the 15th century the world's attention shifted to the seas and this led to a revival of the Spice Route, suddenly made all the more viable and profitable by huge leaps forward in naval technology. The fall of Constantinople to the Ottomans in 1453 sounded the death knell for the Silk Road (though the city and the route had long been in decline) and in 1514 the first Portuguese ships sailed into Canton harbour. Trading by sea had its own problems – most notably scurvy and pirates (especially the hundreds of Japanese pirates in the South China Sea) – and the journey still took a year. Nevertheless, the middlemen were removed, along with all the local taxes and charges, and as ships grew in size they could carry far more goods than a camel caravan and enough cannon and weapons to ward off all but the fiercest Blackbeards.

Life struggled on along stretches of the Silk Road and local trade carried on as before but the big caravans of a thousand camels or more were never seen again. The cities that had lit up the world became poor backwaters, occasionally grabbing the headlines (as during The Great Game between British India and Russia in the 19th century and the exploration of the Taklamakan around the same time) but more often disappearing into the sands, or the snows, of time (though as late as the 1930s Cable and French reported seeing 'the old travel road, wide and deeply marked, literally cut to bits by the sharp, nail-studded wheels of countless caravan carts'). The Silk Road was left instead to intrepid travellers, history buffs, archaeologists – and the hippies who used it as their cannabis trail to India in the sixties.

# PART 3: THE MIDDLE EAST

## Facts about the region

### GEOGRAPHICAL BACKGROUND

What actually constitutes the Middle East is an argument that will run and run (see box below) and this guide will do nothing to simplify the debate. The three countries we have included were chosen only because they are on the Silk Road and political practicalities prevented us choosing others.

In Syria, various arms of the Silk Road ran from the Euphrates in the east, through the major trading centres of Palmyra, Damascus, Hama and Aleppo, and on to the Mediterranean coast. While here you will see much of the Syrian Desert, the fertile plains of western Syria and the Jebel Ansariyya mountain range which separates Syria from Lebanon.

In Turkey our route follows the main arm of the Silk Road in Turkey that ran from Istanbul in the west to Mount Ararat in the east. If you take the west-coast detour you will find lots of rocky bays and sandy beaches but otherwise you will be surrounded by Anatolia's rugged, mountainous, almost lunar landscape. This can be just as fascinating, however, and you get to see Mount Ararat's 5137m peak.

In Iran most Silk Road caravans cut across the north of the country and our route does too, predominantly following the southern curve of the Elborz

> **Where am I?**
> The question of where the Middle East begins and ends is a constant headache. Technically the phrase dates back to 1900 and General Sir Thomas Gordon, a British intelligence officer who used the term to cover Persia and Afghanistan. Two years later, a US naval officer, Captain Alfred Mahan, used it to denote not just those two countries, but the Persian/Arabian Gulf and its coasts as well. A series of articles in *The Times* in 1902-03, entitled *The Middle Eastern Question*, pushed the boundaries further to include anywhere to the west of India which might be a threat to the empire (Tibet even came under this umbrella).
>
> In the beginning, there was a 'Near' East and a 'Far' East sandwiching the 'Middle' East but now the term 'Near East' (like that area's other moniker, 'the Levant') is rarely used. After WWI, the Royal Geographical Society proposed using the term to refer to all Arabic-speaking countries (including those in North Africa), plus Turkey; during WWII, Iran and Eritrea were added. President Bush, too, has been typically keen to put his oar in and now talks of a 'greater Middle East', which includes much of Central Asia and the Caucasus.
>
> To be continued....

Mountains whose highest peak is Mount Damavand at 5671m. Most of Iran is an arid desert but if you cross over into the Caspian region you will encounter a wetter and cooler climate. The other detours we outline will take you into the Zagros Mountains and the triangular desert plateau that sits in the middle of the country (roughly pointing south-east towards the Arabian Sea).

## HISTORY

### Prehistory

The Middle East has a strong claim to be the cradle of civilization, with many of its towns and cities having been inhabited for thousands of years. One of the reasons for this was the Fertile Crescent which broadly ran from the Persian Gulf to the Red Sea (see map opposite pp32-3) and gave much of the entire region a different climate from what it has today – to give you an idea, the Pyramids at Giza in Egypt were surrounded by lush gardens when they were built and the area between them and central Cairo was fertile land rather than the desert of today.

The main inhabitants of the Levant (roughly speaking, those countries bordering the eastern Mediterranean) during this early period were the **Amorites** and the **Canaanites**, while to the west the pharaohs continued to rule Egypt as they had done for centuries. At around 1800BC, Abraham is thought to have been born in Ur in Mesopotamia (which means 'The Land between two Rivers' ie the Euphrates and the Tigris) and moved up to Canaan via his old family holdings in Harran (on the Turkish/Syrian border). He then, more famously, set out for Palestine. At around this time, the **Hittites** built up their empire over the entire area, defeating the Egyptians at the **Battle of Kadesh** (on the Orontes River) around 1300BC. Soon after, in about 1250BC, the Greeks went to war with the Trojans as the Hittite empire fell into decline. However, the next major powerhouse were the **Phrygians**, who built an empire centred on their capital at Gordion and whose rulers included King Midas of the famed golden touch (8th century BC), while along the eastern Mediterranean coast the **Phoenicians** were establishing themselves as the prime traders in the region from their string of coastal cities. This period also saw the arrival of the **Philistines** (the ancestors of the Palestinians) on the plains around modern-day Gaza and the Arameans to the north; both were rivals to the extant kingdoms of Judea and Israel.

The 7th century BC saw the rise of the **Medes** in Persia, the **Assyrians** in Egypt and the Levant, and the **Babylonians** in Mesopotamia (Nebuchadnezzar's Hanging Gardens were built in around 590BC), while in 550BC Cyrus the Great became Persia's leader. He was part of the **Achaemenid dynasty** that included Darius I (521-486BC) and Xerxes (486-466BC) and went on to conquer all of Mesopotamia, Egypt, the Levant and Anatolia before finally being defeated by the **Greeks** at Salamis in 480BC. That the Greeks managed to build on this victory over the next century and in turn take over the Achaemenid lands was down to one man: Alexander the Great. He defeated Darius III and stormed through this region and many others, adding each territory to his empire as he went.

But on his death an inevitable fragmentation occurred. The three main dynasties that followed were the **Seleucids** in the Levant, Mesopotamia and Persia, the **Ptolemies** in Egypt and the **Antigonids** in Greece. These dynasties in turn succumbed to internal rivalries and the whole region descended into petty kingdoms and almost continual warfare until the Parthians and the Romans arrived.

The **Parthians**, under their great king, Mithridates (171-138BC), took over what in effect were the old Achaemenid lands between the Euphrates in the west and Afghanistan in the east. (In turn they were overtaken by the Sassanids in the 3rd century AD; see p44.) By 188BC **Rome** had conquered most of Turkey as well as Greece and over the following hundred years they proceeded to take Syria, Palestine and North Africa, concluding with victory over their last main rival, Carthage, in 64/63BC.

## Christianity and Islam

The Jews were expelled from Jerusalem by the Romans after their revolt in 66AD and in 313AD Emperor Constantine adopted Christianity as the state religion. In 395AD the Roman empire split, with Constantinople becoming the more powerful capital. But for most of this period the region's major theme was the war between the Romans (or, after 395AD, the **Byzantines**) and the Sassanids.

This war was still going strong when Mohammed was born in 570AD. By his death, 52 years later in 632AD, he had united the peoples of the Arabian Peninsula behind his new religion, Islam. There was a split when his succession was disputed (see p68) but within a century the victorious Umayyads had conquered Palestine, Egypt and Persia and their empire stretched from the Indus to the Iberian Peninsula (an area larger than that ever controlled by Rome). In 750AD, however, allegations of massive corruption, high-living and despotism led to a wide-scale Shi'ite rebellion and the Abbassids were able to seize control of the Persian territories, setting up a new capital in Baghdad and ushering in an era that provides the backdrop for some of the greatest stories ever told (see box p56).

The Abbassids must also be thanked for much of our European culture as the scholars in Baghdad were encouraged to record the histories of other cultures, not just their own, and these records became invaluable when so many of the European originals were destroyed in the Dark Ages. While the Umayyads were famous for their beautiful mosques and palaces, the Abbassids will be

❏ **Christianity in the East**
Many think of Christianity as a Western religion but, originally at least, it was very much an eastern one. After all, aside from Rome, Christianity's main intellectual and political power bases in its early years were Jerusalem – where the faith was born – Antioch, Alexandria and Constantinople, these five cities being the homes of the religion's five patriarchs. Furthermore, at the Council of Nicea in 325AD, when church leaders hammered out the definitive wording of the Creed, there were more bishops from Persia, Central Asia and India than from Western Europe. Indeed, if it had not been for the split and ultimate breakaway of the Nestorian Church (see box 44), modern-day Christianity would have a completely different outlook.

> **The Thousand and One Nights**
> These tales, many of which are set in Baghdad and Damascus under Haroun al Rashid (caliph from 786 to 809AD), are iconic. The heroes, including Ali Baba, Sinbad and Aladdin, as well as reams upon reams of magic carpet, are introduced by the beautiful Sheherezade as she tries to escape execution by evil King Shahriyar. Exactly which tales make up the 1001 is unclear because many were in fact updated forms of age-old myths and legends and it seems that every scribe who has sat down to record the tales has chosen the ones he liked best. That said, 271 of the most famous tales seem to come up in every collection. But if you are thinking of checking out the tales, you might want to think again – there is a saying that suggests that you will die before you finish them!

remembered for their innumerable intellectual achievements and Baghdad earned the reputation as the 'scholastic capital of the world'.

It could not last, however, and Haroun's son, al Ma'mum, was challenged by his younger brother who had been awarded some of the empire in his own right. Al Ma'mum had the support of the army and they helped him to destroy his brother. But the help came at a price. At the core of the army was a fierce band of Turk mercenaries and when al Ma'mum died, these Turks took it upon themselves to assert even more authority over the new caliph. This trend continued with every succession until the caliph was little more than a political puppet, despite the considerable religious influence he held. In 980AD most of the Levant was ceded to the **Fatimids of Cairo** and in 1038 the Turks decided to end the sham and seize control of the empire outright; their dynasty became known as the **Seljuks**. They pushed the boundaries of the empire out towards the Central Asian steppes where they had originally come from and, in doing so, took control of Afghanistan, the Caucasus and Anatolia.

### The Crusades

This final acquisition was the most significant for the region as it brought about the backlash of the Christian world known as the Crusades. Not that the Christian inhabitants of this area necessarily wanted liberating. In fact, many preferred their new Seljuk overlords because they allowed Christians to keep their religion and did not persecute those who belonged to sects such as the Nestorians and Armenians. Nevertheless, in 1095, in response to pleas from Byzantium, Pope Urban II called on European leaders to gather their armies, march on Jerusalem and regain the Holy Land (a loose term for most of the Levant) from the infidel. The plan was for these Roman Catholic forces to join with the Orthodox forces of Byzantium in order to defeat the Muslims. In reality, however, the two Churches had very different agendas: the Byzantines wanted help only to regain their lands, whilst the European leaders – to whom the Byzantines were as much 'foreigners' as the Muslims – planned to keep any conquered land for themselves. As a result, the alliance was soon shattered.

The Europeans were known as the 'Franks' even though they comprised many nationalities, particularly the Normans of France, England and Sicily and the naval powers of Italy. They enjoyed early success, notably the capture of Jerusalem in 1099, but just how chaotic and fractured the situation had become was demonstrated by the near total massacre of the city's inhabitants, Muslim, Jew and Christian alike. Nevertheless, the Franks went on to establish a kingdom stretching the length of the Mediterranean's east coast. Further Christian successes were achieved by the kings of Georgia who did much to remove the Muslims (mostly Kurds) from the Caucasus.

One of the reasons for the Crusaders' early success is that the Seljuk Sultan, Malik Shah, had died in 1092. This led to the break up of his empire at a time when a strong leader was needed to unite the Muslim world. Worse still, each time one did appear he became the latest victim of the Assassins as they wreaked havoc from their secret hideouts in the mountains (see box p133).

### Islam

Mohammed began preaching his new religion in Mecca in 612AD based on revelations from God (these revelations were later recorded and compiled into Islam's holy book, the **Koran**). In 622AD, however, he and other believers were forced to flee to Medina amid heavy persecution, a flight that is known as the **Hejira**. There he moulded his followers into an army and returned to take Mecca by force in 630AD. They soon took over all of the Arabian Peninsula and within a hundred years Islam's influence stretched from southern Spain to Central Asia. True Muslims are expected to observe the five 'pillars' of Islam:

- *Shahada* Say, understand and believe the *Azan*. This is the Muslim call to prayer and the words are always the same: ' Allah is great! There is no god but Allah, and Mohammed is his prophet'. Traditionally a *muezzin* would climb to the top of one of the mosque's minarets to issue the call but nowadays you will usually hear taped recordings played over loudspeakers.
- *Salat* Pray five times a day (only three times if you are Sh'ite, see box p68): at dawn, noon, mid-afternoon, dusk and after dark.
- *Zakat* Give alms to the poor.
- *Sawm* Keep the fast of *Ramadan* (see box p12).
- *Haj* Make a pilgrimage to **Mecca** once in your life. Mecca, in Saudi Arabia, is Islam's 'capital' and all mosques are designed so that worshippers face Mecca when they pray. The *mihrab* is the niche inside a mosque or room indicating the direction of Mecca.

Islam forbids gambling, the eating of pork and the drinking of alcohol amongst other things. Most Muslims also consider the left hand unclean and will not use it to eat or accept food which has been touched by someone else's left hand. In most Islamic countries women are required to dress modestly and wear the *hejab* ('veil'; this term is also used to describe the custom of 'dressing modestly' as a whole) and in some they are required to wear a *chador* (an all-covering black cloak) and a *burqa* (a mask with a tiny slit for the eyes). Those countries governed completely by the Koran are said to be following *Sharia* law. *Madrassahs* are Islamic universities and *mullahs* are their teachers/leaders (there is no ordained priesthood as such). *Jame* is Arabic for 'Friday' so you will come across many mosques with this title. A *minbar* is the pulpit inside a mosque. *Salaam aleikum* ('Peace be with you') is the universal Muslim greeting; you will also hear *in Sh'Allah* ('God willing').

For Islamic holidays, see box p12.

Finally, in the middle of the 12th century, one leader, Zengi, began a concerted fightback. His son was **Nur ed-Din** who, aided by rulers from within the old Seljuk empire – most importantly the Emir of Damascus – and with a devastating army recruited largely from the newly displaced Kurds, took on the Franks and their Second Crusade of 1146. One of the Kurds was his star General, Shirkuh, and he gained the even bigger prize of Egypt for his master by defeating the Fatimid Caliph there. Upon Shirkuh's death Egypt passed to his nephew, **Saladin**, and the defeated Fatimids had to give up their position as head of the Shi'ite world. All the Muslims in the Middle East were once again united under the Sunni Caliph of Baghdad, even if many Shi'ite believers remained.

Saladin's relationship with Nur ed-Din, however, was, to say the least, strained, for the truth is Saladin wanted power for himself. What's more, the odds favoured the younger man and, sure enough, Saladin was able to outlive Nur ed-Din and usurp his young son's title of Sultan (though the Caliph of Baghdad remained the nominal head of the empire). Having polished off all his other opponents in the Muslim world, Saladin set about reconquering the Frankish kingdoms, which he did in one fell swoop with his victory at the Battle

---

### The Crusader knights
The Crusades gave birth to a series of military Orders whose mission was to champion the faith and protect Christendom from the infidel. The Knights Templar were the only Order to wear the famous red cross on a white background, however, as other Orders wore black or white crosses on a black background.

**Knights Hospitaller** This tradition (also known as the **Knights of Saint John**) began around 1100AD to protect pilgrims visiting Jerusalem after the First Crusade. A hospital run by the Benedictine Order had existed on the site of Saint John the Baptist's monastery since 600AD, and the knights attached themselves to that. They evolved into one of the key fighting forces in the Crusades and held many strategically important lands and castles, notably the Krak Des Chevaliers (see box pp111-13), Margat and Acre. Following the loss of Christian territory in the Holy Land (the knights at Acre were the last to fall in 1291) they retreated to Rhodes, before Suleiman the Magnificent drove them back to Sicily (from where they moved to Malta).

**Knights Templar** This is perhaps the most notorious of the military Orders (they were also known as the **Poor Fellow-Soldiers of Christ and the Temple of Solomon**). It was founded in 1118 to protect the Christian territories in the Holy Lands following the First Crusade. On the instructions of Bernard of Clairvaux, they were incorporated into the Cistercian Order but they quickly developed into a crack fighting force answerable only to the Pope. Like the Knights Hospitaller, they became great landowners both in the Holy Lands and in Europe. They also became key members of the banking world before the Order was dissolved under pressure from the kings of Europe in the 14th century.

**Teutonic Knights** This was a German military Order formed in Acre in the 12th century. They left the Middle East in the 13th century, however, and spent the rest of their time in eastern Europe where they established their own state before being defeated by a combined Polish-Lithuanian army in 1410 at the Battle of Grunwald.

of Hattin in 1187. All the major cities fell to him, including Jerusalem and Acre (which had recently eclipsed Aleppo and Antioch as the favoured destination for Silk Road traffic). Not that he could rest on his laurels, however, as the Pope used the fall of Jerusalem as a rallying cry for the **Third Crusade** which brought together the three great kings of Europe: Richard 'the Lionheart' of England, Philip of France and Barbarossa of Germany.

*Immensely impressive, Krak des Chevaliers (see pp111-13) is the Crusaders' greatest legacy and well worth a short detour off the Silk Road in Syria.*

They didn't take back Jerusalem but they did regain all the key coastal ports. For many involved in the campaign, these ports had always been the true goal anyway (particularly those Crusaders from the Italian states of Venice, Pisa and Genoa) because for them Jerusalem was just another city and not a very rich one at that, whereas the ports gave them access to all the treasures of the Silk Road. Richard withdrew in 1192 and the following year Saladin died.

With the Muslim leader gone, his power structure was replaced by a very unusual group of men: a slave army from Egypt known as the **Mamelukes**. These men gradually chipped away at the Crusaders' territory and, despite – or perhaps because of – the **Fourth Crusade** (which was hijacked by the Venetians and turned against Constantinople) and the Fifth Crusade (which was turned against Alexandria), the Europeans lost most of their land. The Seljuks managed to keep hold of central Anatolia, which became their Sultanate of Rum (see p60). But they, too, were spent as a real force. The region was now in a sorry state with no strong leaders – which was particularly unfortunate as forces were coming from the East which would demolish all but the strongest.

The first to arrive were the **Khorezm** armies who had recently seen their leaders smashed by the Mongols and their empire (in Central Asia and Persia) torn apart. Rather than sit and wait for more punishment, they had fled on a campaign of looting and pillaging which had taken them right across to the Mediterranean coast and, in 1244, to the gates of Jerusalem. Unfortunately for the Khorezm, the Mongols weren't far behind and they soon wiped the Central Asians out. The Mamelukes managed to defeat a small Mongol army at Ain Jalut in 1260 which kept Egypt independent but the rest of the Middle East was quickly brought into the Mongol empire. What was left of the Seljuk army was defeated at Kose Dag in 1243, Syria fell in 1253, and Persia and Baghdad in 1258. Fortunately, the Mongols retreated in 1335 when the Il Khanate ruler, Sultan Abu Said, died leaving no successor and the Mamelukes, under **Baibars** (their greatest sultan), were able to restore some order (the last of the Crusaders had already been driven out by this time, having been forced to flee with the capture of Acre in 1291). Peace was shortlived, however, as **Tamerlane** returned in 1401 to sack Aleppo and Damascus.

There was a new force now emerging in Turkey too...

## The Ottomans

The Ottomans began as a small tribe of mercenary soldiers from Central Asia who offered their services to the Byzantine emperors. However, as one disaster after another befell their employers (especially in its Balkan territories), the Ottoman leaders took control of these lands in lieu of payment for their services. Soon Bulgaria, Serbia and Bosnia lay in their power and they were able to absorb the Seljuks' Sultanate of Rum into their territory as well. Constantinople was now isolated in the middle and it was only a matter of time before it, too, fell. Two or three centuries earlier it had been the biggest city in the Western world with a population of over a quarter of a million people (in comparison with the contemporary cities of Paris and London which both had just over ten thousand) but it had never recovered from the attacks of the Fourth Crusade. Thus, in 1453, it was the walls of a mere shell that Mehmet the Conqueror breached to fulfil the 800-year-old Muslim ambition of seeing the city fall. One of the many consequences of this capitulation was that the age-old techniques employed in the creation of the purple dyes, which had originally been developed by the Phoenicians and later monopolized by the Byzantines, were lost for good. So, too, was the secret behind 'Greek Fire', perhaps the world's first chemical weapon, which had done so much to stave off the Muslims until then.

It didn't all go the Ottomans' way, however: Tamerlane had already defeated them at the Battle of Ankara in 1402 and Persia never fell to their attacks. Nevertheless, they defeated the Mamelukes at Aleppo in 1517 and their Syrian, Palestinian, Egyptian and Western Arabian territories all came under Ottoman control. Furthermore, 1520 saw the arrival on the throne of one **Suleiman** and in 46 years he earned himself the epithet 'the Magnificent', thanks largely to further victories in Europe (he got as far as the gates of Vienna), North Africa and the Arabian Peninsula. Yet Suleiman's reign proved to be the peak of the Ottomans' power and for the next three hundred years they steadily declined through poor leadership and internal wrangling.

The Persians, meanwhile, prospered under the **Safavids** (1502-1736), whose greatest leader was Shah Abbas I (1587-1629), the man behind much of Esfahan's magnificence. He, however, was followed by as many bad rulers as good. The Abbassids were overthrown by **Nadir Shah**, a warmonger in the style of Tamerlane, who in his eleven years of blazing glory invaded Central Asia, Afghanistan and India (where he made off with the Peacock Throne from Delhi). He even attacked Moscow. Unfortunately, the next two dynasties, the Zand and the Ghajar, were ultimately weak and ineffectual. Both dynasties were established by brave, strong founders but they were succeeded by spoiled and lazy descendants who allowed the country to become corrupt and wasteful.

> **Reza Khan**
> The Ghajar dynasty was Iran's worst and, unsurprisingly, its last. During the 19th century, successive shahs sold off many of Persia's resources to finance their lavish lifestyles and the country was slowly strangled by mismanagement and foreign intervention. During WWI both Russia and Britain occupied great areas of land and, in the north-west, Turkey regularly raided across its neighbour's borders. The last straw came in 1920 when the Bolsheviks inspired the west-Caspian region of Gilan to break away and form its own Soviet republic of Kuchuk Khan.
>
> The young Shah Ahmed was powerless to react and it was left to the army general, Reza Khan, to lead the fightback (with a little help from his British friends). He retook Gilan for Persia and rode the wave right into Golestan Palace in what was essentially a bloodless coup. His dream was to drag Persia into the 20th century and many of the reforms he instigated did just that (particularly concerning the status of women in Iran). Unfortunately, another less altruistic dream was to establish himself as the founder of a new dynasty and in 1925 he did just that, too, declaring himself the first shah of the Pahlavi line.
>
> He did much to restrict the power of the religious establishment and promote Western trends and values but he lost as many friends as he gained in the process. In 1941, following one too many outbursts supporting Nazi Germany, he was ousted at the request of both the Russians and the British and was forced into exile in South Africa.

## European domination

European military expansion eventually began around the Mediterranean, especially Egypt, but soon France, England and Russia considered all parts of the Middle East to lie within their 'Spheres of Influence'. Therefore the Ottomans, despite being nominal overlords of the region, found themselves playing an increasingly superficial role, with Tsar Nicholas I even labelling their empire 'The Sick Man of Europe'.

The outbreak of WWI was the Ottomans' last roll of the dice. But by siding with Germany they succeeded only in uniting their three European enemies into an alliance against them. At the end of it all, the Ottoman empire was carved up in 1918 by the French and the English, who divided the empire between themselves. France took Syria and Lebanon whilst England took Palestine, Transjordan, Iraq and Egypt. Only the Arabs of the Peninsula managed to establish independence. This, however, was a long way short of the Arab League they had been promised to rule the entire Middle East. The first foundations for a Jewish heartland were also laid at this time in the Balfour Declaration and the **Sykes-Picot Agreement**, much to the dismay of a certain TE Lawrence who became famous at this time as Lawrence of Arabia and did more than any British officer to champion the cause of the Arabs.

Turkey bounced back, though, under the guidance of its revolutionary hero Atatürk (see box p63). In the same year, another soldier, Reza Khan, overthrew the Ghajar dynasty and re-established much of Persia's independence, changing its name to Iran (derived from *Aryan* which means 'Of noble origin') in 1934.

WWII largely passed the Middle East by, although Egypt and the Suez Canal remained pivotal throughout. The horrific events that took place in the Nazi concentration camps, however, forced the Allied leaders' hand into creating a Jewish homeland in Palestine (the alternative had been an area of land in northern Uganda), almost as compensation for their suffering. Palestinian opposition to this plan was fierce because it was their land that was being sacrificed, not Allied land. The State of Israel came into being in 1948 and almost immediately war broke out between the Arab world on one side and Israel and its Western backers on the other. The problems such a new state was bound to cause (the number of Palestinians who lost their homes and their lands overnight ran into millions) have been with us ever since.

In 1946 Syria gained its independence from France and in 1952 Nasser seized power in Egypt but politics remained dictated by events in Palestine. Nasser was able to out-manoeuvre Britain and France in the Suez Crisis of 1956 but the plan to unite Syria and Egypt into one Arab nation in 1958 failed and a similar plan to unite Egypt, Syria and Iraq in 1963 was aborted. In 1967 Egypt tried to go on the offensive again against Israel but was let down by Syria who failed to mobilize its troops as agreed. The Egyptians were humiliated in six days by devastating attacks from the Israeli air force that wiped out all the Egyptian planes. The result was that Israel took the Sinai Peninsula, the Gaza Strip, the West Bank of the River Jordan, East Jerusalem and the Golan Heights as a buffer around its original territory.

## Modern Turkey

Being the closest Muslim country to Europe, Turkey has always been less fundamentalist than its Arab neighbours and has refused to get involved in the wars against Israel; but it has been far from plain sailing. By the end of the '70s, the whole Near East region was in a state of flux despite the two oil booms which had brought so much wealth – or perhaps it was *because* of it, as the leaders of the oil-rich nations seemed to be living the life of luxury while many of their people and the people of the neighbouring oil-less countries could only look on in envy. Many Palestinians, Egyptians, Jordanians and Syrians had become migrant workers in the oil-rich states. However, it is indicative of Turkey's idiosyncratic position that most of their workers headed for Europe, notably Germany, France and England.

Nevertheless, as tension mounted in the region and the Shah of Iran was toppled by a revolution, so pitched battles broke out in Turkey between left- and right-wing militants. The army moved in and the government was overthrown in 1980. For the next twenty years, despite a return to democracy, Turkey never quite achieved any position with which she was entirely happy. The age-old conflict between her and Greece continued, with Cyprus (divided since the invasions of Greece and Turkey in 1973/4) the main sticking point. There was also increasing tension with the Kurdish minority who, under Ocalan's PKK party, rose up to be a serious force (over 30,000 people died in the fighting), claiming the south-east corner of the country as their own homeland before Ocalan was captured and sentenced to death.

> ### Atatürk
> Mustafa Kemal (1881-1938) was one of the few Turkish generals to come out of WWI with his reputation intact, as he had successfully commanded the defence of the Gallipoli Peninsula. In the aftermath of the war, and with Greece seizing Turkish land, he decided the Ottoman sultans could no longer be trusted to protect the country and set about organizing his own resistance. Together with a group of officers known as The Young Turks, he waged The Turkish War of Independence between 1920 and 1922. He succeeded in expelling the Greeks and renegotiating the humiliating treaties the sultan had been forced to sign in 1918. In 1923 the republic was declared with Kemal as its leader and major reforms were begun. Islam lost its status as the state religion, Arabic was replaced with a Latinized alphabet, Ottoman symbols such as the fez were prohibited and names of towns and cities were Turkified: Constantinople became Istanbul, Smyrna = Izmir, Angora = Ankara, Antioch = Antakya and so on.
>
> In 1935 Kemal was declared Atatürk ('Father Turk') and the legend was complete. Following his death in 1938, the whole country went into mourning and ever since his hero status has continued. You will see countless statues to this great man throughout Turkey and his sayings are regularly repeated. On November 10 at 09.05 the whole country comes to a standstill to commemorate his passing.

The last few years, however, have been dominated by Turkey's desire to join the European Union, a desire that has instigated several major changes. The elections in 2002 brought victory for a previously unknown party, the Islamic Justice and Development Party, led by the ex-mayor of Istanbul, Recep Tayyip Erdogan. In order to qualify for membership his government has significantly improved its human rights record as well as its relationship with Greece and has made concessions to its Kurdish minority. It has also embarked on a massive programme of privatization. Not everybody in the country is happy with the progress though and there seems to be an increasing polarization between the pro-European west of the country and the more traditional and religiously conservative east.

Events in Iraq have also had an impact. Now that the Kurds in northern Iraq have virtual autonomy their cousins in Turkey are again pushing for similar independence. The year 2005 saw a series of bombings aimed at economic infrastructure in the east and, more worryingly for travellers, the tourist industry in Istanbul and on the west coast. The Pope's tour in 2006 went off without incident, however.

## Modern Syria

The mess of '67 ushered new leaders into power in Syria (as it did in Egypt) but their stance was no less confrontational than their predecessors had been. Anwar Sadat was now the man in control of Egypt and in Syria it was the turn of Hafez al Assad. They combined to attack Israel in what is known as the **'Yom Kippur' War** of 1973. For once they had a chance of winning and Egypt crossed the Suez Canal into the Sinai, taking Israel completely by surprise; but again bad leadership let them down. The Egyptians simply couldn't believe it was so easy and, suspecting a trap, they stopped. This gave Israel the chance to see off the Syrian forces in the Golan Heights and then come back down to face the Egyptians. By the end of the conflict, Israel had more land in its possession than at the beginning and the US Secretary of State had to be called in to broker a deal.

Assad managed to hold onto power, however, and before his death in 2000 he set a record as the longest-serving post-independence Syrian leader. He was not particularly liked by the West because for many years he (not so) discreetly backed the Hezbollah in Lebanon which only prolonged that country's plight. Nevertheless, in his last few years he did begin to soften his stance and today even those who never agreed with him politically profess respect. Israel's withdrawal from southern Lebanon in 2000 also eased the situation considerably but it wasn't until 2005 and the murder of Lebanon's former Prime Minister, Rafiq Hariri, that Syria finally withdrew its troops from its neighbour's lands. Much of what happens next to Assad's successor, his son Bashir, depends on the outcome of the investigation into Hariri's death in which Syria's president and his government are allegedly implicated. Syria is also accused of supporting insurgents in Iraq and as events unfold there they are bound to affect the situation in Damascus. In the meantime, Syria remains a heavily militarized country and the Mukhabarat (secret police) are still very active.

### Modern Iran

Just how compliant Mohammed Reza was to his father's downfall we will never know but after the war he pushed out the Russians and, with the help of the British (and their new allies, the Americans), assumed absolute power. This was not always a straightforward process, however, and in 1953 he had to rely on his new 'partners' to squash the proposed nationalization movement led by the parliament's enormously popular prime minister, Mohammad Mossadegh (the first in a long and sorry line of democratically elected leaders toppled by the CIA).

His control, however, slipped during the oil booms of the '70s as he wasted countless millions on US weaponry and jet-setting weekends to Paris. His enemies began to fan the flames of discontent. Thousands of immigrant workers had arrived in Iran and, like the majority of Iranians, many were Shi'ites; Reza's apparent lack of respect for this branch of Islam only worsened the situation. Blinded by his successes in other areas – like his father, he had done much to emancipate women, redistribute land to the poor, dramatically improve the health and education systems of the country and oversee a massive leap towards modern industrialization – he refused to believe his people would turn against him, but in 1978 they did.

A heavy-handed response to popular demonstrations in Tehran, Qom and Tabriz (Reza introduced martial law) only speeded up his downfall and by January 1979 he was forced to flee (although he took as many of his riches as he could with him). The mood was ripe for a religious backlash and, back from exile in Paris, a cleric named Ayatollah Khomeini swept to power on the back of a promise to create a pure Islamic State governed by the Sharia laws of the Koran. His status was almost mythical before he arrived because he had been banished from Iran over ten years previously, first seeking refuge in Turkey,

---

**(Opposite) Syria**: Magnificent Roman ruins at Palmyra (see pp114-17), a key city on the trade route between Baghdad and the Mediterranean coast. It is now a World Heritage Site.

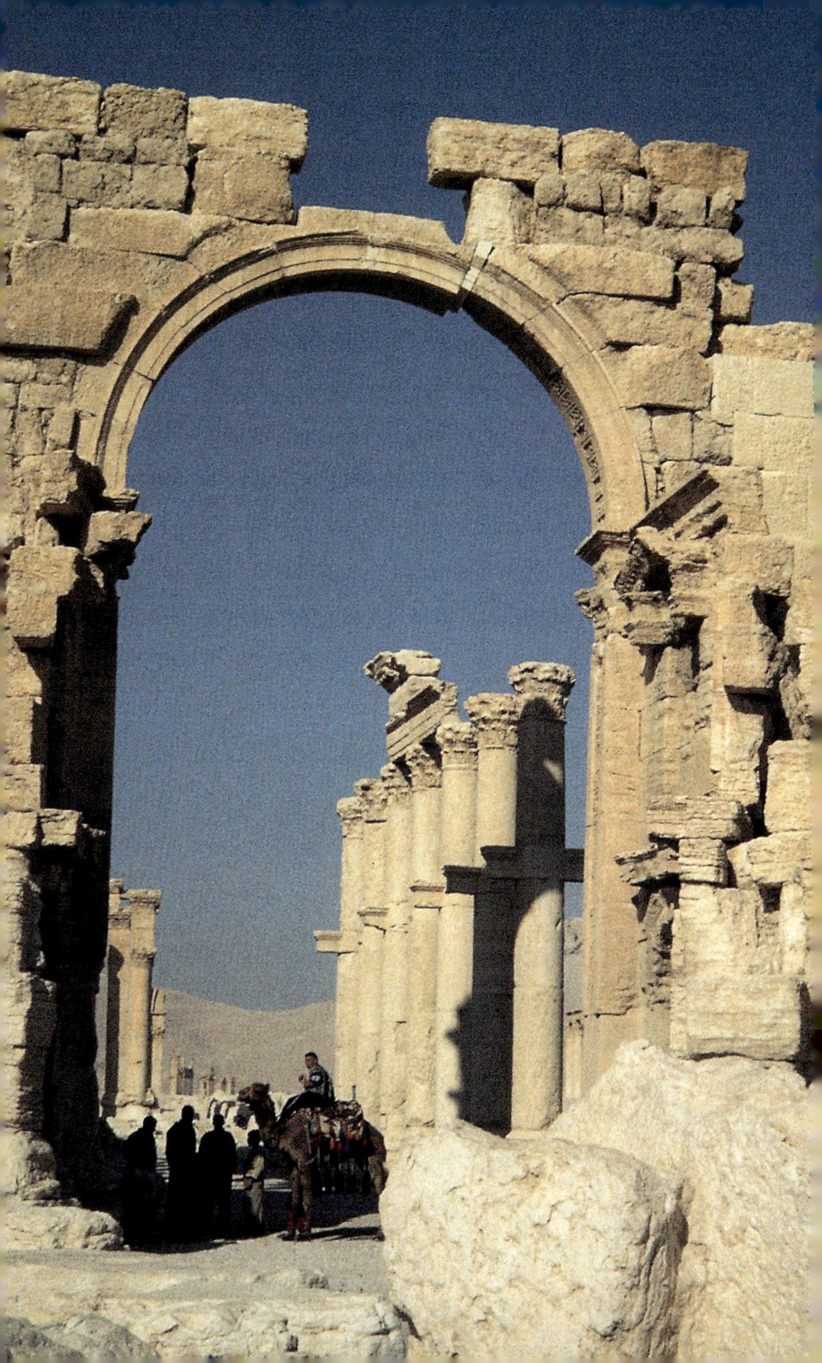

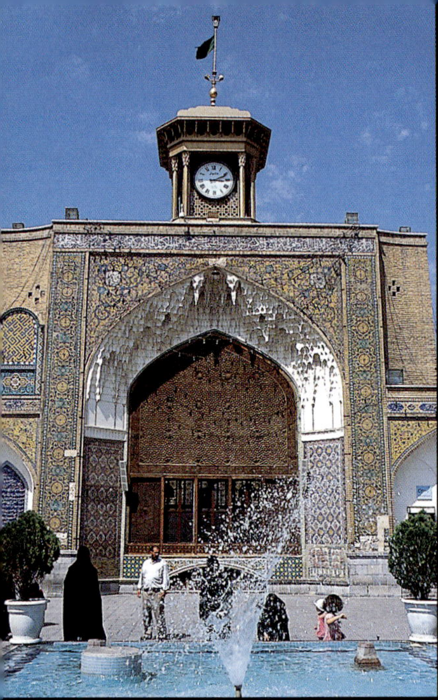
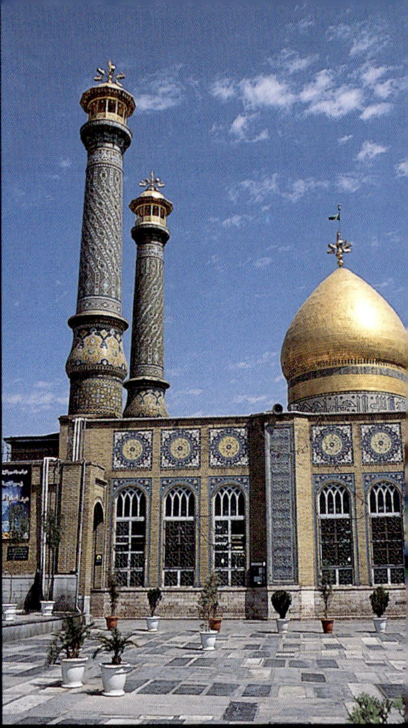
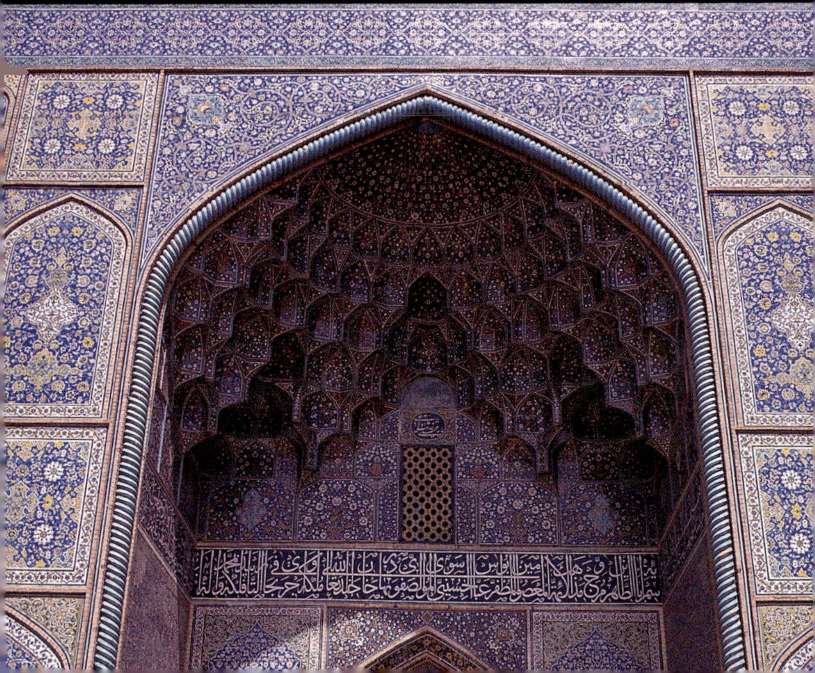

then Iraq, and finally France. If his popularity is to be judged by the millions who welcomed him back into Iran on February 1, 1979, or attended his funeral in 1989, he was the nation's most worshipped hero.

On April 1, 1979, the world's first Islamic Republic was born. This, coupled with the Iran-Iraq War, which broke out in 1980, enabled Khomeini to consolidate his hold on the reins of power and, by ruling with an iron-fist, stamp out any possibility of dissent. The US Embassy was stormed in 1979 (52 hostages were taken for 444 days before being released) amid further allegations of CIA plotting and the war with Iraq continued until 1988. Iran's army bore the brunt of this as its generals made up for their lack of weaponry by pouring more and more men onto the front line; the result was millions of casualties on both sides in trench warfare on a scale not seen since WWI. Few Iranians thought Khomeini was going to lead them so far down the fundamentalist path; fewer still are glad that he did.

Opposition has continued to be ruthlessly suppressed following Khomeini's death and the appointment of Ayatollah Ali Khamenei as his successor. Khamenei maintained the fanatical element in charge of the army and hundreds of newspapers and anti-government groups were closed down and outlawed, whilst many of Iran's leading journalists and political commentators were put in jail. Nevertheless, some progress was made by Hojjat ol Eslam Rafsanjani, surprisingly elected as President in 1989. At the time the post was considered little more than ceremonial but, through years of political brokering, he established enough power to challenge the cleric-run government. The successes of the even more liberal Seyed Mohammed Khatami in the 1997 and 2001 elections were seen as further steps forward but in reality the mullahs were able to block most of his reforms. Lack of progress lead to disillusion, particularly amongst the middle classes, and America's role in Iraq strengthened support for the hardliners.

This combination spelt defeat for Rafsanjani's comeback campaign at the 2005 election, beaten by the former Mayor of Tehran, Mahmoud Ahmadinejad, a supporter of ultra-hardline Ayatollah Mohammed Taghi Mesbah Yazdi. A former Revolutionary Guard commander, Ahmadinejad was involved in the storming of the US Embassy in '79 and to judge by his first years in office, he is dead set on a collision course with his enemies. Labelled part of Bush's 'axis-of-evil', Ahmadinejad has used this tag to unite much of the country if not behind him, then at least against 'the Capitalist Devil'. The country's nuclear ambitions are increasingly a cause for concern, as are its involvement in the Iraq war (where it hopes to see the establishment of a Shia theocracy similar to its own) and Ahmadinejad's call for Israel to be wiped off the map. Nevertheless, talk of the US invading Iran like it did Iraq should be taken with a pinch of salt. We hope.

## THE PEOPLE AND THEIR RELIGION

Islam (see box p57 is the predominant religion throughout this region but it is by no means the only one and there are many theologies, sects and schools.

---

**(Opposite) Iran**: The ornate mausoleum of Shah-e Abdi (**top left and right**), Rey (see p135). Exquisite mosaics on the Sheikh Lotfollah Mosque (**bottom**) in Esfahan (see p143).

## Turkey

Not all 'Turks', of course, live in Turkey. In fact, Turkish is spoken in one form or another by over 150 million people worldwide (from the Balkans to Chinese Turkestan), making it one of the most common languages. Inside the republic, though, most of the 50 million citizens outside the country's south-east corner are ethnic Turks and predominantly Sunni Muslim. However, there are an estimated 12 million Kurds (and virtually no Turks), in the south-east, many of whom want their own independent state (see box below). Few Armenians (see box opposite) still live in the north-east and, during the hostilities with Greece and Cyprus in the '70s, most Greeks/Christians were sent to Greece as part of a mass people swap.

Throughout the country, rural areas are becoming increasingly underpopulated as young Turks head to the big cities or abroad. There's also an increasing

### The Kurds

It is estimated that Kurds have been living in the Near East for well over three thousand years, with their homeland located where the Turkish, Syrian, Iraqi and Iranian borders meet. Nevertheless, they have never had their own state and many have left the region to find a better life. It is estimated that there are over 20 million Kurds in this region today, with over half that number living or taking refuge in Turkey (over one million Iraqi Kurds fled over the border during Saddam's rein). They are Sunni Muslims (unlike most of the Muslims in Iran and, to a large extent, Iraq) which has often added to their 'outsider' image, despite (like the Sikhs in India) being traditionally seen as great warriors and valuable members of many armies.

In 1961, a major campaign was begun to establish an independent Kurdish state in northern Iraq but the movement soon split bitterly between the Patriotic Union of Kurdistan Party and the Kurdistan Democratic Party. Successive Iraqi governments were able to play one side off against the other and thwart any real progress. The situation deteriorated in 1991 when Saddam used the Gulf War as cover to launch further attacks on the Kurds. One good thing that came out of that war, however, was that an almost autonomous region was established for the Kurds with UN protection, which brought with it increased stability and prosperity. In the elections of 2005 the Kurds campaigned for a federal system to be installed in Iraq in order to fortify these gains but their wish to have Mosul included in their territory remained a major sticking point.

In Turkey, the Kurds did not have the right to even call themselves Kurds (on registration forms they were labelled 'Turkish hill-people') and their language was banned in schools and other government institutions. Perhaps unsurprisingly, therefore, their campaign for independence, led by the PKK (the Kurdistan Workers Party), has been bloody and bitter. In the mid-'90s their strongholds, centred on Diyarbakir, posed a major threat to tourism, particularly when PKK members took tourists hostage to draw attention to their struggle. Following the arrest of their leader, Ocalan, in 1999, and certain concessions from the Turkish government, the area returned to an uneasy peace, only to flare up again in 2005.

In Iran, their treatment has been much less prejudiced but if the dream of an independent Kurdistan is ever realized (and a reasonable amount of territory is marked out for it), it is only reasonable to assume that the Iranian Kurds would want themselves and some of their land included, a demand which could cause yet further problems.

The future for the Kurds remains unclear as few Western governments see political or financial gain to be had from openly backing their cause outside of Iraq.

### The Armenians

Armenia has had an eventful history and this is reflected in its people. Originally centred on the southern hills of the Caucasus, it was a small kingdom famed for its merchants. The kingdom often expanded, however, to include parts of present-day Turkey, Azerbaijan and Iran. Indeed, in the 10th century it reached as far as the Mediterranean. Unfortunately, this coincided with the arrival of the Seljuks in Anatolia, who smashed their way through Asia Minor and effectively split the kingdom in two: the northern half became known as Greater Armenia; its southern satellite, centred on the city of Sis (modern-day Kozan), became Lesser Armenia.

The next four centuries witnessed the unusual scenario of Greater Armenia shrinking under increasing foreign pressure while the junior branch of the kingdom (Lesser Armenia, also known as the Kingdom of Cilicia) flourished. In terms of trade, Lesser Armenia could not have been better placed and its first ruler, Prince Reuben, began the trend to maximize the geographical advantage his land had over Greater Armenia. The prince was also quick to adopt European ideas and trends. Later, during the Crusades, Cilicia was an important safe haven on the way to the Holy Lands, while Greater Armenia slipped into anonymity. The Cilicians did a deal with the Mongols through their prince, Bohemond of Antioch, thus hanging on to their lands, and this whole period is regarded as the high point for Armenian art and culture. Today, many manifestations of this golden age can be seen in the lavish Armenian churches spread out across the region.

It was only in the 14th century that the kingdom declined, before disappearing altogether following defeat to the Mamelukes of Egypt. Greater Armenia fared little better, being easily swallowed up by an expanding Russia. The result of all these upheavals was hundreds and thousands of 'homeless' Armenians scattered around the region.

During WWI Armenians in eastern Turkey took advantage of the Ottoman's weak position and rose up in the hope of winning their freedom. They invited Russian forces into the region to consolidate their position and in 1915 an Armenian Republic was proclaimed. In retaliation, the Ottoman government ordered the 'removal' of all Armenians from land still controlled by Turkey and the result was a horrific cycle of massacre and counter-massacre. Armenians claim that between 1.2 and 1.5 million men, women and children died between 1915 and 1923 (those that weren't killed were force-marched to Syria) and want this 'genocide' to be acknowledged. Turks admit many Armenians died but dispute the number (they claim the figure to lie somewhere between 300,000 and 500,000) and claim Armenia refuses to acknowledge the thousands of Turks that were massacred too. What's more, many Turks regard the whole episode as a civil war against 'traitors' rather than a massacre of innocents. With the founding of the Turkish Republic, the country's new leaders also refused to take the blame for the actions of their predecessors.

Following Armenian independence from the USSR, the Turkish/Armenia border area (particularly Mount Ararat) became a subject of dispute once again and few Armenians remain in Turkey today. There is still the odd pocket to be found in Iran, however (see p146).

---

divide between the young, secular urbanites and the older more conservative/religious generation. Nevertheless, Turkey is one of only seven countries which is self-sufficient and the standard of living is rising everywhere. Sitting at the top of this money tree (in what sometimes feels like a world of its own) is Istanbul with its noise, organized chaos and 12 million inhabitants.

## Syria

Syria has over 17 million people and the population is growing fast. Over 90 per cent are Arab but only 80 per cent are Muslim; Christians form a significant minority. The biggest ethnic minorities are the Kurds (see box p66), the Armenians (many of whom fled from Turkey during the massacres of WWI – see box p67), some Turks and an estimated 100,000 Bedouin nomads. Just how many Palestinian refugees there are, however, is almost impossible to calculate because the official figure varies depending on which political institution you consult (some want to exaggerate the figure while others deliberately underestimate).

For a small country, Syria must have one of the most complicated religious mixes in the world. The majority of the population may be Muslim but there are considerable divisions within this group. Alongside the Sunni majority and the usual Shi'ite minority, there are thousands of Ismailis, Druze, Alawites and others. On top of this, the Christian community (about 10 per cent of the total population) is divided amongst Greek Orthodox, Greek Catholic, Roman Catholic, Syrian Orthodox, Armenian Orthodox, Protestant and Maronite. The Jewish population, however, has almost entirely emigrated.

## Iran

Despite losing millions of men during the Iran-Iraq war of the '80s, the population of Iran is still over 70 million and the total is rising fast, with a massive

---

### Shi'ites

Following Mohammed's death in 632AD, Muslims were divided over who should succeed him as leader of the Islamic world. The majority backed the prophet's closest companion and father-in-law, Abu Bakr (his daughter Ayesha was Mohammed's second wife), rather than Mohammed's cousin and son-in-law, Ali (married to Fatima, daughter to Mohammed by his first wife, Kadijah – Shi'ites don't recognize his later wives including Ayesha). Abu Bakr's supporters became known as Sunni Muslims, whilst Ali's followers became known as Shi'ites. Abu Bakr triumphed but his becoming caliph did little to settle the dispute as Ali continued to press his claim, eventually becoming the fourth caliph in 656AD. His assassination five years later drove the wedge deeper and his sons, Hassan and Hussein, were forced to flee. Tensions continued to mount and in 680AD came to a head at the Battle of Karbala. Here, Hussein's death (or martyrdom, depending on your point of view) at the hands of the Sunni Caliph's troops split the sides permanently.

Shi'ites believe that, starting with Ali, there have been (or will be) twelve *imams* or leaders, the most important others being Hussein, Ali's second son and third imam (Ali's first son, Hassan, was the second imam but he died in exile), and Reza, the eighth imam. Reza is said to have disappeared into a cave under a mosque in Smarra in Iraq in 878AD, and is waiting to return as the twelfth imam, the ***Mahdi*** (hidden leader). The Mahdi will guide the world to peace and true happiness. Shi'ism dictates that only the imams can interpret the Koran with the mullahs acting as their representatives until the Mahdi returns. Ayatollah Khomeini was given the honorary title of imam on his death. Shi'ism's mourning ceremonies are unique within Islam. Look out for Ashura, which commemorates the death of Hussein on the ninth and tenth days of the Islamic lunar month of Muharram (the first month in the Islamic lunar calendar).

proportion under the age of 21. More than 14 million people now live in Tehran because hundreds of thousands of the rural population have been migrating here for decades, causing chronic urbanization. Thousands more have left Iran altogether and although some are slowly coming back, many, many more are waiting to emigrate as the massive gap between rich and poor grows ever wider.

Over 60 per cent of Iranians are ethnic Persians and descendants of the Aryans, an Indo-European people who settled here 4000 years ago. The other big ethnic group is the Azari (25 per cent), known as 'Turks', who live in the north-western wedge of the country between Turkey, Iraq, the Caucasus and the Caspian Sea. They have many ties with Azerbaijan and have occasionally sought out independence but as Shi'ites they now integrate well with the rest of the country. Alongside the Azari in this region are the Kurds (10 per cent). The number of Turkmen (2 per cent) in the north-east of the country is also significant, as are the thousands of semi-nomadic Baluchi in the south-eastern province of Baluchistan (the original region known as Baluchistan was twice the size but it was split between Iran and the British during the 'Great Game', with the British half now belonging to Pakistan); they consider themselves independent and tend to operate as a law unto themselves.

Virtually all Persians and Azari are Shi'ite Muslims, although all the other minorities tend to be Sunni. Sunni numbers have been swelled by Pakistanis, Sri Lankans and Arabs of various nationalities who have come to the Gulf to seek work (although these numbers are small compared to the number of immigrants in the other Gulf states). Non-Muslims are very rare in Iran, however there are occasional Armenian and Zoroastrian communities. Despite strong historical ties (see p118), virtually the entire Jewish population emigrated following the Revolution.

# Practical information for the visitor

## THE ROUTE

The options for following the Silk Road in the Middle East are endless. This book starts in Istanbul before moving on to explore the various Silk Roads in Anatolia and the Syrian Desert, though any number of ancient Mediterranean ports would have been just as appropriate starting points for your trip. The important part is that you physically touch the Mediterranean Sea at some stage before heading east and thus allow yourself the opportunity to cross Asia 'coast to coast'.

Ideally, the best route from a historical point of view would take you from Syria to Iran via Baghdad, which was so important to the Silk Road for so long, before travelling along the banks of the Euphrates and Tigris rivers (similarly prominent Silk Road landmarks). Unfortunately, this is of course currently impossible. Our route, therefore, crosses Turkey diagonally, loops through Syria and then heads north-east to the Iranian border.

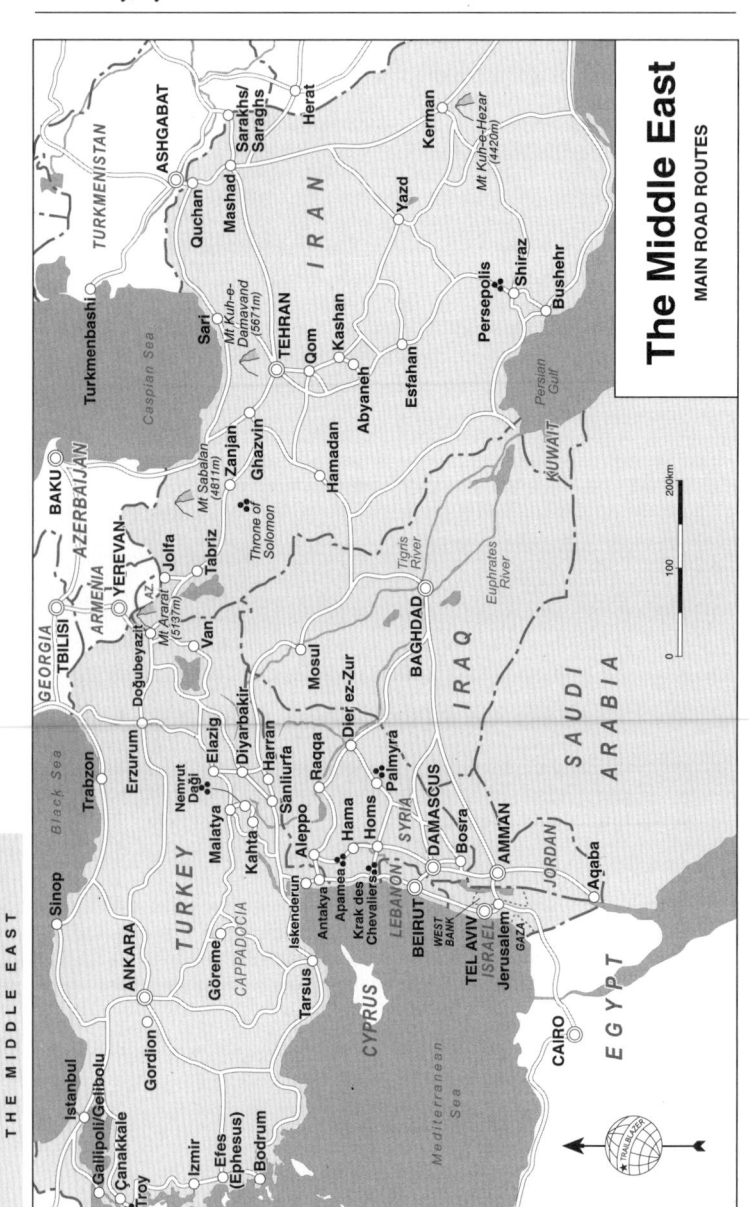

# 70 Turkey, Syria and Iran – Practical information

From Mount Ararat, the journey across the north of Iran is quite straightforward. When you reach Tehran, you can cut north through the Elborz Mountains (through a pass known as the Caspian Gates) to the shores of the Caspian Sea, or carry on straight for the holy city of Mashad. Note, however, that not all Silk Road routes stuck to the north. In particular, a number of cities in central Iran became important trading centres and these are also included in our guide.

If you want to miss out Central Asia altogether, you can make your way to Pakistan from Shiraz and rejoin this guide at Islamabad (see p274).

From Mashad, one branch of the Silk Road carried on east through Afghanistan (see box p10) but the political situation there and the country's roads (or lack of them) made this impractical if not impossible at the time of writing. Our route, therefore, takes you into the heart of Central Asia, which was just as popular a choice for Silk Road traders, and in Turkmenistan merchants would meet up with others who had come from Tehran via the Caspian.

## DOCUMENTS

See pp15-18 for details about **visa requirements**. Overland visitors are neither Syria's nor Iran's favourite type of tourist but the rules and regulations are quite straightforward once you have entered each country. In Syria you will be given an **entry card** – keep this as you will need it for visa extensions and also when leaving the country.

Some hotels might take your **passport** when you check in to save waking you if there are any police checks but don't forget to pick it up in the morning! The Middle East is where you will make your biggest savings if you have a **student card** as it will halve nearly every entrance fee.

### Customs declaration form

The old rules, which meant you had to enter and leave these countries via the same airport or border crossing, have been scrapped. Passing through customs is now a simple procedure, although you may be asked if you have bought any large handicrafts (particularly rugs) when leaving Iran. If an item is very expensive they will tax you for it but otherwise don't let them bully you as it is legal to take out two rugs and 150g of gold.

It is, however, illegal to export antiques from any of these countries without government permission. It is also illegal to take alcohol into Iran. You may need to fill in a declaration form or a disembarkation form when entering each country, in which case, keep it until you leave.

## CLIMATE

All three countries are very hot and dry through the summer; indeed, just how dry is a cause for concern because global warming seems to be having a particularly acute effect. Many dams have also been built in eastern Turkey as part of a programme to revitalize farming in this region but this has lead to increasing aridity downstream, particularly in Syria and Iraq. Eastern Turkey and northern Iran have the advantage of being at a higher altitude, which lessens the ferocity

## Temperature charts – max/min °C centigrade

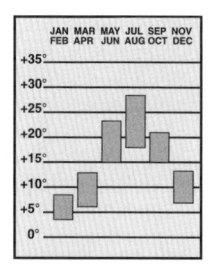

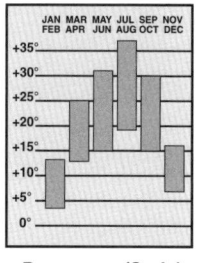

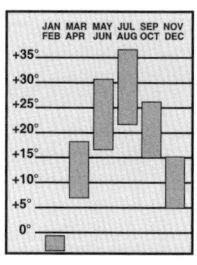

**Iskenderum (Turkey)**    **Damascus (Syria)**    **Tehran (Iran)**

of the heat. In the winter, these same altitudes mean considerable wind, rain and snow (skiing is on the increase here!). Autumn and spring are both very pleasant all over but the Caspian and Black Sea regions can be pretty wet.

## ACCOMMODATION

### Turkey

Turkey has got by far the most sophisticated network of hotels of these three countries but don't expect as many options in the east as you will find in Istanbul or the tourist resorts on the coast.

At the bottom end there are cheap and friendly backpacker hostels in most places (breakfast and free Internet are sometimes included and are worth haggling for) and camping is often (but certainly not always) an option (see box opposite). Things can get really busy in summer so you might want to book ahead (especially in Istanbul). The mid-range is in short supply but what there is gets good reports. The top-flight is really catered for only in the tourist resorts and the capital. If you do want to stay in this type of accommodation it is worth booking beforehand through a travel agent back home or one of the various Internet agents – they always get better deals than individuals and sometimes the savings can be substantial, particularly out of season. Type 'cheap hotels' alongside the city name into any search engine and all the main players should come up.

### Syria

Syria has increasingly good accommodation and all sizes of wallet are catered for, although camping is not really an option.

The budget end is cheap and cheerful and reminiscent of Egypt's budget options although, be warned, there are not as many of them here so you may find you need to book a day or two in advance. Single travellers should find plenty of dorm-bed options to keep their costs down.

The mid-range is probably the weakest area, so you may well find yourself in the most expensive budget option or the cheapest upper-range. At the top end you might be surprised to learn that Syria has its own four- and five-star chain

– the **Cham Palaces** – which covers all the main cities and sights. While they may not compare to many Hyatts and Sheratons around the world, they are a better choice than their Western-owned rivals here.

## Iran

Hotel prices in Iran are set by the government and have gone up quite dramatically in the last few years. Despite a drop in the number of foreign visitors recently, this trend shows no sign of abating. Nevertheless, you still couldn't call the accommodation on offer expensive.

Like eastern Turkey, Iran's budget options, particularly dormitories, are aimed at the local market rather than backpackers (and often refuse foreigners because of this) but this is slowly changing. The mid-range tends to be dominated by hotels that were once top of the range but since the Revolution have deteriorated rapidly. The new high-class hotels springing up, however, are impressive and (outside Tehran) not too pricey.

One thing you might encounter in your hotel room is a large cloth wrapped around a small, round soapstone. The cloth is in fact a prayer mat and Shi'ites place the small stone on the ground in front of them whilst praying so that their forehead will not touch the potentially 'unclean' ground. There will often be a *mihrab* (see box p57) signalling the direction of Mecca.

---

### Camping on the Silk Road

Camping has yet to really take off along this route. Some locals do it but it tends to be an impromptu affair so campsites are few and far between – if they exist at all. Most Silk Roadsters, therefore, see little point in lugging all the necessary gear around just for a few nights (unless they are cycling, see p157, or have their own vehicle, see box p74). If you are planning on trekking, see box p265.

**Middle East** Turkey is the most advanced, camping-wise, so we have listed the odd campsite and, in the countryside, you can often pull off at the side of the road and pitch your tent without too much trouble. Syria and Iran are far less accommodating and camping without permission could cause problems.

**Central Asia** Camping is not an option in Turkmenistan but the landscape in Kyrgyzstan is a camper's dream. There are no organized campsites as such but many hostels will let you camp in their grounds and you will see lots of yurts pitched around lakes up in the mountains. In the Uzbek countryside you can often pull off at the side of the road and pitch your tent without too much trouble, though after recent events in the Ferghana Valley campers there should be cautious.

**China** Camping in the mountains of Xinjiang can be as rewarding as in Kyrgyzstan but elsewhere it is not really an option.

**Pakistan** This is definitely the best country on the route for camping. There are campsites in all the trekking areas and most guesthouses along the KKH will let you pitch your tent in their grounds. Camping gear is also available to hire/buy cheaply in Pakistan (see the 'Orientation and services' sections in that chapter), so readers wanting to give it a go might find it simpler to pick up what they need *in situ*.

## TRANSPORT
### Buses
The road networks in all these countries are impressive, even if the driving skills aren't, and you will find yourself almost entirely reliant on four wheels to travel from one stop to the next. Bus services between towns and cities are regular and cheap and you shouldn't find yourself with too many problems. The quality of buses varies: in Turkey all are modern and efficient (with air-conditioning), while in Syria and Iran such buses exist but you must pay a premium. Bus stations ('*otogars*' in Turkey) can be some way out of town and finding the right local bus to take you into the centre (like deciphering which local bus to take around town) can be difficult.

In Syria, **minibuses** and **microbuses** run alongside most bus routes and can often be quicker and cheaper (if less comfortable).

### Taxis and share-taxis
Taxis are cheap in all these countries and although most towns are small enough to walk around you will probably prefer to take a taxi rather than a local bus for the longer hikes. Share-taxis (*savaris* in Iran) are cars or, occasionally, minibuses which race around/between towns and cities, often duplicating the bus service routes and charging only a little extra.

---

**Driving the Silk Road**
Since 1907 and the great Peking to Paris Raid (see p26), drivers have always considered driving across Asia to be the ultimate challenge. Every year new enthusiasts try (with varying degrees of success) to emulate their heroes but, realistically, driving the Silk Road is not the most practical option.

Bringing your own **vehicle/motorbike** into any single Silk Road country is not too difficult, except for China where it is impossible for standard foreign visitors. Few will entertain this option, however, because the red tape/bureaucracy/costs for entering so many countries on one trip can be overwhelming. Insurance, driving permits, spare parts, repairs and bootleg petrol are the major concerns and many drivers come unstuck. The other major problem is that with most **carnet de passage en douane** insurance schemes, you must pay a large bond (often the resale value of the vehicle) and promise to take your vehicle/motorbike *out* of every country you enter. This means you can neither sell nor dump the vehicle along the way without forfeiting the bond which, in effect, **forces you to drive *back* to your home country** or pay the penalty for breaking the agreement.

Those still keen should consult their national motoring organization for advice (there are also a number of national touring and automobile clubs along the way) and take a car/motorbike they know inside out. You might also consider contacting fellow drivers on the Internet for tips. There is no Silk Road Rally yet despite various attempts to get one off the ground but the Mongol Rally (🖥 www.mongolrally.com) is an annual three-week fun 'race' for amateurs rather than professionals that runs from London to Ulan Bataar and often covers many of the cities on our route. Those on a motorbike might want to contact 🖥 www.globeriders.com, who organize a month-long Silk Road Ride.

For more information on **motorbiking** in Asia see *Adventure Motorcycling Handbook* (see p383), also from Trailblazer. For **Cycling the Silk Road**, see box p157.

> ❑ **The Paykan**
> This Hillman Hunter derivative is an Iranian phenomenon. Up until recently it was almost the only car on the road and even today your taxi is still likely to be one. Unfortunately, it is also one of the worst pollutants on four wheels and despite promises by the government to improve their efficiency/stop making the car altogether, they look set to belch out toxic fumes for many years to come.

### Cars and motorbikes

**Car hire** is not a problem in these countries: Hertz is represented by the Cham Palace group in Syria, Turkey has many of the European networks and Tehran has a couple of outlets. Few will want to use this mode of travel, however, because it is expensive and you usually have to return to your start point to drop the car off. Driving your **own vehicle** (see box opposite) is possible but can be difficult: once off the beaten track, especially in the desert areas, you would be struggling without a four-wheel drive. **Hitching** is not very common in the Middle East (see 'Hitching the Silk Road', p181).

### Train

Theoretically you could do much of this section of the trip by train (see 'Silk Road by Rail', pp8-9) but in reality trains are now used mainly for goods transportation because the passenger service has become so slow and unreliable. For example, the train from Istanbul to Lake Van takes almost two days whereas the bus takes only 24 hours. Nevertheless, the express train between Istanbul and Ankara is excellent and in Iran the line between Tehran and Sari is an engineering marvel.

### Air

The distances between stops in Syria and Turkey are so small that they make air travel as unnecessary as they are undesirable for this land-based trip but in Iran, especially if you are taking the side trips to Esfahan and Shiraz, you should seriously consider flying. Iran Air has a cheap and efficient internal service linking all its major cities, although it must be said its recent safety record is not great. Bookings can be made at any of the travel agencies we have listed.

## TRAVEL AGENCIES AND TOURIST INFORMATION

Turkey has lots of independent tours and tour guides and your hotel should have plenty of brochures and details. Out of season, though, things do dry up, especially in the east. Travel agencies in Syria and Iran tend to be similar to package-holiday agents in the West and they are usually of little use to independent travellers. They can be invaluable in helping with your visa requirements, though, so we have included some of the better ones in the Damascus and Tehran 'Orientation and services' sections. Tourist information offices are not always very helpful (Tehran hasn't even got one!) but the situation is improving.

## ELECTRICITY

Mains electricity supply in these countries is 220V and virtually all sockets take the round two-pin plugs.

## TIME

Syria and Turkey are two hours ahead of GMT and Iran is an unusual $3^1/_2$ hours ahead of GMT. Each country operates the daylight saving system.

## MONEY

In Syria and Iran you will witness the annoying habit of dual-pricing goods and entrance fees with one rate for locals, the other for foreign visitors. There is little you can do except haggle for your life, which can become very tiring and doesn't always have the desired effect.

### Turkey

Financially, you can treat Turkey like any other European country. It has all the facilities you'll need. You can change money and **travellers' cheques** in any bank and most **credit/debit cards** work in most ATMs. The black market is therefore redundant and Turkey is pretty cheap.

The major development to note is that 2005 saw the old Turkish lira (TL) replaced with the new Turkish lira (YTL). This should bring much-needed stability to the currency as part of the country's push for EU membership but it also means that you no longer become an instant 'millionaire' every time you make a withdrawal. There are 1YTL coins; notes come in denominations of 5, 10, 25, 50, 100 and 500.

### Syria

Syrian pound notes (S£) come in denominations of 5, 10, 25, 50, 100 and 500. Syria is a difficult country in financial terms, however, because the Commercial Bank of Syria (CBS) has few links with the outside world and you will have to wait until you arrive in the country to change your money into Syrian pounds; the **US dollar** is by far the most accepted foreign currency and there are plenty of private and CBS exchanges in most towns. Inside Syria it is very difficult to exchange Syrian pounds for any foreign currency.

**Travellers' cheques** are now welcome – both at CBS branches and in top hotels – but advances on **credit/debit cards** are difficult and expensive: the CBS can't help so you must negotiate with hotels/shops that accept Visa/MasterCard (they will charge a hefty commission). There is an ATM at the airport and in the Damascus Cham Palace but you can withdraw money only from certain foreign savings accounts. The **black market** is not worth the hassle as it offers only the same as the official exchanges.

### Iran

Iran's currency is the Iranian rial but many Iranians work in *tomans* which is slang for 10rials. There are coins for the small values but you will mainly deal in 100, 200, 500, 1000, 5000 and 10,000 rial notes. Cash advances are unavailable on **credit/debit cards** as Visa and MasterCard are not accepted in Iran. **Travellers' cheques** can be changed at the main Bank Melli branches but you're unlikely to get a favourable exchange rate.

It is, therefore, best to have a large supply of **US dollar bills** but be careful to check your exchange rate. The banks' official exchange rates are slightly lower than those available from the money exchange kiosks in the street.

Finally, remember to have enough US dollars in cash to last your **entire stay** in Iran!

### ❑ Exchange rates

| | Syria (pound) | Turkey (lira) | Iran (rial) |
|---|---|---|---|
| US$1 | 46.43 | 1.43 | 9248.25 |
| €1 | 60.26 | 1.85 | 11,925.83 |
| £1 | 91.48 | 2.80 | 18,097.13 |
| Can$1 | 39.40 | 1.21 | 7835.05 |
| Aus$1 | 36.10 | 1.11 | 7143.01 |
| NZ$1 | 32.49 | 0.99 | 6412.30 |

For the latest rates of exchange visit:
- www.oanda.com/convert/classic
- www.xe.net/currency
- www.exchangerate.com

## Tipping
Demanding a tip (*baksheesh*) is like a religion in Syria but Iran and Turkey are relatively easygoing and you should tip as you would back home.

## COMMUNICATIONS
Where this region is particularly divided is in its communications.

### Turkey
Most of Turkey cannot wait to catch up with the future and even in the more conservative eastern provinces the **Internet** has had a massive impact with Internet cafés springing up in every town. The **post** and **telephone** networks in Turkey are as good as most European countries and privatization should bring the exorbitant cost of international calls down (Internet cafés often offer cheaper international rates). Most international GSM networks have coverage in Turkey and mobiles are everywhere.

### Syria
In Syria, by contrast, the **Internet** was frowned upon until the arrival of Bashir Assad in 2000. That year saw the country finally open its doors to cyberspace but few locals can afford to log on (it typically costs US$2/hr). Internet cafés are becoming more commonplace but downloading is slow and access is heavily monitored/censored.

❑ **Telephone access codes**
Turkey ☏ +90  Syria ☏ +963  Iran ☏ +98.
See individual 'Orientation and services' sections for local codes.

Both the **postal** and **telephone** services are notoriously slow but the introduction of phonecards (available at most shops) has helped enormously; be careful, though, for each card works only on its own phones and **can't be used in the next town**. Mobile phones are on the increase and most international GSM networks have coverage in the big cities.

Syria has a daily English-language newspaper, the ***Syria Times***, but like its Arabic counterparts it is heavily censored.

### Iran

Iran has taken a similar, if less draconian, approach to that of Syria. The **Internet** is legal but as many cafés seem to close down as open up, mainly because many religious clerics see the whole network as American propaganda and put pressure on the government to prevent access becoming too widespread. Having said that, you should find at least one outlet in each town.

Iran has a good **postal service** and a much improved **telephone system**. Mobile phones are extremely popular but international GSM networks don't yet cover Iran. International calls are relatively cheap (particularly from an Internet café) and domestic calls cost almost nothing.

## NATIONAL HOLIDAYS

The main holidays in this region are the Islamic festivals (see box p12) but there are national holidays too. Finding a room at these times can be tough, expensive or both.

**Turkey**: The Kurban Bayrami festival lasts for a week in February/March, April 23 is National Sovereignty Day, August 30 is Victory Day, October 29 is Republic Day, November 10 commemorates Atatürk's death (see box p63) and December 10-17 is the Mevlana Festival.

**Syria**: 'Commemoration of the Revolution' (March 8), Commemoration of Independence' (April 17) and Martyrs' Day (May 6) are the main secular holidays. There is a **Silk Road Festival** held every year in late September, when Damascus, Aleppo and Palmyra host events along with other cities.

**Iran**: February 11 is the anniversary of Khomeini's rise to power, March 20 is Oil Nationalization Day, April 1 is Islamic Republic Day, June 4 is the anniversary of Emam Khomeini's death and September 8 is the Day of the Martyrs of the Revolution. There are also various other Shi'ite festivals which move around the calendar and Iran has its own Persian calendar with *its* own festivals, most notably *No Ruz* (New Year), which begins on the spring equinox.

## CUSTOMS AND ATTITUDES

**Turkey** is very open and you will receive a warm welcome wherever you go, although eastern Turkey is home to some of the strongest fundamentalist voices in the country and you should act accordingly. Many there call for the law to be changed to bring back the veil and certainly if you come here in Ramadan (see box p12) you will notice a much stricter observance of Islamic law than in the rest of the country. As a visitor passing through at any other time, however, the only difference that you are likely to notice is that here more women wear headscarves (though foreign visitors are not expected to).

English is widely spoken and Western pop music adored (the naffer the better) but men should swat up on their football as it will occupy ninety per cent of all their conversations with locals. Women are usually ignored in football conversations and, unfortunately, this is indicative of many Turkish men's attitude to women. You may also be propositioned or harassed in some of the more touristy areas. Finally, don't forget you are passing close to the Kurdish heartland of south-east Turkey and if that situation does turn violent once again, beware, as foreign visitors have been prime hostage targets in the past.

As for **Syria**, while the Syrian government may not be very popular with its Western counterparts at the moment, the Syrians themselves (like their Lebanese neighbours) have always been considered the friendliest and most welcoming of the Arab nations. Through centuries of extensive trade and travel they have developed a broad understanding of the rest of the world and you will rarely feel ill at ease in this country. There is a massive military presence, however, which can take a bit of getting used to. English is quite widely spoken as is French, although an understanding of Arabic, of course, will help.

**Iran**, like Syria, has a very bad reputation in the West but, again like Syria, the Iranian people have always been known for their friendliness and generosity. Most Iranians are well educated (chess is the national pastime) and the high level of sophistication amongst the middle class under the late Shah has largely survived the Revolution. The fundamentalists still hold much of the power and the army takes a firm anti-Western stance but you will not experience any open hostility as long as you operate within the expectations of an Islamic society, especially regarding their dress code (see box p19), and steer clear of any 'political' events or gatherings. Women will find Iran quite hassle-free, apart from the obvious clothing restrictions and the fact that women are not expected to make eye contact with men; if you do you may well find them all staring at you.

Despite the total ban on alcohol, many Iranians drink and in the big cities a clandestine network allows locals to order beer as we would pizza (the Armenians brew a rough vodka for domestic consumption but most drinks are smuggled into the country from Turkey and Central Asia). Visitors will have little opportunity, however, and anyone caught drinking can get into serious trouble. Recreational and hardcore drugs are an increasingly virulent problem with the vast majority of Iran's estimated one million addicts living in the capital.

Many of the Iranians you meet will speak English and nearly all of them go out of their way to help you and be friendly.

## FOOD

These three countries have some of the best and most famous food in the Middle East and few people, even vegetarians, come away hungry, although you will have to spend a bit more money than you might expect if you are to sample the full range of dishes on offer. Almost all the food you eat will be locally produced; Turkey is one of only seven countries in the world that is entirely self-sufficient.

**Street food** is everywhere and, as often as not, it centres around kebabs (also called *shwarmas*), meatballs (*kofte*) and grilled meats, although the meat in these countries can range from the sublime to the fatty ridiculous. *Falafel* (balls of fried, spicy, mashed chickpeas) are also popular. Pizza (*pide*) is also very popular, particularly in Iran.

The restaurant favourite is ***mezze***, which can be a starter or a banquet depending on how many snack-type dishes you order in your 'mix'. Staple dishes include hoummos, tabbouleh, mini cheese-and-spinach pasties (*borek*), fried chicken livers, olives, stuffed vegetables (*dolme*) such as aubergines or peppers, *shinklish* (a devastating cheese), pancakes (*golzeme*) and lots of fresh salad. Most people fall for mezze in a big way as there is something for everyone.

Most **bread** is flat bread, freshly baked that day. Along with the fresh fruit and vegetables it usually tastes far superior to your local supermarket's offerings at home. In Turkey a particularly popular type of bread is the *simit*; this looks a bit like a bagel but is bigger and covered in sesame seeds. Breakfast usually consists of bread, cheese and honey.

In eastern Turkey and western Iran there are a lot of **stews and hotpots** (especially outside the hottest summer months), which make a welcome change, and as you get further into Iran the food changes again. You might not be able to afford the caviare (which is now generally regarded as being as good as its Russian cousin because the southern half of the Caspian Sea is less polluted; caviare from the beluga – white – sturgeon is considered to be the best) but fish should play a big part in your diet, as will rice and soup.

The Middle East caters for some of the sweetest teeth in the world and the choice of **pastries**, biscuits and sugared delicacies has ruined many a good figure and quite a few sets of molars over the years. The choice is endless; simply go to a sweet shop or stall (they are all over the place and are almost sacred) and have a taste of a few of the treats on offer before you buy.

## DRINK

### Non-alcoholic drinks

In Iranian and many other restaurants the only drinks on the menu are non alcoholic. **Coffee** is king and strong-coffee lovers will be in heaven. Almost everybody takes sugar; many place a sugar cube or wafer in their mouth first and then sip. Each country has pleasant variations of flavoured coffees (cardamom is very popular) as well, so enjoy. If coffee is king, **tea** is queen and although Lipton is making inroads here as much as anywhere, green tea is still the favourite and, like coffee, it will often come in a variety of flavours.

Decent **fruit juices** are available and will often be freshly squeezed but check before you order. **Milkshakes** can be equally delicious. All the **soft drinks** you can think of are here (mostly local brands although international brands are represented too) and once you have tried Iran's non-alcoholic beer you will be glad to return to them.

## Alcoholic drinks
You won't experience many hangovers in Iran (see p129) but beer and spirits *are* available in Syria and Turkey. There are quite a few breweries in the region but the dominant brand is the Turkish Efes. You will come across local wine in Turkey, too, which isn't that bad (Sarafin is a brand worth looking out for) and, surprisingly, you could even be offered a secretive glass around Shiraz in Iran where the art of wine-making is not quite dead (Shiraz vines are thought to have been first taken to France during the Crusades).

Local Armenians brew illicit vodka in Iran and Efes beer is regularly smuggled into the country from Turkey but both are best avoided as the risks/punishments involved are too great.

# Istanbul

If you are beginning your trip in Istanbul and have never been here before you are in for a treat. Yes it's mad and yes it's bad (particularly the traffic congestion) but as Napoleon said: 'If only one state existed on earth, Istanbul would be its capital'. It is one of the few cities in the world that can rightly claim to have something for everyone and you should prepare for a mesmerizing assault on all your senses.

## HISTORY

In Silk Road terms, Istanbul was something of a late developer, although for many it has come to symbolize the route's western terminus.

### The Byzantine Empire
The original city was founded by a group of Greek colonists led by Byzas (hence its first name, Byzantium) in the 7th century BC and prospered as a port because of its remarkable harbour (known as the Golden Horn). Its big break came in 324AD when Emperor Constantine decided to shift his capital here from the declining Rome and laid out a magnificent new city worthy of this new status (the city was renamed Constantinople in 330). Much remains of Byzantium and Constantinople today, including churches, palaces, cisterns and the hippodrome.

> ❏ **Smoking the hubble-bubble**
> Throughout this region, but particularly in Turkey, you might finish your meal by smoking a communal pipe with your fellow diners. These contraptions, variously known as hubble-bubbles, hookahs, qalyans and narghiles, allow you to draw the smoke through the water in the bong, making it much smoother than a standard pipe or cigarette. The tobacco is also mixed with various herbs and natural flavours to improve the taste and smell.

Over the next one thousand years it eclipsed all the other capitals in the West and as such became a major sponsor of trade along the Silk Road and beyond. The size of the empire grew and shrank depending on the abilities of the emperor (the Byzantine court was famous for its cut-throat politics and intrigue) but commerce never ceased and all of Europe's merchants depended on its markets.

The city's geographical position as the gateway between East and West did have its drawbacks, however, not least because it placed it on the frontline in the battle against the 'infidel'. Muslim forces from the Crusades onwards were determined to drive back the boundaries of Christendom and time and again Constantinople was targeted as the key prize and besieged. The Ottomans finally achieved the feat of taking the city on 28 May 1453, with the help of the biggest cannon ever seen. The last Byzantine emperor, Constantine XI, died fighting on the city walls.

### The Ottoman Empire

Mehmet II, now crowned Mehmet Fatih ('The Conqueror'), started to remodel his new capital and set it out, like Rome, on seven hills, with the Fatih Mosque his greatest legacy. His work was further improved by the Ottoman's greatest ruler, Suleiman the Magnificent, and several others until it became known as the 'Paris of the East'. The palaces lining the Bosphorus all date from this period. Even when the Ottomans declined, Constantinople retained a certain allure and was the unquestionable destination for the first-ever luxury train, the Orient Express.

### The republic

Atatürk chose to distance his government from the city, however, in an attempt to cut all ties with Turkey's imperial past. He made Ankara his political and administrative capital and renamed Constantinople 'Istanbul'. Inevitably, over the next few decades, the city lost much of its wealth and glamour.

### Istanbul today

Such a great city was bound to bounce back and bounce back it did. As oil and gas brought new wealth to the region, the city's position at the mouth of the Black Sea again became crucial. Thousands of tankers chug through the Bosphorus every year and with them they bring trade.

As Turkey's most cosmopolitan city, Istanbul is also the public face of the country's bid to join the EU and as such has received major investment over the last few years. The city is also young: 60 per cent of the population is under 24. The fact that in 2005 the city's new national football stadium hosted the Champions League Final and in 2006 Turkey's second ever Formula 1 Grand Prix was held on a new course in Istanbul Park is testament to the city's resurgence.

## WHAT TO SEE

### In Sultanahmet

**Aya Sofya** This unique building has the fourth largest dome in the world after Saint Peter's (Rome), Il Duomo (Milan) and Saint Paul's (London). It began life as Sancta Sophia when Emperor Justinian ordered a great church to be built as a centrepiece for his newly revitalized Constantinople. It was completed in

537AD and was the world's largest church for the next millennium (although it became better known by its Greek name, Haghia Sophia). After the city fell to Mehmet II, it was converted into a mosque and remained so until 1935 when Atatürk decided it would be more politic to transform it into a museum. Admission is YTL15.

From the entrance you will pass into a long corridor (narthex). This takes you to the main entrance, which is divided into three doorways. Above the central door is the ornate mosaic of Christ. Inside you will be blown away by the towering dome. Unlike the Blue Mosque there are no enormous pillars to hold this dome up, rather the dome is ribbed with a brick lining resting on supports hidden within the walls. The paintings on the ceiling are slowly being restored but the scaffolding cannot detract from the interior's splendour.

Most of the interior design has been added under Ottoman rule, such as the elevated Sultan's lodge in the corner, the ornate library on the west wall and the large gold discs with Arabic calligraphy. The mosaics on the ground floor and up in the gallery are from the building's Christian era.

Outside, by the original entrance steps, you can see the foundations of an even earlier (4th-century) church built by Emperor Theodosius, while opposite Aya Sofya are the **Baths of Lady Hurem**, built in the 16th century to accompany the mosque (the building now houses the state carpet shop but feel free to wander around inside).

**Blue Mosque** First-time visitors might be disappointed to find that the outside of this mosque is not blue. Few remain disappointed once inside the building, however. This mosque was built by Sultan Ahmet I (1603-17AD), whose tomb is out the back, and was deliberately positioned to challenge (and, it was hoped, surpass) the glory of the Aya Sofya. The exterior is big and bold with six minarets and an enormous courtyard (the best view is from the main entrance on the hippodrome). The interior is an intricate mix of blue Iznik tile mosaics and stained-glass windows (the tiles are original, the windows replicas). This is still a working mosque so admission is free but non-Muslims usually have to use a side entrance.

**Hippodrome** Originally used for chariot racing, the Hippodrome was once festooned with triumphant statues and monuments, though most of these disappeared when the soldiers of the Fourth Crusade sacked the city. The **Obelisk of Theodosius** (carved around 1450BC) does remain, however, having been brought over from Egypt in 390AD. **The Spiral Column** is also here, although it is now missing its three serpent heads; it was made to celebrate the Greek's victory over the Persians at Salamis in 480BC and originally stood outside the Temple of Apollo in Delphi before being brought here by Constantine the Great.

**Basilica Cistern/Yerebatan Saray** Built in the 6th century, this is one of the few buildings to survive from that period (entrance costs 15YTL; open 9.30am-7.30pm). It is cavernous below ground and is lined with ornate columns. The **Million Pillar** outside is all that remains of the arch from which all distances in the Byzantine empire were once measured.

**Topkapi Palace** Following their conquest of the city in 1453, the Ottoman sultans took it in turns to live in this magnificent palace and extend and elaborate on the original design laid out by Mehmet the Conqueror. It became a den of intrigue and vice with each new inhabitant seemingly determined to outdo his or her predecessor: one sultan drowned in his bath here, another was caged up for four years before going mad. The palace is a series of courtyards whereby the sultan could retreat further and further from public gaze, the inner sanctum being the harem. The three things most treasured by a sultan were water, flowers and trees, as these provided him with refreshment, perfume and shade; the harem was deliberately designed with all three in mind. Admission (15YTL; open Wed-Mon 9am-5pm) includes a map, though entry to the Harem and the Treasury is extra (12YTL each, though a guide is included in the Harem tour).

Below the palace is the peaceful **Gülhane Park** where, at the far end, you can have a relaxing drink on a café terrace with amazing views of the Bosphorus.

**Museums** The **Great Palace Mosaics Museum**, behind the Blue Mosque, has some incredible 5th-century mosaics which originally formed part of the entrance to the emperor's Grand Palace, which stood where the mosque now stands. The **Museum of Turkish and Islamic Arts** is housed in the palace of Ibrahim Pasha, for many years the favourite crony and Grand Vizier of Suleiman the Magnificent; the carpets and Korans are particularly delightful. The **Istanbul Archaeological Museum** in Gülhane Park has a wonderful, if neglected collection. Most museums are open Tuesday to Sunday.

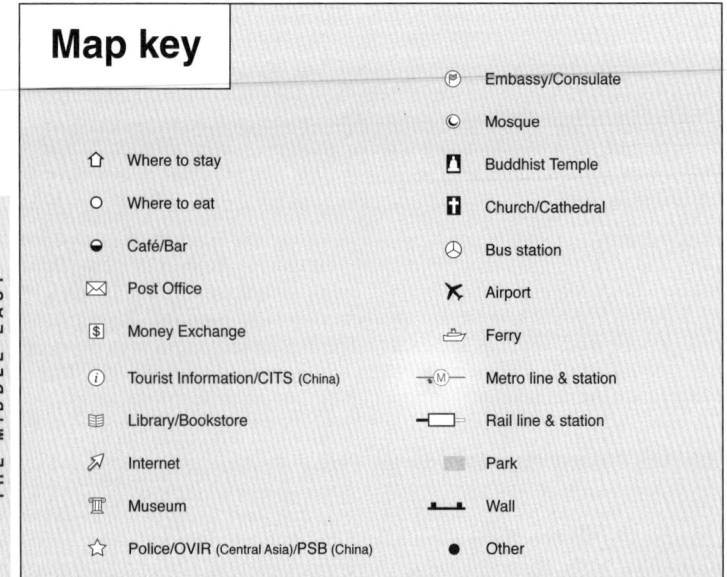

## Map key

|  |  |
|---|---|
| ⇧ | Where to stay |
| ○ | Where to eat |
| ◐ | Café/Bar |
| ✉ | Post Office |
| $ | Money Exchange |
| ⓘ | Tourist Information/CITS (China) |
| 📖 | Library/Bookstore |
| ✍ | Internet |
| ⛫ | Museum |
| ☆ | Police/OVIR (Central Asia)/PSB (China) |
| ⓟ | Embassy/Consulate |
| ⓒ | Mosque |
| ⛩ | Buddhist Temple |
| ✝ | Church/Cathedral |
| ⊕ | Bus station |
| ✈ | Airport |
| ⛴ | Ferry |
| —Ⓜ— | Metro line & station |
| —▭— | Rail line & station |
| ▓ | Park |
| ▪▬▪ | Wall |
| ● | Other |

## Istanbul – What to see

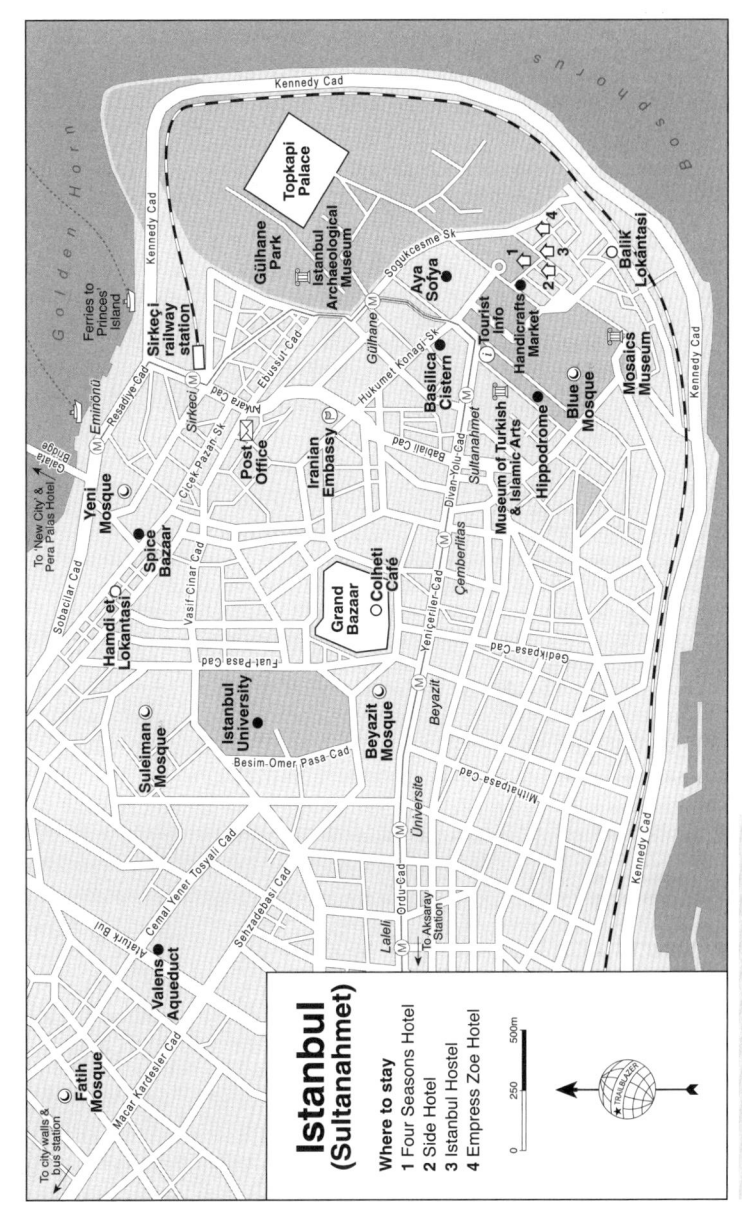

**Istanbul (Sultanahmet)**

Where to stay
1 Four Seasons Hotel
2 Side Hotel
3 Istanbul Hostel
4 Empress Zoe Hotel

> ❑ **Turkish delight**
> This 'comfortable morsel' (*rahat lokum*) is the most popular in Turkey and comes in all sorts of shapes and flavours, although pistachio and walnut are the classic fillings. Ali Muhiddin, the sultan's confectioner, claimed to have invented it in the 18th century and that his shop still stands at 83 Hamidiye Caddesi (near the New Mosque) is testament to him and his creation. Next door, Hafiz Mustafa is a worthy rival.

### In the Old City
**The Grand Bazaar** Some complain that this place has lost some of its charm and become a sanitized clone of the old bazaar; certainly it has been cleaned up and made tourist-friendly but it still knocks most shopping malls into a cocked hat. The indoor streets are as maze-like as ever, although the tradition of each trade having its own quarter is dying out as many shops now sell the full range of souvenirs.

**Beyazit Mosque** Next to the Grand Bazaar this mosque, from the reign of Sultan Beyazit II, may not look too smart from the outside but it dates back to 1501 and is chock full of white and green marble, porphyry rock and granite.

**Suleiman Mosque** Like Rome, Constantinople was built on seven hills and seven mosques crown them. Suleiman was the Ottoman's greatest ruler (hence his epithet, 'the Magnificent') and he commissioned the Ottoman's greatest architect, Sinan, to design this mosque; and many consider it to be his masterpiece. The mosque may not be as ornate as many of its neighbours but it is this simplicity that appeals. Sinan is said to have perfected the mosque design: a front courtyard is surrounded by stone pillar arcades on three sides and a two-storey porch on its fourth; the porch leads into the mosque proper, with its large central dome surrounded by several smaller ones. Suleiman's tomb is in the rear cemetery.

**Yeni Mosque** This is the 'New Mosque', so-called as it wasn't begun until 1597 and was not completed until 1663. Although several sultans were involved it was the mothers of Mehmet III and Mehmet IV who were the real driving force behind this grand edifice.

**Spice Bazaar** Whilst here, look out for 'Sultan's spice': this is a supposed aphrodisiac and considering that many a sultan is said to have gone through ten or twenty of his harem in one night on his return from battle, you shouldn't discount its potency.

**Fatih Mosque** This contains the **tomb of Mehmet the Conqueror**, a much more ornate affair than Suleiman's. The original mosque (1470) was destroyed by an earthquake and its replacement burnt down in 1782 but this latest construction (1785) is a worthy successor. Nearby is the ancient **Valens Aqueduct**.

**Istanbul University** The university buildings themselves are not that remarkable but they occupy a dominant position in the city and the **Fire Tower** in the

Istanbul – What to see 87

> ❏ **The first flight on the Silk Road**
> In 1768 Ahmet Celebi made the first flight along the Silk Road, winging his way from the top of the Galata Tower across to the Bosphorus's Asian bank by means of a primitive type of glider.
> Unfortunately, it appears Celebi was too far ahead of his time, as the sultan became jealous and the would-be pilot was exiled to Algiers for his pains.

middle of the grounds serves as a useful landmark. Also known as the 'Beyazit Tower', it is 85m tall, made of stone and dates from 1828.

**The city walls** Constantinople's walls, stretching from the giant **Yedikule Hisan** (the original 'Golden Gate') in the south to **Ayvansaray** in the north, were, prior to 1453, deemed impregnable. The city has many walls, such as those in the heart of the Old City around Sultanahmet, but the key to defending the capital were these enormous battlements protecting the city against land attacks from the west. Over the centuries they have been severely damaged by earthquakes although restoration is now being carried out on many key sections and it is hoped the work will be completed by 2008. Along the way, drop into the **Mihrimah Sultan Mosque**, built in honour of Suleiman the Magnificent's daughter. **Kariya Church/Museum**, dating back to the 11th century, is also worth a look for its early Byzantine mosaics.

You can just about follow the walls the whole way but new roads and building projects make this rather hazardous – it's better to take the metro out to **Topkapi Gate** and follow the walls north before heading back to town along Fevzi Pasha Caddesi.

## In the New City
**Galata Bridge** Technically the Old City stretched to the northern shore of the **Golden Horn**, but most modern visitors consider this bridge and the water that flows below it to be a more convenient and obvious dividing line between 'New' and 'Old'. A walk across the bridge at sunset is a must for all romantics and the anglers who fish off the side could hardly pick a more evocative spot. The bridge itself is new as the old one burnt down in the 1990s; the cafés below have never been able to recreate their old magic.

Incidentally, Galata Bridge is not just any old bridge, it is *the* bridge: the bridge after which the card game was named. British soldiers invented or at least learnt of this card game whilst stationed in Istanbul during the Crimean War. Each night they crossed the 'bridge' to test their mettle in the local coffee houses, and so the game was christened.

**Galata Tower** This is the major landmark on the northern side of Galata Bridge; the first tower was built in the 6th century AD but the whole area was later given over to the Genoese and this was their offering, constructed in 1348. It measures only 61m high but its position on the hill ensures that it dominates the skyline on this northern side of the river. Admission is YTL8.

## On the Bosphorus

**Çiragan Palace** Originally built in the 17th century, this building has had many uses over the years including being home to the Ottoman parliament. It now has a swanky hotel next door.

**Dolmabahçe Palace** This grandiose wonder was built in the 19th century by Sultan Abdul Mecit in an attempt to convince the rest of Europe that his empire was as 'modern' as they were. Atatürk lived out his last days here and all the clocks are still set to 09.05, the hour of his death. Admission is YTL10; open Tue, Wed, Fri-Sun 9am-4pm.

**Boat trip** A journey along the Bosphorus is a must: there are (expensive) cruises but the public ferry is just as good. The ride to **Andolu Kavagi** takes about 90 minutes. On the way you will see both Çiragan and Dolmabahçe palaces on the western shore plus several other palaces and stately homes on the eastern side. The first bridge you come to is the **Bosphorus**, built in 1972 (before that you could cross the straits only by boat!); the second is **Fatih Bridge**, while a third is still on the drawing board. Just before Fatih Bridge are two magnificent fortresses, **Rumeli Hisari** (on the European side) and **Anadolu Hisari** (on the Asian side); they date from the 14th and 15th centuries and were actually built by the Ottomans to attack the city rather than by the Byzantines to defend it.

Have lunch/a beer at one of the many seafood restaurants in Andolu Kavagi (the best ones are on the town square) before attempting the sweaty hike (20-30mins) up to the **mediaeval castle**, **Andalou Kavagi Kalesi** – you can follow the switchback road or cut your own way straight up through the village. The views of the city, the Marmaris and the Black Sea are spectacular, even if the castle is crumbling somewhat.

Ferries (YTL8/round-trip; allow five hours) to Andolu Kavagi leave three times a day from Eminönü's terminal 3 (get there at least half an hour early to get a good seat); most visitors make a day of it and take the morning ferry. A night cruise is equally majestic and perhaps even more romantic – remember you need to get back though (the regular boats between **Karakoy** and **Kadikoy** are probably best for night cruises).

## The Princes' Islands

These islands have been favoured getaways for centuries; coming here today you feel you are stepping back in time, especially as no cars are allowed on them. There are four main islands: **Kinaliada** is/was the local Armenians' favourite and has a church to go with the obligatory mosque, as well as some

---

❏ **Walking on water**
Incredibly, it has been possible to walk across the Bosphorus at various points in history, the most recent occasions being in 1929 and 1954. The water itself flows too quickly to freeze but on both occasions enormous blocks of ice floated down from the colder reaches of the Black Sea and wedged themselves into the straits, allowing ice to build up around them and enabling locals to walk across.

small beaches; **Burgazada** is/was the Greek favourite but is of little other interest; **Heybeliada** is much bigger and has shops, cafés and the picturesque **Haghia Triada Monastery**; **Büyükada** is the biggest, has the islands' only **tourist information office**, most of the hotels and the Greek **Monastery of Saint George** (although the views from here are more striking than the monastery itself).

Sunday is by far the busiest day for the islands so try to go some other time. You can stay overnight on the islands but the hotels are all overpriced for what they are. The *Monastery of Saint George Restaurant* on Büyükada is the place to have lunch or enjoy a beer. Many ferries (YTL2.5/1hr) run every morning from Sirkeci's 'Adalar Iskelesi' quay, stopping at Kadikoy before moving on to each of the islands. Ferries between the islands also cost YTL2.5, as do the return ferries.

### PRACTICAL INFORMATION
### [☎ code 0212]
### Orientation and services

Modern Istanbul is divided into three parts. It is definitely worth seeking out one of the tourist board's **free maps**: there are **tourist offices** at the airport and by the hippodrome. (See Local transport for details about arriving at/leaving Istanbul's airport.)

On the European side of the Bosphorus are the 'Old' and 'New' cities, separated by the Golden Horn. The **Old City** contains most of Istanbul's historical sites; the **New City** is the commercial hub and home to the capital's most fashionable residents. The **Asian side** of town originally grew up to cater for those who could not afford to live on the European side but has now developed an 'alternative' culture of its own.

There are **Internet** facilities in most hotels/hostels but the cheapest are to be found near **Sultanahmet** in the Old City. There are **telephone** kiosks here as well for cheap international calls. The central **post office** is near the central railway station (Sirkeci). Banks and **ATMs** are all over the city and there are exchange bureaux in the airport and around the major tourist sights. There are plenty of **hammams** (see box p105) in town but they tend to be overpriced compared to the rest of Turkey.

If you are staying for a while pick up a copy of *Time Out Istanbul*, the monthly listings magazine covering the city's nightlife and events.

The **Iranian Embassy** (☎ 513 8230; Mon-Thurs 08.30-11.30 and 14.30-16.30) is near Sultanahmet at 1/2 Ankara Caddesi – the relevant Bank Melli is across the street and a photocopy office is round the corner. The **Syrian Embassy** is way up in the north of the New City, 59/5 Macka Caddesi, Tesvikiye (☎ 232 6721). For visa requirements, see p18.

### Local transport

The Old City, centred on Sultanahmet, is best viewed on foot as it is small and compact. For the New City, Galata Bridge is the easiest way to cross the Golden Horn and, again, your feet will be your preferred mode of transport unless you intend to go further than Taksim Square.

There is a **tram network** and a **metro**, both of which are fast and efficient, but you will rarely need either once you are in the city centre. **Taxis** and **buses** are best avoided because of Istanbul's chronic traffic congestion. Two great bridges span the Bosphorus but dozens of **ferries** also link both sides (and many other parts of the city) and are a cheap and fun way to get around. At Eminönü there are three ferry terminals (orange letters) and two **sea-bus** terminals (blue letters).

If you are arriving at the **airport** the easiest way into the city centre is by taxi (US$15). A **train/tram combination** is not that much harder, though, and during rush hour can work out quicker: take the 'Rapid Transit' to **Aksaray Station** (YTL1), walk round the corner to the **Yusufpasa** stop on Turgut Ozal Caddesi and take the tram to Sultanahmet or Eminönü.

If you are travelling to the airport, the easiest option is to take one of the shuttle buses offered by all travel agents (US$3). Unfortunately, these shuttle buses do not provide a similar service back into Istanbul for new arrivals (although some hostels and hotels can arrange this). Instead, catch the metro to Zeytinburnu and change onto the tram to Sultanahmet.

### Where to stay
The most convenient place to stay is in Sultanahmet. Places here can be fairly touristy during the summer season and mid-range accommodation may sometimes be a bit cheaper elsewhere in town (though Sultanahmet's backpacker hostels remain the cheapest places to stay in the city), but as you will be spending most of your time here, it definitely makes sense. Visitors staying in the New City or on the Asian side often waste a lot of time having to travel to and from Sultanahmet.

There is a **backpackers' strip** along Akbiyik Caddesi but many budget travellers prefer to stay in one of the hostels just off it. *Istanbul Hostel* (☎ 516 9380; YTL12/pp in a dorm), at Kutlugun Sokak 35, has a beer garden on its roof and clean rooms. *Side Hotel* (☎ 517 2282; 🖳 www.sidehotel.com; YTL40-75/Db), Utangac St 20, is split within one large building and has cheaper pension rooms and more expensive hotel rooms; its rooftop terrace, with its views of the major sights both east and west, is perfect for morning breakfast as well as watching the sunset with an evening beer.

*Empress Zoe* (☎ 518 2504; 🖳 www.emzoe.com; YTL160/Db), Adliye Sokak 10, is a more romantic hideaway around the corner. For something upmarket and different, try the *Four Seasons* (☎ 638 8200; 🖳 www.fshr.com; US$400/Db) at Tevkifhane 1. This used to be a prison (*Midnight Express* was set here) before a former inmate (who had made millions following his release) decided to buy it and convert it into a hotel in a final act of revenge. It is very, very luxurious.

Another nostalgic option is the *Pera Palas Hotel* (☎ 251 4560; 🖳 www.perapalace.com; US$230/Db) in the New City at Mesrutiyet Caddesi 98-100. Built in 1892 by Georges Nagelmackers, the Belgian founder of *Compagnie Internationale des Wagons-Lits et Grand Express Europeens*, this became the final stop for his Orient Express train (first run in 1868); Agatha Christie wrote *Murder on the Orient Express* in room 41, Mata Hari stayed here and so did Greta Garbo; Atatürk always took room 101. If you can't afford to stay here, at least have a drink in the bar and take a closer look at the hotel's magnificent interior.

### Where to eat
It's worth getting out of the Old City to eat, as there are only a couple of really good restaurants in Sultanahmet, the rest being just tourist traps. *Balik Lokantasi* (☎ 458 1824; US$70/lunch for two), at Seyit Hasan Koyu Sokak 1, is the serious exception, one of the best seafood restaurants in Turkey and one with a delightful courtyard.

Food is one of Istanbul's passions so you should never find yourself too far away from a good café or food stall but for the best **snack food** head to Eminönü in the evening and meet the boatmen coming in with their catch; their vessels have built-in griddles and within minutes they are serving up some very tasty fresh fish sandwiches.

Inside the Grand Bazaar there are many cafés but few are licensed, making the ornate *Colheti Café* (Sandal Bedesteni 36), which is, even more attractive. *Hamdi Et Lokantasi* (☎ 528 0390) by Galata Bridge at Kalcin Sokak 17 has tremendous views from its roof garden dining area and food to match (booking is recommended).

In the New City, the famous **Çiçek Pasaji** ('Flower Passage') off Istiklal Caddesi is still many people's favourite. Try *Leb i Deryakanta* (☎ 293 4989), Kumbaraci Yokusu 115 in Tünel, one of Istanbul's swishest places with a classy bar boasting enviable views; or *Sofyali 9* at, unsurprisingly, Sofyali Sokak 9, which has great food (particularly mezes) at very reasonable prices.

Some, however, say this area has been overtaken by **Nevizade St** (Beyoglu district) as the main eating hotspot. Try *Krependeki*, Nevizade Sokak 24, or *Haci*

## Whirling Dervishes

All around Istanbul you will see advertisements for these performing dancers. The tradition stems back to **Celaleddin Rumi (Mevlana)**, one of the world's great mystic philosophers, born in 1207 in Balkh but a citizen of the Seljuk Sultanate of Rum. He wrote his poetry and religious works mostly in Persian (the literary language of the day) and is most remembered for ***Mathnawi*** (*Mesnevi* in Turkish), regarded as his greatest poetic work, and ***Divan I Kebir***, a collection of his finest pieces.

He died in 1273 but his followers organized themselves into a brotherhood called **Mevlevi**, or 'Whirling Dervishes'. Over one hundred lodges were founded throughout the region and even Ottoman sultans became Mevlevi Sufis (mystics). Atatürk, however, saw the brotherhood as an obsolete remnant of Turkey's imperial past and outlawed the Order but the tradition was revived in the fifties and is as popular as ever today.

The dance (*sema*) represents man's union with God and the dervishes dress in long white robes, which billow out into full skirts as the dancers spin round. The black cloak represents the dancer's tomb and the fez their tombstone. The ceremony begins with the leader calling out a prayer for Mevlana and reciting a verse from the Koran. Kettledrums and flutes then play as the dancers are led in a circle around the hall. After three circuits they drop their cloaks, then one by one they spin into the centre with their arms folded across their chests. As they achieve union with God they raise their right arms and the whole floor continues to spin until the leader calls a halt to proceedings and intones more passages from the Koran.

**Practicalities** The best place to see dervishes whirl is actually **Konya** in central Anatolia, the capital of the Seljuks and home to Mevlana for most of his life. There is even a Mevlana festival there in December. In Istanbul, try the **Mevlevi Monastery** on Sundays (Galipdede Caddesi 15; YTL25) for a more authentic experience than that offered by cafés and restaurants.

---

*Abdullah* at Sakizagaci Caddesi 17, an Istanbul institution famed for serving all your traditional favourites. Both areas are crammed full of eateries and bars.

All international cuisines are represented in the New City, particularly in **Besitkas**, which is also home to the most fashionable joints in town; if you have the money you can really splurge.

### Nightlife

Again the Old City around Sultanahmet is a bit touristy but it is worth having a few beers up on one of the many roof terraces here to watch the sun go down and get some of the best views of Istanbul. The backpacker strip (see p91) has about as many bars as hostels. For anything more sophisticated, you need to head over to the New City: the **Tünel** end of Istiklal Caddesi is where much of the action is but some prefer the bars around **Nevizade St** (see p91). If you're really glam try the **Reina Complex** of restaurants, bars and clubs underneath the Bosphorus Bridge (Muallim Naci Caddesi) – they are as sleek as they are chic but come with a hefty blow to the wallet.

### Things to buy

If you are finishing your trip in Istanbul you will probably be ready for a shopping frenzy and are unlikely to be disappointed. If you are just beginning your trip you will have to be restrained or prepared to ship box-loads home.

The obvious place to start is the **Grand Bazaar** but it tends to be the most expensive – try the surrounding side streets instead or keep your eyes open as you wander around town; shopping is an Istanbul institution and there are shops and markets everywhere. Remember that haggling is compulsory! The best buys are often handicrafts, ceramics and leather goods; if you are after a carpet see box pp136-7.

**Istanbul Handicrafts Market** (on Kabaskal Caddesi, Sultanahmet) is a good place to watch artisans at work.

## Moving on

Istanbul's **Haydarpaşa Train Station** (which serves all the regions on our route) is over on the Asian side of the city. Although there are convenient express trains to Ankara few choose to use this option as the bus is easier and cheaper.

As for the **buses**, if you buy your ticket from one of the many ticket agencies in Sultanahmet it may cost a few more lira than if you bought it at the station but they will provide a free **shuttle bus** for the 10km journey (which saves you a lot of time and hassle). **Taxis** to/from the station are about US$8. Rapid Transit trains run to Aksaray Station where you can change for Sultanahmet.

There are buses running to everywhere in Turkey and to quite a few international destinations as well including **Ankara** (5hrs/YTL40), **Göreme** (11hrs/YTL45), **Bodrum** (13hrs/YTL60) and **Damascus** (33hrs/YTL65). The standard of coach and bus service can vary dramatically so it is often worth sticking to the big national outfits such as **Kamil Koc**, **Ulusoy** and **Varan Turizm**.

If you are flying out of Istanbul, most travel agents/hostels/hotels have cheap **shuttle buses** running throughout the day.

### Side trip to the Aegean coast

Many Silk Roadsters are stuck in Istanbul waiting for the visa 'Godot' for up to three weeks. Istanbul should keep you busy for six or seven days but after that you might want to venture further afield. One excellent solution is to take a trip down Turkey's west coast. It has two of the Seven Ancient Wonders of the world, some of the country's finest beaches and lots of great places to stay.

The most efficient plan is to take an overnight bus from Istanbul to your most southerly destination (in this case Bodrum) and then slowly work your way back up to the capital; and this is the way we have described the route below. The following itinerary is good for about ten days but there are plenty more places to stop off in between if you wish.

**Bodrum** This town is touristy but certainly still worth a visit. The bus station is right in the centre and there are plenty of pensions in the nearby streets providing good-value accommodation. To avoid the overcrowded main beach and resort hotels, head straight to the glorious Crusader **Castle of Saint Peter**. This is a pure gem, even if it can be a touch crowded, and the views are magnificent. From here it's easy to explore the old harbour and from there it is a short walk to the site of the **Mausoleum of Halicarnassus**, one of Pliny's Ancient Wonders. It was built to house the body of the Persian satrap, King Mausolus (376-353BC); not much is left now but the remains are inspiring nevertheless.

Like any resort, Bodrum is not short on **accommodation** or **nightlife** but it's best actually to move around the peninsula once you have seen the main sights and stay in the much less spoilt **Türkbükü**, 20km away (minibuses run from Bodrum's bus station all day). Admittedly, this is the playground of Istanbul's rich and famous and many of the hotels are at the top end of the market but there are a couple of cheaper pensions advertising rooms in the village. The bay here is gorgeous and all the hotels are happy for you to use their sundecks during the day even if you are not staying there; *Maca Kizi* (☎ 0252 377 6272; 🖳 www.macakizi.com) is top of the range and has, without doubt, the best spot.                    *(Continued on p94)*

## ❑ Side trip to the Aegean coast

*(continued from p93)* The ***Ship Ahoy*** is a great place to spend the night and there are a number of other excellent restaurants and chilled-out bars along the strip. Many people who plan to stay just a couple of days end up spending a week here.

**Efes** From Bodrum it is a three-hour coach trip north to Selçuk. This is the best base for visiting Efes as there is plenty of accommodation here to suit all budgets. Our recommendation would be ***Homeros Pension*** (☎ 0232 892 3995; 🖳 www.homerospension.com), Atatürk Mah, 1048 Sokak 3, a very popular hang-out and if they are booked up they will let you stay on their roof. The bus station is central and most hotels/hostels are within walking distance of it.

You can probably catch a lift to the **ancient city of Ephesus** but a walk or cycle ride there is more rewarding. Try to arrive at the site either very early or late (after 15.00 is ideal) to miss the crowds and have the place almost to yourself. The world famous amphitheatre is rightly lauded but the remains of the city as a whole are also amazing. Admission is 15YTL.

Back in the city there is not much to do at night but many visitors take an extra day to have a look around. The **Temple of Artemis** is the region's second Ancient Wonder, although the remaining column does little to suggest that the monument once outshone the Parthenon. The **Basilica of Saint John** was erected by Emperor Justinian to house the tomb of the apostle and Gospel writer (John is said to have come here with Mary and written his text sitting up on this hill).

**Troy/Gallipoli** From Efes it is a six-hour bus journey to Çanakkale. This is another great base for visiting sights, although the town itself is pretty ordinary. There are plenty of backpacker hostels that rely on Anzac Day to make their money so as long as you avoid the end of April/early May you should have no problem finding a cheap room/dorm; try ***The Yellow Rose Pension*** (☎ 0286 217 3343), which has free Internet access – follow the signs from the clock tower.

Most accommodation runs tours to the **Gallipoli Peninsula**, scene of the disastrous WWI campaign where tens of thousands of allied troops were hopelessly cut down trying to land on the beaches. Interestingly, many more British and French soldiers died in the main landings than Australian and New Zealand (Anzac) men, yet it is the latter two countries who are most associated with the horrors. Some complain that the thousands of 'pilgrims' who descend each year are more interested in the all-night beach parties than they are in the commemoration service. At any other time of year you will probably have the peninsula to yourself for what can be a deeply moving experience.

Those in search of remnants of a more ancient conflict should head to **Troy** (entrance 10YTL). Again most hostels have reasonably priced tours to the site. There are in fact the foundations of six cities to explore here but none of them is as impressive as the ruins on offer at Efes. Nevertheless, just to stand where Trojan commanders would have stood, looking down towards oncoming Greek ships, is enough for many.

**Sea of Marmara** Rather than catch the bus straight back to Istanbul, a more scenic alternative is to take the bus to Bandirma, walk down to the port and catch the ferry across the sea. The approach to the port south of Sultanahmet is splendid.

# Cappadocia

'The Land of Beautiful Horses' has become an increasingly popular destination over recent years and deservedly so, yet there are never the crowds here that you get in Turkey's coastal resorts. A volcanic region of spectacular landscapes, just how Cappadocia came by its name is unclear. We know that Hittites settled in the region in the second millennium BC, that during the Roman period its caves became hideouts for persecuted Christians and that during the Byzantine period many monks and hermits built monasteries here, attracted by the solitude.

The travel industry has put Cappadocia back on the map and expanded it to include much of central Anatolia when, geographically speaking, it only really covers the triangle between Nevşehir, Avanos and Urgup. **Göreme**, in the centre of that triangle, has become the base for most visitors. Many try to cram all the sights into one or two days but you could easily spend a week here exploring the many valleys and trying out the various adventure sports on offer.

## WHAT TO SEE

### Göreme Open Air Museum

This World Heritage Site (TYL14) is amazing and certainly unlike anything else on the Silk Road. The gorges and rock formations alone are impressive but it is the churches, hermitages and monasteries carved out of and into the caves that are truly incredible. They date from the Byzantine period and were built into caves as much to disguise their whereabouts as for the aesthetic qualities such solitude provided. There is a pre-planned route to follow, so it is pretty simple to take everything in. You can spend a few hours wandering around the whole valley but some of the caves charge additional entrance fees. Most visitors walk up to the museum from Göreme town; the walk takes about half an hour.

---

### Ankara

Ankara is a typical bureaucratic capital and as such is ignored by most travellers, particularly because most embassies have a consulate in Istanbul. That is not to say there is nothing to see here. It does, after all, have a lengthy history as **Angora** and has long been famed for its **goats' wool** but compared to Turkey's premier attractions this city is a dull suburb.

If you do stop, make sure you check out the **citadel area** and the magnificent **Museum of Anatolian Civilizations**. Nearby is the city of **Gordion**, capital of the **Phrygian empire** (see p54) and home of the **Gordian Knot**, which Alexander dramatically cut in 333BC.

Nowadays, there is a museum and various tumuli (one is said to belong to **King Midas**) to see here. ***Otel Pinar*** (☎ 0312 311 8951; YTL50/Db) at Hisarparki Caddesi 14 in Ankara's Ulus district (near the museum) is a recommended budget option.

### Hot-air ballooning over the Silk Road

Although the Silk Road is strictly a land-based route, it is definitely worth making an exception in Cappadocia. This area is now firmly established as one of the prime hot-air balloon destinations in the world because of its favourable wind conditions and agreeable geography. The bird's eye views of the region's valleys, fairy chimneys and pigeon houses are unforgettable, while the skill with which the balloonists maneuvre their craft is breathtaking. Be careful of some operators as they often shoot up to great heights and spend the majority of their trip racing over wheat fields, whereas the best flights wind their way in and out of the valleys.

Almost all the companies are based in Göreme although they take off/land from/at various sites. If you're going to spend this amount of money, it is worth going for the full 1½hr/2hr trip (US$180-200) rather than the cheaper 1hr trip (US$100-120). ***Kapadokya Balloons*** (☎ 271 2442; 🖥 www.kapadokyaballoons.com) are the longest-running outfit and have by far the most sophisticated operation as well as the best balloons (they even helped Richard Branson train for his round-the-world attempt). ***Ez Air Balloon Safaris*** (🖥 www.ezairballoon.seyahati.com) are also recommended.

## Göreme Valley walks

Göreme town lies in **Göreme National Park**, an area crammed with gorges, valleys, caves and footpaths. Take a couple of days to sightsee in order to wander along some of the more spectacular walks – there are dozens of recommended walkways but it's just as pleasurable to stray where your fancy takes you as almost everywhere is interconnected. The maps available in your hotel/hostel are not the most accurate but if you allow plenty of time it is pretty hard to get too lost.

## Underground cities

Troglodytes (cave dwellers) have been inhabiting this region for thousands of years, partly in an attempt to keep cool and partly as a means of defence against marauding invaders. It is one thing to live in a cave but quite another to live in an underground city and that is what makes **Kaymakli**, **Ozluce** and **Derinkuyu** so mind-blowing (not that they are alone in this region – locals reckon at least

### Fairy chimneys

These rock structures look as if they belong in a cartoon or sci-fi movie. They can be tall (up to 40m) or squat but the physics and geology behind all *peribacalar* are the same. The whole area is volcanic and much of the top surface here is little more than hardened ash; this has been eroded over the millennia by wind and rain but some patches have been protected by isolated, harder stone boulders (often granite). While this harder rock has been altered but little by the wind and rain, the ground underneath has been whittled down to the stumps and trunks we see now. For centuries, locals have carved pigeon holes into the side of chimneys and other cliff-faces as pigeon droppings are an extremely valuable source of fertilizer for crops in an often-barren region.

(**Opposite**) **Top**: The Blue Mosque (see p83), an icon of Istanbul. **Bottom**: Ballooning over the fairy chimneys of Göreme.

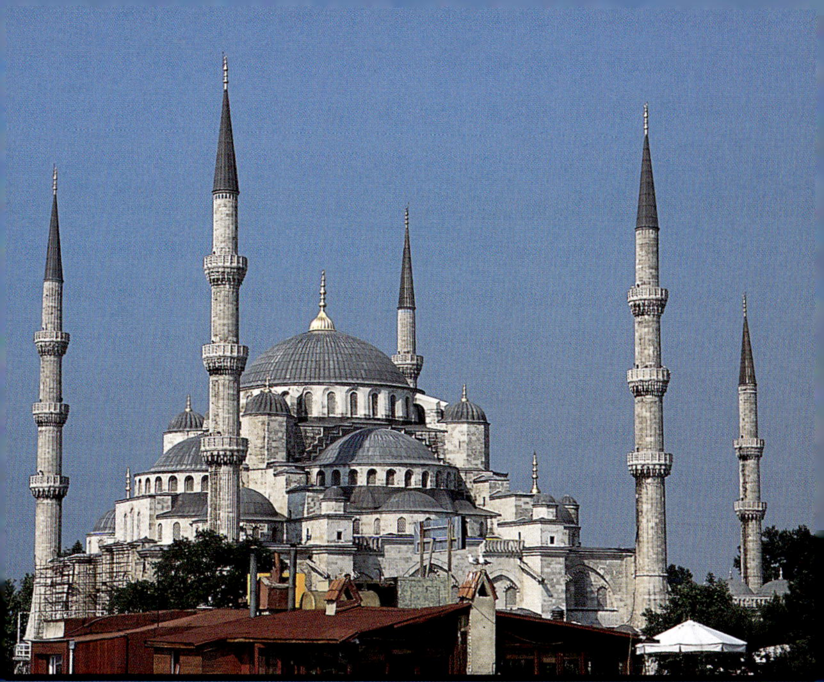

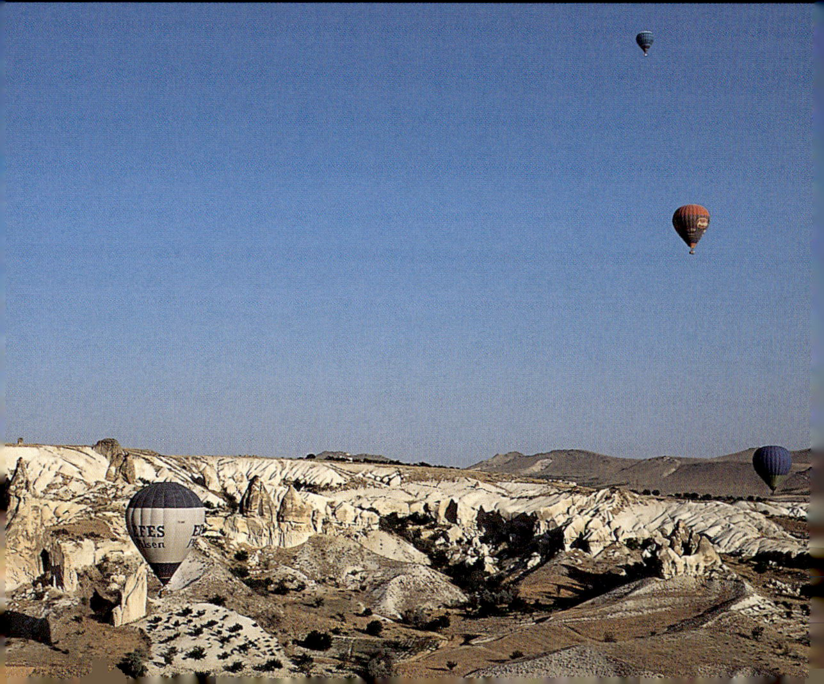

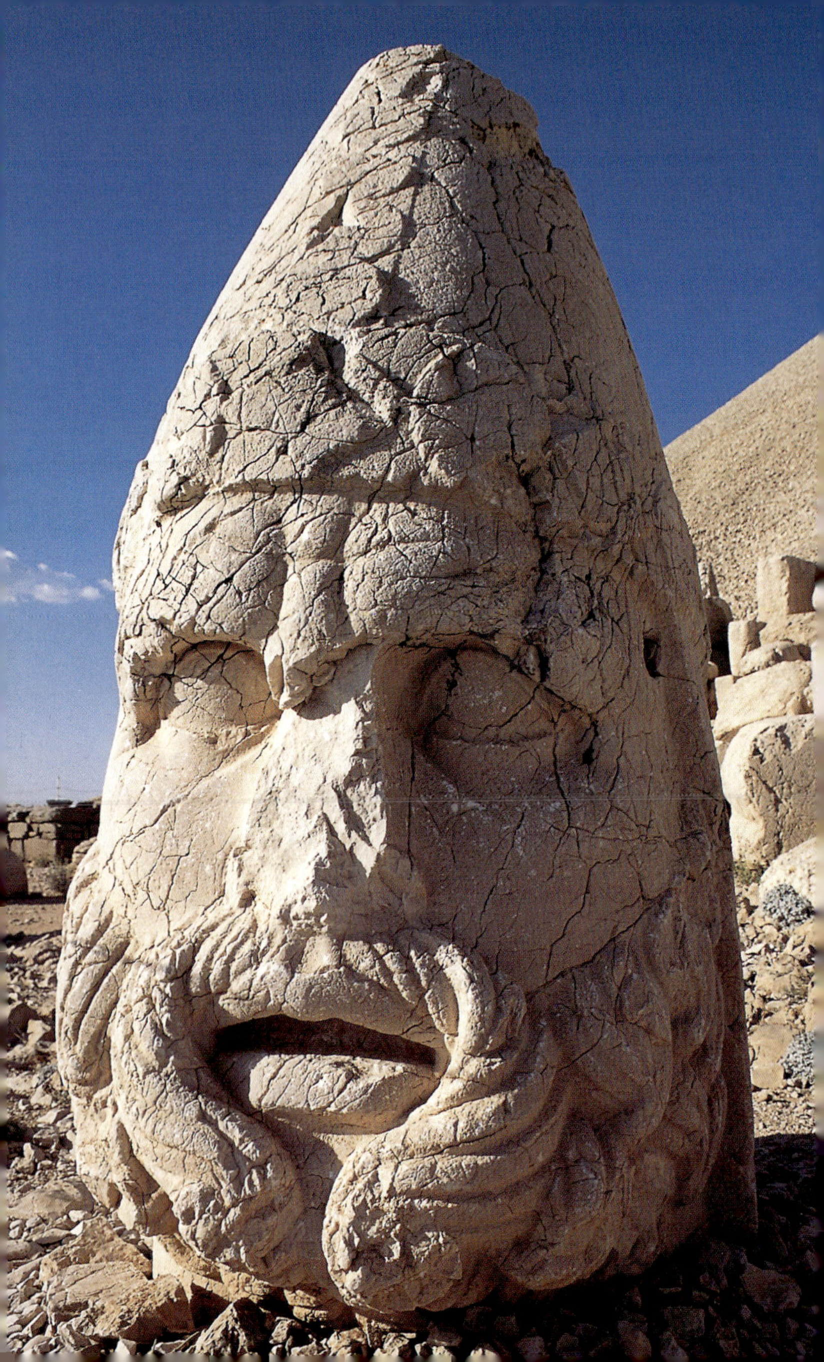

fifty underground cities have been built over the centuries). Your tour will probably dictate which one you visit but Kaymakli is the busiest, Ozluce is the least developed and Derinkuyu is the most extensive.

All the cities go deep, deep underground (often seven or eight storeys deep) and have all the rooms and 'buildings' you would expect to find in an ancient city (they even brought their animals below ground). The enormous stone wheels that act as doors to block tunnels against intruders are straight out of an Indiana Jones movie.

Ozluce is still free to enter but the others cost YTL12. Most visitors find it cheaper to visit the cities as part of a tour.

### Ihlara Valley

Traditionally this was not part of Cappadocia but is still definitely worth a visit while you are here. The valley lies nearly 100km away from Göreme and was a peaceful sanctuary for monks throughout the ages because of this. It is home to dozens of extraordinary monasteries and churches built into caves or cut out of the cliffs that line the valley walls. The **Melendiz Suyu River** flows 16km through the valley and splits it somewhat into two but it is easy to cross from one side to the other via numerous wooden bridges. Most tours allow you only a few hours to walk through the southern half of the valley but those with their own transport or wanting to stay in **Ihlara village** should try to walk the whole route from Ihlara to **Selime** (7hrs). *Akar Motel Pansiyon Restaurant* (YTL40/Db; Ihlara village) is the most convenient place to stay but you can camp at all the restaurants along the way. Entrance to the valley is YTL5.

### Soganli

The twin valleys of Soganli are like a cross between Göreme National Park and Ihlara Valley, except they are hardly visited by anyone and you are likely to have a valley to yourself if you visit. There are some absorbing churches here and plenty of pigeon houses. It is almost impossible to get here by public transport but you should have no problem finding a tour out of Göreme. Entrance is YTL2.50.

---

### Caravanserais

All along the Silk Road, staging posts (known as *khans* in Syria) evolved, where merchant caravans could stay the night or longer to recuperate and prepare for the next day's journey. In key trading cities the authorities built whole complexes to entice traders and persuade them to stay a little longer. These would have rooms for the merchants, stables for the animals and easy access to the markets (which were often next door). With so many routes for merchants to chose from, attracting them was important for a caravanserai – and indeed a town's – survival and, as we can see from their remains, many caravanserais were lavish affairs. In Anatolia, the Seljuks built enough caravanserais to ensure that no caravan need travel more than a day's march (15-25km) before encountering the next caravanserai. Most tours out of Göreme should take in at least one, the best being the ones at Sultanhami, west of Aksaray.

---

(**Opposite**): Enormous stone statues of Commagene kings and gods, such as this one of King Antiochus, sit atop Nemrut Daği (see p125) in eastern Turkey. They're over 2000 years old.

## PRACTICAL INFORMATION
[☎ code 0384]
### Orientation and services
Göreme is tiny and everywhere is within walking distance. Every hotel/hostel is allied to one of the local tour operators who run day tours around the region (YTL50) and 2- to 3-day tours to Turkey's south-east (see box p126). They are much of a muchness but check that your tour takes in all the sites in which you are interested. Try **Zemi Tours** (☎ 271 2576; 💻 zemitours@kosepension.com). **Adventure sports** are a growing business in the area, too, and most tours have links to the various operators.

There are **banks** in the main square where the buses arrive/leave. **Internet facilities** are everywhere.

### Where to stay
There's a whole host of budget options in town. *Kaya Camping* (☎ 343 3100; up from the Open Air Museum; YTL7/pp) is well equipped and offers a free pick up from the otogar.

*Köse Pension* (☎ 271 2294; 💻 dawn@kosepension.com; YTL12/pp), is highly recommended. Run by a Scottish/Turkish couple, it has great shared rooms, a small restaurant and a swimming pool.

*Flintstones* (on the outskirts of town; YTL12/pp) is the backpackers'/partygoers' favourite. Most visitors, however, will want to stay in a fairy chimney. *Kelebek Pension* (☎ 271 2531; 💻 www.kelebekhotel.com; YTL50/Db) does fairy-chimney rooms in style with an excellent rooftop terrace. *Elif Star Caves* (☎ 271 2479; 💻 www.elifstar.com; YTL40/Db) has more caves than chimneys but is very welcoming and does great food.

### Where to eat
*Orient* (Adnan Menderes Caddesi), with its outdoor eating area, offers probably the most charming dining experience in the region and the food is pretty impressive. *Alaturca* (Muze Caddesi) has built up a reputation for style and sophistication and shouldn't be dismissed as merely a hangout for beautiful people – the food is delicious.

The café under *SOS Restaurant* (Bilal Eroglu Caddesi) has free Internet and is a mellow place to relax in the evening (although at weekends it can get quite frisky). *Flintstones Bar* (see column opposite) is the best place for late-night action.

### Moving on
**Buses** leave everyday to **Malatya** or **Kahta** (6-7hrs/YTL20). If you are heading south, you might want to stop off on the coast (see box pp93-4) en route to **Antakya** (7hrs, though you may have to change at **Adana**; YTL20). Many buses go daily to **Istanbul** (11hrs/YTL35) and **Ankara** (4hrs/YTL15).

---

### Saint George
Historically, it is held that George was a Palestinian conscript in the Roman army who served in England and was executed in 203AD for defying Emperor Diocletian's ban on Christianity. The dragon slaying myth came later, with a number of possible locations suggested: some say it took place in Libya, some Cappadocia and others Beirut. But the gist of the story is usually the same: a town was terrorized by a dragon demanding virgin sacrifices, until George got wind of the problem and offered to slay it – which he did, rescuing a fair maiden as he did so. Interestingly, in some stories the old English word used to describe the dragon is 'worm', which nullifies the achievement somewhat – the truth, if there is any, was probably that the beast was some sort of giant crocodile.

Crusaders took the legends back with them to England and George became a romantic hero. Edward III chose him as the patron saint of his newly established Knights of the Garter in the 14th century and from there he became patron saint of England. He is also the patron saint of Turkey, Beirut and Moscow.

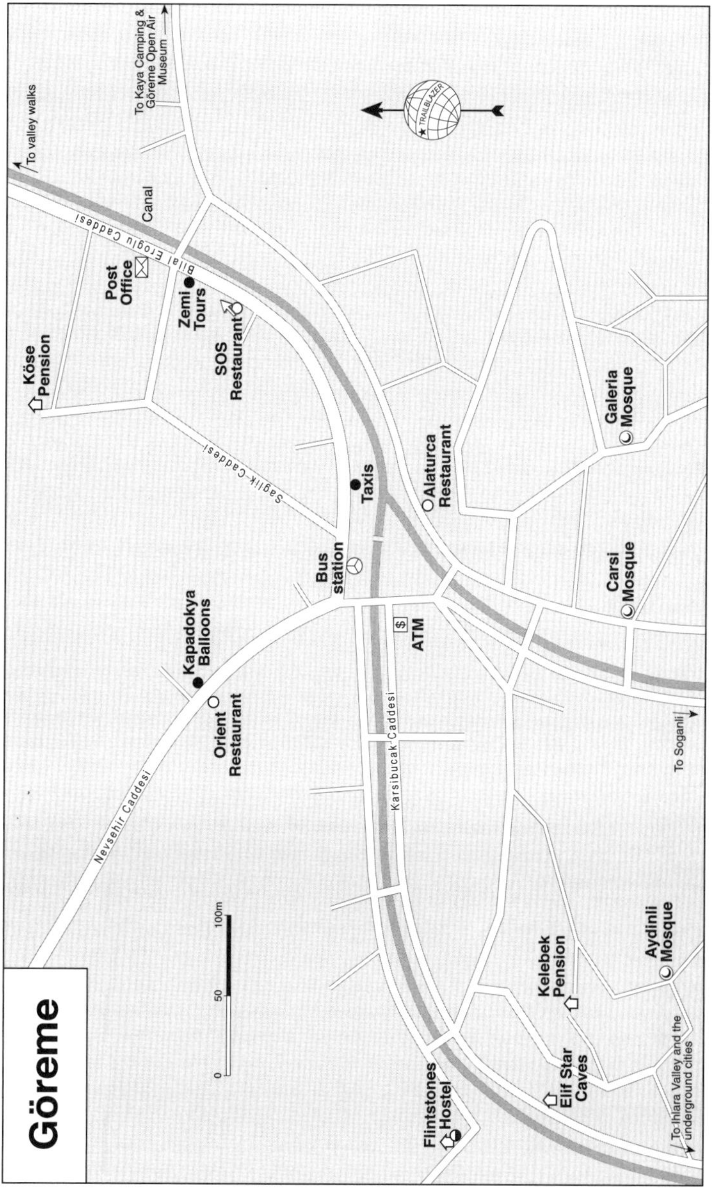
Göreme
0
50
100m
To valley walks
To Kaya Camping & Göreme Open Air Museum
Canal
Bilal Eroglu Caddesi
Post Office
Köse Pension
Zemi Tours
SOS Restaurant
Saglik Caddesi
Taxis
Bus station
Alaturca Restaurant
Galeria Mosque
Carsi Mosque
Kapadokya Balloons
Orient Restaurant
ATM
Karsibucak Caddesi
Nevsehir Caddesi
To Soganli
Kelebek Pension
Aydinli Mosque
Elif Star Caves
Flintstones Hostel
To Ihlara Valley and the underground cities
TRAILBLAZER

> **Iskenderun**
> For a bit of relaxation on your way to/from **Antakya**, you might want to stop off around Iskenderun. This city was founded by Alexander the Great but don't be attracted here by tales of this being the site of Alexander's historic victory over the Persians in the Battle of Issus (this actually took place 30km up the coast, at Issos). This side trip is a good opportunity to have a dip in the Mediterranean Sea, thus setting up the possibility of one of the world's longest 'coast to coast' trips across to the Pacific Ocean. Iskenderun itself isn't very nice but catch a *dolmuş* south to **Arsuz** where the beaches and nightlife are a considerable improvement.

# Antakya (Hatay)

As the capital of **Hatay province** (the wedge of Turkey between Syria and the Mediterranean coast), Antakya, like most cities in Turkey, has been swept up in the desire for all things modern and much of its ancient charm has been swamped in recent years. If you are prepared to dig a little deeper, however, you will be rewarded, though compared to Aleppo this city's a disappointment considering its previous importance to the Silk Road and a couple of days is more than enough.

## HISTORY

The city was founded as **Antioch** in 300BC by Nicator I, a Seleucid king and former general of Alexander. Previously the site had been a religious centre for the worship of Zeus. Under the Romans it was established as *the* destination for all Silk Road caravans coming from the East and completely eclipsed Aleppo. It gained a reputation as the hedonistic capital of their empire and the epithet 'Fair crown of the Orient'.

Yet it still maintained its religious appeal and Saint Peter is said to have preached here; a grotto remains in the nearby Saint Peter's Church, which is thought to be the only Christian structure in the world that has survived from the early period of the religion. Indeed, Antioch was one of the five patriarchal centres of the early Christian world alongside Rome, Alexandria, Jerusalem and Constantinople. It was also sacked by the Sassanids (540AD), however, and shattered by several earthquakes (the biggest in 526AD killed 250,000 people). With the coming of Islam it found itself a prime target and in the face of this aggression traders moved back to Aleppo; Antioch, as a result, lost its shine.

It regained some of its glory during the Crusades, however, when it was restored to its pre-eminent position on the Silk Road and in the 13th century its prince, Bohemond (son-in-law to the king of Armenia), managed a real coup by travelling to Mongolia to offer himself as a vassal just before the Mongol armies decided to smash their way through western Asia. Bohemond became Hulegu's chief Christian advisor and Antioch boomed during the route's last hurrah. He did not account for the Mamelukes, though, who, once they had defeated the Mongols in 1260, proceeded to take the entire Levant for themselves; Antioch fell to a killer three-pronged attack led by the great Mameluke leader, Baibars, himself.

The city, indeed the whole region of Hatay, remained outside Turkish control until the Ottomans took it back but their hold was always shaky. The French claimed control of the territory as part of their Syrian protectorate and it was only in 1939, when it was annexed from Syria, that the city came under Turkish control once more, which is why Arabic can still be heard on the streets.

Modern Antakya (the city's name was changed from the Greek 'Antioch' after independence) is split in two by the Asi (Orontes) River. On the east bank is the old town of **Antiocheia** and on the west bank is the new town of **Antakya**. Locals often refer to the city itself as Hatay; this is also true of bus timetables/noticeboards. Unlike the Turkish coast further west, tourism is far from being the mainstay here and few people speak English.

## WHAT TO SEE

**Saint Peter's Church/Cave** is the highlight for most people. It was declared a place of pilgrimage in 1963 by Pope Paul VI; June 29 is the day of celebration. You can walk up here from town (about 2km) or take a taxi.

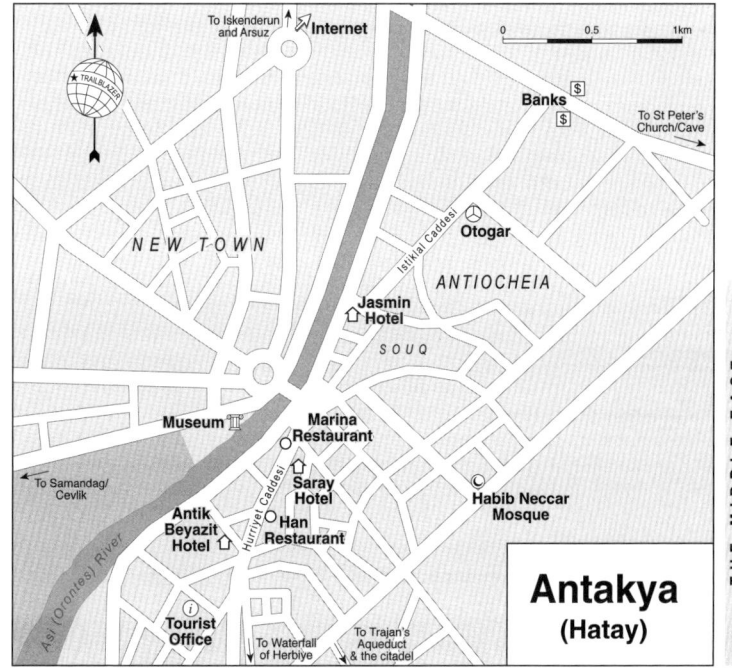

The **museum** in the centre of town has a very good collection of mosaics and local finds from the Roman period and it's well laid out (YTL5; 08.00-12.00 and 13.30-17.00 Tue-Sun). There are various mosques of which the most important is the **Habib Neccar**. There is virtually nothing left of the ancient **citadel**.

Outside the city is an **aqueduct** built by Emperor Trajan in the 2nd century AD which still has many parts of its original 9km intact. You can walk but it is a long way and you will probably prefer to take a taxi.

### Excursions from Antakya

Antioch was always famous for its laurel soap because of a myth surrounding the **Waterfall of Herbiye** (7km away). This is the spot where Apollo is said to have chased Daphne, the beautiful nymph, who, rather than entertaining her new suitor, set new standards in playing hard to get. She begged Mother Earth to save her, and Mother Earth complied by turning her into a laurel tree. It was because of this that Apollo subsequently always wore a laurel wreath, which led to the same symbol being awarded as a prize of honour to poets, musicians and generals who excelled. The waterfall, which still flows, is said to be fed by Daphne's tears and is a popular spot for visitors and locals alike to have a picnic. To get here by public transport is quite tricky but during summer the tourist board runs regular buses to and from the falls.

If you began your trip in Damascus and have yet to see the Mediterranean Sea, a day trip to **Çevlik** and **Samandağ** is worth considering if only so that, by the end of your journey, you can say you have travelled from one coast of mainland Asia to the other. Take a *dolmuş* (minibus) to Samandağ, the new port serving Antakya, and then walk along to Çevlik (**Seleuceia ad Pieria**), the old harbour built in 310BC by the Seleucids; minibuses leave from a variety of stops in Antakya so check with the tourist office as to which one is best for you. Saint Paul began his first voyage back to Tarsus here after his conversion and, in the same century, Emperor Vespasian built a 1330m **tunnel** to bring clean water from the mountains into the estuary and prevent it from silting up – the water that the Asi River brought contained large quantities of alluvium. From the coast you can still make your way up to the tunnel and follow it inland, though now it is more of a gorge as the roof has mostly collapsed.

### PRACTICAL INFORMATION
[☎ code 0326]

#### Orientation and services
The **otogar** (bus station) is pretty central and as you come in you will see a whole host of **banks** on the main street (many with ATMs). There are plenty of **Internet cafés** in the centre of town, with most charging YTL0.5 an hour.

The **tourist office** keeps changing location so be careful and don't believe any signs on the roads as they are probably out of date. If they have moved again from the office marked on the map (see p101), ask at the museum as they are usually clued up.

#### Where to stay
Most hotels cater for local migrant workers or businessmen rather than foreign visitors, so expect your accommodation to be friendly and cheap but a little boring.

*Jasmin Hotel* (Istiklal Caddesi; YTL20/Db) is clean if basic. Off the south side of the main square, **Saray Hotel** (YTL30/Db), above the eponymous restaurant, is a little smarter and includes breakfast in its tariff. Up the hill south of Saray Hotel at Hukumet Caddesi 4 is the *Antik Beyazit* (☎ 216 2900; 🖥 www.antikbeyaz itoteli.com; US$90/Db), which is as plush as you would expect for the price.

### Where to eat
The choice of food is not fantastic. There are plenty of **kebab shops** dotted around both sides of the river. *Marina Restaurant*, opposite Saray Hotel, is probably the most imaginative restaurant in town and is recommended for its fish but some diners have been disappointed. *Han Restaurant* (Hurriyet Caddesi 17) has two well-placed terraces and a good if simple menu.

The **souq** (market) is a great place to stock up on olives, bread, feta cheese, pastries and whatever else you might want for your bus journeys – though watch out for the pickled chillies, they're hot!

### Moving on
Buses for **Malatya** and **Kharta** (see p124) run at least twice a day from the otogar but it's best to buy your ticket the day before to check the times. Those heading to **Göreme** might have to change at Adana (3hrs/YTL8). If you want to have a break on a beach for a couple of days go via **Iskenderun** (see box p100). If you want to explore more of **Turkey's south-east**, see box p126. If you are heading to Syria you can cross over to **Aleppo** (see box below) or take a bus all the way to Damascus and then work your way back north.

---

> **Crossing the Turkish/Syrian border**
> The Turkish side of the border is quite straightforward. Coming into Turkey, the bus conductor will show you which office to go to. There are money exchanges here beside the duty-free shops opposite the visa office; the exchanges are official and offer pretty good rates but you will probably get a better rate for dollars in Aleppo. Change all your Turkish lira at the border because they are worth little inside Syria. **Buses to Aleppo** (3-4hrs/US$8) regularly leave from Antakya's otogar each day.
>
> Coming the other way, **buses for Antakya** leave Aleppo from a parking lot (see map p107). Several companies here run services to Turkey so choose the one with the time to suit you (S£250/3-4hrs). At the Turkish border you may have to buy a visa (if you do it is US$16 and can be paid for in US dollars, Syrian pounds or Turkish lira).
>
> Remember to change all your Syrian pounds when leaving the country as they are worthless outside.

---

# Aleppo

Called Haleb in Arabic, Aleppo is the second largest city in Syria, although from the top of the citadel it looks larger than the capital. The city, like all great trading centres, is a mix of nationalities and, perhaps surprisingly for those who have not visited Syria or Lebanon before, a mix of religions. About 40 per cent of the inhabitants are Christian and of these many are Armenians, the great traders on the western half of the Silk Road (although today the biggest deals are likely to be struck by visiting Russians).

## HISTORY

Aleppo rivals Damascus's claim to be the oldest continually inhabited city in the world and remnants of a settlement dating back to the 9th century BC have been found at the archaeological site of Tell al Mraebet, with the promise of older findings to come. As a result of this longevity, Aleppo has witnessed all the ancient empires come and go, though it really came to prominence under the Islamic rulers who conquered and ran it from 637AD. Many of the towers, walls, castles and schools were built in this period and the city took over from Antioch as the most important destination for Silk Road traffic arriving from the East.

The area occupied by the citadel was a defensive fort as early as the 3rd century BC but what we can see today dates largely from the 13th century AD. Unlike the Silk Road, Aleppo never really went into decline (apart, perhaps, from a small period following the collapse of the Ottoman empire) and it is still held by many to be the third city of Islam. The **Old City** is a World Heritage Site.

## WHAT TO SEE

Much money has been recently spent on restoring Aleppo's sights and improving the Old City as a whole. If you find the streets too crowded, come back on Friday when there is a peaceful calm.

### The Citadel

The Citadel is Aleppo's outstanding landmark and the small hill on which it is set has been home to a fort since 312BC and the Seleucids; Saladin described Aleppo as 'the eye of Syria, with its citadel the pupil'.

You enter the citadel through its 12th-century **gates**, which look so big and bold that you doubt they could ever be stormed. Inside, the **throne room** above the keep is a treasure of artisanship, especially the ceiling, and if this is a model for the eventual restoration of the whole site future visitors are in for a treat.

Unfortunately, the rest of the area within the defensive walls was nothing but a mass of rubble for many years. The government is slowly setting about rebuilding the area and there is a new small amphitheatre, although it is not particularly authentic.

The two small **mosques** that have survived from the 13th century have been considerably smartened up, as has **Ayyubid Palace**. The only downside is that the rubble has been poured onto the already filled-in moat and this is now showing signs of becoming a rubbish dump.

The entrance fee is S£300. It is open 09.00-18.00 daily. There are plans to turn the street circling the citadel into a pedestrianized area with cafés and shops.

### The Great Mosque and the Souq

This Umayyad-period **mosque** is considered to be Aleppo's finest, which since the city has over one thousand is no mean feat. It is notable for its elegant courtyard and square minaret.

It also marks one entrance to the **Souq**. Still occupying the original site that it has stood on since the Silk Road's heyday, the Souq is as interesting for its architecture as its stalls and is definitely worth a couple of hours of wandering. Highlights include many **khans** (caravanserais, see box p98) which are not signposted, though you should come across at least three (the best are to the south-west of the Great Mosque); you know it is a khan by the break in the stalls for a large set of heavy, wooden doors which will lead into a courtyard. These often have a small pool or a fountain inside them. The floors might be dirty but if you scuff them with your foot you should be able to make out the original marble underneath. The khans, like the souq, date from the Ottoman period rather than the heyday of the Silk Road. **Khan al Wazir**, just outside the souq, is a masterpiece.

## Others

Aleppo's **National Museum** (09.00-13.00 daily except Tues) charges S£300 and has some unique finds from the very earliest periods of history but the trouble is these don't tend to be very spectacular, making this museum one for the purists. The **Christian Quarter** is worth a look but be prepared to get lost in its maze of alleys. Lauded by the tourist board as the centre of a new café-society district where tourists can come and watch the world go by, this is over-stretching the mark by quite a bit, though it contains some of the city's best bars and restaurants and the 15th-century **Forty Martyrs Cathedral**, founded by Armenian traders.

---

### Hammams

Travelling by public transport will always take its toll on your body but at least in the Middle East you can treat yourself by indulging in the wonderful experience of a hammam (Turkish bath) to soothe your aches and pains. The steam bath is actually a Roman practice that passed through the Byzantines to the Turks.

A full-on visit to a Turkish bath goes something like this: go into the large lounge area and undress in one of the cubicles (leave all your clothes in the wardrobe but place your valuables in one of the safe boxes); put on your *pestamal* (the proper name for the towel) and your flip-flops (which are provided) and head down towards the sauna. On your way in pick up your bowl, soap and back-scrub and, if you prefer, wash yourself in any of the antechambers; once in the steam room stay and sweat for as long as you want or can bear (it's common to go in and out a few times). Be careful not to splash your neighbour as for Muslims washing is a religious ritual (especially on a Friday) and being soaked by a non-Muslim means you have to start cleansing yourself all over again.

When you are ready, come out to your masseur; he/she (men massage men, women massage women) will bathe you, scrub you with a coarse mitten, knead you, lather you, shampoo you and pull you until you are as loose as a rag doll (this usually takes place on a great marble slab beneath the hammam's central dome); then you can give yourself one last shower; wrap yourself in two body towels and a head towel and make your way back to the lounge where you can recline on one of the many *chaises longues* and relax over coffee or tea. You can stay for as long as you like before changing back and moving on, feeling great and with the clearest sinuses you've had in years. Check before you arrive, though, as there are separate opening times for men and women (with many hammams catering for men only).

> **Syrian Orthodox Church**
> In the 6th century AD **Jacobus Baradeus**, the patriarch of Edessa, fell out with the patriarch of Constantinople over the divine nature of Christ. The official line was that Christ had two forms, being both divine and human at the same time, but Baradeus claimed that Jesus could only ever have one, the divine. He was excommunicated and so formed his own church, which is also known as the **Jacobite** church. Similar movements led to the creation of the **Armenian Orthodox Church**, the **Coptic Church** in Egypt and the **Ethiopian Church**, although (as ever) politics wasn't far behind doctrinal differences in instigating these secessions.

## PRACTICAL INFORMATION
[☎ code 021]
### Orientation and services
Wherever you go in the city the citadel is likely to be in sight and it is the perfect landmark for orientation. The city is large but most sights can be visited on foot.

You should have no problem finding somewhere to change money as there are plenty of **money exchanges**; most of the hotels also offer this service and there is a branch of the **Commercial Bank of Syria (CBS)**. **Internet cafés** are becoming more and more commonplace.

The **Immigration Office** (open mornings Sat-Thurs, Sharia al Qalaa) will extend your visa for an extra 30 days (S£25).

**Hammams** (see box p105) are plentiful in Aleppo and the one we recommend is Yalbougha an Nasry, near the citadel; a full session costs S£350 (with women-only times on Mon, Thurs & Sat).

### Where to stay and eat
There is no shortage of accommodation – there must be 20 hotels just in the square grid of streets north-west of the **clock tower**. Our choice, the *Tourist Hotel* (☎ 221 6583; S£700/Db), is on ad Dala Sharia, a clean and tidy establishment. *Al Jawaher* (☎ 223 9554; S£650/Db) on al Faraj Sharia is also recommended and has a communal area popular with travellers.

For the romantics, there is only one choice: *Baron Hotel* (☎ 221 0880, US$40/Db) on the street of the same name. It may not have maintained much of its former elegance (though some of the rooms have recently been modernized/upgraded), but where else can you say you've slept in the same bed as Lawrence of Arabia, Agatha Christie, Atatürk or Teddy Roosevelt (to name but a few of the former guests). Even if your budget can't stretch to staying here, pop in for a drink in the bar, which doesn't seem to have changed a bit since the hotel first opened.

For modern five-star treatment, some very fine boutique hotels have recently been built: *Beit Wakil* (☎ 221 7169; US$100/Db) on Sharia as Sissi and *Dar Zamaria Martini* (☎ 363 6100; US$115/Db) are both in the Christian Quarter; *Diwan Rasmy* (☎ 331 2222; US$65/Db) is 400m north of the citadel.

The food in Aleppo never quite lives up to expectations but there are a few good **restaurants**. The *al Andalib* (just north of Baron Hotel) is a popular place in the centre of town with a rooftop terrace. In the Christian Quarter, *Beit Wakil* (see above) and *Beit as Sissi* are recommended.

### Moving on
Buses to **Hama** (2½hrs/S£65) and **Damascus** (5hrs/S£150) leave from the **bus station** (Ibrahim Hanano Sharia). Ignore the touts and use one of the more reputable operators (Karnak – the state operator – is cheap but slow; Qadmous, Al Ahliah and Al Rayan are the recommended private operators). For crossing over to **Antakya** (see box p103), buses leave from a parking lot on Sharia al Maari, west of the National Museum.

Aleppo 107

# Aleppo

> **The Dead Cities excursion**
> Between Hama and Aleppo are the remains of about 600 ancient sites with some quite remarkable sights. Just why they came to be deserted is unclear, although the most common theory is that with the demise of the Incense Road (see box p45), the lifeblood of this area simply drained away. Hundreds of relics are sitting here in the sun and an inspection of at least a few sites is worth the effort.
> The easiest way to see these remains in one go is through a tour (see *Cairo* and *Riad* hotels below); try to get a largish group to drive the price down.

# Hama

Hama is famous for its giant, wooden waterwheels (*norias*) along the Orontes River but these days the spectacle is limited by a lack of water. As a base for seeing Krak des Chevaliers (see box pp111-13), Hama is much better than Homs (even though it is further away) as it has a much wider choice of hotels.

## WHAT TO SEE

Apart from the **norias** there isn't much to see specifically in Hama, although **Azem Palace** (built by the same man – As'ad Pasha – who built the Azem Palace in Damascus) is exquisite. Instead, Hama has become popular as a base for some of the best excursions in Syria.

### PRACTICAL INFORMATION
**[☎ code 033]**
**Orientation and services**
Hama is small and almost everything you need is within walking distance of the clock tower in the central square.

There is a branch of the **Commercial Bank of Syria (CBS)** next to the **post office**. If you need to extend your visa go to the new **Immigration Office** (Sharia Ziqar; 08.00-14.00, Sat-Thurs) near the central Norias. Both *Cairo* and *Riad* hotels have **Internet** facilities and there are other cafés in town.

At the end of April, Hama is host to a large **Spring Flower Festival**. This is a very colourful time and ideal for seeing the waterwheels turning as the sluice gates are ceremonially opened.

### Where to stay and eat
You shouldn't have a problem finding accommodation in Hama as there is plenty. All the hotels are gathered in the centre and a few hotels offer 'roof sleeping' as an option, including the two listed immediately below.

On Sharia Shoukri al Quwatli you'll find *Riad Hotel* (☎ 239 512; S£400/Db) and *Cairo Hotel* (☎ 910 537; S£450/Db), two of the best backpacker places in Syria. Rooms include air conditioning, a fridge, a TV and a shower and in the off-season they automatically discount rates. The owners (although fierce rivals) are also very friendly and can organize just about any tour you want.

Up the road is the more expensive *Noria Hotel* (☎ 512 414; US$30/Db), run by Badr Tonbor (who also owns the Cairo) and the best of the mid-range options. By the river is the usual *Cham Palace* offering (☎ 525 335; US$140/Db): it's pleasant enough although a bit soulless and caters mainly for tour groups.

Hama 109

# Hama

- Four Norias Restaurant
- Norias
- Orontes River
- Clock Tower/Central Square
- Shoukri al Quwatli Sharia
- CBS/Money exchange
- PO
- Riad Hotel
- Al Buhturi Sharia
- Jamal Abdl'Naser
- Sadik Avenue
- Cairo Hotel
- Noria Hotel
- Cham Palace
- Norias
- Azem Palace
- Norias
- Abu al Feda Sharia
- Immigration office
- To minibus station
- Citadel Mound

THE MIDDLE EAST

In the same quarter as most of the hotels there is a good selection of cafés and small restaurants. *Four Norias* restaurant is definitely a cut above these, however, and has a patio overlooking four of the biggest wheels – though it's a bit further out.

**Moving on**
Different **bus** services leave from different ticket offices: the offices are between the square and the main road. Buy a ticket the night before you plan to leave.

There are plenty of buses to **Aleppo** (2½hrs/S£65), **Homs** (45mins; from here you can get a bus/minibus to **Palmyra**), and **Damascus** (2½hrs/S£80). The **minibus station** is a ten-minute walk to the south of the city.

### Excursion to Apamea

All that remains of this city, built in the 2nd century BC by Seleucis (one of Alexander's successors), is the long main street of the city centre but the detail on the columns that line this way is as incredible as the length of the street. The standard refrain is that if Palmyra wasn't down the road, Apamea would be famous throughout the world and while Palmyra benefits from a more impressive setting, this archaeological treasure-trove is more than worth the trip.

**History** The city was built in celebration of the marriage between Seleucis and Apamea, a local beauty, and the main road, which you can imagine the celebratory procession passing along, stretches for two kilometres, although most of the best ruins are within the kilometre between the café in the middle and the north end. The city was still rich enough to be sacked in the sixth and seventh centuries by the Sassanids but under Islamic rulers it fell into terminal decline until it was finally destroyed by an earthquake in 1157.

**What to see** At the north end, recent archaeological digs have unearthed water canal pipes, a sunken olive jar and various stone carvings on a wall but you will probably need to tip one of the local, self-appointed guides to find them. On either side of the street, set back from the columns, are the fronts of various shops and stores which serviced the city. There are the remains of a bathhouse about halfway along and two temples, one to Bacchus and one to Venus. On the lintels at the top of the columns you can see more carvings, ranging from flowers and women to more phallic symbols (again, the best examples seem to be about halfway down the street and on the east side).

**Practicalities** If you have your own private transport you can see Apamea on the way between Aleppo and Hama. One alternative is to take a tour (see *Riad* and *Cairo* hotels in Hama, p108). Another is to take a minibus to Suqeilibiyya from the centre of Hama (ask your hotel for the nearest bus stop) and then another to the small town of Qala'at al Mudiq. This is set beneath a steep hill with a medieval citadel on top and you need to climb this hill to reach Apamea itself. Once at the top you will see the columns.

If you are on a tour you will probably be dropped at the southern end of the ruins, near the café, but if you have a choice ask to be dropped at the northern end and picked up at the south end. The ticket for the site is S£300 and although there is no fencing to stop you walking straight in without paying, a man on a scooter will more than likely catch up with you if you try to dodge the fee.

### Excursion to Krak des Chevaliers

This castle has little to do with the Silk Road – although many of those involved in the Crusades (especially the Italians) were here only in order to expand their trading empires and break the Muslim monopoly on the western end of the route. Nevertheless, you would be foolish to miss out on an opportunity to see what Lawrence of Arabia deemed 'the finest castle in the world'.

**History** In the 11th century, the Crusaders arrived here from Europe (see pp56-60) and came up against a small fort known as Hisa al Akrad ('Castle of the Kurds'). The Emir of Homs had stationed a crack garrison of Kurdish troops here to protect the road to the coast (the castle overlooks the Homs Gap – the key break in the Jebel Ansariyya Mountains running alongside the coast). In 1110 Tancred, Prince of Antioch, managed to drive out the Muslims and occupy the fort and in 1142 it was given to the Knights Hospitaller (see box p58). What we see today was not built in one go but in a series of enlargements and modifications completed over centuries. Yet by 1163, when Nur ed-Din attacked, and 1188, when Saladin laid siege, it was strong enough to withstand these Saracen aggressors whilst all around other Christian strongholds collapsed.

In 1271, however, the fortress finally fell. This time it was attacked by the Mamelukes who brought vastly improved siege equipment with them. The knights still held out for months but when the Mamelukes, impressed by their enemy's fortitude, offered them a safe passage in return for surrender, they accepted these very generous terms – at this time it was commonly accepted that if the besieged held out for a long period, only the women and children (at most) would be spared.

The Krak remained an important fortress and more parts were added by its new owners – you can clearly see the dividing line above the front entrance, where the new sections are made of a different coloured stone – but as time went on its location became less strategic and, under the Ottomans, it fell into a state of neglect.

Up until 1934 locals lived inside the castle's walls, quite indifferent to the site's heritage, and this has left the odd inevitable scar. Over the past few decades, however, the fortress as a whole has been restored to virtually all of its magnificent former glory and you will struggle to find fault with the work they have done – although the locals still live right up against the car park which slightly spoils the view. Looking west on a clear day you can see the Mediterranean Sea.

**The exterior wall** Before you actually enter the castle, walk right around the outer battlements to get an idea of just how impregnable this place was. Once inside, the fortress is divided into two defensive sections with a **moat** built in between them. Over the years the moat has been filled in on three sides with rubble and waste (much of it from the removal of the houses in the 1930s) but the south side gives you a clear picture of the original moat's depth. The **sunken baths** that you can see in the south-eastern corner are an Arab addition built below the level of the moat so as to use its water.

On the east side, the archers' positions on the top level of the outer battlements seem impossible to reach: in fact they would have used moveable stairs. At the north end, as you walk along the moat's path you will see that a **drawbridge** would have been lowered from the inner battlements to the outer; the exit from the outer battlements seems too low until you remember that the level of the moat would have been at least ten metres lower than where you're standing. On the south side, there are the remains of a base for a **second drawbridge** which would have served the small arch in the outer wall above.

*Continued on p113*

112 Syria – Krak des Chevaliers

# Krak des Chevaliers

## Excursion to Krak des Chevaliers
*(Continued from p111)* What look like stone frills on the tops of many of the walls are actually machicolations used to support large vats of boiling liquids as their contents were poured through the gaps onto invaders below.

**The interior wall and the castle** The inner fortress is about the size, in area, of the original, pre-Crusader fort, though the Franks did much to build the defences higher and higher and introduce more and more living space. There are whole series of halls, cellars and living chambers to explore with each section cleverly connected to the next through secret passages and narrow staircases.

The **chapel** in the centre of the courtyard was later converted into a mosque and it was probably at this time that its main entrance was blocked by the stairs running up to the battlements, themselves perhaps a later addition.

The gothic **cloister** or corridor opposite couldn't be more European and gives you an idea that, even in a military fortress, presentation was everything in this time of chivalry. Behind the cloister is a large meeting room and behind that an even larger area which seems to have been the **kitchen** (you can see the remnants of a large brick oven and a well). Even further back is a secret corridor which served all the defensive positions within the inner wall at this level.

To the south of the courtyard is a raised platform supported by a grid of pillars which form their own room, possibly the dining room. At the back of this are two more **storerooms** with the remainders of massive oil jars sunk into the floor. There is also an original mill for grinding olives. On top of the platform you can still make out the base of the round meeting table. The round tower in the south-west corner would have served as lodgings for the castle's master.

### The Convent of Saint George
If you are on a tour or are staying overnight, try to make a detour to this convent (the locals will point the way if you don't want to take a taxi for around S£100); it's about 4km from the Krak. A convent was first thought to have been founded here in the 4th or 5th century and there are some very old remains, including the grotto, although most of what you can see dates from the Middle Ages and the upper chapel wasn't built until 1837.

### Practicalities
Give yourself at least three hours to see all of the fortress and **bring a torch**. For the best pictures, walk around the back of the Krak and up the hill towards the restaurant that juts out from the slope. Entrance to the castle is S£300. *Restaurant al Qalaa* is a good place to have lunch whilst admiring the view; it serves a ten-plate mezze for S£250 a head, although the options in the village are cheaper. If you want to stay by the Krak, there are a couple of options nearby. *Hotel of the Round Table* (S£500/Db) is overpriced and dirty. *Bebers Hotel* (20mins walk from the castle, US$25/Db) is new and clean.

Otherwise, make your way down to the Convent of Saint George where there is the modest *al Fahd* (US$20/Db) or the flashier *al Wadi Hotel* (US$70/Db), complete with swimming pool and tennis courts.

Take a bus/microbus to Homs (45 mins) and change at the bus station for the bus/minibus to Tartus (45 mins). Get off at the turn for Krak (you will see the castle from quite a way off) and wait for a local bus/car/taxi up to the castle. Otherwise, you can join a tour from Hama where the Cairo and Riad hotels (see p108) provide a good service.

… Syria – Palmyra

# Palmyra

Palmyra literally means 'City of Palms' and if you are here in the autumn you can treat yourself to some of the most delicious dates in the world. Yet no matter what time of year you arrive, the Roman ruins, which have been so perfectly preserved by the desert, will be a highlight of the entire trip. The city is a World Heritage Site.

The road to and from Palmyra cuts straight across the Syrian Desert. Though it looks inhospitable these days, in ancient times much of this area formed part of the Fertile Crescent. Caravans were therefore confident of finding oases necessary for a direct crossing, rather than paying the taxes imposed by the towns along the banks of the Euphrates. There were still bandits, however: if there was enough water for caravans, there was more than enough for local raiding parties.

## HISTORY

Originally known as Tadmor ('City of Dates'), Palmyra attracted the attention of the Romans early on as it lay directly on the trade route between Baghdad and the Mediterranean coast and its geographical isolation gave it protection from military attack.

As the Roman empire and the Silk Road prospered, so did Palmyra. Indeed, when Rome went into decline in the 3rd century AD, Palmyra was strong enough to go it alone and create its own independent kingdom under King Odenathus the Younger. He managed to defeat the Persians twice before he was assassinated in 267AD and succeeded by his second wife, Zenobia. Despite initial successes that brought Zenobia control of Syria, lower-Egypt and Asia Minor, reports of Rome's decline had been exaggerated. Rome's new emperor, Aurelian, raised a massive army that swept through Syria and stormed Palmyra in a matter of weeks. Zenobia was taken prisoner and led through the streets of Rome as part of Aurelian's Triumph in 274AD. Palmyra was stripped of all its titles and privileges and Aleppo, Antioch and Damascus took over as the prime trading destinations.

In the 17th century, Emir Fakhr Ad Din decided to revitalize Palmyra and use it as a training centre for his army but the idea didn't catch on despite the building of the magnificent fortress we can see today.

## WHAT TO SEE

One of the most refreshing things about Palmyra is that although entry to the **Temple of Bel** costs S£300, the rest of the Roman ruins are free, which makes Palmyra a good place to spend an extra day or two just chilling out and soaking up the atmosphere. If you want to have the ruins to yourself, however, you have to get up at dawn and go for a walk before the day-trippers arrive – it's an early start but the changing colours of the stones at this time make it worth it.

# Palmyra

## Palmyra map

**Where to stay**
1 Zenobia Hotel
4 Ishtar Hotel
5 Citadel Hotel
6 Baal Shamin Hotel
9 Umayyad Hotel

**Where to eat**
2 Pancake House
3 Palmyra Restaurant
5 Citadel Restaurant
7 Traditional Palmyra
8 Spring Restaurant

Labels on map: To the bus stop (at Sahara Café) 2km; To the Arab fortress/citadel; Ar Rais Sq; Al Quwatli St; Money exchange; Museum; City Wall; Marona House Tomb; Basilica; Temple of Baal-Shamin; Nymphaeum; Baths of Diocletian; Monumental Gateway; Temple of Bel; Temple of Nebo; Amphitheatre; Tetrapylon; The Great Colonnade; City wall; Piazza; Decumanus; Funerary Temple; Temple of Allat; Diocletian's Camp; Temple of the Standards; To tombs & funerary towers

THE MIDDLE EAST

The Temple of Bel is a shrine to the Babylonian equivalent of Zeus and dates from around 32AD. It was built as the final stop on the Victory Way, which you can still see marked out by the columns.

This street is notable for the fact that not only are so many of the columns intact but it is not straight, a rarity in the extreme for the Roman empire. There is a slight kink in the middle where the **tetrapylon** disguises the change in direction and at the **monumental gateway** there would have been an even bigger shift to bring the processions to the doors of the temple but this has been obliterated by the modern main road.

The **amphitheatre**, on the south side of the street, is in a good condition even if it is not in the same league as the one in Bosra (see box p122). Take time to appreciate the delicate carving and artistry lying all around you.

To the south of Palmyra are a series of tombs perched high one on top of another to form funerary towers. They date back to the first century AD but most of the interesting finds have been moved to Palmyra Museum. There are also some underground tombs (**hypogea**) here but you need to join one of the museum's organized tours to see inside them.

The **citadel** (S£150), at the top of the hill, is just as beautiful a sight as the Roman ruins even if it is nowhere near as grand. A trek up there is worth it; the views are particularly impressive at sunset but get there well before then because the citadel itself shuts before the sun goes down.

## PRACTICAL INFORMATION
[☎ code 031]
### Orientation and services

Pliny tells us that 600,000 people lived here in the 1st century AD but today Palmyra is a small town tacked onto the end of the historical sites.

The main sights are clustered together, making them easy to walk around, and the hotels are also gathered together at the start of the town proper, a few hundred metres from the sights.

Surprisingly, as this is Syria's number one attraction, there are not that many facilities but you can **exchange money** next door to the museum. There isn't that much to do after dark either and the majority of cafés don't sell alcohol.

Minibuses will probably drop you in the middle of town but scheduled buses will drop you at the Sahara Café **bus stop**, a 2km walk from the centre.

In late April/early May every year the **Palmyra Festival** is held, which has camel racing, folk dancing and music amongst its attractions.

### Where to stay

Despite the huge numbers now coming to Palmyra, most visitors are Syrians who come for the day only so there are not that many hotels. This means that just as the ruins can get pretty packed in summer, so can the hotels. It's best to leave one of you with the luggage by the museum while the others scout around the short main drag for the best deal (beware of rip-offs including exorbitant extras for hot water and breakfast).

In the budget range, some hotels (try *Baal Shamin Hotel*) let you sleep on the roof for a small consideration. *Umayyad Hotel* (☎ 910 755; S£300/Db with an en suite shower) on Saahat al Jamarek has a nice courtyard but check the price carefully and haggle if necessary. *Citadel Hotel* (S£500/Db) is reasonable and has a good café downstairs. On al Quwatli, *Ishtar Hotel* (☎ 913 073; US$30/Db) is more expensive but has a basement bar and a rooftop café, while *Zenobia* (☎ 910 107/ US$78/Db) is the best-placed hotel in town, right beside the ruins.

### Where to eat

*Mansaf* is the Palmyran speciality dish but don't get too excited: it's just another Middle Eastern version of rice, vegetables and meat. If you are looking for a nice beer after a hot and dusty day it's pretty straightforward: those cafés that have a licence will advertise the fact heavily and those that don't, won't.

***Traditional Palmyra*** has been going since 1940 and still comes up trumps with most of its customers, whereas the food at ***Spring Restaurant*** is quite plain. ***Palmyra Restaurant***, opposite the museum, is a tourist trap and should be avoided. Palmyra is Syria's closest thing to a backpacker hangout, as signalled by the ***Pancake House*** (you'll see the sign).

### Moving on

There are regular buses to **Damascus** (3hrs/S£115) and **Homs** bus station (2½hrs/S£65; change here to take a bus up to **Hama**) but there is **no bus station** in town so you need to trek 2km up to the bus stop at **Sahara Café** (taxi S£25). Minibuses/microbuses to Homs sometimes leave from the central square.

# Damascus

The mere mention of Syria's capital arouses a whole host of romantic images and memories and if this is the first stop on your journey it won't let you down. The modern city stretches for miles into the foothills of the Jibal Lubnan Ash Sharqiyeh (anti-Lebanon) Mountains but the Old City is tight, compact and full of treasures. Allow yourself at least two days to explore and a day for the trip to Bosra.

## HISTORY

Just how Damascus got its name is a constant source of argument. Some say the name came from Damaskos, son of Hermes, others from Damas, who accompanied Dionysus and was given a 'skene' by him, hence 'Damascene'. Cain and Abel are also said to have fought in the surrounding mountains and Abraham is supposed to have hidden in one of the caves here but as you would expect from a place that calls itself the oldest continually inhabited city in the world, the number of anecdotes is fairly comprehensive, even without the Saul/Paul conversion.

Whatever the case, there is evidence of a settlement here as long ago as 5000BC and by the end of the second millennium BC the Aramean King, Rezon, had made it his capital. Alexander took it for his empire in the 4th century BC and the Nabataeans (an Arabic tribe) seized it in 87BC, yet the Romans preferred to destroy it and build Bosra as their new capital.

It remained in Roman/Byzantine hands until 635AD when the Muslim armies of the south overran the region. Following the dispute over Mohammed's successor, the Syrian governor, Mu'awiyah, was able to seize power and establish his Umayyad dynasty with Damascus as his capital; it was during this period that most of Damascus's outstanding buildings were erected.

Over the following centuries the city earned itself a nickname which is still used today – 'Cham'. The word comes from the Bedouin word for a facial beauty spot: *chamay*. For the Bedouin riding in from the Syrian Desert, the oasis of

Damascus stood out against the backdrop of the mountains like one such beauty spot and they gave it this name as a mark of their joy for safely crossing the desert.

Richard Burton (the explorer rather than the actor) was British Ambassador here in the 19th century before his daring undercover journey to Mecca.

## Damascus today

Damascus has over four million inhabitants but most are found in the New City, which has engulfed the old. Indeed, such a tightly packed Old City was (and is) totally impractical for cars so in the second half of the 20th century the middle and upper classes moved away into the roomier suburbs, leaving what were once magnificent houses to be chopped up into living quarters for four or five families. No one would begrudge a family the right to a roof over its head but this situation is a reflection of the government's reluctance/failure to intervene and protect the Old City. Having said that, the city is a World Heritage Site.

## WHAT TO SEE

### The National Museum

The museum is laid out around a beautiful courtyard full of various archaeological finds brought to the capital over the years and it makes a very pleasant spot to sit and watch the world go by. Inside, if you go immediately to your left, the first room you enter has remnants of Chinese silk found at Palmyra and dating from the 1st century BC, so you can feel that you are hot on the Silk Road trail! There are plenty of other impressive artefacts all well laid out and with English labels but the highlight for many is the synagogue at the back, brought from Dura Europus on the Euphrates and rebuilt piece by piece. It was this synagogue that the Jews built after being exiled from Jerusalem by Nebuchadnezzar (Cyrus the Great famously liberated the Jews from Nebuchadnezzar in 579BC and gave them lands in his empire; he even married a Jew, Esther, of Biblical fame). It was the priests from this time who first sat down to create a definitive history of the Jews based on their oral traditions, myths and legends, mixed in with those of other tribes in the region. The finished product was the Old Testament.

Entrance to the museum costs S£300. It is open 09.00-18.00 (to 16.00 in winter) Wed-Mon. The entrance is on Qasr al Heir al Gharbi.

---

## DAMASCUS – MAP KEY

**Where to stay**
1 French Tower Hotel
6 Cham Palace Hotel
8 Omayad Hotel
13 Sultan Hotel
16 Al Haramein Hotel
17 Al Rabie Hotel
20 Beirut Hotel

**Where to eat and drink**
2 Al Kamal Restaurant
4 Damascus Worker's Club
19 The Karnak Bar
27 Coffee houses
31 Al Khawali Restaurant
32 Oxygen
33 Marmar
35 Elissar Restaurant
37 Piano Bar

**What to see**
9 National Museum
11 Takiyya as Suleimaniyya
21 Al Adiliyya Madrassah
22 Az Zahiriyya Madrassah
23 Sayyida Ruquyya Mosque
24 Tomb of Saladin
25 Jupiter Temple
26 Umayyad Mosque
28 Azem Palace
29 Hammam Nur ed Din
30 As'ad Pasha Khan
34 Hammam Bakri
36 Chapel of St Ananias
38 St Paul's Chapel

**Other**
3 Tourist Information
5 CBS
6 Chamtour
7 Cinema
10 Tourist Information
12 Baramke bus station
14 Airport Bus Stop
15 Internet
18 Money Exchange

Damascus 119

# Damascus

## Takiyya as Suleimaniyya
This beautiful old mosque and pilgrims' hostel was designed by Sinan, Suleiman the Magnificent's – indeed, the entire Ottoman empire's – outstanding architect; he would later build the great Suleiman Mosque in Istanbul. The Takiyya now houses a **craft market** and small **Army Museum** but the building itself is the main attraction.

## The Old City
The Old City is fantastic and surrounding it is a massive **city wall**. As you come in from the west you will only see reconstructed sections and the renovation work around **the citadel**. Around the east side, however, are quite a few original sections but they are currently in a state of neglect. Have a walk around the walls if you can (there is no dedicated path) and check out the many beautiful **gates** (there are more remaining in the northern sections than the southern).

The Syrians, like many Arabs, are very private people when it comes to their family and their houses, so for much of the day you will see only whitewashed walls interspersed with snatches of the life behind them – which is a shame, as some of the old **Damascene houses** in the city are fantastic (the tourist office has a list of houses recently restored and made open to the public).

The government's attitude to preservation in the Old City is epitomized at the far end of the Souq al Hamidiyya, where the shops and the houses beside the Roman-era **Jupiter Temple** use the columns as part of their supporting structure.

## Umayyad Mosque
Built in 705AD, this was intended to be the world's greatest mosque and along with the Dome of the Rock in Jerusalem it stands as one of the most important Muslim sites in the region. The three minarets rise above the Old City and inside the courtyard the renovated green mosaics (made of glass rather than tiles) are tremendous. Inside the mosque is the **tomb of John the Baptist**, while out the back is another courtyard with a small museum and the **tomb of Saladin**, the Islamic hero who defeated the Crusaders. Entrance to the complex is a compulsory S£50 for non-Muslims but this includes a useful booklet guide.

## Al Adiliyya and Az Zahiriyya madrassahs
Go inside the school and the library of **Az Zahiriyya** (which the caretaker will open for a small tip) and you will be amazed at the collection of books inside, although saddened at their precarious state. Baibars, the great Mameluke sultan, is also buried here. In **Al Adiliyya**, opposite, it is hard to tell whether they are restoring it or knocking it down but at least the work gives you a real glimpse of how the original tile-work has been covered by layer after layer of plaster and paint over the years. Fortunately, it is still there waiting to be rediscovered.

## Azem Palace
In 1749 when this palace (S£300; Wed-Mon 09.00-18.00, to 16.00 in winter) was built, Damascus was a clear case of black and white: black from the volcanic and basalt rock, white from limestone. Nowhere is this more beautifully illustrated than in Azem Palace, which shows how the wealthy houses were built in days gone by.

## As'ad Pasha Khan
The khans of Damascus tend to date from after the heyday of the route and often from the 18th century, as this one does. The design has hardly changed in two thousand years, however, so this khan still offers a reasonable glimpse of the Silk Road's past. As'ad Pasha Khan, like most khans in the region, is right in the middle of the city and like the Azem Palace it is a classic from the Damascene 'Black and White' school. Nowadays it holds concerts and cultural events and when we were there it also held a fascinating collection of old photographs of the city.

## Others
**Sayyida Ruquyya Mosque** (dedicated to the daughter of Hussein, son of Ali, leader of the Shi'ites) is gaudy in the extreme compared to Umayyad Mosque but get used to the shiny mirrors on the inside because there are more to come in Iran and, by the time you get to Mashad, you will realize this is a common theme.

Mark Twain wrote that 'As long as there is the river, there will be Damascus' but, unfortunately, the **Barada river** is suffering heavily from the recent lack of rain and is nothing like the sight it was in Twain's day. Your best views of it are in the north-west of the city.

Of the many **hammams** (see box p105) in the Old City where you can get a Turkish bath, **Hammam Nur ed-Din** is set in a magnificent building and is the most user-friendly (Souq al Bzouriyya; open daily 09.00-23.00; S£240 for the works; men only). Women will struggle to find a good Turkish bath but try **Hammam Bakri** in the Christian Quarter (Kanayet al Hattab St; S£190).

In the **Christian Quarter**, **Saint Paul's Chapel** is a modern structure but it marks the spot where he supposedly escaped over the city walls by being let down in a basket. The **Chapel of Saint Ananias** sits in what is thought to be the cellar of this early disciple's house. This quarter is also where you are more likely to be allowed into the courtyards of the old Damascene houses, many of which have often been converted into small shops, bars and restaurants.

## PRACTICAL INFORMATION
[☏ code 011]
### Orientation and services
The Old City is small and easy to walk around in a few hours, as is the heart of the New City, so there is no need to worry about local transport. Taxis, if needed, are plentiful. The city is also very safe, although whether this is because there are so many secret policemen about is open to debate.

There is a small **tourist information** office near the National Museum and a larger one north of Saahat Yousef al Azmeh Square. Many **Internet cafés** have sprung up in the capital; they come and go but Martyr's Square is always home to one or two. There are several places to exchange foreign currency as well as numerous branches of CBS (see p76).

You shouldn't need a travel agent in Syria unless you are buying a plane ticket home but if you do **Chamtour** (☏ 223 2300; 🖳 www.chamhotels.com), inside Cham Palace Hotel, and **Silk Road Travel and Tourism** (☏ 223 0500; 🖳 www.dm.net.lb/silkroad/) on Fardos St are reliable.

The **Immigration Office** (open only in the mornings – apply one day and pick up the next) is west of Baramke bus station on Filasteen St; you need three photos and S£25. The **Turkish Embassy** is at 58 Ziad bin Abi Soufian St, in the north-west of the city. The **Iranian Embassy** (Autostraad al Mezze) is not recommended as its service is

## Excursion to Bosra

Bosra is a World Heritage Site. The 2nd-century **Roman theatre** here is almost perfect and considered the best of its kind in the world. It is made even better by being housed in a citadel that, under any other criteria, would be a spectacle in itself. Appreciate the acoustics from the top seats (the theatre holds 15,000 spectators). The views from the top are as impressive outside as in because the volcanic-red soil of the surrounding countryside lights up against the desert and it is this fertile land that produces all the tomatoes sold at the side of the road during autumn. Entrance costs S£400. Give yourself plenty of time to wander around the complex (the remains of the **old Roman town** surround the theatre); few are disappointed by what was once the capital of the Roman province of Arabia.

**Practicalities** Buses (2hrs/S£70) leave from Damascus's Baramke bus station but it's quicker to take a **minibus** from outside the station to **Der'a** and then change for the next minibus to Bosra. If you have plenty of time, try to visit Bosra via **Shahba** and **Suweida** (buses run through Shahba to Suweida from Baramke). Shahba was the birthplace of Philip the Syrian (who was Emperor of Rome from 244 to 249AD) and the town has an impressive amphitheatre. It is also the site of the oldest-known baths in the country (dating from the 3rd century BC). Suweida's museum has some of the best-preserved Roman mosaics in the world. Both towns are also home to a large **Druze** population and you will instantly notice their distinctive, long-flowing clothes.

---

slow, unreliable and 4km west of the city centre. For visa requirements, see p17.

**Damascus's airport** is small and easy to negotiate and you will probably receive more attention from the taxi drivers outside than from the customs officials. Buses into the city centre run every half-hour and take 45 minutes. They will drop you right in the middle of the New City and, whichever hotel you pick, it should be within walking distance. Buses to the airport leave from the same place (see map p119).

If you are coming into/leaving from **Harasta bus station**, take one of the many microbuses to/from Martyr's Square; if you are coming into/leaving from **Baramke bus station** you can walk to/from the same square in about 20 minutes.

## Where to stay

As you will spend nearly all your time in the Old City it makes sense to stay as close to it as possible, although actually staying inside is not really an option as there are very few places which allow foreign guests.

*Al Haramein Hotel* (☎ 231 9489; S£395/Db, S£175/dorm, S£100/roof) is an old townhouse converted into a hotel on Sharia Bahsa; on a good night it can be very atmospheric but is often full, even out of season, so do book in advance.

*Al Rabie* (☎ 231 8374; S£395/Db), next door, is an almost identical set up and some prefer it (it is certainly beautiful inside), although others complain that the beds aren't as comfy.

For other cheap options, scout around Martyr's Square but be warned, this area is also home to most of the local prostitutes and dodgy dealers, so a full inspection of your room is recommended before committing. South of the square, *Beirut Hotel* (S£300/Db) seems cleaner than most.

Of the many mid-range options, *Sultan Hotel* (☎ 222 5768) on Mousalam al Baroudi St has doubles for US$30 and

*French Tower Hotel* (☎ 231 4000) on 29 May St has doubles for US$35. Both get good reports for clean, comfortable rooms and friendly service.

The top end of the market is being added to every year but the Chamtour group have three five-star options, of which *Cham Palace* (☎ 223 2300; US$160/Db) on Maysaloun St is the most central and, with its restaurants, bars and swimming pool, is generally regarded as the best in town. However, *Omayyad Hotel* (☎ 221 7700; 🖥 www.omayyadhotel.net; US$105/Db) has perhaps the most character.

## Where to eat

Martyr's Square has the usual collection of *kebabis*, if you're looking for a cheap snack but none is particularly good.

The falafel and mezze in *Al Kamal* are very good as are the various Western dishes (at very reasonable prices) but no alcohol is served here. It is, however, worth paying a little extra and sampling some of the excellent restaurants on offer in the Old City (particularly the Christian Quarter).

On ad Dawamneh St, *Elissar* (☎ 542 4300; dinner for two from around S£800) offers the finest dining in the Old City and is very popular (it's a good idea to book), if a little expensive; you can't beat the setting and few are disappointed with its traditional Syrian cuisine. *Al Khawali* (off Straight St) is an excellent example of a fine old Damascene house converted into a restaurant. For a less formal arrangement, go to the two **coffee houses** below the eastern gate of Umayyad Mosque. These are where you're most likely to bump into fellow travellers and locals as everybody enjoys a couple of hours sipping coffee and sucking on hubble-bubbles (see box p81). Food is available from the stalls next door.

## Entertainment

For nightlife, you are best off in the Christian Quarter where alcohol is more readily available: *Piano Bar* (Hanamia St) is pleasant but expensive; *Oxygen* (nr Bab Touma St) is where the local trendies hang out. *Marmar* (Dawamneh St) is the closest thing to a nightclub and is big at weekends.

Back in Martyr's Square, *The Karnak Bar* is held up as the big drinking den and perhaps if there is a group of you it could be fun but make sure you get blind drunk as quickly as everybody else or you might wake up to the fact that you are sitting on plastic chairs and tables in the Syrian equivalent of a motorway service station.

A better option in the New City is the *Damascus Workers Club* (An Nadi al Umal) where you can eat and drink to your heart's content in a large garden. Alternatively, there are some good **off-licences** on the south side of Martyr's Square where you can buy a few bottles and retire to the courtyard of your hotel. There is a **cinema** showing English-language films across the road from the Cham Palace.

## Things to buy

Souq Al Hamidiyya, at the entrance to the Old City, is one of the best places in the world to buy **gold**, if you know what you are doing. All the gold sold here is 22 carat, rather than the 9-, 12- and 18-carat you see in Europe. The other notable souvenir on offer is, of course, **damask**, which is cloth embroidered on both sides to give it a rich heavy feel. **Straight St** is also worth a look for souvenirs.

## Moving on

Direct **buses** from Damascus's Harasta bus station (about 6km north-west of the city) to **Palmyra** (4hrs/S£100) run on most days, otherwise you must go via **Homs** (2hrs) and change there. Buses also run regularly to **Hama** (2½hrs), **Aleppo** (5hrs) and even **Antakya** and **Istanbul**. Ignore the touts and use one of the more reputable operators (*Karnak* – the state operator – is cheap but slow; *Qadmous*, *Al Ahliah* and *Al Rayan* are the recommended private operators).

**Minibuses** and **share-taxis** regularly run both of the Homs–Damascus and Homs–Palmyra routes and, even with the necessary change, they are often quicker than the buses. They leave from outside Baramke bus station (see map p119).

**Trains** are slow and impractical although there are international services to **Amman** and **Tehran**!

> **A trip back in time**
> Aramaic was the language spoken by Jesus and the *lingua franca* for much of the western Silk Road during the Roman era. Nowadays it is rarely spoken in its ancient form so if you want to hear it, consider a visit to the hill-town of **Maalula**. The town itself is also quite a sight, hewn out of the surrounding cliffs, and it provides a pleasant retreat from the hustle of Damascus. Minibuses run to/from **Maalula Garage** in the north-east of the city.

# Malatya and Kahta

*'Malatya, Malatya, you're unmatched,
Your moon and sun fill our souls.'*

So the Turkish song goes, though we can only presume the creator of this ditty had been drinking. Today **Malatya** is famous for its apricots, which about says it all, though to be fair this is because locals moved here only in 1839 when the town's old site, the ancient town of Eski Malatya, was destroyed. **Kahta**, if anything, is worse but both towns make a convenient base for visiting Nemrut Daği.

## WHAT TO SEE

There is nothing to see in either town, except the **museum** in Malatya, perhaps, though this is more of a time killer than a 'must-see', so book your trip to Nemrut Daği for the day after you arrive.

## PRACTICAL INFORMATION
### Orientation and services
**Malatya** (☎ code **0422**) Buses drop you off at the **otogar** 2km west of town, so you need to take a minibus into the centre (ask for the 'Vilayet' or 'centrum' dolmuş on the main road outside the station). The town is tiny and easy to find your way around. There is an **Internet café** at the otogar – handy if you have a long wait for your bus – and there is also one in town (both charge YTL0.5/hr). The **tourist office** is in the corner of the central square and runs tours to Nemrut Daği and Turkey's south-east (see box p126); it is open every day but tours are limited outside the summer season.

**Kahta** (☎ code **0416**) In reality this town is just one long main road. There is **no tourist office** but all hotel/hostels run tours to Nemrut Daği. They also claim to run tours to Turkey's south-east but you will need to get a group together. There are a couple of **Internet cafés** on the main street.

### Where to stay and eat
**Malatya** This town sees even fewer foreign visitors than Antakya and the accommodation on offer reflects that. *Park Hotel* (Atatürk Caddesi 17; YTL30/Db) is the most basic option but well placed. About another 200m up the street, *Yeni Sinan Hotel* (☎ 321 2907; YTL40/Db) is much cleaner, more comfortable and has en suite showers. There is little in the way of restaurants so many visitors just pick up something from the stalls on Atatürk Caddesi. *Nostalgi*, over the road from the tourist office, is worth a look for traditional Turkish fare.

## Malatya

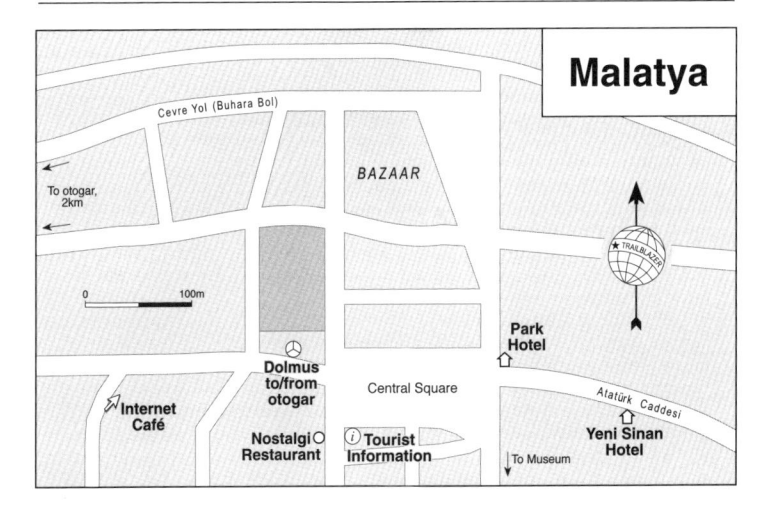

*[Map of Malatya showing Cevre Yol (Buhara Bol), Bazaar, To otogar 2km, Internet Café, Nostalgi Restaurant, Dolmus to/from otogar, Central Square, Tourist Information, To Museum, Park Hotel, Atatürk Caddesi, Yeni Sinan Hotel]*

**Kahta** Wherever you are dropped on the main street you are likely to be approached by a guy from at least one of the hostels. None stand out so haggle hard and take the cheapest on offer: most go to *Commagene Hotel* (☎ 725 7614; YTL40/Db) at Mustafa Kemal Caddesi 1. *Bogazicl Aile Restaurant* (up the road, past the bus station and opposite the police station) is good.

### Moving on
From Malatya, buses for **Erzurum** leave regularly (9hrs/YTL25); from Kahta you will need to take a bus to Malatya first (3hrs/YTL10).

Buses to **Antakya** (6hrs) and **Göreme** (5hrs/YTL20) leave once or twice a day from both towns.

### Excursion to Nemrut Daği
This attraction is another to have assumed the 'Eighth Wonder of the World' tag and really is impressive. Set atop a 2150m mountain, this World Heritage Site is thought to be a 2000-year-old sanctuary for the ancient Commagene King, Antiochus. The original statues here must have been massive but now we are left merely with the heads of the king, Zeus, Apollo, and synthesized local/Persian/Greek gods. On your way, you will also see many of the dams built here to revitalize farming in the region. So far this has worked very effectively but the Euphrates and Tigris rivers are suffering further downstream, making it harder than ever for Syrian and Iraqi farmers (bring your swimming things as most tours stop at one of the rivers for a break).

**Practicalities** In the summer the tourist office in Malatya runs excellent trips to the site for US$30. This includes transport to the stones in the afternoon, time to watch the sun set over them, a night in a motel near the site, another trip to the stones for the sunrise and transport back to Malatya. Food and drink is not included so bring your own, as the café is very expensive.

Tours (YTL40) go from Kahta year-round. Some visitors take a sleeping bag and stay the night at the top and hitch or negotiate a return lift.

> **Turkey's south-east**
>
> As well as being home to some interesting Silk Road cities, Turkey's south-east is home to the vast majority of Turkey's Kurds (see box p66). The region as a whole is one of tremendous natural beauty with scores of rocky mountains, extinct volcanoes and extensive lakes but because of increased unrest in the 1980s and '90s it is the least visited part of the country. The PKK (see box p62) announced a return to violence in 2004 and though its main targets are government/economic infrastructure and the main tourist resorts on Turkey's west coast, you should take care. If the situation doesn't improve it is probably worth joining a tour, either from Göreme (see pp95-9) or Malatya and Kahta (see pp124-5) rather than trying to go it alone.
>
> If you do go, **Harran**, with its beehive houses and its history (Abraham lived here) is many people's highlight. The mosques of **Sanliurfa** are also worth seeing; this city was originally known as Urfa but was renamed Edessa by Alexander the Great and was battled over for centuries by Christians and Muslims. The biggest city in the south-east is the fortress town of **Diyarbakir**, often referred to as the Kurd's capital; it has been the centre of Kurdish resistance throughout their struggle and therefore, perhaps unsurprisingly, is not the most picturesque of cities but it is certainly the place to get a taste of authentic Kurdish life and its 6km city walls give dramatic views of the **River Tigris**.

# Erzurum

The area around Erzurum was known as 'Roman country' by the Persians even though, by the time they came into contact with them, these 'Romans' were Byzantines. The name stuck and when the Seljuk empire collapsed, the chunk of Anatolia that remained in their grasp became known as the Sultanate of Rum (Rome). Erzurum itself was the great garrison city of the area and the city's setting, in almost a complete ring of mountains, is impressive (in the winter, when all the mountains are covered in snow, it is spectacular although extremely cold). There is still a bit of a feel of a border town to Erzurum (and the army still has an important base here) but it's an enjoyable place to spend a day or so.

## WHAT TO SEE

The small **Arts and Ethnography Museum** (YTL2), housed in a 14th-century madrassah, has an interesting selection of local carpets. **Ulu Cami Mosque** (1179AD) is the oldest in the area and is fantastic inside, especially the layered wooden roof, which has portholes cut in around the top. Next door is **Cifte Minareli Madrassah**; the colours and designs on its Seljuk minarets are equally striking. The old **Citadel** (built by Emperor Theodosius in the 5th century) has seen better days but is worth a poke around for its clock tower and the tremendous views of the countryside.

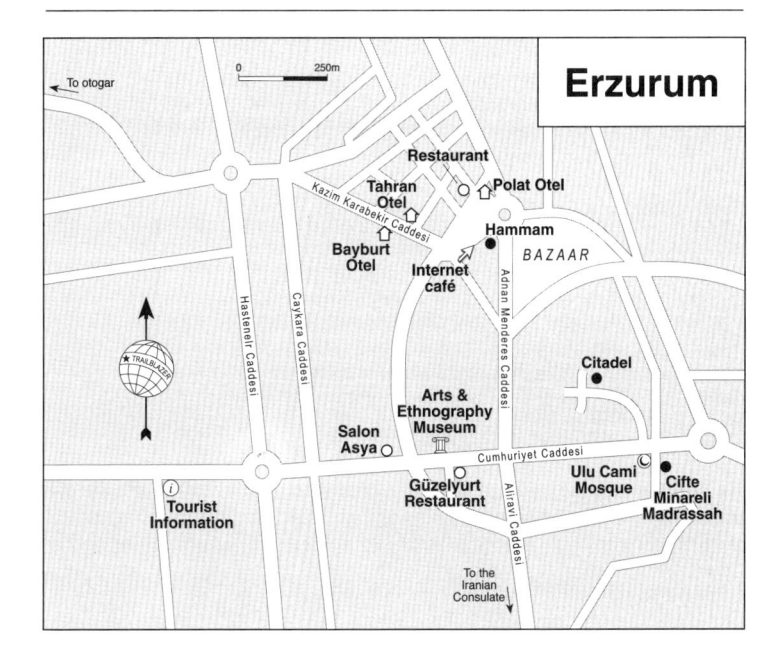

## PRACTICAL INFORMATION
[☎ code 0442]

### Orientation and services
The **otogar** is a little way out and although you can walk it's easier to take a bus from outside the station into the centre (YTL0.6) as this drops you near the best hotels.

If you still haven't obtained an Iranian visa, you need to go to the **Iranian Consulate** (open every day except Friday; off Atatürk Bulvari) in the far south of town (you'll need to take a cab) and hope they will issue you with a transit visa.

There are plenty of **Internet cafés** on and off Cumhuriyet Caddesi. The **tourist information office** seems to open when it pleases and is of little use outside summer.

The **hammam** (see box p105; YTL8 for the full works) on Adnan Menderes Caddesi is a welcome relief.

### Where to stay and eat
Erzurum has quite a few options, mostly gathered together in the northern part of town. *Bayburt Otel* (Kazim Karabekir Caddesi; YTL15/Db) must be one of the cheapest clean and habitable hotels in Turkey, though *Tahran Otel* (☎ 233 9041; YTL25/Db with shower), opposite, seems worth the little extra. Around the corner is the quite upmarket *Polat Otel* (☎ 235 0363; YTL40/Db).

There are two good **restaurants** on the high street, *Güzelyurt* (Cumhuriyet Caddesi 51), a long-time favourite, and *Salon Asya*. There are also numerous nameless cheapies around town; try the one behind Polat Otel, its food is delicious.

### Moving on
Buses to **Doğubeyazit** (4hrs/YTL15) officially leave five times a day but check departure times when you arrive.

Going to **Malatya** is straightforward (9hrs/YTL25), as buses run at least twice a day.

# Doğubeyazit

To reach this border town (called 'Dog Biscuit' by most travellers) you need to travel over high barren mountains and, in the past, conditions and locals were so notoriously inhospitable that many caravans looped up through Armenia and Azerbaijan rather than plough straight across. As far back as the 19th century this area was dangerous, as Robert Curzon, an English traveller, tells us on his 1854 trip: 'Dead bodies were frequently brought into the city (from the roads) and it is common in the summer, on the melting of the snow, to find numerous corpses of men, and bodies of horses, who had perished the preceding winter.' *(Armenia; A Year at Erzurum, and on the Frontiers of Russia, Turkey and Persia)*.

## WHAT TO SEE

No matter which way you come into town you will be treated to spectacular panoramas of **Mount Ararat** and it's easy to catch more glimpses from various points in the centre. If you are planning on doing any serious **trekking** in this region, Mount Ararat is a very 'doable' three-day trek but you must apply for a permit at least 45 days in advance (see Murat Camping below).

The man-made highlight is **Isak Pasha Palace** (YTL5), 5km from town. Built in 1784 by Isak Pasha when he was the governor of the area, the palace sits on the route of the old Silk Road, 1700m up in the hills to the south-west of the city. It has been well restored and looks wonderful. On the other side of the gorge are the remains of an even older citadel, perhaps as much as 3500 years old. A taxi up to the palace is about YTL7 but it's a pleasant stroll back down.

### PRACTICAL INFORMATION
**Orientation and services** [☎ code 0472]
Try not to leave Doğubeyazit with more Turkish lira than you will need before the border as it is a weak currency when exchanging money in Iran; the many **banks** or **bureaux de change** in town offer better rates than the touts at the border. **Internet cafés** have opened in town but most hotels/hostels have access, too. If you still haven't got an **Iranian visa** MesFur Tur (☎ 312 6772; Bekediye Caddesi 6) should be able to arrange one in five days (for about $100).

The new **Yeni Hammam** (see box p105, YTL10 for the full works) has opened; its Jacuzzi and sauna provide welcome relief after a long time on the road.

### Where to stay and eat
This is a transit town so accommodation tends towards the practical. At Büyük Agri Caddesi 124, *Tahran Hotel* (☎ 312 0195; 🖵 www.eastturkey.com; YTL15/Db) is comfy, offers free Internet and some rooms have views of Mount Ararat; they'll also do your washing for YTL3. *Erzurum Hotel* (☎ 312 5080; Dr Ismail Besikci Caddesi 26; YTL15/Db) is also worth considering. *Murat Camping* (☎ 312 0367; 🖵 murat camping@mynet.com.tr; YTL3-5/pp), up

---

**(Opposite) Top left**: Isak Pasha Palace (see above). **Top right**: Making giant bowls of plov (see p185), the Uzbek national dish, on Independence Day. **Bottom**: This tiger in the Registan in Samarkand (see p217) is a rare example of a living creature depicted in Islamic art.

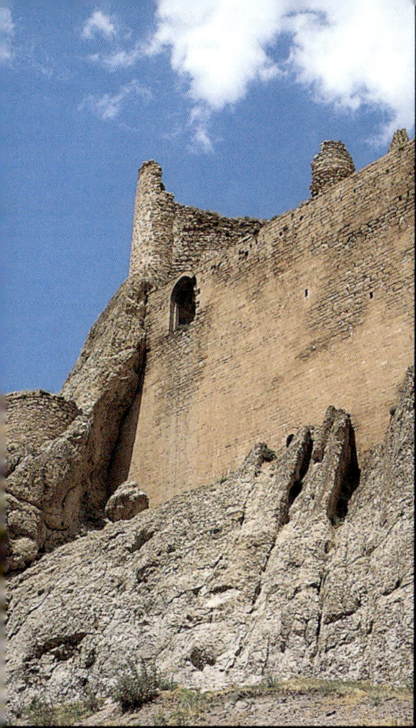
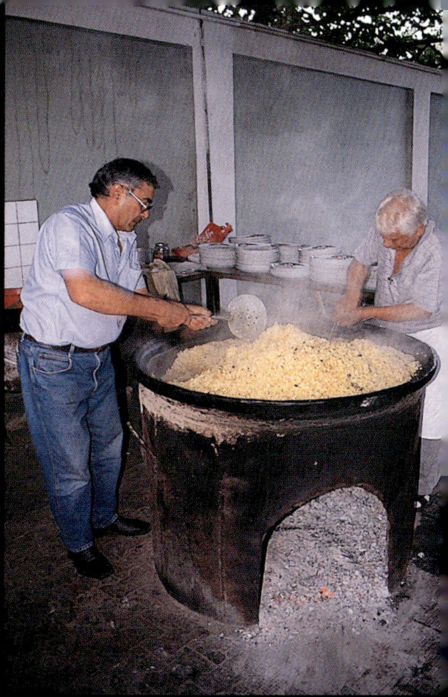
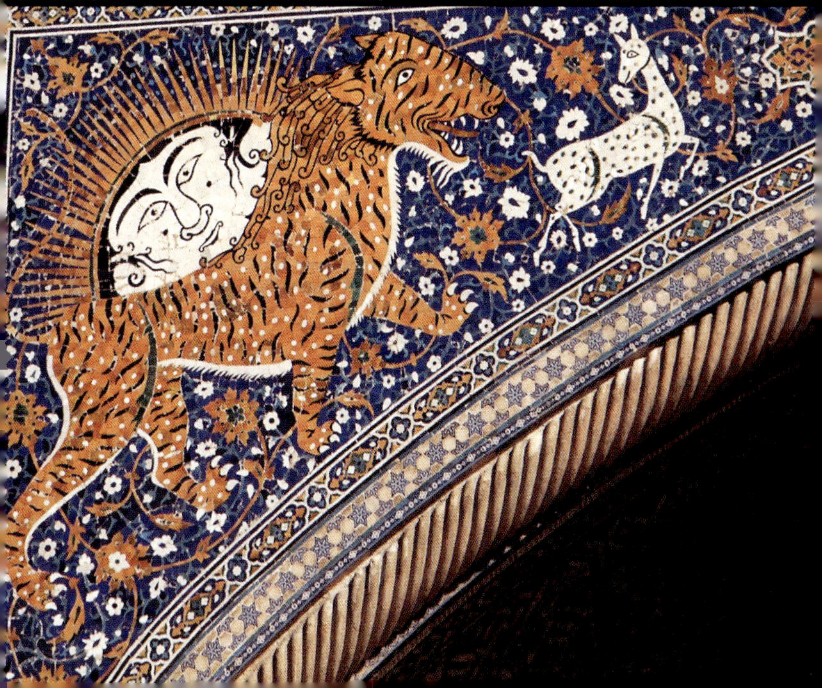

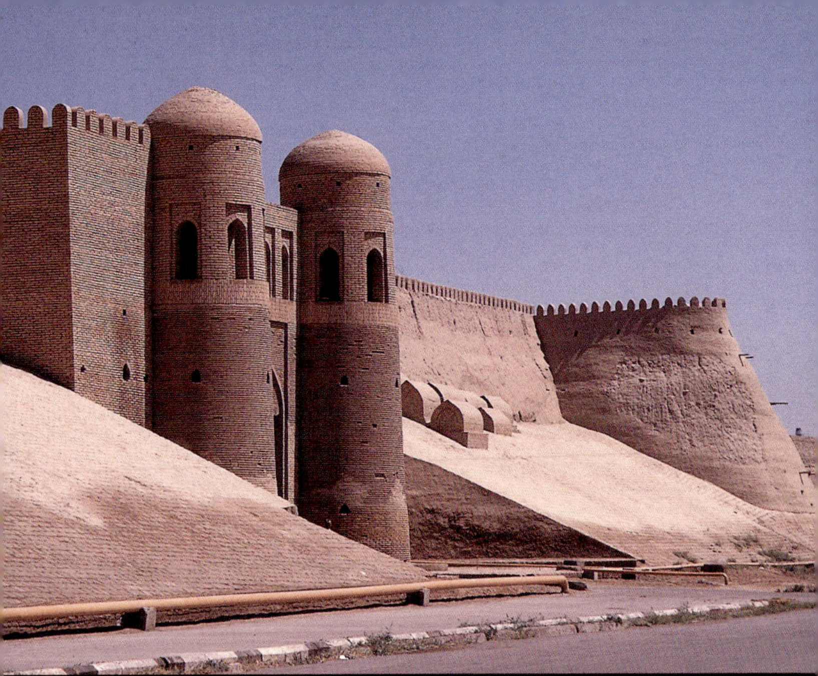
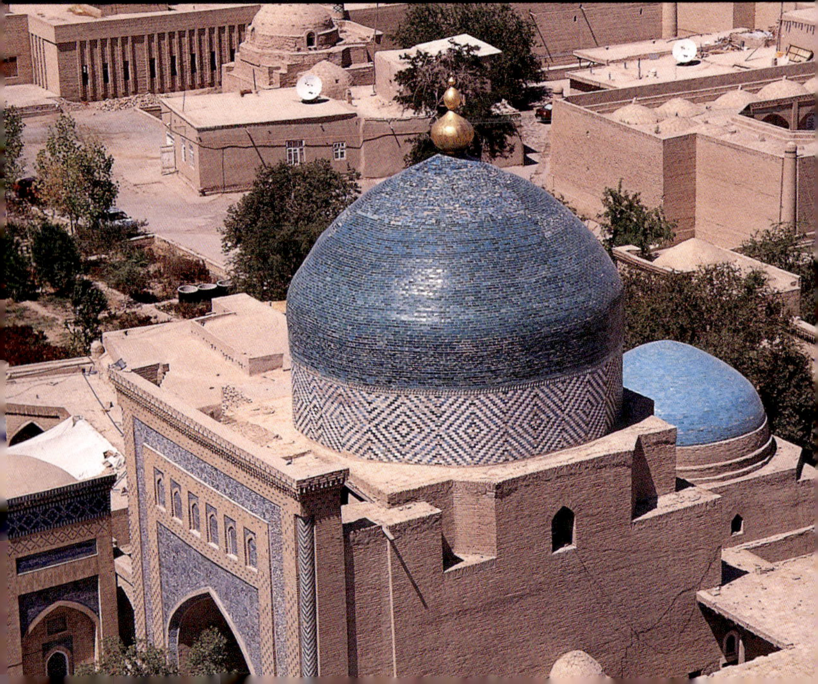

# Doğubeyazit

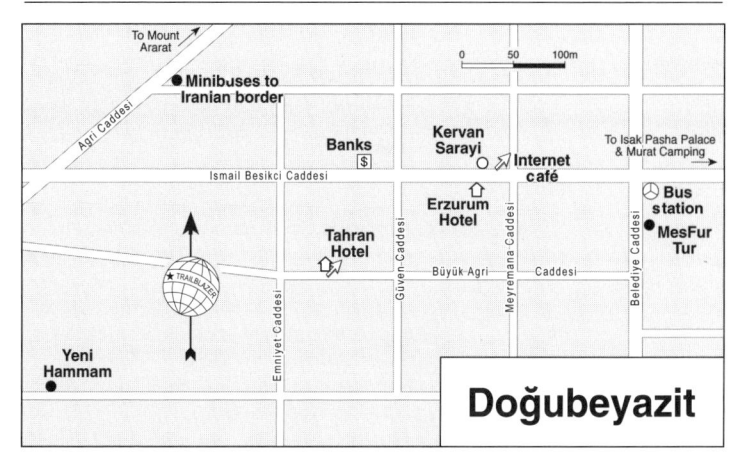

by the palace, has superb views, a decent restaurant and some share-rooms inside the main building. They offer free rides to and from town and, if you're interested in trekking (see box p265), these are the people. *Urfa Kervan Sarayi*, Dr Ismail Besikci Caddesi 77, serves good-value food and has a great rooftop terrace with comfy cushions.

## Moving on

Buses to Erzurum (4hrs/YTL15) leave regularly from the bus station.

---

### Crossing the Turkish/Iranian border

This border is commercially busy and often there are enormous queues of local traders on both sides but as a foreigner to both countries you should be able to bypass them. Minibuses (YTL2) from **Doğubeyazit** to the border at **Gurbulak** are supposed to run from the main bus station but more often than not leave from wherever the driver parks his car; this tends to be near the big red petrol station 400m east of the bus station. They drop you at the Turkish checkpoint. Cross this and walk across the border; ignore the offers of a ride in another minibus (YTL0.5) and any offers to change money into Iranian rials, for you will definitely get a better rate on the other side of the border.

At the Iranian customs you sometimes have to fill out a declaration form (available in both English and Arabic) and you might be asked to unpack your bags: don't forget, **no alcohol can be taken into Iran**.

After passing through the Iranian immigration (you might have to wait 'in limbo' for quite a while in a concrete hall) you need to walk down the hill (or catch a bus, 1000rials) to **Bazargan** where all the share taxis wait to take you into **Maku**.

The share taxis charge 5000rials per person for the ride into Maku where they will drop you at the bus station. It might be getting late now, but don't worry: many Iranian buses travel by night and you should have no problems getting one to **Tabriz** (4hrs/10,000rials). If you are stuck in Maku, *Hotel Lalah* is a recommended cheapie.

Going the other way, you need to leave Tabriz early but once you are through the border there are always minibuses to Doğubeyazit.

---

**(Opposite) Khiva** (see pp199-205). **Top**: The imposing city walls. **Bottom**: Looking down on the Jame Mosque, parts of which date back to the 10th century.

# Tabriz

*'The city has such a good position that merchandise is brought thither from India, Baudas (Baghdad) and Gemesor (Persia) …. it is a city where merchants make a large profit.'*

This is what Marco Polo had to say for the place and sure enough Tabriz became one of the most important stops on the Silk Road during its later years. It was also – and still is – the centre of Iran's Azari population, who have a reputation for being great businessmen. Furthermore, in the 16th century, the city was established as the national capital under the Safavids but now it struggles to maintain any of its former glory. There is not a lot to see in Tabriz and what there is seems to be continually under restoration but you will probably want to spend at least a day here to break your journey.

## WHAT TO SEE

Tabriz's biggest enemy over the centuries has been the land it sits on as this area is particularly prone to earthquakes. They have wreaked havoc on the city and many of the sights; the worst, in 1727, killed over 75,000 people. The hardest hit has probably been the 15th-century **Kabud Mosque** ('Blue Mosque'), although it still boasts some beautiful tile-work and houses a small museum.

Another big sufferer has been the **Citadel**. This is slowly being pieced back together but essentially all that is left is the front gateway. The **museum** also has a habit of being shut, though you won't miss too much if it is.

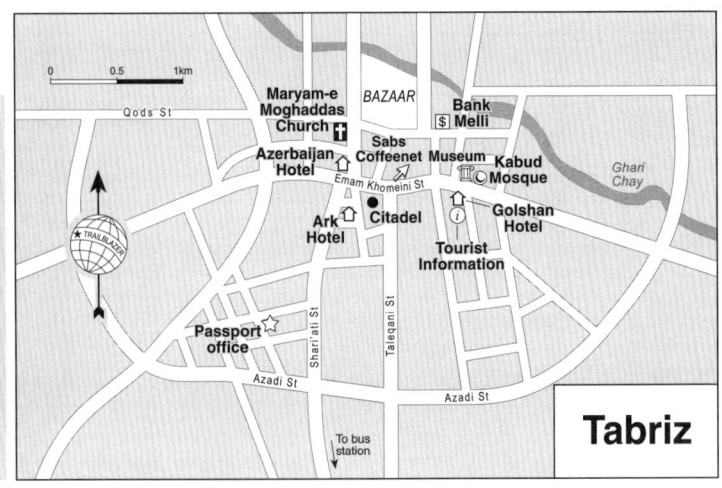

The **bazaar** is as big and well-stocked as you would expect from a town with such a commercial background but most of the goods are aimed at the local market. Henna is particularly plentiful in these parts. Sections of the bazaar are said to date back to pre-Mongol times but most of what you can see was built in the 15th century or later.

Outside the bazaar is the **Maryam-e Moghaddas Church** which dates from the 12th century and was mentioned by Marco Polo in *The Travels*.

## PRACTICAL INFORMATION
[☎ code 0411]

### Orientation and services
Sometimes you will be dropped off at the ring road as many buses for/from Tehran don't come into the **bus station**. Even if they do it is a bit of a hike to or from the south of the city; most people therefore choose to take a **taxi** (6000rials) to their hotel, as the local bus system is indecipherable. **Share taxis** also run between the bus station and a stand opposite Azerbaijan Hotel.

If you have received only a short **transit visa** for Iran, Tabriz is a very convenient place to obtain an extension. The **Passport Office** (☎ 477 6666; 07.30-13.30 Sat-Thur) on Saeb St can sometimes issue your extension on the same day (go through the 'Foreign Affairs' door and up two storeys).

The **tourist information office** is not the biggest in the world but the staff are friendly and can help you with tours. **Changing money** shouldn't be a problem (if not at your hotel then at **Bank Melli**). There are a few **Internet cafés** in town; try *Sabs Coffeenet* in the Tarbeyat shopping centre.

### Where to stay and eat
As a major stopover on the way to or from Turkey, Tabriz has a fair selection of hotels. The most central budget option is *Ark Hotel* (behind the citadel; 90,000rials/Db). There isn't really an upper range but *Azerbaijan Hotel* (☎ 555 9051; 140,000rials/Db), Shari'ati St, is consistently considered to be the best mid-range option. For a cheap bed in a dorm, try *Golshan Hotel* (25,000rials) opposite the museum. *Guesthouse Darya* (☎ 554 0008) on Mohagege St and run by Ahmad Pishva has also been recommended – phone ahead and he will come to meet you.

There aren't any fantastic **eateries** in Tabriz but there are plenty of fast-food outlets and cheap cafés on and off Emam Khomeini St.

### Moving on
As long as it is not winter your next stop heading east will probably be **Ghazvin** (7hrs/30,000rials) but it is just as easy to catch a bus to **Tehran** (9hrs/40,000rials). Buses leave from the station. If you are heading to **Doğubeyazit**, see box p129.

---

### Throne of Solomon
Those with private transport can take in this natural fortress (known locally as Takht-e Soleiman) on their way between Tabriz and Ghazvin but for others it is a long detour and you'll need to set out early. The site sits on a crater lake inside a ring of volcanic mountains and was a key centre of Zoroastrianism in the 3rd century. It has no link to the Solomon of the Old Testament (locals used the name to fool the Arabs in the 7th century so that they wouldn't destroy it) but is a World Heritage site and worth the detour. Over the centuries this site has been used by various ruling clans as a summer retreat and you can still see remains of a Mongol palace built in the 13th century. The setting is what makes the place so special, however, along with the dramatic drive through Iran's northern mountains to get there.

Entrance costs 30,000rials. Alight from your bus at Zanjan and hire a taxi for the day (US$50/4 people) to take you on the round trip, dropping you back on the main highway to pick up the next bus east/west.

# Ghazvin (Qazvin)

Most visitors come to Ghazvin to use it as a base to visit the many Assassin castles in the area. Once the bad weather sets in, however, the roads up to the sites get bogged down and you might not be able to find anyone to take you up there (quite a few of the hotels close then as well). The city has enough to fill at least a morning, if not a full day, as, like Tabriz, this was once Persia's capital under the Safavids. Ghazvin is well known amongst Iranians for its sexual activities (both homo- and heterosexual) but this is not something you are likely to come across.

## WHAT TO SEE

Some of the **Jame Mosque** dates back to the early Islamic period and there are plenty of Seljuk and Safavid additions. **Nabi Mosque** is another favourite for visitors, with its small pools set in a massive courtyard.

The **Shrine of Hussein** is as beautiful as it is sacred: it is the shrine of the son of Hazrat-e Reza (the eighth Imam). There is also a selection of bazaars of which **Saraye Bazaar** has perhaps the finest tile-work.

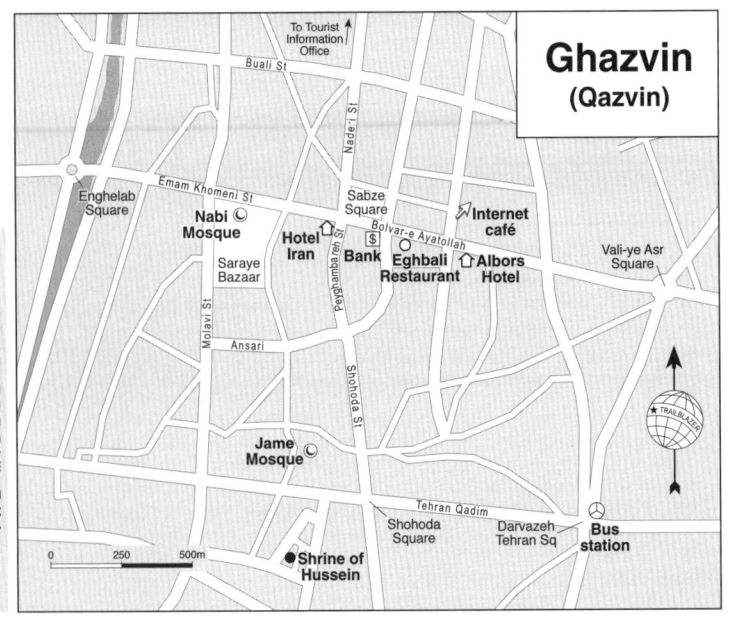

## Excursion to Alamut and the Assassins' castles

To serve their purpose, the locations of the Assassins' castles had to be obscure, secretive and difficult to reach. Today, many are no easier to visit and access involves up to a day's worth of hiking. If you have time, however, this is a very enjoyable way to spend a few days and the views are magnificent. In about a week you can cover most of the castles in the area (see 'Trekking the Silk Road', box p265). There are several villages along the way but unless you speak Farsi you will want to take a guide as well as food, a tent and all your hiking gear (Hotel Iran, see p134, can usually provide most of the things you might need).

Alternatively, you can visit the castles at **Alamut** (known as Gazor Khan) and **Lamaisar** on a day trip from Ghazvin. Either hire your own taxi for the day

---

### The Assassins

The Assassins were Shi'ite extremists of the Ismaili sect who came to prominence in the eleventh and twelfth centuries. They built impregnable fortresses in the mountains of northern Iran and considered it their duty to wipe out all Sunni Muslims (in particular, the Sunni caliphate of Baghdad). Originally the plan was to join forces with the Fatimid rulers of Egypt, who were the nominal Shi'ite caliphs, but this alliance broke down before it began and the Assassins' leader, Hasan Sabah, found himself the enemy of both caliphates.

Not that he let this worry him. Instead, he established his headquarters at Alamut, near Ghazvin, and built up a network of hideouts all over the mountains of northern Iran. Hasan Sabah became infamous as 'The Old Man of the Mountain' and, although no one is quite sure how he recruited his men, he soon built up a small army of disciples known as 'The Fida'i' ('Those Ready for Sacrifice') who were pledged to murder anyone whom Sabah marked out for death.

Marco Polo confirms how these select men were given plenty of hashish and beautiful maidens in the build up to an assignment, along with promises of eternal life in heaven should they have to sacrifice their own life in claiming their victim's (which was nearly always the case). It was the hashish ceremonies that led to the Crusaders' term 'hashishins' which has mutated into the modern word 'assassins'.

It was not a life of total luxury, however, as Sabah trained his men scrupulously in the art of disguise and sometimes years were spent infiltrating a victim's world before the final attack. Their effectiveness was legendary and such groups spread to Syria and even India, striking real fear into rulers' hearts everywhere; both the Crusading King of Jerusalem and Count of Tripoli fell victim to the sect, as well as countless Sunni rulers.

Even Saladin was scared of them and called off the siege of the Syrian Assassins' headquarters at Masyaf when he woke up to find hot cakes (of a kind baked only by Assassins) resting on his pillow.

The branches that sprang up in Syria and other countries appear to have been rival sects rather than colonies; for, ironically, Sabah himself became a target, with the Syrian Rashid ad Din being sent to Alamut to carry out the deed. Fortunately for Sabah, he managed to die of natural causes before Rashid could pounce.

Alamut and its surrounding fortresses were eventually destroyed by the Mongols in 1256, in retaliation for the assassination of one of Khan Hulegu's sons, and the sect died out, although the Syrian version seemed to carry on for a few more decades.

(US$30/four people) or ask for help from Hotel Iran. Unfortunately, there isn't much left of either castle but the Elborz Mountains make up for that by providing a splendid backdrop.

## PRACTICAL INFORMATION
[☎ code 0281]
### Orientation and services
Ghazvin is quite spread out and your bus could drop you outside of town so you will have to take a **taxi/share taxi** to **Sabze Square**, the town's centre, where you will also find **banks** and **Internet cafés**. The **tourist information office** (Naderi St) is a half-hour walk from the square but has an excellent free guide to the city in English as well as other languages.

### Where to stay and eat
By far the most helpful hotel is *Hotel Iran* (☎ 222 8877; 90,000rials/Db) on one side of Meidun-e Sabze on Peyghambareh St, as the owner is geared up for independent travellers and can organize trips to Alamut.

On Bolvar-e Ayatollah, *Albors Hotel* (☎ 222 6631; US$50/Db) is popular with those travelling on a bigger budget and looks smart and comfortable.

The restaurant selection is disappointing but you shouldn't starve; *Eghbali* is worth trying as the smartest place in town.

### Moving on
The bus journey to **Tehran** (9,000rials) shouldn't take more than two hours but it depends on the traffic. There are plenty of buses from the bus station to **Tabriz** (5hrs/6000rials).

# Tehran

Two days is more than enough for the modern Iranian capital, as most visitors come away disappointed. Traditionally, Persia's capital lay elsewhere and before the Qajar dynasty (1776-1925) Tehran was famous only for its mild climate. Today, the city is home to 14 million people (more than Greater London) and is so massive that there is one road running 20km from north to south. As you might expect, traffic congestion is a nightmare.

North Tehran is home to Iran's wealthy elite and can often seem like a different world with all its security-guarded mansions, boutique shops and flashy motors.

## WHAT TO SEE

Note: Everything is closed on Friday and most museums on Monday.

### Museums
The **National Museum** and **Islamic Arts Museum** (09.00-13.00 and 14.00-17.00) are next to each other in the centre of town and covered by the same ticket. This is still an expensive 60,000rials (30,000rials/students), however. Both museums are small although they do have some stunning pieces and the exhibits are well labelled in English.

The **Glass and Ceramics Museum** (09.00-17.00; 30,000rials) is set in a beautiful building nearby and houses an interesting collection. The **Carpet**

> **Excursion to Rey**
> The reason why Tehran has so little to offer historically is because, prior to the Mongol invasion, the major city in this area was actually a few kilometres south in Rey. Unfortunately (like so many cities you are about to encounter if you are travelling eastwards), the Mongols didn't leave much after sacking Rey and it never recovered.
>
> In recent years, therefore, as the capital has expanded so Rey has been absorbed into Greater Tehran and today it is little more than a suburb. Nevertheless, those historical sites that survived the Mongols are still here. The **Mausoleum of Shah-e Abdi** and the 12th-century **Toghoral Tomb Tower** are in the town centre and are most impressive. The **Tabrak Fortress** is up on the hill and the mineral springs which attracted early man to the area in the first place can be found at **Cheshmeh Ali**.
>
> To get to Rey, take the metro to Rey station. You can walk to the mausoleum complex but negotiate with a local taxi driver to see the more distant sites (you'll need about two or three hours).

**Museum** (09.00-18.00; 30,000rials) near Laleh Hotel has as outstanding a collection as you would expect from a country synonymous with carpet making.

The **Jewels Museum** (Sat-Tues afternoons; 30,000rials) is housed in the basement of the central Bank Melli on Kheyabun-e Ferdosi and is a worthy rival to London's Crown Jewels. We have some ardent revolutionaries to thank for not letting the shah's soldiers storm the bank and take the jewels on the day he left. There is one slight disappointment, however: the Peacock Throne on display is not *the* Peacock Throne which Nadir Shah took after sacking Delhi in 1739, but another one constructed later (the original was probably broken up and divided as loot).

The Koh I Noor diamond (which also came from Delhi) is no longer part of the collection, either. Given to Queen Victoria as a present, it now sits in the crown of the late British Queen Mother. The Dah I Noor diamond (another Delhi trophy and the largest pink diamond in the world) is here though, as is probably the world's most extravagant globe.

### Palaces

South of Imam Khomeini Sq, **Golestan Palace** is really a set of remarkable buildings housed in a discreet park. The buildings are free to look at but inside there are various collections of art, diamonds and old photographs that nearly justify their entrance fees; the Shams Al Emarat (20,000rials) probably has the best collection if you can afford only one. The nearby **Shahr Park** is also a welcome spot for some tranquil relief from the noise and hassle of the city.

**Sa'd Abad Museum** on Valiasr Ave, Kheyabun-e Taheri, is actually the last Shah's former residence. Up here, it is easy to see how he became isolated from his people, for the surrounding trees and gardens completely shut out the poverty afflicting the rest of the city. The number and size of the carpets and chandeliers on display are quite phenomenal, although many claim that the Shah left much, much more which has since disappeared to line somebody's pockets.

*(continued on p138)*

## Buying a carpet

If there is one souvenir you should really try to take home with you from this trip, it's a carpet. The Silk Road passes through every country that is famous for making carpets, either now or in the past, and the choice is endless.

**History** Today, Persian carpets are the most famous and Iran certainly does have some great buys, especially now its currency is so weak. Historically, however, Persian carpets came to prominence only in the 16th century (Shah Abbas I's reign, 1587-1629, marks their peak); before then, the best carpets were made in Central Asia and it was this region that was first known as the Carpet Capital of the World. Bukharan carpets are particularly famous and have a distinct, rectangular design, usually in a dark red colour. Going further back, what is now western China was actually the original home of carpets and during the first millennium AD a Khotan carpet was considered supreme, though nowadays most of the carpets in this area tend to be made in factories.

**Silk** If you are going for a silk carpet you should be able to really haggle the price down as most vendors find these harder to sell. Make sure the base is pure silk as well as the carpet itself and check the knottage; that said, silk is so fine the knottage is bound to be exceptional so it's really down to which one you like the best. Be warned though: if you do buy a silk carpet think twice about putting it down on the floor – even shahs and emirs would reserve their silk carpets for decoration rather than everyday use as they are very difficult (and expensive) to clean.

**Wool** For a pure wool carpet with a wool base, the three primary factors when establishing its worth are its design, its age and its knottage. If it was made by a cooperative or factory it will probably carry a standard design. If it has been made by an individual or family (often the case if it's from a small village or from nomads) the design will follow a general theme but will have certain idiosyncrasies which make it unique and therefore more valuable.

The chances are that because it has a wool base in the first place it is quite old (modern practices tend to use a cotton base). Anything over 30 years old is considered valuable purely because of its age but if you are going to use the carpet on a floor where it will be regularly trodden on, you might not want to buy one that is too old.

**Knottage** For knottage, you will have to trust the vendor to a certain extent, because unless you have a very strong magnifying glass with you, you cannot count individual knots with the naked eye. Most vendors quote their knottage in knots per square inch. Anything made in the last 50 years will probably be 350 knots, 500 knots or 750 knots, though the latter is quite a rarity. If the carpet is a real antique, the knottage could be an irregular figure as each maker would choose the knottage according to how long he could afford to spend making it. The more knots per square inch the more a carpet is worth. If you go to see a carpet being made you will see that a 'knot' is literally a knot – the maker will wrap a piece of wool around two strands of the base, tie a knot and move on; when he has finished his row he will trim the loose end (hanging on the front side of the carpet) and reveal the pattern that the knots have made. If a carpet maker is only producing a low-knottage carpet, he will tie his knot around four strands of the base, or six, and so make his job quicker. A high-knottage carpet will take over a year for one person to make. One way to check just how well-made a carpet is, is to turn it over; the pattern on the back should be tight and precise and almost as clear as the front – the better defined the pattern is, the more knots will have been used and the carpet will last longer without losing its shape. Don't expect too high a knottage from nomads' carpets – their unique designs are their strengths.

*(cont'd from p136)* **Cotton** For cotton-based carpets, the same rules apply but there is one other thing to look out for. The strands of cotton that form the back matting are not actually individual strands but three thinner strands wound together. These three strands are also, in fact, made up of very skinny strands wound together, too. The important thing is how many skinny strands are used. If it's three, 3x3 equals nine so the carpet is called a 'nine line' carpet; if it's four, 4x3 equals twelve so it's a 'twelve line'. Obviously, a 'twelve line' strand is thicker than a 'nine line' so fewer knots are need to complete a row and these are cheaper. Cotton is thicker than wool and keeps its shape much better, making it easier to work with, which is why cotton backs are favoured today.

**Patterns** Trust your instinct and go for the pattern you like best – the chances are you are not going to sell it when you get back so don't think of it as an investment but rather as a piece of furniture for your house. Make sure you fully unroll the carpet and that it lies flat on the floor, for bumps and misshapen ends are signs of bad workmanship or wear and tear (if the rug is really old, it is very likely that it will have been put to good use at some stage in its life so don't worry about the sides being perfectly straight; wool by its nature tends to stretch and change its shape; cotton-backed rugs, however, should be perfect). Try to avoid modern dyes as they will fade much quicker than traditional dyes, especially in sunlight: modern dyes should be obvious because they are so bright but sometimes you can't tell (although, by definition, older carpets will have been made with wool coloured with natural dyes). Old carpets might have been washed to make the colours bright again but this isn't a problem – newer carpets, however, might have been washed to fade their colour so they can be sold as older carpets, so beware.

**Styles** Different countries have different styles in the design and feel of their carpets. This might be because of the type of wool they use – different sheep breeds have different wool – or the way the carpets are cut. If a carpet is really soft, almost silk like, it might have been made from the wool cut from a sheep's neck, which is finer; if it's really thick and firm it might have been made from camel hair – thick carpets are actually better for everyday use because they'll last forever. Turkmen tend to cut their carpets short so that they're almost oily to touch but how long the wool is doesn't matter.

If you can't afford a carpet, you can opt instead for a **Kilim** which is a bit like an unfinished carpet. With no back they are so much thinner and have loose knots on the reverse. As a floor covering these won't last as long as a carpet but can look good on your wall (you'll find them in most places you find carpets, especially bazaars).

**Buying** The first decision you need to make is how much you want to spend as this will dictate which type of rug you go for. For a silk carpet expect to pay a US dollar sum in four figures, even for an average-sized, 6ft x 4ft (1.8m x 1.2m) piece. For a pure wool carpet on a wool base (back) you will be looking at around US$400. For a modern, handmade (but in a factory) wool carpet on a cotton base, you can pay as little as US$100-150. Pakistan has the best selection of all the countries en route because its buyers gather carpets both locally and from Iran, Afghanistan and Central Asia and the prices are still cheap. Bazaars will always be cheaper than shops. Try to get down to half the opening price in bazaars, whereas in shops you might have to settle for two-thirds.

**Getting your carpet home** Whichever you choose, do make sure you check out the export regulations for the country you intend to buy in. As long as your carpet is not considered an antique, you should be allowed to take a 6ft x 4ft from any of the countries along the Silk Road but this may change. Most carpet shops will offer to ship your purchases to your home but it's much cheaper to take it home yourself.

*(cont'd from p135)* The 30,000rials entrance fee includes the gardens but only one of the museums (the choice is yours – most people choose the main palace – or you can pay extra to see all of them). Even if you do not go inside the Green Palace, walk up here for the best views of the city but don't be surprised if the smog (which is notorious) prevents you from seeing more than a few metres.

A taxi up to the palace from Khomeini Square is 20,000rials.

### Other things to see
**Emam Khomeini Mosque** is crammed into the middle of the **bazaar**, which is pretty chaotic and not particularly tempting; Esfahan has a much better selection of goods. **Sepahsalar Mosque and Madrassah** are off-limits for non-Muslims, although their external architecture can be appreciated by all.

What used to be the complex for the **US Embassy** is worth a look. In 1979 it was stormed by rioters and 52 hostages were taken for 444 days. Since then the US has pulled out all its representatives in Iran and the building has been handed over to the crack troops of the Revolutionary Guards. The walls are now home to some macabre murals reiterating Iran's stance against the US (our favourite is 'The day USA praises Iran we should mourn') and lots of 'down with USA/Israel' posters. When talking to locals, however, you soon realize that this is just propaganda from the fundamentalists which virtually the entire population ignores – while we were there some local youths walked past the murals fully clad in (admittedly fake) American designer labels. Be careful taking pictures, though, because this can still get you into trouble around here.

---

### Excursion to Sari
The road north to Sari takes you past Kuh-e Damavand, a volcano which at 5671m is the highest mountain in the Middle East, through the natural break in the Elborz Mountains known as the Caspian Gates and down to the shores of the Caspian Sea; the views en route are, as you can imagine, sensational. The train is equally spectacular, passing through the heart of the mountains via a network of stunning tunnels. Iranians will tell you how beautiful the Caspian region is but what they mean is how green it is – compared to the rest of Iran, rain falls abundantly north of the Elborz. Sari is a small town with little to see but it's the journey itself that makes the trip so special.

**Practicalities** Buses to Sari (5hrs/20,000rials) or **Amol** (pronounced Armool; 4hrs) leave from Tehran's eastern terminal; from Amol take a minibus or share-taxi to Sari (1hr). Trains (7hrs/16,000rials for first class) leave daily at around 09.00 from Tehran's train station (in the south-west of the city, near Shoosh metro stop). In Sari, *Sarouyeh Hotel* (☎ 0151 324 5600), Danesh St, is central – you can walk from the station – and clean; there are two buildings, one for the hostel and one for the hotel (80,000rials/Db up to 250,000rials/Db). There are cafés and an **Internet centre** nearby.

From Sari you can return to **Tehran** by either of the above routes (buses leave from the bus station, while more convenient share-taxis leave from Imam Khomeini Sq). You can also carry on east instead. Buses go to **Quchan** (via Gorgan) from where you can cross over to **Turkmenistan** (see box p156), and there are also buses direct to **Mashad** (12hrs/27,000rials).

# Tehran – What to see

## PRACTICAL INFORMATION
[☎ code 021]
### Orientation and services
There have been a few changes to Iran's capital since the Revolution (Winston Churchill Avenue, for example, is now Bobby Sands Avenue after the IRA hunger striker) but locals say they have mostly been for the worse; and as there is still **no tourist information office**, you can see their point. The one major piece of good news is that the **metro** has finally opened and while there are only three lines at present, it is a start.

The city slopes down from the foothills of the Elborz Mountains and the higher up you are the nicer your surroundings tend to be as the richer classes have all moved into the less crowded hills while most Tehranians are squashed into the southern half of the city.

**Khomeini Square** (Meidun-e Emam Khomeini) is as good a place as any to start a tour of the city but remember that Tehran is enormous so you will want to use the metro where possible. Otherwise, the traffic is so bad that it is much quicker (and cheaper) to flag down one of the many **motorbikes** rather than take a **taxi**. **Share taxis** run up and down all the main roads: just shout out an obvious square/road/landmark near to where you are going and they will stop if they are heading that way. The **local buses** are a waste of time and effort.

All buses from western Iran come into Tehran's **Western Bus Station** but this is quite a way out of the city and doesn't have a metro stop yet. Catch a local bus towards the city (they leave from the other side of the huge white Azadi Monument roundabout) and get off at the first metro stop you come to. Alternatively, a taxi will demand 40,000rials for the trip but should settle for 20,000rials.

If you are flying in/out make sure you know which airport you are using. The **new airport** (which caters for most international flights) is over 30km away and takes an hour to get to. The **old airport** is much closer. Either way, there are buses running into the centre but, annoyingly, not the other way so if you are travelling to the airport you will have to take a taxi until the planned metro extension is finished.

**Internet cafés** are springing up quite quickly but many have been closed down by the government. *Pars Internet*, opposite the British Embassy, is your best bet (they also have phone booths for cheap international calls) or ask your hotel. Kheyabun-e Ferdosi has plenty of **bureaux de change**, giving a better rate than the banks.

The most organized travel companies tend to be situated in the foothills and **Holiday Co** (☎ 270 6871, 🖳 holiday@sama.dpi.net.ir) is particularly friendly. If you want to take the strain out of visiting Iran, they can easily put a package together for as many days as you require. They also book flights.

The **Turkmenistan Embassy** (☎ 254 2178) is at 39, fifth Kheyabun-e Golestan; take a taxi as apparently there are more than eight Golestan streets, or 'Kheyabune-e Golestan', in Tehran). Those travelling east are best off obtaining their Uzbek visas

---

### Tehran's metro system
The good news is that Tehran now has three metro lines up and running, and all of them are quick and cheap. The bad news is that one of them (the green line) is of little use to foreign visitors and the other two stop short of key destinations such as the bus terminal and the airport. Extensions are planned, however, as are three more lines but don't hold your breath – the first three took many years longer than promised. A single ticket anywhere costs 750rials – you can buy a few at a time to save queuing up. Women-only carriages are at the front but women can travel in the mixed carriages if they wish.

For more information, go to 🖳 www.tehranmetro.com.

## Tehran Metro

**Line 1 (Red):** Mirdamad, Shahid Hemmat, Mosalla, Shahid Beheshti, Shahid Mofateh, Haft-e-Tir, Taleghani, Darvazeh Dolat, Sa'di, Mellat, Imam Khomeini, Panzdah-e-Khordad, Khayyam, Molavi, Shoosh, Terminal-e-Jonub, Khazaneh, Ali Abad, Javanmard-e-Ghassab, Shahr-e-Ray, Fathabad, Shohada, Haram-e-Motahar

**Line 2 (Blue):** Tehran (Sadeghieh), Tarasht, University-Sharif, Azadi, Navab, Meydan-e-Hor, Majles, Hassanabad, Imam Khomeini, Mellat, Baharestan, Darvazeh Shemiran, Emam Hossein, Shahid Madani, Sabalan, Nezamabad, Golbarg, Sarsabz, Dardasht

**Line 3 (Green):** Golshahr, Mahdasht, Karaj, Atmosfer, Garmdarreh, Vad Avard, Iran Khodro, Chitgar, Varzeshgah-e-Azadi, Ekbatan

---

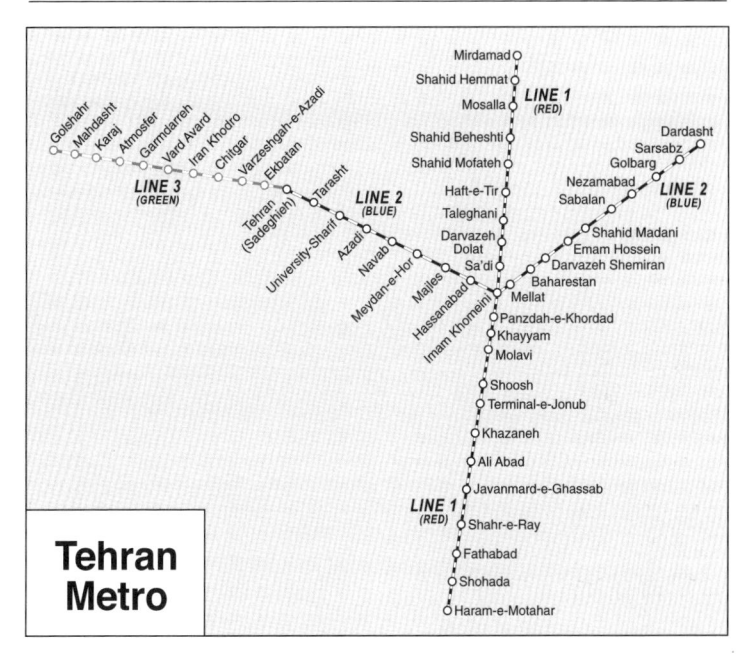

here, too, as they will probably have only a short time in Turkmenistan; the **Uzbek Embassy** is at 6 Kheyabun-e Nastaran but you will need the **Uzbek Consulate** (☎ 229 1519) at 15/4 Kheyabun-e Pasdaran). Those travelling west might want to visit the **Syrian Embassy** (☎ 205 9031) on Afriqa Highway, Arash Boulevard; the **Turkish Embassy** is at 314 Kheyabun-e Ferdosi. For visa requirements, see pp15-18.

### Where to stay

Like any capital, Tehran is not short of places to stay and all budgets are well catered for.

*Khazar Sea Hotel* (☎ 311 3860; 40,000rials/Db), on Kheyabun-e Amir Kabir, is popular amongst backpackers and locals alike although it can be a bit scruffy.

*Markazi Hotel* (☎ 391 7980; 80,000rials/Db) on Kheyabun-e Lalehzar is better and has both Internet access and a laundry service.

On Kheyabun-e Mellat, *Asia Hotel* (☎ 311 8320; US$25/Db) is much cleaner and is very friendly – rooms come with shower and breakfast. *Atlas Hotel* (☎ 890 0286; 55/Db), Kheyabun-e Taleghani, is the best mid-range option.

*Laleh Hotel* (☎ 656 021; US$130/Db), on Kheyabun-e Dr Hosein Fatemi, is the top hotel in town and if you want to treat yourself to a good meal, try one of its three restaurants.

### Where to eat

Surprisingly for a capital, Tehran isn't very good for restaurants. The best ones are in the rich areas of town but if you go up there by yourself you are likely to spend more time and money getting there than you will on eating.

There are restaurants in most of the hotels, however, and apart from those listed above you should try *Bolour Hotel*. *Khayyam* (Kheyabun-e Khayyam; come out of Khayyam Metro and head south for

250m) is worth seeking out if you are in the south of the city – it's in a classic converted mosque and serves food worthy of its surroundings. There are plenty of *kebabis* all over the city and pizza is also popular. The many **teahouses** in Tehran's parks may be a bit more expensive than others but they are a welcome break from the noise.

## Moving on

Before heading east you should take the opportunity to see more of Iran and visit at least Esfahan, Kashan, Shiraz and Persepolis. **Luxury coaches** for all destinations leave from the **Central Bus Station** by Arzhantin Sq (in the north of the city).

For **Kashan** (see p148) and **Esfahan** (6-7hrs/9000rials), buses leave from the **Southern Bus Station** (take the metro to Terminal-e Jonub station). On your way south you will pass the **Holy Shrine of Ayatollah Khomeini**, a massive complex that is intended to be one of the greatest Islamic centres in the world but looks a bit like something thought up in Las Vegas. The main road also passes by Iran's nuclear energy/bomb facility, although there is little to see and you are not allowed to stop.

Heading east, the Silk Road would have gone two ways. For the northern route via **Sari**, see box p138. **Mashad** is best reached by bus (the train is too slow and unreliable). Take the metro to Emam Hussein Square and catch the electric trolley bus to the **Eastern Bus Station** from where the regular Mashad buses (15hrs/35,000rials) leave – it is such a killer journey, however, you are better off going by luxury coach (55,000rials).

Buses to **Ghazvin** (2hrs/10,000rials) and Tabriz (9hrs/40,000rials) leave all day from the **Western Bus Station**.

# Esfahan

Esfahan was known by the Abbassids as 'The Garden of Art' and it is one of the most beautiful cities you will ever visit. It suffered heavy shelling during the Iran-Iraq war of the 1980s but an impressive restoration programme has brought back much of the city's former glory.

## HISTORY

Because of the local Zayande River there have been settlements in this area for thousands of years and the town built up an impressive reputation as a trading centre. Silk Road caravans from Herat would head here on their way to Baghdad, whilst others came up from the Persian Gulf with goods from the Spice Route.

Unlike many of the Silk Road cities, however, Esfahan did not go into decline upon the demise of the Mongols but instead continued to grow and in 1587 Shah Abbas I (the founder of the Abbassid dynasty) set out to make Esfahan the jewel in his newly united Persian crown.

For the next hundred years it became more and more spectacular and so it would have remained if it had not been for the 19th-century Shah Nasreddin. His desire to move his capital here threatened his brother, the Governor of Esfahan, who had previously enjoyed virtual autonomy. Rather than hand over his wealth, the brother ordered twelve of his palaces be destroyed. It was all in vain, however, as Nasreddin came anyway.

## WHAT TO SEE

### Meidun-e Emam Khomeini

This central square (originally known as Naqsh-e Jahn – 'Pattern of the World') was first built as a garden (1602AD) and is the largest enclosed square in the world (Tiananmen Square is larger but it is open). It is also a World Heritage Site. Historically, it doubled as a polo field and at either end you can still see the stone goalposts (they look like four-foot-high bollards).

The main **Emam Mosque** dates from the early 17th century when it was known as the Shah Mosque. It was designed by the same architect who built the Taj Mahal. Its cool-blue dome is the lasting image of Esfahan, though there are in fact two domes, one inside the other.

If you crouch over the black stone marked in the centre of the hall and clap, you will hear seven distinct echoes as the sound reverberates off the two shells. You must crouch, though, because if you clap standing up the metre height difference is enough to distort the symmetry and lessen the number of echoes.

In the north-eastern corner of the mosque's central square is a corridor leading off to a well and the remains of an old pool. This was where the dead were brought for their final cleansing before burial.

**Sheikh Lotfollah Mosque** is particularly noteworthy for the fantastic tilework on its dome and the fact that it has no minarets: virtually every other mosque in the world has at least one tower from where the muezzin can call the people to prayer. The reason this one doesn't is because it was originally meant only for the queen and the ladies of the city. Their lives were expected to revolve around those of their husbands so when the men were called by the muezzin of the Emam Mosque this was meant to be signal enough.

Just how **Ali Ghapu Palace** earned its name is unclear. Literally the title means the 'Big Door' Palace which would fit with the fact that its large door also served as a gateway into the main square for important visitors; but pronounced differently it could mean 'Ali's Door' and there is a legend which says the Shah went to Iraq to the tomb of Ali, Mohammed's son-in-law and head of the Shi'ite sect, and took the door from there.

The palace is beautifully constructed, particularly the top floor which has a double ceiling, with the lower ceiling intricately carved in the shapes of musical instruments. This was the music room and the double ceiling was designed to enhance the acoustics, which are excellent.

Note at the front of the palace how the name of the Shah has been 'bluewashed' over since the Revolution.

Each of the mosques and the palace charges a separate 30,000rials entrance fee. They are open daily between 07.00 and 19.00.

Take a closer look at the arches set in the walls around the square and you may be in for a surprise. Although the ground floor arches lead into workshops and bazaars as you would expect, the top floor arches are 'false' and where some of the stonework has fallen away you can see blue sky. This is not the case at the north end, however, which leads to the main **bazaar**; on its first floor is a **teahouse** worth half-an-hour of anybody's time because of the views it commands.

> **Calligraphy**
> Arabic calligraphy decorates many walls, doors and arches in mosques and madrassahs. It usually contains verses of the Koran or prayers to Allah. In most Sunni mosques the prayers contain the words 'Allah' and 'Mohammed'; in Iran, however, the name of Ali is also incorporated into the swastika-like designs – these are particularly prevalent on the various corner pieces. Not every design is the same because, like the Roman script, Arabic has many different calligraphic styles. For centuries many of the surrounding madrassahs here were dedicated to this art. The Emam Mosque in Esfahan is considered to have the finest examples of Arabic calligraphy in the world.

## Chehel Sotun Palace

Chehel Sotun means 'Forty Pillars' in Farsi and if you look at this building from the other side of the long pool there do appear to be 40 pillars (include the reflections in the water) but the reference might not be as simple as that (see box p146).

Originally, all the pillars were painted and the whole palace was covered in mirrors but much was destroyed by a severe fire. In between the pillars large silk curtains would have hung down and formed walls. Fortunately, the paintings inside aren't damaged and you can see, amongst others, Nadir Shah's victory over the Indian king and his elephants in 1738 – note also the miniature-style paintings underneath (see 'What to buy', p147) and the semi-Chinese features of the women. At the other end of the pool you can still smell traces of the wine that was kept in the big jars.

## Rud-e Zayande (Zayande River)

Esfahan was always famous for this river, one of the few in the world that comes out of the ground (rather than from down a mountain) *and* goes back into the ground (rather than into a lake or sea). When Tamerlane besieged the city for six months and still had no joy, he resorted to building a massive dam that diverted the river away from the city and gave him the new angle necessary for a successful attack – once inside he took no prisoners.

The lovely bridges are still here, as is Tamerlane's dam, but if there has been little rain you might not see any water at all. The oldest bridges are at the very east and west of the city and, although they have been rebuilt over the years, the Sassanid foundations are still

Beached boat on the dry Zayande River

# Esfahan

*To Kaveh bus terminal*
*To Minaret*

- Jame Mosque
- Qeyam Sq
- Jamal od'Din Abdolrazagh St
- BAZAAR
- Amir Kabir Hotel
- Internet café
- Akbar Keshani Carpets
- Reza Sedighee Fard workshop
- Money exchange
- Teahouse
- Kheyabun-e Sepah
- Tourist Information
- Sofreh Khaneh Restaurant
- Kheyabun-e Hatef
- *To Shaking Minarets & Zoroastrian Temple*
- Meidun-e Emam Hussein
- Kh Shahid
- Ali Ghapu Palace
- Sheikh Lotfollah Mosque
- Chehel Sotun Palace
- Kheyabun-e Beheshti
- Meidun-e Emam Khomeini
- Emam Mosque
- Chahar Bagh Abbasi
- Kheyabun-e Sa'di
- Fallahi Miniatures
- Abbasi Hotel
- Chahar Bagh Madrassah
- Kheyabun-e Amadegh
- Restaurant Shahrzad
- Internet café
- Safir Hotel
- Aria Hotel
- Kheyabun-e Abbas Abad
- Kheyabun-e Sayyed Ali Khan
- Meidun-e Enghelab-e Eslami
- ★ TRAILBLAZER
- Bolvar-e Mellat
- Chahar Bagh-e Bala St
- JOLFA
- Esmail St
- Meidun-e Khaju
- Zayande River
- Khaju Bridge
- 0  250  500m
- Kheyabun-e Nazar
- Vank Cathedral & Museum
- *To Sofeh bus terminal*

Esfahan 145

> ❏ **Forty winks?**
> Traditionally in these parts 'forty' was used to signify 'many' or 'a large amount of': the same theory has been used to explain the English phrase to 'take forty winks', which means to have a nap (ie lots of winks), and the section in the Bible that recounts Jesus entering the desert to fast for 'forty days and forty nights'.

there. **Khaju Bridge** is a favourite and the centre of the construction was actually a royal palace where its instigator, Shah Abbas II, would bring his family when they wanted to enjoy the river. The whole bridge also doubled as a dam and you can still see the sluice gates. You can also see head-high notches in each of the central pillars to support wooden gates, which in turn dam the river to a level high enough to irrigate the surrounding land.

## Jolfa

This quarter in the south of the city was and still is purely Armenian and its non-Muslim nature is quite startling when compared to modern media images of Iran. Shah Abbas I did much to rid his country of foreign political influence but he was wise enough to realize that he still had much to learn from the great powers of the day on a practical level. To this end he encouraged artisans to come to his capital from all over – not just his lands but the surrounding countries too.

In Armenia, which at the time was also much larger than it is today, there was a town called Jolfa (it is now in Iran) and its inhabitants, like many of their compatriots, were skilled craftsmen in weaponry and industrial tools. Shah Abbas invited the people of the town to move *en masse* to his capital where he promised them their own quarter, their own church and freedom to practise their religion. They accepted. The church is still there although it is now **Vank Cathedral** and inside are the original murals depicting scenes from the Bible (the gold is real!).

Opposite the cathedral is a fascinating **museum** (entrance 30,000rials; open 08.00-17.00 except Sunday) containing heirlooms from the community over the last four hundred years and a small tribute to the victims of the little publicized Armenian holocaust of WWI – within four years the Turks had forced all the Armenians living within their empire to flee and those who didn't go quickly enough were massacred in a vicious precursor to modern ethnic cleansing.

> ❏ **Zoroaster**
> This prophet is difficult to pin down, with many differing accounts supporting many different versions of his life. Neither where nor when he was born can be said for sure but most scholars now agree it was some time in the 6th century BC. His followers, Zoroastrians, did not actually worship fire (as is often presumed) but were monotheists who used fire in their ceremonies to worship their Supreme God or Wise Lord, Ahura Mazda. They believed the world was a struggle between good and evil and left their dead on stone piles to be eaten by birds and animals so as not to defile the earth.

Today about 7000 Armenians live in Esfahan, quite peacefully, and they are still noted for their mechanical expertise; look out for the prize exhibit, a human hair engraved with the artist's name (you can view it through the understandably large microscope).

## Other sights

At the northern end of the long bazaar is the beautiful **Jame Mosque**. It has buildings from the eleventh, twelfth and fourteenth centuries and each prayer hall is different. Further out from the mosque is a very tall **minaret** which acted as a beacon for all the caravans coming out of the desert. Back near Abbasi Hotel, the **Chahar Bagh Madrassah** has recently been restored to its former beauty.

## Around Esfahan

Just outside the city is the mosque known as the **Shaking Minarets**, which is more famous than it is impressive. The left minaret does shake if you shake the right minaret, but that's about it. A bit further on, however, the remains of a **Zoroastrian temple** can be found up on a hill. There are not too many of these left in the world, so you might want to take a look.

### PRACTICAL INFORMATION
[☎ code 031]

### Orientation and services

**Soffeh bus terminal** is a long way out to the south of the city, although there are plenty of buses and share taxis into town – ask for Meidun-e Enghelab-e Eslami. **Kaveh bus terminal** is not quite as far out and lies to the north of the city but you will still need to take a share-taxi.

Once in the centre you can happily walk to all the different sights although you will need to hire a **taxi** for any excursions.

The **tourist office** can be found next door but one to the Ali Ghapu Palace in Emam Khomeini Square. Most hotels/hostels have **Internet access** (Amir Kabir is the cheapest) and there are a couple of Internet cafés around town (carpet shops often tempt buyers with free access). The best **bureaux de change** are on Sepah St.

### Where to stay and eat

The most beautiful place to stay is *Abbasi Hotel* (☎ 226 009; US$120/Db), a converted caravanserai (see box p98) on Amadegh St – though service is said not to be up to scratch. About 100m from the Abbasi, *Hotel Safir* (🖳 www.safirhotel.com; US$60/Db) is a pleasant mid-range option but as with the rest of Esfahan is a bit overpriced. On Chahar Bagh-e Pa'in St, *Amir Kabir* (☎ 296 154; 90,000rials/Db, 40,000rials/dorm) is the nearest thing to a backpacking hangout in Iran; there's no bar but everything else is here. *Aria Hotel* (☎ 222 7224; US$20/Db) on Shahid Medani St is a step up in comfort and each room has an en suite shower. The café is pleasant, too.

Food options in Esfahan are surprisingly poor and are centred on the hotels, although *Sofreh Khaneh*, beside Sheikh Lotfollah Mosque, is well placed. *Restaurant Shahrzad* (Abbas Abad St) comes recommended for food, décor and ambience.

### What to buy

Esfahan is rightly considered the arts capital of Iran. There are some beautiful items to buy here and some unusual ones too. The **bazaar** lasts for over a mile from the north end of Emam Khomeini Sq to Jame Mosque.

The skill of **miniature painting** came originally from China but has taken hold here as you can see in Chehel Sotun Palace. A true master, Mr Fallahi, has three shops – and many students – in Esfahan; try his gallery, Fallahi Miniatures (🖳 www.miniatureart.org), at Kheyabun-e Sa'di 5. The best miniatures are painted on slices of ivory but camel bone is more often used now as ivory is illegal. Actually, it doesn't seem to be illegal here, just expensive. The brushes that are used are tiny and the detail is fantastic. Only natural colours are used so green comes from real leaves, black from ground fish-bones and blue from lapis lazuli. All the work is original and you can buy a framed work for US$60-70 (even the prize pieces are less than US$150).

The next thing Esfahan is famous for is its **hand-printed cloth**. This is ideal for tablecloths; if you turn right as soon as you enter the bazaar from the north of Meidun-e Emam Khomeini and go through to the small courtyard you will come to **Reza Sedighee Fard workshop** where you can see old granddad pressing away. Again, all the dyes they use are natural but beware of modern replicas sold elsewhere in the bazaar (genuine printers have a big round guarantee seal which should be stamped on any piece you buy). A two square-metre cloth costs about US$20. **Akbar Keshani Carpets**, downstairs in the carpet bazaar, is a very good place to buy nomadic styles (see pp136-7).

### Moving on
Having come this far, it's foolish not to carry on to Shiraz and Persepolis. Buses for **Shiraz** (8hrs/30,000rials) leave regularly from Soffeh bus terminal. Buses back to **Tehran** (7hrs/30,000rials) leave from Kaveh bus terminal.

---

### Excursion to Kashan and Abyaneh

You can stop off at **Kashan** on your way between Tehran and Esfahan but most visitors prefer to visit these two towns as part of a separate trip. Tours can be arranged from Tehran but it is quicker and cheaper from Esfahan. No one can say for sure but Kashan claims to be the departure point, and perhaps the home, of the Three Wise Men. It was certainly a prominent settlement as early as the fourth millennium BC and continued to grow sporadically until the Seljuks developed it into something of an artisan centre in the 11th century AD. Shah Abbas I ensured that the town's prosperity continued and was so smitten he chose to be buried here rather than Esfahan.

The town is full of grand **merchant homes** and houses dating from the last two or three hundred years. Look out for the two knockers on each door – one for men, one for women, so that ladies within knew if it was appropriate for them to open the door. The **Agha Bozorg Complex** houses a stunning mosque and madrassah, set in a magnificently cool sunken garden.

**Abyaneh** is a secret waiting to be discovered. This small village is unique in its population (look out for the women's bright flowery headscarves) and design (most of the houses are mud-built with wooden lattice windows and beamed balconies – they are built on top of one another for protection against the elements, so one person's front patio is another man's roof). There are some beautiful mosques here too, with stunning views of the valleys; it is hard to believe you are so close to one of the most barren stretches of desert in the country.

**Practicalities** There are good **restaurants** in Kashan, particularly *Delpazir* (☎ 0361 27276) on Kheyabun e Ayatollah Kashani, run by an Anglo-Iranian couple. If you want to stay the night try *Golestan Guesthouse* (80,000rials/Db) on Motahhari Sq, a recommended budget option. *Abyaneh Hotel* (US$40/Db inc breakfast), on the hill as you come into town, is about your only choice for staying the night there – it has a café and restaurant too but is aimed at the mid-range pocket.

A **taxi** for the day from Esfahan (see Amir Kabir Hotel, p147) should cost around 400,000rials and can take four passengers. Buses run to Kashan regularly from Tehran (3½hrs) and Esfahan (4½hrs); buses to Abyaneh from Kashan, however, are irregular.

# Shiraz

Shiraz has always been known as a city of culture and before the Revolution it was also known for its wine but now it is used mostly as a base for visiting the ancient city of Persepolis. The city does have a few sights of its own, however, mostly dating from the Zand dynasty (which made Shiraz their capital from 1750 to 1779).

## WHAT TO SEE

The Shiraz authorities have begun to appreciate the tourism potential of their town and have drawn up a programme of restoration and regeneration that should turn the city into a worthy rival of Esfahan. Quite a lot of work is already underway and, eventually, a huge complex incorporating bazaars and mosques will replace all the run-down areas in the centre – there is a model on display in the corner of the Shah-e Cheragh Mausoleum. Most sights are open daily.

### The Citadel
The 18th-century **Karim Khan Citadel** was unfortunately used as a prison for 50 years under the last shahs and heavy restoration work was being carried out at the time of writing. It dominates the centre of town and is open 08.00-18.00.

### Hafez and Sa'di mausoleums
Hafez and Sa'di are two of Iran's cultural icons (see box p151) and in Shiraz both have an exquisite tomb to celebrate their memory. Hafez's burial chamber of alabaster marble is particularly fine and has some of his poetry inscribed on it. There is also a lovely teahouse here. The underground fishpond at Sa'di's resting place is a delight. You will need to take a taxi to visit Sa'di Mausoleum. Both mausoleums are open during daylight hours.

### Eram Gardens
Shiraz earned a reputation in Iranian history as being man's 'Garden of Paradise' and these botanical gardens do their best to keep the tradition going for the 'city of roses and nightingales' (as Hafez referred to it); there are some beautiful cypress trees here as well. The gardens (open during daylight hours) are a longish walk (about 45 minutes) from the centre of town.

### Shah-e Cheragh Mausoleum
This mausoleum houses the tomb of Sayyed Mir Ahmed (the brother of Emam Reza) who was killed in Shiraz in 835AD. It is therefore sacred to all Shi'ites. The building is enormous and the entire interior is covered in mirrors. In the far left corner of the courtyard is the tomb of another brother. At the back of the main courtyard is a rather smaller one dating back to the 14th century. The model for the new town development is in the larger mausoleum and the plan is

150 Iran – Shiraz

to link this complex with the Jame Mosque (which was being restored at the time of writing) via the new bazaar. It's open 07.00-22.00.

## Other sights
The **bazaar** sells handicrafts similar to what you see in Esfahan. The quality is not as good but the caravanserai in the middle courtyard is superb.

**Vakil Mosque** has a winter prayer hall on one side, a summer prayer hall on the other and a giant alcove at either end. It is interesting to see how tastes in the colour of a mosque's tile-work had evolved by the time this was built with pink, yellow and black replacing the blues so dominant in earlier decoration (such as those you see in Esfahan).

## PRACTICAL INFORMATION
[☎ code 071]
### Orientation and services
The **bus station** is within walking distance of Shiraz's city centre. You will have little problem finding your way around, as everything is within close proximity of the main street (Khan-e Zand, known as **Zand**).

The **bureaux de change** on Zand give the best rates and are better than the banks. The **Internet cafés** on/just off the same street are quick and cheap; some also offer cheap international phone calls. The **tourist information office** outside Karim Khan Citadel is very helpful and it's worth paying them a visit if you want to spend some time here. For trips to Persepolis you can also try **Pars Tourist Agency** (☎ 222 3163; 🖳 www.key2persia.com) on Zand.

### Where to stay and eat
*Esteghli Hotel* (☎ 222 7728; 65,000rials/Db) on Dehnadi St is the main backpacker hangout; it runs tours to

---

### Persian poets
Iran has a venerable tradition of writing poetry and has produced some of the world's greats. Even non-Persians, such as Maulana, have historically chosen to write in Persian because of its connotations as a romantic and culturally sophisticated language.

**Omar Khayyam**, or Omar the Tentmaker, was born in about 1407 and is probably Persia's most famous poet. Many of his best works, such as the *Rubaiyat*, became particularly popular in the West after they were translated into English by Edward Fitzgerald. In Iran he is equally remembered for his mathematical, astronomy and history-writing skills, which were similarly impressive.

**Ferdosi** became famous for his brilliance in the art of 'epic' history poems. He was born in 940AD and his best-known work is *Shahnamah* ('Book of Kings'), which reportedly took thirty years to write. Today he is regarded as the saviour of Farsi as his decision to write in his own language gave it much needed credibility at a time when it was in danger of being driven out of the region by Arabic.

**Hafez** was a 14th-century poet and scholar who lived in Shiraz all his life and is still held very dear by its present inhabitants. His real name was Shams uddin Mohammed but he was given the nickname Hafez which means 'Memoriser of the Koran'.

**Sa'di** travelled the world in the 13th century but he always returned to Shiraz. His poetry, including *Golestan* ('Rose Garden') and *Bustan* ('Garden of Trees'), is said to be particularly popular with young couples in love.

### Excursion to Persepolis

Many of the best artefacts that were discovered on this site have been taken to museums around the world but the remains of the Persian capital which Alexander razed are still a wonder and deserve at least half a day. The city is now a World Heritage Site.

This mini-city was built by the Achaemenid King Darius I (the Great) as his summer capital – the winter capital being Susa (Shush), on the Kersan River. It also became the ceremonial capital of the Persian empire. The city was called Parsa (Persepolis was the Greek name for it) and under successive Persian kings it became one of the richest cities in the world; each year, envoys from all across the empire brought their offerings for the Festival of Tribute. Alexander described it as 'The most hateful city in the world' as it represented all the Persian extravagance which the Greeks abhorred and in January 330BC, despite the surrender of the Persian governor, he gave the order for his troops to begin an orgy of looting.

Remember that under the Persian kings, all the stones would have been polished to a black shine like the double-headed eagle you probably saw in Tehran's National Museum. The gaps between many of the pillars would also have been filled by walls or curtains (remnants of which are on display in the small museum). The roofs were made of mud and cedar wood brought from Lebanon but these were all burned by Alexander's troops.

The three languages that are used in the inscriptions are Old Farsi, Babylonian and Elamite. On the **grand stairway** leading up to the palace are carvings of all the different tribute-paying peoples of the empire: Medes, Parthians, Syrians, Arabs, Afghans, even Ethiopians. Xerxes's and Cyrus's temples have carvings of waiters bringing them food. In the Central Palace (see map opposite) some of the massive pillars show the king fighting with lions, bulls and eagles to demonstrate his invincibility.

The complex was still being added to when Darius was defeated by Alexander (as you can see in the area marked '6' on the map). **Xerxes's Palace** seems to have come in for the worst treatment, perhaps in revenge for his invasion of Greece in the 5th century BC.

The small **museum** has a few relics but not many; the highlight being a whisk handle which you can see the whisk bearer holding in many of the carvings (he's the man behind the king, next to the parasol bearer).

Entrance to the site is 50,000rials and on Thursday and Friday evenings there is a (not very good) light show. The massive tents you can see behind the nearby trees were erected for the '2500 years of Iran' celebrations but many were burned during the Revolution.

On the way back you might want to stop off at the **Naghsh-e Rostam Tombs**; these are the tombs of Darius I, Xerxes I, Artaxerxes I and Darius II, although when they were discovered, locals thought they were the tombs of Rustam, the Iranian mythical hero. You can no longer enter them, unfortunately, because when a child fell into one tomb and broke his arm the curators were ordered to remove the steps up to the entrances set high in the cliffs; you can also see two other tombs in the cliffs behind the main site at Persepolis.

Tours can be arranged from Shiraz (see 'Orientation and services' p151) or you can take a taxi to Persepolis, in which case try to team up with others to fill it and share the cost.

Persepolis. ***Darya Hotel*** (☎ 222 1778; 65,000rials/Db) is good fun and the showers (shared) are always hot.

There are plenty of alternatives on Piruzi St and Zand but they tend to be tatty and noisy. On Tohid St, ***Ghane Hotel*** (☎ 222 5374) is nice but we're not quite sure it's worth the 160,000rials it's asking for an en suite double.

On Rudaki St, ***Sadra Hotel*** (☎ 224 740; US$30/Db) seems to be the most attractive mid-range option. It has a good restaurant downstairs.

There are plenty of other mid-range options on Rudaki St and the new ***Aryo Barzan Hotel*** (☎ 224 7128; US$50/Db) has been recommended. On Meshkin Fam St, ***Homa Hotel*** (US$140/Db), a bit further out

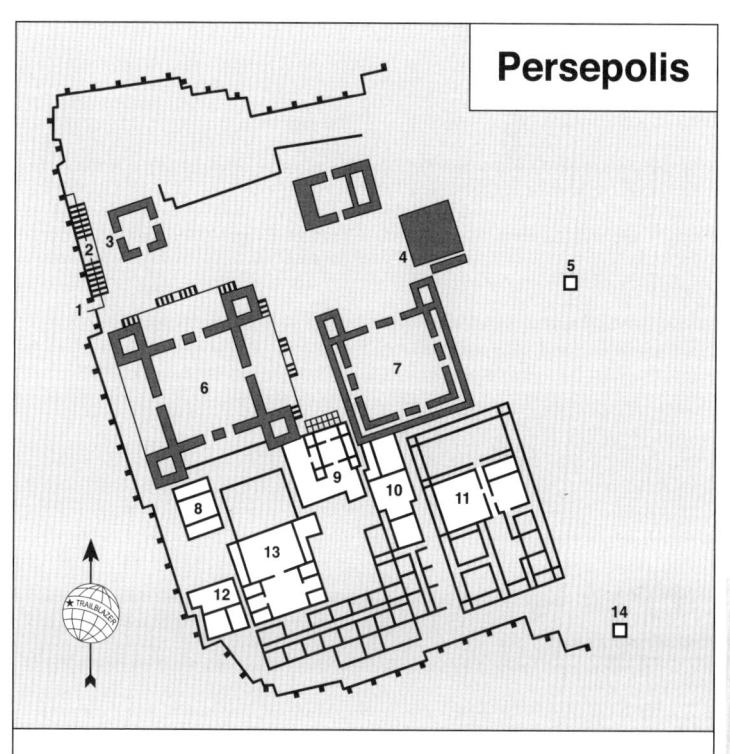

# Persepolis

1 Entrance
2 Grand Stairway
3 Xerxes Gateway
4 Hall of 32 Columns
5 Tomb of Artaxerxes II
6 Hall of Apadana Palace
7 Palace of 100 Columns
8 Palace of Darius I
9 Central Palace
10 Museum
11 Darius's Treasury
12 Xerxes's Palace
13 Artaxerxes's Palace
14 Tomb of Artaxerxes III

> **Yazd**
> Yazd is famous for its silk weaving and has always been a major commercial centre for the region, even if it wasn't always a primary Silk Road stop. Marco Polo came through here and described it as 'a very fine and splendid city' and it is still a beautiful city to look at, even if it is excruciatingly hot in summer. Today it is also famous for its **wind-towers** and **Zoroastrian temples** (it is the centre of Iran's dwindling Zoroastrian population). The **Jameh Mosque** is also a remarkable piece of architecture.
>
> The best place to stay is *Silk Road Hotel* (☎ 0351 625 2730; $30/Db), 100m from Jameh Mosque. There are plenty of buses to/from Mashad, Shiraz, Kerman and Tehran.

from the centre, was built under the shah as the Cyrus Intercontinental and, together with its sister hotel in Persepolis, the Darius Intercontinental, became the showpiece of the '2500 years of Iran' celebrations in the 1960s. It has been refurbished and is now rather plush.

Apart from the hotel restaurants there are few good places to eat other than those you see on Zand. One exception is the elegant *Hammam-e Vakil* in the restored baths within the Vakil Bazaar, although the food is not always up to scratch.

Shiraz has gone pizza crazy like the rest of Iran but none of the pizza restaurants is that great – you are better off sticking to a shwarma/kebab.

## Moving on

The bus back to **Tehran** is a gruelling 16 hours and you should choose your bus wisely even if it does cost a bit more (upwards of 40,000rials). Another option is to go to **Yazd** (see box above) for a couple of days, and then head on (by bus again) to **Mashad**.

The alternative is to fly and as Iran has some cheap internal flights you may be tempted. If you are determined to complete your trans-Asia trip overland, you can fly back to Tehran (two hours, 230,000rials) and rejoin your east–west route; if you are more concerned for your back's well-being you can fly straight to Mashad (320,000rials). To get to the airport take the No 10 bus from behind the citadel.

> **Crossing the Iran/Pakistan border**
> If you are missing out Central Asia you can head into Pakistan and pick up the route again at **Islamabad** (see p274). This detour is quite straightforward, though you will pass through **Baluchistan**, which is very hot and not very exciting scenically. Take a bus to **Kerman** (8hrs) and then another to **Zahedan** (6hrs). There are a few places to stay in Zahedan, though most are reported to be grotty. From Zahedan, take one of the many share taxis to **Mirjave** (they may well run you right up to the border crossing).
>
> The actual crossing is usually a quick procedure and once on the other side you can take one of the many buses from **Taftan** to **Quetta** (14hrs).
>
> From Quetta there are plenty of buses and minibuses to Islamabad. You will probably want to explore southern Pakistan on your way, however, in which case we would recommend picking up a copy of *The Pakistan Handbook* (see p254).

# Mashad

Because of the holy shrine of Emam Reza, Mashad ( the 'City of the Martyr') is an important pilgrimage site for all Shi'ite Muslims. There is little else to see or do, however, so you probably won't want more than a couple of days here.

## WHAT TO SEE

### Astan-e Ghods-e Razavi

Muslims come to this 75-hectare marvel on pilgrimage from all over the world and it is amazingly busy year-round. If you don't go with a guide, however, you will need to report to the International Visitors Office (an usher will take you

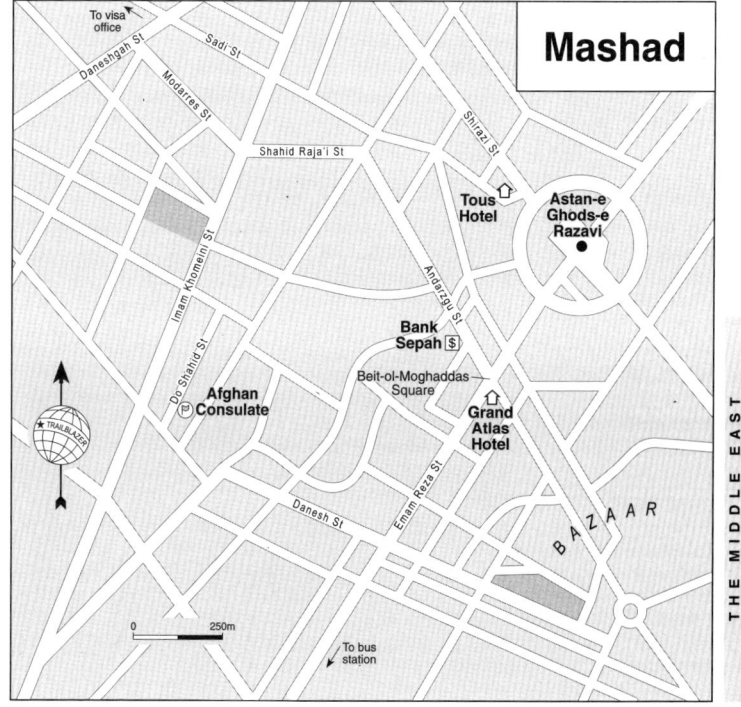

## Crossing the Iran/Turkmenistan border
Buses once ran from Mashad bus station right through to Merv but the company which did this has gone bust so you need to improvise slightly. From Mashad's main bus station, take a bus to **Sarakhs** (3½hrs/6500rials) where you will be dropped in the centre of the village. Walk around to the border crossing or share a taxi (it's not far). **You must pay a US$10 fee to enter Turkmenistan**. If you have paid for a full tourist visa/package your guide will meet you at the border checkpoint (known as **Saraghs** in Turkmenistan). If not, change as little money as you can with the dealers hanging around the Turkmen side as they offer poor rates. You must get a taxi to **Mary** so try to get your driver to accept payment on arrival and change your money there.

Coming from Turkmenistan get a taxi to the border from Mary, cross through the checkpoint and try to get a share taxi into Sarakhs with any fellow crossers. From Sarakhs it should be easy to get a bus/share taxi to **Mashad**.

One other alternative is to take a taxi (US$2) from Ashgabat to the border (20km), cross at **Gaudan** and take a taxi (US$3) to **Bajgiran** (20km) or **Quchan**, from where you can get a bus to **Sari** or Mashad (2½hrs). This can also be done in reverse.

Your *manat* and *rials* are worthless on the other side so have as few left as possible.

---

there from the main gate); unfortunately, there is not always someone in the office (it's generally manned 09.00-17.00), so you might have to come back later.

The complex surrounds the tomb/shrine of Emam Reza who was buried here in the 9th century, though what you can see today has mostly been built since the Revolution or dates from Shah Abbas's reign in the 17th century. As well as the mausoleum there are two mosques, four museums, twelve halls (divans), six madrassahs and several libraries. **Azem-e Gohar Shad Mosque** is the most impressive with its blue dome. Of the museums, **Moghaddas Museum** is probably the most unusual as it houses all the gifts Ayatollah Khomeini received during his years in power.

The shrine itself is out of bounds to non-Muslims but feel free to walk, with due respect, around the rest of the complex.

### Omar Khayyam and Ferdosi Gardens
These two greats of Iranian poetry (see box p151) are buried in enormous separate gardens outside Mashad. You will need a taxi to visit them but both are perfect for a picnic; ask at your hotel for help getting out there.

### PRACTICAL INFORMATION
[☎ code 0511]
#### Orientation and services
The bus station is quite a way out of town at the very end of the 2km-long Emam Reza St. The walk from the station into the town centre is straightforward, if a little tiring. The golden domes of the shrine complex are visible from just about anywhere so it is hard to get lost.

If you've just come from Turkmenistan and have a transit visa, you can pay for this to be extended at the **Visa office/Aliens office** (Meidun-e Rahnama'i – the relevant Bank Melli is about 750m down the street); this is a long way out to the west of the city so you'll need to take a taxi (5000rials).

The **Afghan Consulate** is on Do Shahid St.

Most of what you need (including **Internet cafés**) is on or just off **Emam Reza**. Most banks **change money**; the pick is probably Bank Sepah off the main drag.

### Where to stay and eat
Most accommodation is aimed at Muslim pilgrims so don't expect too many English-speakers around.

*Tous Hotel* (☎ 222 4385; 70,000rials/ Db) on Shirazi St is the best budget option. *Grand Atlas Hotel* (☎ 854 5061; US$40/Db) on Beit-ol-Moqaddas Sq is comfortable and affords great views. Apart from hotel restaurants, **food** options are limited to *kebabis* on Emam Reza St.

### Moving on
Buses to **Tehran** are plentiful but the journey is very long (15-16hrs). If you are heading for **Shiraz** you might want to stop off at **Yazd** (16hrs, one or two buses a day) or **Kerman** (16hrs). If you are heading for **Sari** you will have to change buses at **Gorgan** (10hrs). If you want to explore **Afghanistan**, see box p10.

---

### Cycling the Silk Road
More and more foreign visitors are opting for pedal power to explore our route, even if fewer and fewer locals are using a bike in the Silk Road countries (especially China, where everyone is becoming obsessed with cars). The benefits are enormous, even if the distances are equally extreme. It's one of the finest ways of escaping the crowds, particularly in China where foreign visitors are not allowed their own motorized vehicle or motorbike. Trailblazer's *Adventure Cycle-Touring Handbook* (see p383) provides essential practical information for any such trips.

**Practicalities** Most roads are in good-enough condition to take bikes but you need to plan carefully to find the least hilly route. Many cyclists are forced to camp at least some of the time (see box p73), with long distances between accommodation. Water can be another major headache as the route is so hot and you are so exposed. There are bike/repair shops in most big towns but local shapes and sizes tend to be incompatible with most foreign bikes – even bikes from other countries along the Silk Road. Cyclists we met recommend taking at least two spare chains, four spare inner tubes and two spare tyres, extensive repair equipment – plus front and back panniers for all your gear.

You should have no problem bringing your bike into any Silk Road country as, unlike cars and motorbikes, they don't need separate paperwork or clearance (it's a good idea to take out a **comprehensive insurance policy**, however, both for bike and rider). **Visas** can be tiresome as you often need more time than countries will give you to complete your journey in full (most cyclists are forced onto buses or trains at some stage); sometimes as a cyclist if you apply in your own country and explain the situation you might be given longer than a standard tourist visa (but don't count on this). You will also need detailed maps (much more detailed than the ones we can provide here – see box p29) but this is no longer the impediment it once was.

If you want to go it alone, try the Internet for the latest blogs from fellow Silk Road cyclists as these are far more useful than the information provided by local cycle groups which, if they exist at all, have different agendas. If you want to do it as a group, contact the organizers of the **Tour D'Afrique** (🖳 www.tourdafrique.com), the annual cycle 'race' through Africa from Cairo to Cape Town. They are launching the first-ever Silk Road Cycle Rally, pedalling from Istanbul to Beijing, in August 2007 and will go again in 2008, arriving in time for the opening ceremony of the Olympics. It's open to amateurs and professionals alike and aims to complete the 11,000km or so in 110 days.

**NB Tandem riders beware!** Technically, bikes in China are permitted to carry only one person to prevent accidents. A Western couple on a tandem were turned back at the Chinese border by an over-zealous official bent on upholding the letter of the law.

# PART 4: CENTRAL ASIA

## Facts about the region

### GEOGRAPHICAL BACKGROUND

These days, the term 'Central Asia' usually refers to Kazakhstan, Turkmenistan, Uzbekistan, Kyrgyzstan and Tajikistan. Historically, however, many of these lands formed part of 'Turkestan' which, as a cultural and political entity, also included a massive area to the east of the Tien Shan Mountains (now known as the Xinjiang province in modern-day China). This book falls somewhere in between as it includes Turkmenistan, Uzbekistan, Kyrgyzstan and Kazakhstan in this section, and Xinjiang in the next.

Turkmenistan, Uzbekistan, Kazakhstan and Kyrgyzstan represent a clear cross-section of nearly all the different types of geography to be found in Central Asia: in Turkmenistan there is the Caspian Sea coastline offset by the devastatingly hot Karakum ('Black Sands') Desert; the lush Ferghana Valley runs from Kyrgyzstan into Uzbekistan; in the east of Kyrgyzstan you find the mighty Tien Shan Mountains; the great Amu-Darya and Syr-Darya rivers flow right across your path and in north-west Uzbekistan you can be witness to what remains of the Aral Sea. The whole area is a major earthquake zone as the Indian subcontinent continues to crash into the Asian crustal plate.

### HISTORY

#### Prehistory

The Uzbek plain is thought to have been home to the earliest forms of man in the region, with the remains of a Neanderthal dating back roughly 50,000 years, having been discovered in the Aman-kutan Cave near Samarkand. Recent excavations in Turkmenistan also point to a Bronze Age civilization growing up around the Margiana Oasis. Although this dates from about 2000BC it is as old as any other urban development that archaeologists have discovered and would place Turkmenistan alongside China, Egypt, Mesopotamia and India as a cradle of civilization.

#### Early history

By the time of the Achaemenids, the area was roughly split into three: Sogdiana (between the Oxus and the Jaxartes rivers); Khorezm (below the Aral Sea, to the west of the Oxus) and Saka (to the east of the Jaxartes but without any other fixed borders).

Alexander had his hands full turning these client kingdoms into part of his empire but, after nearly two years of fighting, the Sogdians finally succumbed and their legendary fortress at the Rock of Sogdiana fell (just where this fortress was remains a mystery, though we know it lies somewhere in the Hissar Mountains in western Tajikistan). As booty, Alexander took Roxanne, the beautiful Bactrian princess, and a chain of cities including Alexander the Farthest (modern-day Khojand in Tajikistan).

### Northern invaders
As successive tribes swept out of the Mongolian Steppes (driven south by the increasingly arid climate), many headed for Central Asia. The results were mixed. Some, like the Yueh-Chih, settled down and flourished – it was they whom Zang Qian sought out as allies against the Hsiung Nu and who gave him 'Heavenly Horses' (see box p230). Others were happy to simply plunder and move on.

The first wave of Turks fell into the latter category but in the 6th century AD a branch known as the Blue Turks (after the colour of their helmets) came with more permanent ambitions and ousted the Huns who had ruled the region for the previous two centuries. (These Huns should not be thought of as an appendage of Attila's army; instead, the Huns were a loose confederation of individual armies whose leaders took them where they pleased from their homeland in the Mongolian steppe.)

### Islam
The success of the Turks can be seen today in the lasting impressions they have left on the gene pool and languages of Central Asia. Despite significant gains by the armies of Islam, the Turks managed to retain some sense of independence while the rest of their neighbours collapsed. Indeed, the Muslims turned to the Turks as allies in order to defeat the Chinese army at Talas (in the valley between Kazakhstan and Kyrgyzstan) in 751AD.

Gradually, the Turks prospered and although the Samanid dynasty, which controlled Central Asia by the 9th century, was allied to the Sunni caliph of Baghdad, its rulers continued to sponsor Turkish talent alongside Persian. The

> **The Caspian Sea**
> Depending on whom you talk to, this 370,000 sq km stretch of water is either the biggest lake in the world or one of the Earth's many seas. Normally, this would be of interest only to geographers but since the discovery of oil and gas (the Caspian region as a whole is estimated to be sitting on top of 200 billion barrels of crude oil) it has become a major political hot potato.
>
> Under the USSR system it was simple: Moscow controlled all of it except a small strip of southern water that belonged to Iran; but just as the USSR has broken up into disputed fragments, so too has the Caspian. If it really is a sea, each littoral state (Russia, Kazakhstan, Azerbaijan and Iran) gets its own territorial slice and all the fish/natural resources it can find within that. If, on the other hand, it is a lake, all the water's fish and natural resources are shared equally.
>
> Whatever it is, the waters are some of the dirtiest/most polluted in the world. Underwater volcanoes and industrial waste add to the pollution every day, as does the ongoing gas and oil exploration – at 27m below sea level, the waters will never be drained. The effect on sturgeon (the slow-growing fish from which caviare is taken) has been catastrophic. The beaches have also become discoloured.

> **Thinking outside the box**
> The Samanids gave rise to some of the world's greatest thinkers: **Al Khorezmi** (better known in the West by his Latin name, al Gorismi) 787-850AD. He was the inventor of algorithms (rather than 'alkhorezms'). His other major work was *al Jabr*, or as we call it, Algebra; **Al Biruni**, 973-1046AD, was the leading astronomer of the day, correctly espousing the theory of the Earth rotating and circling the sun; he also estimated the distance to the moon to within 20km; **Abu Ali Ibn-Sina** (Latin name, Avicenna), 980-1037AD, was the greatest medic of his and many other times, whose *Canon of Medicine* was like a bible to European doctors until well into the 17th century.

result was a cultural golden age, with Central Asian cities becoming cultural centres to rival any in the world; Bukhara earned the epithet 'Pillar of Islam'. They were also important business centres providing key services such as banks, brokers, creditors, caravanserai (see box p98) and, of course, markets.

## Seljuks

The Samanids gave way in the 10th century and were replaced by the Ghaznavids (in the south and the west) and the Karakhanids (in the east as far as Kashgar). Then, in a classic manoeuvre, the Seljuks (a third but much smaller Turkic group) promised allegiance to the Ghaznavids to help them beat the Karakhanids and then turned on their allies once the initial victory was secure.

In common with most empires born out of the steppes, the Seljuk star was a shooting one but during their century of power they managed to take *de facto* control of the entire Abbassid caliphate, making them masters of all the land from Xinjiang to the shores of the Mediterranean.

Just as the Seljuks seized power from the inside, however, so they lost it to one of their closest vassals, the Khorezm. This tribe set up its capital at Gurganj (modern-day Konye-Urgench) and its leaders were cultivating a very successful empire of their own when suddenly they found themselves in the path of a whirlwind on horseback.

## Mongols

There was no way the Khorezm could have predicted just how devastating the Mongols would prove to be and without the benefit of hindsight they thought it a good idea to defend their lands as robustly as possible. Unfortunately, it was this stiff resistance which encouraged **Genghis Khan** to be particularly brutal in his destruction of the Khorezm lands. Some cities, such as Bukhara, recovered but many, such as Merv and Bactria, were destroyed for good.

One subject people in this region did benefit from Mongol rule, however: the Uighurs. In the 9th century this tribe had been driven south from their traditional grazing grounds in the Altai Mountains by the Kyrgyz (themselves on their way further west). The Uighurs took advantage of a weak China and pushed on into the Tarim Basin which one way or another they made their home. It was during this period that the Tarim Basin and the other lands surrounding the Taklamakan Desert became known as East Turkestan, and the lands between the Caspian Sea and the Tien Shan mountains became West Turkestan.

Unfortunately, the Mongols chose East Turkestan as their first target and the Uighurs were no match in military terms. They did, however, have highly sophisticated reading and writing skills (whereas the Mongols were illiterate and largely uneducated), so a deal was struck whereby the Uighurs were spared in return for them establishing an efficient administration system for the Mongols' newly won lands. The bonus for the Uighurs was that their language became the *lingua franca* of the empire and their merchants found themselves at the centre of the economy.

Soon after Genghis's death, the Mongols in this region divided when the more conservative eastern and northern tribes rejected a plan to convert to Islam.

## Tamerlane (Timur the Lame)

It was from amongst the newly converted Muslims of the south that one clan leader rose up to carve out his own empire. Tamerlane actually claimed descent from Genghis Khan but this seems as unclear as his religious beliefs (from most accounts he was only nominally a Muslim). As so often, however, perception was more important than reality and he managed to win over Mongol troops with promises of unlimited riches.

By conquering all the land from the Caucasus in the west to northern India in the east (Delhi fell in 1398), the Persian Gulf in the south (Baghdad followed in 1401) and the Kazakh steppe in the north, he delivered these riches and much, much more. Only his death in 1405 prevented him from testing his mettle against the Chinese.

Tamerlane has gone down in history as a baby-eating tyrant (over one million people died during his campaigns – after storming Baghdad, he erected one hundred and twenty towers containing 90,000 skulls) but he also achieved several cultural successes, particularly in science and architecture. They were built upon by his

This impressive statue of Tamerlane has replaced the old monument to Lenin in Shakrisabz.

grandson, Ulugh Beg, who, despite being no match for his grandfather's military prowess, built one of the greatest observatories in history and sponsored scientists to come from all over Asia and join him in his research.

## Uzbeks

The next major players in West Turkestan were the Uzbeks, another outcast of the steppes (probably the Southern Siberian Steppe). They had split in two when in 1468 one faction (later known as the Kazakhs) refused to move any further south and defeated the leader, Abu al Khayr, in battle. The main body, nevertheless, came to settle on that ever-popular stretch of land between the Oxus (by now known as the Amu-Darya) River and the Jaxartes (Syr-Darya). By this time, though, the Silk Road was all but finished and less and less trade was coming through the region. The Ottomans were now the major power in western Asia and they were more interested in the riches to be had in Europe following the fall of Constantinople in 1453. The Uzbeks settled into a domesticated way of life but the cities they inhabited continued to decline. Typically, the Shaybanid dynasty of the 16th century was famous for its piety but not, unfortunately, for its wealth.

In East Turkestan, the more conservative arm of the Mongol Khanate struggled on but they were soon under pressure from the Kazakhs, the Kyrgyz and the Dzungarians (who controlled an empire in western Mongolia which lasted from 1635 to 1758).

In reality, both regions descended into petty squabbling and remained that way until larger powers once again deemed them worthy of interference.

## Russians

Iranian rulers in the 18th century had tried to flex their muscles and bring West Turkestan under their jurisdiction but they were not strong enough and the region remained in the control of ad hoc rulers who held little sway outside their capitals. Officially the land was split between three khanates – Khokand, Bukhara and Khiva – and the inhabitants of each were split between Turkic-speaking Uzbeks and Persian-speaking Tajiks. Outside the major towns, however, Turkmen nomads were a law unto themselves and happily captured prisoners from all sides before selling them into slavery.

To Russian merchants this was a backward land but they hoped that its traders might be persuaded to buy their inferior mechanical goods (which Europe so disdained) and, in exchange, sell their cotton, silk, tea and rhubarb (these last two products had recently become extremely popular in Europe). Similarly, this 'blank canvas' was seen by Russian politicians as potential new land for the empire. Although the colonization of Siberia during the previous two centuries had been an epic success, rulers such as Peter the Great and Catherine the Great still wanted more; of course, they also wanted to be much more European in their outlook but they knew that European luxuries cost money. They may have paid only sporadic attention to the 'hawks' who called for a campaign of 'Mongol bashing' similar to that under Ivan the Terrible but they liked the idea of expansion south-eastwards and encouraged contacts to be made.

In fact, they were left with little choice as the other European states succeeded in establishing their own empires around the world and put a stop to any

Russian expansion to their west at the Congress of Vienna in 1814 (this despite Russia's victory over Napoleon), while expansion in the Near East was checked by defeat in the Crimean War against the British.

## Expansion

The first to suffer were the Kazakhs who were closest to Moscow and before long, their Inner, Middle and Outer hordes had been conquered and the concept of a Great Horde quashed forever.

The next series of moves, however, were far from being part of a coherent strategy. Moscow wanted to expand its empire (by the mid-19th century, despite official protestations, there can be no doubt of that) but it wanted to avoid a conflict with Britain even more (Britain now controlled India and wanted to expand into Central Asia as well). On the ground, generals knew that they would rarely receive the back-up necessary for a full offensive but would nevertheless receive commendation if opportunistic gains were made.

In 1865 Tashkent was just one such gain, with General Chernyaev earning the moniker 'Lion of Tashkent'. As each gain was met with little more than bluster from the British, the Russians grew in confidence. They had one main advantage: logistically, the Central Asian khanates were in the middle of nowhere, so by the time the British had heard about another Russian offensive to take a city, it was too late. The three khanates fell under a hail of cannonballs and broken promises and the last resistance, from the Tekke Turkmen, was crushed in the annihilation at Geok-Tepe in 1881.

## Colonization

The Great Game (see p206) carried on for another quarter of a century but the theatre shifted to Afghanistan and Xinjiang as Central Asia was conceded to the Russians. They began to build the Trans-Caspian Railway from Krasnovodsk (their newly founded port on the Caspian Sea) to Tashkent. Two more rail lines came down from Astrakhan and Orenburg as they looked to maximize economic gains. The first problem they had to tackle was the population: they needed loyal subjects with European skills who could drag the region out of the past.

Fortunately for the politicians, millions of ideal candidates had just been created by limited land reforms back in Russia proper which had abolished serfdom. Newly emancipated Russians came in their droves (mostly from present-day Russia and the Ukraine) to claim the new land for themselves. The old systems of irrigation were revived on an enormous scale and production grew exponentially. All this success, however, came at a price.

## Uprising

Much has been written about the growth of a 'Pan-Turkic' movement at the turn of the nineteenth and twentieth centuries, spurred on by a new sense of national identity. Scholars, such as the great Kazakh Shoqan Ualikhanov, have been held up as founding fathers of this 'movement' but, in reality, it was little more than straightforward resentment against Russian domination and exploitation which sporadically erupted into violence (don't forget that had the Russians not been here, the local tribes would no doubt have quite happily carried on fighting each other). Indeed, Islamic leaders still held more sway over the people than any nationalists, as was demonstrated by the mullah-led holy war against the Russians in 1897.

Therefore, when a mass uprising broke out in 1916, it should be seen in this context, especially as the Russians were placing exorbitant demands on the region for cattle and men to hold up the tsar's flagging armies in WWI. True, there were organizations such as the Young Bukharans and the Young Khivans (who modelled themselves on the Young Turks movement which had made so much progress in Turkey since 1908) but these groups were small and of little day-to-day consequence. The majority of the participants were intent simply on revenge. Most 'strategies' went out of the window as Kazakh and Kyrgyz nomads tried to reclaim some of the lands which had been slowly absorbed into Russian territory for decades. In the cities, rioting and looting were the main weapons as colonists were butchered and their homes and belongings burned.

Unfortunately for the nomads, the tsar was still strong enough to order a crackdown on the dissent, the brutality of which was startling. Whole communities were slaughtered or forced to flee (many tried to go to China, though they received little comfort there). This episode still burns bright in the minds of today's Kazakh and Kyrgyz populations – despite it being merely a taste of what was to come.

### Revolution
Any hopes that the end of the tsar would herald a new beginning for Central Asia were quickly dashed. If anything, the Russians living in this region were those most opposed to the Revolution because many were the cotton magnates whose vast land holdings were prime targets for any redistribution of wealth. An independent state of Kokand was declared in 1917 but its leaders (who spoke of a holy 'jihad' to build a pan-Turkic state) relied on money from the Russian cotton magnates to bankroll their programme which largely defeated the object. They were also attacked by the mullahs who saw their Westernizing, educating ways as a direct threat.

Unsurprisingly, it didn't last and the new Red Army proved just as ruthless as the old regime. It came south in 1918 to make it absolutely clear how it was going to be and Kokand was smashed (Khiva and Bukhara had less gloriously reverted to feuding between themselves upon the fall of the tsar, and both offered little opposition to the forces of the Red Army's commander, Mikhail Frunze). The emir of Bukhara fled to Afghanistan (famously taking his dancing boys but leaving his harem) and for a while it looked as if all the heroes had disappeared.

### Enver Pasha and Paul Nazaroff
That the first leader to raise his head above the parapet was a White Russian shouldn't surprise us. **Paul Nazaroff** was an idealist rather than a pragmatist but he managed to stir up enough support to lead a counter-revolution at the end of 1918. His supporters, including local Uzbeks and Tajiks, managed to seize control of a string of towns and cities (most notably Tashkent) and for a while there was genuine rejoicing. Once again, however, the heavy hand of the Red Army came down on the region and Nazaroff was forced to flee to Xinjiang.

A more popular figure in modern Central Asian folklore is **Enver Pasha**. He was in fact a Turk and had served as the Ottoman Empire's Minister of War (against the Russians). He managed to flee to Moscow as the Turkish army collapsed and convinced the Bolsheviks that he had been fighting the Russians only because he too hated the tsar. He styled himself as a potential rival to Atatürk and asked Lenin to help him seize power in what was left of Turkey's lands. This, however, was merely a smokescreen: knowing how discredited he was in Istanbul, he was now looking for a new stage upon which he could achieve his end. Lenin was rightly sceptical about just how solid Bolshevik power was in Central Asia and when Pasha offered to rally an army to the Revolution's cause, wipe out any White Russian cells of opposition in the region and maybe throw in some loot from India, Lenin was in the perfect frame of mind to be fooled.

Pasha left for Bukhara in 1921 but managed to give his Red Army comrades the slip and put feelers out amongst those tribesmen known as the *basmachi* (Russian for 'bandits') who were still carrying out a guerrilla war of sorts from secret mountain bases. His timing couldn't have been better because the one thing the tribesmen lacked was a leader. Again Pasha changed his story to emphasize how he, a true Turkic Turk, representative of the Prophet and relative of the caliph, had been fighting the Russians all his life. He was fêted like a prodigal son and soon over 20,000 men were said to be at his command with money and support pouring in from the emir of Afghanistan and the exiled emir of Bukhara. Dushanbe was captured and established as their new capital and many of the old Bukharan lands pledged allegiance.

Lenin was not about to be outmanoeuvred twice, however. He sent 100,000 troops down to deal with Pasha's men and at the same time reinstated many of the mullah's powers (a guaranteed source of support against any new secular nationalism). He also offered tax cuts to key sectors of the population and even returned some previously confiscated land.

As quickly as Pasha's supporters had come to praise him, so they melted away, although Pasha himself was determined to have a hero's final curtain. He took a hard core of his best men and hid out in the Pamir Mountains in an attempt to return to the guerrilla tactics of before. Even there, though, he was not safe and on August 4, 1922, he was ambushed by a Russian patrol. Legend has it that rather than flee, he turned back his horse to face the ambushers and, sabre in hand, charged headlong into the machine-gun fire.

### Bolshevik control grows

Bolshevik control in Russia soon grew to strangling proportions and Central Asia became one of the worst victims. The traditional nomadic way of life of so many of the population was an anathema to the Bolsheviks' totalitarian dreams, as were the patchworks of small family farms in areas like the Ferghana Valley.

Millions were starved to death, directly and indirectly, as Moscow initially requisitioned enormous quantities of food to feed the cities and then began to appropriate land for its collective-farming programme. Many Kazakhs and Kyrgyz slaughtered their herds and ate what they could rather than give up their prized animals but this only weakened their position for the following years. The enormous collective farms that were introduced onto the grazing land, like those created to replace the family homesteads, were equally disastrous. With each five-year plan, production dropped and famine increased.

For the Bolsheviks, control of the industrial cities was the key to success, so the countryside's welfare was sacrificed to shore up urban support. If this policy was objected to, the dissenters were brutally dealt with: millions disappeared. Particularly hard hit were the religious leaders: Stalin led the 'Movement of the Godless' between 1932 and 1936 in which mosques were smashed and mullahs persecuted – by the 1940s only 2000 of an estimated 47,000 mullahs remained.

### New boundaries

In another attempt to make the local inhabitants conform, Stalin created Socialist Soviet Republics into which the whole area could be divided. Even this system, however, was perverted. Rather than divide the territory along ethnic or tribal grounds, Stalin manipulated the borders in such a way so as to pay little consideration to cultural boundaries, indeed, often to deliberately spite them. The Uzbek and Turkmen SSRs were proclaimed in 1924, the Tajik in 1929 and the Kazakh and Kyrgyz in 1936. This divide-and-rule tactic became typical of the rest of Stalin's reign and it is little consolation that such programmes enabled Stalin to maintain the absolute power which ultimately saved the Russians against Hitler. That over half the 1.5 million conscripts called up from Central Asia are said to have deserted during WWII cannot come as a surprise.

After WWII many soldiers from the European front were offered homes in the region in an attempt to import their manufacturing skills. To their surprise they met another collection of recent exiles – Chechens, Russians and Ukrainians of German descent, Koreans and any other ethnic minority suspected of being potential fifth columnists.

### The upside

Surprisingly, perhaps, there were some significant improvements in the region during this period compared to some of the neighbouring areas and these must be credited to the Russians. Most obviously, the education and literacy levels are outstanding compared to Afghanistan, Pakistan and even Iran. The whole area is also much more industrially developed, thereby giving it greater potential now that communism has fallen. That each country has retained a secular government is also seen as a positive by all but the most ardent Islamic fundamentalist.

There has been some violence in each of the republics but since the break up of the USSR, the 'ethnic' unrest which saw running battles between, for example, Uzbeks and Kyrgyz in Osh in 1990, has virtually disappeared. Many say the initial violence was stirred up by hard-line communists anyway, in a last ditch attempt to revive the divide-and-rule tactic.

There is still much to debate, however, and the most intriguing arguments surround the new Commonwealth of Independent States (CIS). In 1991 all the old SSRs were offered complete independence but those in Central Asia refused to go it alone and demanded to be part of the CIS which was originally intended only for Russia, the Ukraine and Belarus. Was this because Russia had raped its republics so hard that they had no choice but to stick together? Or were there genuine feelings of regret? Certainly we have met many who hark back to the 'good old days' and it is true that Kazakhstan has seriously considered reunification with Russia. Or is it just that the Russian immigrants of the past fifty years speak with the loudest voices?

As it is, this section of your Silk Road trip will take you through at least three republics, each with a unique post-USSR history.

## Turkmenistan

Turkmenistan's history since the demise of communism has in many ways been the history of one man, Saparmurat Niyazov – or Turkmenbashi ('Head of all Turkmen') as he has proclaimed himself and is referred to by the entire population (they have little choice).

Niyazov was the Communist Party boss at the time Moscow began to encourage semi-independence in its republics and he managed to swing an election for the new post of president which gave him 98 per cent of the vote. In 1991 he campaigned to keep his country within the USSR and victory in the referendum came with an overwhelming majority. Unfortunately, the wishes of the Turkmen were irrelevant as Moscow had decided that the USSR was no more and Turkmenistan, whether it liked it or not, was independent.

**Independence** They didn't like it because for decades the entire economy of Turkmenistan had been designed around supplying Moscow and there was virtually no crop diversity to support the new nation. Whatever happened next, it was going to be a severe uphill struggle but Niyazov grasped the opportunity with both hands and tried to drag his country out of the poverty trap. His first moves were to cut Ashgabat's dependence on Moscow and to this end new foreign relations were quickly cultivated.

The most obvious new partner was Iran to the south, home to over one million Turkmen. Iran suddenly became interested when it was revealed how much oil and gas is potentially under the Karakum Desert and the Turkmen-controlled area of the Caspian Sea. One pipeline for Turkmen gas has already been built across Iran to the Gulf (from where it can easily be exported around the world) and a new much larger pipeline is planned.

The other, more surprising choice of partner has been Turkey: apart from their names the two countries have little in common but Niyazov sees Atatürk as his ideal role model as he builds a Turkmen nation. Turkey also has access to the West, through NATO and Europe, and Niyazov's greatest dream is to build pipelines across the Caspian Sea and into Turkey from where it can be exported via the Mediterranean at even greater profits.

There is only one problem: between the Caspian and Turkey lie the Caucasus and in particular, Azerbaijan. Niyazov has tried to cultivate a new partnership with Baku but with every step forward, there is a step back – the major problem is who owns what in the Caspian (see box p158). That said, the first of these pipelines has finally been laid and, with the oil price soaring, money is beginning to talk.

> **The cult of Turkmenbashi**
> Everywhere you go you will see posters and statues bearing Niyazov's inane grin. You will also see his ubiquitous slogan *'Halk, Watan, Turkmenbashi'* which translates as 'People, nation, Turkmenbashi'. He has promised his people a Turkmen Golden Age, *'Altyn Asyr'* – though it will be an age dictated by him. His book *Rukhnama* ('Book of the Soul') is compulsory reading and you cannot enter a Turkmen university without taking a *Rukhnama* test. The only problem is most of it is nonsense: a Turkmenbashi skewed portrayal of Turkmen history, culture and spirituality.
>
> He has made more enemies than friends since taking absolute power, both inside and outside the country, and even his daughter and son have washed their hands of him and left the country.

**Ships in the desert** So Turkmenbashi charges on. He is desperate to tap into this natural wealth to create what he terms a 'New Kuwait' and refuses to let anyone stand in his way. This came to a head in 2002 when he survived an assassination attempt and retaliated by purging his party and closing up his country's borders (the then opposition leader, Boris Shikhmuradov, has not been seen since).

In this state of limbo his actions are becoming more erratic: one day new mosques will be built to please Tehran, the next day a statue of Atatürk is erected. Meanwhile, the majority of Turkmen remain below the poverty line in an increasingly arid land. Here again, however, Turkmenbashi is convinced – or convinces himself – that he has the answer.

Since the 1950s the massive (it is 1100km-long) Karakum Irrigation Canal has run from the Amu-Darya River across southern Turkmenistan in an attempt to turn wasteland into cotton fields. Seventy per cent of the water is lost through evaporation but as long as some gets through it is considered a success and a similar canal has been built across the north of the country. This has had the unexpected effect of creating a huge, new lake in the Sarykamish Depression from where, once again, the water evaporates. Nevertheless, some water reaches the thirsty farms so the scheme is considered a success. Indeed, now Turkmenbashi's advisors have spied another large depression near the Kaplangyrsk Reserve and new canals are being dug out to flood this area as well.

With a ban on all opposition parties and newspapers, dissenting voices are seldom heard (furthermore, Turkmenbashi has forced the Turkmen parliament to extend his term of office indefinitely). The situation is not quite as bad as North Korea but it's getting there. One source of comment which cannot be stifled, however, is the black market which values (or doesn't value) the *manat* at a quarter of the official rate. Inflation is also galloping away.

**Turkmen culture** What no one can deny, however, is that Turkmenbashi has cultivated a massive revival of all things Turkmen. He may not be a true Turkman himself but all things indigenous, from the arts to the Turkmen language and history, have been encouraged.

> **Stop Press!** As we go to press, it has just been announced that Turkmenbashi died suddenly of a heart attack on 21 December 2006. This leaves a potentially dangerous power vacuum in the region.

This has ranged from the building of a monument in memory of the victims of the devastating earthquake which hit Ashgabat in 1948, killing over 100,000 people including Turkmenbashi's mother and brothers (Stalin refused to acknowledge such a catastrophe, claimed only a few thousand had died and sealed off the city until repairs were complete), to the endless promotion of the poetry of Magtymguly, Turkmenistan's Shakespeare.

## Uzbekistan

Uzbekistan's break from the USSR has been more radical than most with all things Russian being replaced or attacked, from the grand statue of Lenin in Tashkent's central square to place and street names.

The irony is, however, that the old Communist Party and its leader are still very much in charge, having merely changed the party's name; this shouldn't be that surprising, though, because during the Brezhnev era (he was a local boy) the republic was legendary for its corruption and nicknamed the 'Sewer of the USSR'.

**Independence** As the break up of the USSR became obvious, Uzbeks led the way in voicing criticism of Moscow. A new movement called Birlik ('Unity') was formed and quickly gained strong popular support, as did the fundamentalist Islamic Renaissance Party. Yet in the presidential elections of 1991 they were both barred from entering a candidate and Islam Karimov (the old Communist Party boss) won by a mile as head of his newly named Popular Democratic Party of Uzbekistan.

Karimov continued to consolidate his position and over the next ten years held a series of similarly biased elections, though this has not been taken lying down. In 1998, Tashkent witnessed several bombings attributed to the Islamic separatists, which lead to a crackdown on Islam in general and the banning of the *Azan* (call to prayer) throughout the country.

Prior to September 11 the same groups (supported by fundamentalist Uzbek minorities in Tajikistan and Afghanistan) invaded from bases across the Tajik border and entered the Ferghana Valley: government troops were killed and one

> **The Islamic caliphate**
> The dream for many of the more radical Islamic groups in Central Asia is to create an Islamic super-state stretching over all the lands that once made up Turkestan. Secular government would be abolished and Islamic law would be imposed, as it was in Afghanistan under the Taliban. There are supporters of such a state in all the former Soviet republics and even amongst the Uighur in Xinjiang but the fall of the Taliban put an end to any realistic hopes of ever bringing it to fruition.

unit got within 100km of the capital. After September 11, though, opposition parties found it even harder, as any criticism of the government was instantly labelled as part of the fundamentalists' plot. Karimov was similarly helped by the war in Afghanistan as, in return for huge amounts of aid, he allowed America to build airbases in the south of the country.

Everything came to a head in 2005 when several business leaders connected to the Islamic movement were arrested and put in prison in Andijan. Locals rebelled, stormed the prison to free their leaders and took temporary control of the streets. The government responded by sending in the troops: up to seven hundred people (including many civilians apparently running away to escape the carnage) were massacred. So far the show trials into the events have done little to improve the situation (fifteen leaders of the uprising have been sent to jail for twenty years) and, although peace has been restored in the area, the situation remains tense.

In response to Western criticism of his human rights record (the British Ambassador, Craig Murray, has been unusually vociferous), Karimov has ordered America to close down its airbase in Khanabad and is even looking back to Moscow for protection.

**The economy** Looking at Tashkent and some of the food markets in the Ferghana Valley you might think that Uzbekistan was on its way to prosperity but UN figures paint a bleak picture as the economy remains both unsophisticated and overly dependent on primary resources. It is also corrupt and foreign investors are unwilling to commit money while it remains subject to the whim of the president and his increasingly power-hungry daughter Gulnara Karimova. A classic example is Coca-Cola: while the local head of the company was married to Karimov junior this couldn't have been rosier; upon their divorce Coca Cola was thrown out of the country and all the Coke you will drink here now has to be imported.

That the autonomous province of Karakalpakstan has not demanded independence should be taken more as a sign of their desperate poverty (it is they who have been hit the hardest by the destruction of the Aral Sea) than Karimov's popularity. With many Russians and Slavs still returning to their homelands every year, Uzbekistan is also suffering from the same drain of skilled workers as the rest of the region, yet the inefficient bureaucracy inherited from the USSR shows no signs of disappearing.

One hope is that if the war in Afghanistan is really over, a new trade route can be opened to the south. Essential to this has been the rebuilding of the Friendship Bridge on the border at Termiz and the projected new road to link Central Asia with the booming markets of the Indian subcontinent. With this complete, Uzbekistan's cotton (like Kazakhstan's cereals) could once again be in high demand.

### Kyrgyzstan

If the Silk Road is a 'necklace of cities, strung out like pearls across the Orient' as it has been described, then somebody put Kyrgyzstan in the wrong jewellery box. There are only two cities of any size in the country, Bishkek and Osh, and even these have only recently been joined by a proper metalled road and public transport. But it was not always so (the Chuy Valley at the western end of Issyk Kul was home to many key Silk Road cities, including Ak Beshim, Balasagun and Navekat) and the country's idiosyncrasies might just be its saviours.

**Independence**  In the initial stages of the USSR's disintegration, it appeared that the leader of the Kyrgyz Communist Party, Absamat Masaliev, would join his fellow party leaders of the other republics and twist control of the country into his hands. He was thwarted, however, when ethnic violence erupted in Osh between the city's majority Uzbek population and the Kyrgyz minority. Tension seems to have been stoked up by official bodies and Masaliev carried the can. In his place, a surprisingly liberal academic was nominated and elected president.

Askar Akaev may have been a compromise candidate but he did more than any of the other presidents in the region to introduce electoral and political reforms. Significantly for us he also made his country the most open to visitors. That is not to say everything was perfect: the economy struggled to cope without the old subsidies from Moscow; Bishkek earned itself something of a reputation for seediness and violence and the police seemed to be unashamedly corrupt. Akaev won another term in office in the 2000 elections but in 2005 fell to what has been dubbed the 'Tulip Revolution'. Following the 'Orange Revolution' in the Ukraine, the 'Cedar Revolution' in Lebanon and the 'Rose Revolution' in Georgia, the Kyrgyz people clearly thought it was their turn for a change but so far little seems to have altered and even the new president's name, Bakiyev, sounds the same as his predecessor's.

**The economy**  While a rural economy may not make a country rich, many of Kyrgyzstan's people seem satisfied to be able, at last, to return to their traditional shepherding way of life. The old collective farms are therefore being dismantled. The problem with this, however, is what do those people (notably the young) who don't want to return to this way of life do instead? Many are increasingly attracted into the towns but here they are as likely to still be employed in some type of agriculture as in industry – although unemployment is an increasingly regular third option as the proportion of people out of work has risen to over 20 per cent.

Many hopes are pinned on the mining potential of the mountains. Large deposits of coal and gold have been detected but since the withdrawal of Soviet technology many mines have seen their production collapse and the country's primitive banking and financial systems have deterred much-needed foreign investors. The Soviet legacy has also left a series of mini-environmental disasters which need to be thoroughly tackled if the nation's largest resource (pure glacial spring water) is to be exploited.

**Culture**  With such a diverse collection of tribes within its borders, Kyrgyzstan needed something or someone to pull the country together and this has been achieved to a certain extent by the resuscitation and almost deification of an epic hero called Manas. He is the ancient leader who took on his barbarian neighbours and carved out a homeland for his people, the Kyrgyz. In fact, it is quite a bit more complicated than that, as the story of Manas we have today is an amalgamation of many of the traditional myths and legends told by the wandering bards in days gone by – a bit like Robin Hood, King Arthur, Peter Pan and the Loch Ness monster all rolled into one. The whole collection of Manas poetry is twenty times longer than *The Iliad*, to which it has also been likened, and those few bards still capable of reciting verses by heart are given the esteemed title *manaschi*.

The oral tradition has typically declined as the advent of literacy and new forms of communication have taken their toll but Manas is still cherished by the entire country, to such an extent that UNESCO joined the Kyrgyz government in declaring 1995 the 'International Year of Manas'.

## THE PEOPLE

No matter which of the republics you visit, you are bound to see the whole array of nationalities that have gathered in the region over the centuries. The most obvious division is that between the town and the countryside: traditionally the Kazakhs, Kyrgyz and Turkmen were nomads while the Uzbeks and Tajiks were sedentary town dwellers.

Under Stalin, however, these last two peoples were joined in the cities by Russians, Ukranians, Slavs and Germans. Most men make it easy for you to identify their background by wearing their own distinctive national hats and the women's clothing can be equally indicative.

Despite seventy years of communism, Islam is still strong in all the countries covered in this section. Mosques are springing up or being rebuilt everywhere you go and nearly everyone you meet will be Muslim – at least in principle. In reality, however, each state is secular and the brand of Islam being practised owes as much to pre-Islamic cultures, traditions and beliefs as it does to Mohammed (less than ten per cent of the region's population are practising Muslims). One common practice you will witness (particularly in rural areas, where Islam is strongest) is the regional ritual of ***amin***, a gesture of thanks whereby men and women cup their hands together and pass them down over their face as though washing.

### Turkic languages
Many of the languages of Central Asia are Turkic-based and are remarkably similar. There are over 140 million Turkic speakers, from Turkish Turks in the west to steppe Mongolians in the east, making it the fourth most spoken language in the world.

### Turkmenistan
Turkmenistan's population is tiny and since the country is second in size only to Kazakhstan in this region, all the land, including the capital Ashgabat, seems sparsely populated. The population is also very polarized, a situation that has not been helped by many of the Stalin-era immigrants packing up and going home.

Those who have stayed, despite official spin-doctoring to the contrary, now keep themselves even more to themselves and stick close to Ashgabat – recently at a marriage within the Russian community we noticed that not only were there no Turkmen guests, there wasn't even a Turkmen member of staff at the reception (and it wasn't a small wedding).

On the other hand, many Turkmen whose forefathers fled to Iran and Afghanistan in order to escape the Russians are beginning to return. Most Turkmen tend to keep out of the city centres except for market day. They are also the most non-Islamic people in the region – despite most of them being officially Muslims – and tend to obey the traditional ways of their forefathers and their forefathers before them.

Turkmen make up 82 per cent of the 5 million or so population while Russians have shrunk from 13 per cent to 3 per cent. As economic realities have set in, the rate of population growth has slowed to a moderate 1.5 per cent per annum. The centre of the country, of course, is all desert and virtually uninhabited but you are unlikely to run into crowds anywhere as only a few hundred visitors come to Turkmenistan each year.

### Uzbekistan

The Uzbeks have always considered themselves to be the most sophisticated of the region's peoples, tracing their Turkic roots back to Ozbeg, great khan of the Golden Horde (1313-40). With its position at the centre of the region, however, this country has also become the most diverse ethnically – a situation not helped by Stalin's gerrymandering.

Of the estimated 24 million people, 80 per cent are Uzbek while about a million are Kazakhs (mainly in Karakalpakstan province), with a similar number of Tajiks (see box p176) in cities such as Samarkand and Bukhara (these were major centres within the Samanid empire and maintained much of their Persian/Tajik culture even after the Uzbeks arrived). The number of Russians has dropped dramatically, although you will still notice their strong presence in Tashkent.

Another major area of complication is the Ferghana Valley – this was always considered the Uzbek heartland, especially in the east around Osh, yet this city, along with all its Uzbek inhabitants, was placed within Kyrgyzstan's border. An estimated four million Uzbeks live outside Uzbekistan, mostly in the towns of neighbouring countries (it was Uzbek Afghanis who formed the Northern Alliance which defeated the Taliban).

### Kyrgyzstan

Bishkek used to be famous for being the only city in Asia to have a daily newspaper printed in German but since 1991 the exodus of Germans, Slavs and all sorts of Soviet-era immigrants has been near total.

Kyrgyzstan has remained the most rural of all the former republics but it is not just Kyrgyz living in the hills – there are an estimated 80 different ethnic tribes. The total population is just under four million of which three million are Kyrgyz. Kyrgyz and Kazakhs share many customs and traditions and have a similar language; in a way they are mountain (Kyrgyz) and steppe (Kazakh) versions of the same people.

Kyrgyzstan's diversity, together with the fact that so much of the population lives in remote mountains, has helped it withstand most of the ideological brainwashing that has taken place elsewhere – whether in the name of Stalin or Mohammed. The result is that Kyrgyzstan, on the whole, has the most relaxed population in the region, with women in particular given a freer and more prominent role. Most people are very keen to have foreign visitors in their country and give them a warm welcome.

# Practical information for the visitor

If you are travelling west to east, start to think about your crossing of the Torugart Pass (see box p242) now – you'll save yourself quite a bit of money by planning ahead.

## THE ROUTE

As explained earlier, there was always more than one route to choose from for the Silk Road caravans (see maps opposite pp32-3) and nowhere is this more true than Central Asia.

In order to see as much as possible our route is more of a zigzag across the region but if you are short of time you can skip some of the side attractions and head in a straight line from Mashad to Merv, Bukhara, Samarkand, Tashkent, Bishkek, Naryn and Kashgar (but don't forget that the road from Tashkent to Bishkek runs through Kazakhstan and you will need to buy a Kazakh visa – the easiest way around this is to fly).

We have also included an alternative route by rail through Kazakhstan (see box p229) in case the road routes through the Torugart and Irkestan passes are closed by the weather, and a new option through Tajikistan (see box p176) to explore the recently completed Pamir Highway.

## DOCUMENTS AND FORMALITIES

In the old days, all the republics in the region allowed you a little leeway whereby you could spend 72 hours in transit in any of the countries as long as you had visas for the country you had left and the country you were visiting next. Unfortunately, this whole system has been officially scrapped.

On entering all of these countries you should fill out a customs form, **in duplicate**! This is considered your responsibility so ask for a second form and keep it for inspection when you leave – this can be a particularly difficult task if you are crossing a border by train as the customs officials tend to sit in their carriage rather than actually issue you with forms, as they are supposed to do. Declare all your foreign currency on your forms as otherwise you might find it confiscated when you leave. Keep hold of all your currency exchange receipts as they may well be needed on exit.

If you are using **Tashkent** as an exit/entrance point for your trip, the customs procedure at the airport is a lottery: you may sail through or you may be

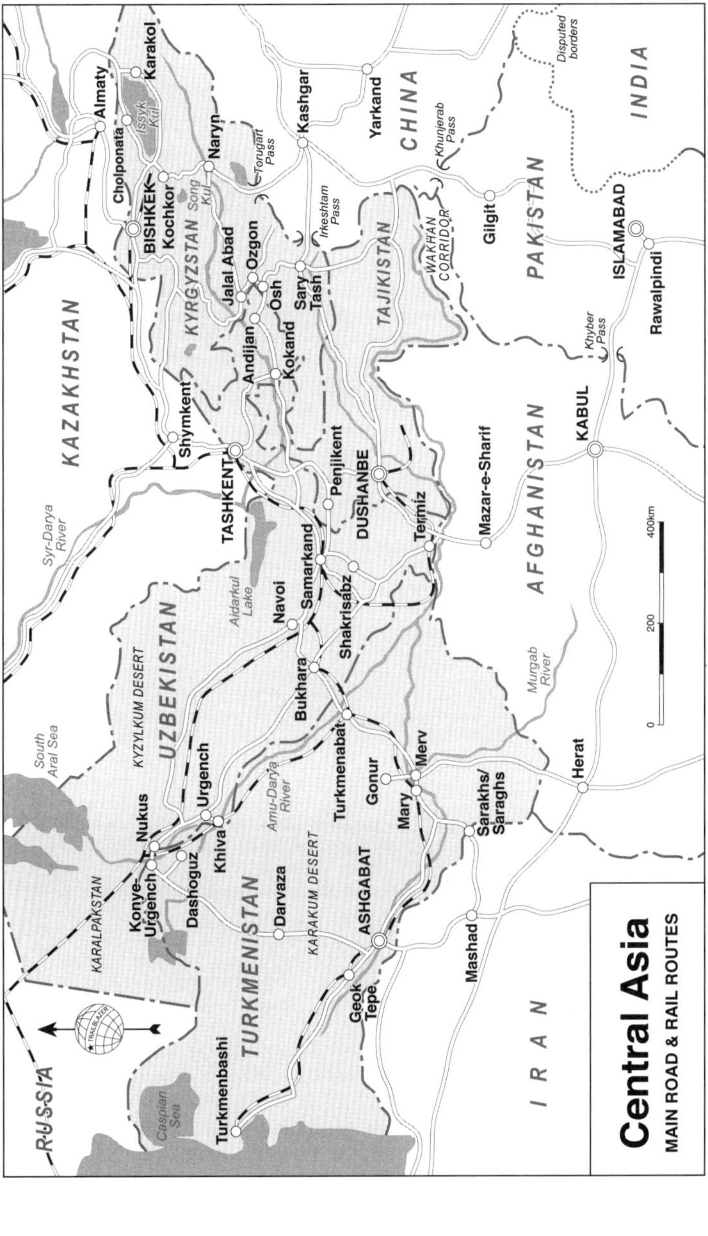
Central Asia
MAIN ROAD & RAIL ROUTES
RUSSIA
KAZAKHSTAN
UZBEKISTAN
KYRGYZSTAN
TAJIKISTAN
TURKMENISTAN
AFGHANISTAN
PAKISTAN
INDIA
CHINA
IRAN
KARALPAKSTAN
KYZYLKUM DESERT
KARAKUM DESERT
WAKHAN CORRIDOR
Disputed borders
Caspian Sea
South Aral Sea
Issyk Kul
Song Kul
Aidarkul Lake
Syr-Darya River
Amu-Darya River
Murgab River
Torugart Pass
Irkeshtam Pass
Khunjerab Pass
Khyber Pass
Almaty
Karakol
Cholponata
BISHKEK
Kochkor
Naryn
Kashgar
Yarkand
Gilgit
ISLAMABAD
Rawalpindi
Jalal Abad
Ozgon
Osh
Sary Tash
Andijan
Kokand
Shymkent
TASHKENT
Penjikent
DUSHANBE
Termiz
Mazar-e-Sharif
KABUL
Samarkand
Shakrisabz
Navoi
Bukhara
Turkmenabat
Urgench
Nukus
Khiva
Konye-Urgench
Dashoguz
Darvaza
Gonur
Merv
Mary
Sarakhs/ Saraghs
Herat
ASHGABAT
Mashad
Geok Tepe
Turkmenbashi
TRAILBLAZER
0
200
400km

## Tajikistan

Tajikistan is still Central Asia's unknown quantity and in many ways the odd one out. It has also suffered the most since independence from Moscow. All the Central Asian republics had their borders gerrymandered by Stalin to suit his political needs but Tajikistan bore the brunt (it became the smallest and the poorest). The statistic that there are as many Tajiks (roughly 4.5 million) outside Tajikistan as inside its borders may not be that surprising (there are more Jews in New York than Jerusalem, more Irish in America than Ireland), but what makes it so peculiar is that the Tajik people themselves haven't moved; instead, it is their homeland that has been annexed and appropriated by others, leaving those populations stranded in foreign countries (there are 3.5 million Tajiks in Afghanistan alone).

It is also an incredibly mountainous country (**Peak Koh I Samani**, formerly *Pik Communizma*, is Central Asia's highest mountain at 7495m), where pocket valleys are cut off from one another for days, weeks, even months. Furthermore, what constitutes a 'Tajik' is open to debate. Most trace their history back to Sogdians, Bactrians and Samanids but **'Tajik'** was often a term used merely to denote **'Persian speaker'** (the Tajik language is Persian rather than Turkic based). In the mountains you will in turn encounter green eyes and red hair descended from Aryans, white skin descended from the Russians (although most of the 600,000 USSR-era Russians have now left), black-hatted Uzbeks and a multitude of Turkic tribes.

The clan system is therefore very strong as is Islam (particularly in the south and east) and few were surprised to see the country descend into civil war once Moscow withdrew in 1991.

Peace was finally patched together in 1997 and since then foreign aid has slowly begun to rebuild the country but 50 per cent of all economic activity is still connected to the drug trade (mainly heroin and opium from Afghanistan) and sixty per cent of Tajiks are still living in abject poverty (the legal minimum wage is US$1 *a month*).

**Practicalities** The most important news for visitors is that the country is now more or less safe. You will probably need a letter of invitation to get a visa but applications in Tashkent and Bishkek are pretty straightforward. The **Gorno-Badakhshan** region also needs a separate permit but these are easy (if expensive) to obtain through an agency in Dushanbe.

**The Pamir Highway** is back in business, too, and despite its innumerable checkpoints must be the most exhilarating drive in the whole of Central Asia. You will probably want to go through a local agent (**Great Game Travel**, Dushanbe, 🖳 www.greatgametravel.co.uk, comes recommended; **Stantours**, see p192, can also put most things together) as you will need your own transport to even begin to explore this country. But your time and effort will be rewarded. Tajikistan is also an emerging trekker's paradise (for advice on trekking, see box p265).

If you have the time (minimum three weeks) you can do the entire Pamir Highway drive from **Dushanbe** to **Osh** via **Khorog**; if you just want a small taste try coming in at **Penjikent** and looping around to Dushanbe. Either way, Dushanbe's **Museum of Antiquities**, home to Central Asia's largest-surviving Buddha, is a must see.

Finally, the **Qolma Pass** is now open to freight travelling between the Pamir region and the KKH in China; it shouldn't be too long before it is open to foreign visitors as well. The road from Dushanbe to Kabul (see box p10) is also open to visitors.

stuck with a bureaucrat for over an hour. The main restrictions on what you can take out are what are classified as 'antiques'. These are usually goods over thirty years old and the rule is particularly aimed at carpets.

If you buy anything from a government shop your receipt will be enough to waive this rule and other shops are usually willing to write whatever you want on a receipt. That said, unless you are buying more than one major item or you hit upon an official looking for a kickback, you should be fine whatever you buy. All these rules also apply when crossing from one republic to the next.

In **Uzbekistan** you are supposed to register every night with the OVIR office but in effect this is done for you when you check into a registered hotel or guesthouse (make sure you keep the receipts as you may be asked for them by police or at the border on departure). If you are staying in a 'homestay' you are technically breaking this law – so try to get your next hostelry to tack those nights onto their receipt. In **Kyrgyzstan** you no longer need to register with an OVIR office at all.

In all countries, but particularly **Turkmenistan**, be prepared to be regularly stopped at **road checks** no matter how you are travelling. Keep your passport handy or, if you have to leave it with an embassy while you apply for a visa, make sure you carry a photocopy of your passport and the visa for whichever country you are in.

**Student cards** are again a big plus here as they drastically reduce the admission prices of all the sights.

## CLIMATE

If you are heading east and hoping for a respite from the heat of the last few weeks, Central Asia will let you down badly (the bureaucracy of these countries can also give you a headache). The climate has been made even more extreme over the past fifty years by both the draining of the Aral Sea (see box p178) and pollution.

Contamination is a major problem in the region, mostly from the pesticides and fertilizers used to increase cotton production, the use of low-grade coal in

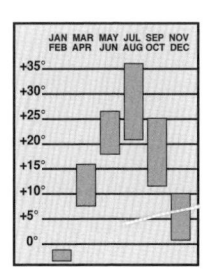

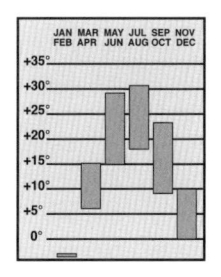

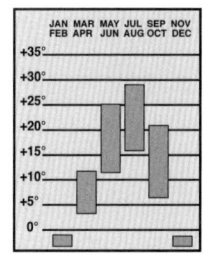

**Ashgabat (Turkmenistan)   Tashkent (Uzbekistan)   Bishkek (Kyrgyzstan)**
**Temperature charts – max/min °C centigrade**

> **The Aral Sea**
> By bleeding the Amu-Darya (and to a lesser extent the Syr-Darya) almost dry, the canal systems introduced into the region by the Russians in the 1950s to promote cotton production are systematically destroying once and for all the Aral Sea, previously the fourth largest lake in the world and home to one of the rarest ecosystems on the planet. Already the sea has shrunk to half its size of 20 years ago (leaving fishing boats and fishing villages stranded kilometres from any water). Indeed, it has now split into a South Aral Sea fed by the Amu-Darya and a North Aral Sea fed by the Syr-Darya River.
>
> Almost all the fish have been driven to extinction and the 60,000 fishermen living by the lake's former shores have all lost their jobs. Summers are hotter and winters colder, with the average number of rainless days in the area rising to between 120 and 150 per year compared with 30 to 35 days per year just fifty years ago. Of the 173 animal species around the lake, only 38 survive. In human terms, the salt and dust are blamed for respiratory illnesses and cancers, while the area has the highest mortality and infant mortality rates in the former USSR.
>
> Turkmenbashi (the biggest modern culprit) responds with 'everybody else is doing it' (which is true) and 'the Aral Sea isn't in my country so it's not my problem'. In fact, the environmental damage and gradual salination of all the surrounding land is hurting northern Turkmenistan just as much as it is Uzbekistan and Kazakhstan.
>
> Despite the legions of scientists who have studied the area, no one is seriously considering restoring the Aral Sea to its former levels and repairing the damage done. The best that can be hoped for is that the northern sea will be saved (the small channel linking the two seas was permanently blocked in 2003 to prevent water loss from north to south) while the southern sea will continue to shrink, split and disappear.

power stations, untreated waste from metal smelters and leaks from up to 100 abandoned uranium mines (as an example, around Osh 94 per cent of the soil contains DDT). Even sparsely populated Turkmenistan has a choking smog cloud that often sits over Ashgabat.

Rainfall is minimal throughout this region except for in the mountains. The inhabitants rely instead on a massive network of irrigation canals to feed their lands. Even in the highlands, don't expect much rain outside of March/April and October/November. Little rain means a lot of sun and temperatures on the flat plains of Turkmenistan and Uzbekistan can be unbearable in the summer: it's regularly over 40°C (you know you are in a hot country when houses have huge fans **outside** to cool you while you sit on the veranda!) and can push 50°C in July and August. From October, however, it turns cold in most places and in the winter heavy snowfall in the mountains can block off roads and leave temperatures in the minuses (the average temperature in the Kyrgyz hills during winter is -24°C).

## SAFETY

The police in Central Asia have a bad reputation and unfortunately it's probably a fair one (although they are nowhere near as bad as they used to be). They are usually looking only for a kickback but they can turn nasty. If any police officer asks to see your passport, ask to see their badge first. The likelihood is that they will be straight but this tactic seems to dispel any temptation they might have to corrupt the rules.

Prostitution is also rife in each of the capitals in Central Asia and foreign visitors are their number one target (they will commonly approach you on the street as well as in bars and clubs).

Remember that all emails in Turkmenistan can be monitored and many buildings, hotels and restaurants are bugged.

## ACCOMMODATION

This whole region is not the best for accommodation. It is improving, however, as a number of budget options have now opened and there are a few gems, even if they do seem overpriced when compared to the rest of the economy and the other countries you will visit. At least most places provide a laundry service at a reasonable price. For camping, see box p73.

### Turkmenistan

Turkmenistan gets so few visitors each year that demand for hotel accommodation is low, making any serious improvements difficult. The top end is catered for in Ashgabat because the oil companies have just enough researchers and clients to fill them (there is even a Sheraton Hotel here) but the rest of the country can be tricky.

If you are visiting on a full tourist visa your agent will make all your accommodation bookings for you so you won't really have much choice.

The mid-range is inadequately filled by the old Intourist establishments and the budget range is almost non-existent – in some places you will have no choice but to seek out your own homestay. You must fill out a registration form at each hotel and can often choose to pay in US dollars or local currency.

Hotels in Turkmenistan are overpriced for visitors (locals pay one-tenth of what you are charged) but this pricing system is standard and accepted so don't go mad about it, although you can try to haggle.

### Uzbekistan

Uzbekistan has the widest range of accommodation in the region but everywhere is more expensive than it should be considering the cost of living here.

The upper end has seen the arrival of quite a few new establishments with impressive facilities. Most of the old Soviet monoliths have changed hands but are usually still depressingly ugly and malfunctioning.

The mid-range and B&B sectors are Uzbekistan's highlight, as a significant number of families have opened guesthouses (particularly in Bukhara and Samarkand). You still pay quite a bit (US$20 is the going rate for a double room) but the rooms are clean and modern with showers that work and you often have a sauna or breakfast included.

The real budget end is once again made up of homestays and the odd cheapy but most visitors choose to enjoy the decent mid-range accommodation while it's available.

## Kyrgyzstan

Thanks to two remarkable programmes, Kyrgyzstan is the easiest country in the region to find cheap accommodation or stay with local families. Shepherd's Life and Community Based Tourism were both inspired by the Swiss development-based programme Helvetas (the Swiss have long been coming to Kyrgyzstan, particularly Issyk Kul, because of its alpine feel and look) and both organizations have set out to establish a network of homestays, drivers and guides. The results so far are tremendous with Kochkor providing the central base and offices operating throughout the main tourist areas.

As well as accommodation, both programmes act as tour operators and can put together almost any type of trip you require (see the relevant 'Orientation and services' sections).

Kyrgyzstan also has a Hyatt Regency in Bishkek for the high-rollers, so most visitors find something they like. US dollars are again the preferred currency and little English is spoken in the cheaper options.

## TRAVEL AGENCIES AND TOURIST INFORMATION

In the old Soviet days all tourism was controlled by Intourist and the organization was famous for its rudeness, incompetence and its habit of ripping you off. Since the collapse of the USSR, local offices have attempted to reform into a Western-style national tourist bureau for each of the republics but they have largely failed. Fortunately, as an independent visitor travelling overland, you should hardly come across any of them.

Instead there is quite a good selection of local tour operators who can rustle up just about anything from visa support letters to a week-long camel safari, usually at very competitive rates. They are generally clued up and are often run (at least in part) by someone with international experience. Virtually all of them are based in the capital cities and we have listed them under the relevant 'Orientation and Services' sections.

## TRANSPORT

The infrastructure in Central Asia is a hangover, in more ways than one, from the Soviet era. Not only is much of the network out of date, most of its design was completed under Stalin in such a way as to make it largely inoperable outside a USSR framework. For example, roads and railways were built to deliberately criss-cross the borders of the newly created republics.

When the region became independent, each country was left in the ridiculous position of having to travel through another's territory in order to visit parts of their own lands. The most striking example of this was the railway line running along the Turkmenistan–Uzbekistan border; though even more annoying is the main road linking Tashkent with Bishkek which still runs through Kazakhstan (see p228). Attempts have been made to improve certain areas and many new roads have been built but the transport situation away from the main tourist cities can be a real headache.

## Train
On paper the train looks a viable option (see box pp98-9), but in reality the network has been run down from what was already a creaking monster under the Soviets. With the end of Moscow subsidies and a simple lack of funds, train travel has been demoted to the bottom of the pile as far as public transport is concerned. Goods trains still run and, officially, there is at least one passenger train per day on each route, though journeys are very slow and the timetables erratic. We do not want to add to the vicious downward spiral, however, and therefore recommend you travel by train at least once: they are far more pleasant than cramped coaches or minibuses, very cheap and you will be travelling on a piece of history: try the overnight train between Bukhara and Tashkent.

## Bus
Buses are the most convenient way to travel and quite easy to find and use. You don't need to book in advance and some, especially between Bukhara and Tashkent, can be of a surprisingly high standard. Fares are cheap but expect to breakdown at least once on your travels in this region. The only other drawback is that most bus stations are quite a way out of town.

## Minibuses and share taxis
Wherever there are buses you can expect to find minibuses and share taxis. They are slightly more expensive and usually a bit more cramped but they go as soon as they are full and therefore can be quite a bit quicker. The only drawback is that they are nearly always made to stop at roadblocks, whereas the larger coaches are usually allowed to drive through.

## Taxis
Taxis are still cheap in this region but not as cheap as they used to be, so haggle hard. On short journeys you can only gamble but for a full day (which is often your only option for getting to out-of-the-way places in Kyrgyzstan and

> ### Hitching the Silk Road
> At one time, hitching a ride (often illegally) was the only way to see much of the Silk Road. Today, the situation has improved tenfold making hitching unnecessary for most foreign visitors. It is a brave man or woman, therefore, who attempts to hitch the entire length of the Silk Road but in most of the countries it is possible, and in some remote areas it can be the only method of getting where you want to go when you want to go there.
>
> The major problem, however, is that most people who stop will expect you to contribute to the petrol costs, often making it little cheaper than taking the bus. You will see many locals standing at the side of the road, thumbing a ride, but they are expecting to pay for their ride and usually they are just looking for short lifts into town. Indeed, most of the lifts you will be offered will be for short journeys.
>
> Technically, hitching is not sanctioned in China, although many people do it (and you will probably have to if you wish to complete the Southern Taklamakan route, see p320). Your biggest problem here, as in most of the other countries, is getting to the outskirts of town so that you can begin.

## 182 Turkmenistan, Uzbekistan and Kyrgyzstan – Practical information

Turkmenistan) you can 'guestimate' the fare at double the price of the petrol (most cars will do just under 10km to a litre).

In city centres virtually everybody will be your taxi if you flag them down and this can be very cheap, although most will not speak English **so make sure you have agreed the price and that they know where they are going** (this is a real problem as most drivers are more concerned with getting you into their car than in actually taking you where you want to go). The newly popular Uz Daewoo cars are a big improvement on the old Ladas.

### Cars and motorbikes
**Car rental** is not advised for this region as hiring a driver with a car usually works out cheaper. **Bringing in your own vehicle** is similarly warned against (see box p74). **Hitching** is not common here either (see box p181).

### Air
Because of Kazakh visa requirements for road travellers, flights between Bishkek and Tashkent do have their advantages (see p228). Internal flights are quite cheap in all three countries but they are largely as unnecessary as they are undesirable for this land-based trip. If you do need to book a flight, all the travel agencies we have listed will be able to help. Planes are rarely full.

## ELECTRICITY

The normal supply is 220V using European two-pin plugs. Adaptors are available in the main cities.

## TIME

All three republics operate five hours ahead of GMT although Kyrgyzstan has Daylight Saving Time in the summer when it is six hours ahead.

## MONEY

Officially, all three countries have a stable currency with an official rate of exchange but in reality all three of the currencies are very weak and liable to fluctuate wildly. Turkmenistan is the worst offender and the **black market** is rife here.

If you are using a **credit/debit card**, ask

❑ **Exchange rates**

|  | Turkmenistan<br>Manat | Uzbekistan<br>Sum | Kyrgyzstan<br>Som |
|---|---|---|---|
| US$1 | 5200/22,000* | 969.36 | 41.45 |
| €1 | 6762 | 1256.40 | 53.90 |
| £1 | 10,275 | 1906.91 | 81.90 |
| Can$1 | 4404 | 819.77 | 35.10 |
| Aus$1 | 4079 | 757.63 | 32.52 |
| NZ$1 | 3633 | 675.02 | 28.96 |

To get the latest rates of exchange visit 🖳 www.xe.net/currency, 🖳 www.oanda.com/convert/classic or try 🖳 www.exchangerate.com.

\* street rate

to withdraw US dollars rather than the relevant local currency because if you withdraw local currency on a credit card you will get a poor rate. If you are bringing **travellers' cheques**, make sure they are in US dollars.

For cash exchanges the **US dollar** is king but make sure your notes are new (at least post 1996) and not scruffy, or they will be considered less valuable. You can always pay for things like taxis and hotels in dollars but make sure you have small denomination notes as no one ever has change. Poor rates of exchange are offered for neighbouring currencies so try not to have too much local currency left over by the time you reach the border.

### Turkmenistan
The unit of currency is the *manat* (M) but it is the weakest in the region and is continually devaluing. The denominations are 10,000M, 5000M, 2000M, 1000M and 500M.

The 'official rate' of exchange is about 5200M to US$1 but in reality you are likely to get around 22,000M.

Do not exchange money at banks, official bureaux de change or hotel exchanges as you will receive only the official rate. There are plenty of money-changers on the street and most will approach you as a foreign visitor.

### Uzbekistan
The currency is the *sum* and all banks and exchange offices offer a similar rate. The denominations are 200, 100, 50, 20, 10, 5 and 1sum. In reality, you are likely to receive a massive wad of small denomination notes wherever you exchange.

### Kyrgyzstan
The unit of currency is the *som* and its denominations are 100, 50 20, 10, 5 and 1som. All banks and exchanges offer a similar rate.

## COMMUNICATIONS

The state communications systems in all three countries are a mess. There are private Internet cafés in Uzbekistan and Kyrgyzstan but only in Ashgabat in Turkmenistan. Mobile phones are expensive but commonplace; most international GSM networks have limited coverage in Central Asia.

Making international telephone calls is very expensive even with a phone card and often involves going through an operator, which can take forever. The postal service is also considered to be very slow, although things tend to get there in the end – and it is cheap.

---

❏ **Country access codes**
Turkmenistan ☎ +993     Uzbekistan ☎ +998     Kyrgyzstan ☎ +996
See individual 'Orientation and Services' sections for local codes.

## NATIONAL HOLIDAYS

Islamic festivals (see box p12) are increasingly significant in the region. The rest are peculiar to the individual countries. These are all genuine!

| | | |
|---|---|---|
| **January** | 7 | Orthodox Christmas (Kyrgyzstan) |
| | 12 | Geok-Tepe anniversary (Turkmenistan) |
| **February** | 19 | National Flag day (Turkmenistan) |
| **March** | 8 | International Women's day (all) |
| | 21 | Navrus (all). This is the major spring festival like *No Ruz* in Iran and is celebrated over two days. It used to coincide with the vernal equinox but now is normally fixed to March 21. |
| **April** | 6 | Drop of water is a drop of gold day (Turkmenistan) |
| | Last Saturday of the month | Horse day (Uzbekistan) |
| **May** | 1 | International Labour day (all) |
| | 5 | Constitution day (Kyrgyzstan) |
| | 9 | Victory day (all) |
| | 18 | Day of revival and unity (Turkmenistan) |
| | 19 | Day of Magtymguly the poet (Turkmenistan) |
| | 25 | Carpet day (Turkmenistan) |
| | 29 | Armed Forces day (Kyrgyzstan) |
| **June** | 13 | Commemoration day (Kyrgyzstan) |
| | 21 | President's day (Turkmenistan) |
| **July** | 10 | Melon day (Turkmenistan) |
| | 14 | Turkmenbashi day (Turkmenistan) |
| **August** | 31 | Independence day (Kyrgyzstan) |
| **September** | 1 | Independence day (Uzbekistan) |
| **October** | 6 | Remembrance day (Turkmenistan) |
| | 27-28 | Independence day (Turkmenistan) |
| **November** | 17 | Student Youth day (Turkmenistan) |
| | 30 | Harvest Festival (Turkmenistan) |
| **December** | 7 | Good Neighbourliness day (Turkmenistan) |
| | 8 | Constitution day (Uzbekistan) |
| | 12 | Neutrality day (Turkmenistan) |

## FOOD

*'Then from the cauldron comes out the liver, which is cut into slices in addition to chunks of fat – all their sheep have fat tails – and the table is laid. The meal is eaten with the fingers by making small sandwiches of liver and fat. When I came to stop at last, my knife, cheeks, and all ten fingers are swimming in grease. Instinctively I use the rich white fat to grease my shoes and lo and behold! Our host does the same.'*
**Ella Maillart**, early 20th-century Swiss explorer, describes a Kyrgyz dinner, *Turkestan Solo*.

Central Asian food is not up to much and if you are a vegetarian you are going to struggle to find variety; but if you like kebabs morning, noon and night this is your region! Having said that, the meat in **kebabs** (*shashlik*) and other meat dishes is very fatty. This is because the locals consider the fat to be the best bit: they are treating you if they offer you giant globules of the smelly white stuff with just a shard of meat attached to one end. A preferable snack is the *samsa* (a pastie-type pie filled with meat and vegetables).

You can find **pork** in Russian-style restaurants and **beef** and **sausages** are quite common but the staple dish throughout the region is *plov* – a mound of boiled rice dotted with a few grilled or roasted vegetables and bits of meat/fat.

If it's not *plov*, the chances are it's *laghman* – a noodle soup where the noodles are thick and greasy. There will be the odd bits of meat and vegetables in this dish too but the main advantage it has over plov is that this soup is a bit more spicy and takes away some of the burned fatty taste. **Fish** is rare outside Ashgabat and the Issyk Kul area but if you are offered some, take advantage. You may also find yourself offered entrails, horse, camel and goat. **Soured milk** is used to make yoghurt which is then strained and dried into disgusting marble-shaped balls.

The sad thing is, if you go to a local produce market you will see a huge array of good **fresh fruit** and **vegetables** but no one seems to use them. Admittedly, they are all available only in season so after a few days they too might become monotonous – but it would be nice to be given the option!

**Foreign foods** are restricted to restaurants in the capitals where they have a fair (if Russian-dominated) selection.

## DRINK

### Non-alcoholic
**Tea** (*chay*) is the major staple in all three countries. Hosts tend to pour only a little at a time but regularly refill your cup to ensure that the tea is always hot. If you manage to stay in someone's home or yurt, the tea will flow constantly. Like in China the tea is usually green rather than black. Decent **coffee** is a rarity although you can buy jars of instants such as Nescafé at exorbitant prices.

All tap **water** is best avoided but bottled mineral water and soft drinks are readily available and cheap. The only problem with these is that they are rarely chilled as a Russian old wives' tale says that if you drink cold drinks from the fridge you will get a cold yourself – and most people believe this, even in the 40°C heat of summer!

### Alcoholic
As with any self-respecting former USSR member, alcohol is where each of the republics comes into its own: alcoholism is one of the top killers in all these countries. **Vodka** naturally leads the way; there are numerous brands but don't go too far down the price scale as things can get nasty. Toasting is a serious business here, especially within the Russified communities, and if you are invited to a session don't expect to walk home straight.

Russian **beer** and **champagne** are less notable highlights, as are the local beers (*piva*). All beer in Central Asia is strong but don't be confused by the percentage labels on the sides of the bottles (7 per cent, 9 per cent, 12 per cent etc), as these refer to the length of the fermentation period rather than the beer's strength. Lots of Western brands are now on sale in off-licences and in bars – but at a price. ***Jarma*** is a home-made wheat-based beer popular in the Ferghana Valley – it is weak and tastes revolting. ***Kumys*** is fermented mare's milk and is also an acquired taste.

# Mary & Merv

**Mary** is the new town the Russians built in the 19th century as a stopover for where their new train line crossed the Murgab River. As this might imply, there is little in the town of any interest. The reason for making this a key stop on your journey, however, is that a few kilometres down the road is the old city of **Merv** (see p188), once the 'Queen of the World'.

## HISTORY

Merv's actual beginnings are unclear. It was known as Margiana or Margush to Alexander the Great and certainly has remains which date from this period but 'Margiana' has also been used to refer to another, older site further north (Gonur; see box p190), making historical references ambiguous. The picture has been further clouded by claims that Zoroaster founded the city as his capital.

The oldest of the cities that we can see today, however, was definitely built in the Achaemenid period and a new larger city was designed by the Sassanids in the 3rd century AD. It was built here because the Murgab River ran close by and a channel could be dug to bring water to the city. Over the following centuries fortresses were built on the other side of the river and new channels were constructed. Under the Seljuks, the whole city was moved across.

This city seems to have been expanded three times, reaching its zenith as capital of the Seljuk empire in the eleventh and twelfth centuries. It was a city famous throughout the world. Sultan Alp Arslan was probably the Seljuks' greatest leader, conquering the whole of western Asia in 1072, and he brought wealth into Merv from all over his lands in order to build libraries, observatories and many, many palaces. It all came to an abrupt end for Merv, however, with the arrival of the Mongols.

By this time the Khorezm had replaced their masters the Seljuks as the dominant force in the region and when Genghis Khan arrived demanding tribute (mostly beautiful women) they innocently refused. That was in 1218 and by 1221 all their major cities, including Merv, lay in ruins. Tuluy, Genghis's youngest son, was responsible for this front during the Mongol sweep across Asia. He seems to have had a particular dislike for Merv for, after sacking it in 1221, his men were ordered to decapitate over 300 civilians each despite their peaceful surrender; three days later he returned, smashing anything he had missed the first time and murdering anyone who had dared to go back to their homes.

Following this, the city was understandably deserted and it remained largely this way until the 18th century when, during a struggle over land with the emir of Bukhara, a Persian noble, Bairam Ali Khan, saw the political potential of having a military base here. He rebuilt the dam on the Murgab and began reconstructing the channels. But it was all in vain for in 1795 the emir managed to break the dam and lead an army into the city to destroy it once more.

The site returned to little more than a nomad camp until the Russians annexed the area in 1884. They had no interest in what they considered to be a pile of rubble and built a new town a few kilometres away, nearer to the Murgab which over the centuries had altered its course. They took the name Merv with them and the few shacks remaining around the ruins were given the name Bairam Ali. In 1937 the Russians renamed their town Mary and a town by the name of Merv technically ceased to exist.

## WHAT TO SEE

In **Mary**, the short answer could be 'nothing' but this is slightly unfair. Mary's saving grace is its **Regional Museum** (US$1; closed Mondays). This is a good way of warming up for Merv as it houses a large collection from both there and Gonur. It also has scale models of the sites and a beautiful collection of carpets. They sell a handbook, *Ancient Merv*, which is the definitive appraisal of how the city took shape. **Tikinsky Market** (now also known as Tekke Bazaar) is worth visiting if you are here on a Sunday but not worth delaying your trip for. The carpets are even cheaper than in Ashgabat (see box pp136-7 for tips on buying a carpet). The market is a few kilometres out of town so take a cab (US$1).

### Merv

Try to come here early because you might be lucky enough to catch these fantastic remains shrouded in morning mist – then they really do look like a mythical lost city (the mist also helps to block out the ugly modern edifices which have been cobbled together on Merv's outskirts).

Some people might complain that there is not that much to see but, in fact, there are the remains of five different cities, none of which has undergone much restoration or beautification, so for the purists Merv is a gem. In recognition of this the city has been made Turkmenistan's one and only World Heritage Site.

The oldest of the cities is the Achaemenid **Erk Kala**, a circular earthen fort which over the years has eroded to resemble a dried-out rubber ring. Nevertheless, at over 20m high, its walls are the tallest of all the remains and offer the best views of the site in its entirety.

Using this as its northern fort, the next incarnation of Merv (**Giaur Kala**) was much larger. Originally built by the Sassanids, it received impressive additions from each empire that brought the city into their fold. A **mosque** sits on the crossroads in front of the fort, while in the south-east corner is a **Buddhist stupa** and the outline of its surrounding monastery.

On the site to the west of the old water channel are the remains of **Sultan Kala**, built by the Seljuks as their capital. Again this city seems to have evolved and grown over the years from the original construction known as the **Shahriyar Ark** and its *koshk* or fort. In the middle of Sultan Kala is the **Mausoleum of Sultan Sanjar**, the grandson of Alp Arslan. Captured by nomads in 1150, he was taken to Khiva while his capital was looted and smashed but he managed to escape and make his way home only to die a broken man, devastated by what had happened to his city (perhaps he was lucky, then, not to live and see the destruction carried out by the Mongols). The mausoleum was begun in 1157 (the same year as the Notre Dame in Paris).

Outside Kala's walls are what's left of three more small forts: **Kyz Bibi**, **Great Kyz Kala** and **Little Kyz Kala**. To the north is the **Mausoleum of Mohammed Ibn Zeid** which dates back to the 12th century. The shrine is in an enchanting setting but of more interest are the trees that surround it in the hollow. Ribbons have been tied to many of the branches by Turkmen women hoping for a child and if the practice is successful, the new mother must return on each anniversary of her first visit and offer a sheep in sacrifice – such practices give you an idea of how Islam still plays second fiddle to older ways in so much of Turkmen society. The **Mosque of Yusuf Hamadani** is nearly all modern restoration and is open only to Muslims. On your way back to the village, the beehive-like cones are **icehouses** which would preserve their stock for weeks.

There are two ways to see this fantastic lost city. You can go to the Mary Regional Museum (see opposite), see its collection and ask the curators for help (they are used to acting as impromptu tour guides and will arrange a driver and a guide for a small fee) or you can hire a taxi. Obviously the latter is a much cheaper option (about US$5 for the morning between four people). You do not actually have to pay to look around the ruins and what is there is quite straight-

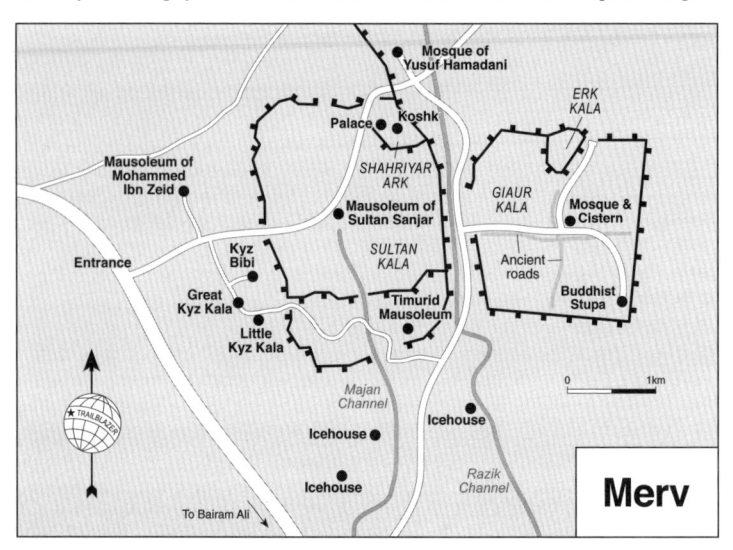

## Mary

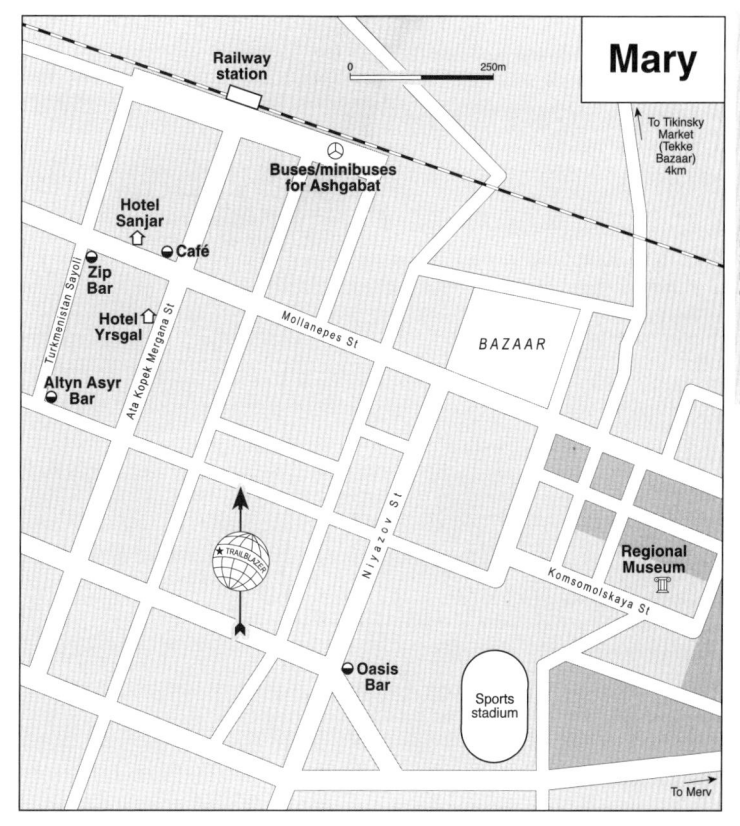

*[Map of Mary showing: Railway station, Buses/minibuses for Ashgabat, Hotel Sanjar, Café, Zip Bar, Hotel Yrsgal, Altyn Asyr Bar, Turkmenistan Sayoli, Ala Kopek Mergana St, Mollanepes St, Bazaar, Niyazov St, Regional Museum, Komsomolskaya St, Oasis Bar, Sports stadium, To Tikinsky Market (Tekke Bazaar) 4km, To Merv]*

forward, although walking around the whole site (which sounds good on paper) should not be entered into lightly: the area is massive and in summer you could really suffer from the sun and the heat, so it's better to be driven from one section to the next and spend more time at each one. A taxi driver probably won't know his way around but all the major sections are signposted from the main dirt track/road. You will probably enter the site from the west.

### PRACTICAL INFORMATION
**Where to stay and eat** [☎ code 522]

You cannot stay in Bairam Ali so you have to stay in Mary. *Hotel Sanjar* (☎ 57 644; US$30/Db) on Mollanepes St is the main choice. *Hotel Yrsgal* (US$25/Db) is nearby and gets good reports, as does the *Hotel Caravanserai* (US$40/Db), a homestay-style place on Nisimi Kocesi 25. Alternatively, you could ask your taxi driver if he knows of any **homestays**, though this may well lead to you being driven round to the house of his unsuspecting sister or ending up in the Sanjar after all.

> **Excursion to Gonur**
> This site is really one for the archaeologists but what Victor Sarianidi and his team have been digging up here is revealing Gonur (often referred to as Margiana) to be one of the original cradles of civilization. There are traces of life dating back to the Bronze Age and in some of the later finds Zoroastrianism (see box p146) has a prominent role; some of the fire temples that have been dug up are incredible. Whether the man himself was born here, however, is another matter.
>
> You really need the help of the Mary Museum to visit Gonur, as the site is 80km north of Merv and many locals don't know where it is. The museum curators should be able to arrange transport and a guide for your visit (US$40). You could squeeze Merv and Gonur into one trip but it would be a long day.

There is nothing in the way of a good restaurant in town so most visitors stick with the *café* next to the Sanjar.

There are two restaurant/bars, *Altyn Asyr* and *Zip* (both on Turkmenistan Sayoli), but just how entertaining they are remains open to debate.

**Moving on**

If you're short of time or have a transit visa you may need to head straight to **Uzbekistan** (see p197). For **Ashgabat**, either take a bus from outside Mary's train station or, quicker, one of the minibuses (4hrs/US$3). For crossing to **Mashad** in Iran, see p156.

# Ashgabat

The Turkmen capital appears very Soviet, especially if you have just come from Iran, and few people (apart from Turkmenbashi) have ever got excited about it. It does, however, have all the major facilities you might need and, after Iran, the sight of a proper bar is enough to make you very glad to be here.

## HISTORY

Ashgabat (which translates from the Arabic *Ashkabad* as 'City of Love') has not been the luckiest town over the years but somehow it has struggled through. In the 1st century BC it was flattened by an earthquake at a time when it was a prosperous wine-producing town in the Parthian empire.

The Silk Road came to its rescue, however, as the town lay directly on the route skirting the Kopet Dag Mountains to the north and was also just above the last gap in that mountain range if caravans wanted to divert onto, or from, the more southerly route.

The town was rebuilt under the name of Konjikala and survived until the 13th century when, along with all the other main power centres in the region, it was razed by the Mongols.

The town was reduced to little more than a nomad camp and when the Russians arrived there was nothing to see. At that time, however, this was often considered an advantage as the Russians could build their own city from scratch and avoid Turkmen politics. Strategically it was also well placed as it lay on the Trans-Caspian Railway and was close to Persia.

A very European-looking city sprung up with all the trappings of a regional capital and Thomas Cook even included it on one of his early tours. But in 1948 disaster struck again. Another earthquake hit the region and the epicentre was nearly smack bang on Ashgabat. Over 100,000 people (two-thirds of the population) died as the entire city was levelled in a matter of minutes. Stalin refused to acknowledge the tragedy and claimed that only 14,000 people had died. To hide any evidence to the contrary, he had the city sealed off for five years as it was rebuilt.

Turkmenbashi, alas, has not learned much from the failures of the Soviet era and modern Ashgabat has become a rash of oversized, over-expensive projects designed to flatter Turkmenistan's industrial prowess and the president's ego.

## WHAT TO SEE

A trip up Turkmenbashi's monument (officially the **Arch Of Neutrality**) has to be done but it isn't very inspiring (though the café is OK). From the first level you can take another lift to the top for a small fee. You will probably have heard about this monument before you arrive and how the statue rotates to greet the sun in the morning and say goodbye in the evening but, whichever way you look at it, that is not much of a rotation and it won't look as if it's moving at all unless you spend hours staring at it. From the top you can see the enormous white marble, golden-domed **Turkmenbashi Palace** and, next to it, the similarly awful **Parliament**. To the east is the **War Memorial** and the old **Russian Palace** while back in the square at the foot of the arch is the **Earthquake Monument**. The fountain next to the arch does nothing except remind you of the hypocrisy of a country where so many families don't have access to clean water.

Yet the centre of Ashgabat is nothing compared to another of Turkmenbashi's projects: **Berzengi**. In the '90s, he ordered a series of futuristic hotels to be built a few kilometres out of town (no one stays there as they are so far away) and he has since added a whole suburb of marble tower blocks, shopping centres and parks. The area has been crowned with '**The Largest Fountain In The World**'. Apparently it does merit its title but it's still hard to be impressed. You need to take a taxi out to see these 'masterpieces'.

A trip to the **Russian Bazaar** is worth it if you want some cheap vodka or some fresh vegetables but there is little else you will want to buy here or in any of the other shops. To meet Turkmens and buy their local crafts you have to go to the **Tolkuchka Market**, one of Central Asia's most flamboyant and an impressive rival to Kashgar's Sunday market. This is held every Saturday, Sunday and (on a smaller scale) Thursday. It's a few kilometres out of town (take a taxi for US$0.50) and is a real highlight for visitors and locals alike. It sounds quite mercenary but the economy is in such bad shape that most of the vendors have little choice but to haggle. Hats and carpets are the best buys (see 'Buying a carpet', pp136-7). Expect to pay about US$10 for a telpek hat (a kind of wet shaggy afro) and up to US$20 for a genuine Russian fur hat.

The **National Museum of Turkmenistan** houses a fine collection of early treasures found at Merv, Gonur and Nisa but most visitors balk at the US$10 entrance fee (try for a student discount) and the fact you need to take a taxi to get here. The **Carpet Museum** is exactly what it says it is, though its thunder has recently been stolen: previously it used to house the largest rug in the world but a larger one has since been unrolled in Dubai.

## Excursion to Nisa

Unfortunately, what was left of Nisa by the Mongols has been further eroded by the elements over the centuries so it is hard to picture just how splendid this city, the Parthians' capital, once was. Nevertheless, this was a big player in the shaping of the region during Seleucid and Roman times and must have been the base for countless merchants on the Silk Road.

Signs with English explanations are few and far between so you might want to hire a guide. The road by which you approach the city is the original entrance and the ridges around the outside were the fortress walls. Inside are the remains of the street networks and their houses (now one big archaeological dig).

A trip here (including the journey) should take a couple of hours in all and shouldn't cost more than US$2-3 (either take a taxi or ask one of the agencies below to fix you up with a guide or tour). Entrance to the site is US$3.

### PRACTICAL INFORMATION
[☎ code 012]

### Orientation and services

One landmark you can hardly miss is Turkmenbashi's rotating gold statue of himself. From this central point in **Azadi Square** the town grows outwards in a grid pattern, which is easy to follow. In 2002 the president renamed all the streets with numbers (many had already been renamed – sometimes twice – after independence!) but most people still use the old Russian names. Be aware that streets and whole districts are regularly demolished to make way for the latest of Turkmenbashi's pet projects.

Like other Central Asian capitals, all cars here are potential **taxis** so you should have no problem finding a ride ($0.25 to anywhere in the city centre) but it's much easier to walk around what is really little more than a small town. If you do need a taxi, flag down a civilian rather than a registered taxi as the latter are often crooked and will charge foreign visitors anything up to ten times the local price.

The **Internet cafés** which sprung up around 2000 were all **closed** during the post-2002 clampdown. The only Internet access available is in the Sheraton and Nissa hotels and they are expensive.

There are several **travel agencies** who can organize your stay, provide visa support letters and arrange tours and trips. The best inside the country is **Ayan Travel** (☎ 352 914, 🖥 ayan@online.tm), on the first floor of Magtymguly Ave 108. You may be better off, however, using **Stantours** (🖥 www.stantours.com). This company is now based in Almaty but began in Ashgabat, has plenty of local contacts and is run by a European who knows what he is doing. If you can afford a full tourist visa for one or two weeks, they can arrange a really interesting trip taking you all over the country.

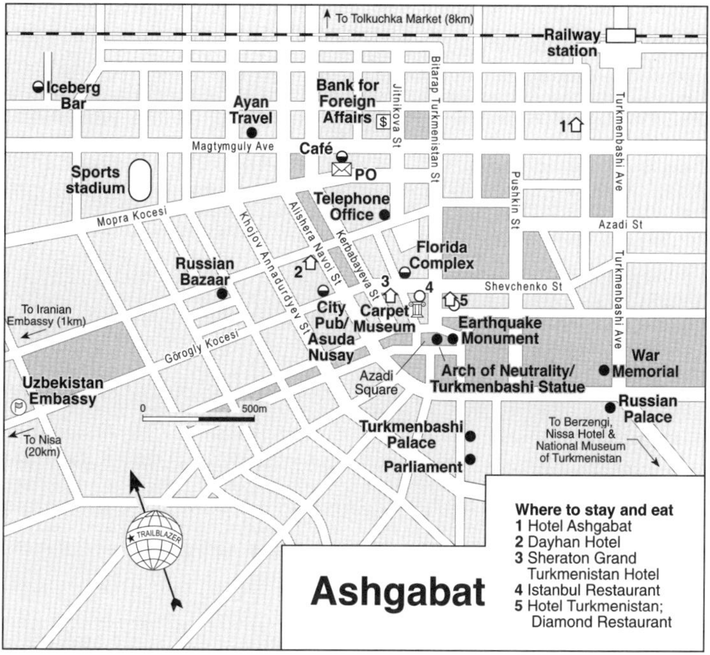
To Tolkuchka Market (8km)
Railway station
Iceberg Bar
Ayan Travel
Bank for Foreign Affairs
Jitnikova St
Bitarap Turkmenistan St
Turkmenbashi Ave
Magtymguly Ave
Café
PO
Sports stadium
Pushkin St
Telephone Office
Mopra Kocesi
Alishera Navoi St
Khojov Annadurdyev St
Kerbabayeva St
Azadi St
Florida Complex
Russian Bazaar
Shevchenko St
City Pub/ Asuda Nusay
Carpet Museum
Earthquake Monument
To Iranian Embassy (1km)
Görogly Kocesi
War Memorial
Azadi Square
Arch of Neutrality/ Turkmenbashi Statue
Uzbekistan Embassy
0
500m
Russian Palace
To Berzengi, Nissa Hotel & National Museum of Turkmenistan
To Nisa (20km)
Turkmenbashi Palace
Parliament
TRAILBLAZER
Ashgabat
Where to stay and eat
1 Hotel Ashgabat
2 Dayhan Hotel
3 Sheraton Grand Turkmenistan Hotel
4 Istanbul Restaurant
5 Hotel Turkmenistan; Diamond Restaurant

To withdraw US dollars on a credit card go to the **Bank for Foreign Affairs,** which is the large green building on Jitnikova St. They give advances for a 5 per cent commission. The **National Bank of Pakistan** (within the Sheraton complex) also provides this service. Both banks have **ATMs**, which have been known to dispense US dollars. To exchange money at the 'street rate' wait until you are approached outside the **Florida Complex** where moneychangers openly tout for business (although to be more discreet you might want to inquire at a bar or restaurant).

The **post office** and the **telephone exchange** are round the corner from each other in the middle of town but neither service is recommended.

Applying for visas (see p15-18) whilst in Turkmenistan is not recommended as you either won't have enough time or won't want to waste the time you do have queuing in embassies. The **Iranian Embassy** (☎ 341 452), Tehranskaya St 3, and **Uzbek Embassy** (☎ 360 006), Görogly St 50A, are both in the west of town. Both are open only in the morning and demand watertight documentation.

### Where to stay

On Azadi St, ***Dayhan Hotel*** (☎ 253 078) charges US$20 for a double and is the best bet for budget accommodation as the similarly priced ***Hotel Ashgabat*** is something of a Soviet relic. If you are really pushed for money, ask around for homestay accommodation; ***Amanov Homestay*** on Shaumyana St has been recommended.

A very pleasant alternative in the mid-range is ***Hotel Turkmenistan*** (☎ 350 63; US$50/Db), Shevchenko St, which used to be the top joint in town in the Soviet era and has managed to change with the times without losing its classical style.

The Sheraton Group bought the *Grand Turkmenistan Hotel* a few years ago but it's already going downhill; if you're serious about staying here, their US$175 'walk-in rate' usually collapses under persistent haggling as they are never anywhere near full.

### Where to eat and drink

*Istanbul Restaurant* is said to be the best of the Turkish-type restaurants in town but if you are heading east you may be tired of this food by now. *Diamond Restaurant* in the Hotel Turkmenistan serves a wide selection of Russian food in very elegant surroundings and is not too expensive.

The **Florida Complex** as a whole is an ex-pat rip off, with its *British Pub* ($3 for a small beer) the worst offender. While the *club* downstairs seems to have some sort of party night every weekend, it can be little more than a pick-up joint.

Quite a few smaller bars, however, are opening up of which the *Iceberg Bar* is probably the best. It has tables inside and out and serves its own locally produced beer, which isn't too bad. They also serve a wide selection of snacks/bar meals although you might need a bit of Russian to understand exactly what's on offer.

The *City Pub* and *Asuda Nusay Restaurant* share the same premises (Alishera Navoi St 54a); they are both popular and busy, despite being a little expensive.

### Moving on

Minibuses (*marshrutka*) and share-taxis to and from **Mary** leave from and arrive at Ashgabat's train station. Travel to the rest of the country requires a little bit of improvisation and a lot of patience, unless you put yourself in the hands of one of the local agencies.

If you are going it alone to **Konye-Urgench**, transport leaves from **Dashoguz Bazaar** (you need to take a taxi to get here). Buses, minibuses and share-taxis go to Konye-Urgench or **Dashoguz** depending on demand. They run straight through the Karakum Desert, described in 1888 by George Curzon (the future Viceroy of India) as 'The sorriest waste that ever met the human eye'. Little has changed so be prepared for a journey that will last at least 12 hours: bring lots of water and sunglasses.

You used to be able to break your journey and stay at **Darvaza** to see the burning gas craters but this is no longer possible (unless you have your own transport) as Turkmenbashi drove the nomads away, accusing them of drug-trafficking. As a result, the campsite/stopover has been abandoned and the bus no longer stops.

If you are on transport headed to Dashoguz, ask the driver (or your fellow passengers) to drop you at the junction with the road to Konye-Urgench. You can quite easily hitch a ride into town from here (although you will probably have to pay a contribution to petrol).

If you are heading for **Iran**, see p156. If you couldn't get a visa for Iran and you are determined not to fly, you could try going to **Turkmenbashi** on the Caspian Sea, taking a boat from there to **Baku** (Azerbaijan) and continuing to Turkey via the Caucasus.

# Konye-Urgench

The first city to be built here (known as Avesta-Urva) seems to date from the 6th century BC and entering this city is a little like entering a living museum with odd relics from all over history popping up around you. The town became known as Urgench in about the 10th century but it is now called Konye-Urgench (Old Urgench) because it was deserted in the 17th century when all the inhabitants upped sticks to move to the modern-day Urgench in Uzbekistan.

You shouldn't need too much money between now and Nukus so try to keep your *manat* to a minimum and have a few low-denomination dollars as back up.

## HISTORY

Like Khiva, Konye-Urgench is on the branch of the Silk Road that ran around the top of the Caspian Sea. Therefore, despite the age of this city, it did not see its glory days until the Silk Road's later years, when the routes taken by the different caravans were at their most varied. Before the Silk Road arrived this area depended on the Amu-Darya River for its wealth and it was at Konye-Urgench that the river turned sharply westwards and ran into the Caspian Sea along the Uzboy Channel (at this time the Karakum Desert was not in fact a desert but a highly fertile alluvial plain constantly fed by the river – a bit like the Sarykamish Lake area today).

It was always considered a regional capital by the Khorezm but like the branch of the Silk Road it controlled, this tribe spent most of history in the shadows. By the end of the 10th century AD, however, a new leader, Mamun, had managed to gain some independence for his people and by the 12th century they were finally in a position to challenge their latest overlords, the Seljuks, who were beginning to crack under the strain of maintaining their enormous empire.

The result was a new Khorezm empire with Konye-Urgench as its capital and for a while all the riches of Asia flowed into the city. Even after 1210 when the then ruler, Mohammed II, moved the capital to Samarkand, Konye-Urgench was still considered a jewel of the Islamic world and an important centre for learning. The Amu-Dayra no longer flowed past the city into the Caspian (an earthquake had changed its course so that it ran into the Aral Sea) but a large dam ensured that the city was well-watered and prospered.

In 1216, Genghis Khan paid tribute to the Khorezm's strength and sent an envoy to Mohammed offering peace, a trading treaty and many lavish gifts but Mohammed gave no reply. Then, in 1218, when the first of the Mongols' trading caravans arrived, local Khorezm killed the entire 450-strong party. Genghis gave Mohammed a last chance but he killed the first of the khan's messengers and burned the beards of the other two.

Mohammed lived to regret his mistake – but not for long. Konye-Urgench was flattened, along with all the other Khorezm cities, in 1221. Konye-Urgench's end was particularly harsh. The city held out for months behind its strong defences until Genghis's son, Tuluy, realized the potential destructive power of the Amu-Dayra. By smashing Mohammed's dam, he directed the river back along its old course to the Caspian and straight through the heart of the city. Nevertheless, over the following century, the inhabitants managed to piece together some of the remains and in 1321 it became part of the Golden Horde's territory. Under this new protection the town once more became a semi-independent state (ruled by the Sufi dynasty) but Tamerlane considered it too much of a rival to his capital, Samarkand, and proceeded to smash it a record five times by 1388.

Some life was breathed back into the area after the demise of the Timurids but in 1646 the Amu-Dayra changed its course for the last time following another earthquake. Now, not only did the river flow back into the Aral Sea but its new course also ran some fifty kilometres away, forcing the city to be abandoned. The settlement was only reinhabited (albeit on a very small scale) with the building of massive canals in the eighteenth and nineteenth centuries.

## WHAT TO SEE

The main group of buildings is quite near the centre and they are grouped around the **Mausoleum of Nedjmeddin Kubra**. This was built for the founder of the Kubravid school of Sufism and was rebuilt after the Mongol invasions; there are two tombs now, one for his head and one for his body which, thanks to the Mongols, parted company. The mausoleum's portals are its most attractive feature and this building is still the most sacred in the area. Opposite is the **Mausoleum of Sultan Ali**, a 16th-century ruler of Urgench. The **City Museum** is also here (around the corner) but it's not always open.

The remaining sights are dotted all over but your taxi driver should know them. The **Mausoleum of Turabeg Khanym** is said to be the most perfect building in Central Asia and it may well be that it was initially built as a palace and then converted. There are 365 sections of the mosaic covering the inside of the dome (one for each day of the year), 24 small pointed arches (one for each hour of the day), 12 larger arches (one for each month in the year) and four big windows (one for each of the seasons).

Cross the road and walk through the cemetery to the **Kutlug Timur Minaret** (you can't miss it). At 64m it is the highest minaret in Central Asia and is said to date back as far as the 12th century. Next is the **Mausoleum of Sultan Tekesh**, popularly referred to as 'The Blue Dome', which gives you an idea of what you are about to see. Tekesh (the father of Mohammed II) was the man who truly made the Khorezm great. The nearby mound of graves known as the **Kirkmolla** was where the Khorezm made their last stand against the Mongols.

The **Mausoleum of Il Arslan** is the tomb of Tekesh's father (Il Aslan ruled from 1156 to 1172) and is the oldest building still standing in the city. The **Caravanserai Gate** may not have been part of a caravanserai (see box p98) at all but one of the gates to the city used by the traders, although it might also have been the entrance to a palace – no one is really sure.

### PRACTICAL INFORMATION
#### Where to stay and eat
Your biggest problem in Konye-Urgench is accommodation – the only official option, *Gurgench Hotel* (Dashogus Kocesi, US$6 a bed) is awful and out of town. You should manage to find a **homestay**, however, by asking around. Whoever you stay with should be able to put you in touch with a taxi driver to take you around the sights. The *Mekan* is the only place resembling a proper restaurant but there are a couple of **cafés** and **food stalls** near the sights.

#### Moving on
Buses and *marshrutkas* (minibuses) run regularly to **Ashgabat** (10-12hrs/US$4) from the car park out near Gurgench Hotel.

> **Crossing the Turkmenistan/Uzbekistan border**
> **Konye-Urgench** is less than half-an-hour from the border at **Hojeli**, so you should be able to see the town's sights and take a taxi (US$0.50) to the checkpoint all in one day. Crossing is straightforward but the biggest problem is money: there should be some moneychangers hanging around the taxi drivers but they will try to rip you off; establish what the dollar/*sum* exchange rate is with either the other locals crossing the border or the guards. Your *manats* are worthless outside Turkmenistan so try not to have too many left. From here you need to take a taxi to **Nukus**; you shouldn't pay more than US$4.
>
> If you are heading west your accommodation in Nukus should be able to help with transport to the border. On the other side take a taxi and ask your driver if he knows anywhere to stay in Konye-Urgench.
>
> **From Mary**, take a bus, marshrutki or share-taxi (forget about the train option – it's too slow and unreliable) from outside the train station to **Turkmenabat** (3hrs/US$2), from where you will need to take a taxi (about US$4) to the border (sometimes they can take you only to within 2km of the border, in which case you can walk or take a shuttle bus – US$1). Cross the border by foot. On the other side, take another taxi to **Karakul** or **Alat** (also about US$2), and from here take a bus, minibus or share-taxi to **Bukhara**. You should complete the whole trip in less than a day.
>
> Coming the other way take a share-taxi (US$4) from Bukhara's **Bolshoy rynok bazaar** to Alat, then take a taxi to the border and follow the above instructions (in reverse) to Mary.
>
> **Note: You have to pay a US$10 fee to enter Turkmenistan.**

# Nukus

Nukus is not a pretty town and most people would, understandably, stop only to change buses or say 'I've been to Karakalpakstan' (literally 'The Land of the Black Hat People' – although no one is sure as to which black hat they are talking about). Something quite amazing has taken place here, however, making it worth at least a few hours of your time.

## HISTORY

As we know from Konye-Urgench, people have lived in this part of the Amu-Dayra Delta for thousands of years but Nukus gives few hints of such ancestry. This town was built by the Soviets to serve the Soviets and, unsurprisingly, such a pedigree has brought with it a catalogue of unmitigated disasters. As you enter or leave the town you will probably cross the river at least once and by looking at the larger trees and mud banks you will see how wide the river used to be before all the irrigation canals began to bleed it dry. This irrigation gave Karakalpakstan two decades of unprecedented harvests in the sixties and seventies – but at a price.

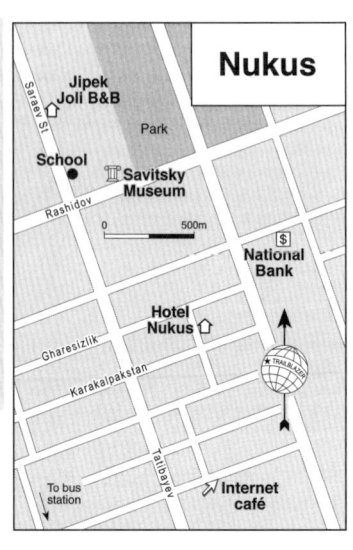

Now, not only is the Amu-Dayra severely depleted but the chemicals used to increase the crop yields have seeped right into the ecosystem.

Some land, even with irrigation, is refusing to be fertile and great swathes of land further downstream have dried up altogether now the river can no longer feed them. This combination has meant that not only has the Aral Sea shrunk but also the newly dried-out lands are prone to sandstorms as there is nothing to bind the earth together.

These sandstorms pick up and disperse a cocktail of poisonous chemicals, which are also beginning to show up in the water supplies.

What the final results will be are unclear but for the moment the immediate effects on the population are obvious: Karakalpakstan has some of the world's highest rates of birth deformities, infant mortality, cancer and hepatitis.

## WHAT TO SEE

At this stage you could be forgiven for thinking 'this had better be good, now that I've just wiped ten years off my life' but if you have any interest in art you will be rewarded. Nukus is home to the **Savitsky Karakalpakstan Art Museum** (127 Doslyk; www.savitsky.museum.uz; US$4, Mon-Sat), a unique art collection. It contains avant-garde Russian and Uzbek art assembled between 1918 and the 1930s, a period that saw most non-government-approved art destroyed by Stalin during the purges and many of its artists sent to Siberia. The man responsible for preserving these works is Igor Savitksy, an archaeologist and artist in his own right. There are an estimated 80,000 pieces in the entire collection, so even though a beautiful new museum has been built to house it, only a fraction (3 per cent) is on display at any one time. The quality and range on offer are nevertheless incredible. The old museum is still open and houses more pieces if you are interested.

### PRACTICAL INFORMATION
[☎ code 061]

**Orientation and services**

The town is set out on a uniform grid, with the Museum in the centre and the accommodation nearby. The **National Bank** here advances US dollars on credit/ debit cards.

### Where to stay and eat

*Jipek Joli B&B* (☎ 222 3452; jipek_hotel@rambler.ru; US$25/Db), 29 Saraev St, is the best option, has a café and is convenient for the museum (they have their own small family museum, too). Otherwise you can stay with the local businessmen in the rather run-down *Hotel Nukus* (☎ 222 8941; US$20/Db) at 4 Lumumba. There are a couple of **cafés** near the museum but little else.

**Moving on**
Two or three minibuses and buses (US$3) leave for **Urgench** each day from in front of Hotel Nukus (they stop at the **bus station**, too, to pick up more passengers); you may need to change at **Biruni**. On your way, look out for the enormous **Chilpyh Kala** fort (about 40mins south of Nukus).

From Urgench, catch the local bus or a share-taxi (US$0.50) to **Khiva** (it's not worth breaking your journey at Urgench as the town has little to offer).

For crossing over to **Turkmenistan**, see box p197.

# Khiva

Hungarian traveller Arminius Vambery visited Khiva in 1863. One of his first encounters was with eight old men lying in a line on their backs having their eyes gouged out by the khan's executioner, who wiped his knife clean on each victim's beard before moving on to the next. Mosques, minarets and mausolea reign supreme here and as you wander through Khiva's maze of dusty, cobbled streets surrounded by towering Islamic architecture it's almost as though you have stumbled onto the set of an Indiana Jones movie.

## HISTORY

Nobody seems quite sure exactly when Khiva was founded. One popular myth attributes it to Noah's son Shem, who started building after a vivid dream of torches burning in the sand here.

The Greek historian, Herodotus (484-425BC), mentions the kingdom of Khorezm, noting its subservience to Darius's Achaemenid dynasty, yet at this time Khiva was still just a village compared to Konye-Urgench.

As a fully fledged city, Khiva was probably founded in the 5th century AD and we know for certain that by the 6th century it was famous for its Kheivak Well and soon became an important rest-stop/fortress on this section of the Silk Road. It was also noted as an intellectual centre by the 9th century, having produced many great mathematicians, astronomers and chess players.

Khiva really came to prominence, however, once Konye-Urgench had been abandoned and soon after that it began to earn its notoriety as a trade centre for Persian slaves. So much so that when the Persian king, Nadir Shah, invaded in the early 18th century, he singled the city out for a special drubbing; 20 years later the place was still almost totally deserted.

### The arrival of the Russians
The Russians discovered this prosperous kingdom at around the same time as the Persians invaded and there are records of a number of Cossack-led plundering raids: on one occasion 1000 Khivan women were carried off, only to be recovered when the raiders were killed in an ambush shortly afterwards.

> **The Rhubarb Road**
> The Chinese had sung the praises of rhubarb for many centuries and considered it to be essential to the balance of a human body (Marco Polo even took some home with him and left a bag of rhubarb to one of his beneficiaries in his will). In the 17th century these "medicinal" qualities became the talk of Europe and soon the large-leaved plant became a highly sought-after commodity. Peter the Great instructed his Chief Apothecary officers to buy up a monopoly on all the rhubarb passing out of China, which they did. This trade route, around the Caspian to Astrakhan (near the old Golden Horde capital of Sarai) and up the Volga River to Moscow, became known as the Rhubarb Road.

The first real Russian push, however, came in 1717. Fuelled by reports of gold in the area and the certainty of treasure in India to the south-east, Peter the Great dispatched a force of 3500 men under Prince Bekovitch Cherkassky. To his surprise, Bekovitch was welcomed into the city by the khan. He was then persuaded that, since food could not be provided for such a large army in one place, his men would have to be split up. He fell for this and subsequently had the dubious pleasure of watching his entire army slaughtered. Finally, he was flayed alive and his head sent to the emir of Bukhara as a trophy.

But it was not all bad news for the Russians. During Peter's reign (1682-1725), the branch of the Silk Road that had looped up around the Caspian Sea suddenly took on a new significance. Peter was much more fond of Europe than Asia but he knew that if his European cousins were to take him seriously, he must have in his grasp something which they wanted. Silk, of course, had long lost its novelty (if not its value) and the European courts were instead eager for a new fad. The answer, somewhat fantastically, was rhubarb; see box above.

Russian success couldn't last forever, though, and catastrophe was only narrowly averted in 1801 when Tsar Paul I, rapidly losing his sanity, sent a force of 22,000 Cossacks to take Khiva in mid-winter; luckily they were recalled upon the news that Paul was dead, having covered only 600km. The next Russian attempt to gain a hold on the area came in January 1840 with a bold campaign under General Perovsky but he was turned back by severe weather (over 1000 men died on the retreat alone). Finally, in 1873, it was General Kaufman who simultaneously mobilized 10,000 troops from Orenburg, Tashkent and Kranovodsk and took the walled city with hardly a struggle. In theory, Khiva was taken to stop the slave trade here though in fact trading continued for another 50 years.

## Khiva today
With a population of around 40,000, Khiva is now in effect two towns but you will spend most of your time in the old walled city (the Ichan Qala, or *Shakhristan*). The reason that the monuments look so good is that they have all been restored with Russian/Uzbek patronage and hand in hand with this restoration has come the notion of Khiva as an 'outdoor museum'. Consequently, many locals have been forced out to live in the new town. This 'museumization' of the city is the cause of much controversy: many believe that it should have

been left in its crumbling state and that the atmosphere of the place has gone. The Ichan Qala has been made a World Heritage Site.

## WHAT TO SEE

The Old City is pretty spectacular, particularly in the late evening or early morning light. You can buy a US$5 ticket from any entrance (this gives you unlimited access to all the sites in the Old City), or you can pay separate entrance fees (500-1000som each) for those you particularly want to see.

### Kunya Ark

Immediately to your left as you enter the Ichan Qala through the **West Gate**, this is the former residence and court of the khan. Building started in the 17th century and work was pretty much continuous.

The entrance to the Ark is particularly ornate, as was noted by the Russian envoy, Nikolai Muravyov, who was imprisoned outside for nearly two months before finally being allowed to enter in 1819. If you take the first right after entering, you will find the lovely Summer Mosque and, opposite this, the royal mint (now a tiny museum). Also in here is the reception hall; look for the three entrance arches side by side. The left-hand entrance was for use by all the non-officials and was built smaller than the others to make them stoop before the khan as they entered. In front of this hall is a raised circular brick pedestal, which is where the ruler's winter *yurt* (a circular felt tent used by nomadic steppe-peoples) was rigged. Muravyov describes the scene here nearly 200 years ago:

'*...on reaching the end of this corridor, we had to go down two steps into a fourth courtyard, larger than the other three, but surpassing them all in filth, and covered here and there with weeds. In the middle of this stood the khan's yurt.*'

### Zindan

Just outside the Kunya Ark in the large square is the jail, now converted into a grisly showpiece. Pictures inside depict favourite methods of execution: impalement, burial alive and tying people inside sacks with fierce wild animals were all favourites in their time. Muravyov comments that '*sometimes an impaled man will live for two days on the stake, only dying when the point comes through his shoulders or back.*' These atrocities took place in the square outside.

### Mohammed Amin Khan Madrassah and Kalta Minaret

This madrassah was built in 1852-5 and is easily recognized by its large arched entrance. It stands to the right of the West Gate as you go in and now houses Hotel Khiva. The courtyard of the hotel is worth a look around as is the stubby, multi-coloured tower beside it: this is **Kalta Minar**, the 'Short Minaret' which was commissioned in 1852 to be the tallest minaret in Central Asia.

There are two theories as to why it was never completed: one is that the khan died; the other involves the emir of Bukhara, who apparently contacted the architect and persuaded him to build an even bigger one in Bukhara when this one was finished. The Khan of Khiva, hearing of this treachery, ordered the architect to be executed and had him thrown from the top of his own minaret. Unfortunately the Kalta Minar stands only 29.4m tall (it was intended to be 79.5m), and he was not killed immediately. The khan then ordered the hapless architect to be hauled up to the top and thrown off repeatedly until he did finally die.

## Islam Khoja Minaret

Khiva's tallest minaret stands 44.6m high and is in immaculate condition. This is partly due to the fact that it was built only in 1908; Islam Khoja was the Grand Vizier of Asfandiyar Khan (ruled 1910-20) and was a benevolent, popular man. The khan saw him as a political threat, however, and one night, after declaring a curfew in the town, summoned him to the palace alone. On the way, he was murdered by hired bandits. Asfandiyar then proceeded to dispose of the evidence by having the bandits publicly executed the next morning. It's possible to climb to the top for an aerial view of the city.

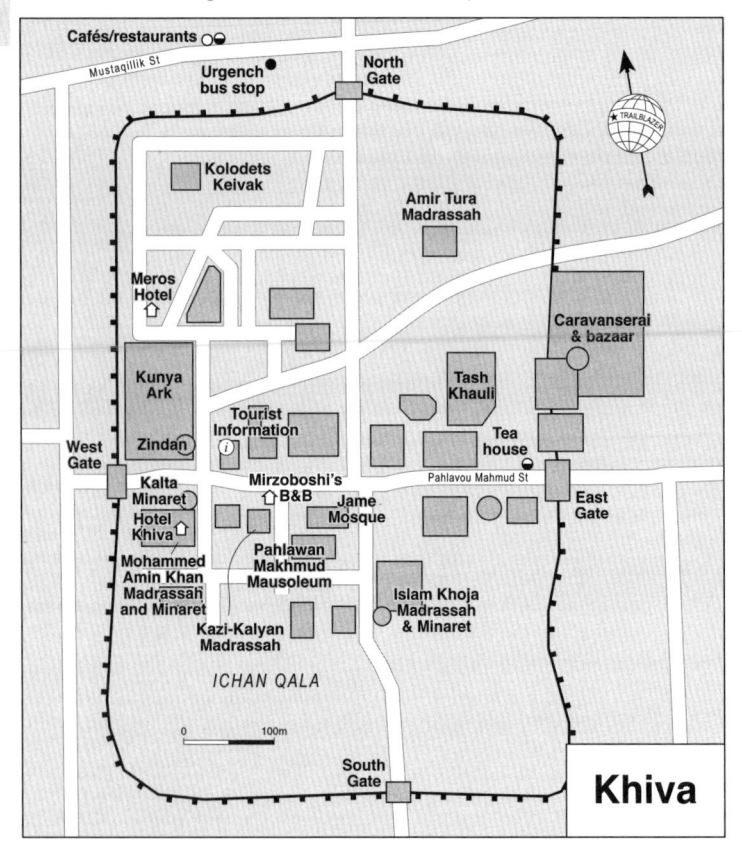

## Pahlawan Makhmud Mausoleum

Pahlawan ('Hero') Makhmud was a furrier who helped the poor, wrote poetry and was the strongest man in the kingdom. Since the 12th century he has been canonized as Khiva's protector. This mausoleum was constructed in 1810 on the site of his fur shop but there has almost certainly been some kind of monument here since his death. Following Makhmud's burial, numerous wealthy traders and khans staked their claims to be buried near him and hence there are a number of other tombs here. As you walk through the arch you will see a well to the right, the water of which is supposed to have miraculous properties. It is traditional to make a wish as you drink from it.

Inside the prayer hall directly ahead lie the tombs of three khans from the 17th century, and in the hall to their left is Makhmud's; note the groups of devotees who will, no doubt, be posting money through the grille. The inscription above is from one of his poems and translates roughly as: 'It is easier to spend one hundred years in jail or to climb one hundred mountains than it is to persuade a fool of the truth'. Remember to take off your shoes before going in.

## Jame Mosque

This mosque's most notable features are its pillars: there are over 200 of them, of which the oldest (some have been replaced) dates right back to the 10th century. It is extremely airy inside and if you're too hot this is a good place to sit and cool down. The carriage here was a gift to the khan from Tsar Nicholas.

## East Gate (Paiwan Darwaze)

Located in the oldest part of the city, this entrance was known as the Executioner's Gate. Its association with slavery is hard to miss as it contains small alcoves once used as cells and the slave market was just inside to the right.

The Khivan slave trade is described by Muravyov:

*'A young Russian (up to 25 years of age) fetches from fifty to eighty tillas. The Persian slaves are much cheaper. Of the latter there may be 30,000 in Khiva, but there are not more than 300 Russian slaves there. The Persians come into the market in batches of five, ten, and even thirty at a time. Their captors do not trouble themselves about them on the road, and, if they get exhausted, leave them without compunction to die on the steppe. On arrival at Khiva their owner sets himself down with them in the market, and purchasers surround him, inspecting and examining the poor wretches, and haggling about their price as if they were horses. Masters have the power of putting their slaves to death, but seldom avail themselves of this right from economic considerations. They therefore punish their slaves, as a rule, by putting out an eye, or cutting off an ear...'*

If this gate was not a very happy sight for slaves on arrival, it could be a considerably more unpleasant one for them later on: when a slave was suspected of trying to escape he was nailed to it by his ears and left there for a couple of days. The majority, already weak, battered and undernourished, died blistering deaths in the heat.

When the Russians arrived in 1873 they counted 29,300 slaves still in bondage and over 6500 that had managed to buy their freedom.

## Tash Khauli

Tash Khauli literally means 'Palace of Stone'. It was built as a replacement for the aging Kunya Ark between 1830 and 1838 under Mlah Kuli Khan (1826-41). Inside you will find a number of courtyards, each decorated with beautifully crafted majolica tiling. Do bear in mind that every one of these tiles was made, glazed and fired individually, and only then were they assembled, rather like a jigsaw. They say that each tile is unique but with complex geometrical patterns like these it is difficult to tell. Certainly, assembling the jigsaw would have been nearly impossible without the help of the small numbers painted in the corner of each tile. Unfortunately the architect was never able to see the results of his work: having been given two years in which to build the palace, he was beheaded the day after that limit was up. While this may have satisfied the khan's impatience to some degree, it didn't accelerate the building process: Tash Khauli was another six years in the making.

The quarters to the right were for the emir's harem, whose inhabitants wandered about with their faces uncovered inside the courtyard, knowing that any non-court official caught looking at them would be executed. The women were never permitted to leave. Note the swastika-like symbols at the feet of the pillars on the left, symbols of Zoroastrianism (see box p146).

## Caravanserai and bazaar

Directly opposite the entrance to the Tash Khauli is the old caravanserai (see box p98). The long covered corridor, rather like a cloister, which you have to pass through to get there is called the *Tim*. The caravanserai is now a covered market and the writing around the side is political rhetoric. Just beyond the market you step outside again to find the bazaar. This is open daily; Sunday is best.

## Around Khiva

There are a number of extremely significant **forts** in the area around Khiva. A taxi (US$30-40 between three or four people depending on the vehicle) is the best way of seeing them – the trip should last all day and take in at least four of the main sites. The surrounding lakes used to be famous for their migrating swans (Genghis Khan was so impressed he ordered a number of birds to be delivered to his palace in Karakorum every year) but environmental damage has seen them off. If you are on your own put a note up in the tourist office and try to gather a group together.

### PRACTICAL INFORMATION
**[π code 0362]**

#### Orientation and services
From Urgench you will pass through the new town but there is no reason to stop. Instead, you are likely to be dropped off just by the **North or West gates**. Once inside, keep an eye out for the Islam Khoja Minaret as an orientation point.

There is a **tourist office** in the main square that has a helpful messages board; the manager is also happy to double up as a **guide** (US$5/hr). You can **change money** in Hotel Khiva.

#### Where to stay and eat
It is definitely worth staying inside the Old City to experience the atmosphere once the majority of tourists have departed and you have the place to yourself. *Meros Hotel*

(☎ 375 7642; US$20/Db) at 57 Abdulla Baltaev is very hospitable – try to get a room with a terrace. Next to the Kazi-Kalyan Madrassah, *Mirzoboshi's B&B* (☎ 372 753; US$10/dorm) is the cheapest. *Hotel Khiva* (☎ 375 4945; US$50/Db), Mohammed Amin Khan Madrassah, has been restored and is the most authentic place to stay.

You can usually eat in your hostel or, given enough warning, any other guesthouse. There are also several **cafés/restaurants** outside the North and West gates.

**Moving on**
There are frequent minibuses/share taxis to **Urgench** from the North Gate. From there you can change for buses to **Nukus** (US$3, though you might need to change at **Biruni**) or Bukhara (7-10hrs/ US$15).

It's not worth taking the train as it's too slow and unreliable. You'll hit the Kyzylkum Desert on this leg, which means few towns to stop for refreshments so bring lots of fluids.

# Bukhara

Bukhara is a prime example of the whole being more than a sum of its parts. Everywhere you go there is something that will add to your visit and although the sights could be taken in within two days, give yourself three or more to soak up the atmosphere.

Just the **Labi Hauz** is worth an afternoon to sit and watch the world go by over a few beers and some kebabs. If you don't believe us, listen to Lord Curzon. He visited Bukhara (equipped with his inflatable 'India-rubber' bath) and called it 'the most interesting city in the world'.

At the same time, however, Bukhara has always been considered the most violent of the Central Asian states. Its emirs' tyrannical ways were notorious and following the gruesome deaths of two English army officers here in 1842, this infamy spread to the West. Yet, hand in hand with this notoriety has gone Bukhara's reputation as a key centre of Islamic scholarship and as a consequence it is liberally endowed with mosques and madrassahs.

## HISTORY

According to the Persian poet, Abdul Hassim Firdausi, Bukhara was founded by a Kanian prince, Siyawush, who lies buried here. The story tells of Siyawush's sticky end: when he refused to respond to his stepmother's amorous overtures she suggested that her husband, the king, should have him beheaded. Hearing this, Siyawush fled to Turan where King Afrosiab (the founder of Samarkand in another myth, see p216) betrayed him. Siyawush's stepmother, you will be glad to hear, was later put to death by Rustam, whose huge six-stranded whip used to hang over the main entrance to the citadel, or 'Ark'.

Actually, the first agricultural settlements located around modern Bukhara date from the 8th century BC but nothing of real significance has survived. Alexander the Great took Bukhara by siege in 328BC and tells us that at this time it was already heavily fortified (not heavily enough, obviously) but this seems

### The Great Game

Peter the Great was the first Russian ruler to have the idea of taking over Central Asia and he set a precedent for all future tsars. Indeed, by the early 19th century, it seemed the aim was not just to take over Central Asia but to use this land as a base to threaten the British in India (if not take India altogether!). Napoleon actually proposed a joint Franco-Russian alliance that would march the length of Asia and attack India through Afghanistan (this plan, like many others, never materialized).

Few politicians in Britain believed Russia would dare to invade but all agreed that the 'no-man's land' lying between the two great empires was a mystery that needed to be solved – particularly as this was a 'no-man's land' that was shrinking (down to just a few kilometres in some places).

Thus began the Great Game (or as it was known in Russia, The Tournament of Shadows), a battle of espionage and intrigue played out across the deserts and mountains of Central Asia, Persia, Afghanistan and China. While the Russians sent agents to prepare the way south, the British sent spies to chart the territories, assess the risks and forge links with the local rulers. The spies themselves were generally young officers of exceptional bravery and linguistic ability. They travelled for months disguised as holy men or traders, sure in the knowledge that if they were discovered they would die gruesome deaths – as some inevitably did. (See also box opposite.)

---

to have been largely ignored by early historians. They refer to the city as Numijkat and tell of its foundation in the 1st century AD, though in their defence the first real archaeological evidence dates only from the 1st or 2nd century BC.

By the 7th century, construction of the Ark on its present site was underway and by the eighth the living quarters around the fort were surrounded by a 25km-long protective wall. However, this wasn't enough to keep out the Arabs, who invaded in the 8th century.

Their leader, General Kutayba ibn Muslim, introduced a religion to the city that was to take such a firm hold as to make Bukhara one of the most zealous cities in the Islamic world; yet when he built the first mosque in 712, interest was slight. So slight, in fact, Kutayba had to bribe the inhabitants to give up their old ways and attend Friday prayers (two *direms* per man).

### The first flourishing

The Samanids succeeded the Arabs as rulers in the 9th century and Bukhara, now capital of the area, flourished both industrially and intellectually. Most prominent among the scholars who studied here was Abu Ah Abn Sina (980-1037), better known to the West as 'Avicenna', whose 'Canon' of medicine was the authoritative medical textbook throughout Europe until the 17th century.

The golden age was not to last for long though: Avicenna was thrown out of Bukhara amidst allegations that he had set fire to the city's extensive library. Moreover, Bukhara was invaded numerous times before being obliterated by Genghis Khan in 1220. After Genghis's men had taken everything of value he ordered the city to be razed to the ground; residents who did not remove themselves fast enough before the incineration were executed on the spot.

Although the Timurids brought wealth and prosperity in the fourteenth and fifteenth centuries, their capital was actually at Samarkand and the dynasty was short-lived. Yet by 1500, under the Sheibanids and then the Janids, Bukhara had made a comeback. It is estimated that 30,000 students flocked in to study at the 360 mosques and 80 madrassahs.

The expansion of the Russian empire eventually put paid to Bukharan autonomy, however, and the city was absorbed in 1868. On 2 September 1920, the Soviets, under Mikhail Frunze, stormed the town, sending the emir, Said Ah Khan, into exile in Afghanistan.

## Modern Bukhara

At Russian insistence all pictures depicting torture or death (so common under the cruel emirs) were removed from the museums. They also drained the many pools and canals which had watered the town. When the water disappeared, the bugs disappeared too, as intended, but this also led to the demise of the storks, which had famously built their nests on the high minarets. Although you will still see the odd nest perched up high, they all are empty now that the storks' main source of food has been removed. The Ark, 80 per cent of which was destroyed by Frunze, is now restored but the Registan, where so many atrocities took place, is empty. The whole of the Old City is a World Heritage Site.

## WHAT TO SEE

Before attempting any sightseeing, spend at least a day just wandering around but be prepared to get thoroughly lost. As Geoffrey Moorhouse notes, '...because these alleys twisted and doglegged erratically, it was very easy to lose all sense of direction and return to a starting point without the slightest inkling that one had gone astray. It was like trying to find a way through some gigantic maze made of baked mud' *(Apples in the Snow)*.

### Stoddart and Connolly

Two Great Gamesters stand out as visitors to Bukhara: Colonel Charles Stoddart and Captain Arthur Connolly. It was Connolly who first coined the phrase 'The Great Game' (not Kipling as some would have it); Connolly was a boy at Rugby in the 1820s when a certain William Web Ellis first picked up a ball and ran with it, so perhaps it was rugby he had in mind (rather than chess as has often been supposed) when he conjured his sporting analogy.

Stoddart was dispatched to Bukhara in 1839 in order to foster good relations with Nasrullah, the legendarily cruel emir. Nasrullah was not at all impressed by the English officer, however, and had him incarcerated. After the best part of three years as a lone prisoner, Stoddart's spirits received a huge boost with the arrival of another emissary, Connolly, intent on securing his release. Unfortunately, Connolly, as he had been warned by other local rulers, fared no better and was thrown into the 'bug pit' to keep Stoddart company. Worse was to come as, following Britain's defeat in the First Afghan War (1842), Nasrullah felt powerful enough to openly shame his enemy by having its two officers dragged out into the Registan and publicly beheaded.

208 Uzbekistan – Bukhara

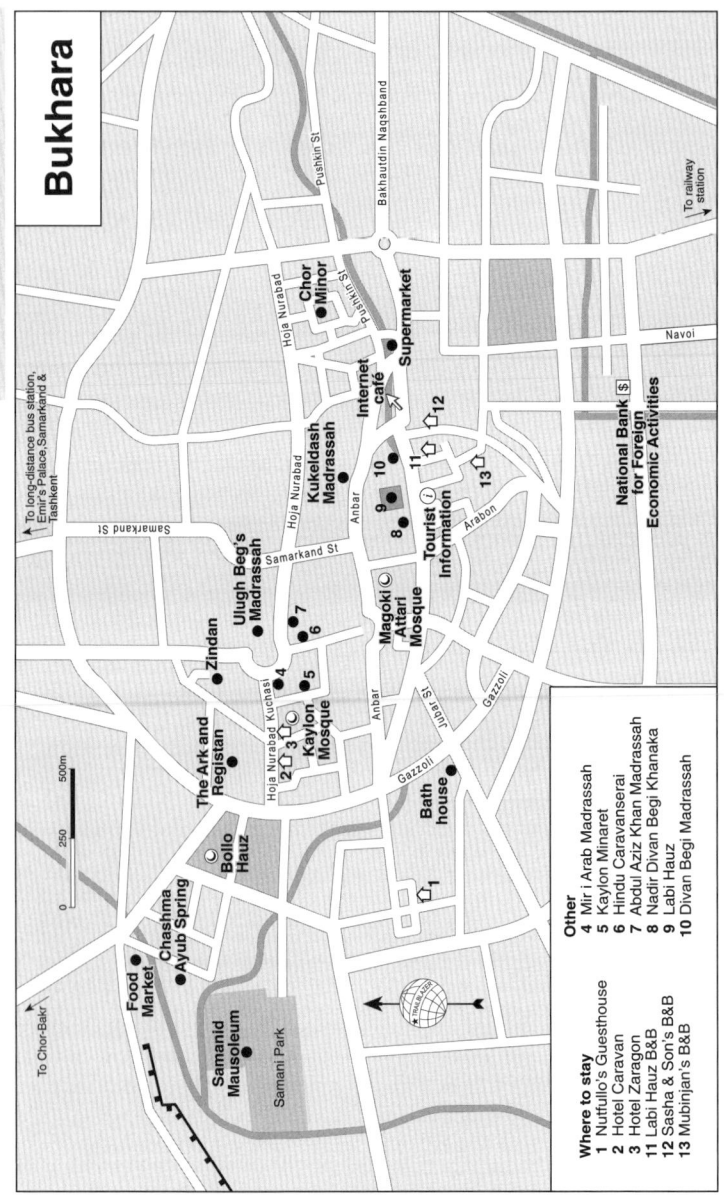

# Bukhara

**Where to stay**
1 Nutfullo's Guesthouse
2 Hotel Caravan
3 Hotel Zaragon
11 Labi Hauz B&B
12 Sasha & Son's B&B
13 Mubinjan's B&B

**Other**
4 Mir i Arab Madrassah
5 Kaylon Minaret
6 Hindu Caravanserai
7 Abdul Aziz Khan Madrassah
8 Nadir Divan Begi Khanaka
9 Labi Hauz
10 Divan Begi Madrassah

## The Ark and Registan
Although the buildings you see today are either recently restored or date back only to the 16th century, there has been a large fortress here ever since the 1st century. The West Gate was originally one of many entrances but only this one, leading to the main square, or Registan, has been restored.

The **Ark** (entrance 2000sum) was the fortified residence of the emir. Hanging above the archway until 1920 was a huge six-tailed leather whip signifying justice. Emir Nasrullah commissioned a great clock to be mounted there too. Italian watchmaker Giovanni Orlando built it, only to be promptly executed over some triviality. The whip is in the museum inside the fortress but the clock has disappeared. As you walk through the entrance note the prison cells on the left, strategically situated under the stables so that when the yard was washed down all the effluent would flow into them.

The Ark was more than just a home for the emir though: it was also his barracks, mint, place of worship (there is a mosque inside) and prison. About 3000 people lived inside its walls. Each building has now been converted into a museum and although there is no English labelling it's fairly easy to work out what's what (the guides who offer you their services are unnecessary). There is an especially valuable 10th-century Koran in the Friday Mosque. If you wander up directly above the West Gate you can see the spot where the emir would sit to watch floggings and executions in the **Registan** below – this is the square where Stoddart and Connolly were beheaded 150 years ago. Their remains are probably still buried somewhere here. The best views are from the parapets and a perfect time to go is in the evening when it is cooler and quieter. You can climb onto the back wall and sit on the ramparts for tremendous panoramas across the whole city. Be careful though, for the guards don't like you doing it and if you get caught you'll be severely shouted at, at best.

The Ark is open all day every day but the museums open from 09.00 to 17.00 and are closed on Wednesday.

**Bollo Hauz Mosque** When the emir went to worship in this Mosque (built in 1712) opposite the Registan, the whole square was carpeted. The small minaret here has been leaning since an earthquake in 1976. The pond *(hauz)* is one of only two remaining in Bukhara today (there used to be more than 80).

## Zindan
The most sinister relic of the days before Russian rule lies at the north-eastern corner of the Ark. Zindan, meaning 'Alive' in Tajik, was the city jail. Inside are three cells, two of which were for debtors who were compelled to work for the jailers in order to redeem their debts. They were not fed, relying entirely on the charity of friends and relatives. The third cell, for more serious offenders, is simply a hole in the ground known as the 'Bug Pit' because the guards used to sweep vermin and insects on top of the prisoners. (One recent commentary suggests that tarantulas, specially bred for their size and venomous bite, were released into the pit but this seems unlikely.) This is the cell where Charles Stoddart spent six months of his life, later to be joined by Arthur Connolly for a final three months before they were both beheaded. Entrance is 1000sum.

## Samanid Mausoleum

Further west from Bollo Hauz is **Samani Park** which leads to what's left of the Old City walls. In the middle of the park is the Samanid Mausoleum. This is generally considered to be one of the greatest pieces of Central Asian architecture. Built on the orders of Ismail Samani (who reigned 892-907) for his father, it ended up as the family vault. It is one of the oldest surviving buildings in Bukhara thanks to the fact that Genghis Khan didn't find it (it was either buried or concealed by trees, depending on whom you believe).

Despite all the superlatives it is small and deceptively simple but these are not necessarily negative attributes in a city whose other buildings are huge, flamboyant creations. The two squares above each doorway are supposedly aerial plans of the building. Note also the **crypt** inside with a hole at each end: after it was discovered in the 1920s, resident mullahs spread it around that the mausoleum was an oracle. Locals placed their question, wrapped in a wad of banknotes, in one hole, and picked up the oracle's 'advice' from the other the next day. A large **ferris wheel** also stands in the middle of the park and offers great views of the various minarets and mosques.

## Chashma Ayub

Very close to the mausoleum is Chashma Ayub, an ancient spring created, according to local legend, by the Biblical character, Job, during a drought. The building housing it has been remodelled a number of times over the years, notably in the twelfth, fourteenth and sixteenth centuries, resulting in a mishmash of architectural styles (the 12th-century conical cupola is considered particularly unusual). The spring has long been supposed to be curative and analysis shows that its water is potassium-rich.

## Kaylon Minaret

Probably the most impressive sight in Bukhara, the **Kaylon Minaret**, built in 1127, is 46.5m high; in 1220 Genghis Khan was so impressed that he left it standing. The second tallest minaret in Central Asia, its foundations go down 13m; it's said that its strength comes from special mortar in which blood and camel's milk were used instead of water. Note the intricate bands of decorative brickwork, 14 in all. It has had a number of uses, including the calling of the righteous to prayer (pity the poor muezzin who had to climb the 105 steps five times every day), a lighthouse, and a launching pad for criminals tied up in sacks. It was this final usage which led to its nickname 'The Tower of Death' (the last execution here was in 1884). It costs 3000sum for a trip to the top.

The minaret is flanked by the **Kaylon Mosque** to the west and the **Mir I Arab Madrassah** to the east. The mosque was completed in 1514 and covers exactly one hectare. It can easily accommodate more than 10,000 people, making it the second largest in Central Asia – after the Bibi Khanum in Samarkand.

The madrassah, meanwhile, is one of the few in Bukhara still in use. It was built by Ubaidullah Khan with the money he received from the sale of 3000 Persian slaves. The name Mir I Arab means 'Prince of Arabs', the soubriquet of Abdullah, Sheikh of Yemen, who lies buried here.

> **Bride before a fall**
> Local legend has it that the only person ever to have survived a 'fall' from the Kaylon minaret was a young woman who had recently married a wealthy businessman. Just before the executioner was to push her from the top, she asked, as a last request, that she be allowed to wear the dress that her husband had bought her for her wedding day. Not knowing which outfit to bring, the servant sent to her house brought the whole wardrobe – 40 dresses in all. Calmly she put on all 40, one on top of the other, and then allowed herself to be thrown from the top.
>
> The padding cushioned her fall and she survived, whereupon the emir was so impressed he spared her life. It is now a Bukharan tradition that every man must give his bride 40 dresses as a wedding present – just in case.

The square beneath the minaret is usually home to a merry band of children selling hats and other knick-knacks and while these might not take your fancy, they may also offer to take you home for lunch in their parents' house, for a small consideration, which can be fascinating. The parents are used to the practice and will happily welcome you into their home. It's a real chance to see behind the mud walls and take a look at ordinary Uzbek life. The house we entered, like most Uzbek houses, was made up of a courtyard centring on one large room with carpets on the walls and cushions on the floor. This is where they eat, live and sleep, with the cooking done on an open fire in the courtyard.

Perhaps the most telling observation was the mother's: she couldn't understand her previous Western guests' obsession for diving in for the meat on top of the plov first, explaining that Uzbeks always start from the outside of the plate and work their way in, saving the best for last. Finally, pay your 'tip' to the child after you've left the house: to give it straight to the mother will be taken as an offence.

### Ulugh Beg and Abdul Aziz Khan madrassahs

**Ulugh Beg's Madrassah**, completed in 1417, is a magnificent example of the kind of architecture Central Asia has to offer. Yet one wonders why Ulugh Beg should have built a madrassah here in Bukhara before he built one in Samarkand, since that was where he lived. It is also famous for its inscription, 'The desire for sciences is the duty of both men and women' – a statement which caused great offence to the misogynistic mullahs of the time.

The **Abdul Aziz Khan Madrassah** opposite is a copy made 250 years later (1652) but never finished; note the beams still protruding from the walls. This building reveals the architect's poor sense of balance and proportion and his attempted rejection of the Islamic prohibition of animate images.

If you can get inside, look for the man-made optical illusion to the right of the entrance: in the right light, the silhouette of a man is clearly visible but this fades away as the light changes.

Just to the south of these two, you can still see the remains of a Hindu traders' **Caravanserai** (see box p98), proof not just of the importance of the Silk Road to the city but how widely traders and their religions travelled across Central Asia.

## Labi Hauz and surroundings

Bukhara's water supply originally consisted of a series of tanks scattered around the city. Since the water in these was used for washing, laundry, horse-watering and drinking, it all became a bit of a health risk, so the Bolsheviks drained them. It is still possible to find some of the empty pools around the town but the Labi Hauz, right in the centre, has been maintained, minus the pollutants. It was commissioned by Nadir Divan Begi in 1620, is five metres deep and is surrounded by ancient mulberry trees (planted in 1475). It provides a lovely shady haven; there is no better place in Central Asia to drink tea/beer, contemplate life, or just sit.

Helping to create the mellow atmosphere are three major buildings flanking the *hauz*. The most colourful of these is **Divan Begi Madrassah**, to the east, with its remarkable portal: the mosaic covering the arch, featuring two large birds beneath a sun, consists of over 11 million ceramic tiles. This madrassah was originally intended to be a caravanserai. Shortly before it was finished, however, Khan Imamkuli rode by and commented that it was a beautiful madrassah. Not wishing to imply the khan had been mistaken, Divan Begi altered the building's function accordingly.

Directly opposite the madrassah on the western side of the hauz is the **Nadir Divan Begi Khanaka** (1620), which was designed as an inn for Muslim dervishes. It is now an arts and crafts gallery and gift shop. On the north side is the **Kukeldash Madrassah** (1568-9), once the key religious school in Bukhara and the largest in Central Asia. With the arrival of the Russians it was closed down and now houses the city's archives.

The old **bathhouses** dotted around Bukhara have mostly been converted into mini bazaars, although a couple seem to be ticking along (the one on Juba St is said to be the best).

## Magoki Attari Mosque

Of all the mosques in Bukhara, this is probably the most intriguing because its origins are shrouded in mystery. It was renovated in the 12th century, although the main façade is 10th-century work. The reason that it sits so low in the ground is not that it was built underground but rather that, over the years, the dust has accumulated around it: Bukhara is slowly being buried.

Nobody really knows much about this mosque; archaeologists have found evidence of previous worship beneath the building and some reports state that this area was already considered sacred by the Sogdians as early as 500BC. This is possible but difficult to prove. Remains have also been found of Buddhism and Zoroastrianism. Go into the main entrance and turn 180 degrees sharp right or left to see the extent of the excavations.

## Chor Minor

This building, constructed in 1807 as the entrance of a madrassah, is particularly worth a visit if only because of its originality. An old proverb relates that he who manages to climb the steps of the building and then make it back down without being bitten by the snakes inside is 'sinless'. In fact, the chances

> **Nasreddin**
> The statue at the eastern end of Labi Hauz represents the Islamic comic hero, Hoca Nasreddin. One of the many stories surrounding him tells of his solving of a local dispute: one afternoon, three men were standing underneath the Kaylon Minaret arguing heatedly. They could not agree on how it had been constructed; the first thought it had been built upwards with bricks, rather like a house. The second thought that this was impossible: obviously it had been carved downwards out of a huge chunk of stone. The third, meanwhile, disagreed again: the only way to create something of this magnitude was to assemble it on the ground and haul it upright to its present position.
>   Nasreddin happened to be listening from behind the minaret. 'Gentlemen, you are all wrong' he said emerging with a grin. 'It took only two very simple steps. First they dug a huge well and then they simply turned it inside out'.

of actually meeting a snake inside are remote. It's very photogenic and for some reason pictures always seem to make it look much bigger than it is.

## Around Bukhara

**Emir's Palace (Sitori Makhi Khosa)** Opinions vary: local people tend to rave about this as the most beautiful building in Bukhara, while visitors generally consider it as little more than an exercise in kitsch. Built at the turn of the 20th century, it reflects the emirs' attempts to keep up to date with modern European styles. It is now a museum and guides here show you the pool and tell you that the last khan (Said Ah, exiled to Afghanistan in 1920) would sit in the small pavilion (still here) watching his harem frolic in the water. This is unlikely since the pool is within full view of common land and if there was any frollicking to be done it would have been done out of sight. The palace is open 09.00-16.30 daily and is 3km out of town.

**Chor Bakr** A 20-minute drive from Bukhara, this necropolis is not really on the tourist map but it should be. It's the resting place of Abu Bakr Said, a 'descendant' of Mohammed, and has become something of a pilgrimage destination. 'Chor' means beauty or purity, while 'Bakr' is the name of one of the wealthy families whose burial vaults lie here. With the arrival of the communists, however, the families left and have never returned, apart from one clan who carried out a secret burial here one night in 1921.

You will find the tomb of Al Bakr Said if you look carefully; the tree beside it is decked with ribbons and faded pieces of string indicating supplications to the 'saint'. Orthodox mullahs look upon this with disdain.

The mosque here has been under restoration since 1987 but it looks as if they left it too late: there are massive cracks down one side. The site is fairly overgrown and there are snakes here, so watch out.

To get here you will need to take a taxi; get the driver to wait for you, otherwise you'll be stuck. The best time to go is in the early morning or evening, when the ruins look particularly romantic.

## PRACTICAL INFORMATION
### Orientation and services
(☎ code 065)

From the **railway station** (*Kagan*), virtually all minibuses will take you to the town centre (US$0.50; 10-20 mins). From the **bus station,** there is little option but to take a taxi to the old town's Labi Hauz, which lies within walking distance of most things you'll want to see. Old Bukhara is small and easily taken in on foot. New Bukhara is about a kilometre to the south but unless you need to visit the bank (see below) you won't venture that far.

The **tourist office** opposite Labi Hauz is helpful but overworked. They can arrange **homestays** and also **guides** (US$5 a day). If you're staying at Labi Hauz B&B, ask Mubinjan to put you in touch with Zinnat Ashurova, who has been recommended by several readers.

There is an **Internet café** in the main square to the east of Labi Hauz.

The **National Bank for Foreign Economic Activities** changes money and gives cash advances on credit cards (for 5 per cent commission). If you just need to change money (cash) you can do this in any hotel.

### Where to stay
Bukhara has probably the best selection of accommodation in Central Asia and new places are springing up all the time. For the cheapest **homestays** (US$5/pp) go to the tourist office and be directed from there. The best hotel and hostel options are to be found in the old town. Base yourself at Labi Hauz and scout around for the best deal.

*Mubinjan's Guesthouse* (☎ 224 2005; US$10/pp in the off-season including breakfast), 4 Ishoni Pir St, is a traditional Uzbek merchant's house and the rooms, arranged around a shady courtyard, are wonderful; the only drawback is the flies. *Nutfullo's* (☎ 244 5151; US$25/Db) is away from the centre on Vavilova St but it has a beautiful small courtyard; they will usually drop you off free of charge at the bus station, and overall is a good option in peak season. *Labi Hauz B&B* (☎ 224 8424; 🖳 www.lyabi-house.com; US$40/Db), at Husainov 7, and *Sasha & Son's* (☎ 224 4966; US$50/Db), at Eshoni Pir 3, are beautifully restored but increasingly expensive.

*Hotel Zaragon* (☎ 224 5821; 🖳 zaragon@mail.ru; US$50/Db) at 3-4 Haqiqat St is the pick of all the hotels in the city; the rooms are modern and well appointed, while the roof bar/restaurant terrace has the best view in town. *Hotel Caravan* (☎ 224 6144; US$50/Db) is only slightly less impressive.

### Where to eat
Wherever you are staying, a variety of meals will be offered and these are usually pretty good. Otherwise, most people settle for one of the **cafés** around Labi Hauz or the main square a bit further east, which can be very enjoyable. Bukhara is pretty quiet at night and most places shut fairly early. There is a **supermarket** in the main square.

For cheaper food try the **market** (near Samanid Mausoleum) where you can gorge yourself on anything from pistachio nuts to whole fried chickens.

### What to buy
Bukhara is famous for its rugs but you won't find many bargains here today. There are other local crafts, though: inside old madrassahs you may find arts and crafts stores where you can watch the craftsmen at work. Particular favourites are brass or copper plates and wooden boxes; some of the embroidery is very fine, too. Try the Nadir Divan Begi Khanaka for a browse. Be extremely careful when buying 'antiques'.

There is a good quality jewellery and souvenir shop in the Hindu caravanserai but it's fairly expensive.

### Moving on
If you can't find a 'camel' (see box opposite), the overnight train to **Tashkent** (12hrs/US$10) is a pleasant alternative to the bus but not very practical for Samarkand as that city is only seven hours away. Buses to **Samarkand** (4-6hrs/US$3) leave from the bus station, as do buses to **Urgench** (9hrs). Share-taxis wait outside the bus station. If heading to **Turkmenistan**, see box p197.

# Samarkand

Of all Central Asian cities, Samarkand is the one which most fires the imagination. Alexander the Great was moved by its beauty, Marco Polo lavished it with praise and Tamerlane made it the capital of his empire. European poets dreamed of it and for the West it became a symbol of all that was forbidden and mysterious about the East. Things have changed, however, and much has not survived. Nevertheless, what is left is astonishing both in scale and intricacy. Two or three days are needed here to see all the main sights.

## HISTORY

Samarkand officially celebrated its 2500th birthday in 1970 though it is probably much older than this. Reliable evidence is scarce but archaeologists have unearthed traces of a large human settlement dating before the 6th century BC.

> ❑ **The Golden Road**
> 'Sweet to ride forth at evening from the wells
> when shadows pass gigantic on the sand,
> And softly through the silence beat the bells
> Along the Golden Road to Samarkand.'
> *The Golden Journey to Samarkand*
>
> James Elroy Flecker's poem evokes much of the romanticism associated with the next leg of your journey.
> If ever there was a time to hire a 'ship of the desert' and attempt to emulate past travellers, this must be it (ask the tourist office for help).

The Greek historian, Strabo, writes of this city as Marakanda, the capital of Sogdiana and records the arrival of Alexander the Great in 329/8BC (who commented that it was 'even more beautiful' than he had imagined).

It was here, in a famous drunken brawl, that Alexander killed Cleitus, one of his own generals, with a spear. Plagued with guilt afterwards, he was reconciled to this act only by his friends' insistence that his drunken outburst was punishment from Dionysius (the God of Wine) for not having made the correct sacrifices earlier.

### Ten centuries of invasions

Alexander's empire crumbled shortly after his death and in the following centuries Samarkand was invaded by the Seleucids, the Graeco-Bactrians, the Kushans and the Turks.

The Arabs brought Islam with them in the 8th century and as their empire fragmented in the 9th century, the Samanids became rulers of the first independent Islamic state in Central Asia. Their most famous son has to be Mohammed Ibn Musa al Khorezmi (see p160). Power struggles and invasions continued until the arrival of Genghis Khan in March 1220. He wrecked the city so comprehensively that the original site, now Afrosiab, was abandoned altogether and the whole town was shifted to a patch of wasteland immediately to the south. Sources indicate that over 300,000 of the 400,000 inhabitants were killed or forced to flee. The city recovered quickly, though: by the time Marco Polo arrived 50 years later, he noted that Samarkand, on its new site, was 'very large and splendid'.

## Tamerlane

It was to become even bigger, however, under its greatest ruler, Tamerlane. Born in nearby Shakrisabz (in 1336), Tamerlane decided that Samarkand was to be the heart of his empire, the 'centre of the universe'. Artists and architects were recruited from all over Asia to develop it and they didn't mess around, building magnificent mosques, madrassahs and palaces, each covered in the fabulous turquoise blue tiles that stick in our mind today. Inside these buildings were some of the finest schools and workshops on the planet, attracting a second tier of finery which combined to truly create a 'Mirror of the World', 'Garden of the Blessed' or 'Fourth Paradise', as Samarkand has variously been called over the centuries. It shouldn't be forgotten that Tamerlane is estimated to have been responsible for 17 million deaths; but for Samarkand his rule meant untold riches as it became the capital of an empire that stretched between Russia in the north, the Mediterranean in the west, the Persian Gulf in the south and Delhi in the east.

Tamerlane's grandson, Ulugh Beg, a noted intellectual, maintained the artistic traditions even if he shunned military glory. He matched Tamerlane's achievements in the arts and added cutting-edge developments of the sciences: Omar Khayam (author of *The Rubajyat),* Al-Biruni (who suggested that the Earth might revolve around its own axis) and Avicenna (see p160) all lived here as Samarkand reached its zenith.

By the 16th century the ruling Sheibanids had moved their capital to Bukhara, leaving Samarkand in decline until 1868 when the Russians arrived. On 15 May, 1888, the first train pulled in, shunting it back onto the map. Restoration of monuments began under Lenin in 1921 and the city was declared capital of the Uzbek Socialist Republic in 1925, only to be replaced by Tashkent in 1930.

## Samarkand today

You can't fail to notice the Russian influence. From being a relatively backward Islamic city in the last century, Samarkand has come a long way. According to the official figures, the surrounding region currently produces 500,000 tonnes of cotton per year, which is more than the entire state of Uzbekistan produced before 1917 (though such figures may be suspect: Uzbekistan is notorious for its fraudulent crop statistics). The downside of this Russian input, however, is that main roads now converge on Registan Square, one of the greatest Islamic architectural ensembles in the world, and the traffic can be noisy.

Restoration never seems to stop on one building or another, however, and the city centre has been recognized as a World Heritage Site.

## WHAT TO SEE

### Registan Square

This square constitutes the heart of the city. The Registan (literally 'Sandy Place') seems always to have been busy; originally it was the bazaar with a caravanserai (see box p98) on the northern side. Skirting the square today are three madrassahs and a mosque, and the effect of this combination is sublime: the 'noblest public square in the world' according to Lord Curzon.

The earliest of the three buildings is the **Ulugh Beg Madrassah** to the west (left as you face the central building). It is widely acknowledged to be the best of the three. Built at the command of this great ruler between 1417 and 1420, it housed up to 200 students studying sciences, mathematics, astronomy, law, languages and theology. Ulugh Beg himself taught here. The fact that it has been restored is most easily seen by looking at the minarets, which were leaning precariously until fairly recently. Soviet engineers were called in and in 1938 the right-hand minaret was rotated through 180 degrees (no mean feat considering its size). The left-hand minaret was straightened in 1965. To see the curve, look along the right-hand wall.

The minarets are not purely decorative but have steps leading up their insides. Although not officially permitted, if you come early and slip some money to one of the guards (1500sum) he will show you the way up. Inside the madrassah there's a small art gallery and a bronze statue of Ulugh Beg and his courtiers around an Astroglobe.

Directly opposite Ulugh Beg is the **Shir Dor Madrassah**. Built at the order of 'Little Timur', Amir Yalangtush Bahadir, between 1619 and 1636, this was meant to be the mirror image of the Ulugh Beg Madrassah. Clearly it is not identical but apparently if you were to tip the fronts of the two madrassahs towards each other they would exactly touch along the centreline of the Registan. Shir Dor means 'Lion-bearing'; the lions (they look more like tigers) above the entrance represent the rising sun, thus exempting themselves from the Islamic prohibition of animal images. Inside is a musical instrument museum, entry to which is free.

Between the two are the **Tillya Kari Mosque and Madrassah**. 'Tillya Kari' means 'Decorated with Gold' and the buildings date from 1646 to 1660. The inside of the mosque was restored in 1979 and is now so blue and gold it is breathtaking. Patches of water are already rising up the walls, however, fading the colours as they go. In the room next to the dome is a tiny museum with photographs of how the town used to look pre-1940s. These give you a good impression of the city before the recent restoration.

Entry to the Registan costs 2500sum; this gives you access to all four buildings. Its opening hours change with the season but it is always open during daylight. Note that access to the buildings has been steadily restricted over the years so you will need to come early (around dawn) if you want to bribe your way up one of the minarets.

Outside the Registan you can see a bronze statue in memory of the traders and camels of the Silk Road and it's nice to feel part of it – though if you have come from China you might be sick of these by now.

218 Uzbekistan – Samarkand

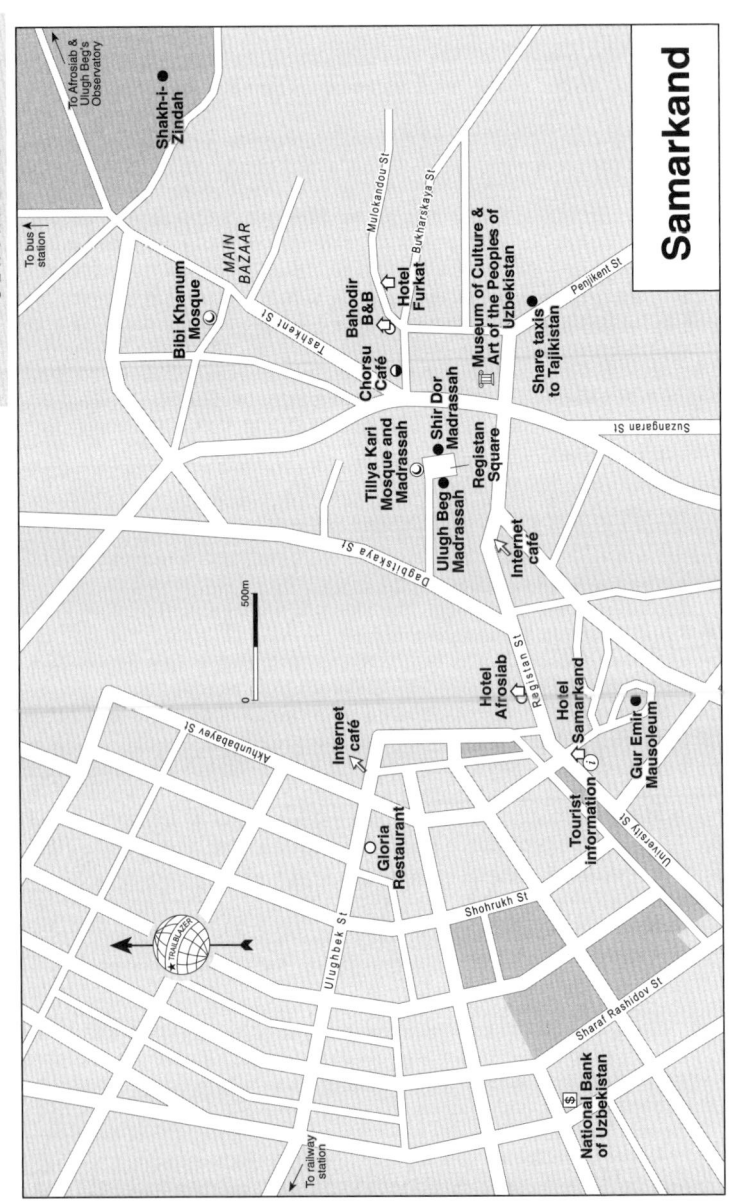

## Museum of Culture and Art of the Peoples of Uzbekistan

The contents of this museum do not live up to its grand name. It's so close to the Registan, however, that it's worth a look – and there are toilets here if you need them. When we visited, we had the whole place to ourselves, apart from the curators who were busy trying to sell us the exhibits. It is open daily (except Wednesday) from 09.00 to 17.00. Entry is US$2.

## Shakh-i-Zindah

This necropolis is in its original condition (Genghis Khan's troops refused to touch it) and one of Samarkand's highlights. Legend has it that Qutham ibn Abbas, either the cousin or the nephew of the Prophet Mohammed, was beheaded here by infidels. Instead of dying, he picked up his severed head and disappeared into the depths of a well, where he still lives today. Since then aristocrats have clamoured to be buried near the grave of this 'saint', resulting in a narrow alley of highly decorated mausoleums nicknamed 'City of the Dead'.

Abbas's tomb is at the top end on the right and although excavations revealed that there is actually no body here, the gravestone (which can be seen through a lattice grille) is the original, listing his death as occurring in 676/7. The inscription above the door reads, 'The gates of Paradise are open wide for the believer'. Modern legend says that he still makes the odd appearance and there are further rumours telling of a city of catacombs beneath the site.

Most other tombs date to within a century or so of Tamerlane's time. The second mausoleum on the left (that of Tamerlane's niece who died in 1372) is regarded as the best. Keep an eye out for the architects' signatures on the portals of the tombs. Remember that this spot is considered sacred by many (you are likely to see people praying in Abbas's tomb) so dress and act appropriately. Entry is 2000sum and it's open daily 08.00-18.00.

## Gur Emir Mausoleum

This is the mausoleum of many of the key members of the Timurid line including the Big Man himself and, despite its mediocre size, it is breathtaking. Originally built for a favourite grandson, Mohammed Sultan, Tamerlane was laid here because he died unexpectedly in 1405, before his real tomb in Shakrisabz (see box p221) was completed. He lies at the foot of his spiritual guide, Sheikh Mirs aid Bereke, with his grandson Ulugh Beg beside him. The entrance is marked by a long pole sticking out of a tomb opposite. While digging the mausoleum's foundations, workmen found human remains. Not willing either to find a new site or to desecrate the grave they reburied the individual as a holy man in the crypt of the king.

The tombs were opened in 1941 and it was confirmed that Tamerlane was lame (and that he had had tuberculosis) and that Ulugh Beg had been murdered (beheaded by his own son). A time capsule was included when the tombs were closed once more. The jade stone over Tamerlane's grave was originally one slab, brought back from Mongolia by Ulugh Beg, but it was stolen by Persian invaders under Nadir Shah. They took it to Mashad, only to return it, in two pieces, because it had brought them bad luck. Numerous modern myths surround the unsealing of Tamerlane's tomb. An inscription was said to have been found warning that the opening of the crypt would release the spirit of war. Germany marched on Russia the day after the opening. It is sometimes possible to get into the crypt beneath the building (this costs 2000sum; wait to be approached by the vault keeper). Descending into the crypt is similar to entering the pyramids in Egypt – although obviously on a smaller scale.

There is a large slab of carved marble in the courtyard outside the mausoleum which is supposed to be the Kok Tash, the stone upon which Tamerlane's throne sat. This is unlikely but it has certainly been used for coronations since. The large stone bowl beside it was part of Tamerlane's pre-battle ritual: he would have it filled with pomegranate juice (dark red) and then his army would file past, each man taking a swig of the 'blood' of the enemy.

### Bibi Khanum Mosque
Designed to accommodate over 10,000 people, this mosque was to have been Tamerlane's *pièce de résistance*. Unfortunately, it started to collapse as quickly as it was built; some say it was just too big, others too hurriedly built; others blame seismic activity. Whatever the cause, shortly after it was finished in 1404 cracks started appearing.

The huge stone lectern you see in the courtyard was placed in the mosque by Ulugh Beg but was moved outside in 1855 when it became clear that the building was no longer safe. It collapsed in an earthquake in 1887. Restoration started in 1974 but has only recently been completed. The main gate is the focus of this restoration and it is worth a closer look. It was designed to face the prevailing wind in an attempt to keep the courtyard cool and if you stand underneath the portals you realize just how successful the plan was, sucking in any breeze that is about.

Legend has it that the head architect working on the mosque fell in love with Tamerlane's wife, Bibi Khanum (hence the name). He beseeched her for a kiss but that fabled kiss left a permanent scar on her lips. Tamerlane was not at all happy when he discovered this and called for the executioner, whereupon the architect promptly climbed to the top of a minaret, sprouted wings, and flew home to Persia! Open daily; entrance is 2000sum.

### Around Samarkand
To see these sights, hire a taxi. It won't take much more than a couple of hours and you can hire a cab from outside Chorsu Café (it should cost 2000sum for the round trip).

**Ulugh Beg's Observatory** As well as being Tamerlane's grandson and ruler of Samarkand, Ulugh Beg was one of the greatest intellectuals of his time. Although a noted theologian, mathematician and poet, his real passion was for astronomy. In the 14th century he compiled the first star atlas since the Greek astronomer, Hipparchus, and managed to include over a thousand stars, a massive improvement on his predecessor. Unfortunately, his great passion for science was out of kilter with the religious authorities of the day and, in league with his son, they organized a coup: Ulugh Beg was beheaded and his observatory torn down by a mob of dervishes. Legend holds that his extensive library was saved and lies hidden to this day but all we know for sure is that the star chart survived and made its way to Istanbul, where it became the basis for all navigational charts in the 17th century. The remains of his observatory lie a couple of kilometres north of the bazaar.

The observatory was a circular three-storey building containing a sextant which stood 55 metres high. In 1437, using this unique instrument, he compiled his atlas and calculated the length of a year to within one minute of what we now know it to be. All that remains of the observatory is an 11-metre sextant arc underground (which was discovered by a Russian archaeologist in 1908) and the running track for the instrument around the circle but these are enough to give you an idea of the size of the thing. There is a small Ulugh Beg museum here, too (2000sum; open 09.00-18.00).

**Afrosiab** This is the site of Maracanda, ancient Samarkand, where Alexander stopped to camp. Although there isn't that much to see, it's fun walking around a place that could double as a Star Wars set. The **Afrosiab Museum** (US$2) here is poor on the whole but the fresco inside the lower hall is marvellous and well preserved by a humidifier. On the other side of the hill is **Daniel's Tomb** (US$1). This is the tomb of the Old Testament prophet Daniel (Tamerlane brought his body here) and a myth says that each year the body grows half an inch so the sarcophagus has to be regularly extended – it certainly is surprisingly long.

### Excursion to Shakrisabz

This small town, the birthplace of Tamerlane, is well worth a day trip although the sites are mostly in ruins. It is a quiet, pleasant place and the two-hour ride through the mountains makes the journey worthwhile.

To the south of the town is the **Kok Gumbaz Mosque** (built in 1435-6 by Ulugh Beg in honour of his father, Shah Rukh). A small entry fee is charged to see the remains of the blue dome but the place is rather decrepit. Not far from here is the **Mausoleum of Jehangir** (Tamerlane's eldest and favourite son, who died aged 22) and behind this is the site of **Tamerlane's Tomb** (in the end, of course, this was never used as he was buried in Samarkand): look for the small, sunken, whitewashed building with the green door. It is unlikely to be open unless you are in a tour group. All that remains of Tamerlane's **Ak Sarai Palace** is the huge skeleton of an arched doorway, but this is excellent for those arty 'crumbling relic' photos.

Shakrisabz is famous for its embroidery and if you know what you are looking for you may be able to pick up something really valuable in the **bazaar** here. If you don't, be careful. Try the wonderful black figs, but caution is advised since too many can lead to a nasty stomach upset.

You will have trouble getting a bus here, although share-taxis (US$2) leave from Penjikent Kuchasi. Many find it easier to take a taxi and book it for the day, or join one of the day trips run by the travel agencies in Samarkand (US$35/pp).

## PRACTICAL INFORMATION
[☎ code 03662]

### Orientation and services
Basically: for the old town, head east, for the new, west. Samarkand is not a difficult city to find your way around. Most hotels and sights are within walking distance of the centre of town, Registan Square.

The **Uzbektourism Office** is at Hotel Samarkand and offers the usual array of sightseeing tours. Your hotel/hostel can put you in touch with others.

The **bus station** is quite a way to the north of the city and a taxi into town costs 350-400sum. There are various cheap **Internet cafés** near the Registan.

The main branch of the **National Bank of Uzbekistan** has been known to swap old dollar bills for new (for no charge) and give dollar advances on credit cards.

### Where to stay
Beware that electricity and water can cut out at any time, even in some of the better establishments. *Bahodir B&B* (☎ 358 529; ✉ b&bahodir@yahoo.com; US$18/Db, US$8/dorm) at 132 Mulokandov St has become the undisputed budget favourite. Nearby at No 105, *Hotel Furkat* (☎ 353 261; US$30/Db) has a good central position, a nice courtyard for breakfast, clean (if small) rooms and an annex down the street if it gets full. *Hotel Samarkand* (☎ 358 812; US$25/Db), the Uzbektourist hotel at 1 University, is another mid-range option but is a bit shabby. At Registan 2, *Hotel Afrosiab* (☎ 231 2080; US$150/Db) has a swimming pool.

### Where to eat
Considering how many tourists come to Samarkand, the city is distinctly short on bars and restaurants. The most upmarket food is at the *Afrosiab*. Otherwise, try *Gloria Restaurant* (Ulughbek 5), which is pretty good although the menu is all in Russian and little English is spoken.

*Chorsu Café*, on the corner near Bahodir B&B, has been renovated and has lost some of its character but is still good for *chai*, kebabs and shashlik (even the bread is freshly baked and specially decorated in intricate patterns). *Bahodir B&B* does an unbeatable communal dinner for US$1.

### Moving on
Buses and share-taxis depart from the bus station every hour to **Tashkent** (4hrs/US$2); departures to **Bukhara** (5hrs/US$2.50) are every other hour. Two buses a day go to **Urgench** (15hrs/US$4.50). The trains out of Samarkand are not worth taking as they are too slow. The city is only 42km away from **Tajikistan** (see p176) and historically it has always been linked to that culture. If you are thinking of visiting **Penjikent**, share-taxis leave from Penjikent Kuchasi, 500m to the east of the Registan.

# Tashkent

With its wide boulevards and tree-lined streets, Tashkent can give the impression of being a quiet, provincial European town of 50 years ago but its people, Soviet-style monolithic buildings and fleets of Ladas soon remind you that you are definitely somewhere a bit more unfamiliar. Old women sit out with sets of scales, which other old women use to excitedly weigh themselves, while young girls sing to karaoke machines in the street, unperturbed by the lack of an audience. It's also hard to convince yourself that the streets weren't designed to accommodate a convoy of Russian tanks if ever the need arose.

You will probably want to spend only a couple of days here to recharge your batteries and stock up on supplies but if you want a longer break or are forced to take one while awaiting visas there are some good treks and other outdoor activities in the hills outside Tashkent, especially in Chimgan (see the local travel agencies, p226). If you are heading east, it might be an idea to call ahead to Bishkek in order to set the ball rolling for the crossing into China (see p242).

## HISTORY

Tashkent is in fact a fairly ancient city, dating back at least to the 2nd or 3rd century BC. Over the years it has been known by a number of names, including Dzhadzh, Chachkent, Shashkent and Binkent, its fortune coming mainly from traders passing through on the Silk Road.

The origins of the settlement are, like that of other Uzbek towns, difficult to trace since there have been numerous invasions and annexations. What we can say is that, like the others, it was taken by the Arabs in the 8th century; that they brought Islam and a largely civilized outlook with them; that the Mongols arrived in 1220 (it is also fairly safe to assume that they left very little standing); that they were succeeded by the Timurids, who were followed by the Sheibanids, and that Tashkent was ruled independently by either Uzbeks or Kazakhs until it was absorbed into the Khanate of Kokand in 1815.

### The Soviet era

The Russians arrived in 1865 and Tashkent was earmarked for great things: in 1867 it was made capital of Turkestan and with the arrival of the Trans-Caspian railway on 1 May, 1899 it became the administrative centre of Uzbekistan (except for the brief period between 1925 and 1930 when Samarkand was the capital). During the Great Patriotic War it served as host for thousands of refugees, among them such Soviet luminaries as Ivanov and Pogodin.

Although the city grew fast throughout the 20th century, its only moment of real fame occurred in the winter of 1965, when, through the mediation of Soviet Premier Alexei Kosygin, the Pakistani and Indian prime ministers Lal Bahadir Shastri and Mohammed Ayub Khan signed a treaty here, ending their 17-day war over Kashmir. Shortly after this, on 26 April 1966, an earthquake ripped the city in two, leaving over 300,000 people homeless. A whole new city had to be built which is why, today, there is such an air of modernity and order while little of any real antiquity remains.

### Tashkent today

Tashkent is still very much at the heart of Uzbekistan and rightly so; it was the fourth largest city after Moscow, Leningrad and Kiev in the USSR. It is a big, sprawling Westernized urbanization with very little feel to it and a population of over two-and-a-half million. Nevertheless, while it is developing fast (the first metro lines were completed in 1977), the underdeveloped areas have remained poor so the Old Town is increasingly cramped and squalid. When you wander through the green parks and fountains, admiring their sophistication, just remember about the demise of the Aral Sea (see box p178).

## WHAT TO SEE

### Old Tashkent
Definitely not the place to visit if you're planning on doing anything else that day, the Old Town is Tashkent the way it used to be before the Russians arrived; ie, a maze. The streets are cramped and dirty but it's full of character. Go early in the morning so that you have plenty of time to take everything in – take the metro to Chorsu and walk.

One item worthy of note is the 7th-century Koran (reputedly the world's oldest) in the Khast Imom Mosque on Zarkainar St; everyone knows where this street is though they'll all disagree on how to get there. Entry is free, although someone might try to charge you (a new museum is being built to house the book).

### Amir Timur Square
There isn't much to see here but it's pleasant enough to wander among the food stalls and sit in the garden around the statue of Uzbekistan's national figurehead. This park used to be called Revolution Garden and a statue of Marx had pride of place. Now the huge statue of Tamerlane dominates the place, with 'Strength in Justice' inscribed on the plinth.

### The Courage Monument
This monument on Sharaf Rashidov Prospekti commemorates the courage of Tashkent's citizens following the earthquake that devastated the city in 1966. An impressive statue stands alongside a block of stone that was supposedly shattered by the earthquake; the monument itself stands at what is believed to have been the epicentre.

### Museums
Tashkent's museums are generally of a high standard. The **State Museum of the History of Uzbekistan** is housed in an impressive new building on Matbuotchilar St, directly opposite Mustakillik (Independence) Square. It is open daily (except Monday) 10.00-18.00 (US$2).

The **Fine Arts Museum** (open daily 10.00-17.00, except Tuesday; entry US$0.90) at 16 Movarounnakhr St has exhibits drawn from, among other places, a collection formerly owned by a member of the Romanov family.

The small **Railway Museum** (US$0.10; open Wednesday to Sunday 09.00-17.00) next to the main train station (Sevirny Vokzal) has locomotives from Russia, Czechoslovakia, USA, Germany and Hungary.

**Navoi Literary Museum** (open daily 10.00 to 17.00; US$1) on Navoi Prospekti, just after the intersection with Pakhtakor, contains manuscripts, paintings and numerous books by the man himself but since this 15th-century Afghan writer is virtually unknown in the West and labelling is in Cyrillic, this museum might be a bit boring for some. Navoi's main work, *Mahakamat-al-Lugatayn (The Trial of the Two Languages),* is available in translation.

---

**Opposite**: Ulugh Beg Madrassah (see p217). The majolica tilework on Samarkand's mosques and madrassahs is outstanding.

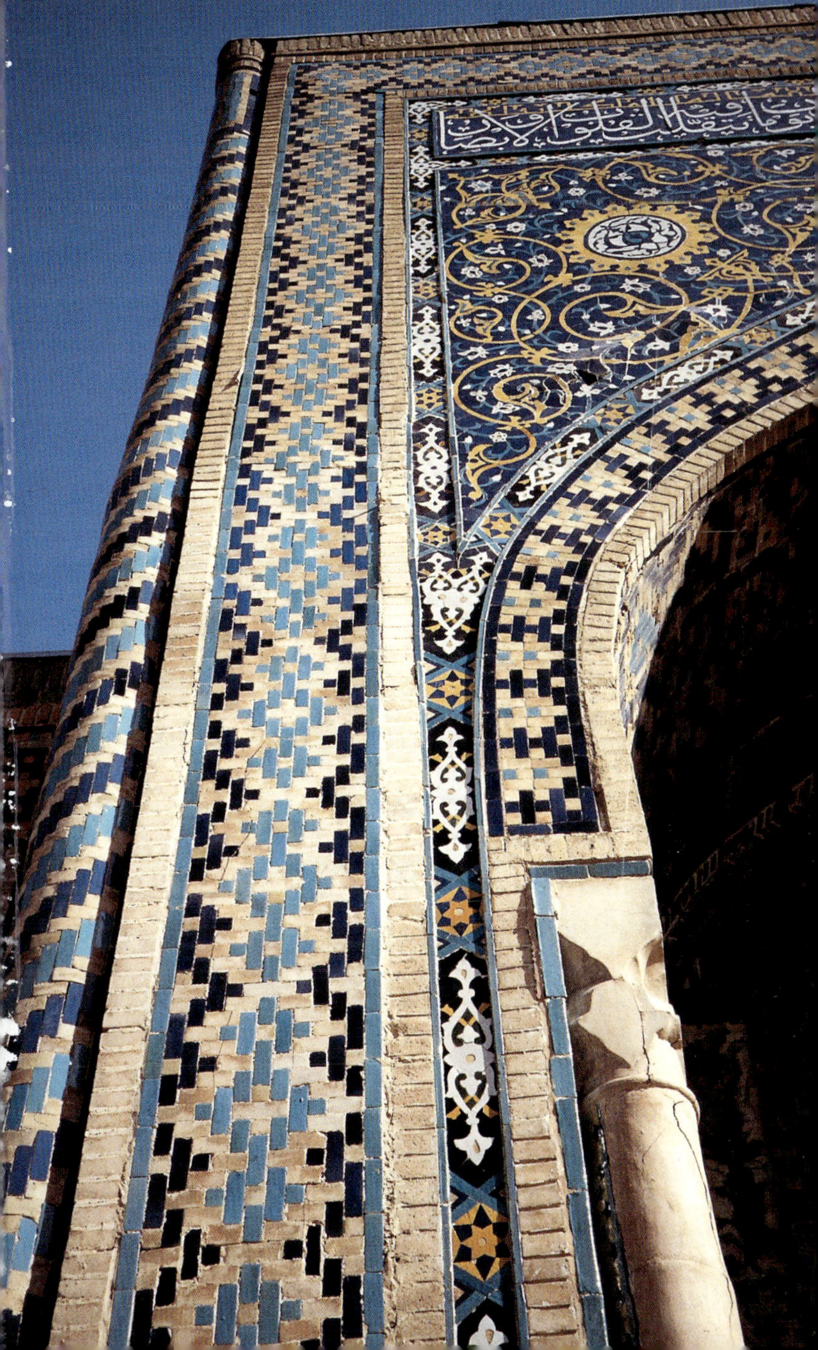

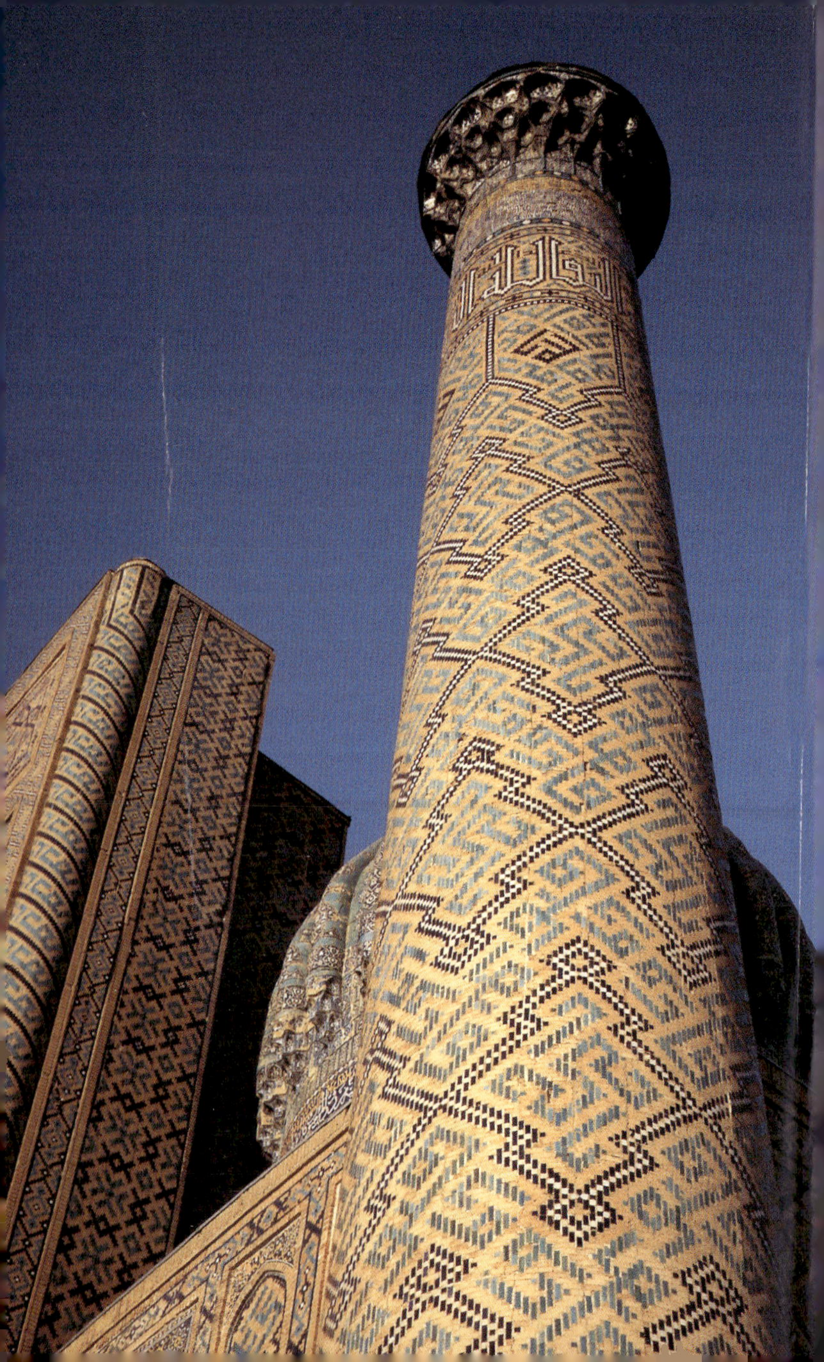

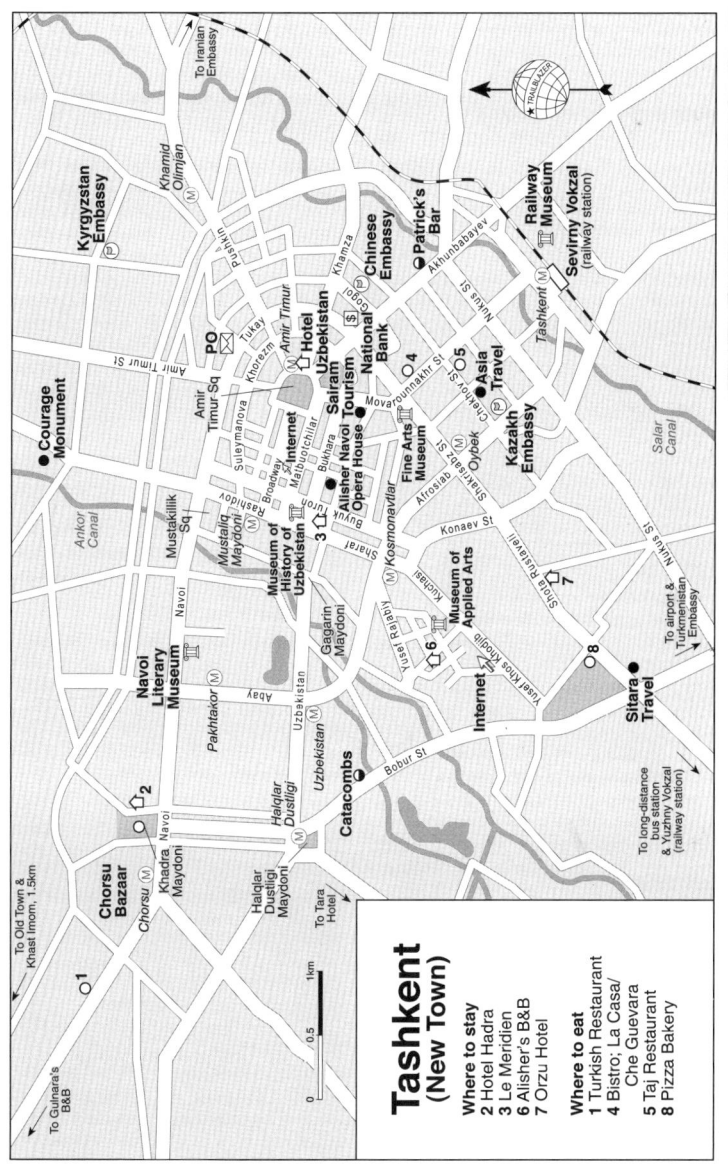

**Opposite**: The minarets in Samarkand's Registan (see p217) provide the best views of the city.

## PRACTICAL INFORMATION
[☎ code 071]
### Orientation and services
In a town this size it is a good idea to buy the biggest **map** you can find: the shop in Hotel Uzbekistan sells an excellent map with English labels, or try the **bookshop** on Pushkin St; get a map with a metro plan and the bus routes marked on it.

The modern heart of the city is in the east, with **Broadway** and the Amir Timur statue at the centre, while the old town is to the west. Orientation in Tashkent, however, has been complicated by a massive restructuring of street names. In a show of independence all the streets in the city are being renamed after Uzbek figureheads or landmarks and the old Soviet signs are being replaced; unfortunately, no one seems to have told the locals this. Almost all of them still use the old Soviet names (especially taxi drivers) and you can really get frustrated over a simple journey. Having said that, central Tashkent is compact and not too demanding to walk around (though some streets are still unnamed as replacement signs have not been put up). Hopefully, as everyone gets used to the changes, the problems will subside.

There are lots of **Internet cafés** (900sum/hour) but the biggest and best is near Alisher's B&B.

The main **post office** is to the north of Amir Timur Square on Tolstoy St and **international phone calls** can be made from here, though they are still very expensive. You can change money at any hotel and the **National Bank for Foreign Economic Activities** (23 Yuldosh Okhunboboev St) gives dollar advances on credit cards.

Of the local travel agencies, **Sitara Travel** (☎ 152 7109, 🖳 www.sitara.com) at Dom 45, office 42, Shota Rustaveli St, is by far the most efficient. They can help with visa support letters for Uzbekistan, Kyrgyzstan, Turkmenistan and China and also offer a wide selection of day trips and activities. Sitara has an office in Pakistan so are a good source of information if you are heading, and also an office in Canada.

Other agencies include **Asia Travel** (🖳 www.asia-travel.uz) and **Sairam Tourism** (🖳 www.sairamtour.com).

If you do not already have your Chinese and Kyrgyzstan visas this is the best place to apply (Chinese visas are also available in Bishkek but the service there gets bad reports). The **Chinese Embassy** (☎ 133 3779), Yakhyo Gulomov St, opens for visa applications only on Monday, Wednesday and Friday from 09.00 to 12.00 (having said that, the gates are often not opened until 10.00). The **Kyrgyzstan Embassy** (30 Samatova St) issues visas the same day, as does the **Kazakh Embassy** at Chekhov St 23. The **Turkmenistan Embassy** is at 10 One Katta Mirabat and the **Iranian Embassy** is at 20 Parkent. For visa applications, see p15-18.

### Local transport
Despite being home to over 2.5 million people, Tashkent always manages to appear quiet and empty, for which much credit must be given to the transport system. There is an efficient metro and tram service as well as cheap buses and taxis.

**Taxis**, in fact, are so cheap (generally 250sum to anywhere within the city centre) that most visitors use them for every journey; the **buses** and **trams** are always overcrowded and not easy to work out. If you do take a taxi and the driver is unsure of the street (probably because he knows it by its old name), try to direct him rather than showing him your map as it usually only confuses him more. Most 'taxis' who stop to pick you up will be locals looking for a bit of extra cash.

The **metro** (see map opposite) is quick and your best bet for longer journeys, especially out to bus and train stations. Take a look at **Kosmonavtlar Station** with its dramatic homage to Yuri Gagarin.

### Where to stay
Hotel prices in Tashkent seem to have gone up across the board in the last few years, and this can make it an expensive city to visit if you're on a tight budget, especially if you have to hang around waiting for

# Tashkent Metro

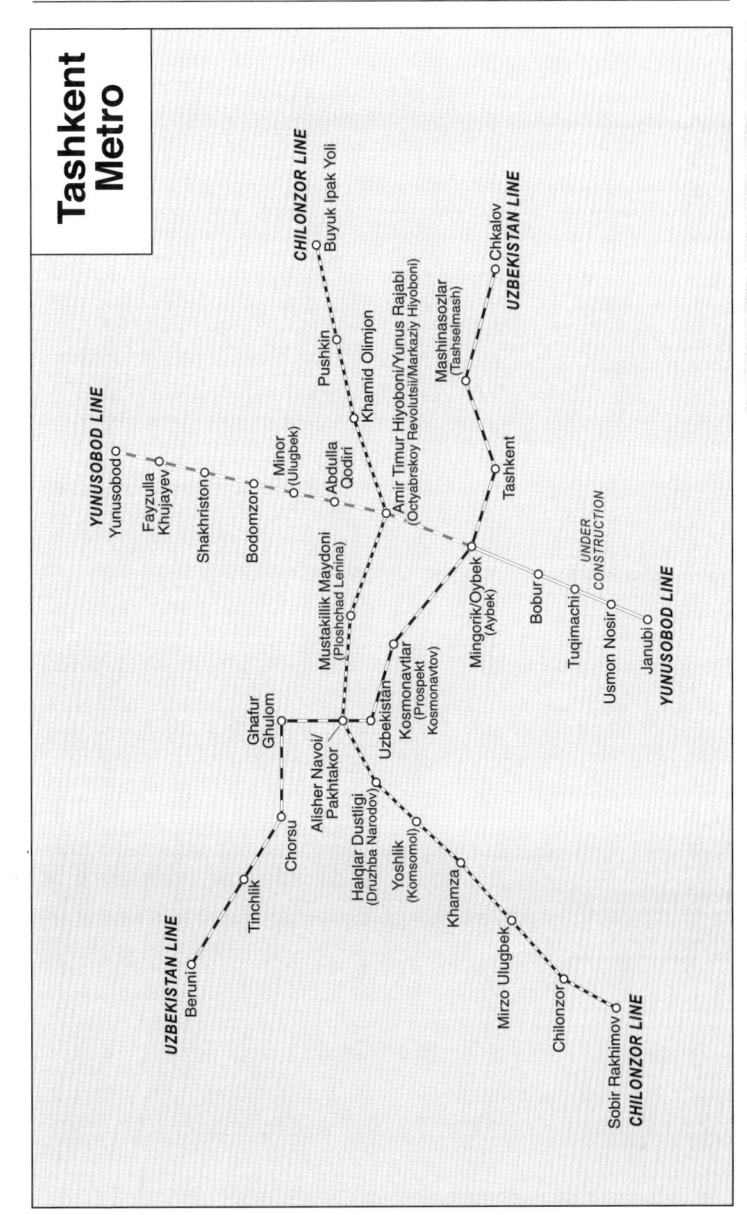

**YUNUSOBOD LINE**
- Yunusobod
- Fayzulla Khujayev
- Shakhriston
- Bodomzor
- Minor (Ulugbek)
- Abdulla Qodiri
- Amir Timur Hiyoboni/Yunus Rajabi (Octyabrskoy Revolutsii/Markaziy Hiyoboni)

**CHILONZOR LINE**
- Buyuk Ipak Yoli
- Pushkin
- Khamid Olimjon
- Mashinasozlar (Tashselmash)
- Chkalov

**UZBEKISTAN LINE**
- Beruni
- Tinchlik
- Chorsu
- Ghafur Ghulom
- Alisher Navoi/Pakhtakor
- Uzbekistan
- Kosmonavtlar (Prospekt Kosmonavtov)
- Mingorik/Oybek (Aybek)
- Tashkent

**CHILONZOR LINE**
- Mustakillik Maydoni (Ploshchad Lenina)
- Halqlar Dustligi (Druzhba Narodov)
- Yoshlik (Komsomol)
- Khamza
- Mirzo Ulugbek
- Chilonzor
- Sobir Rakhimov

**YUNUSOBOD LINE** (UNDER CONSTRUCTION)
- Bobur
- Tuqimachi
- Usmon Nosir
- Janubi

visas. One possible solution is to make contact with a local guide and see what they can offer in the way of **homestays**.

*Orzu Hotels* (☎ 120 8077; 🖥 www.sambuh.com; 27 Makhmud; US$30-50/Db) have a few options in town and are the best mid-range choice.

For something of a unique experience try *Alisher's B&B* (☎ 152 6308; 🖥 www.ali-tour.narod.ru; US$25/Db) at 26 Vakhidov/Vosit Vohidov St. Alisher is the 'Hospitality King of Tashkent' and will be more than happy to see you – you will probably end up having a large vodka session with him. His son, Anwar, will also help you find your way around the city.

A bit cheaper, *Gulnara's B&B* (☎ 144 7766; US$10pp) is at 40 Azad. To get here, take the metro to Chorsu Station and walk to where Chorsu St meets Beruni St. From here walk north to Ozod Kuchasi and turn right where you see the Coke signs; Gulnara's is the two-storey cream house.

If you are really cutting it tight, ignore **Hotel Hadra** next to the Circus (it's a dump); instead take the metro to Sobir Rakhimov Station and follow the tram tracks left to Chilanzor D20A, Dom 16 and *Tara Hotel* (US$2.50/dorm)

*Le Meridien* (☎ 120 5800; US$180/Db), Buyuk Turon 56, is the refurbished version of Hotel Tashkent and is pretty smart. Its position is unbeatable and it has retained some of its old-world charm.

### Where to eat
In the centre of town there are **cafés** and **food vendors** all over the place. Head to Broadway (one block west of Amir Temur Square) for shashlik, fast-food, cold drinks and ice creams.

On the way to/from Gulnara's B&B, the *Turkish Restaurant* is friendly, clean and dishes up heaps of great food for a reasonable price, or try Chorsu Bazaar.

If you fancy a change, try the *Pizza Bakery* (Shota Rustaveli), up the road from Sitara Travel. The *Taj* (☎ 711 33 5392) at Chekhov St 5 is a good Indian restaurant. *Bistro* at Movarounnakhr St 33 has good Italian food and *Omar Khayyam* (next door) serves more traditional cuisine.

### Entertainment
**Opera** **Alisher Navoi Opera House**, just south-west of Amir Timur Square, was built in 1947 by the same architect who built the Kazin Sky Station and Lenin's Mausoleum in Moscow. There is a regular programme of music, opera and ballet and tickets (US$1-8) can be bought on the day of the performance from the ticket windows at the front of the building. If it is closed (June-August), seek out the cleaning lady and she will let you explore inside for 2000som.

**Bars and nightclubs** It is time to get your gladdest of rags on as Tashkent actually has a proper nightlife scene. *La Casa/ Che Guevara's* is part of the Bistro building and is big at the weekend. *Catacombs* (near Haqlar Dostligi metro) is part owned by Karimov's daughter, has a very late licence and was the 'in' place in 2006. *Patrick's* (Akhunbabayev) serves a goodish pint of Guinness.

### Moving on
Those wanting to travel directly to **Bishkek** should note that buses there (13hrs) pass through Kazakhstan so **you must have a Kazakh visa/transit visa** – it often works out cheaper and quicker to fly.

There are **two railway stations** in Tashkent. Trains to/from the north (eg Moscow) use the main station (Sevirny Vokzal) next to Tashkent metro. Trains to/from **Samarkand** and **Bukhara** (this overnight train is highly recommended) stop at the more distant south station (Yuzhny Vokzal; the easiest way to get here is by taxi). **Direct trains no longer run to Almaty or Bishkek**.

The **bus station** is more of a car park to the south of Sobir Rakhimov metro station (which is at the southern end of the Chilonzor line). From here there are buses to many destinations including **Kokand** (5hrs), **Samarkand** (6hrs) and **Bukhara** (9hrs). Overnight buses also run to **Bishkek**.

For **Osh** see box p231. Share-taxis wait outside the bus station.

**Tashkent Airport** is smart and new and is Central Asia's hub. The **customs and immigration** procedures are still a hit-and-miss affair but increasingly visitors are being treated swiftly and with little hassle. There is a **money exchange** inside the terminal and a quick **bus service** (Nos 67 & 77) from outside the old domestic terminal (across the car park from the international terminal) into the city centre. If you are leaving Tashkent, bus No 67 runs to the airport from just south of Amir Timur Square on Movarounnakhr St. A taxi to the airport should cost about US$4.

Many airlines fly in and out of here, so flights home (and flights to neighbouring capitals such as Bishkek) should be reasonably competitive; hunt around the travel agencies listed above – Uzbek Airlines are the best of all the Central Asian fliers in terms of fleet and service.

---

### Kazakhstan

Kazakhstan has a rich nomadic history but most of its steppes lay well off the Silk Road. The only areas of real significance for Silk Roadsters are the coastal region around the Caspian Sea (through which The Rhubarb Road ran, see box p200), and the south-east corner around **Almaty**, **Shymkent** and **Lake Balkhash** (where a major arm of the Silk Road passed).

Today, most visitors to Kazakhstan are rich businessmen there for its oil (the Kashagan oilfield probably holds the world's second-largest oil reserve, some 300 million barrels) and the tourist facilities reflect that.

Almaty is a cosmopolitan (if expensive) city with plenty of nightlife and the route through Kazakhstan to China is a useful alternative to those through Kyrgyzstan, especially in winter when the Torugart and Irkeshtam passes can be closed/blocked.

**Practicalities** Buses and share-taxis run between Bishkek and **Almaty** (3-4hrs) daily. From Tashkent take a taxi to the border (US$4), which is quite straightforward to cross, then take a share-taxi to **Shymkent** (US$6). Overnight trains (US$20-30) run three times a week to Almaty but tickets (particularly sleeper tickets) can sometimes be hard to come by and you may need to talk the conductor into letting you on.

If you need to stop in Almaty, *Transit Hotel* (US$20/Db), outside the train station, is about the only budget option. There are plenty of **banks/bureau de change** and **ATMs** that accept Western credit/debit cards (you can even withdraw US dollars). If you want to see a bit more of the country, contact **Stantours** (see p192); they can also arrange travel and accommodation.

The **Uzbek Embassy** is at 36 Baribaev St. The **Kyrgyz Embassy** is at 57 Amangeldy St. The **Chinese Embassy** (137 Furmanov St) is not recommended as the service is unreliable and slow.

**If you stay in the country for more than five days you must register with Immigration Police Department.**

Overnight trains (36hrs/US$60) leave for **Ürümqi** on Monday and Saturday evenings. There is a separate ticket office for international tickets out on the platform. There is also an erratic bus service (24hrs/US$40) that leaves from the main bus station at around 07.00 most mornings; arrive at 06.30 to try to find out what's happening that day. Sometimes if there is no scheduled bus you can squeeze onto a tour bus going that way; sometimes the bus will take you only as far as the border or **Yining**, in which case you must change and grab the next bus through. For Ürümqi, see p318.

# The Ferghana Valley

The Ferghana Valley is seen by the Uzbeks as their heartland and a major branch of the Silk Road wound its way through here. Geographically, it stretches eastwards from the plains south of Tashkent far into the Ferghana Mountains. To the north of the valley are the Chatkal Mountains and to the south are the Fan Mountains but for the most part these are so far away it is hard to consider yourself in a 'valley' at all. Moreover, when you do get to where the mountains meet, and where the purest dialect of the Uzbek language is considered to be spoken, you suddenly find yourself in Kyrgyzstan! The gerrymandering of the valley was Stalin at his worst (a large chunk of the western valley was sliced off into Tajikistan, as well) and these splits are the source of great unrest today.

## HISTORY

The valley first came to prominence over two thousand years ago because of its 'Heavenly Horses'; see box below. The fertility of the valley ensured that, like today, it was always heavily populated but as new empires came and went, the

### Heavenly Horses
Man has always wanted to fly but, in the past, the closest he could get to it was on the back of a horse. The finest stallions were not just magnificent to ride, they were great weapons in war and as such were doubly valuable. Horses and the breeding of horses took on an incredible significance in many ancient cultures and a myriad of myths and legends sprung up around them, with some notably featuring flying horses. The animal was also worshipped and ornate sculptures (including statues of winged beasts) have been discovered in various archaeological sites (see p334-5), with Chinese mythology depicting the horse as the magical 'vehicle' that escorted the souls of legendary emperors to their final resting place in the Western Paradise.

The most important steeds on the Silk Road were the 'Heavenly Horses' of the Ferghana Valley. They were bigger and stronger than all their contemporaries, were said to sweat blood and were famous as far away as Xi'an – China had its own horses but because the land there was not very calcium-rich its horses tended to be weak and small. In the 2nd century BC the Chinese Emperor, Wu, even sent his best general, Zhang Qian, over the Tien Shan to try to bring some prize specimens back (see p40).

Horses continue to be revered along the Silk Road today, the most famous (and endangered) being the tiny **Przewalski horse** (see box p238) and the *akhal teke* of Turkmenistan (the forefather of the modern Arabian steed), which even have a national holiday named after them. Other breeds include the stocky *lokai* of Tajikistan and the *karabair* of Uzbekistan, which are both used in the spectacular sport of *buzkashi* (the anarchic polo-like game played with a headless goat carcass). In Kyrgystan, shepherds still refer to their steeds as their 'wings'.

> **Crossing the Uzbekistan/Kyrgyzstan border**
> Don't be too surprised if your journey encounters complications – like your bus breaking down. Most transport, whether bus or share-taxi, leaves early in the morning. Take the earliest bus possible from **Tashkent** to **Kokand** (5hrs). On arrival in Kokand (the **bus station** here is by the main bazaar but away from the town centre), change onto the next **Andijan** bus or ask about a share-taxi (they leave from outside the bus station). The trip to Andijan takes three to four hours depending on the number of melon stops. This border crossing should be no problem but with the increased tension and military activity this may have changed; expect to see a higher than normal military presence.
>
> There is no bus to take you to the border from Andijan so you will need to take a share taxi (2000sum per car). On your way out of Andijan, try to get the driver to stop at **Babur's Mosque** and **Monument** which are worth a look. The taxi drivers at the border have you over a barrel so expect to pay 100som for a cab into Osh (it's useful to have a few low-denomination dollar notes to change at the border).
>
> Coming the other way it's the same except, of course, in reverse. You should make it to Tashkent as there are more buses running that way in the afternoons but you may well arrive late.

cities of the plains took all the glory and the valley was regarded merely as a source of food. Even its greatest son, Babur, found his fame in another land (see p245).

In the later centuries the valley became the powerbase of the Kokand khanate but in 1876 the whole khanate collapsed under Russian pressure and its lands were quickly absorbed into their empire.

### The Ferghana Valley today
To the modern traveller the valley is, unfortunately, a major disappointment. It is now the most densely populated region of Uzbekistan (around eight million people live here) yet its cities are grey and boring with little evidence of their former greatness. Following the Andijan massacres and previous social unrest (see p169) you can also feel an unpleasant edge, especially after dark. The region is the most Islamic in Uzbekistan so visitors should dress and act appropriately.

**PRACTICAL INFORMATION**
**Orientation and services**
Most visitors try to complete the journey from Tashkent to Osh (see box above) in one go but many fail. If you plan to break your journey or are caught out, the most practical stops are **Kokand** and **Andijan**. Despite Kokand's history, Andijan is a better place to stay, though Kokand has both a **bank** that changes money and an **Uzbektourism Office**, while Andijan has just a **bank**.

**Where to stay and eat**
Kokand has only fleapits on offer; *Hotel Kokand*, the least bad, is very central; US$10/Db. *Nulifar Restaurant* nearby serves OK food and beer but isn't keen on foreign visitors.

l Andijan boasts *Hotel Andijan* (very central, US$12/Db); it is nothing special but it is clean. The nearby *Golden Chicken Restaurant* serves edible food.

**Moving on**
See box above.

# Osh

Osh is an ancient town seated at the head of the Ferghana Valley and was a key stop on the Silk Road for all trade coming over the Pamirs, crossing the Kyrgyz Mountains and heading onto the plains below. In 1990, however, it became a byword for ethnic conflict as clashes between local Uzbeks and Kyrgyz hit the headlines.

In October 2000, it celebrated Osh 3000 but in fact it is probably older than that (according to one saying, 'Osh is older than Rome'!). The highlight of the festival was a two-week cultural extravaganza but they have yet to give the city a much-needed facelift. There is no sense of an old city at all, just a pile of concrete houses crammed together beside a dirty river.

## WHAT TO SEE

Depending on your point of view, **Jayma Bazaar** is little more than a large flea market selling lots of things no one seems to want to buy or one of Central Asia's most dynamic treasure troves. By the bridge on Alisher Navoi St it is, however, a good place to buy a felt hat. Sunday is the biggest day.

The one sight definitely worth seeing is **Solomon's Throne**, the large rock mass on the west bank of the river. It's a steep climb so bring plenty of water. At the top is the '**House of Babur**', where the future ruler of India (see p245) is said to have taken refuge whilst on the run from Samarkand. From here you also get the best views of the Ferghana Valley. At the back of the building (which also houses a mosque and is a place of pilgrimage for Muslims) is a natural slide worn smooth in the stone by visitors who test the myth that you will be blessed with good fortune if you slide down it seven times.

The **Silk Road Museum** was built as part of Osh 3000 but is as unrewarding as the Soviet-era **Historical-Cultural Museum** around the back of the mountain.

### PRACTICAL INFORMATION
[✆ code 03222]
### Orientation and services

Osh is split by the **Ak Buura River** but there is little difference between the two sides of town. Everything you will want to do or see is within walking distance of the river so it's pretty easy to get around.

**Internet cafés** have been set up around town; try above the Istanbul Bistro (60som/hr, 30som/hr after 21.00). The main **telephone office** and **post office** are on Lenin. There are many **banks** and money-changers in town, all offering roughly the same rates so changing money is not a problem. **Bank Bakai** and **Demir Kyrgyz Bank** (both on Kurmanjan Datka St) offer advances on credit/debit cards.

The **CBT** office (see p235; 🖥 www.cbtkyrgyzstan.kg) here is inconveniently positioned (58 Kurmanjan Datka St) but in its favour it can arrange **homestays** and day trips.

## Where to stay and eat

The ***Taj Mahal*** (☎ 396 52), Zaina Betinova St, is a hotel (600som/Db) not a curry house and probably offers the best mid-range deal. English is spoken and there's even an official translator. ***Eta's Hotel*** (☎ 566 45; 600som/Db) at Kyrgyzstan 44 is modern and clean, with a good restaurant.

A cheaper place on the same street at No 88 is ***Osh Guesthouse*** (☎ 306 29, 🖳 oshguesthouse@hotbox.ru; US$4/dorm bed) but this is tricky to find and cramped. Another option is the very friendly ***Hotel Sara*** (450som/Db) on the other side of the river at Kurmanjan Datka 278.

***Café Ala-Too***, around the corner from the Taj Mahal, is a recommended teahouse. ***Golden Coast*** by the river also has a fair selection of food (though the menu is in Russian) and this is probably the best of the various riverside establishments. When we say 'riverside', however, don't think Henley Regatta as, even with the sun shining and the wind whistling through the trees, the river is brown, dirty and full of litter.

There is a large **supermarket** across the river from the Golden Coast if you want to buy your own supplies.

## Moving on

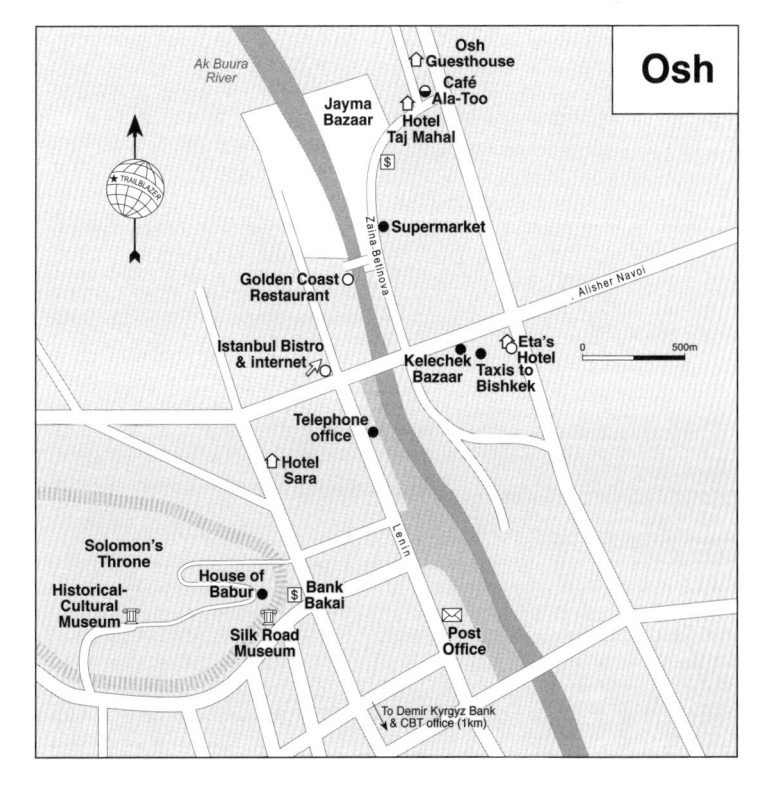

Buses for **Bishkek** leave from the **new bus station** but most people take a share-taxi (15hrs/500som pp) from behind Kelechek Bazaar. The new road took a long time to be built but now the journey is largely incident-free. There are towns such as **Jalal Abad** on the way but few visitors without their own transport care to stop. If you are in a share-taxi ask your driver to stop at **Ozgon** to see the foundations of Alexander's Camp and a squat minaret beside some beautiful mausoleums (their matt colour is all warm terracotta as they were built before the art of glazing had been mastered). The rest of the journey offers some tremendous views, especially around **Lake Toktogul** and up through the passes.

There is a road between **Jalal Abad** and **Naryn** but it is in a bad state of disrepair and is only for 4WDs. Similarly, the route south-east of **Ozgon** has fallen into disrepair and peters out at Kok Art (at the Silk Road's height this popular branch would have carried on through to Kashgar). **South-eastern Kyrgyzstan** is still well off the beaten track and although roads run that way, it is the least safe area of the country.

Buses for **Kashgar** (see box below) leave from the new bus station. If you are heading into **Uzbekistan**, see box p231. If you are heading for **Tajikistan**, see box p176.

---

### Crossing the Kyrgyz/Chinese border 1: The Irkeshtam Pass

This border crossing is much simpler than the Torugart Pass (see box p242), as you don't need a permit and there is no no-man's land. It is therefore becoming more popular (it is definitely the best crossing for cyclists) but that is not to say it is without problems of its own.

There is a twice-weekly overnight bus in both directions between Osh and Kashgar (18hrs/US$50) but the service was halted because of SARS and non-locals are always in danger of being kicked off. Alternatively, you can take taxis from Osh/Kashgar to the border (US$50).

If you are driving your own vehicle or cycling, the road between Osh and **Sary Tash** is now part of the new Pamir Highway and much improved but from there on it is still unpredictable, especially in winter (the border is theoretically open year round).

From Kashgar, you can hire a taxi to the border, cross under your own steam and then take a share-taxi or bus to Osh.

---

# Bishkek

Bishkek is a modern city and if any part of Kyrgyzstan can be called developed this is it. It is also the most Russian city. In fact, before the Russians arrived in 1862 there was little more than a clay fort here. At that time it was known as Pishpek but in honour of its most famous son it was renamed Frunze by the Bolsheviks – General Mikhail Frunze was largely responsible for ensuring the whole Central Asian region remained loyal to the Bolsheviks.

You won't be enthralled by this capital but for its restaurants, bars and limited nightlife, you'll be glad you made the stop. There are some decent treks around the capital too, particularly in Ala-Archa.

## WHAT TO SEE

The large **statue of Lenin** is still here but has been moved to a smaller square behind the museum. Ala-too Square now plays host to the **Erkindik** ('Freedom') **monument**. This typifies Bishkek, which has little to offer visually. The **State Historical Museum** has all its labels in Russian so it's difficult to appreciate everything but the views across the city from the top floor are good and the collection of handicrafts and carpets is the best in the country. The tribute to communism and Lenin is enjoyably outdated propaganda. Entrance is 50som.

There is a large **monument to Frunze** outside the train station and a **memorial** to WWII heroes in Victory Square.

There are several **theatres** in the city, many of which have an impressively high standard of operas and plays. Ask one of the agencies for the latest programme of events.

### PRACTICAL INFORMATION
[☎ code 312]

#### Orientation and services
Bishkek is set out on a **grid pattern** so it is simple to find your way around but at night the lighting is poor and the city has a reputation for being dangerous. **Jibek Jolu Prospekt** (Silk Road Ave) used to be the main drag but now the centre of town has shifted south to **Ala-too Square**.

US dollar cash advances on credit/debit cards are easy at quite a few **banks**, as is exchanging currency (if you are heading east over the Torugart Pass and are relying on a credit/debit card, take out plenty of cash as the next facility is in Kashgar). Try **AKB Bank** at 54 Togolok Moldo St.

**Taxis** cost only 20som to anywhere in the centre, so they are worth using, especially at night. **Internet cafés** are widespread: **Shakrus** at Kiev St 58 is open 24hrs and offers cheap international phone rates. The English-language *Times of Central Asia* is worth a look.

The **Uzbek Embassy** is at 213 Tynystanov St (☎ 226 171; see p15-18 for visa requirements). The **Kazakh Embassy** is at 10 Togolok Moldo St. The **Pakistani Embassy** is at 308 Panfilov St. The **Chinese Embassy** at 196 Toktogul St is not recommended as its service is slow and unreliable.

#### Travel agencies
If you are heading east across the Torugart Pass (see box p242), your best bet is **Celestial Mountains Tours** (☎ 212 562, 🖳 www.celestial.com.kg), 131-4 Kiev St, run by a Scotsman, Ian Claytor. His full package might not be the cheapest but he has the distinct advantage of also running the Celestial Guesthouse in Naryn (see p241) and therefore you can arrange to meet him there. He also had a 100 per cent success rate for getting clients across when we met him. Having said that, it is still expensive: even in a group of four it's about US$50 per person for the jeep from Naryn to the border, US$50 per group for the crossing permit and US$90 per person for the taxi from the Chinese border to Kashgar.

**CBT** (☎ 622 385, 🖳 www.cbtkyrgyz stan.kg) has an office around the back of 4 Kiev St. They can put you in touch with all the other CBT offices around the country and are your best bet if you want to spend some time in Kyrgyzstan.

**Novinomad** (☎ 221 335, 🖳 www.nov inomad.com) offer a trans-Torugart Pass service (and their prices at US$100/pp are very tempting) but they don't specialize in this trip. What they do specialize in is accommodation and trekking, both in the mountains and on the lakes on the way up to Naryn. They work with CBT and Shepherd's Life (see p241) and offer homestays, trekking, horse riding and shepherding tours.

**Alpine Fund** (☎ 665 567, 🖳 www.alp inefund.org), Erkindik Prospekt 2, is a youth charity organizing **treks** in Ala-Archa National Park, with trekking gear for hire.

## Where to stay

If you are looking for a **homestay** or something **mid-range** try one of the agencies above.

*International Business School* (☎ 623 101) at 237 Panfilov St might sound like an odd place to stay but it is the most popular budget choice (US$10/Db with a shared bathroom).

Nearby, *Hotel Sary Chelek* (☎ 662 627) at 87 Orozbekov St is certainly cheaper (US$8/Db with en suite shower) but is also deteriorating in quality.

*Hotel Semetey* (☎ 218324; US$20/Db) at 125 Toktogul St is a bit of a hangover from the Soviet days but has a great location for the price.

Celestial Tours own the *Silk Road Lodge* (☎ 661 129) at 229 Aldymomunov St. It has well-equipped rooms, high Western standards and a swimming pool but the price (US$85/Db) reflects that.

## Where to eat and drink

Bishkek is turning into a little gem when it comes to wining and dining. There are curry houses, pizzerias, American burgers, fries and beer imported from all over the world! Many places have pleasant outdoor seating areas too. Most people start at *Fatboys* (104 Chuy Prospekt). This provides exactly what you'd expect from its name and is one centre for the ex-pat crowd. *Bar Navigator* (103 Moskva St) is the other but it is slightly more upmarket and trendy. The prices are high but the choice of good, back-home-style food and familiar beer brands usually prove too tempting. *Johnnie's Pub* (Chuy Prospekt 209) is also popular.

*Yusa Restaurant* (14 Logvinenko St) is Turkish but has a menu in English and good pizzas. *Steinbrau* (5 Gertse St) offers a combination of German beer and food. *Planet Holsten* on Dobovy Park is good for an outdoor beer and pizza.

*Khanguk Koan* (Shopokov St) has great Korean food. *Indus Valley* (105 Sultan Ibraimov St) and *Bombay* (110 Chuy Prospekt) do mean curries.

All sorts of new restaurants are opening around the Kiev St/Soviet St area so wander around and pick your favourite. *Astana Café* (Kiev St) and *Café Faiza* (Jibek Jolu Prospekt) are good options for cheap local food.

If you are up for it, there are quite a few **nightclubs** and you'll usually find some budding accomplices in Fatboys or Johnnie's to share a taxi.

## Moving on

**Domestic** If you are heading to **Osh** (15hrs) you need to get a taxi out to Osh Bazaar (it's not worth going here for the market) and from there get a bus/share taxi.

If you are going east you have to go to the long-distance bus station (this is called *zapadny* or 'west' station). Buses go to **Karakol** (8½hrs/145som), **Cholponata** (100som), **Kochkor** and occasionally **Naryn**, but you are better off taking a share-taxi from outside the bus station, as they are much quicker and more reliable.

**International** Two or three overnight buses leave the **long-distance bus station** for **Tashkent** every evening but you might want to consider flying (see p228).

The bus to **Kashgar** via the Torugart Pass (see box p242) leaves from the long-distance bus station, as do the ones for **Almaty** and the route to China via Kazakhstan (see p229).

Bishkek 237

# Bishkek

**Where to stay**
1 Silk Road Lodge
2 International Business School Hotel
3 Hotel Sary Chelek
10 Hotel Semetey

**Where to eat**
4 Planet Holsten
5 Indus Valley Restaurant
6 Khanguk Koan Restaurant
7 Fatboys Restaurant
8 Bombay Restaurant
9 Johnnie's Pub
11 Yusa Restaurant
12 Bar Navigator
13 Steinbrau Bar

# Issyk Kul (Lake Issyk)

The name Issyk Kul means 'Warm Lake'. It is so named because it never freezes, despite being surrounded by snow and ice for many months of the year. This is largely due to its great depth (695m, making it the fourth deepest lake in the world). The largest town is **Karakol** (at the eastern end) and most independent travellers make this their base.

## WHAT TO SEE

The north shore was where the old Russian bosses used to take their holidays and is home to a string of towns with beaches (**Cholponata** is the biggest). There are also quite a few **sanitoria** operating here, with bathhouses and promenades. The mountains on the north side have the easier hikes and if you want to explore the area on your own, that area is your best bet.

The south shore, however, has the more beautiful hills and is the real homeland of the **Kyrgyz shepherds** (the north side was gradually colonized by Russians and Slavs in the old days). On a reasonably lengthy trek or ride you can expect to see hawks, eagles and Marco Polo sheep, as well as meet shepherds who still live most of their lives at this high altitude.

On both sides of the lake you can also see traces of civilizations dating back to the 5th century BC and **caravanserais** (see box p98) built for the arms of the Silk Road that ran between Bishkek and Xinjiang.

---

### Przewalski

There has been much written about the explorers of Central Asia but in many ways they all started with Nikolai Mikhailovich Przewalski, born into an army family in Smolensk in 1839. He persuaded the Russian Imperial Geographical Society to sponsor his first expedition, to the Usuri River, in 1867. In 1870 he set off on the first of four major expeditions in Central Asia, Mongolia, China and Tibet. He not only discovered various new routes through the region but also new mountains, lost cities and, of course, his very own breed of horse.

He died on the shores of Issyk Kul in 1888, on the way back from his last expedition, on which he had finally met the then Dalai Lama. Having come down with typhus, he wrote to the tsar asking to be buried in his full expedition uniform (he was also a major-general in the Russian army) and his grave, together with a monument and chapel, are still here today.

Of particular interest to Silk Roadsters is the **museum** opened in his honour in 1957. It contains a huge map indicating Przewalski's expeditions, as well as a fine collection of his belongings. To get here take a bus from Karakol to **Pristan Prahevalsk** (7km).

# Issyk Kul

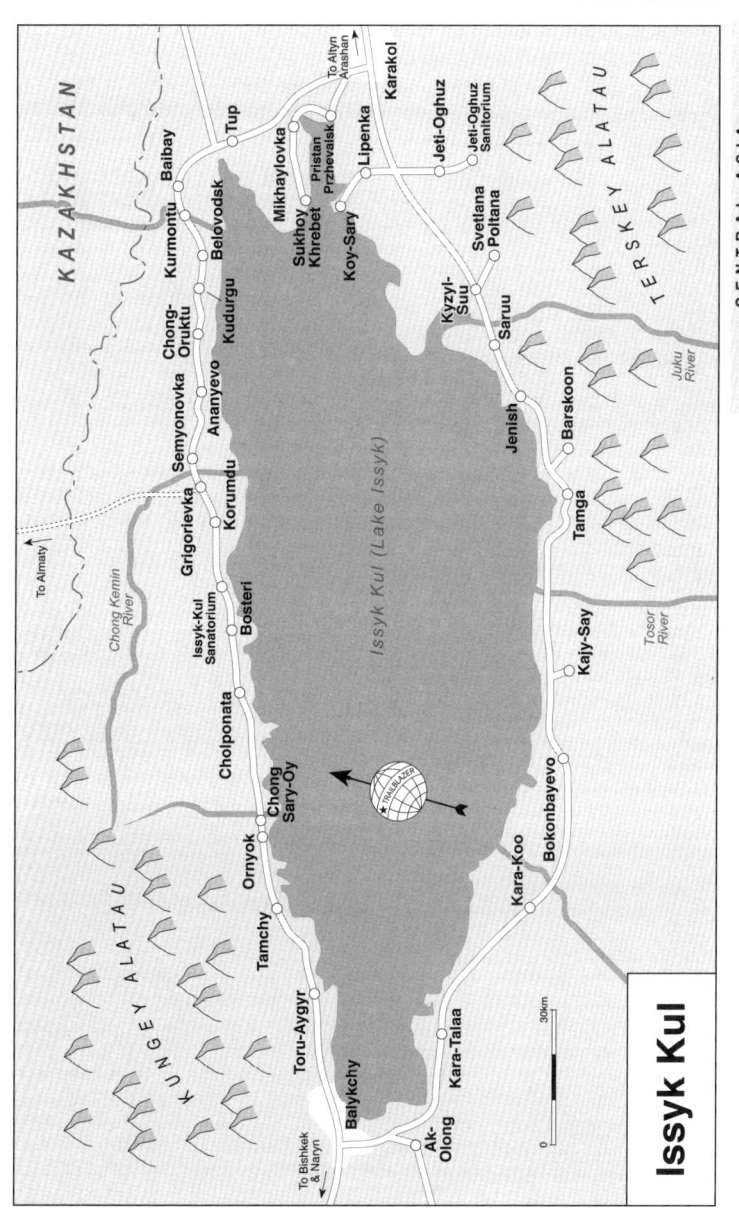

Trekking (see box p265) is the area's big draw card and there are plenty of great routes in and around Karakol Valley (the main trekking season runs from June to early October). Information is easy to pick up at any agency or hostel (see below). The hot springs at Altyn Arashan are also popular.

## PRACTICAL INFORMATION
### Orientation and services
Facilities are limited, though if you're with an organized trip that won't be a problem (there are a few places to change US dollars). **Investbank** in Cholponata and **AKB Bank** in Karakol give advances on credit/debit cards. Karakol has a few Internet cafés.

**CBT** (🖳 www.cbtkyrgyzstan.kg) have an office in Karakol (55 Korolkova St) and can organize great homestays, transport and treks. **Tourist office** (TIC, 🖳 ticigu@net mail.kg), 130 Jusup Abdrakhmanov, provides the same and are equally recommended (they can also arrange visits to local craftsmen and if you are after a *shasdyk*, a handmade felt rug, this is the place to buy one).

In **Barskoon**, *Shepherd's Way Trekking* (🖳 shepherd@infotel.kg, www.kyrgyztrek.com) is run by a wife-and-husband team, Gulmiera and Ishen, together with his brother and father (who is one of the few shepherds who can still catch and train young hawks and eagles for hunting).

They have nine horses for hire and charge US$5 an hour. They can organize anything from a day's trek to a week-long camping trip (rates come down with the size of your party and the length of your trip).

### Where to stay and eat
In **Karakol**, as well as several **homestays** there is *Yak Tours Hostel* (☎ 03922 569 01, 250som/pp including one meal) at 10 Gagarin, probably the first backpacker place in Central Asia and, at 166 Jamansariev, *Neofit Guesthouse* (☎ 03922 206 50, 🖳 neofit@issyl-kul.kg, 100-300som/pp); the courtyard here is popular with trekkers seeking to unwind over a beer.

Most visitors eat 'in-house' as the traditional food is good and cheap but there are a couple of **cafés** in town too.

In **Barskoon**, *Shepherd's Way Trekking* (see column opposite) has a guesthouse (US$8/pp) that sleeps four but also has room for tents in the garden.

### Moving on
The **long-distance bus station** in Karakol (Przhevalskogo St) has services to **Bishkek** (8hrs), **Barskoon** and **Balykchy** (change here for **Kochkor** and **Naryn**).

**Share-taxis** also run most of the bus routes and leave from outside the station. Minibuses run from the centre of Karakol to the bus station.

# Song Kul (Lake Song)

At 3016m, this alpine lake is breathtakingly beautiful. In the summer the local shepherds pitch camp around its shores and welcome visitors to stay with them. For those going over or coming from the Torugart Pass, it is the perfect point to break the journey between Naryn and Kochkor; for others it is just the perfect spot to relax and explore the summer pastures (*jailoos*).

## WHAT TO SEE

Song Kul is a natural paradise, pure and unpolluted (and teeming with fish). All around are hills in which a wide variety of animals live and up to 66 species of waterfowl visit to nest each year; one thing you won't see, however, is a tree: you are too high up. You are welcome to wander around the hills and often you can ride the shepherds' horses, before being called in for a freshly caught meal.

Kochkor and Naryn have little to see but make excellent bases to stock up on provisions for Song Kul.

## PRACTICAL INFORMATION
### Orientation and services
Remember that no English and only a little Russian is spoken by most of the people you will meet in this region. At Song Kul, your driver may well stay the night with you but if not, he will come and pick you up in the morning. Costs can vary dramatically depending on petrol prices, the size of your party and your vehicle, so shop around and check exactly what you are getting.

**Kochkor** CBT (🖳 cbt_kochkor@rambler.ru), Pioneerskaya 22a, and **Shepherd's Life** at Kuttuseyit Uulu Shamen 111 both have offices here and can provide transport, horses, guides and accommodation. They will also arrange yurt-stays at Song Kul. **Jailoo** (Orozbakova 125/3, 🖳 www.jailoo.com.kg) is a privately run competitor. There is **Internet** access at the telephone office. **Kredobank** will change US dollars.

**Naryn** CBT (🖳 naryn_tourism@rambler.ru), Lenina 8, is the most helpful agency here, offering much the same as its Kochkor office. The **AKB Bank** will change US dollars. There is an **Internet** service beside the telephone office.

### Where to stay and eat
**Kochkor** There are more **homestays** opening up every year and they are all connected to one programme or another, so they are easy to come by. Most offer dinner and breakfast as part of their package (250-300som/pp).

**Naryn** As well as the **homestays** offered by CBT (300som/pp including meals) there's the *Celestial Guesthouse* (☎ 03522 50412; 🖳 www.celestial.com.kg, US$36/Db) at Razzakova St 42. This is more modern than you might ever think possible for somewhere stuck in the middle of nowhere; a great place to settle down and watch a video (in the video lounge) with a couple of bottles of wine from the fridge.

**Song Kul** There are two tourist **yurt camps** (US$26pp/full board) on the lake which are best avoided. Instead, the **shepherds** connected to CBT and Shepherd's Life are more than happy to have guests, even though your arrival will be unannounced. You will immediately be welcomed into their yurt where tea, bread and triple cream will be served. Inside these massive felt tents are lots of rugs and cushions to keep you warm, along with the odd stray child or hen. After dark, the table is removed from the yurt, more mattresses are put in its place and you all line up in bed for lights out. Lodging and all food costs US$5 per day per person but it's not just the prices that tempt you to stay for more than one night. The only drawback is the lack of toilet facilities (and there are wolves in the hills in winter too!).

### Moving on
**Kochkor** Share-taxis leave every morning from the bazaar to **Bishkek** (200km; 150som), and **Naryn** (100km;120som).

**Naryn** Buses run daily to **Bishkek** (6hrs/150som), stopping at **Kochkor** along the way; they are a better option than the share-taxis unless you are prepared to haggle for your life. For the **Torugart Pass** you need your own transport (see box p242).

**Song Kul** There are **two roads** leading to the lake from the main highway, making it possible to enter along one and exit via the other (ideal if you are breaking the journey here between Kochkor and Naryn) but the southern road is suitable only for 4WDs. There is no public transport to the lake so you are reliant on the transport arranged through your agency.

### Crossing the Kyrgyz/Chinese border 2: The Torugart Pass

Technically, this border crossing is considered a Class II crossing, meaning that it is closed to all except citizens of Kyrgyzstan and China. The problems for travellers crossing via this route stem from this rule; that and the fact that a bus was attacked on its way over the pass in 2002, resulting in over 20 deaths.

You can get permission to cross from the Chinese Department of Foreign Affairs in Ürümqi but, unsurprisingly, this costs money. The crossing's Class II status also means non-locals cannot use public transport to cross it: buses do the 48hr journey between Bishkek and Kashgar every week to coincide with the Kashgar Sunday market but foreigner visitors trying to take them are usually kicked off – sometimes in the middle of nowhere (check with the agencies at either end to see if this is still the case, as obviously once bus travel is an option the prices will come tumbling down). Furthermore, the border is closed at weekends and on public holidays.

It is planned to upgrade the crossing to Class I but until they do you must hire private transport the entire way (it is virtually impossible to hitch). It is safer to put yourself in the hands of a reliable agency (see p235 and pp307-8) as stories of transport not turning up from the other side abound: this problem is not as common as it used to be but that will be no consolation to you – even the US ambassador was once refused permission to enter China here because he didn't have the right papers!

**Coming from Kyrgystan** You can cross from Naryn to Kashgar quite easily in a day but it is worth setting off at dawn to take in **Tash Rabat**, a picturesque caravanserai (see box p98) dating back to the glory days of the Silk Road. You are likely to arrive there before it is officially open but a key will be found, often for no charge. It's another hour to the Kyrgyz side of the border but nothing opens until 10.30 and the Chinese side doesn't open until 13.00 so be prepared to hang around. The Customs officials here have an English translation of their declaration form if you ask for it.

You then have another 45-minute drive up to the famous arch in the middle of no-man's land where you will meet your transport from the other side – your Kyrgyz driver has to turn back here. **NB You will not be allowed to drive up to the arch until your Chinese transport has arrived (and vice versa if you are coming from Kashgar)**. Once you've crossed under the arch and shaken hands with all the green uniforms on the other side, you can officially say 'I am in China' which, after all the aggravation, feels very, very good.

It's not over yet, though. Now your Chinese driver will drive for about an hour-and-a-half to the official Chinese Customs where everything, and we mean everything, will be searched thoroughly but very politely. It's another hour down the road to passport control and a final check for seditious material (such as maps showing Taiwan to be a separate country). Finally, you are free to enjoy yourself and the two-hour drive to Kashgar.

The views from Torugart Pass (3752m) are not as spectacular as you might have hoped for (they are certainly nothing compared to those on the Karakorum Highway) but it is the completing of the journey itself that makes this so special.

**Coming from Kashgar** It is much the same but in reverse. There are a number of agencies offering this service, although you might find it more difficult to stop off at Tash Rabat.

**NB The Torugart Pass is theoretically open year-round but is regularly blocked by snow between October and April.**

# PART 5: PAKISTAN

## Facts about the country

### GEOGRAPHICAL BACKGROUND

Nothing is unequivocal about Pakistan. That includes its borders. Officially, Pakistan is only 803,940 sq km but in practice the 83,000 sq km of the Northern Areas plus Azad, Jammu and Kashmir can be included. Although the terrain can be flat and desert-like in the south, all the areas covered in this guide are mountainous – because the Himalayas, the Karakorum, the Hindu Kush and the Pamirs all converge here. These mountains are big too: of the ten mountains in the world over 8000m, five are in northern Pakistan, including K2 (8611m) and Nanga Parbat (8125m).

### HISTORY

#### Prehistory
Evidence of Stone Age man has been found in the Punjab and by the third millennium BC the Indus River valley was the centre of a flourishing civilization that lasted until around the 18th century BC when it came to an abrupt but mysterious end about which historians are still uncertain.

#### Indo-Aryans
Around this time, however, new peoples were coming in from Central Asia through the Hindu Kush and turning from their nomadic lifestyles to the more settled practices of agriculture. This migration began a trend that would last for

---

**The Khunjerab Pass**
Despite its name (Khunjerab means 'River of Blood' in Tajik) this pass is more of a plateau than a pass and sits on top of the enormous **Karakorum** ('Black Gravel') mountain range. It should not be confused with the **Karakorum Pass** on the other side of K2, at the disputed border between Jammu and China. The plateau is home to wild Bactrian camels, yaks, marmots and ibex, all of which you should be able to see during the summer. That the pass is also home to a few Tajik families, however, is more of a marvel.

The pass has as good a claim as any to be the physical centre of the 'Pamir Knot', the term coined during the Great Game to describe the complexity of this region's politics (see p206). The name **'Pamirs'** means 'Wide, open plateau' and it is these mountains you can see on a clear day climbing off north-westwards into Tajikistan; the **Hindu Kush** (literally 'Hindu Killers') also begin to climb from here, south-westwards into Afghanistan.

thousands of years and bring this area much closer to its northern and western neighbours than to its southerly ones, despite the apparent geographic contradiction. The newcomers also brought with them a Vedic religion based around the worship of cows (this is seen by many as the precursor to Hinduism) and a type of caste system. There was no overall unity, however, rather a mishmash of tribal kingdoms, the most famous of which was that of Ghandara (controlling parts of Afghanistan as well as the Peshawar and Swat valleys). All of them, however, fell to the mighty Persian leader Cyrus the Great (see p36) and remained under the control of the Achaemenids until they in turn were toppled. It was about this time that Buddhism (see box pp38-9) emerged.

## Alexander the Great

In 327BC, Alexander led his troops over the freezing Hindu Kush to take control of the final pieces of the Persian empire jigsaw. He was keen to continue and win new lands but even his most loyal Macedonian troops were reaching breaking point. They mutinied at the Indus (near present-day Amritsar) and, rather than push on, they sailed down the river to the ocean and headed home.

Governors were left to control the area, however, and no doubt some troops decided to stay and build a new life as Alexander colonized towns wherever he went; if you go up into Chitral and the Swat Valley you still might be surprised by the number of people who talk with such pride about this part of their heritage, and the abundance of distinctive European features such as blue eyes and blond hair.

## The Mauryans

Alexander's empire was almost bound to break up upon his death and this area was one of the first to go. In 321BC the king of northern India, Chandragupta Maurya, challenged Seleucis, Alexander's successor in the east, for the Ghandara lands and the Greek leader was powerless to stop him. In fact, Seleucis was almost glad to be rid of this area so long as it remained in friendly hands and trade continued to flow into his empire, so he officially handed it over in return for a peace treaty and 500 elephants.

Chandragupta's grandson, Ashoka (ruler from 272 to 235BC) went on to take most of the Indian subcontinent and his capital, Taxila, seems to have reached new heights of wealth and sophistication at this time. Ashoka disinterred the ashes of the Buddha from stupas in the Ganges valley, divided them up and had them sent to the eight most important cities in his empire; in Taxila, the Dharamarajika stupa (see p276) was built to house its portion. Everything, however (apart from the strength of Buddhism), collapsed upon his death.

The Bactrians of northern Afghanistan were the first to fill the gap in northwest India but they were overrun by the Scythians coming down from Central Asia, who in turn succumbed to the Parthians. This didn't do much for stability but it did wonders for trade, as this area became a firm player in the boom initiated by the Silk Road. There is archaeological evidence in the Hunza Valley and surrounding areas that the route over the Karakorum to and from Yarkand was very much up and running at this time.

## The Kushans
Finally, in the 2nd century AD, yet another tribe from the steppes above Lake Balkhash arrived. They were known as the Yueh-Chih or Kushans. They initially set up a kingdom based in Bactria that stretched from Uzbekistan in the north to Ghandara in the south with frequent additions being won and lost in Xinjiang. Slowly their attention turned further south and they moved their capital to Peshawar, extending their lands to the Ganges. Nevertheless, they maintained control of the key middle section of the Silk Road and earned themselves the reputation of being the consummate trading race, even once their political superiority had diminished. Their lands were reduced to Ghandara and Kashmir in the 3rd century AD and when in turn these lands fell it was to Persian Sassanids, rather than the Gupta dynasty of north India which had taken Sind and much of the Punjab.

The 5th century, however, saw a return to invasions from the north. First were the White Hun and then the Turkic Shahi. Fa Hsien (see p44) arrived at this time on his Buddhist Pilgrimage from China and he was followed in the 7th century by Xuan Zang (see box p345). In the 9th century the ruling king was deposed by his Brahman minister and the whole region was set to turn to Hinduism; as it turned out, the timing couldn't have been worse...

## The coming of Islam
In 709AD an Arabian ship had been seized by pirates off the Sind coast. A punitive expedition was sent to reassert the authority of the country's now all-powerful Muslims. At the same time, a section of the Muslim army that was busy conquering Central Asia was deployed through Afghanistan to Peshawar.

At first the Arabs were content with appointing a governor to control their gains in the Indus valley and the Hindu Shahi dynasty was allowed to remain in control of the north. By the end of the 10th century, however, the Muslim Sultan of Ghazni wanted the throne for himself and his son, Mahmud of Ghazni, set about annexing the Punjab, converting the civilians as he went. His successors reached as far as Delhi but there were also setbacks: first the Mongols sacked Lahore and Peshawar before turning their attention to Delhi in the 13th century, then Tamerlane repeated their invasion in 1398.

Nevertheless, Buddhism struggled on in the mountains, although the religion's epicentre shifted north to Tibet. Islam did not truly penetrate areas such as the Hunza Valley until the 16th century.

## The Moghuls
Going by his pedigree you can be forgiven for calling Zahir-ud-Din Babur's desire to rule an empire 'predictable' – he was descended from Tamerlane on his father's side and Genghis Khan on his mother's – yet, initially, he looked likely to let his ancestors down: he became ruler of the Ferghana Valley following his father's death but was then kicked out by rivals in 1500, aged only seventeen.

Nevertheless, he washed up a few years later in Afghanistan and was able to manipulate himself into a position of power, ruling Kabul for two decades. In 1524 his army burst out of the mountains and took Lahore before marching across to Delhi and defeating its last sultan in 1526: the sultan's swords were no match for Babur's new firearms. The Moghul empire was founded ('Moghul' is a corruption of 'Mongol' and was the name given by Indians to any invaders from the north) and it soon controlled the whole subcontinent.

Babur is said to have been a great poet but, unfortunately, little has been translated out of Uzbek. Nevertheless, one line that he is famous for is his sad reflection at the end of his life: 'It's better to be a beggar in your own country, than a king in a foreign land'. It is difficult to say that he was the originator of this sentiment and he certainly wasn't the last, but there can't be too many more striking examples considering his ultimate power and wealth.

Under his descendants, the Grand Trunk Road was built and during the reign of perhaps the greatest Moghul leader, Akbar (1556-1605), the capital was moved to a new palace/fort built in Lahore. His grandson, Shah Jahan (1628-1658) built the Taj Mahal, Lahore's Shalimar Gardens and commissioned the famous Peacock Throne (see p135), as the empire reached new heights in opulence and cultural extravagance. It is important to remember that all these Moghul leaders were Muslim.

It wasn't until the Persian opportunist, Nadir Shah, invaded in 1738 that the dynasty's power was challenged. He took Afghanistan, Kashmir and the Punjab, and, on his death, these lands were in turn seized by the Durrani Pashtun leader, Ahmad Shah. The rest of the subcontinent, however, faced a very different threat.

## The British

Queen Elizabeth I granted the East India Company its first charter in 1600 and soon the one-off expeditions to trade in the Bay of Bengal for cotton and spices became part of a more permanent strategy. Competing efforts from France, Holland and Portugal were edged out and the company began to establish territories of its own in coastal areas. These grew in size and influence until Robert Clive was in a strong-enough position to take on and defeat the Moghul forces at Plassey in 1757.

By now the lands were becoming too big for the company to handle, so a governor-general was appointed by the Crown in an attempt to tighten the reins. London was so far away, however, that the effectiveness of this post was limited. The company still sponsored any incursions into Indian territory that would help bring in financial profit, sure in the knowledge that the governor-general was unlikely to oppose any territorial expansion if presented with a *fait accompli*.

### The Sikhs
Sikhism was founded as a hybrid of the main religions of Islam and Hinduism in an attempt to cut away man-made elaborations and return to the true spirit of worship. As such it attracted many followers but at the same time its leaders were persecuted as a potential source of unrest. As a response, Gobind Singh (all Sikhs took the added surname of 'Singh'), the last great Sikh guru, founded the Khalsa, a brotherhood of 'holy warriors', which soon had a whole series of units across the country.

In 1799 the governorship of Lahore was granted to a Khalsa leader, Ranjit Singh, and he exploited the Moghuls' weakness to carve out his own Sikh kingdom covering not just the Punjab but also Kashmir, Ladakh, Baltistan, Gilgit and the Peshawar Valley.

He made a treaty with the British to stay out of their territory if they stayed out of his. After he died in 1839, the agreement broke down and the two Sikh Wars of 1846 and 1849 were fought. The British won and with victory came Kashmir, Ladakh, Baltistan and Gilgit. They sold this new land, now called the State of Jammu and Kashmir, to a Jammu prince, Gulab Singh (who, despite his name, was a Hindu). He was created the Maharajah of Kashmir in a move that is still having repercussions today. The fighting qualities of the Sikhs, however, were noted and many were drafted into the British army.

### The First Afghan War 1839-42
With the Great Game (see box p206) hotting up and Russia expanding into Central Asia, Britain wanted to make sure that whoever was on the Afghan throne, which was seen as lying in the British 'sphere of influence', remained loyal. Doubts had arisen by 1839 about the leanings of the latest incumbent, Dost Mohammed, and Britain took the typically bullish approach of marching into Kabul and placing their man, the previous ruler, Shah Shuja (who had been exiled because he was so unpopular), back on the throne. Unsurprisingly, it did not work and Britain suffered one of its worst losses when the tribal leaders revolted. The British force sent to prop up Shah Shuja was massacred (there was one survivor out of 16,000) as it tried to retreat to the British garrison at Jalalabad. Dost Mohammed returned as ruler and Britain was shame-faced. Like a school bully it reacted by picking a fight with a weaker target, Sind, and this previously independent region was taken in 1843.

### The Great Mutiny and the Second Afghan War 1878-81
In 1857 there was the first major uprising in India against British rule. It began in the Bengal Army and, although short-lived, the soldiers managed to take Delhi. The British response was again brutal but this time was, at least, effective. In an attempt to prevent anything like this happening again, the Crown took complete control of the country. A Viceroy of the Raj was appointed and India became a formal part of the British empire. Moghul government practices were abandoned and a completely British structure was introduced from the railways to the legal system.

The second attempt to install a British puppet in Kabul was as unsuccessful as the first but what it did achieve was the formalizing of the British/Afghan border in the north-west Pashtun district. The precise position of the border was dictated by the Durand Line (1893) but, in fact, neither the British nor the Afghans had much control over the Pathans who lived here so Durand had little to go on: the result was a predictable mess. The Pathans began to revolt immediately and in 1901 a separate North-West Frontier Province (NWFP) had to be created to give the Pathans near autonomy – a province and policy that still exist (in tribal areas, federal law applies only to the roads and ten yards on either side of them).

In 1907, as the Great Game drew to a close in this area, the Wakhan Corridor was officially pronounced Afghan territory to ensure that British and Russian lands would never have to share a common border.

## The independence movement

In 1885, the Indian National Congress was formed to press for constitutional reform. From the very outset, however, it was regarded with suspicion by the Muslim minority within India who considered it merely a Hindu mouthpiece. The All-India Muslim League was therefore convened in Dhaka in 1906. The British tried to exacerbate the divisions within the independence movement but when Britain declared war on Muslim Turkey in WW1, the Congress and the League joined forces in the historic Lucknow Pact of 1916.

A new leader had emerged for the Muslims, Mohammed Ali Jinnah, who together with Gandhi and Nehru pushed for more reforms. In 1919, British soldiers massacred hundreds of unarmed protestors at Amritsar and the revolution

> ### Kashmir
> The status of this province has been by far the most difficult conundrum for the region since India and Pakistan's independence and today resolution is still, unfortunately, a long way off. Problems began when the Hindu Maharajah of Jammu and Kashmir, Hari Singh (a direct descendant of the first Maharajah), realized that the majority of his civilians were Muslim and that, given the choice, they would probably side with Pakistan. As he was a Hindu, he knew this would probably mean the end to his reign. On the other hand, he was quite happy with the virtual autonomy afforded to him by the British and had no desire to suddenly hand his lands over to an Indian Congress. He prevaricated and prevaricated and what the true will of the people was, we will never know.
>
> In October 1947 a band of Pashtun Afridi tribesmen invaded Kashmir and declared a *jihad* or Muslim holy war, having heard a rumour that the Maharajah was going to sell out to India; the Maharajah fled to Delhi to do exactly that. Mountbatten washed his hands of the affair (issuing the ambiguous verdict that Indian troops could assist Singh against the rebels as long as a full vote was held once the fighting was over) and Pakistan and India were at war.
>
> In 1949 the United Nations ordered a ceasefire and another province was divided. Pakistan was given the Gilgit area, Baltistan and the western rim of Kashmir while India received the much larger areas of Jammu, Ladakh and the larger part of Kashmir. Both sides, however, were given only temporary charge over these lands – they would not officially become part of one country or the other until a referendum was held. We are still waiting for this referendum and even though India has now claimed its lands for itself, Pakistan refuses to acknowledge that its lands are officially part of Pakistan (as that might be seen as an acceptance of India's actions) and is still demanding that the original vote is carried out. The UN's inaction on this has been one of its major failures of the past 50 years.
>
> Pakistan has also provided arms (directly or indirectly) to those fighting inside Kashmir against the Indian government, although this practice seems to be dying out now that the two governments are slowly beginning to work together to find a solution. That said, few would claim to know what the true wishes of the majority of Kashmiris are now anyway.

was under way. Jinnah resigned from the Congress in 1920, believing that Muslim demands were being ignored, even though the Lucknow Pact had promised separate Muslim electorates. Yet it wasn't until 1930 that the concept of a totally separate Muslim state was proposed, by the poet-philosopher Dr Allama Mohammed Iqbal. The name 'Pakistan' was suggested for this state by a group of Muslim intellectuals in exile at Cambridge University – it is an acronym for Punjab, Afghan, Kashmir, Sind with *stan* (meaning 'land') tacked on to the end, and means 'Land of the Pure'.

Everything continued to drag on, however, and with the outbreak of WWII independence was again put on hold by the British. One thing was now clear, however: the Muslims were not going to accept the compromise, suggested by the British, of autonomous Muslim regions within a united India – only an independent Muslim state would do.

## Partition

In February 1947 Britain appointed Lord Louis Mountbatten as viceroy, after Jinnah refused to join Nehru in a power-sharing government. Mountbatten declared that independence would come in June 1948 when elections would be held. Tension mounted, however, as the form Indian independence would take remained unclear and soon this erupted into Muslim versus Hindu violence. Mountbatten panicked, as he knew he was swiftly losing control, and agreed to Muslim demands for a separate Pakistan. Each province and princely state would vote whether to join India or Pakistan and those provinces where there was a fine balance between the two sides (Punjab and Bengal) could vote to split themselves in two. The date for the election was also brought forward to August 1947, leaving just ten weeks to decide how these states would be split up (it being almost a certainty that both these states would indeed be divided in two).

The man handed this thankless task was Sir Cyril Radcliffe. Ignoring all the political advisors around him, he did what any self-respecting civil servant would do and drew two arbitrary lines on the map. One roughly followed the east bank of the Indus and its feeder rivers, dividing the Punjab but placing the Sikh holy city of Amritsar in India; the other was a very rough semi-circle around the flood plains of the Ganges Basin. The Bengalis managed to make the best of their bad job and millions of Hindus still live in what is now Bangladesh but in the Punjab the ordinary people on both sides were terrified. Muslims living in the areas designated for India fled one way, as Sikhs and Hindus in the designated Pakistani areas fled the other. Over six million people migrated in each direction and, unsurprisingly, such massive migrations created a disaster area in the middle. Riots frequently broke out and massacres were carried out by both sides: as many as a million people are estimated to have died.

## Coups and counter-coups

Just when it seemed things couldn't get any more complicated for the fledgling Pakistani state, new divisions quickly appeared after independence and this time they were on the inside. Jinnah had died of tuberculosis in 1948 and without their Quiad I Azam ('Great Leader') Pakistan's politicians began to flounder.

West Pakistan, as present-day Pakistan was known, may have been by far the larger constituent in terms of landmass but East Pakistan, as Bangladesh was known, had a substantially larger population.

As debate descended into petty squabbles between East and West (and between those in favour of a secular state versus the religious hardliners), the country was ripe for a coup. In October 1958 President Iskander Mirza was happy to oblige. A former army general, he declared martial law and in 1961 shifted his capital from Karachi to the newly built city of Islamabad (conveniently next door to the army headquarters in Rawalpindi). Yet almost immediately he was asked to stand aside by his own prime minister, General Muhammad Ayub Khan.

Ayub Khan maintained martial law and dismissed all calls for a separate Bangladesh but he did manage to turn the country around economically. He won backing from the World Bank and the United States and developed a new partnership between Pakistan and China, epitomised by the idea of building a highway across the Karakorum (see p256) – China had gone to war with India over the position of a common border in 1962 and had heavily defeated Pakistan's enemy. In the end, however, he became over-confident and in a two-and-a-half week renewal of the war with India in Kashmir, he took a beating. In 1968 an attempt was made on his life and in 1969 he handed over power to General Agha Mohammed Yahya Khan who called for fresh democratic elections.

## Bangladesh

Not for the first time, the election didn't go the way it was supposed to. Virtually all the East Pakistani seats on offer for the new assembly went to Sheikh Mujib's Awami League and, because of East Pakistan's superiority in population, this gave the League a majority (even though hardly a single vote was cast for it in West Pakistan where Zulfiqar Ali Bhutto's Pakistan People's Party won the majority of seats).

Bhutto and Yahya Khan conspired to prevent Mujib forming a government and East Pakistan went on strike; Mujib had campaigned on an independence platform after a cyclone had devastated East Pakistan in 1970 and the government in West Pakistan had virtually turned a blind eye.

The army tried to clamp down on the strikers and arrested Sheikh Mujib but that lead only to civil war. India characteristically joined in to take advantage of Pakistan's weakness, under the pretext that millions of refugees were flooding into its territory (which they were). Pakistan's army was forced to surrender once more. In January 1972, Bangladesh was proclaimed an independent country and Bhutto was left in charge of the demoralized remains of West Pakistan.

## Bhutto and Zia

Following Bangladesh's independence, Pakistan's governmental policies were (and to a certain extent still are) very much dictated by events in India. Bhutto managed friendly terms with the Indian Prime Minister, Indira Gandhi, but once an Indian nuclear-testing programme was initiated, demands came for a Pakistani programme which the country could ill-afford. This meant investment much-needed elsewhere was often side-tracked.

Bhutto was accused of fixing the 1977 election (which he won) and General Mohammad Zia al Huq carried out a bloodless coup. Despite a massive international outcry, Bhutto was hanged in 1979 on a series of trumped-up charges. Zia held on to power, though, as now the US needed him as an ally against the USSR in the Cold War. The USSR had invaded Afghanistan and the USA ploughed millions of dollars into Pakistan, usually in the form of weapons, as long as Zia continued to support and arm the rebel *Mujahideen* in Afghanistan.

By 1986, however, Zia was under severe international pressure to restore the rights of opposition parties and the main beneficiary was Benazir Bhutto who returned from exile in England to lead her father's party, the PPP.

Zia himself died, along with five of his generals and the US ambassador, in a very convenient plane crash in August 1988 and Benazir did just enough (including an arranged marriage) to win the election and be proclaimed prime minister.

## Modern Pakistan

Rajiv Gandhi visited Islamabad as India's leader in 1989 but by the end of the year Kashmir was again heavily occupied by Indian troops. Further unrest broke out as tribal conflicts flared up within Pakistan itself: Sindhis in Karachi and Hyderabad turned on Pashtuns and Mohajirs (those Pakistanis who had fled from India after the 1948 partition). The millions of Afghan refugees in the NWFP and around Peshawar (together with their guns and drugs) did little to encourage stability.

A new general election was called in 1990 by the president, much to Benazir's dismay. During the build up her husband was arrested on charges of kidnapping and corruption as part of the wider charges the president had cited when dissolving Benazir's government. The PPP unsurprisingly lost.

The new man in charge was Nawaz Sharif, leader of the Islamic Democratic Alliance and a former Zia protégé. He didn't have much luck either, however. The US suspended US$564 million in aid in response to Pakistan's nuclear-bomb programme; the 1990-91 Gulf War stemmed the enormous tide of earnings that usually returned from Pakistani workers in Kuwait, and 1992 witnessed Pakistan's worst flooding in a century, destroying millions of homes and crops. Again, President Ghulam Ishaq Khan demanded a new election and this time the PPP scraped home in a coalition.

Thus Benazir returned to power in triumph in 1993 but the tribal conflicts worsened to almost daily tit-for-tat killings. Now Sunni Muslims turned on Shi'ites, too, in another depressing twist. Nor did the suspicions over Benazir and her husband's corruption disappear as they were accused of buying a US$4 million estate in England on a declared salary of US$25,000. In 1996, as the Taliban's star soared in Afghanistan, Benazir's fell, probably for the last time (she faces arrest if she re-enters Pakistan).

The 1997 election brought Sharif back to power but with one of the lowest turnouts ever (36 per cent) as most, especially the young, stayed away. This was much to the disappointment of Imran Khan, who was counting on them to vote for his new 'Justice' party. In fact, Khan was always up against it as most of his

> **Earthquake 2005**
> The geography and geology of the Pakistan's Northern Areas may be dramatic but it is also highly dangerous for those living there. The enormous earthquake of 2005 has had a devastating effect not just on the rural areas in the country's north-east but the nation as a whole. Thousands of families died or were made homeless and it soon became clear that even with the KKH running through its heart, this is one of the most remote and inhospitable places in the world. Expect to wait a long time for tourism in the region (already badly hit by 9/11) to return to normal.

support is not just young, it is under twenty one, the legal voting age – if it had been just three years lower, eighteen, he probably would have won millions more votes. It was no surprise when General Pervez Musharraf ousted Sharif in 1999 in another bloodless coup.

This led to an increase in tension between Pakistan and India, however, with the escalation of nuclear testing a particular worry. Musharraf had meetings with India and talked about solving the Kashmiri problem but these events were nothing compared to the fallout from September 11.

During the American war against the Taliban, enormous pressure was placed on the Pakistani leader to assist the US against a force he, like many in Pakistan, had previously endorsed and condoned. America accompanied its pressure with enough money, aid and promises to persuade Musharraf it was worth his while and the Taliban were duly removed from power, if not ultimately defeated.

This pro-America stance alienated large parts of the population, however, especially the religious hardliners and several attempts have been made on the president's life. Yet Musharraf continued with the elections he had promised for 2002 and although the outcome wasn't quite as convincing as he had hoped, there was not the widespread unrest many predicted. He has since consolidated his control and is moving forward on negotiations with India in an attempt to boost the economy. The most significant outcome so far has been the reopening of some border crossings and the beginnings of cross-border trade.

Nevertheless, many of the ousted Taliban seem to have fled into the border areas and the NWFP; the situation remains uneasy and attacks against American and Western interests continued in 2006.

## THE PEOPLE

As we have seen, Pakistan has had a complicated past which has resulted in a complicated mix of races and you will probably not be surprised to learn that there hasn't been a proper census since 1981.

It is estimated, however, that there are over 140 million people in Pakistan, with another three million in Jammu and Kashmir and two million in the Northern Areas, making it the ninth most populous country on the planet. Around 40 per cent of the population is under fifteen. Well over half the population is also illiterate and for women in rural areas this figure can grow as high as 90 per cent.

There are all sorts of ethnic divisions in Pakistan but these are the main groups: the Punjabi (Punjab), Sindhi (Sind), Mohajir (Sind), Pashtun (Baluchistan and NWFP), Baluchi and Brahui (Baluchistan). Although Urdu is the national language, less than ten per cent of Pakistanis speak it as their mother tongue. Despite the ending of the war in Afghanistan, thousands of Afghan refugees have preferred to stay in Pakistan rather than return to their homes and this has caused further tensions.

## ECONOMY

The problem for Pakistan has been that, before partition, the regions that form the country today were primarily used only as a source of raw materials; any manufacturing was carried out in what is now India. Therefore, despite an impressive growth rate – one of the highest in Asia during the 1980s – the country was starting from a very low base.

Unemployment is still growing and much of the wealth has been retained by a very narrow group of families. In the Northern Areas the average per capita income is less than US$200 a month. Corruption is still rife, inflation remains high and although the full cost of the earthquake in 2005 (see box opposite) has yet to be calculated, it was an enormous setback which the country could ill-afford.

## RELIGION

Despite being the birthplace of Hinduism, Buddhism and to an extent Sikhism, Pakistan is virtually entirely inhabited by Muslims (see box p57). Of these, a large majority are Sunni Muslim (77 per cent) rather than Shi'ite (20 per cent) but there is a significant number of Ismaili Shi'ites, especially in the valleys along the Karakorum Highway.

The debate, however, still rages as to how much influence Islam should have in the running of the country. Jinnah and the early leaders wanted a secular state where Muslim interests were protected but many want a full Islamic republic and it is these groups that fleeing members of the Taliban have joined. Alcohol has been banned, though not completely, and after a short period of switching the day of rest to Friday, it has been restored to Sunday.

### Ismailis
The founders of Ismailism agreed with the Shi'ites that the descendants of Ali should be their leaders, known as imams, but they disagreed as to which son of the sixth Imam should have succeeded him (they backed Ismail and have given allegiance to his line of descent ever since). Ismailis also believe that each successor has been an Imam like his predecessor whereas most Shi'ites believe that there have been only twelve (see box p68). The present Aga Khan is considered by Ismailis to have the magic touch as the 49th Imam and those of you who have backed one of his many horses may agree.

# Practical information for the visitor

One of the reasons why retracing the Silk Road is so appealing is that you have the added enjoyment of entering each country by land rather than on a plane. Although some borders can be little more than checkpoints in the desert, others, such as the entrance into Pakistan through the Karakorum Mountains (if heading west along the route from China), can take your breath away.

In these mountains you also have the opportunity of going much further off the beaten track than in most of the other countries *en route,* so be prepared for a more physical encounter if you want to reap the most rewards (see 'Trekking the Silk Road', p266). Having said that, there is nothing in this guide that requires too much equipment or exceptional fitness.

We have laid out this section as a trip from Sost (the first village after leaving China) to Rawalpindi but you can easily use it in reverse if you have come from Iran (see p154) or are beginning your trip in Islamabad. If you want to spend more time in Pakistan to explore the likes of the Khyber Pass, Peshawar, Chitral and the Swat Valley (not to mention Lahore and Karachi), we fully recommend *The Pakistan Handbook* by Isobel Shaw (you can easily pick it up in Rawalpindi and Islamabad if you cannot find it at home).

The biggest difference you will notice if you are coming from China or Iran is that in Pakistan nearly everybody speaks English.

## THE ROUTE

This is probably the most straightforward section of the guide as you are sticking to the KKH all the way to Rawalpindi (or Kashgar, if you going the other way). The only decision you need to make is how many times to stop and how long to spend in each area.

Originally, this section of the Silk Road followed a fairly similar path as the KKH does today, although another route also came across from China through the Karakorum Pass (see p9) into Leh and Srinagar. Some historians, however, have mistakenly concluded that these were primary routes for moving silk west to Europe (partly, no doubt, because Marco Polo seems to have visited at least part of the area on his way to Khublai Khan's court). In fact, this was a separate Silk Road in its own right, carrying goods to trade with the many riches of the Indian subcontinent (although, of course, some wares did go on as part of the caravans heading west to Afghanistan and beyond).

What is so special about this section is that as you descend from the Khunjerab Pass on the Pakistani side, you can actually see the original Silk Road chipped out of the cliffs on the opposite banks of the river. This was meant for single-file camel trains, however, and their journey would have taken weeks (in 1877 John Biddulph, Britain's first political agent in Gilgit, tells us that the route

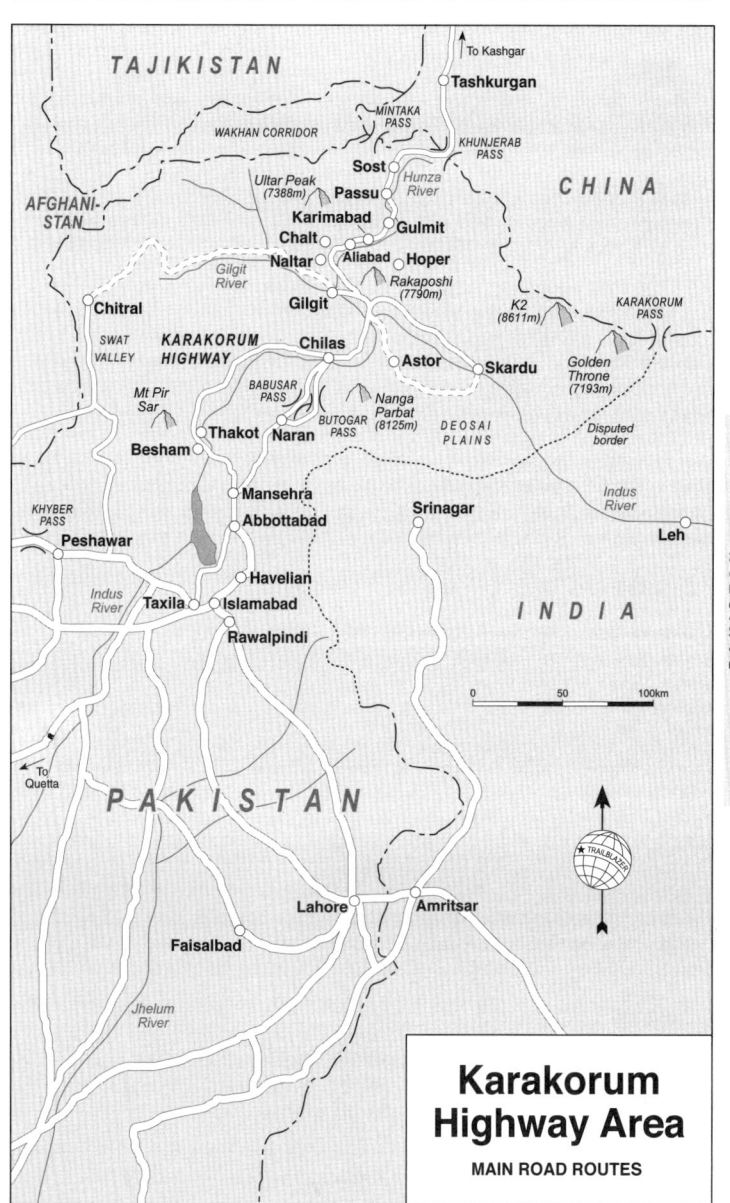

# Karakorum Highway Area
MAIN ROAD ROUTES

> ### The Karakorum Highway
> This road is the main artery for all of northern Pakistan and runs 1200km from Havelian (see map p255) to Kashgar. It was begun in the 1960s as part of a plan by China to strengthen its ties with Pakistan, whom it saw as a natural ally against India with whom it had a disputed border. It was not completed, however, until 1982. Running through some of the most challenging terrain on earth, it is rightly compared to the Pyramids as one of man's most incredible engineering feats. Hundreds of Chinese workers died during its construction (one, it is estimated, for every two kilometres), as a path was literally blasted through the mountains, but it has brought magnificent trade and tourism opportunities to the area.
>
> In 2005 a complete overhaul of the highway was begun. The road has been widened into a dual carriageway on most of the Chinese side and rockfalls are no longer the major problem they once were. The Pakistan side is similarly being upgraded so that bigger trucks can stimulate cross-border trade – but expect this to take a while longer, especially in light of the earthquake in 2005 (see box p252).

was little more than a goats' track which even pack animals found impossible to follow, forcing him to transfer all his possessions onto the backs of sheep). It seems odd that it is now quite a simple journey to organize and that thousands of Pakistanis make the trip every month to stock up on cheap supplies in China.

## DOCUMENTS

If you are beginning your trip in Pakistan you will have obtained your visa in your home country. You can easily apply for your Chinese visa in Islamabad, since relations between the two countries are very good (it should take three or four days only, see p276), but you **cannot obtain a visa (not even a transit visa) at the border**.

If you have come from China and did not get your visa for Pakistan in Beijing, you might be able to get a seven-day transit visa at the border (for free) which will allow time to get down to Islamabad and upgrade it to whichever length visa you require. However, we would rely on this only as a last resort because they expect you to head straight to Islamabad and can be very uncooperative if you stop off, which means you have a gruelling two-day bus ride down and then an equally uncomfortable journey back up.

If you want to stay in Pakistan for more than 30 days you must apply at a Foreigners' Registration Office in the Interior Ministry in Islamabad (see p276).

## CLIMATE

There are enormous differences between the various regions of Pakistan but winter in the north is long and harsh. Get here by September because not only is the KKH closed from late October but also the weather deteriorates dramatically in

---

**Opposite**: Retracing Silk Roads can be a precarious business as this rope bridge (see Walk 1, p264) demonstrates.

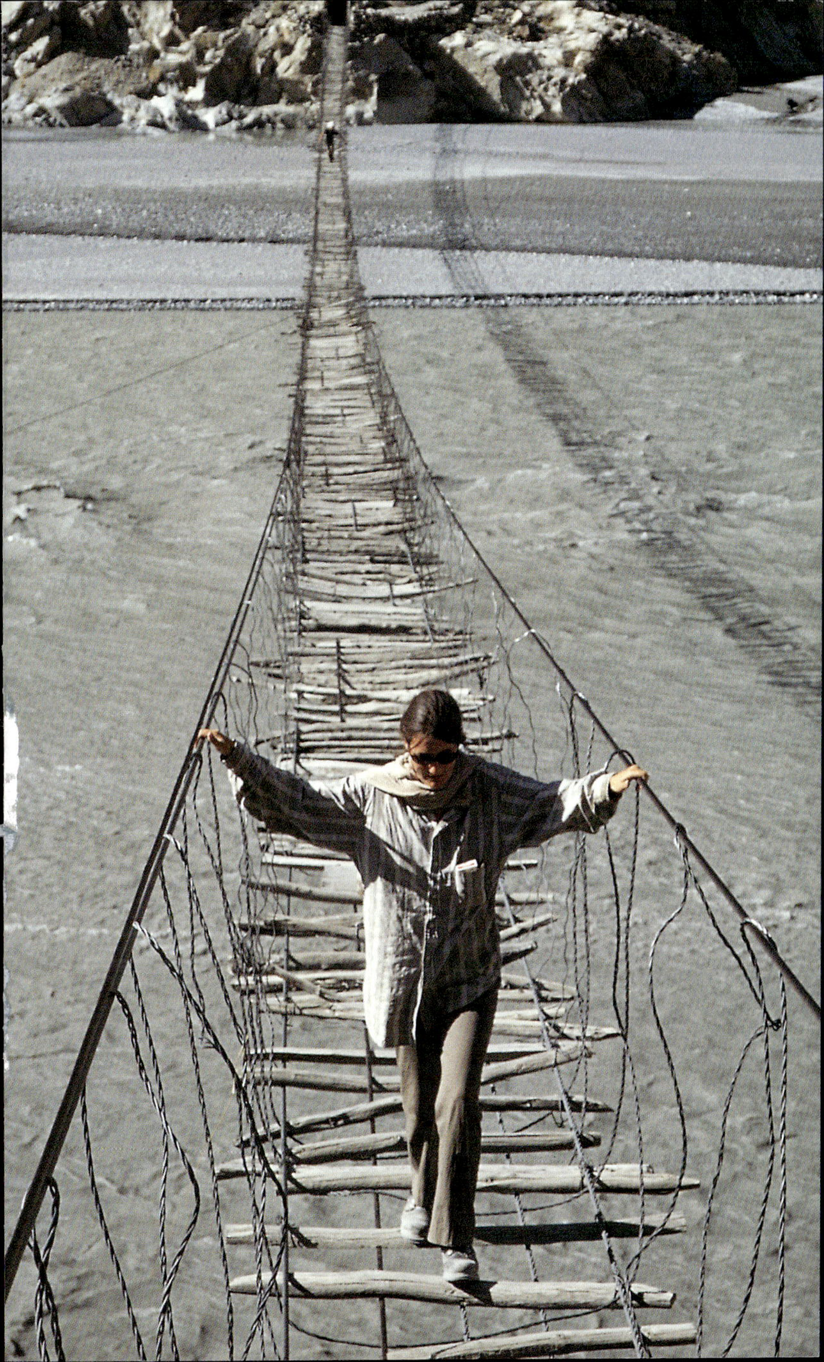

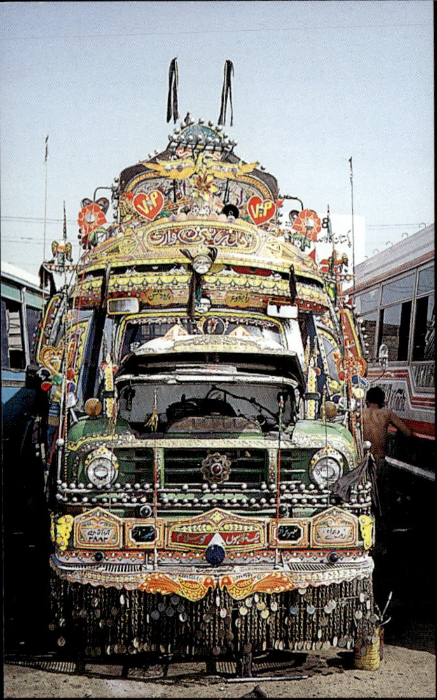

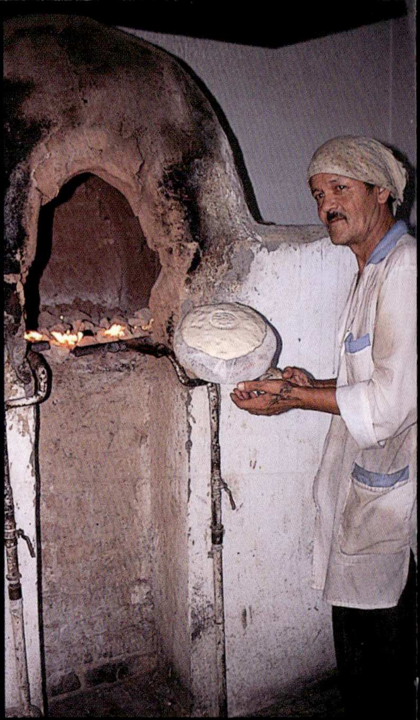

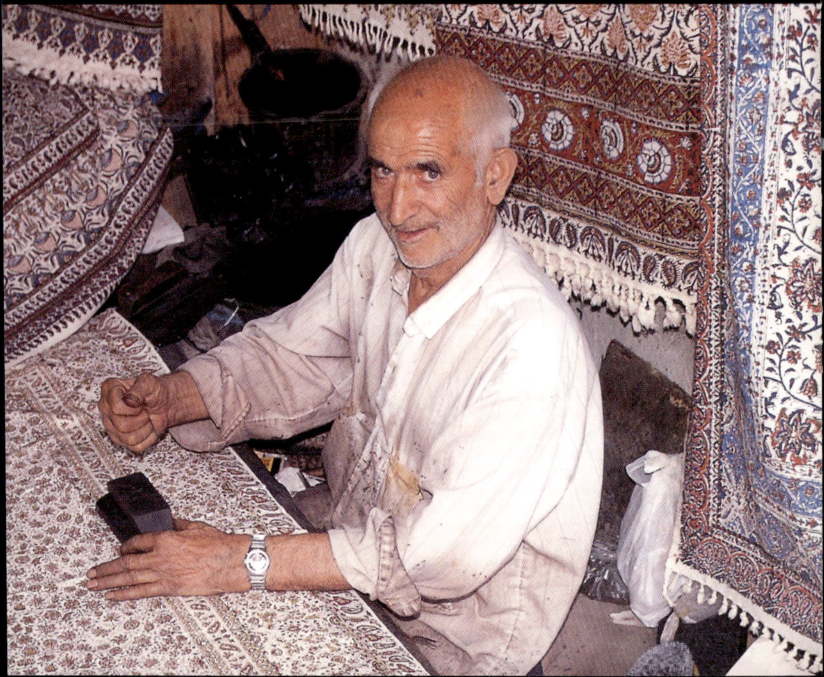

the mountains during the autumn; it's not much fun trekking all day just to get a closer look at a cloud without a glimpse of the snow-covered peaks. Rain can strike from the west at any time during the late summer, so May and June are probably the best months.

## ACCOMMODATION

Tourism in this part of the world really took off before September 11 so there is a good choice of accommodation, although it is mostly aimed at the backpacking/trekking type so don't expect too many luxuries.

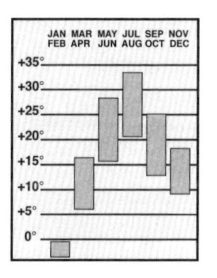

**Max/min °C
Hunza Valley
(Pakistan)**

Dorms are common as are communal showers. Some hotels offer camping accommodation. Most budget hotels will expect you to eat breakfast and dinner in their communal kitchens/restaurants, so it is good manners to inform them early on if you're 'dining out'. Most hotels provide a laundry service for a small charge.

## TRAVEL AGENCIES AND TOURIST INFORMATION

If you are beginning your trip in Pakistan, you may decide to contact the tourist office website (see p30) or seek the help of a tour operator in Islamabad (see p276) though this isn't really necessary as there are groups organizing tours in all major towns and we've listed the best ones in the relevant sections.

## TRANSPORT

### Buses

Virtually everybody in Pakistan takes the bus as their prime means of transport. This might be a state-run **Natco** coach but it is just as likely to be a private minibus, which charges only a little extra. Simply put, wherever you want to go along the KKH, some sort of public transport will be going there (usually the service will be regular, though early mornings are best). Fares are very cheap and although the ride will rarely be a comfortable one, it shouldn't be too slow.

For short journeys, everybody uses the long, thin **Suzuki pick-up trucks**, which can fit about ten on the back.

If you are a woman on any type of bus, you will often be asked to sit separately with the other women; they try to keep one row for women only.

Whichever form of bus you take, you will be struck by how magnificently they are decorated, especially in the big cities. The drivers obviously take great pride in their vehicles and the kaleidoscope of bright greens, reds, yellows and blues is worth a photo on any camera. Unfortunately, Pakistani vehicles are

---

**(Opposite) Top left**: Pakistani bus drivers are obsessed with their vehicles and their rivalry has produced some of the most colourful modes of transport on the planet. **Top right**: Making bread, Uzbek style. **Bottom**: Esfahan (see pp142-8). Artisans have been block printing the city's famous cloth by hand for centuries.

reported to emit 26 times more pollution than their European counterparts, so perhaps a bit more attention should be paid under the bonnet.

### Cars and motorbikes
You can **rent cars** and motorbikes in Islamabad but this isn't very common. Neither is bringing your **own vehicle** (see 'Driving the Silk Road', p74). **Hitching** is common in the Northern Areas (see 'Hitching the Silk Road', p181).

### Other forms of transport
Although Pakistan, like India, has an impressive **rail** network, only the very end of this section is covered by it. Still, you can try it on a ride out to Taxila (see box p276) and if you stick around in Pakistan you shouldn't miss out on the Khyber Pass railway (see 'Silk Road by Rail', pp8-9).

Cyclists are increasingly common (see 'Cycling the Silk Road', p157) although you need to be pretty fit even for the smallest climb – downhill must be fun though!

You can take **internal flights** all over Pakistan, even from Gilgit (which is supposed to have one of the scariest take-offs and landings in the world) but they are largely as unnecessary as they are undesirable for this land-based trip. Bookings can be made through any travel agent we have listed.

**Taxis** are useful in Rawalpindi but even there you will probably see a bus first. For a more eco-friendly option you could take a *tonga* (a type of horse and cart/carriage).

## ELECTRICITY

Mains electricity is supplied at 220V and most sockets take only two-pin plugs, though adaptors are widely available. Most villages you stay in will experience a blackout at least once a week so keep your torch handy!

## TIME

Pakistan is five hours ahead of GMT and the country does not have Daylight Saving Time.

## MONEY

The unit of currency in Pakistan is the Rupee (Rs). Notes come in denominations of Rs1000, 500, 100, 50, 10, 2 and Rs1. The larger-value notes can some-

❏ **Exchange rates**
| | |
|---|---|
| **£1** | Rs119.60 |
| **€1** | Rs78.76 |
| **US$1** | Rs60.76 |
| **Can$1** | Rs51.51 |
| **Aus$1** | Rs47.20 |
| **NZ$1** | Rs42.48 |

To get the latest rates of exchange visit 🖳 www.oanda.com/convert/classic or 🖳 www.xe.net/currency/.

times be awkward to spend as no one ever has enough change.

You can easily change **travellers' cheques** in major banks; the National Bank of Pakistan is the most efficient. **Credit/debit cards** can be used for cash advances in Rawalpindi and Islamabad where there are Western banks such as Citibank. It's best to have enough **US dollars in cash** to last you outside the main cities.

If you are going to/coming from China, you can change yuan and rupees at the border, in Kashgar, in Sost and in Gilgit, though in Pakistan the rates aren't particularly good.

Demanding a **tip** (*baksheesh*) is like a religion in Pakistan.

| ❏ Country codes | access/phone |
|---|---|
| Pakistan | ☎ +92 |
| Islamabad | ☎ (0)51 |
| Rawalpindi | ☎ (0)51 |

## COMMUNICATIONS

The **Internet** is now widespread in the city areas and Internet cafés are even to be found up in the hills but, understandably, the service here is not always flawless. In the cities it is cheap and speedy.

Stamp theft is a major problem: ask for all your letters and parcels to be franked in front of you. Apart from this, the service is quite reliable.

Most of Pakistan has international direct dialling (IDD) now but it's cheaper to go to one of the many private call offices (shop around as prices can vary).

## NATIONAL HOLIDAYS

| | |
|---|---|
| 23 March | Pakistan Day |
| 1 May | International Labour Day |
| 14 August | Independence Day |
| 6 September | Defence of Pakistan Day |
| 11 September | Anniversary of Jinnah's Death |
| 9 November | Iqbal Day, in honour of the philosopher behind the concept of Pakistan |
| 25 December | Jinnah's birthday |

For Ramadan and Islamic festivals see box p12.

## CUSTOMS AND ATTITUDES

If you are beginning your journey here or are coming in from China, be ready for a culture shock. The debate about just how much you should try to adapt to local customs still rages but the majority of Pakistanis don't expect foreign visitors to be as strict as themselves.

### Men

Men should wear trousers and long-sleeved shirts but you can wear shorts and a short-sleeved shirt when you are hiking as these are deemed acceptable for sports (we met a guy who had been cycling around Pakistan for six weeks wearing cycling shorts and a T-shirt and he was only harangued twice – each time by an old-fashioned cleric). Short-sleeved shirts are acceptable in towns and cities when it is hot. Holding hands is normal even between people of the same sex.

### Women

Women are expected to wear 'modest' clothes (see box p19). Don't worry about the colour but make sure they are baggy. Although a headscarf is not obligatory outside holy sites, you might prefer to wear a light one or a shawl at all times to minimize harassment. All these garments can easily be bought or made up for you in the local markets in Islamabad or Rawalpindi (if you are coming from China you should find something in Kashgar).

The local attitude to women is an issue for many international visitors. There is no getting away from the fact that many Pakistani men treat women as second-class citizens and few women pass through the country without at least one major hassle (women often receive complaints and stares just for smoking in public). Various tactics have been adopted to counter this, including wearing a wedding ring and saying you are married to any male that you might be travelling with. Most women we met said they wouldn't like to spend too much time in Pakistan on their own, so if you are a single female try to team up with other travellers as soon as possible. Having said that, Ismaili areas (especially the mountain valleys where you will be spending most of your time) are much friendlier and more relaxed than the rest of the country.

### Haggling

Haggle for everything. Apart from buses, anything you want can be bargained for. Sometimes it's not worth bothering as you will be talking just about a few rupees. But if you have little money and plenty of front, Pakistan is the place for you.

### FOOD

Food in Pakistan is pretty good although in many areas there will be little choice of restaurant and/or menu and what there is will be based around the staples of

---

**Crossing the China/Pakistan border**

**From Kashgar** Buses for Pakistan leave from the **International Bus Station** (see map p308). The full ticket to Sost costs Y270 and the journey takes almost two days but you might want to stop off at Kara Kul (see box p309). Stock up on cash because you won't see another ATM until Rawalpindi, although cashing travellers' cheques is not a problem.

The journey from Kashgar to **Tashkurgan** is said to take nine hours but don't be surprised if it takes two hours just to leave the bus station and price in a few extra stops along the way. When you put your bags on the roof, make sure you keep everything you might need for the journey as you won't see those bags again until the next morning. Most buses stop at *Traffic Hotel* in Tashkurgan, where the rooms have been refurbished with modern beds and bedding (Y10/dorm, Y100/Db). *Pamir Hotel* (Y100-200/Db) is more upmarket.

If you are stuck here for a day or fancy a break, hike up to the **Manchu-era fort** that sits up on the hill and dominates the town. The town is earning a seedy reputation though, as Pakistani traders come up here to drink and meet local women.

The next morning you all troop round to the **Customs office**, where it is a simple procedure but one made extremely time-consuming by the tendency of your fellow passengers to have brought half of Kashgar Market with them. There are no hidden charges or taxes to leave China. You can change your Chinese money here but if you are changing dollars use large notes as small denomination bills get a worse exchange rate.

curry, dhal and chapatti. The following are the highlights of what you can expect (regulars at their local Taj Mahal back home will recognize most of the names but should expect the odd twist here and there).

Meat is called *gosht* and is usually mutton (pork, of course, is out) or chicken (*murgi*); *tandoori* means cooked in a clay oven; *biryani* means cooked and served with spiced rice; *chargh* means steam roasted; *karai* means braised with vegetables and served in its own dish (this is often a favourite with foreign visitors) – a *balti* dish is similar (*balti* is the name for a small metal bowl as well as someone from Baltistan), though it is not necessarily the really spicy dish you might have encountered in Britain (in fact most of the food in Pakistan is less spicy than its relatives abroad); *jalfrezi* means fried with eggs, tomatoes and chillies and is a great morning-after eye-opener if you do manage to have a heavy night; *masala* means cooked in a creamy mild sauce and *dopiaza* dishes come with 'double onions'. *Tikka*, *bhoti kebab* and *tabak* mean grilled. Meals are mopped up with chapatis, rotis and nan breads.

If you are coming from China, just these words will be enough to make you lick your lips. For a long time, Tuesdays and Wednesdays were 'meatless' days everywhere for economic reasons. Nowadays, restaurants will serve you some sort of mutton or beef but the tradition still exists.

Remember that you should not touch or eat food with your left hand, especially when offering it to another person, as it offends the locals.

Vegetables are commonplace and it is quite easy to avoid meat if you want to but be prepared for a lot of lentils and some over-boiled greens.

---

The descent from the plateau of the Khunjerab Pass (see box p243) to Sost (6hrs) is a hell-for leather charge down what must be one of the longest/narrowest/deepest/most hair-raising gorges in the world and you soon realize why the road can be closed for days because of rockslides.

You can pick out the old Silk Road scraping its way up the other side of the river (it crosses where you cross) and see how whole chunks have just fallen away over the years under the pressure of the slides. As you come out of each gorge you are met by stunning views of snow-capped mountains which never fail to impress.

Beware that you will be asked, as a foreigner visitor, to pay the US$4 entry fee (payable in any currency) for Khunjerab National Park when you arrive there (even though you will not be getting off the bus and you will be passing through for less than 1km).

Two punctures and a small landslide used to be about par for the course over the two days but now the new road improvements mean journeys are less eventful (certainly on the Chinese side).

**From Sost** You can buy tickets straight through to Tashkurgan (6hrs) and Kashgar from the bus station, and follow the above advice in reverse.

If you want to visit Kara Kul (see box p309), ask the bus driver to let you out on the way down to Kashgar.

> **Marco Polo map**
> Passu's general store (see p264) has a fabulous map showing the presumed route Marco Polo took as he passed through this area. Polo tells us in his *Travels* that, having fallen ill in Afghanistan, he was advised to go into the neighbouring valleys to recuperate, and this is generally held to be the Hunza area; even today, the locals are famous for their health and longevity.
> In 1981, Harry Rutstein carried out his second expedition to track Polo's route and his map demonstrates what he believed the route to be – it is interesting that he considers it more likely that Polo used the Mintaka Pass (see map p255), rather than the Khunjerab.

### Snacks
Kebabs are prevalent and have an interesting Pakistani twist. Try a *chapli kebab*, which is fried in massive flat pans, or a skewer of *kaleji* – chicken livers. Lots of different types of samosas are here as well, alongside sacks of 'Crispy Nimco' (Bombay Mix) and carts of roasted corn-on-the-cob.

## DRINK

### Non-alcoholic
Tea (*chai*) is the staple but you can buy **Nescafé** in the stores. Pakistanis will as often as not serve tea without milk although green tea is available in restaurants.

**Soft drinks** and **bottled water** are everywhere. Waiters will bring you a pitcher of water when you sit down in a restaurant but most people will want to avoid that (as it is only local water) and order a soft drink. Unfortunately, many waiters won't bring the drink until the meal is ready (anything up to 20 minutes) so specifically ask for the drinks to be brought straight away.

*Lassi* is a yoghurt mix and the perfect antidote for a hot curry.

### Alcoholic
The country is officially dry but, in a breathtaking piece of hypocrisy, there are two breweries in the country. You can sign a form in the cities' bigger hotels to confirm that you are a non-Muslim and order just about anything (although all bars close on Thursday evening and all day Friday). If you are staying for a long time you can also apply for an alcohol licence which allows you to purchase alcohol from a limited number of state-run outlets.

In the hills you may also run into 'Hunza water' (which can be quite lethal) or a sickly red wine from the Pathan areas; any dreams of finishing a long day's hike with a beer as the sun goes down, however, can be scrapped.

# Sost

First things first: *this place is not a town*. In fact, it's not even a village. It is a small strip of shacks where you can get some food, change some money and have a night's sleep: blink and you'll miss it. If you go in with these expectations, you will come out happy but if you have been led to believe, as we were, that it is some kind of Kashgar, you will be sorely disappointed.

## PRACTICAL INFORMATION

Coming from China, the chances are that your bus will arrive after the Customs office is closed so you will have to wait until the morning to unload. Whichever currencies you are changing, the rates are poor, so change only what you need to get by until Karimabad/Kashgar.

The hotel options are much of a muchness but we went for ***Al Mahmood's*** (Rs100 for a bed in a three-man dorm with a hot shower), which is in the middle of the row opposite the bus station. If you have been befriended by any Pakistanis on your bus, you might want to follow them as they probably know one of the hotel owners and will make sure you get a fair price. Each hotel has a kitchen and eating room downstairs; it is expected that you will eat here. There is no menu and little choice but the food is surprisingly good and cheap. Wherever you stay, expect frequent power cuts.

### Moving on

From the bus station you can catch a lift in any one of the minibuses (Rs25) and trucks heading down to Passu (if you are a smoker, stock up in Sost as Passu has banned the sale of cigarettes within its boundaries since 1994).

If you are heading to China see box pp260-1.

# Passu

Again, this village isn't big but its setting is beautiful and it's a great base for exploring the nearby mountains and glaciers. Unfortunately, not all is quite as idyllic as it seems. The village council is keen not just to stop smoking within its boundaries but to keep foreign visitors separate too. There is no open hostility but they would much prefer you to stay on the outskirts of the village rather than in the village itself. To this end, one guesthouse (***Guesthouse No 2***) has been closed and if you opt to stay in ***Guesthouse No 1***, they ask you not to leave the hostel after dark.

Their point of view is understandable as an attempt to minimize the impact on their local culture; you can help by not staying in Guesthouse No 1 (Rs50 for a mattress and duvet on the floor of the dining area), although this does have the best location as a base for all your treks.

The irony is that Passu, like most of the Hunza Valley, is a heartland for the Ismaili sect of Islam, which is usually more relaxed and tolerant than the others.

## PRACTICAL INFORMATION

Your lift will drop you at the **general store** at the top of the village but if you want to stay at one of the hotels on the main road, you can arrange this with the driver as you approach the village – they know where they all are.

For a double room you'll do worse than *Passu Peak Inn* (Rs150/Db), about a mile north of the village. The owner is an ex-army officer and the beds are spotless. The buildings are quite spartan but the food comes in giant portions.

For dorms, *Sheesper Inn* (Rs60), south of the village, gets good reports, as does *Babura Inn* (Rs150/Db, camping is also available here), close to Passu Peak. If you do the walk up to Borit Lake you might want to stay at *Borit Hotel* (Rs50, open only in summer months).

The general store may not sell cigarettes but it is otherwise well stocked. If you have come from China, you can buy some goodies you won't have seen for a while and admire their map (see box p262!

### Moving on

For a ride to Karimabad (Rs40) or Sost (Rs45), wait by the road opposite the general store in Passu and one of the regular minibuses will pick you up; or there's a Natco Bus leaving early every morning.

## HIKING AROUND PASSU

Whichever route you take you will get hot, thirsty and hungry so bring a hat, plenty of water (two bottles per person per day), some food and some sunscreen. If you are camping overnight in summer you can usually get away with just a sleeping bag rather than a tent but check the local conditions. Most hostels have detailed walking books/maps you can borrow.

The villagers see it as their right to be employed by you as a guide or porter but for day walks they are rarely needed and even for tougher walks a porter is usually enough (95 per cent of the time he will be a guide in his spare time).

We did these treks in September so be warned that what for us were dry riverbeds and small puddles might be torrential waters and large lakes when you visit. Nevertheless, all the walks should still be possible.

### Walk 1 (see map opposite)

This walk is easy if done over two separate days. If attempted in one go it will be a long, full day.

Walk through the village past Guesthouse No 1 (see above) and follow this path all the way down and round until you come out near the road by a ravine. Go down the ravine (following the cairns) and up the path on the other side which will take you round the base of the hill and down onto the riverbed near the first **suspension bridge**. This is wobbly but safe.

On the other side of the river, follow the hill straight up as if heading for the black crags, directly ahead from the bridge. As you gain height you will see the remains of a riverbed on your right; you should start picking out cairns but beware, there is more than one path crossing this area. The key is to keep high near the base of the hillside (to the right of the crags) as you cross the riverbed and head south-west. It's not a disaster if you head straight west from the

# Hiking around Passu 265

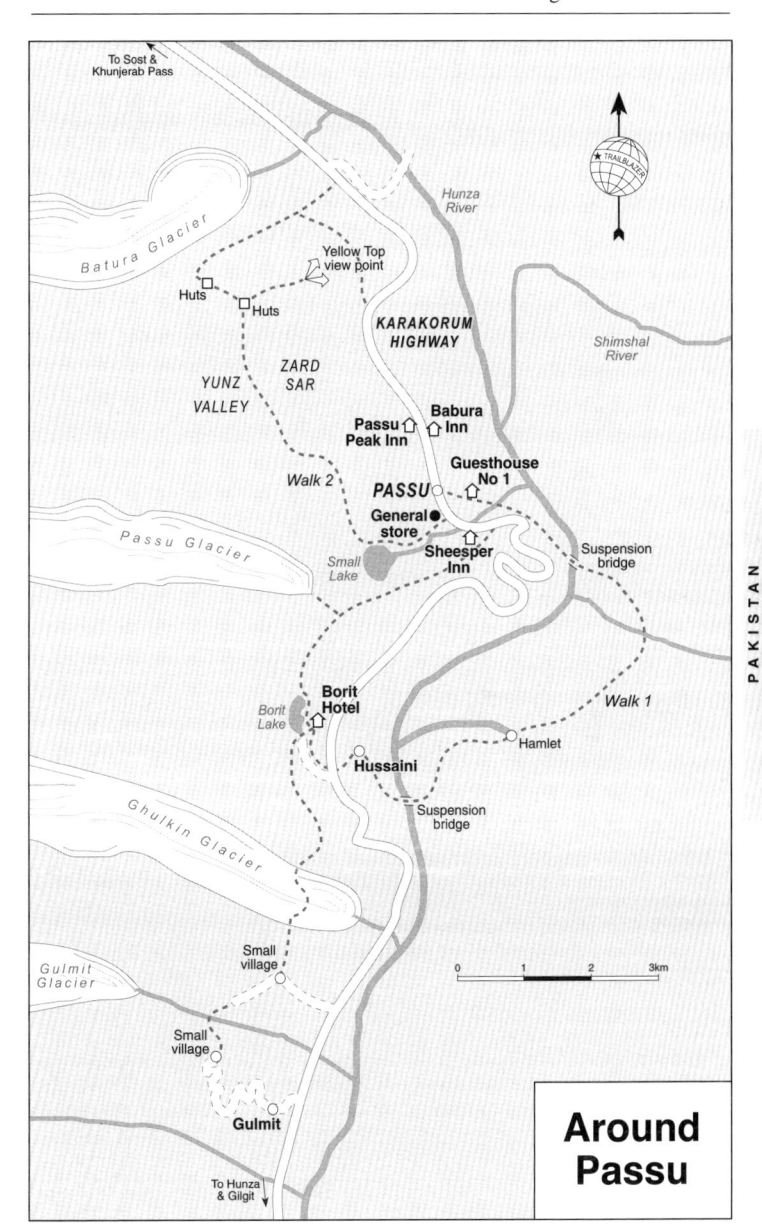

## Around Passu

riverbed but when you come to the huts of a hamlet, you will probably be on the wrong side of a thorny gorge which you will need to cross.

Do not descend to the river yet as you need to follow the path round the base of the cliffs from the huts to the next **suspension bridge**. Once on the other side climb up through the tiny village of **Hussaini** until you hit the main road.

If you are doing this trip over two days, you can now walk or hitch back to Passu – the first part should take about four to five hours.

If you are carrying on, you need to cross the road and ascend the jeep track on the other side to Borit Lake. Depending on where you come out on the main road you might need to turn left or right for 200m before you come to the jeep track. The track is steep but short and at the top is a wonderful lake and the very pleasant Borit Hotel (see pp264). The owner will happily provide food and drinks even if you are not staying there. (If you have any spare cigarettes he is usually very grateful as he can't buy any in the village either.) Down through his garden is the lake – walk to the right towards the big rock as this is the best place to enter for a swim (the locals don't mind you swimming, though ladies should stay wrapped up in a sari or something similar).

From the lake, walk north up to the top of the small saddle in the hill. You will now get a good view of **Passu Glacier**. Keep going up to your left and the views get better and better. On the way back down stay on top of the ridge – don't be tempted to drop down to the dirty small lake in the hollow, for it is a long and difficult descent. Drop down to the road on the left or right of the final spur. (The left is much quicker if you're walking back to Passu.)

### Trekking the Silk Road

Although much of our route passes through desert and across plains, various parts also take in some of the world's most spectacular mountain scenery. Many visitors break their journey and take a closer look. Whichever direction you travel in, you probably won't be carrying the gear necessary for anything much more than a day's hike. Don't let this put you off, however, as the two main trekking regions (in Kyrgyzstan and Pakistan) cater even for the unprepared. The equipment necessary for medium-level treks can usually be hired/bought/swapped whilst there, through a network of tours, agents, hostels and fellow travellers (we have highlighted some of the best options in the relevant places). When you have finished you can usually sell gear on.

The most important items are warm clothes: you will often trek at higher altitudes and even in summer the mornings/evenings can be chilly. Hiking boots are a must and if you are planning to spend a longer time in the hills or want to have a go at more difficult treks, a sleeping bag, tent and cooking equipment are all advisable. It may rain/snow in the mountains at virtually any time of year but if you are planning to trek between September and March you will definitely need waterproofs.

One problem can be maps (or lack of them, see box p29), especially if you are intending on something particularly adventurous, though many treks are well trodden/marked and many trekkers use guides and porters. If you are attempting anything involving snow or ice, you should really coordinate with one of the local mountaineering groups (again, some of the best options are highlighted in the relevant places).

## Walk 2 (see map p265)

This walk gets you close to the glaciers. From the main road head up to the small muddy lake you may have seen on walk 1. Aim north up through the gap between the mountain to the west and the spur in front of you. This takes you up into the Yunz Valley, though it is a hard slog.

When you get to the **huts** (about three to four hours from the lake) you can strike out east up to **Yellow Top** for decent views of Hunza Valley; allow two hours there and back. You might prefer to carry on to the next **huts** at the base of Batura Glacier and then descend sharply to the valley plateau, or walk round the east side of Yellow Top and back south to the road.

# The Hunza and Nagar valleys

Trying to pin the **Hunza Valley** down on a map is not easy since the name is now applied to so much of this region. In the past, however, when it took a day's trek just to reach your next-door neighbour's front door, only the short stretch of the Hunza River between just north of Chalt and south of Gulmit was considered to be true Hunza country, with the centre being the Baltit Fort (around which the modern town of Karimabad has grown).

**Nagar** is even trickier to pinpoint but, approximately, it used to be the land on the south side of the river (opposite the Hunza heartland) plus a wedge in between Chalt and Jaglot on the west bank of the river.

Both are dominated by Mount Rakaposhi (7790m) and both are very friendly places to relax, although the Northern Areas can get quite packed with tourists in the summer. The locals' ability to sustain their crops and terraces means that, in spring especially, it is incredibly beautiful and throughout the year it is surrounded by snowy peaks.

## HISTORY

Feuding between these two valleys has probably gone on as long as man has inhabited the region, though it was events in the 15th century which prompted

---

### Gulmit

In between Passu and Karimabad you may want to stop at Gulmit with its old **polo ground**, **Mir's Palace** and the absorbing **Cultural Museum**, as this was once the capital of the Gojal region. Today this is considered part of the upper reaches of the Hunza Valley but it was very separate up until the building of the KKH. The village is a very short ride from Passu or, for the fighting fit, a good day's march. Gulmit certainly has plenty of history as many Great Game players, and probably Marco Polo, passed through here. Various accommodation is on offer; try the *Hunza Marco Polo Inn*.

all-out war. A royal marriage produced twin boys and one, Maglot, was given Nagar and the other, Girkis, was given Hunza. Before long Maglot sent a band of men to murder Girkis, which they did. Ever since, murder and revenge have been a way of life.

Even at the end of the 19th century the two valleys were still considered too dangerous and were left well alone by the British until there was clear evidence that Russian players in the Great Game were being invited here. In retaliation, British soldiers (actually, they were mostly Gurkhas and Kashmiris) under Algernon Durand were sent in. There was no road let alone a bridge and only a series of daredevil exploits clinched victory for the British.

## HUNZA VALLEY & KARIMABAD

**Karimabad** is the Hunza Valley at its best so it's well worth staying a few days.

### What to see

**Baltit Fort** charges a pricey Rs300 entrance fee but contains some fascinating artefacts (it is also beautifully lit up at night). Having said that, if you climb the hill behind Hidden Paradise Restaurant and cross Ultar River to **Altit Fort**, the ruins there are free and equally impressive.

**Excursion to Ultar Meadow** **Ultar Meadow** above Karimabad is an easy spot to reach as you can walk here from the village yet you still manage to feel completely isolated whilst you're up here and if the season is right the ice/waterfall is exquisite.

Getting here involves a four- to five-hour climb from around the back of Baltit Fort; you could get here and back in a day but it's more enjoyable if you stay the night, especially under a clear sky or a full moon (bring some warm layers).

The shepherds up here are likely to offer you Hunza water (the local jungle juice) and when there is a full moon this can be a great combination. If you don't have a tent or sleeping bag, you can hire them from one of the camping shops in the village or, during May to October, from the shepherds at the *Lady's Finger Campsite*, in the meadow.

From the top of the village take the path that skirts around the left-hand side of Baltit Fort. This will take you to the stream and up its steep west side. It's over 700m up so take it easy, though the end result (access to the Ultar Basin)

---

**The Silk Road Festival**

Over the last few years the Silk Road Festival in Karimabad has grown from a one-off craft fair to a serious event. It now attracts not only all the local crafts of the region but has recently expanded to include a series of traditional polo matches, live music and dancing and a funfair. Organizers cannot confirm the exact dates of the next few festivals but look out for them around September.

It is as much for the locals as foreign visitors, however, so some 'legendary' performances might leave you a little underwhelmed; go for the polo if nothing else.

is worth it. The meadow sits in an enormous hollow surrounded by massive peaks, the best known of which are the sheer vertical stack of Lady's Finger (6000m) and, to its right, Ultar II (7388m).

## PRACTICAL INFORMATION
### [☎ code 05821]
### Orientation and services

Your lift will drop you by the road at the bottom of the hill and you can walk up to the village or get a Suzuki for Rs5.

There is a **telephone office** down by *Hunza View Hotel* but don't pin your hopes on it working.

An **Internet café** has opened but until it faces competition prices will be high and service slow.

**Sitara Travel** (see p276) have an office here and while they specialize in mid- to upper-range tours, they have a head office in Islamabad so you could try to get the ball rolling here if you haven't yet arranged a flight home. This is especially worth it if you want to use up every last day in the mountains.

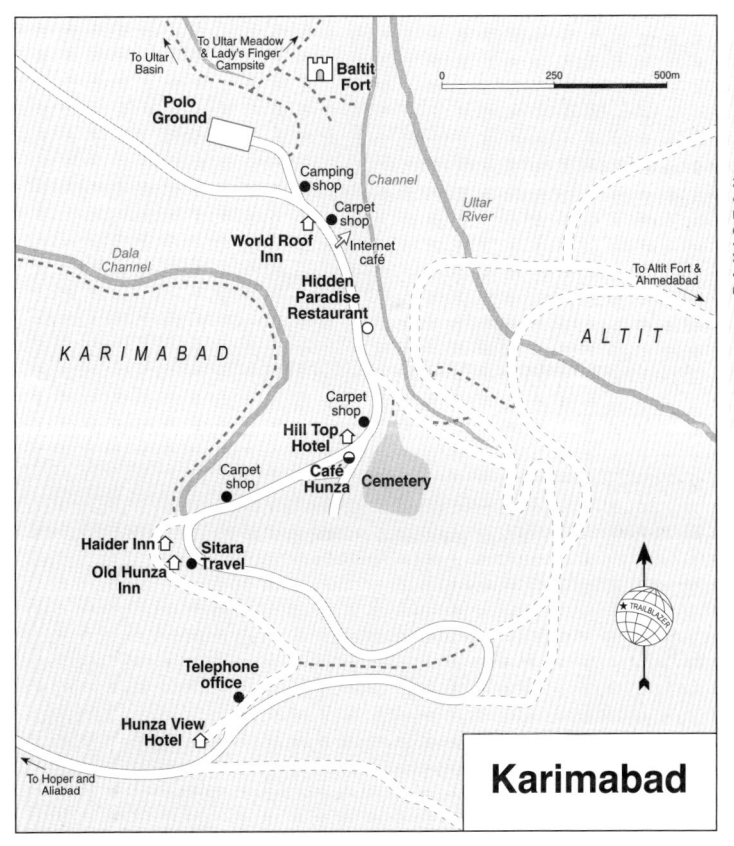

### Where to stay
Karimabad is almost littered with places to stay so this is just a short selection. The oldest hostel in town (and Karimabad is just about big enough to be called a town) is *Haider Inn* (Rs50/dorm) at the bottom of the hill where Old and New Ganish roads meet. The owner used to own *Old Hunza Inn* (Rs50/dorm) next door as well. What he offers is basic but his roof terrace still has the best views of the valley.

For something a little more comfortable, *World Roof Inn* (Rs700/Db) in the centre looks smart and the food is excellent. *Hill Top Hotel* (Rs800/Db) also garners good reviews.

### Where to eat
Most people gravitate to *Hidden Paradise Restaurant* (previously Ultar Restaurant), which has many local specialities and is reasonably priced.

*Café Hunza* is probably the face of what Karimabad is becoming in terms of prices, though their coffee is said to be the best.

### Shopping
Just below the **polo ground** is a great shop for camping and outdoor gear. The owners run tours for the upper-end of the market during the summer and each year they have to buy new equipment for their clients. Once the clients have left they sell the gear (still as good as new) at bargain prices. If they haven't got what you want they usually know someone who has.

Karimabad probably has as good a selection of **carpets** as any town on the Silk Road. They are bought from all over Central Asia, Iran and Afghanistan as well as from local producers (for buying a carpet, see box pp136-7). You will have to really push to get more than 30 per cent off the starting price, however. There are three excellent shops, one each in the upper, middle and lower part of town. Furthermore, if you are desperate for cash, they will also give you an advance on your credit card for 15 per cent commission.

Together with Gilgit, Karimabad is the best place to buy any gifts to take home; a 'Hunza hat' is a common favourite.

### Moving on
For **Gilgit**, take a Suzuki from the main road down to **Aliabad** (Rs5) where you can get a minibus (Rs50).

On this journey you will pass **Chalt**, said to be a pleasant stopover, and the **Naltar Valley**, said to be equally attractive, but for Naltar it is easier (and cheaper) to go down to Gilgit and organize your trip from there (see p272).

For **Passu** or **Gulmit**, minibuses buses run all day along the KKH (from town you can walk downhill to the highway). If you are a smoker, stock up as Passu has banned the sale of cigarettes within its boundaries since 1994.

## NAGAR VALLEY

### Excursion to Hoper
Another good trip is out to Hoper but for this one it's best to group together and hire a jeep because minibuses past Nagar village are infrequent, making this relatively short trip a long journey.

There are plenty of small walks out from Hoper village as well as large treks for the professionals and an overnight stay here is thoroughly enjoyable. Again, if you don't have camping equipment you can hire it up here from *Hoper Inn* or stay in one of their beds. Accommodation is also available at the tongue-in-cheek *Hoper Hilton*. There are quite a few tour operators who do this excursion from Karimabad, so shop around for the best price.

# Gilgit

Gilgit is the hub of the Northern Areas and, with its airport and markets, it has all the facilities you will need but don't expect too much. There are usually plenty of backpackers in town and if you are looking for cigarettes not necessarily filled with tobacco, you should be satisfied here.

## HISTORY

Like the rest of this region, Gilgit's past is more folklore than history but its role in the partition of India is true enough as everyone in the town will tell you.

With the Hindu Maharajah of Kashmir dithering as to what to do, a small group of his Muslim officials was plotting to seize the principality and hand it over to Pakistan. The plot was suspected, however, and its leader, Colonel Mirza Hassan Khan, moved out of harm's way to the small garrison at Bunji (a few kilometres south of Gilgit). Meanwhile, Muslim soldiers in a regiment of the British army, the Gilgit Scouts, were also brewing rebellion and their leader, Mohammed Babar Khan, gathered his supporters outside the Governor of Gilgit's office – a man loyal to the Maharajah.

The Governor knew Babar meant trouble and called for support from the commander of the nearest garrison but that just happened to be Colonel Hassan Khan's at Bunji and the only help the Governor received was in packing his bags. He was arrested on November 1, 1947. The rebels asked that Gilgit be made part of Pakistan and to this day November 1 is celebrated as Independence Day here rather than August 14; look out for the polo (see box p272).

## WHAT TO SEE

The markets are competitively priced and if you are looking for presents this is a good place to stock up. A particular favourite seems to be the shawls: there are silk shawls, cashmere shawls and Kashmiri shawls. This can be confusing as you can also get Kashmiri cashmere shawls: one is where it is made, the other the type of wool it's made from. You can also get Pashmina shawls – a pure Pashmina is made from wool taken only from the wispy beards on the necks of ibex.

### Excursions

The best way to really get to grips with the mountains without having to buy the sort of equipment used to scale K2 is the **Baltistan** trip to **Skardu**, the **Deosai Plains** and **Astor** (see 'Trekking the Silk Road', p266). You will see the **Indus River** churning its way through deep gorges, glaciers aplenty and one of the most beautiful meadows in Asia, all set off by **Nanga Parbat** (at 8125m, the 'Naked Mountain' is the ninth highest in the world).

> ### Polo
> No one can say for sure where polo was born (Pakistan, India, Persia and even China are all contenders, although Persia is the favourite). Few will argue, however, that the most spectacular version is played in Pakistan's northern mountains. In the modern game each team has six players, originally any number was allowed.
>
> There are several festivals of which the finest are the **Shandur Cup**, where Gilgit and Chitral battle it out on the Shandur Pass over four days of exhilarating action (usually in July but dates are not fixed until a month or so beforehand); the **Gilgit Festival**, which begins on November 1, celebrates the Northern Areas Independence day and features a week-long polo tournament. If you are really lucky you might even get to see a wild game of Buzkashi (see box p230)

Take plenty of supplies with you as well because although there are small villages on the way, they have little more to offer than the bare essentials. The trip takes three days and two nights so try to get at least four of you together to split the costs. To save money you can get a bus to Skardu from Gilgit and a bus back from Astor but you may then have difficulty hiring a jeep across the plains.

## PRACTICAL INFORMATION
[☎ code 05811]

### Orientation and services
Gilgit has many **Internet cafés** – the best is in **Northside Tours**' office (💻 Guides@isb.compol.com) on the same road as Madina Hotel. They also organize good tours to the Naltar Valley and surrounding area but there is plenty of competition, so shop around.

There are lots of places to change **money** and travellers' cheques but no credit/debit card facilities.

### Where to stay
Like Karimabad, you should have no problem finding somewhere to stay in Gilgit as the town is very tourist-friendly. *Madina Hotel*, off the main road, is a real Mecca for backpackers and most people gravitate towards it.

There is a decent garden area to sit and eat in, a shop and a tour operator (although this can be more expensive than others in town). They show videos every night and have clean, basic doubles (Rs250) and dorms (Rs80).

For something quieter, try *Mountain Refuge* (Rs200/Db), while for something more upmarket try *Chinar Inn* (Chinar Garden Rd; Rs1650/Db). The top place in town is the picturesque *Gilgit Serena Hotel* (Rs4000/ Db); it's a bit out of town in Jutial but the hotel provides free shuttle buses.

### Where to eat
*Haji Ramzan* serves a variety of dishes that look and smell good but some diners have complained that the food has gone straight through them. If this worries you, you might prefer to stick to the staples offered by your hotel. Those with a strong disposition can have fun eating on the hoof as you shop around town.

If you want to treat yourself, head up to the *Serena Hotel* (see above) and try out its restaurant or its outdoor BBQ.

### Moving on
**To the south** If you are in a rush, buses go straight through to Rawalpindi four times a day (18hrs/Rs360) but this is a killer journey on battered seats and overnight journeys are guaranteed to be virtually sleep-free. The final few kilometres before Rawalpindi take you through dozens of small green villages, home to exclusive bungalows that were once the summer retreats of the British but are now holiday homes for Pakistan's rich and famous.

Gilgit 273

If you are in a real hurry, there are planes everyday to the capital but they are subject to weather conditions and the flight is hairy to say the least. Tickets can be bought from any of the tour agencies (US$30 one way).

**To the north** Buses/minibuses leave for Karimabad (Rs70) all day.

# Rawalpindi and Islamabad

After the magic of the mountains, the twin cities of Rawalpindi (known as Pindi) and Islamabad are a letdown. There is little to see or do in either and if you have not already booked your flight out, you will probably want to arrange one within a few days.

If you have just arrived in Pakistan, you might want to spend a bit longer here to adjust to the culture and buy some suitable clothes but as the mountain areas are much more friendly and, on the whole, more relaxed, you will do well to head straight up to Gilgit and acclimatize there. This is definitely the best option if you are looking to hook up with some fellow travellers.

Islamabad is a more cultured city (and it's greener) than Pindi, as you would expect for a city purpose-built for government officials and international dignitaries. However, like most modern cities (it was built in 1961), the capital is soulless and, for Pakistan, very, very quiet.

## WHAT TO SEE

**Pindi** The permanent markets in both cities are a disappointment to some. All the spices and leather jackets that you might want are here but the markets are designed for locals and most items on sale will probably be of little interest. For

---

### Karakorum Highway (KKH) detour

Rather than charge from the mountains to the capital in one go, it is much better to stop off along the way; see map p255. The best option is to hire a jeep from Gilgit down to **Naran** (Rs7000 between five people) which takes you through the **Babusar Pass** or the nearby **Butogar Pass** and right under Nanga Parbat. You can stay in Naran for a day or two (there are half a dozen cheap hotels), chilling out and enjoying the tremendous views of the mountain. Next, take a bus/minibus south to **Mansehra** (through the idyllic Chagan Valley), where you rejoin the KKH and can pick up the bus to Rawalpindi (there is no need to stay in Mansehra).

The other option is to take the bus down the KKH from Gilgit and get off at **Besham** or **Thakot**. Both are near **Pir Sar**, 'The Peak of a Holy Man' (2160m), the mountain Alexander the Great famously took on one of his last truly great campaigns. Besham is more used to foreign visitors and has quite a choice of accommodation but Thakot is better placed if you want to emulate Alexander and climb the mountain.

Heading north from the capital, it is easy to get buses to Naran via Mansehra but you may have a problem hiring transport in Naran to take you across the pass to Gilgit.

gifts and souvenirs you are better off in Karimabad and Gilgit but if it's too late for that there are a few shops gathered around the corner of Haider Rd and Canning Rd which have a reasonable, if overpriced, selection. In Islamabad there's a better one (see below).

**Islamabad** Visitors who miss out Islamabad altogether don't miss much. The highlight is **Shah Faisal Mosque**, which is huge and no doubt capable of holding the 100,000 people it claims, making it one of the largest mosques in the world. The building's modern architecture, however, is unlikely to inspire you.

**Juma Bazaar**, operating on Sundays, gets good reports and wares come here from all over Pakistan.

### PRACTICAL INFORMATION
[✆ code 051]
#### Orientation and services
Pindi and Islamabad are separated by a 15km stretch of highway (the gap is shrinking every year as both cities expand) but it is simple to catch a **bus/Suzuki** between the two. The centres of both cities are very small and it is hard to get lost (Islamabad is laid out on a perfect grid). However, you will probably spend most of your time in Pindi's **Saddar Bazaar** area, which has everything you need; buses and minibuses run from here (**Haider Rd**) to Islamabad all day.

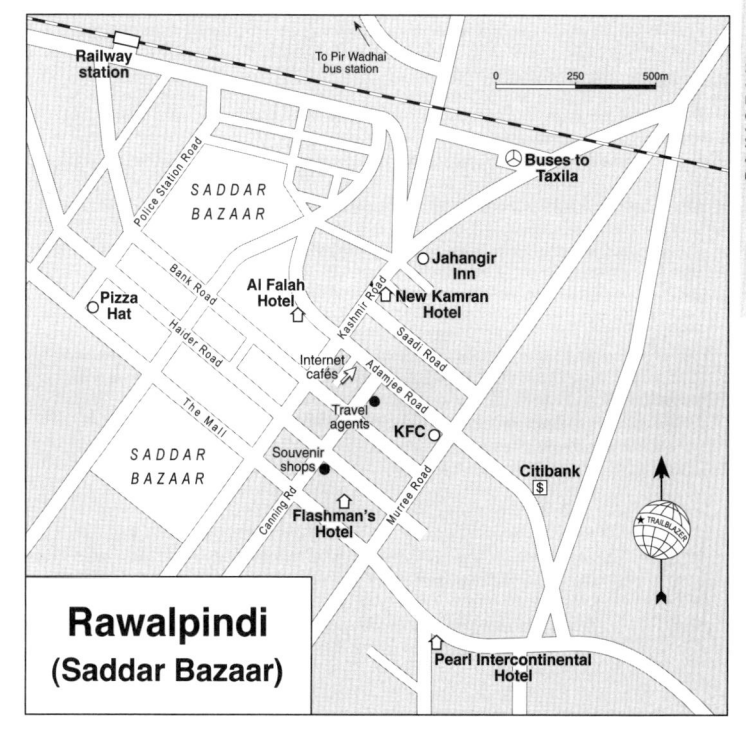

# Rawalpindi
## (Saddar Bazaar)

**Pindi** The city has plenty of **Internet** and **international telephone outlets** offering cheap rates so you shouldn't have a problem finding one; the side alley off Adamjee Rd is full of them. There is also a **Citibank** branch in both cities, which has an ATM for foreign credit/debit cards.

For international and domestic air tickets, there is a string of **travel agents** on the next street across from the Internet shops in Pindi, or see one of the agents below. Pakistan is not a particularly cheap place to fly to or from.

**Islamabad** The main **tourist office** (☎ 920 2766) is in Jinnah Market. The most reliable travel agent is **Sitara Travel** (☎ 287 3372-5; 🖳 www.sitara.com, sitarapk@isb.compol.com) in Waheed Plaza, 3rd Floor, 52 West Jinnah Ave, Blue Area. They can also arrange a variety of tours. The agency is run by one of the founder members of the Pakistani Mountaineering Club, so there isn't much they don't know about trekking. They also have offices in Karimabad (see p269), Tashkent (see p226) and Canada (see p14). Another tour operator that runs good Silk Road tours and some excellent treks is **Panoramic Pakistan** (☎ 225 5838; 🖳 tour @panoramic.com.pk) at Flat 1, 1st floor, Block 19, G-8 Markaz.

If you have come from China on a transit visa you need to visit the **Interior Ministry** (Block R, Civil Secretariat, Islamabad) for an extension. Similarly, for a Chinese visa (see p17) you need to apply at the **Chinese Embassy** (☎ 282 2540); along with most other embassies they are in the diplomatic enclave, G-5, Embassy Rd.

If you want to apply for an alcohol licence (Rs50 per month) go to the **Excise and Tax Department** in Ayub Market.

### Excursion to Taxila

Make space for a day trip to this collection of ancient ruins (now a World Heritage Site) as you are unlikely to be disappointed. The site is actually home to all the various incarnations of Taxila over the centuries, with the oldest remains dating back as far as Alexander the Great and the Persians before him. The most impressive sites are at **Sirsukh**, **Sirkap** and **Bhir**. There is also a selection of outstanding temples and monasteries here (**Dharmarajika Stupa** – see p244 – is perhaps the most impressive).

At the gates to the whole area is a small **museum**. This has only a small collection yet it is fascinating to examine not just the coins and jewellery that have survived but the toys and household items as well.

**Practicalities** The ticket (Rs4) also gives you access to the ruins but as this is so cheap, it's worth buying their small information brochure for Rs15 because this contains a good plan and history of the sites. There is a lovely garden at the back of the museum where you can have a picnic lunch. Each site can be reached by a Suzuki or tonga for a few rupees and refreshments are sold at each stop.

You will also be offered a variety of replica and 'authentic' pieces dug up by locals but it is difficult to say what, if anything, any of them are really worth.

From Saddar Bazaar, walk up to the car park at the top of Kashmir Rd, by the railway track. From here you can catch one of the many **minibuses** to Taxila (Rs10, 40mins). Tell the driver you want the museum and he will drop you on the main road by a roundabout just before you get to the site. It is still too far to walk, however, so catch a Suzuki (Rs3) from the other side of the roundabout, which will drop you off at the museum gates. Alternatively, you can take the slow but very enjoyable train ride (Rs10, 50mins). This requires a trip to Rawalpindi **train station** the day before you go in order to establish train times and tickets (the timetable is notoriously fickle). The station at Taxila is right beside the museum.

> ### The Khyber Pass
> There are few such evocative names in the world as the Khyber Pass. Although it doesn't actually mark the modern border between Pakistan and Afghanistan, for centuries it has been the physical dividing line between Central Asia and the Indian subcontinent. Many a famous explorer and invader have passed through this barren gateway and with a bit of luck you can join in. There's even a golf course at the top though currently play is 'suspended'. Most visitors make their way to Peshawar and begin from there but you can squeeze everything into a day-trip from Pindi.
>
> **Practicalities** There are two ways to reach the top of the pass: by private car or by train. In a **private car** you need a permit from the Khyber Political Agent's Office in Peshawar who will also provide you with an armed guard. A 4WD with driver costs about Rs2000 for a group of four (half-day round trip); try the PTDC Office (☎ 091 286 829) in the Benevolent Fund Building, Saddar Rd, Peshawar.
>
> Public **trains** no longer travel this most romantic of routes though **Sehrai Travels** (☎ 091 272 085; 💻 sehrai@psh.brain.net.pk) at 14c Cantonment Commercial Plaza, Saddar Rd, Peshawar, charters steam trains for its monthly 'Khyber Steam Safari' (Rs5000). This switchback journey is prone to cancellation but remains a treasure.

### Where to stay
It's possible to stay in Islamabad but most foreign visitors prefer Pindi. Islamabad does have a secure **campsite** (Rs50/pp), though, at Shahrah-e Kashmir Rd.

*Al Falah Hotel*, in the Saddar Bazaar area on Adamjee Rd, is about as cheap as it gets (Rs240/Db) but it's worth paying a bit more for a room at the *New Kamran* (☎ 556 6420; Rs350/Db) on Kashmir Rd. The owners here are very helpful, the rooms are clean and there is a good breakfast and lunch café.

*Flashman's Hotel* (☎ 927 2014; Rs1400/Db), on The Mall, is still getting bad press but it does have a liquor licence and thus remains full for most of the year – although we bet old Flashy would turn his nose up (see *Flashman* p29). Also on The Mall, *Pearl Intercontinental* (☎ 566 6011; US$225) has a swimming pool and an alcohol license! Feel free to use the bar even if you are not staying here (just sign a form stating you are a non-Muslim).

### Where to eat
There are plenty of fast-food/Western restaurants in **Islamabad**.

Your best hope for a good meal in **Pindi** is at *Jahangir Inn* (Kashmir Rd); it beats everything else hands down with its great tikka and karai dishes served in the pleasant garden at the back. There is a *KFC* and a replica *Pizza Hat* (sic), which can be a welcome change.

Several hotels also have restaurants or serve food of some description.

### Moving on
Buses to/from **Gilgit** (14-17hrs) use the **Pir Wadhai bus station**, which is quite a way out of both towns so you'll have to haggle for a taxi. There is a VIP bus service (Rs665) and two 'deluxe' buses (Rs400) per day. If you want to stop off on your way to Gilgit, see box p274.

If you are in a real hurry there are planes to Gilgit everyday but they are subject to weather conditions and the **flight** is hairy to say the least. Tickets can be bought from any travel agent (US$30 one way).

A taxi to the new **airport** costs Rs100 (30mins) and **Suzukis** (Rs10) run between Adamjee Rd and the airport gate. There is no departure tax (it should be included in your ticket, though check).

If you are heading to Iran, see box p154. If you want to spend more time looking around Pakistan, see p254.

# PART 6: CHINA

## Facts about the country

### GEOGRAPHICAL BACKGROUND

The People's Republic of China is the third largest country in the world today after Russia and Canada. Incorporating 9.6 million sq km of land, it stretches 5500km from north to south and 5200km from east to west, making it approximately the same size as Europe.

Despite its vast size, however, only around 10 per cent of its land is agriculturally viable (20 per cent is actual desert) and a recent census indicated that over 50 per cent of China's 1.3 billion population lives in urban areas – a percentage that is increasing. For further information, see 💻 www.environinfo.org.cn.

As well as Everest (Mount Chomolungma, 8848m) on its southern border, China is dotted with hundreds of dramatic mountains, many of which are sacred. There are five holy Buddhist mountains and five holy Taoist mountains.

The whole country is prone to earthquakes, particularly Xinjiang where an earthquake near the Kyrgyz border killed over 250 people in 2003.

### HISTORY

#### Prehistory

It is often difficult to separate fact from myth in Oriental history. Although some evidence suggests human activity dating right back to 2,000,000BC, we can be sure that China has been populated since at least 500,000BC (see 'Yellow River' box, p335).

The discovery of Peking Man at the Zhoukoudian site south-west of Beijing in 1921 highlights this and, despite the fact that what remained of Peking Man himself (a part of his skull only) was unfortunately 'lost' during a Japanese invasion, scientists believe that he was a hunter, cooking meat and also eating nuts and berries. Certainly, by 50,000BC his descendants were widespread throughout China, with gathering rather than hunting now the preferred method of collecting food.

The Neolithic era dawned here between the seventh and the fifth millennia BC, well ahead of other parts of eastern Asia and at least 5000 years before Japan. Artefacts are fairly common (the Banpo site near Xi'an has been a particularly good source, see pp346-7), so we have a fairly accurate idea of what sort of pottery and tools were being used.

Agriculture arrived between 6000 and 2500BC. Scientists have identified two types of farming from around this time: the green vegetable cultivation of the north and the rice domination of the south. By 3000BC pigs, dogs, cattle and water buffalo were domesticated. Bronze casting had made its appearance by 2000BC.

### The first dynasties

Chinese legend dictates that the first dynasty, the **Xia** (2200-1800BC), was founded by Emperor Yu, who appeared after a great flood. Historians, however, are not convinced, generally agreeing that the first dynasty was the **Shang** (traditionally 1700-1600BC to 1200-1100BC), whose capital was eventually settled at Anyang. They were a superstitious people who divined by the use of oracle bones. Tomb excavations have revealed evidence of human sacrifice at funerals.

The Shang were overthrown by the **Zhou** in around 1100BC. At first their capital was at Hao near modern Xi'an (historians refer to them in this period as the Western Zhou), while later on they moved it to Luoyi, near Luoyang (the Eastern Zhou period).

Zhou culture was not dissimilar to that of the Shang but politically much was changing: China was now subject to repeated barbarian attacks from the north, the capital was under threat and the empire collapsed into a patchwork of petty kingdoms known as the 'Warring States'. During this period (c500BC) iron casting (1500 years before Europe), mounted cavalry, the crossbow and Confucius (551-479BC) all made their appearances. Feuding continued, however, until the foundation of the first 'imperial' dynasty, the **Qin** (221BC).

The Qin introduced many of the traits we find in later dynasties such as the standardization of weights and measures, a universal script for official documents and an organized judicial system. They also linked up stretches of earthen ramparts, forming what was later to become the Great Wall.

### The Han dynasty

Yet the Qin dynasty lasted only 15 years and after inter-factional fighting Liu Bang emerged in 206BC, adopted the title **'Han'** and began one of the greatest dynasties in China's history. Characterized by territorial expansion, intelligent emperors, Confucianism and progress generally (paper, for example, was invented by Cai Lun in 106AD), this period was a golden age.

In the middle of the dynasty, however, a high-ranking official, Wang Mang, seized power to create the **Xin** ('New') dynasty, although this lasted for just 14 years before Han power was restored. Like the Zhou, the Han rulers before the Xin are known as the Western Han because their capital was in Chang'an, while the rulers after the Xin are known as the Eastern Han because they moved their capital to Luoyang.

With the fall of the Han in 220AD, China was once again split up, this time for four centuries, during the so-called **Three Kingdoms period**. Buddhism (introduced during the Han dynasty) began to flourish despite the conflicts while literature and science made great leaps too, for large areas of China did experience prolonged periods of peace.

## Reunification; the Sui and Tang dynasties

China was finally unified in 581AD by Yian Jian (who took the name 'Wendi'). He was a good ruler despite being subject to fits of rage which, on occasion, led him to personally beat government officials to death. Under his reign civil service, tax collection and the legal system were revamped and he constantly strove to increase the size of his empire. His **Sui** dynasty lasted only for a brief period before collapsing in 618AD but it did oversee the building of the Grand Canal linking the Yellow River to the Yangzi and paved the way for the Tang dynasty (618-907AD).

The **Tang period** is looked upon as a great era and it contained some of China's most famous rulers: Taizong (626-649AD), together with his wise minister Wei Zheng, was seen as an ideal model for government by later Confucians; Taizong's wife, Empress Wu, became the first (and last) legitimate female ruler of China in 690AD; while Wu's grandson, Xuanzong, became known as 'The Brilliant Emperor'. Their reigns are remembered as the 'High' Tang period.

Their two capitals, Luoyang and Chang'an, attracted trade and traders from the Silk Road and with them came a constant influx of new ideas. The empire expanded right up to modern Afghanistan and Central Asia, and culture flourished along with all aspects of science. Buddhism also saw its popularity increase and it was as a subject of the Tang that Xuan Zang (see box p345) made his pilgrimage to India. Unfortunately, by the middle of the 8th century the dynasty was in a decline. It fell in 907AD, leaving China fragmented again.

## Five Dynasties and Ten Kingdoms; the Song dynasty

The period of disorientation that followed is known as that of the '**Five Dynasties and Ten Kingdoms**'. History books tell us it lasted for only 50 years but actually it was longer than this, for feuding began well before the end of the Tang and did not truly end until the final submission of the south to the Song dynasty in 975AD.

The **Song dynasty** was founded by a military leader of one of the Five Dynasties who finally managed to unite the majority of the warlord-run states. It featured rapid military, economic and technical growth and some see it as the formative period for the later imperial era because education, taxation and the civil service examinations were all restructured. Yet the seat of power moved south in 1127 at the threat of more barbarian invasions from the north and thus from this point the dynasty became known as the 'Southern Song'. The north of China, meanwhile, was ruled by the invaders who set up, respectively, the Liao, Western Xia and Jin dynasties.

## The Mongol invasion and the Yuan dynasty

The Mongols eventually swept the country clean of its divisions but it was a gradual process: **Genghis Khan** started it with the unification of the northern tribes in 1206, yet the conquest and reunification of China proper was completed only 75 years later under his grandson, **Kublai Khan** (who founded the **Yuan dynasty**). Kublai's China was the largest single country the world had ever seen.

It was also visited by increasing numbers of foreign travellers: Marco Polo's story is the most famous but Arabs and Venetians became commonplace in Chinese ports and a Russian came top of the Imperial Civil Service exam in 1341.

The Mongol capital was at Khanbalig (on the site of present-day Beijing), and China's population in 1340 was 60-80 million. Such a large territory needed an impressive government; a despatch postal service was introduced, facilitating fast communications throughout the empire. Gunpowder was invented and astronomy took great steps forward; at this time China's technical level was on a par with, if not ahead of, that of the West.

### The fall of the Yuan; the Ming dynasty

Unfortunately, the Mongols were given to feuding among themselves and their Yuan dynasty collapsed in 1368. It was immediately replaced by the **Ming dynasty**, founded by the one-time peasant Zhu Yuanzhang, with its capital at Nanjing. Steps were taken to improve the lot of the farmers, Confucian ethics were reintroduced into civil service recruitment and fine art flourished, particularly porcelain. Seven great maritime expeditions were also launched in the 15th century, the most successful of which reached Aden in 1417. The main themes of the Ming dynasty in its later years, however, were stagnation and isolation, characterized by the 900km extension to the Great Wall during this period (although Portugal was allowed to establish its first base in Macau in 1557). The end came with popular rebellions in the north-west in the first half of the 17th century.

Seeing chaos prevailing, a Manchurian chieftain, Dorgon (1612-50), marched straight into Beijing (supposedly, he was invited to cross the Great Wall by a Chinese general) and established his **Qing dynasty** (1644-1912).

### Qing and the opium problem

The early part of the dynasty was a period of great prosperity, mainly thanks to the efficiency of three particularly strong emperors from 1661 to 1799. In 1683, Taiwan was conquered, in 1751 Tibet was made a Chinese colony, and the Qing did much to bring Xinjiang under its control.

After the death of Qianlong in 1799, however, government corruption increased and foreign opium began to enter the country at large, heralding the collapse of an economy that had already been weakened by lengthy military excursions. A ban on opium imports in 1896 did nothing to stem the flow, for the East India Company simply sold it to independent traders who smuggled it in. As addiction became widespread, demand rocketed and from an average of 4000 chests per year before 1829, the nation's intake leapt to 19,000 in 1830 alone.

Attempts to suppress opium imports by force led to the Opium Wars with Great Britain, each of which ended with ignominious defeat for the Chinese and huge indemnities for them to pay. The 1842 Treaty of Nanking handed over Hong Kong to the British 'in perpetuity'. This period really illustrates China's decline as a result of Western interference.

### Internal confusion – the Taiping and Boxer rebellions

Opium and foreign traders weren't the only problems: the economy was in tatters following a series of natural disasters and silver was pouring out of state coffers into the pockets of foreign governments. There was also a series of popular uprisings, the most famous of which were the Taiping Rebellion and the Boxer Movement.

**Taiping** was led by one Hong Xiu Quan, who believed he was Jesus's younger brother and managed to gain enough support in the south to occupy Hankou and Nanjing in 1853 (the latter of these became the capital of his 'Heavenly City of Great Peace'). His rebellion was suppressed only in 1864, with Western assistance.

The **Boxer Rebellion** was more serious both for the Europeans and the Chinese. This uprising began in the north of China around 1900 as a protest against Manchurian rule and foreign exploitation. Although they had no weapons but their 'harmonious fists', the Boxers believed themselves impervious to Western bullets. Encouraged by the cruel Empress Dowager Ci Xi they laid siege to the foreign legation in Beijing, having first killed a number of foreign missionaries. The Westerners managed to hold out until reinforcements arrived on 4 October 1900, whereupon they occupied the city and wreaked havoc wherever they found anti-foreign feeling. Ci Xi, for her part, fled to Xi'an. Western governments imposed the **Peace Protocol** in 1901, which included yet another huge indemnity to be paid by China.

## Acceleration towards revolution

Effectively China was being divided up between the foreign powers, who were more than happy to abuse their position – Great Britain and France took over Shanghai, Germany moved in on Qingdao, Taiwan was ceded to Japan in 1895 and the Russians, fearing uprisings in territory ceded to them in 1860, started slaughtering the local Chinese before seizing Manchuria (the Japanese subsequently laid claim to Manchuria too, an act which ultimately led to the 1904-5 Russo-Japanese war). The Qing dynasty was falling apart. Ci Xi, having herself usurped the throne from her son, juggled the line of accession so that her five-year old nephew, Guangxu, became heir. Even when he succeeded her in 1875, she kept the real power and eventually had him imprisoned in the Summer Palace in Beijing. She died in 1908 and Pu Yi ('The Last Emperor') was proclaimed emperor at the tender age of two. But for the Qing it was too late.

In 1905 the force for change inside the country found vent in the formation of the Tongmenhui, the Chinese Revolutionary Party, by **Dr Sun Yat Sen** (1866-1925). This party later formed the foundation of the Kuomintang, the Nationalist Party. At the beginning of 1912 there was a brief coup and on 12 February General Yuan Shi Kai proclaimed the abdication of Pu Yi (still only six years old). At the same time Sun Yat Sen, under pressure, handed the general his presidency of the 'republic'.

The Kuomintang was not the only people's party, however. The Chinese Communist Party, fuelled by the USSR, held its first congress meeting on 1 July 1921. In 1922, at Stalin's insistence, it joined forces with the Kuomintang. The alliance was short-lived, for undermining their unity was a disagreement concerning the exact nature of the revolution itself. In 1927 an alleged telegram from Stalin to the CCP, in which he ordered them to seize power from the

> **The Long March**
> This is something of a misnomer as there was not one march but rather a series of them (they were all 'long', though). Mao Zedong had long decided that revolution in the cities was doomed and that the Chinese peasants were the key to any success. China's ethnic minorities make up only around 8 per cent of the population but they inhabit over half the country geographically and Mao hoped to make use of them as a cover for his retreat.
>
> By now a recognized luminary in the CCP, Mao led one group from the south of Jiangxi province using Sun Tzu's ancient *Art of War* as his military gospel. Other groups followed from various communist bases in central China, but most women and children, including Mao's wife, He Zizhen, had to be left behind in friendly peasant villages. The men and women covered 9600km across twelve provinces at a rate of 27km per day through snow, desert, bogs and mountains. Around 86,000 marchers began the trek and they were joined by tens of thousands more along the way but only 4000 survived to reach Yan'an, in northern Shaanxi – approximately 170,000 died or went missing along the way.

Kuomintang, was intercepted by the then Kuomintang leader, Chiang Kai Shek. Ruthless persecutions of communists followed and China, already fragmented and controlled by warlords, had a civil war on its hands.

## Civil war and the Japanese invasion

The communists were severely outnumbered by the Kuomintang at the outset of the ensuing war and barely managed to survive. They relied on guerrilla tactics before eventually setting up camps south of the Yangzi River in Jiangxi Province. After heavy losses there they decided to retreat to a safe haven in Yan'an, Shaanxi Province, resulting in the '**Long March**' (see box above) of 1934-6.

By this time, Japan had marched into Manchuria and installed Pu Yi as puppet emperor of the state of Manchukuo, declaring its independence in 1932. In 1935 the CCP issued a statement appealing for a united front against Japan but Chiang Kai Shek did not respond.

On 12 December, 1936, he was seized by his own men in the so-called 'Xi'an Incident' (see p341). CCP leaders flew in to persuade him to fight the Japanese instead of them. He agreed, although there is some debate as to how much effort he really put into fighting the Japanese. Military and economic aid was sent by the Allied Forces during WWII, together with troops under US General 'Vinegar Joe' Stillwell, who was not at all impressed with the Oriental war effort. At Chiang's request he was removed from office in 1944.

## Communist victory and the Liberation

It didn't take long for the civil war to start again after the Japanese surrender but this time the communists gained the upper hand. Mao Zedong was convinced that the real power lay in the hands of the rural peasants and by mobilizing them he eventually won, forcing the Kuomintang to flee to Taiwan, taking with them as much of the state funds and antiquities as they could carry (to prevent any pursuit from the mainland, US president Truman ordered a protective naval blockade).

Mao, now officially leader of the CCP, proclaimed the foundation of the **People's Republic of China** on 1 October 1949 ('The Liberation') and immediately set about trying to repair its wrecked economy. With Soviet aid he was extremely successful and by 1952 it was back to its pre-war levels. Mao's ambitions for China, however, led him to initiate the '**Great Leap Forward**' in May 1958. This was an ill-fated attempt to stimulate industry and the economy generally by organizing workers into self-managing communes.

Unfortunately, for a variety of reasons (perhaps Mao should have heeded Soviet warnings that the communes idea was too Utopian) the Great Leap was a catastrophe. Its failure, together with a series of natural disasters, resulted in widespread famine. The situation was made even worse when the rift between China and Russia over their respective roles as leaders of the communist movement led to the withdrawal of Soviet aid. It has been estimated that more than 30 million Chinese died in the three years around 1960; some statisticians claim that China's population actually decreased during this period.

## Cultural Revolution

Mao became disillusioned. His failures at home (particularly the Hundred Flowers campaign which had been meant to expose inefficient officials but had resulted in widespread criticism of The Party and its governmental system), together with the new policy of coexistence between the USSR and the USA, convinced him that something was wrong. As he saw it, communism had been corrupted, and something had to be done to restore the revolutionary spirit. As he said, 'You learn to swim by swimming. You learn to make revolution by making revolution'. His right-hand man, Lin Bao, collected Mao's ideas into the compilation known everywhere as the 'Little Red Book', and this spurred on Mao and his supporters to launch the Great **Proletarian Cultural Revolution** (1966-9) to set the country back on its feet.

The initiative was another catastrophe. Its first step involved the removal of the 'Capitalist Railroaders' from the CCP. This was shortly followed by the removal of anything and anyone that could be seen as authoritarian or in any way representative of the old order, because it was here that the bourgeois influences were supposedly hiding. Temples and cultural relics were destroyed as Mao stirred up the country's youth: 'To rebel is justified', he declared, 'bombard the headquarters'.

Schools and universities were closed, their teachers publicly humiliated and sent for 're-education' (usually manual labour in the country). The students formed the Red Guards and travelled (for free) the length of the country, leaving trails of destruction wherever they went and advocating 'Mao Thought'. As their slogan went, 'Everything that does not reflect the thought of Chairman Mao must be burned'. Everyone adopted the new uniform: the blue 'Mao suit'. China was turned upside-down.

## Mao's decline and the rise of Zhou Enlai

Whether Mao really believed in what he was doing or whether he was simply trying to consolidate his own political power is debatable. By the 1970s, however, the tide was beginning to turn and a new line of tolerance and moderation came in, most closely associated with **Zhou Enlai** (who had somehow escaped the party purges). The violence ended only in 1972-3, though, and by this time premiers Liu Shaoqi and Lin Bao had disappeared (the latter in a plane crash after an alleged coup attempt).

Power gradually shifted to Zhou, who helped to thaw relations with the West by inviting President Nixon to visit in 1972 (the interaction between the US and China at this time became known as 'ping-pong' diplomacy and is said to have brought down the equally clichéd 'Bamboo Curtain'). Universities and schools reopened and the obsession with Maoism began to fade. China (rather than Taiwan) was accepted for the first time into the United Nations Assembly.

With Zhou Enlai's death in 1976, a public protest known as the **Tiananmen Incident** once again threatened public security. In early April, Tiananmen Square began to fill up with wreaths and flowers for Zhou; Mao (correctly) considered this to be partly a statement of support for the emerging moderate leader **Deng Xiaopeng**, who had been vilified as China's 'No 2 Capitalist Railroader' during the Cultural Revolution but rehabilitated in 1973. When the military tried to remove wreaths from the square, violence broke out and Deng was removed from office. But in the same year Mao died and the days of autocratic domination were over.

The so-called Gang of Four (including Mao's wife Jiang Qing), responsible for many of the worst excesses during the Cultural Revolution, tried to cling on but popular feeling was too strong: they were given a show trial and finally convicted in 1981 (Madame Mao, under house arrest, committed suicide in 1991). China badly needed scapegoats for the lost decade.

### The democracy movement and the Tiananmen massacre

With the failure of the next Five Year Plan, Deng Xiaopeng was once again rehabilitated and he began to assume much of the responsibility of government. Foreign trade shot up and in 1980 China joined the IMF and World Bank, while at home the 'one child' policy was instigated. This process of opening up, however, was hindered by the widely televised **Tiananmen Square Incident** of 1989.

Pro-democracy rallies started in April, leading up to the rally on 4 May which attracted some 50,000 students. Warnings had been given to officials by students demanding 'genuine dialogue' but they were dismissed as 'naive and impulsive'. The previous day had seen 1000 students commence a hunger strike in Tiananmen Square. Gorbachev arrived for a state visit on 15 May to find over 100,000 protesters there and the Chinese government embarrassed (particularly when a huge rally with over a million participants took place two days later). Martial law was declared.

By the start of June the authorities' patience had worn thin and on 3 June 10,000 unarmed soldiers were sent to Tiananmen Square, only to find their access blocked by throngs of people. Next, armed police arrived and used teargas to disperse the crowds but to little effect. Just before midnight troops opened fire and heavy artillery fire was reported on the outskirts of the city. At around 01.30 on 4 June soldiers started to fight their way to the centre of the square. A vote was held at 05.00, whereupon student leaders decided to disperse but as they did so they were fired upon. Western media reported that hundreds of unarmed civilians were shot in the back as they attempted to flee. Realistic estimates put the dead at 2000 to 5000 but the Chinese official estimate says 300, and some cadres seriously contended that there had been no casualties at all. Blame was put on 'counter-revolutionaries' and the 'brave' soldiers were praised. Footage supposedly showing vicious attacks on the military by civilians was aired.

Within a month over 2500 civilians had been arrested and charged. A number of executions followed. Foreign reactions were strong, and in parliament the governor of Hong Kong suggested that the British Government had a moral responsibility to allow the three million British passport-holding Hong Kong Chinese access to the UK in 1997. The USSR was non-committal but Gorbachev was later reported as saying that he did not believe the students' motives to have been 'evil'.

## One China, two systems

Martial Law was lifted in January 1990 and major efforts were made to restore China's damaged image abroad. Particularly helpful in this direction was the Chinese support of the US military actions during the Gulf War (China is one of the permanent members of the UN Security Council) and their support of the UN peace plans for Cambodia. By the early '90s international contacts were more or less back to normal. Deng Xiaopeng retired but retained most of his influence until 1994, when he bowed out owing to increasing ill health before dying in 1997.

This event did not produce the collapse of the government many had predicted and the **restoration of Hong Kong** (1997) and **Macau** (1999) to mother China went remarkably smoothly. Similarly, Deng's successor, Jiang Zemin, was able to hand over power to Hu Jintao in 2002. China's economic policy is also working better than anyone could have anticipated: the country joined the WTO in 2001, has the fastest growing economy in the world, and in 2005 the private sector accounted for more than 50 per cent of the economy for the first time since the Revolution.

## China today

It's a cliché but China today really is a country of contradictions. On the one hand, the Chinese space programme put their first man into space in 2003, Shanghai's Maglev train is the world's fastest at 430km/h, The Three Gorges Damn project is the most ambitious of its kind, the railway line to Lhasa is an engineering miracle and Jinmao Tower is the world's tallest hotel. On the other, there are still 750 million peasants subsisting in China's rural areas, the country's human rights record is woeful, political progress has been minimal and all over the country cities are becoming increasingly polluted (see 'Climate', p291).

Relations with **Taiwan** (which China still wants to see return to the fold) and the staging of the 2008 Olympics will probably dictate China's position in world affairs for the next decade or two.

## THE PEOPLE

China is the most populous nation on earth with about 1.3 billion people (but no one really knows, even after the recent census). Traditionally, Han Chinese see themselves as the original Chinese race, tracing their lineage back to the successful Han dynasty (206BC to 220AD); they constitute about 95 per cent of the population, while the other 5 per cent belong to any one of over 50 ethnic groups. This means that some 60 million inhabitants are looked down upon as non-Chinese.

China's huge population has been a source of worry for some time now and a birth-control programme has been operating since 1953, although it wavered rather during the Great Leap Forward and the Cultural Revolution.

Originally two children per family was seen as the ideal with a limit of three, but now one is the limit. Larger families are heavily penalized and the pressures on young mothers to conform can be considerable. Ultimately the aim was to limit the population to 1 billion and reduce it to 700 million by 2050 but so far this has failed.

Western concern has been expressed that the 'one child' policy may lead to cases of infanticide (male children are seen as more desirable than female). In an effort to combat this, rural families are now permitted to have a second child after a certain period of time provided their first was a girl. Fears are also growing over the 'little emperor' phenomenon that is developing as these only (often extremely spoilt) children grow up.

The country is divided into 22 provinces, five autonomous regions (plus Hong Kong since July 1997) and three municipalities. The latter are the large cities of Beijing, Shanghai and Tianjin, while the so-called 'autonomous regions' are those densely populated with ethnic minorities (Xinjiang, Inner Mongolia etc). They are allowed some extra concessions, one of which is the relaxation of birth-control regulations for minorities; despite this, numbers remain static.

### Uighurs

Uighurs make up the majority of Xinjiang's population but only just, because each year the government sends/entices more and more Han Chinese to live and work here. Uighurs are descendants of the 'Rock' Turks or Blue Turks (they got the latter name from the colour of their hats) from the Lake Baikal area. Their original capital was at Karabalghasan and they seem to have arrived in the Tarim Basin in about the 5th century AD.

Legend says their founding father was one Wugusi, who could speak from the day he was born and was brought up on raw meat and wine. He had 24 grandsons and they were the founders of the 24 different Uighur tribes. Their ancient writing system was adopted by the Mongols, even though they now use the Arabic script and have a language similar to Uzbek. Today almost all Uighurs are Muslims but in the seventh and eighth centuries they were major proponents of Manichaeism (see box p315) and were mostly vegetarian.

> **Chinese medicine**
> Throughout Chinese society, 'balance' is seen as a key attribute and something to be striven for. The universe is often explained as a world of opposites, which, when combined together equally, bring balance and harmony. This is most commonly portrayed as the black and white, **Yin** (female, passive energy) and **Yang** (male, active energy) symbol, but is also present in the *Feng Shui* used to design and position many buildings.
>
> Huang Ti, the Yellow Emperor (see p35), is said to have written the medical book, *Huang Di Neijing*, in which this balance is highlighted as the cornerstone to treating illnesses. Since then, much of Chinese traditional medicine has been aimed at creating or restoring such balance. Thus Chinese medicine has become as much a philosophy as a school of science and this is centred on a person's *qi*: their 'life force' or 'life energy'.
>
> This energy flows around the body along energy paths ('**meridians**') and acupuncture is used to increase/decrease, block/unblock this flow. Doctors supplement this with 'herbal' medicine (in fact, this includes not only herbs, plants and flowers but also natural animal and mineral ingredients), usually drunk in tea form.

## RELIGION

Confucianism and Taoism are the sources of traditional beliefs in China and, along with Buddhism (see pp38-9), form the foundations of Chinese culture. They were clamped down upon by Mao and The Cultural Revolution stopped all overt religious activity and was responsible for the wholesale destruction of religious centres and symbols. But since his death, their popularity has increasingly returned, particularly in the last few years.

### Taoism

Founded by Lao Tze in the 7th century BC, Taoism posits a sense of all-pervading unity behind objects and their ideal state; this is the Tao or 'Way'. Life should be lived in accordance with the Tao in order to promote oneness and harmony. Various ways of doing this are prescribed, including such diverse disciplines as yoga, meditation, philosophical dispute and magic.

### Confucianism

This is a philosophy rather than a religion and is based around Kong Zi (Confucius), a 6th-century BC scholar who wrote numerous discourses on the art of successful government.

Although he was largely unrecognized in his own lifetime, his writings were adopted by virtually all later dynasties as models for civil service training, recruitment and practice.

Amongst the ethnic minorities, **Islam** (see box p57) is strong, with an estimated 12 million adherents. There are about 50 million **Christians**. Various sects and cults such as **Falun Gong** continue to attract new recruits despite major government opposition. Whatever their religion, however, virtually all Chinese perform solemn ceremonies of ancestral reverence.

# Practical information for the visitor

## THE ROUTE

One of the best ways to see as much of the Silk Road as possible is to cross China twice in a rough figure of eight (see map opposite inside back cover). The advantage of this is that you can see both routes around the Taklamakan.

This guide is set out travelling east from Kashgar on the northern Taklamakan route and stopping at every stop until you hit the coast. If you *are* coming back to Kashgar, you can miss out some of the stops on the outward journey and take them in on the way back along with a different route around the Taklamakan (see box p303).

Another option if you want to visit Pakistan is to fly back from Beijing to Kashgar (or to Dunhuang, from where you can pick up the above detour); this can be a very shrewd move, especially if you are short on time.

## DOCUMENTS

You probably won't need an **extension** to your 60-day visa but if you do (or you got only 30 days first time round) you can apply at any **Public Security Bureau** (the equivalent of a police station). They should issue a one-month visa extension. Be careful, though, as there seem to be massive discrepancies between individual PSB offices. **Turfan** is a good place to try (Y100 for an extra 30 days), while those in Beijing are a nightmare.

Every town has a **PSB**. The general rule seems to be: the smaller the town, the less hassle you get. The other good rule to note is that you don't have to wait until your first visa runs out to apply for an extension, as the extension is valid not from the date of issue but from the day your original visa runs out. A second one-month extension is trickier and after that officials get pretty uncooperative unless you have plenty of mitigating circumstances or letters from the powers that be.

---

**The Chinese zodiac**

Astrology has always been important in China and the lunar calendar dictates many things, including Chinese New Year (although unlike Muslim festivals, see box p12, Chinese festivals stay within the Western calendar framework, so 'New Year' always falls between late January and mid-February).

There are 12 signs which rotate in order in an annual cycle; 2000 was the year of the Dragon and you can work forwards from that using the following formation: Dragon (strong, intelligent), Snake (secretive, greedy), Horse (emotional, clever), Goat (charming, good with money), Monkey (confident, humorous), Rooster (diligent, imaginative), Dog (humble, patient), Pig (materialistic, loyal), Rat (social, insecure), Ox (stubborn, conservative), Tiger (creative, brave), Rabbit (timid, affectionate), and back to Dragon.

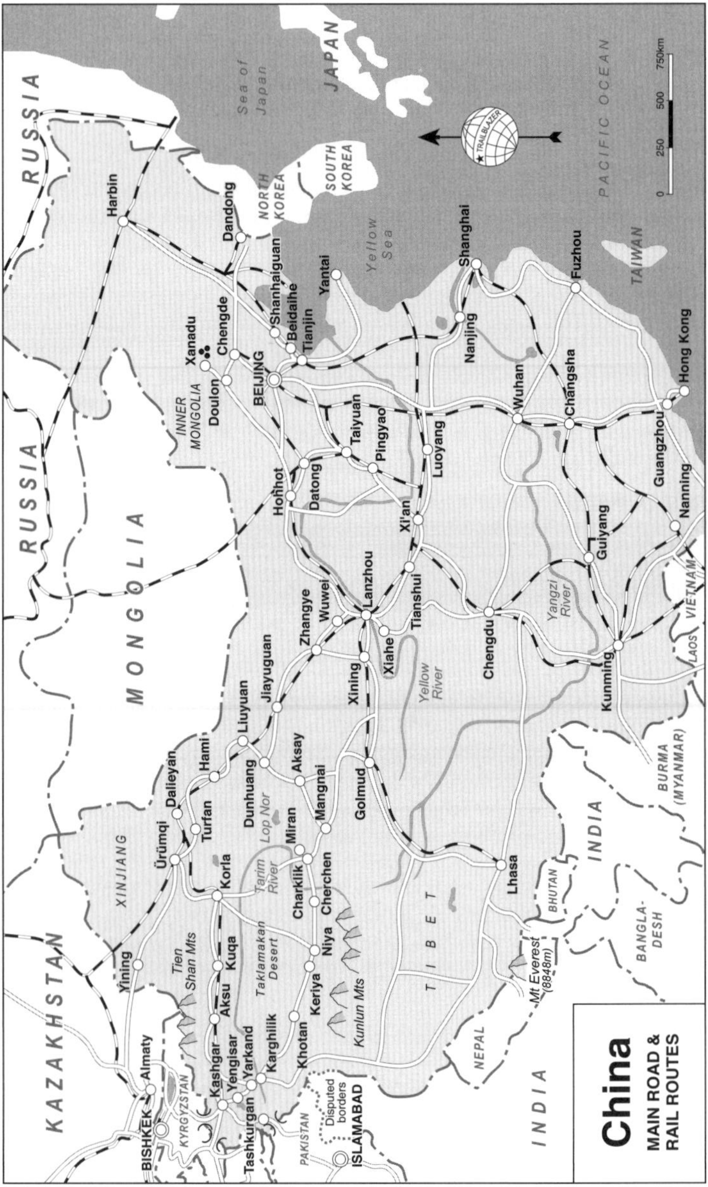
China
MAIN ROAD & RAIL ROUTES
RUSSIA
RUSSIA
MONGOLIA
KAZAKHSTAN
KYRGYZSTAN
PAKISTAN
INDIA
INDIA
NEPAL
BHUTAN
BANGLA-DESH
BURMA (MYANMAR)
LAOS
VIETNAM
TAIWAN
NORTH KOREA
SOUTH KOREA
JAPAN
Sea of Japan
Yellow Sea
PACIFIC OCEAN
INNER MONGOLIA
XINJIANG
TIBET
Disputed borders
Tien Shan Mts
Kunlun Mts
Taklamakan Desert
Tarim River
Lop Nor
Yellow River
Yangzi River
Mt Everest (8848m)
0 250 500 750km
TRAILBLAZER
Harbin
Dandong
Shanhaiguan
Beidaihe
Yantai
Chengde
Xanadu
Tianjin
BEIJING
Doulon
Hohhot
Datong
Taiyuan
Pingyao
Luoyang
Xi'an
Shanghai
Nanjing
Wuhan
Changsha
Fuzhou
Hong Kong
Guangzhou
Nanning
Guiyang
Kunming
Chengdu
Tianshui
Lanzhou
Wuwei
Zhangye
Xining
Xiahe
Jiayuguan
Liuyuan
Aksay
Dunhuang
Mangnai
Golmud
Lhasa
Hami
Dalieyan
Turfan
Ürümqi
Korla
Miran
Charklik
Cherchen
Niya
Keriya
Khotan
Kuqa
Aksu
Yining
Kashgar
Yengisar
Yarkand
Karghilik
Tashkurgan
Almaty
BISHKEK
ISLAMABAD

> **Martial arts**
> Most martial arts have their roots deep in religion and philosophy. As such they were practised and developed by monks and priests throughout the ages. There are hundreds of different forms, schools and doctrines but the most famous is **Shaolin Kung Fu**, as taught by the 6th-century Indian Buddhist monk, Boddhidarma, in the Shaolin Temple on Song Mountain (Henan province).
>
> If you get up early anywhere in China, you will see a large majority of the population practising their traditional **Tai Chi** ('shadow boxing') exercises in the country's numerous parks.

**Identity cards** of any sort can be useful as a deposit (eg for bike hire); anything with your photo on it will do (video cards, old library cards, expired passports etc). If you didn't manage to get an **ISIC card** (see p11) at home you could try to get a Chinese student/teacher's card here, as this will entitle you to similar reductions on entrance fees. Obviously these are 'illegal' unless you are actually studying or teaching in China and a US$100 fine was apparently levied on some recent offenders in Xi'an. Having said that, there are several places in larger cities which offer to 'procure' fake cards at a price and checks do not seem to be common.

## Customs Declaration Form

In China you are required to fill in a Customs Declaration Form on entry into the country; technically you must produce the same form on exit but most foreign visitors aren't checked. If challenged you may be asked to prove that you still have all your valuables and can account for the money that you brought into the country by showing exchange certificates.

Customs officials are quite lax about what you take out but they can be awkward about what you bring in, particularly regarding politically sensitive material. Check your books for maps which show Taiwan as a separate country or in a different colour as they are liable to be cut out and confiscated (if any of your books do contain such maps try to put them in your large rucksack rather than your daypack or cut Taiwan off the corner of the map – apologies to Taiwan residents).

## CLIMATE

During the summer, China is hot, often uncomfortably so. Xinjiang, in particular, can be fierce so be prepared to have a few days 'off' or you'll suffer. Look out for sandstorms, too, as they are common in desert areas and give little warning (the sky turns a very bleak yellow/white but usually the next day will be clear).

You can never have enough water so stock up regularly. Nights can be cold but nothing that a fleece won't handle except, perhaps, for the crossing into Pakistan where you will want to wrap up warm. In the east, especially towards the end of summer, the heat can turn to haze and thunderstorms (although these are not common until autumn), so be prepared to be flexible with your itinerary.

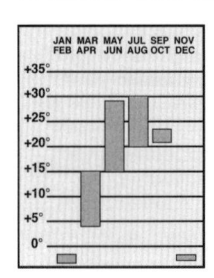

**Max/min °C
Beijing**

The advantage of travelling through China in autumn (and to a lesser extent spring and early summer) is that there are few tourists and the Chinese themselves are not on holiday. This means that the sights and the trains are not so packed (hotels are also more likely to offer you discounts). The downside is that some places are closed and fewer tours are running so it becomes harder and more expensive to see some attractions, especially if you are travelling alone.

China is home to eight of the world's ten most polluted cities and pollution means that many potentially clear days in a city will appear cloudy.

## ACCOMMODATION

All hotels in China are happy to show you your room before you commit and it's a good idea to check that the showers and air-con work and that there's hot water and, if it's important to you, a sit-down toilet. It is also common practice to haggle, especially in the smaller cities. In this guide we have listed only the official price each hotel was charging but with a bit of hard bargaining we paid about two-thirds/three-quarters of this in over half the hotels we stayed in. This applies only to double and single rooms, however: you won't get much of a discount on dorm beds!

In the larger cities a series of hotel touts operate outside the train stations, offering rooms in whichever hotels are short of customers. This system seems to be safe and you can often get a central location for a cheaper price than you might expect, although these hotels cater primarily for Chinese visitors, so English might not be spoken – where we have included these types of hotels, we have referred to them as 'Chinese hotels'. (NB It is particularly important to check the rooms first and haggle in these hotels.)

Check-in requires you to present your passport but they don't keep it, only the slip of paper they give you to complete with your personal details. As in Central Asia you will often be given not a key but a piece of paper which you must present to the floor attendant in order to get into your room.

If you are staying **'upmarket'**, expect hotels to be of a similar standard to those in the West. Rather than ring up and book directly, however, your best bet is to book through a travel agent back home or through one of the various Internet agents. They always get better deals than individuals and sometimes the savings can be substantial, particularly out of season. Type the city you want into any search engine alongside 'cheap hotels' and all the main players should come up.

**Budget** travellers don't get it so easy although rooms are generally hygienic, if basic. The arrival of **YHA** hostels (🖳 www.hostelchina.org) in the last few years has brought about a big improvement. Most budget hotels/hostels have dormitories which can hold anything from two to twenty or thirty beds. They are suitably cheap (US$3-5) and can be very pleasant, though some people are unhappy about leaving their possessions in a room full of strangers. If you check into an empty three-/four-bed room do not be surprised if someone else rocks up at two in the morning. If a bed in a three-or four-bed room seems unduly expensive, make it clear that you want only the one bed rather than the whole room to yourself.

Hotel rooms come equipped with washbowls, spittoons, televisions (sometimes) and plastic slip-on sandals in which you are supposed to potter off to the showers. If it is cold expect high-quality eiderdowns. Every room has its own thermos flask, which is filled by the 'Thermos Lady' – it should be full of piping hot water for tea (tea bags are often supplied) or pot noodles. If the water inside is only tepid it should still be safe to drink, as it will have been thoroughly boiled recently (if you are unsure, ask the 'Thermos Lady' to replace it or go to the communal washrooms where more hot water should be available).

In budget hotels, washing and toilet facilities are often limited (see 'Customs and attitudes' p299): the showers, as often as not, are in a separate block around the back of the building and it may be necessary to take along your room card or a shower token in order to get in.

Virtually all hotels in China provide a left-luggage service free of charge.

## TRAVEL AGENCIES AND TOURIST INFORMATION

Most national agencies like CITS (**China International Travel Service**) and CTS (**China Travel Service**) are state run and annoyingly expensive and useless. Even if all you need is a **support letter** for your visa, these agencies can be inefficient and require of lots of prodding; you are better off trying a private firm; see the Beijing listings (p368).

It is also worth noting that just because CITS is the official tourist organization, this does not mean that their tours will go like clockwork. Some local offices, however, can be useful to the **independent traveller** as most are staffed by foreign-language speakers. They occasionally give away free maps.

Private travel agencies like those in the West are still rare but in most of the tourist centres there are local operators catering for almost all visitors' needs.

## TRANSPORT

There are 1,100,000km of roads in China and a major percentage of freight travels across the country by truck. The number of people with a car has also exploded and cities are often clogged to breaking point, while the bicycle in many regions is becoming an endangered species.

Millions still go by train and even though there are some 53,000km of track, the demand for tickets is high, particularly during the summer when many locals are keen to use their new-found wealth to explore a country they could previously see only on television. The trains themselves are continually improving (Shanghai is home to the fastest train in the world) and you will be as unlikely as you will be unlucky to encounter one of the old green boneshakers. Sadly, the steam locomotives that had hordes of train-spotters queuing up to enter China in the '80s and '90s have mostly been replaced.

Air travel is popular amongst the wealthier Chinese but is still expensive. The inland waterway system is extensive, carrying some eight million tons of freight per year (about half of the total taken by rail).

## Train

The nightmare that was once the Chinese railway system has improved considerably. This is primarily due to the introduction of a **computerized ticketing system** (in the old days you could expect to queue for hours while they checked file upon file) and you will probably find yourself using trains as your primary form of transport. Several of the larger train stations also have a special **foreigners' ticket window** where the teller should speak English, though customer-service skills as a whole are still very much in their infancy!

To **buy a ticket** or to get anywhere in China it helps to have your destination written on a piece of paper in Chinese – ask a receptionist or friend in your hotel to do it for you (including the date, time and class of travel). When you get your ticket it should show the number of the train and the price paid (almost all tickets sold in China are one-way). Unless you are travelling on a 'no seat' ticket (see below), your ticket should have carriage and seat numbers printed on it too, so don't panic when everyone starts charging on to the train – having said that, once away, everyone seems to happily move around from seat to seat, usually in an attempt to talk to you. Always keep your tickets, as you will need to produce them at your destination in order to leave the station. We have quoted the price of a 'hard seat' for all the journeys; 'hard sleepers' cost about twice as much, soft seats and soft sleepers about three times.

There are three **classes of train**: those numbered 1-299 are express trains and are really comfy but carry a surcharge (a prefix of K or Z means they are even more high speed). Numbers 300-599 are standard trains. Those numbered above 600 are the old trains, which go at a snail's pace.

After you've chosen your train (it's definitely worth getting an express if you have the choice) there are five **classes of ticket** available: **'soft sleeper'**, **'soft seat'**, **'hard sleeper'**, **'hard seat'** and **'no seat'** (see p378 for Chinese translations). Express trains in eastern China have all classes available (often on two levels so check your ticket to see if you are upstairs or downstairs), the rolling stock is modern and the seats are comfortable in every class; further out in the sticks, standard seats are little more than PVC-covered planks.

The 'soft' options are as comfortable as they sound but nearly as expensive as flying. The 'hard sleepers' are simple bunk beds which everyone agrees give you a good night's sleep. 'Hard seats' are not as bad as they look and are definitely more fun, especially if you want to meet local Chinese. Anything over 18 hours on a 'hard seat' does, however, take its toll on your back (locals often ignore the spit and fag ends that cover the carriage floor by laying a blanket over them and stretching out under the seats) and your sleeping patterns – Chinese 'classics' tend to blare out over the speakers throughout your journey.

There is a ticket booth on every train (usually coach seven) where you can theoretically **upgrade** your ticket but in the summer the train will often already be full. If you do manage to upgrade (very possible in the low season) you pay only for the kilometres covered while you are in the bed so you can 'hard seat' during the day and bunk bed at night which is a lot cheaper. If you have to resort to a 'no seat' ticket, which can be the only option for 'travel that day' on busy routes, you will find the Chinese very generous in making room for you if you are prepared to join in with the chit-chat. Theoretically, ticket offices cannot refuse you a 'no seat' ticket.

'Hard sleeper' tickets are often gold dust so you might have to employ the help of a local or book up to four days in advance to get one. During summer even these tactics might not work, so be prepared for some hard-seat action.

**Food** is always available on board from trolleys. Platform hawkers also operate at each station. The supply of boiling water in hard-seat class often runs out for your pot noodles so a daring raid into the sleeper carriages to use their never-ending urns might be necessary. There is a buffet car but you can no longer use the ploy of having a few beers and then falling asleep on the tables: you must order a food dish and leave before midnight.

All **trains leave on time** and you will not be allowed to board less than five minutes before departure. In smaller stations you might get away with it but, trust us, they are just as likely to have locked the doors to the platform and enjoy waiting the five minutes with you to watch your train pull away.

## Cars and motorbikes

It is still illegal for foreign visitors to rent cars outside the major cities which is a shame as a road trip across China would be fantastic. Similarly, you cannot bring your **own vehicle** into China as a normal visitor (see 'Driving the Silk Road', p74). **Hitching** is not sanctioned in China although it may be the only option in some places; see 'Hitching the Silk Road', p181.

## Buses

Chinese **long-distance buses** run to every city that trains go to and more, so if you are ever stuck and unable to buy a train ticket, buses are viable alternatives along most of our route in China (even if we haven't listed them). The problem is they are often slow and very, very uncomfortable if you are over five foot two. However, if you need to travel the same day over a shortish journey consider them. In Xinjiang you will need, and maybe even prefer, them for some routes, particularly the Southern Taklamakan. **Bus stations** are quick and simple to use (there are rarely the massive queues you will encounter at railway station ticket offices) and are usually near the train station.

**Local buses** are a nightmare. The problem lies in getting on to the things. As the bus pulls in, its doors open to reveal 80 per cent of China's entire population heaving under thousands of tons of pressure per square inch inside. Despite the fact that half the passengers want to get off, everyone who wants to get on just does. The ensuing struggle can be violent and there is no sympathy for the weak. If you wait, British style, for the other passengers to get off before you get on, you probably won't make it. Equally, don't bother waiting for the next bus as it will be just as bad: elbow your way on.

Chinese buses generally have one or more conductors who sit in the small recesses behind the doors; tell them where you want to go (a written note may help here) and try to make it clear that you would like to know where to get off. Those who can't reach the conductor pass their money to the person next to them who passes it on – if everyone is staring at you and passing you money you are probably right next to the conductor.

Numerous foreigners are pickpocketed on Chinese buses so do be careful. If you are carrying a large piece of luggage (rucksack etc) it is probably better to take a cab.

### Bicycles

The Chinese may have stopped using so many of them but bikes are still a great way to get around town. You will have to leave a deposit to rent one (perhaps Y200, or try one of your ID cards) and they should not cost more than a few yuan per hour. If you want to **bring your own bike**, see p157.

Before you accept a bicycle test it – the old Flying Pigeons can be bone-rattlers – or you could find yourself paying for its repairs (or yours) later on; ensure that the brakes, pedals and wheels all work smoothly. Also check that the saddle can't suddenly tip up, or you could be in for a painful ride. Finally, check the bell (no one takes any notice of them but you will blend in better if you ring it constantly). Never accept a bike without a lock.

There is supposed to be a law against locking bikes to railings but this does not seem to stop the Chinese, though there are so many bike parks you should not need to. Generally, bike-park attendants give you two metal discs with numbers on them: one stays on the bike and you keep the other so that you can reclaim it later. There will be a small fee (usually Y0.10).

You have to be quite forceful when you are riding, especially in the big cities, or you will find yourself waiting for a gap in the traffic that never comes. Most cyclists look for safety in numbers and cross major junctions in a convoy. As the weather is nearly always dry, you can enjoy whole days in the saddle and visit places you wouldn't reach any other way. It is also a pleasure to join those locals who regularly cycle the wrong way down a road or even around a roundabout.

### Taxis

Drivers are very unlikely to speak English so get a friend to write down your destination for you. Before you get in, either negotiate a price or agree to use the meter. **Minibus taxis** are available in some places and these are ideal for groups; **rickshaws** are also common but they are mostly tourist traps these days and you'll spend as much time haggling your driver down to a reasonable price as you will on the journey (although everyone ends up trying them once). Motorbike taxis are catching on amongst the dreadful traffic jams but they are usually unlicensed so be careful.

Generally speaking, taxi drivers are much keener to get you into their cabs than they are to listen to where you want to go, so make your destination clear or you could be in for a slow, expensive ride while the driver stops at random to ask pedestrians where they think you want to go.

## Flights

CAAC is the parent body for the aviation industry and they have worked hard to improve their performance since they were labelled **C**hinese **A**irways **A**lways **C**rash in the '80s and '90s. The network is now comprehensive, relatively cheap and reliable, particularly in the east. If you are beginning or ending your trip in Beijing or Xi'an, more than enough major international airlines fly in and out of these hubs to keep prices competitive.

There are a whole host of internal carriers too, although services vary between them. China is a massive country and if you are short on days, a four-hour flight beats a 36-hour train journey every time. It's pretty simple to buy a flight from one of the many travel agents on the main streets but ask at your hotel if you are having problems.

For international flights, the cheapest tickets are to be had out of Beijing (although, those heading south will find even lower prices in Hong Kong). **Travel agencies** are not China's strong point but we have listed our favourite in Beijing's 'Orientation and services section' p369. Departure tax is Y90.

## ELECTRICITY

The mains electricity supply throughout China is 220V, and two main plug types seem to be in use: North American two-pin and the round three-pin plugs.

## TIME

China operates entirely on Beijing Time (GMT+8). In reality, however, Xinjiang province lags behind by two hours and local watches and clocks may be set either to Beijing time or 'Xinjiang time' (see box p305). All timetables work on Beijing time.

## MONEY

China uses 'People's Money' or 'Renminbi' (RMB). Since 1995 this has officially been pegged to the US dollar at 8.28, although officially this currency is still not valid/available outside the country. Most businesses and hotels are allowed to take only RMB (although airlines and hotels often quote their prices in dollars and take US$). The RMB is still pegged but, because of its strength, not as tightly as before. Exchange rates vary little from one place to another and the currency is stable.

The basic unit of currency is the *yuan* (Y), commonly nicknamed the *kwai*. This is subdivided into 10 *jiao* (which have the nickname 'mao'), and one jiao is in turn divided into 10 *fen* (but fen are worth so little you probably won't come across them). The largest

❏ **Exchange rates**
| | |
|---|---|
| £1 | Y15.30 |
| €1 | Y10.06 |
| US$1 | Y7.77 |
| Can$1 | Y6.58 |
| Aus$1 | Y6.03 |
| NZ$1 | Y5.43 |

To get the latest rates of exchange visit 🖳 www.oanda.com/convert/classic or 🖳 www.xe.net/currency/.

banknote is the Y100 note, after which there are notes for Y50, Y10, Y5, Y2 and Y1, as well as a Y1 coin. There are notes and coins for jiao and fen.

All towns will have a wide choice of banks but often only the **Bank of China** will exchange foreign currency, although larger hotels have exchange counters. The Bank of China also exchanges **travellers' cheques** and the main branch in each town should give cash advances on credit cards at 3 per cent commission. There are **ATM**s in the big cities but not all will accept foreign **credit/debit cards** (again the Bank of China is your best bet) and, despite the signs, ATMs in Xinjiang often don't accept any foreign cards at all.

## COMMUNICATIONS

There are privately run **Internet cafés** in most places you will visit and these are usually cheap and quick; even the smallest towns have some sort of access. Email systems are monitored though and many websites are blocked (the government firewall is often dubbed the new Great Wall).

❏ **Country code** China ☏ +86
See individual 'Orientation and Services' sections for local codes.

The **postal service** is generally reliable, though it's worth noting that international mail to Europe all departs from Beijing or Shanghai, so if you post something from Kashgar it will go thousands of kilometres east before going west.

**Stamps** are sold in post offices and the bigger hotels but they are not gummed; there are pots of glue strategically positioned around post offices.

**China Telecom** is efficient and quite cheap for international calls. IDD is available from all major towns and cities. Phone cards are also widely available for international calls but calls are still not that cheap. Most international GSM networks have coverage in China (at least in cities) and mobiles are everywhere.

*China Daily* (🖥 www.chinadaily.com.cn) is the locally published English-language paper and is available in most cities.

## NATIONAL HOLIDAYS

In addition to the following, in January/February there's the **Chinese New Year** and the related **Spring Festival**. New year is celebrated over two days, the Spring Festival goes on for two weeks. In the countryside it's accompanied by the sound of firecrackers; these are banned in cities so people listen to taped firecracker recordings instead! Everything ends with the multicoloured lantern festival.

| | |
|---|---|
| March 8 | **Women's Day** |
| May 1 | **Labour Day** This is usually a week-long holiday. |
| June | **Dragon Boat Festival** Falling on the fifth day of the fifth lunar month, this is the best time to see dragon-boat racing. |
| September/October by | **Moon Festival** This mid-autumn festival is celebrated giving one another moon cakes. |
| October 1 | **National Day** This celebrates the creation of the People's Republic. The Chinese often take the whole week off to visit their families. |

Banks are usually closed on Saturday and Sunday; museums are frequently closed on Monday.

## CUSTOMS AND ATTITUDES

There are a number of Chinese behavioural quirks that tend to confuse/annoy foreign visitors, so it would be as well to be ready for these, particularly as your route passes through many of the more isolated regions of the country. It is something that the Chinese government is addressing, however, as a recent government official quoted in China Daily testifies: 'The behaviour of some Chinese is not compatible with the nation's economic strength and its growing international status'.

### Spitting
Despite national campaigns to stamp out the habit, the Chinese tend to spit a lot. Spittoons litter most hotel corridors and floors can be positively slippery. As likely as not, when you wake up in a cheap hotel it will be to the sound of four or five individuals hawking in the bathroom, all apparently trying to eject their lungs through their mouths. It is often said that Chinese men stop spitting only to smoke, and vice versa.

### Language
More and more Chinese can speak English (especially students) and many will approach you wishing to practise their skills. But the vast majority still don't and can seem very curt. This is something to do with the Chinese outlook itself, so don't lose your temper, as this won't get you anywhere at all. Unfortunately, the phrase budget travellers are still most likely to remember from their time in China is 'mei yo', which can mean virtually anything, as long as it is negative, from 'No' to 'There are no rooms free at this hotel' to 'This train is full', to 'Go away – we can't be bothered with you, you're a foreigner'. Just try to remain calm and persist with your line of questioning, as they tend to give in, in the end.

If you do speak a little Chinese, it is usually greatly appreciated but far from expected.

### Shouting
Many Chinese people, when speaking in public, have the volume turned up high (in Singapore's airport there is a single sign in Chinese – but no other language – asking for passengers to 'be quiet'!). At first it sounds as if they are vehemently arguing but, in fact, they are just going about their daily business. TVs are usually set to the highest volume too and can be very annoying in next-door rooms.

### Staring
The novelty of a Western person does finally seem to be wearing off in China but expect to be stared at on occasion, particularly in rural areas. Similarly, the absence of a concept of privacy in Chinese society can sometimes get out of hand and really play on your nerves. Many Chinese will repeatedly interrupt you if you are talking with a friend, or reading a book, and might even take the book out of your hands to have a look themselves. It's easier said than done but keep smiling and don't lose your temper.

## Toilets

The practice of going to the toilet in the street is disappearing (at least amongst adults) but Chinese lavatories can still be a little disconcerting. Old-style cubicles have no doors and only low partitions separating you from your neighbour (it is not uncommon to have a full blown conversation mid-squat). Toilet paper is rare so always have your own handy. This is all changing rapidly in the cities (sit-down toilets are increasingly common) but unfortunately not so along our route.

## FOOD

You will probably be surprised by the food you receive here if you have not been to China before. For a start, you will be travelling mainly through the northern half of China, which is the home not of rice but of wheat noodles.

Chinese noodles take a variety of shapes and forms, the most flamboyant being the stretch noodles *(ban mien)*, which you can see being created throughout the country. They are made by pulling the dough into a long strip, shaking this up and down so that it stretches, joining the two ends together, and repeating the process; it's impressive to watch. Apart from noodles, the dough is often made into the ravioli-like *jaotse*, which can be very extravagantly folded before being boiled and then either served fried or in a soup.

That's not to say that rice is not on offer but it is the most obvious example that the food you eat won't necessarily correspond to that of your Chinese take-away back home. Similarly, virtually nothing is off-limits to a Chinese chef, whether it's snake-meat, horsemeat or camel hump! The biggest shame is that many restaurants are scared you won't like more authentic Chinese food and therefore deliberately make your dishes bland.

The best Chinese food is said to come from the Cantonese and Sichuan areas of the south, which aren't covered on this trip, though many emigrés have brought their techniques to restaurants in other cities. Many good restaurants, however, often cater only for the Chinese market and have no English menu.

Something that shouldn't be missed on this trip is a Mongolian hot pot. This is not a hot pot of the Lancashire variety but a huge wok of constantly boiling water into which you dip a selection of vegetables and wafer-thin meats to cook, before coating them with sauce and popping them into your mouth. The closer you are to Mongolia when you order this dish, the better.

In Xinjiang, *laghman* (noodle soup) and shashlik will hold few surprises to those coming from Central Asia (although they're tastier here) and they will become a staple alongside the chicken, peanuts and rice that you'll find in the many backpacker cafés. As most locals are Muslims, however, don't expect pork.

Some travellers like to carry their own chopsticks for cleanliness (or is it vanity?) though most restaurants use disposable ones nowadays.

## Snacks

Snacking is easy and cheap in China: try *baotse*, the wonderful steamed dumplings which contain either meat or vegetables or both. They're spongy, white and very filling. The Chinese are fond of sweet potatoes too (the misshapen objects seen on barbecues in the streets; the flesh inside is yellow and tastes like a cross between a baked potato and a roasted chestnut). Hard-boiled eggs are sold all over the place, usually picked from their mini-charcoal stoves with chopsticks (a real test to see if you have mastered the art!), often having been cooked in tea. In Xinjiang you will enjoy the small samosas (*sam-sam*) and meat-filled bread rolls (*lujabee*) that are available everywhere.

Chinese bread gets progressively more doughy as you head east; there is white bread for sale in railway stations but it tends to be rather spongy and cake-like. Check before you buy that it does not have a sweet filling inside.

There is plenty of fruit around, notably melons, grapes and pomegranates during the mid- to late summer; Hami, just to the north-east of Dunhuang, is particularly renowned for its melons, and Turfan's grapes and raisins are supposed to be the best in China.

## DRINK

### Non-alcoholic
The staple drink is green tea *(chai)* which is always served weak and without milk. Coffee and Western hot drinks are often available in shops or hotels and it is worth buying a small jar of something instant, as eventually you will want something other than tea or hot water.

Fizzy drinks and bottled water are available too, though local Chinese brands often aren't up to much. Always check the seals on bottles to ensure that the contents have not been diluted. Keep an eye out for the excellent fresh yoghurt, which is sold on street corners throughout the country.

### Alcoholic
Chinese **beer** (*piju*) is of a surprisingly high standard and should be quaffed as often as possible (*Tsingtao* is the most popular brand but there are lots of regional alternatives). It is sold by the bottle and at train stops it's common to see small children rush into the carriage hunting for the empties: not that this stops passengers tossing the bottles out of the window, along with the rest of their rubbish. Chinese **wine** (*putao jiu*) tends to be very sweet but there is drier stuff if you search hard (*Great Wall* wine is the top brand!). Watch out for the local spirits, which are very strong and extremely cheap but rather rough for the Western palate.

Caravan on the Silk Route, 13th century
(from *Travels of Marco Polo*)

# Xinjiang

## GEOGRAPHICAL BACKGROUND

Xinjiang is a massive province but boasts few cities or inhabitants. The main reason for this is the Taklamakan Desert (see box opposite) which sits roughly in the middle of Xinjiang. To the south are the Kunlun Mountains (the 'Mountains of Darkness' that form the foothills of the Tibetan Plateau) and to the north lie the Tien Shan ('Heavenly Mountains'). The Silk Road was forced to split around this desert. Initially the more isolated southern route was favoured while the northern route became more dominant as law and order was established.

Further north, on the other side of the Tien Shan mountains, the climate is less hostile and sandwiched between the Tien Shan and the Altai Mountains is the area where most of Xinjiang's population live. This was sometimes used by silk caravans on their way to Almaty or the Dzungarian Gap by Lake Balkhash. Unfortunately, hospitable valleys and increased populations attracted the attention of bandits so, until the Pax Mongolica (see p51) ensured their safety, merchants rarely ventured this way.

## HISTORY

The Chinese first arrived in the region in the 2nd century BC when they drove out the Yueh Chin tribes, though the Chinese were themselves driven out by those same tribes a century later. At the time, Xinjiang was probably not known to the West at all, although Ptolemy (2nd century AD) writes of a 'Scythia beyond the Imaus', a 'kasia regio' ('unknown land'), and this may be where the name Kashgar comes from; little more than this is known about the region's ancient history. It is clear, however, that Xinjiang was the victim of a number of invasions by semi-nomadic tribes for the first few centuries AD. The Chinese then returned in the late 7th century under the Tang dynasty to install a military garrison but the sheer distance between the Tang capital of Chang'an and Xinjiang meant that communications were difficult. They withdrew in 752AD, leaving it again to the wandering tribes. It was then taken and occupied successively by the Turks (10th century), the Uighurs (11th) and the Karakitais (12th). During these three centuries Islam was introduced into the region.

### The Mongols

In 1219 the Mongols arrived, yet the initial destruction wreaked by them was only short-lived. The later unification of the Mongol kingdom under Kublai Khan (1215-94) meant that travel was safe and trade centres flourished. The Mongol rule was not to last for long, however, because it was weakened by internal strife. In 1389-90 Tamerlane arrived to sack Kashgar, heralding an age of unrest until the Chinese returned en masse in 1755. Reports state that they

> ### The Taklamakan Desert
> Taklamakan is a Uighur word meaning 'Enter But Do Not Come Out'. This desert is 450km across, 375km north to south and is filled with red-gold sand dunes up to 100m high. Together with the neighbouring Lop and Gobi deserts, it is estimated that it took up to six months to cross all three by camel (Marco Polo said one year).
>
> The Tarim River flows through the desert sporadically and others, such as the Yarkand, the Khotan and the Cherchen, feed water from the mountains into the Tarim Basin. But in the summer they are scorched by temperatures in excess of 38°C, while in winter they are frozen by -40°C conditions.
>
> Up until the 3rd century AD, one road dared to cross through the middle of the desert – in the east, via the town of Loulan – but the river and the lake (Lop Nor), upon which life depended slowly dried up, forcing the caravans away and the inhabitants to abandon the settlement to the sands; although, ironically, it was a flood which finally did it for Loulan in 330AD.
>
> On train journeys throughout Xinjiang you will repeatedly gaze out onto bleak salty wastelands as you pass through this desert but you will also pass by incredible rock formations, dramatic cliffs and a myriad of different coloured stone. More and more splashes of colour are to be seen too, from water, heather and sheep as well as roads, trucks and houses: all signs of man's gradual invasion of the desert.

carried out 'wholesale massacres' of the locals before installing Chinese settlers and traders to govern the town.

## Yakub Beg

Xinjiang still witnessed several open (often Muslim-inspired) rebellions and revolts, however. One particularly successful attempt to wrest power from the Chinese took place in 1862 with a movement that originally started in Gansu Province. It spread west rapidly and on 10 August 1863 Yarkand (200km southeast of Kashgar) witnessed a struggle that resulted in the deaths of at least 7000 Chinese settlers. The leader to emerge from this movement was Yakub Beg, who seized control by some rather underhand tactics and then proceeded to set up the independent Islamic state of 'Kashgaria'.

In a well-publicized attempt to gain credibility for his 'state', he sent his brother to Great Britain as an ambassador (he made an extremely favourable impression wherever he was received). Meanwhile the Russians, keen to advance in the area, signed a commercial pact with Beg in 1872 and were thus able to occupy parts of Xinjiang Province. The British, worried at this Great Game development, happily signed a similar treaty to try to halt Russian expansion towards India. Thus the shrewd Yakub Beg had managed to gain international recognition for his state.

Not that it did him much good. A Chinese army under General Tso Tsung-T'ang advanced westwards at speed and managed to take Yakub's capital city of Turfan on 6 May, 1877. Beg committed suicide shortly afterwards. His death spelled the end of the revolt, although the local Muslims' desire for independence did not necessarily die with him. Throughout the next 50 years Kashgar remained in the headlines because of its key position within the Great Game (see box p206): a Russian Consulate was set up here in 1882, shortly to be followed by a British 'listening-post' in 1890.

It was in these consulates that the great explorers like Sven Hedin, Sir Aurel Stein and Albert von Le Coq stayed before clawing their way through the desert (see box below). There have been numerous altercations between the locals and their Chinese overlords ever since. A notable one took place in 1928, with the Chinese properly regaining control only in 1943.

## Xinjiang today

Depending on whom you talk to, an independent 'Uighurstan' or 'East Turkestan' is either only a matter of time or nothing more than a pipe dream. There have been several attacks on Han Chinese targets over recent years and a major bomb exploded in a truck in Ürümqi during the summer of 2000, killing 60 people. Responsibility was claimed by Islamic fundamentalists as part of their programme to destabilize the region but it was reported by the Chinese Press as simply 'an accident during which a bus exploded'. Any Uighur rebellion has the full backing of many in the Islamic world, especially Al Qaeda.

The independence movement cannot, therefore, be dismissed lightly but it is difficult to detect any major groundswell of popular protest. Most locals will still tell you that they are Uighur first and Chinese second, but now that oil has been found in the Taklamakan Desert the province has become worth much more to China than just the buffer against the Islamic world that was its traditional role.

### Foreign devils?

Explorers had been coming to 'Turkestan' for centuries and it was no surprise when surveyors and archaeologists were enlisted to help map out the territory for their political masters during the Great Game (see box p238). Towards the end of the 19th century and the beginning of the 20th, however, several men from across the world took it upon themselves to dig deep into the region's countless historical sites and cart off as many wall-paintings, manuscripts, sculptures and other treasures as they could carry.

Sven Hedin of Sweden lead the way, quickly followed by Sir Aurel Stein (see p27 and box p326), a Hungarian sponsored by the British Museum, and Albert von Le Coq of Germany. Paul Pelliot of France, Langdon Warner of the USA and Count Otani of Japan were later arrivals. None of them saw what they were doing as wrong: in their eyes they were saving priceless relics from almost certain destruction (which is half true); nor did their sponsors – the leading governments and museums of the West – find any fault (Hedin and Stein were both knighted!).

Each of them certainly made some remarkable discoveries and contributed greatly to the scholarship of the region but in Chinese eyes they are still thieves and bandits who stole the region of its heritage (which is also half true).

If you find yourself in London or Berlin you should look up their collections in the British or Berlin museums – but remember how they got there. All six men left detailed accounts of their expeditions, which can be found in libraries today.

> **Xinjiang time**
> Locals in this province live on Xinjiang time, which is two hours behind Beijing. This is despite Beijing's official policy that all China is in the same time zone. You can certainly have sympathy for their decision to fall in with nature rather than doctrine. You will find it easier to set your watch according to party rules, however, as trains, buses, planes, banks and hotels all operate on Beijing time. The bonus then is you can lie in until 11.00 and the locals still think you have made an effort to get up at 09.00.

More and more Han Chinese have been encouraged to move here alongside those that perhaps didn't have a choice in earlier years and although they tend to live very separately from the locals, their presence is definitely felt. Uighurs still use Uighur names for their towns and cities, as we have in this guide, but, increasingly, the rest of the population refers to them by their Han Chinese names (which we have given in brackets).

## KASHGAR (KASHI)

Owing to its strategic position at the crossroads of the northern and southern Taklamakan routes, Kashgar has always been one of the major stops on the Silk Road. Marco Polo, who visited Kashgar in 1275, said:

*'The inhabitants live by trade and industry. They have very fine orchards and vineyards and flourishing estates. Cotton grows here in plenty, beside flax and hemp. The soil is fruitful and productive of all the means of life. This country is the starting-point from which many merchants set out to market their wares all over the world. The folk here are very close-fisted and live very poorly, neither eating well nor drinking well. There are some Nestorian Christians in this country, having their own church and observing their own religion'.*

It has always traditionally been more Central Asian than Chinese (it is, in fact, marginally closer to Beirut than Beijing) but each year more and more Han Chinese are moving in, diluting the town's exotic feel.

### Kashgar today

Today, old Kashgar is still a good area to wander around, or simply to sit and relax; unfortunately, it is slowly being swallowed up by the new town. Most foreign visitors don't come to Kashgar for underground shopping malls, MP3 mobile phones and playboy boutiques but they're all here, and even the Sunday market is losing some of its character.

Kashgar is a big town and, especially after the emptiness of the mountains, it feels like a big city – though if you're coming back from eastern China it seems to be nothing more than a village. After Central Asia the Chinese writing on all the huge hoardings and a genuine sense of order and control can be a real culture shock. The massive Chairman Mao statue opposite the park is the most obvious example of Han Chinese attempts at domination.

## What to see

**The Sunday Market** This is not simply 'another' market. It is superior in every way – the hottest, most crowded, most colourful and biggest – and a real assault on the senses. People and their wares come from all over (Xinjiang, Pakistan, Kyrgyzstan, Tajikistan and Kazakhstan), so you can buy almost anything. What makes it unique, however, is the animal market where you can watch for hours as Uighurs inspect the sheep, donkeys, cows and camels (often taking them for test runs). It's hard work fighting your way through the crowds so you might want to take a break mid-morning but you no longer have to get up at the crack of dawn to witness the action as it now tends to last all day (a lesser market operates Monday to Saturday).

Keep a very close eye on your valuables as this must be one of the worst places in China for pickpockets. You can cycle here (though this is not for the faint of heart as the streets all around are swarming) and park your bike in front of the big trade building. Or you can take a donkey-cart (typically Y2 per person) from in front of Mao's statue.

**Id Kah Mosque and Bazaar** This mosque was built in the late 18th century and although it is considered big by Chinese standards (there is room for 5000 people), it's a bit of a let-down compared to the treats of Central Asia.

More interesting by far is the bazaar, just to the south of the mosque, which is always guaranteed to be humming with activity. The maze of alleys is squeezed under the rickety balconies and verandas, with stalls selling everything from hats and carpets to herbs and spices. The streets are still set out according to trades and amongst the fig trees and the old men with wispy beards you can get a glimpse of the Kashgar of yesteryear. Once you enter this area, you are unlikely to resurface for a while, so it's lucky that there are numerous food stalls here. This area is shrinking, however, as the Han Chinese authorities try to modernize the centre of town.

**Renmin Park** This is another good place to wander around, although it offers a stark contrast to the hustle and bustle of the bazaar. These shady gardens are opposite the Mao statue. Unfortunately the soft-drink sellers have acquired ghetto blasters, though the further you get into the park the quieter it is. It's an excellent place for a picnic or an afternoon nap. The zoo, like the others you will come across in China, is a depressing collection of large animals in small cages.

**Abak Khoja Mausoleum** This is quite hard to find (the otherwise useless CITS map comes into its own here if you are cycling) but it is intrinsically the most interesting construction in Kashgar: a square, domed building covered in green majolica tiling. It's not known if Abak Khoja (whose real name was Hidayatilla and who is now revered as a saint) is actually buried here.

The mausoleum is also named the 'Tomb of the Fragrant Concubine' after a local girl who was abducted by Emperor Qianlong's officials and taken to Beijing to be his concubine. The story goes that her fragrance worked on Qianlong who fell hopelessly in love with her and the episode ended, as do all great love stories, tragically, with her death. In fact it is highly unlikely that she is buried here, if she ever existed. More plausible is the rumour that this is the tomb of rebel leader Yakub Beg (see p303).

The mausoleum has been repaired a number of times and around it are several attractive buildings. There is an impressive graveyard next door, with an entrance around the other side (don't climb over the wall).

It is best to cycle the few kilometres here if possible as the scenery is attractive (a taxi is Y30 there and back). Head east over the bridge on Aizirete Lu and keep asking directions. The mausoleum is open daily until 6pm. Entry costs Y8.

### Excursions from Kashgar

A visit to **Kara Kul** (Lake Kara; see box p309) is worth considering even if you are not going to Pakistan. You can expect close contact with yaks, oxen and camels. Two places that might also be of interest are the 'deserted ancient city' of **Hanoi** and the **Caves of the Three Immortals**. A trip to the former involves a taxi ride to the site, whereupon you discover that the stupa you saw in the postcards is all that there is to see. The latter involves a trip of about the same length to see the three caves, situated on a cliff-face. Take plenty to drink for both trips. You can expect to be totally covered with dust by the time you get back.

### PRACTICAL INFORMATION
[☎ code 0998]
#### Orientation and services

Kashgar's **train station** is quite a ride out of town. Take No 28 bus from opposite the Id Kah mosque (Y1.5). A taxi costs Y20.

Kashgar's centre is not too big. Most things are within walking distance of the hotels but by far the best way to get around is by bicycle – the only distant site is the Abak Khoja Mausoleum, 3km away. Most hotels and cafés hire bikes for about Y5/hr. Alternatively, taxis are plentiful and cheap.

The branch of **Bank of China** on Renmin St is the only one to give advances on credit (but at the time of writing not debit) cards but other branches will exchange cash currency, as will hotels and various money touts outside the Qiniwake and Seman hotels.

The **post office** and **China Telecom** are on the same street. **Internet cafés** can be found inside and just outside the Qiniwake and Seman hotels but it's cheaper to use the local ones in town.

The **CITS office** outside Qiniwake Hotel isn't helpful but you can get a map of Kashgar here. If you need to organize the Torugart Pass crossing (see box p242), start

---

**John's Information Cafés**

If you have been to Xinjiang before you will probably have heard of **John's Information Cafés** (there are branches in Kashgar, Turfan and Dunhuang) as havens for backpackers. Nowadays, however, they are overpriced and substandard, especially the Western dishes, but they still have a key location, provide tours and information, and are the first stop for many; the tour guys also can organize transport over the Torugart Pass for US$120-150/pp.

John himself is known to be a bit of an 'eavesdropper' for the local PSB, so it is probably not a good idea to ask for advice here if you are wanting to visit any 'closed' areas of China, especially the direct route from Kashgar to Tibet. That Uighurs are not welcomed in the café lends weight to the rumours. The branch in Ürümqi closed and the branch in Kashgar has retreated behind the steel gates of the Seman Hotel – some say because of lack of customers, some say because of Uighur threats.

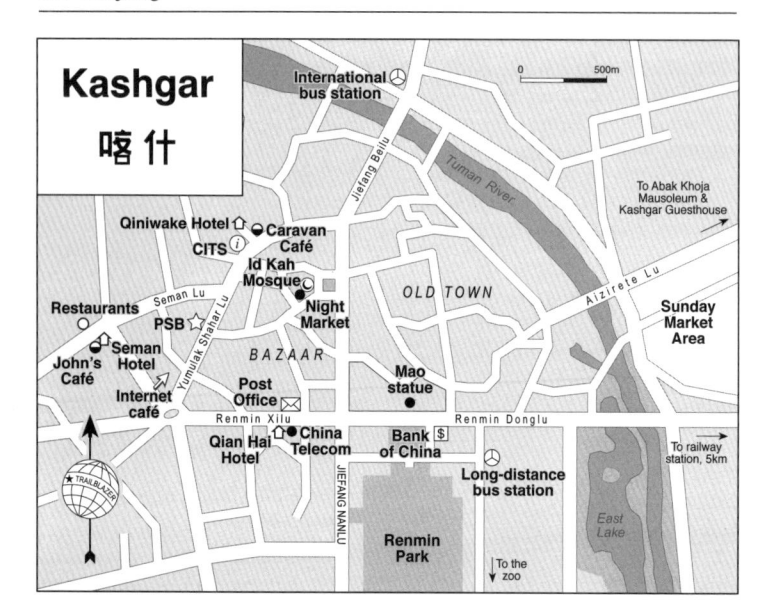

at the noticeboard in your hotel or John's Café (see box p307) – you should meet someone who is organizing a crossing and looking for passengers. Caravan Café also runs local tours and trips over the Torugart Pass.

### Where to stay
*Qiniwake ('Chini bagh') Hotel* (☎ 298 2103; Y35/dorm, Y360/Db inc breakfast) was named after the 'Chinese Garden' created by Lady Macartney during her stay here as wife to the British consul (see p28); forget any hopes of this hotel still resembling that Victorian oasis where intrepid travellers like Sven Hedin (see box p304) were welcomed with open arms, however; the modern hotel is a large tower block, though its new wing is an improvement (if more expensive).

If you venture round the back you can see the old consulate building and even eat in the restaurant inside.

*Seman Hotel* (☎ 258 2129; Y25/dorm, Y180-280/Db) is on the site of the old Russian Consulate; the original buildings are still here, and you can even stay in one of the suites if you have the money; the hotel is actually made up of two separate buildings, differently priced. It is well placed with cafés and tour operators within its grounds.

A more upmarket hotel, *Kashgar Guesthouse* (☎ 265 2367; Y250/Db), 3km east of town, is good but inconvenient, especially as no public buses go this way. *Qian Hai Hotel* (Y350/Db), a large place on Renmin St by China Telecom, is pretty swish but aimed at the Chinese market.

### Where to eat and drink
The restaurants around the main hotels tend to cater for travellers. This means menus in English but not such great food. For a more authentic atmosphere, head for the **bazaar** and its environs or the **night market**.

There is a strip of Uighur and Chinese restaurants outside the Seman. None of them is named but the further away from the hotel you go the cheaper they become. At the entrance to Qiniwake Hotel is *Caravan Café*, which serves the best coffee in town but at Western prices.

> **Kara Kul excursion**
> This area is a particularly beautiful stop-off if you are camping, as you can pitch your tent wherever you want around the lake for free. From there, you can spend as long as you like hiking around the hills, watching the villagers at work around the lake or just enjoying the scenery (see 'Trekking the Silk Road', p265); or you can hike up the hill and over into the next valley to really escape. Stock up well on food and water, though, because the limited supplies that are available are expensive. For those without camping equipment there is a *Lodge* (Y40/dorm) by the lake but the best experience is to be had staying with the locals in their yurts (Y30/pp, Y50 including food) dotted around the shore. From Kashgar's international bus station, **buses** going to Tashkurgan and beyond will happily drop you by the lake (Y45) and it's easy to catch the bus up to Tashkurgan, or back to Kashgar, when you have finished.

Kashgar's night scene is limited and foreign visitors tend to congregate at the makeshift **bars** by the Seman roundabout.

### What to buy
Kashgar is the place to make up for lost time in the souvenir stakes, especially if you are here for the Sunday Market. Particularly popular are ornamental knives (a large knife may cause problems, however, both within China and at customs on departure), hats, shiny metal boxes, skins and boots. You will certainly see pelts of endangered species like the snow leopard but don't buy them. Woven cloth, silk, rugs and carpets are good here but be wary of spending a fortune unless you really know what you are looking for (see 'Buying a carpet', pp136-7).

### Moving on
If you want a 'hard sleeper' ticket in the summer you will probably have to book a couple of days in advance but 'hard seats' can usually be bought on the day or the day before. If this is your first time on a Chinese train, be prepared for some of the best scrums outside New Zealand. The train will arrive about an hour before departure but you won't be let on until there are 20 minutes to go. In the interim the jostling crowds build up into a frenzy until at last the gates are opened and you charge amidst a crowd of maniacs. There are two trains a day heading east: to **Kuqa** (11hrs/Y90) and **Korla** (16$^1$/2hrs) and all the other stations on the way to **Ürümqi** (23hrs).

**Buses** leave from the **long-distance bus station**, follow the same route and are more plentiful than trains but they are more expensive and less comfortable. There are almost daily **flights** between Kashgar and Ürümqi, Dunhuang, Xi'an and Beijing.

For **Pakistan** (see p260), buses leave from the **international bus station**, as do those buses for the Torugart Pass into **Kyrgyzstan** (see p242). For the **Southern Taklamakan Route** (see p320), buses use the long-distance bus station.

## KUQA

Kuqa (Kucha) was described by Aurel Stein as a 'natural fence against that advance of drifting sand' because it was permanently fed by water from the Tien Shan and had a well-developed irrigation system. Xuan Zang (see box p345) was more concerned that it was famous for its 'perfumed women' (it was also famed for its lute players and Kuchan musicians were once to be found all along our route). Either way, this was once one of the great Silk Road cities and a major Buddhist centre. If you found Kashgar too modernized, it's worth breaking your journey here to see the Old Town, which has hardly changed at all.

## What to see

The major **market** in the Old Town is on a Friday and as Kuqa is still heavily Uighur-dominated this is very like Kashgar's Sunday market used to be, although on a smaller scale. It is held on the banks of the river by the bridge between the two halves of town. If you don't catch this, the Old Town is much like a big market in itself and is worth a wander.

Xuan Zang tells us of two enormous statues of Buddha, 27m high, that stood at the gates of the town in the 7th century but these are now long gone, as are most of the remains of ancient Kuqa, known as **Qiuci City**. To reach the few stones/bits of wall that are left, walk away from the new town along the road past Qiuci Hotel until you come to the small river.

## Around Kuqa

The reason Kuqa became a major Buddhist centre was because of a 4th-century scholar, Kumarajiva (known in Buddhist history as the 'Nineteenth Patriarch of Buddhism') who was born here. He was one of the earliest Chinese scholars to make the trip to northern India and learn the true meaning of the scriptures and his fame brought him many disciples. Over the centuries various 'Thousand Buddha' caves were built in his memory, often financed by wealthy Silk Road traders. Problems began, however, when Kuqa was taken over by Muslims from Central Asia in the 9th century and many caves were defaced or abandoned. Worse followed with the arrival of von Le Coq, Stein, Pelliot et al (see box p304) and most of the best finds now sit, like so many others, in Berlin and London.

The **Kizil Thousand Buddha Caves** are the most famous because they housed the best selection of murals and carvings but they were also the worst ravaged so they can no longer be described as a 'must-see'. It's a long way (60km) but the trip itself is quite dramatic and the caves' setting is picturesque. Only a few caves are open to the public, however, making the entrance fee (Y35) expensive. All the paintings that were found, as you can just about see from the fragments that are left, were remarkable for their distinct Ghandaran (Greco-Indian; see box below) look with no Chinese influence at all.

### Ghandaran art

The kingdom of Ghandara was always hard to pin down as its borders were ill-defined but it was centred on what is now northern Pakistan and eastern Afghanistan. When Buddhism seeped into China from northern India its art was mostly Ghandaran, which was a mix of traditional Indian art and the art introduced into the region by Alexander the Great.

The reason this is so significant is that unlike other Buddhist art that used mystical symbols such as a footprint, a wheel, a tree, a stupa or a combination of Sanskrit characters, Ghandaran art depicted the Buddha in human form. Moreover, the Hellenistic influences introduced by Alexander meant that these human forms had a straight, sharply chiseled nose and brow, classical lips and wavy hair; they even wore togas rather than the usual loincloth. Indian influence was not completely removed, however, as the elongated earlobes confirm.

Most hotels run tours to the caves and they should also include (amongst others) the ancient city of **Subashi**. This site is much closer to Kuqa. It was built between the fourth and twelfth centuries (when it was abandoned) and there are still some large pieces intact. A taxi for the whole day is Y300 for four people.

## PRACTICAL INFORMATION
[☎ code 0997]
### Orientation and services
The **train station** is quite a way out of town so it's best to get a No 6 bus or taxi (Y10) to your hotel.

The city is divided into the **old city** (west) and **new city** (east) with a surprisingly big gap between the two. You'll probably stay in the new part but spend most of your time in the old city, or outside Kuqa altogether at the Buddhist sites.

There is an **Internet café** in the centre of the new town near the **Bank of China**.

### Where to stay
Dorms are hard to come by in this town but doubles are pretty cheap. At the northern end of Jiefang Lu, *Kuqa Hotel* (☎ 712 2901; Y200/Db) gets the best reports and, set in its own gardens, is very pleasant.

*Qiuci Hotel* (☎ 712 2005; Y250/Db), on Tianshan Lu on the way out to the ruins of the ancient city, is a step up in price if not class.

*Kala Kuer Binguan* (Y140/Db) is the cheapest place in town but can be a bit noisy.

### Where to eat
Kuqa is known for its fresh fruit in the summer and has lots to offer at its **market** (in the new town) and **Friday Market** (in the Old Town). Restaurants, however, do not seem to have caught on, although there are plenty of small **cafés**.

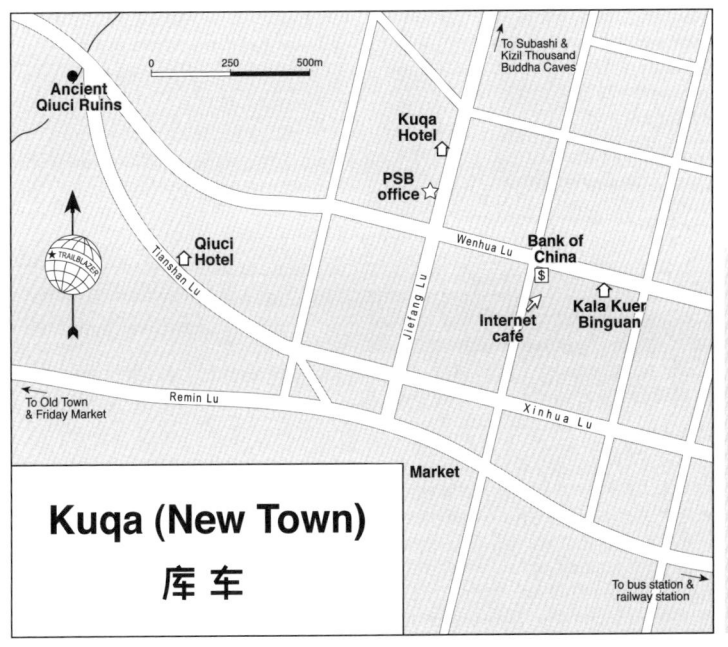

Kuqa (New Town) 库车

### Korla and the Trans-Taklamakan Highway

Few guidebooks pay much attention to Korla and it's no surprise. Unless you are using it to transfer from the train to a bus heading through the Taklamakan (or the other way round), there is no reason to stop in this unfriendly, modern city.

If you do change here, try to do so in the same day as it's an expensive place to stay (if you can find a room – some hotels refuse foreigners). Few people speak English, so get a **taxi** from one station to the other (inconveniently, they are at the opposite ends of town). If you are coming from Khotan you should be able to get a seat on the next **train** to Daheyan/Turfan (12hrs) or Kuqa (6hrs). There are regular **buses** in the morning and evening through the desert to Khotan but be careful – there are two routes! The quickest (20hrs/Y250) goes right through the heart of the Taklamakan to Niya (Minfeng), on the new road built by Western oil companies for exploration. The slower and older buses (36hrs/Y140) take the circular route around the western side of the desert (nearly as far as Kashgar) and through Yarkand (Shache). There are also buses down to Charklik (Ruoqiang) if you want to see more of the Southern Taklamakan route (see p320).

If you are stuck in Korla for the night, there is a **hotel** (Y60/dorm) on your right as you come out of the train station.

### Moving on

**Trains** are your best option: to **Daheyan** (for Turfan; 17hrs/Y175), **Kashgar** (11hrs/Y90) and **Korla** (5-6hrs). Often you can buy only a 'no seat' ticket from Kuqa's train station, so you need to upgrade on the train.

**Buses** run the same routes in similar times from the bus station in the east of town.

## TURFAN

Surrounded by fascinating relics including traces of lost cities, burial grounds and an impressive 37m-high minaret, Turfan (Turpan) is a small, pleasant place with a slow, naturally relaxed pace of life. This may have something to do with the weather: it's the hottest city in China (see box opposite), earning it the nickname 'Dragon Spring'. Luckily for those who don't like the idea of heatstroke, a simple tour of the main sights is easy to arrange and takes a couple of unstressed days. The rest of the time you should spend underneath the vine trellises that cover the main streets (they are as beautiful as they are practical), sipping a cool beer and trying not to expire. Turfan also claims to be further away from the ocean than any other place in the world, so there is no need to unpack the snorkel.

### History

Turfan's history is not well documented, which is rather ironic because the area around the town is loaded with archaeological sites of immense significance. The region's early history is characterized by the ongoing struggle between the Chinese Han dynasty and the Xiong-Nu tribesmen of the steppes to the north of the Tien Shan Mountains. The Xiong-Nu wanted Turfan as a gateway to the lands further south, while the Chinese needed it as a stepping-stone for their policies of westward expansion. Thus we have records of China attacking and taking Turfan in 108BC, but struggles continuing until 126AD, when China was finally able to claim total control of the whole region (known as the **Turfan Depression**).

**Gaochang and Jiaohe** Whenever the controlling Chinese dynasty was in an expansionist mood, Turfan was a rung on the ladder west, hence after losing and regaining it twice, military garrisons were stationed here at Karakhoto (Gaochang) and Yarkhoto (Jiaohe). Both these towns were later mysteriously abandoned, a fact that has thrown up as many questions for modern historians as it has archaeological treasures for the professional diggers who were later to descend on the place. Part of the explanation for their desertion may be linked to the arrival of the Mongols in the 13th century; certainly it would not have been the first time they had been responsible for a city's change of location. Yet the Turfan region came into its own during the ensuing Yuan dynasty, for this was when the Silk Road staged its grand finale and the oases of the Taklamakan became boom towns.

## What to see – in Turfan
**Emin Minaret** Despite its shape you might be forgiven for wondering whether you have seen this 37m-high minaret somewhere before (its 14 different patterns of brickwork certainly do seem reminiscent of Kaylon Minaret in Bukhara).

The minaret was erected in 1778-9 by Uighur architects on the order of local leader, Emin Khoja, at a cost of 350kg of silver. He died six months after its completion. The mosque behind it is no longer functioning. Scattered around

---

### The hottest city in China
Situated in the deepest depression in China (the surface of Ayding Kul sits 156m below sea level), Turfan is actually the hottest, driest place in the whole country. Average summer temperatures of 38°C, a highest recorded temperature of 49.3°C and the fact that it rains 'once every ten years' (Stein) would have combined to make this an extremely scorched patch of bare earth, were it not for an ingenious irrigation system which harnesses water from the snows of the Tien Shan to the north. All visitors will notice this intimidating heat, while a few have written of another problem: the local wildlife. Albert von Le Coq remarked that:

'*insect pests are very much in evidence here. There are scorpions whose sting is a very serious matter, and, in addition, a kind of great spider that, in spite of a hairy body the size of a pigeon's egg, can take mighty jumps with its long, hairy legs. It makes a crunching noise with its jaws and is said to be poisonous, although we have never known any bitten by it....The cockroaches too, are a repulsive pest, in size quite as long as a man's thumb, with big red eyes and formidable feelers. It is enough to make a man uncontrollably sick to wake in the morning with such a creature on his nose, its big eyes staring down at him and its feelers trying to attack its victim's eyes. We used to seize the insect in terror and crush it, when it gave off an extremely disagreeable smell...*'.

Luckily the insect problem is pretty much under control these days and life is dominated by grape harvests and irrigation schemes; anything else is too much effort in the heat.

the buildings are graves littered with broken bottles and bleached human bones, which give the whole place a rather eerie atmosphere.

Compare the minaret with the remains of the one just east of the main **city mosque** (to the west of town). Although the latter was clearly a lot smaller, the style of brickwork is similar. No one knows much about it, except that it was a victim of the Cultural Revolution; also a victim was the city mosque itself, which is why the one you see today is so new.

To get to Emin Minaret, cycle east from Turfan Hotel along the small dirt road for about ten minutes. Just when you think you must have taken a wrong turning you'll come to a field with the minaret in the middle. There's not much to see inside.

**Turfan Museum** The museum contains a lot of written material, both on tablets and paper. All the finds were unearthed in the region. In one display there are five perfectly preserved corpses but, sadly, there is no evidence of the notorious fossilized dumpling that is supposed to prove that pasta was invented in China and not brought over by Marco Polo as the Italians claim. Entry is expensive at Y12 and various displays tend to be closed for no apparent reason.

**Bazaar** This is one of the better bazaars in China, for while small, it is so incredibly crowded and bustling that there is a very intense feel to it. Cable and French wrote that it 'has a much more oriental look than that of Hami. In summer the whole street is covered with red matting and boughs of trees. The earth beneath is always damp, for the young shop assistants are responsible for scattering water many times a day in front of each stall'. Not much has changed. Try it for food and photography – this is an excellent place for taking pictures of locals (ask first, though). It's just opposite the bus station.

### What to see – around Turfan

There are a lot of options around Turfan so if you take a tour make sure everything you want is included. You can just about squeeze everything into one day (Y300 for a car and driver between three passengers) but it's a real slog, especially in the heat. The eight main sights are better seen divided between two relaxed days, in which case you could cycle one day and take a taxi the next – but in this heat cycling is hard. Most sites charge a Y20 entrance fee and cold drinks are readily available.

**Karez Wells and Museum** Turfan's furnace-like climate means that water evaporates fast here, making conservation essential. Water is channelled through the region in subterranean canals called *karez,* which are thought to have originated 2000 years ago in Iran. Such canals were essential for Silk Road towns from here to the Middle East. This underground network consists of 11,000 different canals, all interlinked, covering a distance of over 3000km. Water flows down from the mountains and is tapped by means of wells spaced at regular intervals, with tunnels linking them. The locals are very proud of this system, claiming that it's one of the wonders of the world. The new museum houses models showing how all the canal systems work and you are allowed to go inside one.

Attached is a 'Uighur village' with traditional dancing girls. But it's by no means the real thing and tends to be of more interest to Chinese tourists from the east.

**Flaming Mountains**  Another staple tour sight (they are on the way to Gaochang, so it's no effort to see them), these mountains extend for 100km and are so-called because, in the intense heat of the day, they look as if they are on fire. Legend relates that they came from heaven when the Monkey King, enraged at having been locked inside a stove for a week(!), kicked it over, whereupon the heated bricks supporting it fell to earth. In the Chinese classic *Journey to the West,* Silk Roadster Xuan Zang was here when they were still actually burning, and he had to beat back the flames with a magic fan so that he could pass unharmed. Today, they are more impressive from a distance.

**Grape Valley**  The rare combination of extreme heat and constant irrigation means that local fruit is particularly sweet, hence Turfan raisins are renowned throughout China. They are dried in the square, aerated brick buildings you can see everywhere; because they are shielded from the bright rays of the sun they retain their green colour.

Grape Valley is worth a visit only in season but between July and September it is a treat. From above the valley is a sea of green vines but then you realize that underneath all this is a maze of shaded walkways, restaurants and market stalls. The prices are very good (Y10 for a feast of tea, grapes and chow mein) and it's great to get out of the fierce heat. Set at the bottom of the valley is a small (and not very amusing) amusement park.

**Gaochang**  The history of this deserted walled city, 45km east of Turfan, is steeped in mystery. Originally known as Karakhoto, it was set up as a garrison town by the Chinese in the second or 1st century BC. With the arrival of Buddhism it became a religious centre and was visited in 630AD by monk Xuan Zang, who was made so welcome that he had to go on a hunger strike in order to persuade the king to allow him to leave. By the start of the 15th century the city had been abandoned but whether this was due to war or shortage of water no one knows. Not much remains on this impressively large site, so an active imagination helps when you get here.

---

### Manichaeism

The Babylonian prophet Mani was active in the 3rd century AD. He preached that he was the Chosen One, descended from a long line of prophets including Adam, Zoroaster, Buddha and Jesus. Little else is known about this religion (probably some sort of blend between Zoroastrian and Semitic beliefs) because so few traces of it have survived but it seems that, like Zoroaster, Mani believed the universe and everything in it was made up of good and evil constantly at battle with one another.

Manichaean priests followed a strict vegetarian diet, amongst other things, in an attempt to cleanse their bodies so that they could become beacons of light in the fight against darkness. Manichaeism was a forerunner to the Cathar movement in medieval Europe.

> **Bell of Moderation**
> Ancient Chinese rulers kept these bells in their courtrooms to remind them of their need for moderation. They ordered each bell to be specially designed so that the bell could rotate around a pole running through the middle of the bell (as if they were on a spit). The wide base was made heavier than the rest so that if the bell were empty, it would hang upright. By turning the bell upside down and half filling it with wine, however, the ruler could balance out the weight and provide himself with refreshment. Yet with too much wine, the bell would become top heavy, swing down and spill all its contents. Similarly, not enough wine (because of evaporation, or through excess drinking) also led to the bell toppling. The wine level therefore needed to be monitored each day by the ruler and, as such, acted as a constant reminder to behave in a moderate fashion.

It was here, in 1904, that German archaeologist Albert von Le Coq (see box p304) unearthed a life-size mural of Manes, founder of the heretical Christian sect of Manichaeism (see box p315). This find was particularly exciting because persecution of the sect had been so harsh that virtually nothing was known of it except from manifestos written against it. The majority of extant Manichaeist documents come from this region.

It was also here that von Le Coq noted the widespread destruction of priceless relics: he relates that one of his hired assistants had previously found 'cartloads' of ancient documents perfectly preserved, yet had disposed of them in the river for fear of divine retribution. He himself found a secret library, whose documents had all been destroyed by water as a direct result of the local farmers' irrigation schemes. It's a fascinating place to explore and for the best views, climb the walls at the back (to the left of the monastery ruins) – if you want to join the Chinese on the donkey carts from the entrance it's 10Y but the walk is not far.

**Astana Graves** These burial sites near Gaochang date from the 3rd century AD right up to the thirteenth but the graves have been pillaged over the years. What's left means little, even with a guide. There may be hundreds of chambers here but only three are open, so a visit lasts about 10-15 minutes. The bodies inside the tombs are not mummified but have been perfectly preserved by the arid climate.

Tomb 3 is best with its mural depicting the Confucian belief that gold, jade and stone represented the three sides of man. The God of Gold is in the centre with the God of Jade on his right and the God of Stone on his left. In the bottom left-hand corner of the painting is a bell (see box above).

The tombs are badly lit and the glass cases are very dusty, making it difficult to see the bodies.

**The Bezeklik Caves** The 'Thousand Buddha' cave complex at Bezeklik consists of over a hundred caves but only a handful are open. The caves, hewn and decorated between the sixth and the ninth centuries, were deserted at the same time as Gaochang. Before then, monks used to live in them and the frescoes clearly represent the life work of generations of devotees. Many caves are closed because they are considered 'not interesting' but it is possible to peep through the shutters. Photography is not permitted.

Bezeklik was visited by most of the early Western archaeologists. It was von Le Coq, however, who was responsible for the wholesale removal of murals and sculptures (to Berlin). You can clearly see the cuts he made around the frescoes so that he could insert saws behind them.

Almost without exception the remaining frescoes are in a poor condition: faces and eyes have been picked out and walls and roofs have been smeared with mud by Muslims (for whom the depiction of humans or animals is sacrilege). There are photographs of those murals removed by Le Coq in one of the caves. Outside, there is a perfectly shaped sand dune alongside a statue of Xuan Zang and Monkey.

### Hami

This town was always the gateway to Xinjiang from China proper and as such became a key stop on the Silk Road. On the map it looks easier to travel directly north-west from Dunhuang to Turfan but that route takes travellers through the harshest sections of the Lop Nor Desert, so caravans went either slightly to the south via Loulan or north via Hami.

When the Loulan route dried up and the Southern Taklamakan Route (see p320) fell out of favour, Hami found itself the centre of Silk Road attention and duly flourished. Unfortunately the old traditions described by Marco Polo seem to be dying out:

*'I give you my word that if a stranger comes to a house here to seek hospitality he receives a very warm welcome. The host bids his wife do everything that the guest wishes. Then he leaves the house and goes about his own business and stays away two or three days. Meanwhile the guest stays with his wife in the house and does whatever he will with her, lying with her in one bed just as if she were her own wife; and they live a gay life together.'*

For the two hundred years before 1930, Hami was a nominally independent kingdom but suffered badly during the Muslim revolts of that period (see p303).

Hami is still an oasis between the Lop and Gobi deserts and is still famous for its fruit (melons in particular), but there is little of historical significance to see, except for the **Hui Wang Fen Mausoleum** complex (Y10): this contains the tombs of the 18th- to 20th-century kings (take a forty-minute walk south out of town and across the river to reach the site). As it is rarely visited by foreigners, however, Hami provides an authentic view of local life in this region.

**Practicalities** The town centre is small and the bus station is at its heart but the train station is a bit further out to the north-west (take bus No 1 or 3).

If you intend to stay the night there are various unnamed **hostelries** around the bus station – if these are no good head a bit further south down Jianuo Lu to *Hami Binguan* (Yingbing Lu; Y30/Db). There is an **Internet café** by the Bank of China and a good **night market**.

Trains leave daily for Daheyan/Turfan (12hrs) and Liuyuan/Dunhuang (12hrs), but they are slow.

**Jiaohe** What makes Jiaohe so interesting is that although it was abandoned in the Yuan dynasty it is still largely intact. Whereas in Gaochang you can recognize the odd archway or two and little else, here you can see each building and browse along what was clearly the main street.

Stein noted that this 'lost city', known to early archaeologists as Yarkhoto, marked 'the capital of Turfan down to Tang times' but that, because it was never totally deserted or buried, most of the really valuable items had already been removed or destroyed by the time he arrived. The town housed a garrison of Chinese soldiers in the Han dynasty, hence its safe location between two rivers (and thus its name, which means 'Where Two Rivers Meet'). No one knows exactly why the inhabitants moved out in the 14th century; perhaps there was a fire or the water supplies failed. Then again, this could be the work of the Mongols, who arrived the century before.

Jiaohe is a fascinating place to explore, with sunset a particularly atmospheric time. It is 9km west of Turfan so can be reached by bike; entry is Y13.

**Ayding Kul (Lake Ayding)** At 156m below sea level, this lake is the second lowest in the world after the Dead Sea. It only looks like a 'lake', however, in spring (at any other time of year it is more like a puddle). Many, therefore, find this part of the tour a letdown and regret paying the extra Y150 for the taxi ride.

---

### Ürümqi excursion

Ürümqi is the capital of, and biggest city in Xinjiang but it's not of particular interest to foreign visitors. It is fast becoming an ugly industrial sprawl and the Uighur population is in danger of being outnumbered by Han Chinese. Its saving grace is **The Silk Road Museum** (Y25; Xinjiang Zizhiqu Bowuguan; catch bus Nos 2, 8 or 16 from the train station), which houses one of the best and most relevant collections along our route – there are particularly unusual findings from the Chinese excavations of Loulan.

The beautiful **Tian Chi** (Heaven's Lake) is nearby, where you can stay in yurts (Y40pp including meals) at the foot of the mighty **Peak of God** (5445m). The place has become overrun with Han Chinese tourists lately, however, and is nowhere near as authentic an experience as that on offer in Kyrgyzstan – although if you go hiking/camping in the surrounding mountains, you soon lose the crowds. Take a bus (Y50 return) from the north gate of the People's Park in Ürümqi.

**Practicalities** That the *John's Café* here has closed down gives you some idea of how few foreign visitors now make the detour to come up here. If you need to stay the night, *Ya'ou Binguan* (outside the train station on your left; Y40 dorm, Y120/Db) is the most convenient place to stay.

There are plenty of **Bank of China** branches to change money and advance money on credit/debit cards. The **Kazakhstan Consulate** (open mornings Mon-Thurs) at 31 Kunming Lu should be able to issue you with at least a transit visa if not a three-week tourist visa (see p18 for visa requirements) but foreign visitors are often required to provide letters of invitation and/or medical certificates and there have been complaints that the service can be haphazard.

**Trains** leave for Kazakhstan twice a week (see p229), and to Kashgar and other parts of China daily. **Buses** to Turfan (3hrs/Y29) leave regularly from the bus station.

## PRACTICAL INFORMATION
[☎ code 0995]

### Orientation and services
Coming by train, you will actually arrive at **Daheyan Station** (although your ticket will say Turfan). If you arrive in Daheyan in the middle of the night you can sleep in the waiting room for Y5. You need to take a minibus or share taxi (Y10) to Turfan (32km/45mins). It is wise to book your train ticket out of Daheyan before you head off to Turfan.

Turfan is very small: you can walk to the hotels from the bus station. **CITS** is in Oasis Hotel. They're actually very helpful here and sell maps for Y2.

If you need an extension to your visa, the **PSB office** (Gaochang Lu, in the north of town) is very good. There is a **Bank of China** by the bus station. If you want to take a tour there are plenty of **tours** and tour guides in town, so take a seat in a café, let them come to you and haggle.

There are a number of **Internet cafés** near the hotels so shop around.

### Where to stay
There isn't much choice for a town with so many tourist attractions and those that are here cater mainly for the Chinese market. As such, most people head to 1695 Qingnian South Rd and *Turfan Hotel* (☎ 856 8888; Y450/Db, Y60/dorm); it has raised its prices steadily over the last few years but it still has clean, if dark, dorms down in the cellars at the back, as well as a swimming pool. *Oasis Hotel* (☎ 852 2478; Y500/Db) is more attractive but a bit further away. *Yingyuang Hotel* (no sign in English; ☎ 852 2478; Y160/Db with private bathroom) is a good deal. *Station Hotel* (Y30/dorm) by the bus station is the cheapest.

### Where to eat
The branch of *John's Information Café* (see box p307), opposite Turfan Hotel, is most foreign visitors' favourite in the chain (certainly to look at); it's also the best option for a pleasant drink and chat (and cheap washing) but the menu is overpriced.

Further up, *Brother's Restaurant* is cheap (Y7/lunch) and cheerful, as is the hairdressers and the Internet-cum-convenience shop (Y5/hr for the Internet) next door.

There is a row of **Chinese restaurants** nearby serving good, cheap fare; some but not all have menus in English. There is also lots of cheap food in **Gaochang Market**: corn on the cob, meat soup, noodles or kebabs, as well as a bizarre open-air dance-floor!

### Moving on
**Heading east** there are two **trains** per day from Daheyan to Liuyuan (the closest station to **Dunhuang**; 8-12hrs/Y80). As neither town is near a train line (Dunhuang is two hours away) this is one occasion when you might want to take the **bus** (two a day from the bus station) although it usually ends up little quicker.

You also might want to break the journey at **Hami** (see box p317): there are trains and buses to Hami but the bus (6hrs) is usually quicker.

**Heading west** you can take the train to **Kuqa** (17hrs/Y175) or **Korla** (6hrs). If you are heading to **Ürümqi** (see box p318) it's much quicker to take the bus (3hrs/Y29) from the bus station as a new road has been built that connects the two.

## THE SOUTHERN TAKLAMAKAN ROUTE

*'The Southern route is barren, very stony, and grass and water are exceedingly scarce.'*
From the travelling tales of the Buddhist monk **Ch'ang Ch'un**

Although this is the oldest of the Silk Road's routes around the Taklamakan, it was deliberately chosen for its isolated terrain and hostile climate rather than its ease, as merchants hoped these elements would put off potential marauders. Today it remains isolated and if anything the climate is even more hostile than before. Little of modern-day China's progress has seeped through here and it is much harder and takes much longer than the northern route. Allow a week to ten days to see the most interesting sights and negotiate the unpredictable transport options.

You can travel only by slow buses and even these don't always go the whole way. By taking this route, however, you will have a real opportunity to see how Uighur life exists away from Chinese influence and you can get a feel for what life used to be like.

This trip is an adventure and not for the faint-hearted but if you complete it you will achieve something that not even Dalrymple or Danziger managed.

### Kashgar to Khotan
You can cross this route from either direction but we recommend going west to east as there is a real chance you won't be allowed to complete the crossing, in which case you can take a bus up to Korla from Charklik.

Starting from Kashgar, you need to take a bus (preferably a sleeper bus) to **Khotan** (10hrs/Y56) – these look pretty good until you realize each bunk is for two people and their luggage!

You will pass through **Yengisar**, known for making all the inlaid daggers you see in Kashgar; **Yarkand** (Shache), another famous stop on the original Silk Road, and **Karghilik** (Yecheng), starting point for any attempts on K2 from the Chinese side (Karghilik is also where the road from western Tibet meets our route). You will probably stop in each place for one of lunch/dinner/breakfast but there is little to see and most visitors head straight through. If you are going only as far as Khotan, however, you might want to spend a day in Yarkand.

## Khotan (Hetian)

Your first impression of Khotan, no matter what time of year, will be dusty. Straight away, you realize that you are on the edge, if not the inside, of a desert. On the town's outskirts in the early morning, when dust mixes with the mist or heat haze and families can be seen travelling into town on their donkeys and traps, it's easy to believe you have stepped back in time. Marco Polo tells us that

> 'It is amply stocked with the means of life. Cotton grows here in plenty. The people live by trade and industry; they are not at all warlike.'

Khotan is one of the world's leading jade producers. The town's modern centre, however, has seen a lot of development recently and seems to be heading down the same path as Kashgar.

**What to see** One thousand years ago Khotan was known as the producer of the finest silk carpets in the world but as the technology spread so Khotan was overtaken by carpet makers in Central Asia and Iran. Nevertheless, a fair choice of carpets (see box pp136-7) is available in the shops in the town centre and at the **Sunday market**, the size of which is unpredictable but on a good week it can surpass Kashgar's. Haggle for your life, as starting prices will be high.

Khotan is actually situated between two rivers, the Kara Kash ('Black Jade') and the Yurung Kash ('White Jade'). These unite to form the Khotan River that continues north into the desert. The **carpet factory** is worth a visit, as is the **silk factory** (both are on the other side of the river to the hotels) but the end products are disappointingly lacking in variety. You will probably want to take a taxi for these trips as they are quite far but if you do walk, you can stop to go down to the riverbed before you cross the bridge and join the locals hunting for white jade – though don't expect to make your fortune.

Outside of town is **Melikawat**, the remains of ancient Khotan, once an independent kingdom controlling all passage through this area, not just east and west but south through the Karakorum as well.

You can arrange camel trips into the desert but allow yourself a couple of extra days for this and be prepared for what at times can be an uncomfortable journey: Xuan Zang tells us that as he left Khotan he was 'attacked by tornados which bring with them clouds of flying gravel'.

---

### The Jade Road

Thousands of years before silk began its long journey across Asia, a precious stone was being traded across the east of the continent at enormous profit. It was highly prized for its incredible durability and was seen as a sign of immortality. The best jade came from the Khotan region. White, green, black and yellow jade were all traded; indeed, the tomb of Fu Hao, a Shang dynasty queen who died around 1200BC, contained more than seven hundred jades.

Confucius added to jade's allure in China by giving it a symbolic significance: in his eyes the qualities of jade mirrored those human qualities we should all aspire to, 'its flaws not concealing its beauty, nor its beauty concealing its flaws.'

## 322 Xinjiang

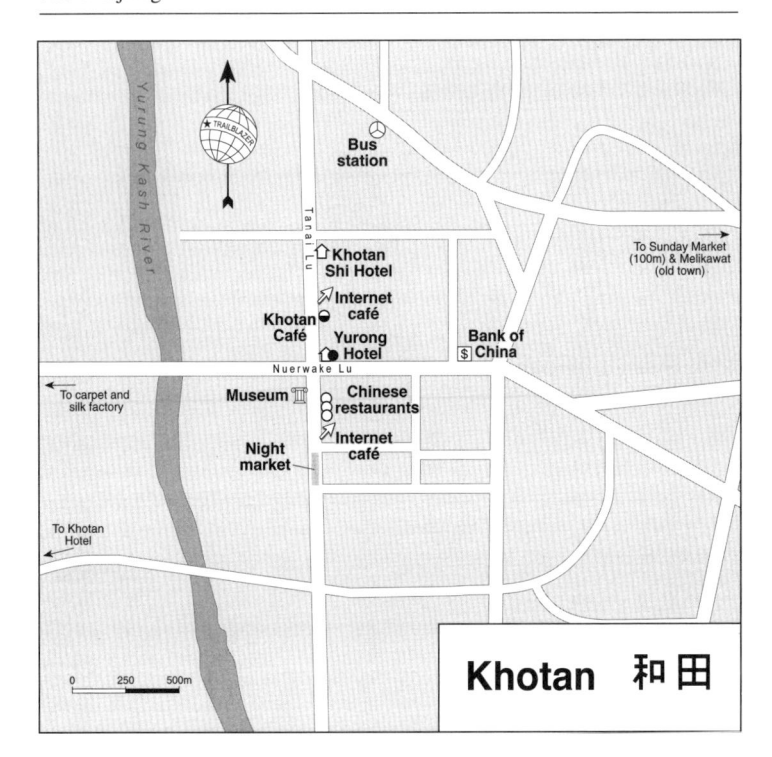

### PRACTICAL INFORMATION
**[☎ code 0903]**
### Orientation and services
Khotan's 'new town' (where you will invariably stay) is small and set around a central crossroads, which is a 15-minute walk south from the bus station.

Most hotels are connected to a travel service that can arrange trips to Melikawat (Y300), camel tours and visits to watch local craftsmen and women at work, which can be fascinating (especially the silk growers). **Hetian City Travel Service** (in room 228 at Yurong Hotel) are particularly helpful and can also organize the rest of your trip to Dunhuang but at a price (a jeep for the necessary three days costs up to Y8000, split between a maximum of three). Judging from their photographs and other services you would have a good trip but, if you have time, you should be able to do it by yourself and for much less money.

There are a couple of Internet cafés on Tanai Lu. The **Bank of China** should be relied upon only to change cash and travellers' cheques.

### Where to stay and eat
On the way into the centre of town from the bus station on Tanai Lu (North) 4 is the no-frills ***Khotan Shi Hotel*** (☎ 202 2824; Y20/dorm, Y90/Db). ***Yurong Hotel*** (dorms Y20), further down on the corner of a crossroads, is also good value. ***Khotan Hotel***, in the town's south-west, is more aesthetically pleasing and not much more expensive.

Nightlife in Khotan is non-existent as Uighurs spend their evenings at home. Still, there's a small strip of **restaurants** on Tanai Lu serving cheap and cheerful food with cold beer. Our favourite was the green-fronted dining-room four doors down. The *Khotan Café* is a useful base for visitors.

## Khotan to Charklik

From Khotan a bus (up to two days/Y72) will take you to **Cherchen** (Quiemo) where you will be dropped outside the only hotel, the *Muztag* (Y20/dorm bed). Buses are not always daily and it might end up being an overnight bus, or you may need to change buses/stay overnight in **Keriya** (Yutian, see box below) or **Niya** (Minfeng).

Marco Polo also tells us that 'Quitting Cherchen, you ride some five days through the sands, finding nothing but bad and bitter water.' Today you can cover the ground more quickly but each leg still takes the best part of a day and timetables are not always reliable.

From Cherchen the twice-weekly bus (13-16hrs) should take you to **Charklik** – the bus should leave early in the morning but nothing is certain so check with the station and your hotel.

## Charklik (Ruoqiang)

This is where it gets difficult because you are now approaching the legendary **Lop Nor** area (Charklik is near the site of the ancient town of Lop and its eponymous **lake**), the modern home of China's Nuclear Testing programme. The government does not want you here, unless you are part of a registered group of which they can keep track.

Another problem is that what's left of the lake actually moves around each year, as the rivers that feed it regularly change their course on their descent from the Kunlun Mountains; most of the rivers will dry up for part of the year and by the time the glaciers begin to melt again in the spring, the old riverbeds have often been filled by windswept sand, forcing the river to find a new path. This can result in whole sections of the road being flooded or washed out.

**What to see** **Kroraina** was a Southern Silk Road kingdom centred on the lost city of Loulan in the Lop Desert. At its height in the third and fourth centuries AD, it stretched south to Miran and west to Niya. They spoke Ghandari (an Indian dialect) and wrote in Kharoshti (a unique script used on the Silk Road only for a short period). They were conquered first by the Chinese and then the Tibetans, who made Miran one of their Silk Road fortresses in the 8th century at a time when Tibet controlled much of this part of the Silk Road.

---

**Keriya**
If you stay in Keriya you might want to heed Marco Polo's warning:
*'The people of Pein (Keriya) have a custom which we must relate. If the husband of any woman goes away upon a journey and remains away for more than twenty days, as soon as that term is finished the woman may marry another man and the husband may marry whoever he pleases.'*

You are unlikely to be able to visit **Loulan** unless you are willing to pay over a thousand dollars, as the authorities consider this their prize site and are very protective of the excavations here, but you can sometimes get out to see the ruined city of ancient **Miran** – your hotel should be able to fix you up with a tour, or there are occasional buses out to Miran town.

## PRACTICAL INFORMATION
### Where to stay
There are three hotels here: *Loulan* and *Altun* are more expensive but *Xinglong Guesthouse* (Y20/dorm) is reasonable.

### Moving on
It's no too difficult getting to **Miran** (75km, see above), the next town along, and from here there is a desert track straight through to **Dunhuang** but this is not maintained and there is no public transport so you can cross this way only in a jeep.

The easier option is to go from Charklik to **Mangnai** or **Huatugou**. There should be a bus but some foreigners have reported not being allowed on and have had to take private transport: minibuses sometimes run this route (9hrs/Y150), otherwise you need to hitch (see box p181) or pay for a ride in a jeep.

There is a **hotel** in Mangnai (Y20/dorm) and supposedly a daily bus to Dunhuang (direct or via **Aksay/Lenghu**) but again you might not get on or it might not be running (the road was closed in 2005 because of a huge flood).

If you have had enough by this stage or can get no further, there is a bus from Charklik that heads north through the desert to **Korla** (see box p312).

# Dunhuang

A major stop along the Chinese leg of the Silk Road, Dunhuang is the setting for the Mogao Thousand Buddha Cave complex, arguably the most spectacular of its kind in China. The town is surprisingly small but there are a number of interesting sights around it, making it a pleasant place to relax and explore slowly.

## HISTORY

The name Dunhuang literally means 'Blazing Beacon' and refers to the time when this small town was at the extreme western point of the Chinese empire and marked the end of the Great Wall (the wall was extended west from Jiayuguan during the Han dynasty) – it was the last stop for Silk Road caravans before they crossed the dreaded Lop Desert.

Dunhuang's other traditional name, Sha-Chou ('City of Sands'), is also apt – the vast dunes here feature in every traveller's account, including that of Marco Polo, who labelled them the 'Rumbling Sands'.

What makes Dunhuang so special, however, is that during the Tang dynasty, when Buddhism was violently suppressed, documents destroyed and temples ransacked, the city was under the control of the devoutly Buddhist Tibetans so escaped unscathed.

## The Mogao legend

'One day, Le Zun, a monk from the East on his way with three disciples to the Western Paradise came to these parts. He had earlier learned that none but those who drank the spring water of Sanwei Mountain would be able to cross the vast Gobi Desert that lay ahead. Eager to drink this miraculous water, Le Zun sent his three disciples ahead to fetch some.

They set out in the sweltering heat of mid-summer but two gave up from thirst and hunger. Only Zhi Qin persisted and drove his donkey forward suffering hardships for several days. At last, before him, he saw green trees in the midst of the barren desert, and he could hear the sound of flowing water.

After Zhi Qin had quenched his thirst, he sat down on the soft sandy bank to rest and watch the sunset. Suddenly the peaks of Sanwei Mountain became iridescent and in the centre of the golden rays sat a giant Maitreya, and emerging out of this radiance were thousands of Buddhas – all at perfect ease. In the golden light, myriads of fairy maidens flitted amongst them, making music on various instruments.'

Chen Yu *Tales from Dunhuang*

The next day, convinced he had found the Pure World of the West, he set about building a cave in which he could carve a figure of Buddha and paint the hosts of attendant spirits. Soon the local animals came to help him: gazelles removed the rubble; wild boars mixed the mud plaster for the walls and birds brought different coloured stones to grind into pigments. As a finishing touch, he incorporated all the animals that had helped him with the cave in his painting and so we have the styles that we see today.

Zhi Qin was joined by many other monks and more caves were begun. They thrived by playing on the fears of passing traders who wanted divine protection for their forthcoming crossing of the Lop Desert and were willing to pay for it.

## WHAT TO SEE

### The Mogao Caves

These 'Caves of a Thousand Buddhas', set in Sanwei Mountain, are probably the finest in China and are a World Heritage Site. They were carved between the fourth and fourteenth centuries, the best work taking place during the Tang dynasty (618-907AD). The caves were abandoned for several reasons, including the decline of the Tang dynasty and the repeated threats of nomadic marauders.

The survival of the caves in such a pristine condition is miraculous. Historians put their longevity down to the fact that this region was taken by the Tibetans in 781AD (see p46). Even the Mongol arrival in 1227 had no effect on these caves, although construction stopped under the ensuing Yuan dynasty.

The greatest threat to these 1000-year-old caves came recently with the arrival of treasure-seeking archaeologists (see p326). Langdon Warner, an American who visited in 1923, saw some of the damage caused by Russian refugees fleeing the Revolution and decided to 'save' as many of the artefacts as possible by shipping them to the USA. Other archaeologists were more reserved, perhaps because the complex was never quite deserted, and thus the caves survived in remarkably good condition.

The size of some of the carved Buddhas is truly amazing. Many caves are not caves as such but rooms hacked out of the rock. The statues were then erected within the caves as the clay rock was too crumbly to carve them out of the walls – the colours have survived because the heat is so dry. You will probably see restoration work being carried out in some caves and even replica statues being modelled out of clay – both of which give you an idea of just how much went into these caves in the first place.

Notice the heavy Ghandaran influence (see box p310) on the statues' features, especially the noses. This is an indication of just how deep the impact of Alexander and his armies was in Central Asia and north-west India. It also demonstrates how much cross-cultural exchange there was between here and other Buddhist centres.

On your way out it's well worth stopping by the **Research and Exhibition Centre** (Y25), which is in the modern building next to the car park. The building contains all sorts of interesting relics from the caves (including documents from the Cave 17 cache not bought by Stein and Pelliot; see box below). There are also displays detailing how the caves were made and full-sized reproductions of some of the caves themselves. They are all beautifully laid out and labelled with clear explanations in English. This is one of the better museums in China.

**Practicalities** Entry to the caves is a hefty Y80 but don't let this put you off. For their protection, strict rules have been laid down concerning visitors: you must be accompanied by a guide, cameras must be left in the left-luggage office (Y2) and several caves now have plastic glass covering the murals for their protection. Guides are generally excellent and tours last about two hours. It's best

### The Diamond Sutra

The story of the discovery of this most famous book is one that the Chinese recall bitterly. The manuscript, along with thousands of other ancient documents, appears to have been rediscovered in the 19th century by one Wang Yuan Lu (or 'Abbot Wang' as Western visitors called him). Wang had set himself up as the custodian of the caves and during his time here he discovered a sealed chamber in cave No 17, which contained a library of ancient documents (some so old they were brought here by Xuan Zang, see box p345) hidden for safety. British archaeologist Sir Marc Aurel Stein (see box p304), hearing of this discovery on his 1907 expedition, went to investigate. After prolonged negotiations he was permitted to view the chamber and thus wrote himself into the history books, for inside was a hoard of documents so great that its discovery is now held to be on a par with Carter's opening of Tutankhamen's tomb.

Stein then earned himself the perpetual hatred of the Chinese by purchasing over 5000 scrolls and paintings for the measly sum of £130, although the missionaries French and Cable reckoned that 'the business transaction with the old priest was done honourably'. So big was the find that when French sinologist Paul Pelliot arrived at the caves one year later he didn't even realize that any manuscripts had already been taken. Among Stein's crate-loads of documents was the Diamond Sutra, printed in 868AD, qualifying it as the oldest known printed document in the world. It is still on display in the British Museum.

to go early in the morning as it's cooler. Don't bother staying on for a second tour in the hope of seeing different caves: it will be substantially similar to the first as only a few caves are open to the public each day. It's not really worth bringing a torch, unless you happen to have a really high-powered one; it's better to hire one (Y3) when you get to the caves.

Buses to the Mogao Caves trawl along Dunhuang's main street, picking up punters and charging about Y10 for a return ticket. The journey takes about 40 minutes. It is possible to catch a morning bus and then return on an evening one but there's not much point as the caves are closed between 11.00 and 14.00.

### Sand dunes and the Crescent Moon Lake
Cable and French reported that 'The skill of man made the Caves of the Thousand Buddhas, but the hand of God fashioned the Lake of the Crescent Moon'. The lake (Y50) is pretty small but its setting is wonderful. It is surrounded by rolling sand dunes that give the area an air of looking, well, as a desert ought to look. There are three 'summits' you can climb but only the fittest (maddest) make it to the third. Just climbing to the second summit is extraordinarily hard work, though well worth the effort.

Coming down is wholly more enjoyable than going up (Cable and French set the trend of sliding down the dunes on toboggans, Y10), and you may even manage to make the sands 'sing' (slipping and sliding triggers off a set of vibrations that penetrate the entire dune, causing it to emit a ringing sound). Be careful with your camera here as fine grains of sand and intricate mechanisms don't mix.

It's best to hire a bike and go in the late afternoon or early morning when it isn't too hot. Allow three to four hours for the whole trip. It has now become quite popular to stay up in the dunes all night – but wrap up warm as it gets cold up there at night.

### Dunhuang Museum
Big signs in English advertise the displays on offer in this museum but inside the English disappears. Still, it's a mostly self-explanatory collection of coins, combs and weaponry unearthed in the region. It's OK for a browse but hardly riveting. Perhaps they should oust the tourist shops and add more exhibits to make the Y10 entrance fee seem worth it. The Mig jet fighter parked outside is an unexpected bonus, though.

### The White Horse Pagoda
This Buddhist temple was the highest building in Dunhuang when it was built in the 4th century and it's a clear example of how the Silk Road brought new religions with it as often as it did new luxuries. You'll need a taxi to find this place but should be able to walk back the way you came.

### The Jade and Yang gates
Little is left of either of the two gates that marked the end of China for traders heading west but their significance to the Silk Road was immense. It split here with one arm going through the Jade Gate and north to Loulan and Turfan and one heading south through Yang (South Pass) Gate to Lop Nor, Miran and the

Southern Taklamakan Route. Both gates are excellent places just to sit down and soak in the surroundings. To the south are the Kunlun Mountains which lead up to the Tibetan Plateau, while to the west is the emptiness of the Taklamakan.

The **Jade Gate** (Y30) got its name because of all the jade which traders brought here (its official name was the Yumen Gate). This site has the remains of a small keep that was once part of a complex the size of a small town. The gate marks the most westerly point of the Great Wall and you can clearly see its mud-and-straw base in the sand.

The desolation of the **Yang Gate** (Y40) can be as beautiful as it is eerie and you can imagine the fears of previous travellers who had no choice but to plough on into the emptiness – 'West of the Yung Pass, there'll be no friends' was how the Chinese saying went.

To reach both gates you have to hire a taxi for the day (Y500-600). Try to team up with others the night before. If you can get enough people you can hire a minibus through Shirley's Café. On the return journey, make sure you stop at the ruins of **Old Dunhuang** where you can see more sections of the Great Wall. Your driver will also tempt you with a visit to the movie set built for the 1991 epic *Dunhuang* (Y15) but it's a bit tacky.

## PRACTICAL INFORMATION
[☎ code 0937]

### Orientation and services
Dunhuang is not on a train line so you must use Liuyuan's station instead. Outside that station are white minibuses and share-taxis doing the shuttle run to Dunhuang (Y10). Each driver seems to have his favourite dropping-off point in town (none of which seems to be the bus station) but wherever you are dropped, it shouldn't be much of a walk to John's Café, a useful base for deciding upon a hotel and getting the latest tips.

Dunhuang is so small that a short cycle ride is enough to acquaint yourself with all its streets. **Bikes** can be hired from the cafés on the main street. The most useful **CITS** office (there are three) is in the International Hotel but tours of all the sights can be arranged in your hotel or one of the cafés below – camel trips into the desert are also available! **Internet access** is available in most of the restaurants/cafés around Five Rings Hotel. The **Bank of China** has an ATM that accepts credit/debit cards.

### Where to stay
Because of the caves, Dunhuang has learnt to accommodate large numbers of tourists and thus boasts quite a few reasonable hotels. Dunhuang Airport has also been upgraded so, as more and more tourists flood in, standards are set to rise yet further. The most upmarket place is *Dunhuang Hotel* (☎ 888 2088; 🖳 www.the-silk-road.com; US$100/Db) out by the dunes – it is pretty swanky. At the other end of the scale, prices for budget rooms are remarkably similar and there is plenty of choice: on Mingshan Lu *Five Rings (Olympic) Hotel* (☎ 882 2620; Y140/Db, Y30/dorm) is the favourite option but *Mingshan Binguan* and *Youhao Binguan* are similar, while *Feitian Binguan* (Y280/Db), almost opposite Five Rings, is smarter.

### Where to eat
The main street (Mingshan Lu) is home to a string of restaurants/cafés offering a similar choice of menus – the pick of the bunch are *Shirley's*, *Moon Crescent* and *Charlie Jongh's*. If you speak Chinese, head further up the street where more variety is available but no English is spoken. The **day/night market** is a great place to try local food, though in the evening you may have to put up with some terrible karaoke. There's also a *John's Information Café* (see box p307) in the grounds of Feitian Binguan, though this is more for drinking than eating.

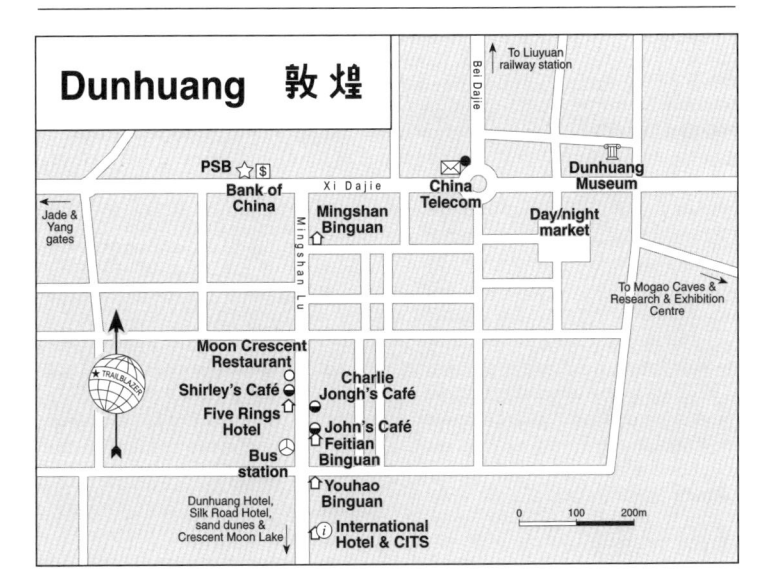

## Moving on

It's easy to get to **Turfan** (13hrs), **Hami** (7hrs/Y60) and **Jiayuguan** (5-7hrs/Y52) by **bus**. Not only will this save you the hassle of getting to Liuyuan and queuing for a train ticket, but it could save time, too. In all, it can take up to five hours longer to travel to Liuyuan, buy your ticket and go by train to Jiayuguan, than it would to catch a direct bus.

**Trains** heading east from Liuyuan go to Jiayuguan (3-6hrs; try to get an express train) and **Lanzhou** (13-19hrs); those heading west go to Hami (8hrs) and Daheyan (for Turfan, 11hrs). Minibuses for Liuyuan's train station run regularly from Dunhuang bus station (Y10-15). CITS in Dunhunag will book 'hard sleeper' tickets for Y50 commission (you'll be doing very well to get these without their help).

If you are attempting to take the **Southern Taklamakan Route**, see p320. There are regular **flights** from the airport to **Kashgar**, **Xi'an** and **Beijing**.

# Jiayuguan

Before the fort at Dunhuang was established, Jiayuguan Fort was the last outpost of the Great Wall proper. In Chinese myths and legends its name had the same connotations as Siberia had for Stalinist Russia: a remote, desolate outpost on the edge of the wilderness. Much of what we now see of the fort is restoration work but it has been done well in the most part and those sections that have been left alone are equally impressive. As you move around you can really get a sense of the isolation, especially when looking out over the Gobi Desert to the east.

## HISTORY

Jiayuguan owes its existence and its importance purely to its strategic position. Located at the western end of the Hexi (or Gansu) Corridor, sandwiched between the Qilian Mountains to the south and the Gobi Desert to the north, it was the natural bottleneck through which all traffic had to pass for centuries and, as such, has been exploited through the ages. We know that settlements here date back to the 2nd century BC and beyond and that tolls on travellers were taken as early as the Han dynasty.

Jiayuguan Pass marked the border between the known and unknown, a desolate spot particularly for those heading west. Yet at the same time it must have been a triumphant sight for travellers coming home from the deserts beyond.

The fact that many of its visitors were in a celebratory mood does not seem to have made this remote spot any more lively: the missionaries tell us 'There is nothing to do here all day but sit and listen to the howling wind'. Some diversions were on hand, though: '...there was constant entertainment for the carters in watching the dosing of desert-tired beasts, the ramming of needles into the tongue of a sick mule, and the more delicate operation of cutting the cartilage of the nostril to cure spasms'.

## WHAT TO SEE

You can take a tour/taxi to see the sights far out of town but for those near to town it's much more fun on a bike: it is not too physically demanding and the way is quite well signposted. If you do take a taxi/tour, make sure the trip includes the rock art found in various mountain caves and some of the many tombs scattered in the area.

### Jiayuguan Pass

Forts have been built here dating back at least to the Han dynasty, but this edifice was constructed in 1372 when it marked the boundary of Chinese civilization. Cable and French wrote that the West Gate was known as the 'Gate of Sighs' and that it was common for miscreants to be forcibly ejected through it

---

**The Gobi Desert**

What translates as the 'Stony Desert' must be one of the most well-known and most feared deserts in the world. It may not reach the temperatures of the Taklamakan but it is perhaps even more inhospitable as, unlike its neighbour, the Gobi has virtually no rivers, lakes, wells or oases to support would-be travellers. As Cable and French noted:

*'Only those who have crossed the Gobi roads can possibly understand the thrill and excitement of the traveller when the first tower of Kiayukwan (Jiayuguan) comes into sight, about 5km before the town is reached. Drivers and passengers always raise a shout at the prospect of once more passing the portal of China'.*

– cast out into the wilderness, as it were. This expulsion was termed *kow wai*, or 'without the mouth', the image called to mind being that of China having 'spued (sic) an unwanted national from her mouth' (Cable and French). The portal used to be covered with mournful graffiti, to which the missionaries added some suitably evangelical offerings. Tradition dictates, so they say, that travellers heading west through this gate throw a pebble at the wall beside it – if the pebble fails to bounce back to its thrower, the journey will end in tragedy. The fort is open all day (entrance costs Y60).

If you are cycling, follow the Gansu Highway out of town until you see a large sign pointing right for the fort, officially known as Jiayuguan Pass. The small hills to the north are the Heishan Mountains and those to the south are the Wensha Mountains (behind the Wensha are the much larger Qilian Mountains which are snow-capped most of the year).

### Overhanging Great Wall
From the fort you will see the Great Wall heading north and south. To follow it north, leave the car park, go directly away from the fort for 100m and turn left. This road takes you all the way to the Overhanging Wall section; or you can take the gravel track that you can see when you are climbing around the fort. Along the way you can clearly see the remains of the original wall, though they are fairly dilapidated. From the top of the renovated section (entrance costs Y9), you can see for miles across the Gobi Desert (see box opposite).

### Beacon Tower
From the fort (Jiayuguan Pass) go back to the main Gansu Highway, turn right and keep heading out of town. The fort will now be on your right and you should be able to take a good photograph from here. Further on you will see the Great Wall on your left heading off to the south. Go past where the road meets the wall, over the railway bridge and then turn left off onto the dirt track, which takes you back to the wall. Follow the wall to the end (make sure you stop or you'll fly off the edge of a 100m cliff!) where there is a ruined beacon. No doubt this wasn't so close to the edge when it was built but has assumed this position as the cliffs have crumbled away; be careful!

### The cave tombs
Discovered by a farmer in 1972 these tombs, some 20km east of the city centre, date back to the Wei dynasty (4th century AD). No one knows how many tombs there are as excavation is still underway. Only one is open to the public.

The paintings in the open tomb (No 6) are perfectly preserved. They are very small and simple: several depict everyday activities such as ploughing and hunting but some are little more than doodles. Quite a few seem simply to be attempts to draw perfect circles freehand. The cave is interesting to visit but expensive at Y30, although this may become better value as more tombs are opened. It can be visited at virtually any time as the custodians live here. If you are not part of a group you will first be taken to the gift shop where it is a good idea to buy the pamphlet on the tombs' history, as English is not spoken here.

### Black Mountain cave paintings

These paintings, considerably older and less sophisticated than those at the Wei tombs, are more difficult to find. Very few people go to see them, since they are little more than primitive scratchings on the rocks dating from the Warring States period (up to 221BC). If you want to go, take a photograph of what they look like with you (pick up a postcard or a brochure from CITS), and show it to your taxi driver before you agree on a price.

### Great Wall Museum

The town museum, located at the southern end of Xinhua South Rd just before it disappears into the desert, is rather disappointing. It is in a modern replica of an old Chinese fort and although the display is reasonably well laid out, it is extremely small. Exhibits here include inscribed bamboo strips, miscellaneous metal and wooden tools and other ancient Chinese relics. There are a couple of paintings from the cave tombs and lots of photos. Look out for the military dress and early firearms, particularly the spears and arrows with explosive charges. Nothing is labelled in English. Entry is Y10.

## PRACTICAL INFORMATION
[☎ code 0937]
### Orientation and services
The **train station** is stuck out at the southern end of town but the No 1 bus will bring you into the centre, which is compact and easy to cover on foot. The **bus station** is opposite Wumao Hotel.

The **CITS** office, at 2 Sheng Li Rd, is pretty good: there are some excellent English speakers here.

**Bikes** can be rented (Y6 per day) from Jiayuguan Hotel. There's an **Internet café** on the corner opposite Jiayuguan Hotel. **Bank of China** is next door.

### Where to stay and eat
There isn't much choice in terms of eating or sleeping but *Wumao Hotel* (☎ 628 0855; Y30/dorm, Y120/Db) on Shengli Lu satisfies most visitors. It's not a pretty building but the views from the fire-escape balcony on the top floor are tremendous. CITS has an office in the lobby but this provides only basic information.

On the main roundabout, *Jiayuguan Hotel* (☎ 622 6983; Y180/Db) offers a smarter deal for a little extra; like Wumao, it has a basic travel service. If you are arriving late or catching a really early train you might want to consider the *Railway Hotel*. They are not used to foreigners but are friendly.

**Food-wise**, your best bets are the restaurants in the Wumao or Jiayuguan. They're not cheap but the few other restaurants on the main street are poor. Of the two **bazaars**, the southern one is better for noodle dishes and fresh fruit, while the northern one is good for *shashlik* and barbecued foods. Particularly good is *malatang*, satays of meat or vegetables broiled Sichuan style – the chilli sauce they daub liberally over them can be particularly fiery.

### Moving on
Cable and French tell us that when they passed through here, the original Silk Road was still plain to see:

'*At the foot of the mountain range lay the old travel road, wide and deeply marked, literally cut to bits by the sharp nail-studded wheels of countless caravan carts. Over this road myriads of travellers had journeyed for thousands of years, making of it a ceaselessly flowing stream of life, for it was the great highway of Asia, which connected the Far East with distant European lands.*'

It has been wiped out now though so you might as well take the **train** or **bus**. To **Lanzhou** (try to get the express train; 9-13hrs/Y65-80) there are 6 trains daily, though you might want to break the journey (see below). If you're heading west, trains go to **Liuyuan** (for **Dunhuang**; 4-6hrs) or take a bus direct to Dunhuang (5-7hrs/Y55).

---

### Zhangye and Wuwei
East from Turfan, **Zhangye** (3hrs from Jiayuguan by train) was another major stop on the Silk Road and is home to China's largest reclining Buddha (34.5m long). The **Great Buddha Temple** (Y21) dates back from 1098AD and the beautiful wooden pagoda (*mu ta*, Y5) one block north, was built in 528AD. This walkable town is centred on a **Drum Tower**. Accommodation-wise there's *Liangmao Binguan* (☎ 0936 824 0162; Y18/dorm, Y80/Db) at Dong Jie, 5 mins east of the Drum Tower, or *Zhangye Hotel* (Y20/dorm) on Xianfu Jie. Leaving, you can buy only 'no seat' tickets to go by **train** and the **train station** is way out of town but minibuses (Y3) shuttle passengers to and fro; **buses** are perhaps more convenient and many run to Lanzhou and Jiayuguan (the bus station is near the Great Buddha Temple).

**Wuwei** (3hrs from Zhangye, 5hrs from Lanzhou) is most famous for its **Flying Horse**, a beautiful, tiny bronze statue now housed in Lanzhou. Catch a minibus from the train station to the town centre and enjoy a few hours of aimless wandering around the streets, people watching. **Hotels are poor** so move on rather than spend the night.

# Lanzhou

Peter Fleming told us that in 1935 'The streets of Lanchow are romantic' but you are unlikely to over-exert your camera finger in this city now, let alone your heart strings. In terms of the history of the Silk Road, however, this place is key (as the statue of Monkey and Xuan Zang, see box p345, on the river testifies). This is because Lanzhou marks where the caravans from the West met the Yellow River (see box opposite) and were presented with all the extra transport options this gave. Unfortunately the river is now a muddy orange colour, though it still forms the city's heart. You won't want to spend more than a couple of days here but the city is a perfect base for trips to the Bingling Si Caves and Xining.

## HISTORY

Lanzhou has been inhabited since at least the 6th century BC but only really became prominent in 81BC during the Han dynasty, when it was established as the seat of power for the surrounding area. This role as the centre of local government was lost and regained several times until 763AD, when invasion by the Tibetans forced a major Chinese withdrawal from the region. It was recovered by the Tang dynasty in 843AD, only to be lost again until 1041 when the Song dynasty stepped in. In fact every new power that passed this way laid siege to the city and established prefectures here until 1666, when Gansu was made a Chinese province in its own right and Lanzhou was declared the capital, a position it retains today.

The city was badly damaged in the Islamic rebellion (1864-1875), which catapulted Yakub Beg (see p303) into the limelight. Repairs were made but they proved temporary as the town was devastated by a huge earthquake in 1920.

Fortunately, recovery was swift and by the time the Sino-Japanese War (1937-45) broke out, Lanzhou was the major distribution centre for all ammunition and supplies shipped into China from the Soviet Union. The strategic significance of this town near the terminus of the Sino-Soviet Highway was not lost on the Japanese who bombed it heavily. Today, Lanzhou is a large, modern city, which plays a major role in China's petrochemical industry; oil from the Yumen oilfield is refined here. It also lies at the heart of the Chinese nuclear industry. With a population of over two million, this is the largest Chinese city you will have encountered if you have come from the West and the modern face of the town ('The East is Red' Square, for example) can only be described as 'grey'.

## WHAT TO SEE

### Gansu Provincial Museum

This is one of the best museums in China and exhibits are labelled in English. Among numerous displays is a large exhibition of 'Historical Finds of Gansu' including some impressive woodcarvings, the famous **bronze 'winged horse'** of **Wuwei,** and paintings from tombs in the Jiayuguan area. There are also some of the handwritten sutras from Dunhuang and, surprisingly, the complete skeleton of a woolly mammoth. Other sections include 'Chinese Art and Economics' and 'Produce of Gansu Province'. The museum is open 09.00-11.30 and 14.30-17.00 (except Sundays). Entry is Y25.

## Baitashan Park and Ququan/Lanshan Park

The **cable car** (Y5)across the river and up the opposite mountain is worth going on if the weather is good but a bit pointless if it's not. At the top is **Baitashan Park**, laid out across a steep hillside. It is small and fairly attractive, but tends to get crowded and noisy at weekends (when the tea shops fill up and the fairground-type games are running at full capacity). If you find a quiet spot, it's a good place for a break, however, and there's a fine view of Lanzhou from the **White Pagoda** at its summit.

### The Yellow River (Huanghe River)

'Whoever controls the Yellow River, controls China.' So said Emperor Yu, founder of the Xia dynasty, over two thousand years before Christ. He seems to have had a point as this river has been central to China's fortunes for as long as there has been a China (bones from the Palaeolithic era, perhaps a million years old, have been found near its banks). It is the dragon of Chinese legend that loops and twists from Qinghai province to the Gulf of Bohai.

This is China's second longest river, measuring over 5400km from its source in Tibet (at an altitude of 4575m) all the way to the Yellow Sea. It drains an area of 745,000 sq km and well over 100 million Chinese live in its basin. It is particularly prone to seasonal flooding and dykes have been built around its banks for thousands of years with varying degrees of success; in 1887 it burst its banks near Kaifeng and covered an area of more than 48,000 sq km. Two years later another flood injured over one million people. The Chinese actually placed explosive charges on the river's banks in 1938 to slow the Japanese advance. This caused the deaths of 900,000 of those who had been unlucky enough to build their houses near its path.

The Yellow River is unusual for many reasons: firstly, its course has changed substantially over the centuries, so much so that its present mouth on the Yellow Sea is 800km from the original one. Secondly, it has a phenomenally high output (up to 48.2 cubic km of water each year), which is partly responsible for its tendency to flood (locals were not able to build the first permanent bridge over the river until 1912 – at Lanzhou); nowadays, dykes run for 1400km on each side of the river in the hope of checking further floods and over half the river water is siphoned off to be used for irrigation. Finally, the river is the world's muddiest, being rich with the loess dust from all over China's plains (it is the loess that makes the plains so fertile). Every cubic metre of this river contains 25kg of silt (compared to just 1.4kg in the supposedly muddy Nile) and this can make up to 70 per cent of the river's volume when it is flooding. It is the presence of this silt that makes the river look so murky, and gives it its 'Yellow' tag.

The Yellow River makes up China's trio of great waterways, the other two being the Yangtzi River (China's longest at over 6300km) and the Grand Canal (this is the world's longest artificial waterway, once stretching 1800km between Hangzhou and Beijing, although today it is heavily silted up and largely unnavigable).

336 Lanzhou

Back on the south side of the river, pop into the **Baiyun Guan**, a still-practising Taoist temple with a massive statue of their founder, Lao Tze, in the back.

**Wuquan/Lanshan Park**, on the south-western side of the city centre, is a lovely place to while away an afternoon. Much bigger than Baitashan, its buildings are far more intricate, there's a large Buddhist temple in the centre and a chairlift (Y10) runs up to Lanshan Park. Art exhibitions are held here, too. Entry is Y6 and trolley buses Nos 31 and 33 run here from the train station.

### Bingling Si Buddhist Caves

The spectacular scenery around this cave complex is Lanzhou's highlight. The caves are cut into cliffs high above the Yellow River and you are unlikely to find a more isolated attraction anywhere. They can be reached only by bus and boat. Unfortunately, you can spend only one or two hours at the caves themselves and the journey is a long one: the round trip from Lanzhou takes seven to eight hours.

The caves (there are some 180 of them) are in good condition. The oldest is thought to be No 169, which features an inscription dating it to the early 5th century. Most of the caves were carved out later, though, with the peak construction period being the Song and Ming dynasties (c960AD onwards). The construction of the Buddha figures is complex: because the rock is not suitable for sculpture, they were built around wooden frames and it is possible to see, as at Mogao, broken limbs displaying their straw and clay contents. The centrepiece of the ensemble is a stunning 27m-high Maitreya figure. The new development around the quay may bring in better facilities but it is doing little for the site's charm.

**Practicalities** The best way to see the caves is to take a tour, though they are expensive (**Western Travel Service** charges Y300/pp). Try to gather a group together or join an existing group as this brings the cost down.

The drive to the jetty takes three hours and on the way you pass Liujiaxia Dam and Hydroelectric Plant. The boat then takes about 45 minutes up the Yellow River. Make sure that you bring some warm clothes as it can be chilly on the boat. Entry to the site is Y20 but this should be included in the tour price. A further Y20 allows you to get right up to the caves but they charge a whopping Y450 to climb the stairs up to the prize caves by the main Buddha's head.

You can organize the trip yourself by taking a taxi to the jetty and waiting for a spare place in a boat (there are plenty) but it rarely works out cheaper. They are opening a **hotel** at the caves in 2007 but expect it to be expensive.

### PRACTICAL INFORMATION
[☎ code 0931]

### Orientation and services

Though a large city, Lanzhou is surprisingly easy to get around. It sprawls along the Yellow River from east to west and getting from one side of the city to the other is not difficult, just time consuming (look out for bus No 1, which runs the entire length of the city). There are three bus stations but only two of them are of interest to visitors: the **main bus station** near the train station and the **western bus station**, which is over 10km west along the Yellow River.

Good maps are readily available at most hotels. The main **CITS** office is on a lane behind Lanzhou Hotel; a 'Travel Service' sign is prominently displayed over the door so it's hard to miss. The staff are fairly capable. Inside the Lanzhou Hotel

### Excursion to Xining and Taer Si Monastery

**Xining**, the capital of Qinghai province, has little to offer though a small branch of the Silk Road passed through here on its way from Lanzhou to the southern branch of the Taklamakan road. The nearby Taer Si Monastery, however, was the former home of the Dalai Lama and is the most important Buddhist centre outside Lhasa – you may already be familiar with its Tibetan name, 'Kumbum'. The countryside in between the two is mesmerizing in summer.

**Taer Si Monastery** was built in 1560 in honour of Tsongkhapa, the founder of the reformist Yellow Hat Sect of Tibetan Buddhism, who was born here. At his birth, it is said some of his blood fell to the ground, causing a tree with a thousand leaves to spring up. Each leaf was shaped in the face of Buddha and his image also appeared on the tree's trunk. Tsongkhapa was identified as remarkable at an early age and so he proved to be as his sect came to dominate Buddhism in China and two of his disciples became the first Dalai and Panchen lamas. Make sure you take in the yak-butter sculptures in the Tantra temple and spend a bit of time watching the pilgrims wear grooves into the wooden floors around the Great Hall of the Golden Roof (you may also see pilgrims studying the fallen leaves from the tree outside the hall, searching for a face of Buddha).

The monks don't mind you taking photos of them outside the temples but be respectful. You will also see pilgrims (mostly from Tibet, Qinghai and Mongolia) slowly circling around the complex in the hills above (often on hands and knees), as part of their bid for religious purification. With the massive revival of Buddhism in China be prepared for big crowds, especially in summer.

One final quirk to note is that nearly all the wholesalers of Buddhist merchandise you will see (priests come from all over China to buy supplies for hundreds of new monasteries springing up) are Muslim locals!

**Practicalities** The train station in Xining is massive. The **train** here from Lanzhou (3-6hrs/Y33-50, try to get the express train) carries on to **Golmud** and since July 2006 you can ride all the way to **Lhasa** along a line which is little short of an engineering miracle. A good idea is to get an afternoon train from Lanzhou, stay in Xining for the night, spend the day at Taer Si and get the evening train back to Lanzhou (buy your ticket back to Lanzhou when you arrive in Xining – it saves queuing).

Most foreigners stay at *Kuslan Hotel* (aka *Yongfu* and *Kunlun*; ☎ 0971 814 0236; Y30/dorm), just over the river from the train station. *Post Hotel* (Y15/dorm) on Huzhu Lu, on your left as you come out of the station, is a cheaper option. In the evening there are lots of food stalls outside Kuslan Hotel but you're better off heading down to the **night market** at Ximen Square. **Minibuses** (Y4/45mins) leave from a private bus station on Xiguan Dajie west of Ximen Square (from your hotel you can walk 3km or take a taxi). You are dropped at the temple gates. You should be able to negotiate a taxi from Ximen Square to Taer Si for Y20-25.

Tickets into the complex cost Y30 (Y15 out of season) and give access to all the temples. Each temple is numbered but these don't seem to correspond with the numbers on the map on the back of your ticket, so just wander around at leisure.

To get back to Xining, walk down the ramped road outside the monastery into town and catch a bus from the main street. There are various **restaurants** here which all serve reasonably priced dishes.

If you want to spend the night at Taer Si, there is *Kumbum Motel* (Y15/dorm) just inside the temple. Primarily this is for pilgrims but they will accept tourists as well. This might be a good idea in the summer when the temples can get packed as you can have them to yourself early in the morning and late in the evening.

complex, **Western Travel Service** (☎ 885 2929) does good tours to Bingling Si Caves. There is an **Internet café** beside the university which charges only Y7/hr and Y3/hr after 21.00 (it's open until 02.00). The **Bank of China** has an **ATM** that accepts credit/debit cards.

The **department store** on Tianshui Lu has English-language books, mostly 19th-century classics (the sweet department on the ground floor is also very tempting). The main **post office** is to the south of the main square, a short way down Pingliang Lu.

### Where to stay
If you wish to stay near the train station the closest place is *Lanzhou Dasha* (☎ 841 7210; Y280/Db). The cheapest place in town is *Yingbin Hotel* (formerly the Hua Yi; Y80/Db) on Tianshui Lu, though the rooms aren't great and the showers work only in the evenings.

The plushest place is *Lanzhou Legend* (🖥 www.lanzhoulegendhotel.com; Y800/Db) on Xiguan traffic circle. Western Travel Service can get you the best price for a room in the mid-range *Lanzhou Hotel* (Y250-500/Db), also on the Xiguan traffic circle.

If you are visiting Xiahe (see box p340), you might want to stay at *Youyi Hotel* (Y250/Db) near the western bus station.

### Where to eat
The **night market** off Tianshui Lu is a scoffer's paradise with stalls selling snails, langoustine, crabs, hot pots, kebabs and stir-fries. Also on Tianshui Lu, heading north from the main railway station, are plenty of smart, clean and attractive **restaurants**.

### Moving on
The ticket office is always packed during the day and has no 'Foreigners' window so queuing to get a ticket can take hours. It opens until after midnight, however, so go late in the evening when everything is calmer. There are eight trains a day to **Xi'an** (12hrs/Y85), but you can break the journey at **Tianshui** (6hrs; see box below). Trains run to **Datong** (25hrs/Y175) via Inner Mongolia – you may want to break your journey in **Hohhot** (see box p354) to have a look around.

If you are heading west your next stop will probably be **Jiayuguan** (9-13hrs/Y65-80) but you can easily break your journey at **Zhangye** or **Wuwei** (see box p333).

---

### Tianshui
This town was another important Silk Road stop, is home to one of China's finest Ming temples and is a good base for visiting the Buddhist caves at Maiji Shan. **Fu Xi Temple** (in Qincheng; Y30) was begun in 1483 and is an ornate wooden temple with artistic wood panelling and painting. It also houses the city's **museum**.

**Maiji Shan Caves** (Y54) are up there with those at Dunhuang, Turfan and Datong. The caves are cut out of a massive rock mountain sticking up in the middle of the forested countryside. The earliest caves date from the fourth to sixth centuries AD and the tallest Buddha is 16m. Next to the caves are some beautiful **Botanical Gardens**.

**Practicalities** Tianshui's train station is way out east in the suburb of **Beidao**. Buses No 1 and 6 run to the town centre (known as **Qincheng**). Minibuses for Maiji Shan (1hr/Y10) leave from in front of the train station when full. *Tielu Zhaodaisuo* (Y20/dorm), on your right as you come out of the train station at 26 Yima Lu, is cheap and cheerful. Staying in Maiji Shan is a pleasant option: try *Maiji Shanzhuang* (Y120/Db), near the car park to the caves, or *Zhiwuyuan Zhaodaisuo* (Y300/Db), at the top of the hills inside the botanical gardens. The best **restaurants** are in Qincheng.

> ### Xiahe
> For an insight into what Tibetan life is like you may be interested in visiting **Labrang Monastery** at Xiahe. This is set in beautiful hills to the south of Lanzhou and has become a backpackers' favourite hangout. Like Taer Si, Labrang (founded in 1709; Y21) is one of the six major monasteries belonging to the Yellow Hat Sect and is home to over one thousand monks.
>
> You can get here only by **bus** (4-6hrs/Y32-44), however, and this costs more than it should as separate **travel insurance** is stipulated (although not always checked); buses leave from Lanzhou's **western bus station**. Travel insurance is available from the PICC office in the bus station in Lanzhou and from opposite the post office in Xiahe.
>
> On arrival, there is plenty of budget accommodation available. ***Tara Guesthouse*** (☎ 0941 712 1274; 🖳 t-dolma@yahoo.com; Y20/dorm, Y60/Db) on Zhouma Lushe is most visitors' favourite because of its roof terrace with gorgeous views. There are plenty of **cafés** and **restaurants** serving 'Westernized' Tibetan food.

# Xi'an

As the old capital of China, Xi'an thinks quite highly of itself and the centre of the city is both a tribute to its past, with its well-preserved monuments, and to the future, with its massive building programme of shopping arcades and five-star hotels. Just outside the city there is also a great number of attractions, the foremost undoubtedly being Emperor Shihuang's Terracotta Army. If you give yourself at least four days to see everything, this city shouldn't let you down, although the number of tourists might get to you if you stay any longer.

## HISTORY

Xi'an was the nucleus of ancient China. Records show that there has been a major settlement here since at least the 11th century BC (some say the evidence dates back to 2205BC). In its early days, Xi'an was referred to as the 'Well-Watered City'. It was more than just another large city, however, for a number of dynasties, notably the Zhou, Han, Sui and Tang, made it their capital.

Having said that, it no longer sits on its original site. In the 11th century BC the Zhou dynasty called Xi'an 'Fenghao' and the city lay some 15km to the south-west of its present location. This site flourished until 771BC when the capital was moved east to Luoyang. By the time of the short-lived Qin dynasty, it had moved back again. They called their capital Xien Yang and its centre was 18km west of present-day Xi'an. It was during this period that the elaborate tomb of Emperor Shihuang was constructed.

### The greatest city in the world
The Han dynasty ruled from Xi'an after first rebuilding it on yet another site, just north of the present-day city. This capital, known as 'Chang'an', was the

greatest that China had ever seen, though that didn't stop the Han from deserting it for Luoyang in 23AD. Following this, the city went into a steady decline until its selection as capital by the Sui dynasty in the 7th century. It was then that Xi'an attained its present-day site, which was adopted and expanded by the succeeding Tang dynasty. The city swelled and was divided into three parts: a palace city for the emperor, the imperial city for the officials, and the outer city for the rest. During this period, with a population of well over a million, it was not only the greatest city in China but also almost certainly the largest in the world. External influences flooded in and Chang'an nurtured thriving foreign religious and merchant communities, including sizeable colonies of Mazdeans, Manichaeists, Jews, Muslims, Uighurs and Nestorians. Evidence of this can be seen today in the various artefacts displayed in the city's museums.

### Chang'an's decline
In 904 the Tang capital moved briefly to Luoyang again and in 907 the dynasty collapsed. Chang'an, although it remained a major Chinese city, was never to recover its status. It was still a thriving community, however, when Marco Polo visited in 1278. He called it Quengianfu and commented:

> 'The people are idolaters and subject to the Great Khan and use paper money. They live by trade and industry. They have plenty of silk and make cloth of gold and silk of many varieties. There are merchants here of wealth and consequence. There is no lack of game, both beast and bird, and abundance of grain and foodstuffs. There are two churches here of Nestorian Christians'.

### The Xi'an incident
The world next heard of Xi'an some 650 years later, when General Chiang Kai Shek was the victim of a coup here in 1936. Following the aggression of the Japanese (who had moved into Manchuria in 1931 and were to invade China proper in 1937), Communist Party chiefs tried repeatedly to make the KMT leader understand that his greatest threat was not from them but this foreign aggressor.

Chiang refused to acknowledge suggestions that the two warring factions should unite to eject their common enemy so on December 12 he was seized by his own men under Chang Xue-Liang. Communist Party leaders flew in to explain their views to him. On Christmas Day, 1936, he was released and given full control of his men again in return for promising to fight against the Japanese rather than the communists. In fact, his efforts in this direction were minimal. All he really did during the following months was to prepare for the civil war, which he knew would restart when the Japanese were defeated. Chang Xue-Liang, for his efforts, was thrown into prison for 40 years.

### Xi'an today
Until recently, Xi'an was simply a large-sized industrial city with a sound pedigree. All this changed with the discovery by some peasants of the long-lost tomb of the Qin emperor Shihuang in 1974. The 'Terracotta Army' found inside catapulted the city to superstardom in the tourist world; the hotels, shops and restaurants in the city are now on a par with most of the major tourist destinations in Asia. For the Chinese it has become the most popular domestic attraction. The

industrial side of the city has not disappeared, however, and Xi'an is very polluted (although more and more businesses are hi-tech chemical works these days).

## WHAT TO SEE

### Inside the walls

**City walls and gates**  The city walls (Y12) dominate Xi'an's centre; much is original from the Ming dynasty and parts date back to the 14th century but the restored parts look equally tremendous. A walk around them on your first day (though you might not want to walk the full 13.7km) really gives a feel for the Old City: you will also see just how far the New City spreads out around beyond the moat. Of the four gates, only the south, east and west are open to visitors. Inside the West Gate is an expensive art gallery where calligraphy and paintings range from Y80 to Y10,000. The rafters of the ceiling are spectacular.

**Bell Tower**  Further in, the Bell Tower (Y15) is the central landmark to get your bearings from and worth a visit, too. Originally built in 1384, the tower was moved from the exact centre of the city to its new (more southerly) home in 1582 and rebuilt brick by brick. It was restored in 1740. Traditionally, an official rang an enormous bell to signal dawn although a local legend maintains it served a different purpose: after a series of minor tremors and earthquakes, a local mystic diagnosed the cause of the problem as a dragon trapped beneath the soil of the city. The bell was to be pealed at regular intervals to scare it away. Inside the tower is a small, badly lit display of Ming and Qing furniture, which is unlabelled. The buildings' Ming design (multi-storied and triple-eaved) is a classic and the rafters are particularly ornate, although the view has been spoilt by the building of multi-storey hotels and shopping centres all around.

**Drum Tower**  This edifice (Y12) on the other side of the main square housed a large drum which would sound at sundown. Like the Bell Tower it contains a large modern replica but it is no longer called into action. It offers better views of the city and its walls. The Drum Tower is peculiar as it has an arch in its base for a road to run right through it.

**Great Mosque**  In the heart of the Muslim quarter is the Great Mosque (Y15). This was founded in 742AD but looks more like a Chinese garden than a traditional mosque. That said, its beauty, continually built on over the centuries, rivals any. Huddled into the narrow streets outside are some of the better souvenir market stalls.

**Shaanxi Provincial Museum**  This is a real treasure-trove with lots of steles and other relics from the Silk Road but if you have to pick between this (Y30) and the National Museum of Shaanxi History (see p344), go for the latter.

### Outside the walls

First stop has to be the **Monument to the Silk Road**. Although it seems rather pedantic to speak of exact starting and finishing points in relation to the Silk Road, this is officially the beginning of the original Silk Road in China (of

# Xi'an – What to see 343

# Xi'an 西安

course, when the capital moved to Luoyang or Beijing, so the Silk Road was extended). It may not be the most awesome monument in the world but if you have come all this way, you deserve a photo of yourself beside it. The fact that the Chinese regard this only as 'the beginning' of the Silk Road, not 'the beginning and the end', gives you an idea of how superior they considered themselves: for them, the Silk Road was all about exporting their success, rather than importing foreign offerings.

**National Museum of Shaanxi History** Even the most ardent non-museum-goers we met admitted that this was great. Since Xi'an was the capital for so many periods of Chinese history, this is like a trip through China's early history rather than just Shaanxi's. The exquisite camel with merry Silk Roadsters on its back is one of many highlights. Try to visit before you go to the Terracotta Army to get a sense of things. Entrance costs Y35 (open daily 09.30-17.30).

**Big Goose Pagoda** Just around the corner from the National Museum is the Big Goose Pagoda (*Dayan Ta*; Y20; daily 08.00-17.00), one-time home of that favourite son of the Silk Road, Xuan Zang (see box opposite).

The Big Goose Pagoda was built by Emperor Gaozong in 648 inside the existing Da Xi'en temple to house Xuan Zang's collection of Buddhist scriptures and give the monk a place to carry out his translation work. At one time there were ten storeys but three burnt down to leave the seven we see today. Climb up the steps inside for unparalleled views from the south of the city. Like the National Museum, the pagoda is beyond walking distance from the city centre so it's best to hire a bike for the day or catch a taxi.

**Little Goose Pagoda** On the way back into the city you can stop off at the Little Goose Pagoda (*Xiaoyan Ta*; Y12; daily 08.00 to 18.00). Not as impressive as Xuan Zang's pad, this temple was built in 684 and became the home of monk Yiqinq, a successor to Xuan Zang who made the trip to India to collect sacred texts in the 8th century. He also used his home to translate the texts and the tower is all the more remarkable in that it is said to have survived over 70 earthquakes, as well as the anti-Buddhist purges of the 9th century.

One earthquake, in 1487, is said to have split the pagoda right down the middle but, fortunately, the earthquake of 1556 is said to have brought the two sides back together.

## EXCURSIONS

The principal sights outside of town can be divided roughly into two trips, one for those to the **east** of Xi'an and one for those to the **west**. Most tours are arranged this way but be careful: many new 'highlights' are dreadful concoctions, which are of interest only to anyone who is still impressed by the special effects in *Thunderbirds*. The best trips are coordinated by the YHAs but most hotels offer something (tours cost Y35-Y50 for a full day but entrance fees will add up to over Y100/pp per day). There is a new toll road opening up, which should greatly improve access to the Terracotta Army.

If you have extra days, tours can be organized to a **Panda Reserve** in the mountains or the **Imperial Tombs** in the surrounding countryside (the latter are a World Heritage Site and date from the Ming and Qing dynasties).

## Tomb of Qin Shihuang

Qin Shihuang, the 'First Emperor', whose reputation is that of a ruthless, ambitious tyrant, ascended the throne in 246BC at the age of only 13. Work on his mausoleum began immediately. The tomb itself, 30km east of present-day Xi'an, has yet to be excavated but has already created great excitement in the archaeological world as preliminary investigations suggest that the tomb has never been looted. According to a 1st century BC chronicle, it took 700,000

---

### Xuan Zang

Xuan Zang is better known to many of us as Tripitaka, that shaven-headed boy with the three funny friends on TV in the eighties (see p25). It seems hard to believe but the exploits as depicted in *Monkey* were actually based on a true story – or rather they were based on a collection of stories (*Journey to the West* by Wu Ch'eng En) which in turn were based on Zang's original book, *Records of the Western Regions*, an autobiographical account of his journey to India. It is because of the success of Wu Ch'eng En's book that Xuan Zang is such a popular figure today, not just in China but all over the Buddhist world.

Zang, in fact, was a celebrated Mahayana Buddhist scholar in the 7th century. Following numerous debates with his fellow Mahayanans and rival Hinayana priests, he set off for northern India to seek enlightenment and collect true scriptures to replace what he considered to be the flawed works that were circulating China – each school and sect, no matter how small, had their own pet theories and over the years these had become incorporated into the main texts via various translations and new editions. He left Chang'an in 629 (despite travel outside of China being illegal at that time) and, overcoming many hardships, made his way to Aksu via the northern Taklamakan route; from here he crossed the Tien Shan and passed Issyk Kul on the way to Tashkent and Samarkand; from Central Asia he passed through the 'Iron Gates' (these were literally iron gates as the only way through the mountains was a gorge so narrow that a huge set of wood and iron doors were built to control the traffic flow) to Balkh; from Balkh, Zang made his way across the Hindu Kush to the Buddhist shrine at Bamiyan and from there to the famous Buddhist university at Nalanda where he stayed to debate and learn for many years.

By a stroke of luck his arrival coincided with the Fourth Great Buddhist Council, conducted under the patronage of the Kashmiri king, Kanishka. Here, the New Logic of Buddhism was written down and the name given to the scriptures was *Tripitaka* or 'Three Baskets' (hence Zang's nickname). The scriptures were in three parts: the sayings of Buddha – the *Sutras*; the Rules of Discipline – the *Vinaya*; and the Systematic Philosophy – the *Abhidhama*.

Xuan Zang received a full copy of all three works and returned over the Pamirs to Yarkand and via the southern Taklamakan route to Dunhuang. Eventually he arrived back in Chang'an, 16 years after he had left. His work was not complete, however, as now he had to translate these new scriptures from Sanskrit into Chinese, which he did in his Big Goose Pagoda, while still finding time to set up the Fa Xiang School of Buddhism before dying in 664.

workmen 36 years to complete. It contains a number of intriguing displays. Rivers of mercury were designed to flow perpetually throughout the mausoleum and the roof was depicted as Heaven, studded with jewels. Most interesting is the assertion that the tomb is protected by mechanical booby traps, including crossbows set to fire upon intruders. It is said that, once complete, all workmen and designers who might be able to reveal the tomb's secrets were buried alive with their emperor's body (as were his wives). Archaeologists are unwilling to unseal the tomb for fear that its contents will crumble on exposure to the air.

Having said that, there's not a lot to see here as, obviously, you can't get in and it's therefore not much more than a large green mound covered in pomegranate trees. The mausoleum (Y26), together with the tombs housing the Terracotta Army nearby, have been made a World Heritage Site.

### The Terracotta Army

What historical records did not reveal, however, was that along with his wives and craftsmen, Qin Shihuang planned on taking an entire army with him to the other side. The army was discovered by some farmers in the summer of 1974 while they were digging a well. It seems that the vaults containing the soldiers, some 6000 of them in all, were originally covered with a wooden roof but that General Xiang Yu, having plundered the tomb in the late 3rd century BC, set fire to it. It collapsed onto the army, burying it for 2000 years. Since the initial discovery of **Pit 1**, another two vaults, **Pit 2** and **Pit 3**, have been unearthed. All three are now open to the public. The buildings housing the warriors are simply vast but that doesn't stop them becoming packed with tourists all the time.

Enough has been written about the Terracotta Army to render yet another list of superlatives unnecessary here. Suffice to say that, with every soldier attired slightly differently, individually painted and perhaps modelled on real members of the imperial guard, this represents a feat of sculpture on an unprecedented scale.

Next to the pits are **two small museums**: one contains some miscellaneous objects unearthed during the excavations, including a number of the warriors themselves. This gives a good impression of their size and of the detail that went into their construction. Opposite this is the Chariot Museum, which contains two beautiful bronze chariots unearthed 20m to the west of the mausoleum's entrance in 1978. Entry to both these museums is included in the price of the main entry ticket.

Outside the site there are numerous stalls selling (surprise, surprise) miniature terracotta warriors. It is debatable whether there are more warriors outside the pits than in them. Still, prices are very low if you bargain.

The site is open daily 08.00-18.00 and entrance costs a hefty Y90.

### Banpo neolithic site

Seven kilometres east of Xi'an is the Banpo Neolithic Village (Y20), which dates back to 4500BC and was discovered in 1953. The site is particularly interesting for archaeologists because it is so well preserved, thus giving an accurate impression of what life was like for prehistoric man here. The village was home to some 300 people, for whom agriculture was the main source of food. They supplemented their diet with fish from the nearby Chan River (caught with both hooks and nets) and also kept pigs, dogs and fowl. While this is no doubt fascinating to the trained eye, it's not quite as fascinating to the untrained: it's certainly hard to work out, for example, what the photographic display of African tribesmen ('The Last Primitive Man') is doing there.

The village is included in many tours but you can get here on your own, either by bicycle or trolley bus No 5 from the railway station.

### Huaqing Hot Springs and Palace

The Huaqing Springs (Y30) have been channelled into royal bathing houses since the Zhou dynasty and it's still possible to bathe here. Royal palaces have been built and rebuilt on this spot since then but most of the pavilions standing today date back only as far as the start of the 20th century.

The palace was the site of the famous Xi'an Incident (see p341) and if you follow the steps up the hill you will eventually get to the small pavilion where the arrest took place; there is no English sign but the view is pleasant enough. Chiang's office and bedroom are also open to the public. Most tours usually stop here for a couple of hours and many complain that they get bored in this time but the palace is very picturesque and is fun to explore – it's only a pity that it gets so crowded.

### PRACTICAL INFORMATION
[☎ code 029]

#### Orientation and services

The **railway station** is on the northern edge of the walled city so getting to a hotel from here is simple. Being rectangular, Xi'an is easy to explore, with all its streets running either east–west or north–south. The city buses also travel east–west or north–south, which makes them quite easy to use, though most visitors hire a bike during the day and take a taxi at night. Good maps are easily available from all hostels/hotels and any of the many **CITS** branches.

The **post office** is in the centre of the walled city near the Bell Tower. There are many branches of **Bank of China** and most in the centre have ATMs. The **PSB** can be found just to the west of the Bell Tower on Xi Dajie. There are **Internet cafés** (Y10/hour) in most hotels and hostels (non-guests are welcome to use the YHA's Internet and laundry facilities). **Tours** to all the major sites run from most hotels/hostels so there is little need for the CITS. **Bikes** can be hired from most hostels.

#### Where to stay

There are plenty of upmarket hotels in Xi'an but for location you can't beat *Bell Tower Hotel* (☎ 8727 9200; see p292 for booking tips) on Xi Dajie, near the actual tower.

The *YMCA* (☎ 876 73000; Y300/Db), at 339 Dong Dajie, is not in the same league as its Hong Kong cousin but is comfortable.

The middle range is more limited but try *Jiefang Hotel* (☎ 8769 8881; 🖳 www.jiefanghotel.com; Y220/Db) at 321 Jiefang Lu, right opposite the railway station. *Shengli Hotel* (aka *Victory Hotel*; ☎ 789 3040; Y200/Db) on Heping Lu is about as close to the centre as you will get without spending a fortune and they also run reasonable tours.

Any of the **YHA hostels** are fine for budget visitors. The *Shuyuan YHA* (☎ 872 87721; 🖳 www.hostelchina.org; Y25/dorm, Y160/Db) on Xi Nanmen St is our choice. They run good tours and have much more central locations than the older backpacker hangouts such as *Renmin Flats*.

### Where to eat
**Western-style fast-food joints** and modern Chinese restaurants are centred on Dong Dajie and Nan Dajie; quantity often beats quality as many restaurants (and hotel restaurants) do 'all-you-can-eat' buffets (the late-night dim sum at *The Palace* is very good).

You're better off in the **Muslim quarter** around the Great Mosque, which has streets full of sizzling spits loaded with all sorts of meat and fish as well as cauldrons full of noodles and soups.

The food (particularly the **breakfasts**) in the YHAs is very good (if you book a tour through a YHA their breakfast is free).

### Entertainment
Nightlife in Xi'an seems, at first, to consist solely of the pool of hostess bars around the main drag and the expensive hotel bars, all of which are a bit dead (for a few beers, you are better off having a session at one of the joints on **Defu Lu**, aka Bar St).

There are, however, a couple of **clubs** and Tuesday night is 'Ladies' Night', when girls get in free (though foreigners are let into most clubs in China for free anyway; even in your sweaty shirt and battered sandals you are still considered a cool asset to impress the punters. Or is it that we drink more than everyone else?) If you can round up a group, this can be a fun night out

---

#### Luoyang
Luoyang, like Xi'an, was often the **Chinese capital** during the Silk Road's heyday. In fact, by the time of the Northern Song (10th century AD), it had been the capital of over a dozen dynasties. After being sacked in the 12th century, however, the city never really recovered, so that by the early twentieth it was little more than a small provincial town with just a few thousand inhabitants. Only the advent of communism and Mao's 'Five year plans' brought about a revival in Luoyang's fortunes and today it is a mixture of old and new: on the one hand, it is an ugly industrial city with over six million inhabitants; on the other, it is home to some ancient treasures, most notably the Longmen Caves (see below), which are in a similar league to those at Mogao and Bingling Si.

The **museum** in the centre of town houses a laudable collection of artefacts taken from the hundreds of excavations that have been undertaken in the surrounding areas. The city is also famous for its **Peony Festival** in spring.

Try to visit the **White Horse Temple**, about 12km east of the city. Founded in 68AD, it was the first ever Buddhist temple to be built on Chinese soil. Tourist minibuses run from outside the train station.

The **Longmen Caves** are about 15km south of the city but many buses (including No 81 from the train station) will take you there. The caves were begun in 494AD by the Wei dynasty. They had just moved their capital here from Datong (where they also built the Yungang Caves) and over the next 200 years thousands of statues and caves were carved into the cliff face running along the bank of the Yi River. The **Ten Thousand Buddha Cave** stands out amongst the carefully renovated sections but sadly much of the complex was either ravaged by Western collectors or damaged by the Cultural Revolution. It is interesting to compare the earlier artistic styles of the caves at Datong with the more sophisticated styles on display here.

**Practicalities** Accommodation in Luoyang as a whole is overpriced but *Mingyuan Binguan* (☎ 0379 390 1377; Y80/dorm, Y175/Db) at 20 Liefang Lu, just south of the train station, is connected to the YHA and is clean and bright. Luoyang's restaurants are famous for their '**Water Banquets**', which can last up to 24 courses. There are regular trains between Luoyang and **Beijing** (8-10hrs), **Xi'an** (6hrs) and **Datong** (via Taiyuan).

(check with your hotel/hostel for the latest hotspot as they change every year). Be prepared for a tombola prize draw halfway through the evening and a crooning slot slap in between the techno! Beers are cheaper if bought in bulk.

## Moving on
The train station has a separate **office for foreign visitors** and although it has annoying opening hours (daily 08.30-11.30 and 14.30-17.30), it does make getting tickets much easier as the local demand at this station (especially in summer) is so high.

Trains go to **Beijing** five times a day (15hrs) but it is one of the busiest routes in the country so you will want to buy your ticket as soon as you can. Check which station you are arriving at as trains go either to the Beijing Central or Beijing West terminal. There are also trains to **Pingyao** (10hrs), **Datong** (18hrs), **Tianshui** (6hrs), **Luoyang** (6hrs) and **Lanzhou** (10-12hrs).

Xi'an has an impressive **international airport** with flights to/from numerous destinations around Asia and links to all cities in China by domestic air services. Tickets can be arranged by any hotel or travel agent.

# Pingyao

Pingyao really came to prominence during the Ming and Qing dynasties when, as the leading merchant town in the area, it gave birth to China's banking system. Most of China's financial institutions had their headquarters here under the Qing but as they inevitably moved to the great coastal trading centres, so the town drifted into obscurity. The downside of this is that the former banking capital of the most populous nation on Earth now cannot boast one single ATM; the upside is that Pingyao has China's only surviving fully intact Ming dynasty city wall and has been listed as a UNESCO World Heritage Site because of this. The city is also closed to traffic daily from 08.00 to 19.00, which makes it even more pleasurable to wander around.

## WHAT TO SEE

### The city walls
These may have been heavily restored but they are a true reflection of what Chinese cities looked like in the Middle Ages. The first set of walls was erected in the 9th century BC but these date from the 14th century AD. You can walk all around the walls but enter only at the North and West gates – admission (Y120) is expensive but this does grant you access to over twenty of Pingyao's lesser sites (those interested only in the walls have been known to access them for free from the South and East gates).

### The Bell Tower
This marks the 'almost centre' of town, near where Nan Dajie meets Dong Dajie. You can climb up the tower (Y5), which at over 18m is the tallest building in town.

## Others

Take a walk around the main streets and you will soon find the other attractions Pingyao has to offer. There are plenty of **Taoist temples** in Pingyao and, perhaps more surprisingly, **churches**. Various **old banking buildings** and **merchant houses** have been converted into small **museums**.

### PRACTICAL INFORMATION
[☎ code 0354]
### Orientation and services
All the sites are within the old city walls but the modern city sprawls all around. You can easily walk from the station to the old city.

As the former banking centre for the entire Chinese empire, it is a bit galling that there are **no banks** here that accept credit/debit cards, though most hotels change US dollars *and* provide **Internet** – but it's cheaper at the local café on Xi Dajie.

### Where to stay
It is worth booking ahead as many hotels will pick you up from the train station, although those who just turn up can haggle for the best prices, as there are usually many more hotel rooms than visitors.

Most of the hotels are restored traditional Chinese townhouses and a real treat to explore. *Tian Yuan Kui* (Nan Dajie 73; ☎ 568 0069; 🖳 www.pytyk.com; 250/Db) is rightly popular. *Xiyucheng* (☎ 568 4917; 🖳 www.pyxyc.com) is similar and dates from the 18th century. *Yun Jin Cheng* (☎ 568 0944; 🖳 www.yyjc.sxty.com.cn; Y60/dorm), 64 Nan Dajie, is the most expensive but it is also connected to the YHA and has cheap dorms at the rear.

### Where to eat
Have a wander around the streets and take your pick. Most hotels have restaurants.

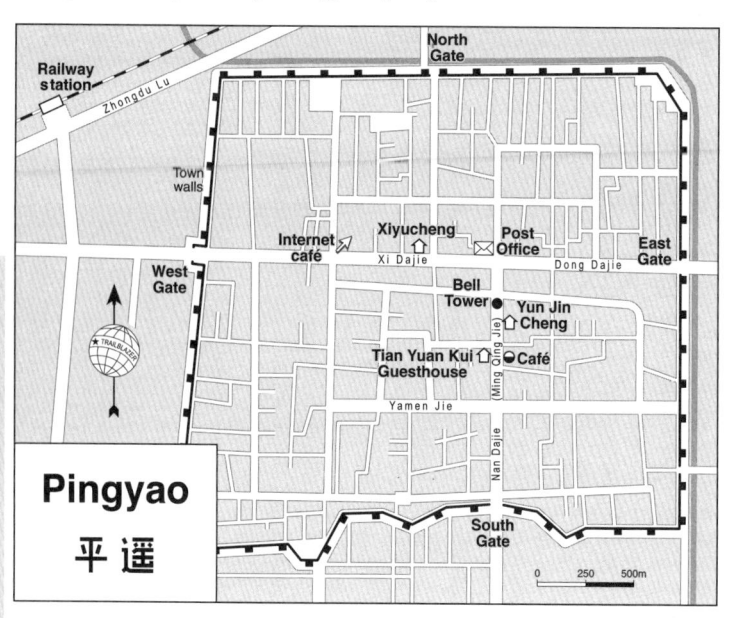

# Pingyao
# 平遥

Some restaurants are overly 'touristy' but most serve good food. There is no outstanding option but we kept going back to the café opposite Tian Yuan Kui Guesthouse.

**Moving on**
There is a day train and a night train to **Xi'an** (10hrs) and **Beijing** (10hrs), despite what your hotel might tell you. You can buy only 'hard seat' tickets at Pingyao station but for a fee most hotels will arrange for a 'hard sleeper' ticket to be bought in Taiyuan and brought down on the train.

# Datong

Datong has little to do with the Silk Road and the town is an unattractive mining community better known for building steam engines and producing coal than anything else. Nevertheless, there are a couple of treasures close by which make this worth a detour.

## WHAT TO SEE

A walk around the centre of the city can occupy an afternoon. Beginning at the **Drum Tower** it is an easy walk to the **Nine Dragon Screen** (Y3), the 12th-century **Huayan Si Temple** and **Buddhist monastery** that are still active, and the **Shanhua Temple**. The Dragon Screen doesn't match up to the one in the Forbidden City but the temple is worth a visit.

Datong, especially in the suburbs, can be very run-down, making a trip to the outskirts to see the crumbling ramparts a poor choice (you will see them when leaving the city on the tour to the Hanging Temple, anyway). This is what life is like, however, for the majority of Chinese city dwellers so it gives you an interesting, if depressing, insight into the 'real' China.

The **Locomotive Factory** tour run by CITS is really only for rail enthusiasts.

## Around Datong

**Yungang Caves** These caves (Y80) are terrific in size and quality and, unlike those at Mogao where the cliffs were too crumbly, here the statues were carved directly from the rocks as the caves were dug out of the cliffside. They mostly date from about the 5th century AD and an estimated 40,000 workmen were involved. Many of these came from northern India, hence the Ghandaran characteristics (see box p310) in the Buddhist statues' faces and also the Persian and Afghan influences. There are 50 caves to see but the central ones are the most dramatic.

To get to the caves, take the No 4 bus (Y2) from opposite Feitian Hotel. This goes to the bus station from where you take the No 3 bus (Y2) to the caves – the whole trip takes 40 minutes. On the way back you can wait for a bus or get a lift into town in one of the many private minibuses that pass by on the highway.

**The Hanging Temple and the Yingxian Pagoda** The **Hanging Temple** (Y36) is smaller in real life than you might imagine from pictures but no less impressive. It is set in the **Heng Shan Mountains**, which contain one of the five holy Taoist Mountains – Heng Shan. The temple clings to the side of a cliff, supported by a few poles in what can only be described as a death-defying act. A dam has been built upstream to remove the threat of floods (it was these that caused the temple to be built so high up in the first place) but, especially from a distance, you still wouldn't give it long to live. The monastery is over 1400 years old but can get a bit touristy in the summer.

The **Yingxian Pagoda** is the oldest wooden building in China, having been built in 1056 (originally without the use of a single nail – although there are plenty to see now). It is an impressive 70m high, with nine storeys all beautifully decorated inside and out. Entrance costs Y36.

A round trip to both sites by taxi costs Y150 (maximum four passengers) and takes the whole day, or you can get to the Hanging Temple by bus from the square in front of Datong's train station. This costs Y5 but it's a long, slow two-hour ride to Hunyuan and from here motorbikes run a quick shuttle service to the temple (Y10 return). It is usually easier to take one of the CITS tours.

## PRACTICAL INFORMATION
### [☎ code 0352]
### Orientation and services
The **old city walls** can still be seen in places around the centre of modern Datong and most of the city's sights are within these walls, except for the Yungang Caves which are a way out of town. The **train station** is in the north of the city and contains three separate buildings: the northernmost hall is where you come out from the platform; the middle hall is the entrance and has a small ticket office and the **CITS** office, while the southern hall has the large ticket office and a counter where English is spoken.

The CITS offer a good service (you are likely to be met by them as soon as you come out of the station), will find you a room in a hotel and run tours to the major sights but they have jacked up the prices and the discount rates they offer for hotels are no lower than those you can negotiate yourself.

For some reason, **laundry** seems to be expensive whichever hotel you stay in but there is a cheap laundry woman to be found just before the Chinese Hotel. An **Internet café** is down the side street by Hongqi Hotel.

### Where to stay
As there is little to see in the town you might as well stay near the station. There are three options here and all are clean and reasonable. *Feitian Hotel* (☎ 281 5117; Y45/dorm, Y180/Db), Chezhen Qianjie, is on your left as you come out of the station; it also has a cheap canteen-style restaurant on the fifth floor. *Hongqi Hotel* (Y290/Db), on your right as you come out of the station, has recently been refurbished and is very presentable; it has two restaurants on the ground floor. Down the small road on your left, between the station and Feitian, is a *Chinese Hotel* (Y80-120/Db).

### Where to eat
The cheaper-looking of the two **restaurants** in Hongqi Hotel does a great Mongolian hot pot and beer for Y30 per person; its food is just as good as the other restaurant but half the price. *Yonghe*

---

**(Opposite) Top left**: Buddhist prayer wheels are turned clockwise to activate the prayers within them. **Top right**: Novice monks at Taer Si Monastery (see p338). **Bottom**: The Hanging Temple outside Datong (see p352) is delicately balanced halfway up a cliff to prevent it being washed away when the river floods.

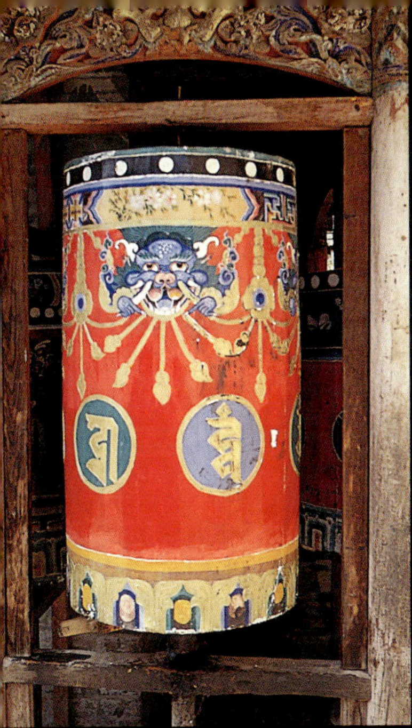
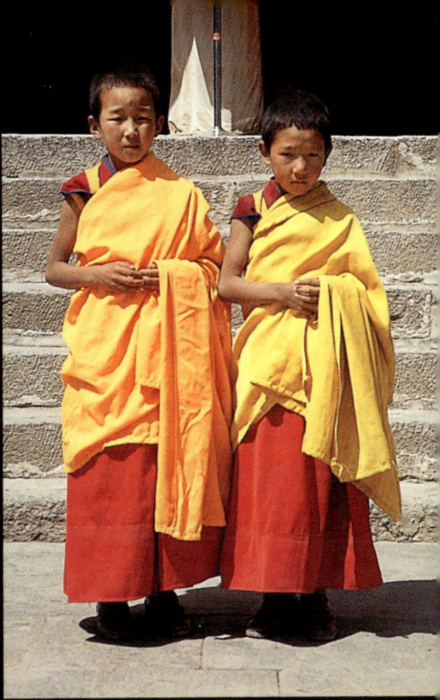
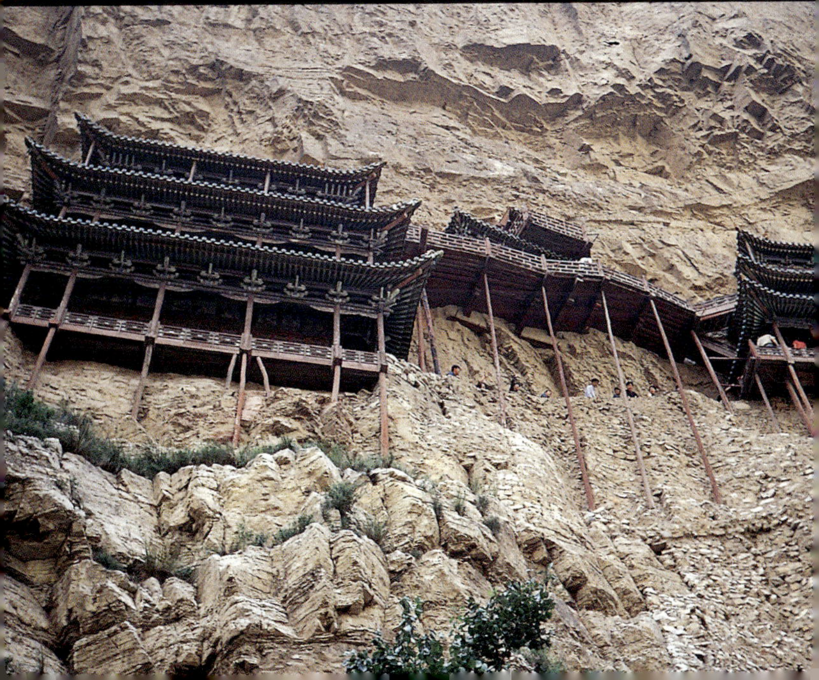

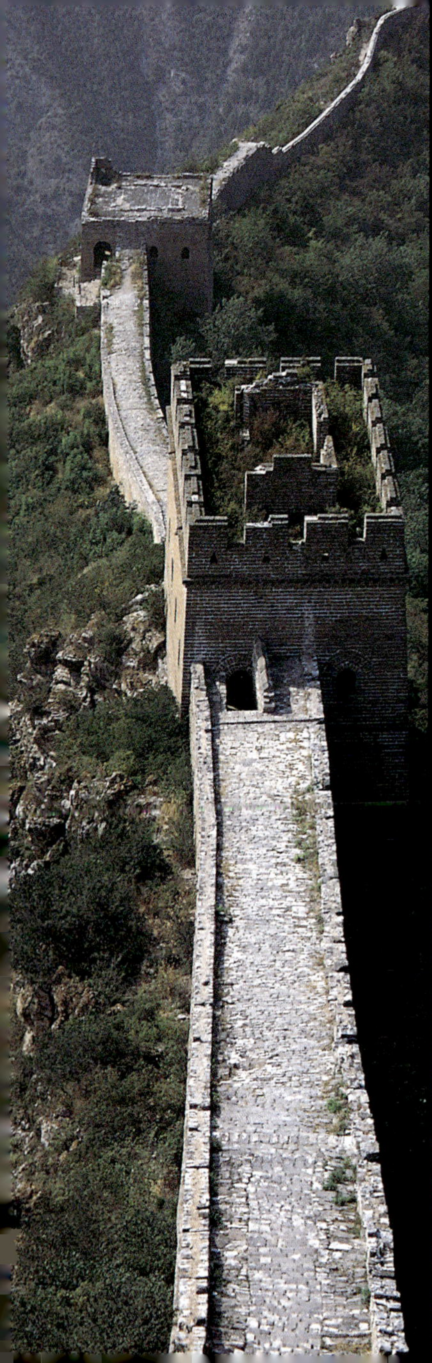
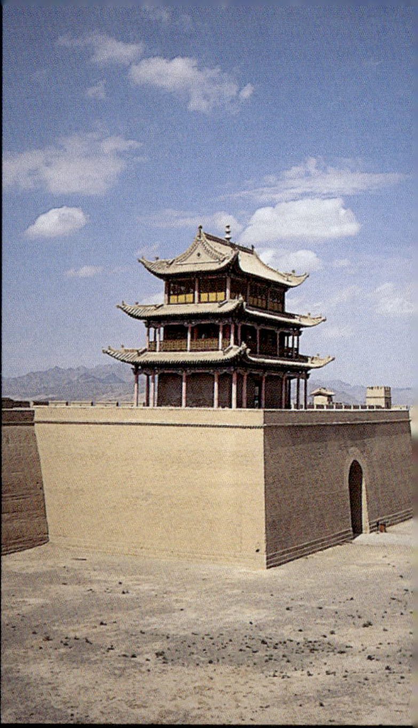
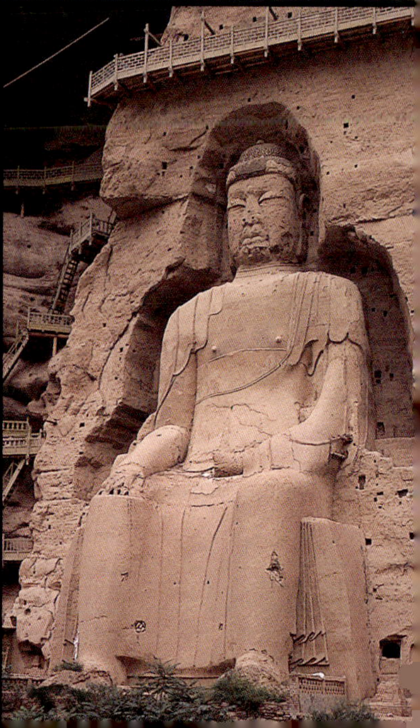

Datong 353

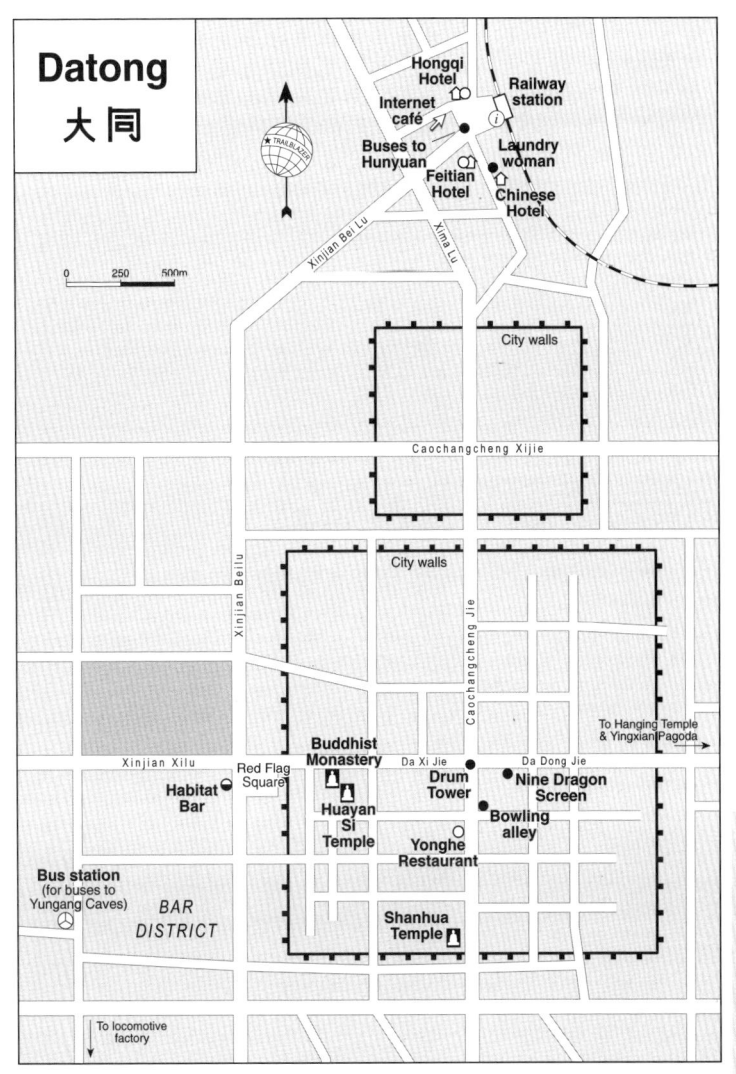

# Datong
# 大同

- Hongqi Hotel
- Railway station
- Internet café
- Buses to Hunyuan
- Feitian Hotel
- Laundry woman
- Chinese Hotel

Xinjian Bei Lu
Xima Lu

City walls

Caochangcheng Xijie

City walls

Xinjian Beilu
Caochangcheng Jie

To Hanging Temple & Yingxian Pagoda →

Xinjian Xilu — Red Flag Square
- Buddhist Monastery
- Da Xi Jie — Drum Tower — Da Dong Jie — Nine Dragon Screen
- Habitat Bar
- Huayan Si Temple
- Yonghe Restaurant
- Bowling alley

Bus station (for buses to Yungang Caves)

BAR DISTRICT

- Shanhua Temple

↓ To locomotive factory

(**Opposite**) **Left**: Near Beijing, one of the best places to visit the Great Wall is at Simatai (see p367). **Right, top**: Jiayuguan's fort (see p331) lies at the western end of the Great Wall. The fort marked the boundary between the Chinese empire and the wilderness that was the rest of the world. **Right, bottom**: At 27m, the Buddha at Bingling Si Caves (see p337) is one of the tallest in China.

> ### Hohhot and Inner Mongolia
> Unfortunately, over the past half century, Inner Mongolia has become a poor shadow of its neighbour, Mongolia proper. Today, 85 per cent of the population here is Han Chinese rather than Mongolian and the nomadic lifestyle has to a large extent been eradicated. Nevertheless, those travelling between Datong and Lanzhou by train might consider Hohhot a worthy stop.
>
> Hohhot, like Ürümqi, is in danger of becoming just another Chinese city but serves as a good base to visit the surrounding **grasslands**. There are two or three major areas that most tours visit and the general rule is the longer you travel to get to your destination, the less crowded it will be (Huitengxile, $3^{1}/_{2}$hrs from Hohhot, gets good reports). Tour operators are all over town and many will come to find you, so haggle (Y200/pp should be about right for the day). If you cannot find anyone running tours to **Xanadu** (see box p368), check with the CITS office. *Beiyuan Fandian* (☎ 0471 226 4222; Y25/dorm, Y120/Db), 28 Chezhan Xijie, is opposite the train station and is considered the best deal in town. Trains leave daily for Lanzhou (18hrs) and Datong (4-5hrs/Y40).

*Restaurant* on Nanguan Nanjie can't do enough for you in terms of service – look out for the Eight Treasures tea, which the waiter will pour into your cups from a long-spouted teapot five metres away!

Datong's nightlife is still very much in an embryonic stage but there is an ex-pat bar, *Habitat* (Xinjian Nanlu), where the beer flows and pub grub is served. The **10 Pin Bowling Alley** near the Drum Tower charges Y24 per person per game and has a pool hall at the back.

### Moving on
If you are doing a figure of eight through China (see p289), you can catch a train to **Lanzhou** (25hrs/Y175) via Inner Mongolia, or you may want to break your journey in **Hohhot** (5hrs, see box above) to explore the Mongolian steppes or take a tour to Xanadu (see box p368).

Otherwise, there are trains to **Beijing** (6-9hrs/Y45, try to take an express train), **Pingyao** (9-11hrs, sometimes via Taiyuan) and **Xi'an** (22hrs) twice daily.

# Beijing

For many, Beijing will be the end of the line and you will feel like celebrating. If you are heading west to Pakistan or Central Asia you should join in with these celebrations as you might not have another chance to party for several weeks. This city was not always part of the Silk Road but as China's capital from the Mongols onwards it is one of the most prestigious and fascinating cities on the route. The sights here are so numerous that no matter how long you stay, you are unlikely to see them all. Nevertheless, most visitors manage to see the main sights in four or five days, though visitors arriving from western China should be prepared to pick up the pace after months in the slow lane. Don't expect too much, however, as the communists chose Beijing for their capital in the first place only because of its conservatism. Even with the 2008 Olympics coming to town, Beijing is still quite some way behind Hong Kong's glitz and Shanghai's glamour.

## HISTORY

The earliest evidence of human settlement around Beijing was found at the Zhoukoudian site, 48km to the city's south-west, in 1921. The remains of this settlement and its most famous occupant, Peking Man, are tentatively dated at around 500,000BC. The first Chinese records of the area, however, are considerably later than this. They relate that a feudal state called Yen had its capital, Chi, on a site close to present-day Beijing during the Zhou dynasty (twelfth to eighth centuries BC).

The state thrived for 500 years until it was wiped out by Qin Shihuang as part of his drive to unify China for the first time. Having destroyed the place, however, he immediately set about rebuilding it. By the time of the Han dynasty (206BC-220AD), the Beijing area had been noted for its strategic significance owing to its proximity to the barbarian threat from the north. Thus, in times of danger its importance grew, though it was never adequately protected from attack. Consequently the city was taken and retaken a number of times by the northern tribes, often becoming the capital of the invaders' kingdoms.

### The Mongols

The most significant of these conquests, of course, was carried out by Genghis Khan in 1215. Having torched the city, they proceeded to build their own capital here, calling it Khanbalik ('City of the Khan'). The Chinese knew this city as Ta-Tu ('Great Capital') and it was during the Mongol rule that the first Westerners entered the city – including Marco Polo, who described the Khan's palace thus:

*'The palace itself has a very high roof. Inside, the walls of the halls and chambers are all covered with gold and silver and decorated with pictures of dragons and birds and horsemen and various breeds of beasts and scenes of battle. The ceiling is similarly adorned, so that there is nothing to be seen anywhere but gold and pictures. The hall is so vast and so wide that a meal might well be served there for more than six thousand men. The number of chambers is quite bewildering. The whole building is at once so immense and so well constructed that no man in the world, granted that he had the power to effect it, could imagine any improvement in design or execution'.*

### The Ming dynasty and the Forbidden City

When the Mongols were finally overthrown in 1368, Zhu Yuanzhang, founder of the Ming dynasty, moved the country's capital south to Nanjing, while the old capital, Ta-Tu, was given to his son, Prince Yen. Yen, however, immediately usurped his father's throne and brought the capital back north. He also renamed the city Beijing ('Northern Capital') and began designs for what eventually became the Imperial City. Unfortunately, there have been a number of fires in the last 500 years and nearly all traces of the old city of Ta-Tu have been demolished; only a couple of parts of the walls and the khan's wine bowl (see p365) remain.

### The Qing dynasty

Beijing's position as capital was partly tactical: the city was suitably close to the Great Wall, so possible invasions could be monitored from here, while reinforcements for the wall garrisons were close at hand. Not that it made much difference:

following a series of civil uprisings, the Manchurians were invited across the wall by a Ming general in 1644. They immediately stormed down to take Beijing and from there they ruled until the abdication of Pu Yi in 1912.

In the meantime the capital suffered greatly at the hands of Western powers: following the Arrow War of 1856-60, the Summer Palace was looted and burnt to the ground by Anglo-French troops. European embassies began to spring up in 1860 and parts of the city were declared foreign areas; the Boxer rebellion of 1900 saw the siege of embassy officials and other foreigners inside their legations for two months. When European reinforcements finally arrived, punitive measures were taken in retribution, including the incineration of the recently rebuilt Summer Palace.

## The Revolution and beyond

After the abdication of Pu Yi, Beijing remained at the heart of the country until the Kuomintang moved the capital to Nanjing in 1928. It was at that time the city was given the name Pei Ping ('Northern Peace') and became known in the West as Peking. The major battleground for the civil war, however, was further south

### Chairman Mao

Mao Zedong was born in Hunan in 1893, the son of a farmer. He taught at the Peasant Training Institute in Guangzhou in the 1920s and became an ardent promoter of peasants' rights. Influenced by Marxist theory, he believed the only way to replace the old order was through mass armed rising.

His mentor in the early days was **Li Dazhao**, a former librarian at Beijing University and one of the founders of the Chinese Communist Party, formed in Shanghai in 1921. At that time the party was made up of two groups, one headed by Li Dazhao, the other by **Zhou Enlai**, but in reality most of the major decisions were dictated by Russian advisors sent by Moscow to assist the Revolution.

Mao was sent from Shanghai to organize the first peasant-worker army in Changsha. This he did and the following **Autumn Harvest Uprising** was a success. The army was able to establish a headquarters at Jinggang Shan on the Hunan–Jiangxi border, where Mao was joined by **Zhu De**, a former Kuomintang commander who had defected to the communists and taken his troops with him. Together their forces became China's first **Red Army** and during the early 1930s they enjoyed considerable success using a variety of guerilla tactics. They were still no match for Chiang Kai Shek's crack troops, however, and all attempts to attack some of China's larger cities ended in disaster. The communists eventually found themselves surrounded by over half a million Nationalist soldiers and were forced to retreat on what famously became '**The Long March**' (see box p283).

Whilst on the march, Mao was elected as the new party leader at the **Zunyi Conference** (1935). His main political allies were Zhu De and **Lin Bao**, another Red Army commander; together they decided to sever links with their Russian advisors. The march cemented the CCP's position in Chinese politics and following WWII, Mao's troops (now known as the **People's Liberation Army**) trounced the Nationalist army at Huai Huai. In October 1949 Mao was able to climb Beijing's Tiananmen Gate and declare the founding of the **People's Republic of China.**

Mao's personal life (particularly the early years) is shrouded in mystery but it is now accepted that he had four wives and several children.

and to a large extent Pei Ping was forgotten about (so much so that the Japanese were able to take the city quite easily in 1937). The civil war recommenced at the end of WWII and it was only following the retreat of the KMT to Taiwan (with hoards of treasure from the Forbidden City) that the city was renamed Beijing. In 1949 the People's Republic of China was officially founded here. Since then it has withstood the stormiest excesses of China's politics, including the mass gatherings of the Cultural Revolution and the Democracy Movement.

## Beijing today

Like most major cities, Beijing can come across as rather impersonal to the modern visitor and it's difficult to avoid the crowds. The tourist sights are particularly busy and rush hour is one big traffic jam you will want to avoid (these days, as many of Beijing's 13 million inhabitants own a car as own a bike). The upside is that Beijing is an excellent place to meet up with others, and you'll find some of the better entertainment in China to fill the nights. For the 2008 Olympics, many of the dirtiest factories around the city have been closed to reduce pollution and a massive construction programme has been undertaken throughout the city (don't be surprised if things have moved or disappeared as nothing seems sacred); almost all the sights have received an extra lick of paint or a good polish.

## WHAT TO SEE

### Tiananmen Square

This is the ideal starting place for a tour of Beijing and most people use it as such. The square is vast (at 40 hectares it is the largest city square in the world) and has been the site of a number of important movements in 20th-century Chinese history, from the declaration of the Chinese Republic in 1949, through the massive fanatical reviews of the Cultural Revolution, to the massacre of the peace protestors in 1989. If you include the Forbidden City to the north, the numerous sights in and around the square will take at least a day.

**Chairman Mao's Mausoleum** Visit Mao's Mausoleum first as it is open daily but only from 08.30 to 11.30. It was completed in May 1977 and is still pulling the crowds in, with well over a million Chinese visitors each year.

The mausoleum is hemmed in north and south by four statues, each representing the historical struggles of the Chinese people (although the artist's style has a distinctly Russian flavour). Queues are astonishingly long, a testament either to the fact that Mao lives on in the hearts of the people, or that the Chinese just love to stare at things in groups. The line moves surprisingly fast, however, so you shouldn't have to wait for more than 20-30 minutes. Inside, guards bark at you if you slow down or look as if you are about to stop for a better view. Utmost respect is expected from all visitors even though there have been suggestions from as high up as Deng Xiao Ping that the mausoleum might have been a mistake (in 2004 a formal petition was presented to the government asking for the body to be removed to Mao's hometown of Shaoshan, in Hunnan; it argued that unless this happened, Beijing would not appear 'civilized' to its

## Tiananmen Square

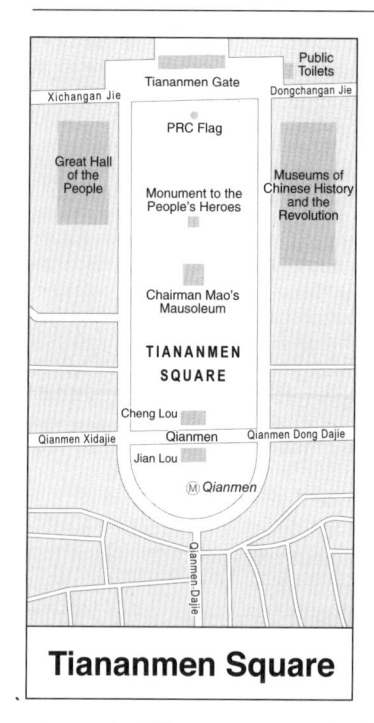

*Map labels: Tiananmen Gate; Public Toilets; Xichangan Jie; Dongchangan Jie; PRC Flag; Great Hall of the People; Monument to the People's Heroes; Museums of Chinese History and the Revolution; Chairman Mao's Mausoleum; TIANANMEN SQUARE; Cheng Lou; Qianmen Xidajie; Qianmen; Qianmen Dong Dajie; Jian Lou; M Qianmen; Qianmen Dajie*

many Olympic visitors). Bags and cameras must be left in the booths (Y10) on the east side of the mausoleum, though the mausoleum itself is free.

**National Museum of Chinese History** On the eastern side of the square, this museum (Y10; 08.30-15.30, closed Monday) contains extensive relics from every period of China's history, with occasional English labelling, making a visit here something of a guessing game.

Easily recognizable are the prehistoric tools, early jewellery and terracotta warriors. Watch out for the gunpowder display featuring flying bombs, and the jade burial suit complete with jade posing pouch.

The building also houses the **Museum of the Revolution**, which contains many hundreds of relics from pre- and post-WWII struggles – everything from photographs, flags and cannons to a cloth cap once worn by Mao. Alongside these is a display of gifts given to the Chinese government by foreign dignitaries, which is less culturally exciting but still pretty interesting: check out the Brazilian tea tray surfaced entirely with butterfly wings and the fearsomely tacky Shakespeare plate from the UK.

**Great Hall of the People** Covering an area of 170,000 sq metres, this hall is used for meetings of the **National People's Congress** but is open to the public from 08.30 to 15.30 when meetings are not being held. Unless you enjoy looking at vast, empty rooms it's probably best to give this a miss and save Y20.

**Tiananmen Gate (Gate of Heavenly Peace)** On the northern side of Tiananmen Square sits the entrance to the Imperial (Forbidden) City.

This famous gate was also used as a podium from which imperial decrees were read and it was from here, on 1 October 1949, Mao proclaimed 'The People's Republic of China has now been founded. The Chinese People have now stood up'.

The front is embellished with a huge picture of the man himself, and the inscriptions read 'Long live the People's Republic of China', and 'Long live the unity of the peoples of the world'.

Inside are an exquisite ceiling, a couple of paintings of Mao and his acolytes and some dodgy 1960s' furniture. Open daily 09.00-17.00, it's not really worth visiting unless you are desperate to spend Y30 on an 'I mounted the Tower of Tiananmen' certificate.

**Qianmen Gate** This was the main entrance to/from the southern half of the city. It was built in 1419 and, at 42m, is the tallest of the old buildings here. It's possible to get inside for Y10 (daily) to see the **photograph museum** (no English labels). Continue climbing for a good view of the square and its surroundings and to visit the huge souvenir shops; although items in here have price tags on them, prices are not necessarily fixed.

**Other sights in Tiananmen Square** The **Monument to the People's Heroes** stands directly north of Mao's mausoleum; this was the centre of the wreath-laying protests in 1976 (see p285). It is decorated with Mao's and Zhou Enlai's calligraphy and the base contains carvings which illustrate suitably revolutionary events in Chinese history.

Directly to the north of this, the **PRC flag** flies from sunrise to sunset and if you get here early or late enough you can catch the Colours ceremony. Finally, note that there are toilets and a bicycle park just to the east of Tianan Gate.

### The Imperial Palace (Forbidden City)

For centuries no Chinese citizens were allowed in the Forbidden City – only members of the Imperial court and the odd visitor who had travelled from afar – and after three hours of jostling with the locals you might agree with the tourist we met who wished the same rules applied today.

It comprises more than 178 acres, 1000 buildings and 9000 rooms and is so vast that it's difficult to know where to start. If you want to explore the whole thing be prepared to spend days inside; half a day is about the most a sane person can take.

The Palace itself, also known as the Purple Forbidden City, was built in the reign of the Ming emperor, Yong Le, between 1406 and 1420, and the next 24 emperors lived there, right up until 1911. It has been destroyed by fire and rebuilt a number of times but the reconstruction always followed the original designs, so the integrity of the place is retained. Maps of the Imperial City are common and many city maps have them on the back. It's worth considering a guided tour, or hiring the cassette tour (Y40) from outside Meridian Gate, because the site is so big; after a tour, of course, there's nothing to stop you exploring other areas on your own. Official guides cost Y80 but unofficial ones outside the gates will settle for Y40 and there seems to be little difference.

The Imperial Palace (Y50; open daily 08.30-16.30 but ticket offices close at 15.30) is a World Heritage Site

**Entering the city** Tiananmen Gate leads into a massive courtyard, which although full of people contains little of interest. Make your way past Duanmen ('Upright') Gate to the enormous Meridian Gate, which is the entrance to the Forbidden City proper. Ticket offices are on the left. *(continued on p362)*

360 Beijing

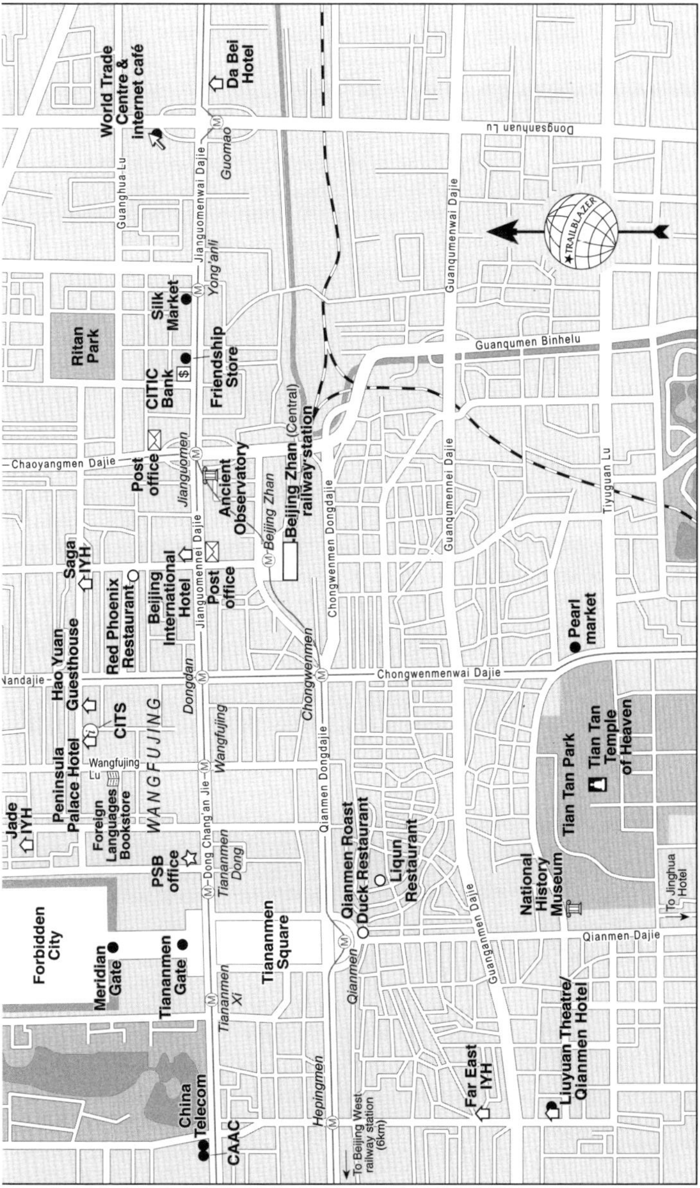
Forbidden City
Meridian Gate
Tiananmen Gate
China Telecom
CAAC
Tiananmen Xi
Tiananmen Square
Tiananmen Dong
PSB office
Jade IYH
Peninsula Palace Hotel
Foreign Languages Bookstore
WANGFUJING
Wangfujing Lu
Dong Chang'an Jie
Wangfujing
CITS
Hao Yuan Guesthouse
Nandajie
Dongdan
Saga IYH
Red Phoenix Restaurant
Beijing International Hotel
Jianguomennei Dajie
Post office
Beijing Zhan
Ancient Observatory
Jianguomen
Post office
Chaoyangmen Dajie
Beijing Zhan (Central) railway station
CITIC Bank
Friendship Store
Ritan Park
Silk Market
Yong'anli
Jianguomenwai Dajie
Guanghua Lu
Guomao
World Trade Centre & internet café
Da Bei Hotel
Dongsanhuan Lu
TRAILBLAZER
Guanqumenwai Dajie
Guanqumen Binhelu
Guangqumennei Dajie
Tiyuguan Lu
Chongwenmen Dongdajie
Chongwenmen
Chongwenmenwai Dajie
Pearl market
Tian Tan Park
Tian Tan Temple of Heaven
Qianmen Dongdajie
Qianmen Roast Duck Restaurant
Liqun Restaurant
National History Museum
To Jinghua Hotel
Qianmen Dajie
Qianmen
Guanganmen Dajie
Hepingmen
To Beijing West railway station (6km)
Far East IYH
Liuyuan Theatre/ Qianmen Hotel

*(cont'd from p359)* Although you cannot see the water from the Meridian Gate, you should be aware that you are crossing over the moat (50m wide) and through the palace walls (7m thick). Once through the gate there are five bridges over the Golden Waters River. The middle bridge and the central path throughout the city were reserved exclusively for the emperor's use. Emperors were not expected to soil their feet with the earth so the path was constructed entirely of marble; this was known as the Imperial Way. Just to be sure that no dirt ever touched the imperial feet, the emperor was carried everywhere in a sedan chair. Emperors used to stand inside the Meridian Gate to supervise the flogging of errant courtiers in the eastern half of the square; records tell of one such session in 1534 when 134 men were beaten here; 17 died.

**Central halls** Heading north, you will pass through the Gate of Supreme Harmony to face the largest structure inside the city, the **Palace of Supreme Harmony**. From the throne in this palace, the emperor surveyed the most important court pageants. Nearly 100,000 state officials could fit into this square and they did so on truly auspicious occasions: when he had a birthday party, for example.

You will then come to the **Hall of Complete Harmony**, which was used as a preparation room for the emperor and for occasional state functions; there are two original sedan chairs in here today.

Behind this is the **Hall of Preserving Harmony**, which was used for less significant banquets and the final stage of the highest civil service examinations. Of the ten shortlisted candidates (drawn from all over China), three would be chosen by the emperor. These three were allowed to tread the Imperial Path through the city once. Behind the Hall of Preserving Harmony, note the vast carved marble slab decorating the stairway: this is the largest single piece of marble in the city, weighing in at over 200 tons. It is 16.5m long, 3m wide and 1.5m thick and it was dragged to the palace in winter, when water was thrown over the roads to make them icy.

**Inner court** To the north of this ramp lie the living quarters of the emperor – the elite part of the city – and there are three successive palaces here. The first, the **Palace of Heavenly Purity**, was the emperor's bedroom until the mid-18th century when it was converted into a meeting room for foreign dignitaries. The second, the **Hall of Union**, was the empress's quarters, while the third, the **Palace of Earthly Peace**, was used, among other things, for the consummation of imperial marriages. It is worth noting the blocked-up hole against the wall of this building, part of a charcoal underfloor-heating system.

Behind the palace you will find the **Imperial Garden**, which was laid out in the Ming dynasty. From here the path leads straight to the **Hall of Imperial Peace** and then to **Shenwumen Gate**, the northern exit from the Forbidden City.

**Other sights** It would be a mistake to wander through the palace only from south to north. Other sights of interest in the eastern part of the city include the **Museum of Clocks**, the **Dragon Screen**, the **Jewellery Museum** (containing two huge elephant's tusks and a most delicate bed-mat made of ivory) and

**Qianlong's Garden** (which contains a tiny artificial river along which cups of wine were floated; whenever the cup stopped moving the individual nearest to it would have to compose a poem or drink the contents).

Also look out for the **Imperial Opera House** and the famous **well** in which Guang Xu's favourite concubine, Zhen Fei, was drowned on the orders of his aunt, Ci Xi (see p282).

## Jingshan Park

Immediately to the north of the Forbidden City is Jingshan Park, built on an artificial hill made out of earth removed to create the palace moat. Most palace visitors go straight into the park after leaving the north gate, as the top of the hill affords a fine view of the city.

If you are not totally overloaded with Forbidden City architecture, there are two interesting buildings on the park's northern side. As Beijing's parks go, however, this is not one of the best, so try elsewhere if you fancy a quiet place to sit.

## Tian Tan Park

**Tian Tan (The Temple of Heaven)** was the site at which the most auspicious imperial ceremonies were held; emperors communicated with heaven here from the early 15th century until the end of the imperial dynasty. Although there were altars on this site for centuries, the temple we see today was built at the order of Yong Le (of Forbidden City fame) in 1420. Since then, emperors have visited regularly to pray for good harvests and to celebrate the winter solstice. Invariably the emperor would enter the complex from the eastern gate, spending at least one night fasting in the **Hall of Abstinence**.

West of this hall stands a marble circular altar. This was constructed in 1530 and rebuilt in 1740 when it was given the name **Temple of the Winter Solstice**. It is worth noting of this altar, as of every building in the ensemble, that construction dwelt upon the sacred numbers three and nine, each being representative of heaven. Thus, virtually any statistic you can think up about the buildings here (apart from their construction dates, of course), will be a multiple of three: try counting the number of tiers, steps, or the posts around the edge.

Just north of the altar is the **Imperial Vault of Heaven** which contained the sacred ancestral tablets, to be produced for each ceremony. The **circular wall** around this vault is said to have been designed for its acoustic properties, which should ensure that a whisper towards the surface of one side of the circle is clearly audible on the opposite side. It's not quite the Whispering Gallery of Saint Paul's Cathedral, however, and on a busy day all you can hear is everyone frantically clapping and shouting at the wall.

To the north is the **Hall of Prayer for Good Harvests**, whose name is self-explanatory: this is the most important building of the complex and it is particularly impressive. When you look at it, remind yourself that it was built entirely without glue or nails.

The Temple of Heaven is another of Beijing's World Heritage Sites. Try to get here as early as possible in the morning or late in the evening when the place will be more or less quiet, otherwise it will be swarming. If that is the case, the tree garden on the eastern side of the temple offers some welcome peace and quiet as well as a rich pine aroma. The parks to the west are similar. The **Big Bell** here is Y1 a dong and the beautiful interlocking **pagoda** nearby is a favourite of the 'young lovers' it is named after.

On your way home it's worth popping into the **Pearl Market** just to the east of the entrance if you're looking for souvenirs.

Entry to the park only is Y10 but visitors are pressed to take the sightseeing ticket, which gains you entry to all of the buildings and costs Y30 (the cheaper ticket, however, is enough for most people and covers the important sights); keep your ticket, as it is needed to access each area. The park is open daily from 06.00 to 22.00, the temple daily from 08.30 to 17.00.

### The Summer Palace

This palace (Y40), together with its grounds, covers an expanse of 290 hectares – four times the size of the Forbidden City. Another World Heritage Site, it could take days to explore if you have the time. Bring a picnic and enjoy a relaxing day off from the congested hustle of the city; it's open daily 08.00-19.00.

**Kunming Lake**, the Lake of Superior Brightness, was originally a small pond but was converted into a reservoir in 1292 to provide drinking water for the area. In 1750, Emperor Qianlong built a garden here to celebrate his mother's birthday and the lake was further dredged and expanded. Since that time the site has been used by the imperial households as a summer retreat. Following the Opium Wars the palace was sacked by Anglo-French troops in 1860. It was rebuilt on its present site by Empress Ci Xi just in time for it to be burned to the ground again in 1900 after the Boxer Rebellion.

As with the Forbidden City there is almost too much to take in but you should try to see the following: from East Palace Gate the visitor steps into the royal residence areas. Here, in the late 19th century, the Empress Dowager Ci Xi lived and received guests. Her unfortunate nephew, Guang Xu, was imprisoned here, despite the fact that he was the legitimate heir to the throne; the wall she built to stop him from escaping can still be seen. In this area you will find Ci Xi's private theatre and a number of living quarters, which have been converted into museums (Ci Xi's car, clothing, carriages and make-up are all on display).

On the left as you reach the lake you will see the small **Perceiving of Spring jetty/island** – so called because the ice melts here first at the end of winter. Passing south along the shore you come to the beautiful 17-arch marble bridge leading to **South Lake Island**, which is the setting for the **Dragon King Temple**.

Heading north and west, meanwhile, you will be approaching **Longevity Hill**. Turning left around the lake you find the **Long Corridor**, which, measuring 730m from end to end, is the longest covered walkway in the world. It is very impressive, with unique artwork on every eave. This brings you to the main architectural structures of the complex, the **Cloud Dispelling Hall** and the **Tower of Buddhist Fragrance**, which at 41m high is the park's dominant non-fluid feature. Ci Xi celebrated her birthdays in the first building. There are a number of museums in this part of the grounds, each of which charges an entry fee;

the famous 1905 portrait of Ci Xi by Dutch artist Voss Hubert is in one of them. Most visitors see about this much and then visit the famous **marble boat** further to the west (this was built by Ci Xi as a two-fingered gesture to her political enemies who said she spent far too much money on wasteful fancies when in fact the country needed to invest in its navy). There is a good deal more exploring to do, however, if you have the time. If you make your way across as many bridges as you can towards the west side, you can find a nice spot to chill out, have a picnic or watch the boaters on the lake (pedalos and row boats cost Y20/hr to hire, electric boats Y40/hr).

To get to the Summer Palace take the metro along its new extension to Zhichunlu station then take a taxi (Y20). There is a good, clear, aerial map of the complex on the right as you go in and many signs in English to guide you round so no guide is needed.

### Beihai Park

Located just to the north-west of the Forbidden City, Beihai Park (Y5) is another pleasant place in which to while away an afternoon, although it can get rather crowded, especially at weekends.

Its history considerably predates the Imperial Palace, for it was on the southern side of the lake here that Kublai Khan lived. Construction of the **lake**, which accounts for over half the park's area, originally started in the 10th century, the rocks being piled up in the middle to form **Qionghua Island** ('Jade Flower Island').

The Yuan dynasty remodelled the place, while the ever-busy Qianlong conducted major reconstructions here too. The buildings were sacked and burned by Western soldiers in 1900 following the Boxer Rebellion. Entering the park from the south you will find all that remains from Kublai Khan's palace: a huge carved **jade bowl** from which, apparently, he used to drink wine (he must have been some drinker because it's about three feet across). This bowl was lost for some time but was rediscovered in 1749.

Behind the bowl, in the **Chengguandian** ('Hall for Receiving Light') is an impressive Buddha figure hewn from a single piece of white jade and encrusted with jewels. The figure came from Burma and was presented to Ci Xi in the late 19th century. Crossing the **Yong'an Bridge** you come to the park's most famous construction, the 35m-high **White Pagoda**, which was built in 1651 to commemorate the first official visit of a Dalai Lama to Beijing. In fact, the top half dates only from 1977 and it had been rebuilt a number of times before this because of earthquake damage.

Other notable sights, both on the island and off it, include the dew-collecting plate, which was used to gather pure dewdrops for the emperor's various potions, and a nine-dragon screen on the northern shore. The **Five Dragon Pavilions** that line the shore are so-called because their roofs look like the spine of a huge swimming serpent. There are also bandstands on the northern side where impromptu music sessions are held and it is possible to rent rowing boats in summer. In winter the lake becomes a huge ice-rink.

## Museums and other attractions

The **Ancient Observatory** (Y15) on Jianguomen Dajie has an interesting outdoor collection of instruments and a small museum with a copy of the Dunhuang Star Map (the oldest star map in the world – the original was 'bought' by British explorers and is in the British Museum, London). You can also buy any size of lodestone from the shop.

**Yonghe Gong** (Y25; just south of Yonghe Gong metro station) is a very bright and beautifully preserved Tibetan Lama Temple which is quite a sight

---

### The Great Wall of China

The image conjured up in most people's mind when you mention the Great Wall of China is that 100-yard stretch of steeply climbing stone used in all the TV clips when a famous dignitary comes to visit. Either that or the tediously overused statistic that the wall is the only man-made object you can see from space (this claim is, in fact, untrue as space missions have testified that the wall is not visible – it was merely Chinese propaganda). Up close, however, as you see time and again on this trip, the wall is a coat of many colours – it isn't even one long wall for a start. The Great Wall is, of course, a World Heritage Site.

**History** Most of what we see today, including the famous sections at Badaling and Dragonhead, date from the Ming period (1368-1644), yet the wall dates back centuries before this: as far back, in fact, as the period of the Warring States in the 5th century BC. The rulers of this era had consistently improved and extended their city walls until they had developed a walled network around most of their territories, so when Emperor Qin united China in 221BC his first logical step was to link up all these networks and establish a singular defence – which, with the help of his expert general, Meng Tian, he did. Under the Han emperors it was extended west to Dunhuang and took on a new role by incorporating towns and garrisons into its structure. These housed soldiers whose task it was not only to police the border against the northern Hsiun Nu invaders but also to colonize the new territories and ensure they would forever remain an integral part of China. This was the development that intrinsically linked the wall with the Silk Road as, for caravans heading west, the end of the wall signified the end of 'civilization'.

The final improvement was the expansion of the wall in terms of width as well as length, as the newly widened tops were then paved with stone to provide a flat 'road' right across the kingdom. This may not have kept the Mongols or the Manchus out but it did provide successive Chinese rulers with the most sophisticated communications system and military-supply line the world had ever known – even if half of it was made with little more than mud and straw because of the lack of any other raw materials in the desert landscapes of the west.

At its height the Great Wall covered some 6300km from Jiayuguan (see p331) in the west to Shanhaiguan (see box pp372-3) in the east, to the Yalu River (separating modern-day China and North Korea) in the north. Yet it did not just run in one straight line; several side spurs protected valleys and passes to the north and south as well. In total, over 50,000km of wall was built.

Most of those 50,000km are still with us today, although many sections have fallen into serious disrepair. Technically it is possible to visit every part of the wall but logistically some areas are too remote for casual inspection. Having said that, don't just limit yourself to those areas around Beijing.

although it can feel a bit artificial as it is so full of tourists. That it is here at all is thanks to Zhou Enlai who is remembered as this monastery's protector against the savagery of the Red Guards when most other monasteries were destroyed.

If you are staying for a long time you might also want to take a tour out to the **Ming Tombs** (40km north-west of Beijing); tours run from most hostels/hotels.

Apart from the museums in Tiananmen Square the best of the rest are the **Museum of Peking Man** (the skull here is a replica), Zhoukoudian, Fangshan District; the **Museum of Buddhist Sutras and Relics (Fayuansi Temple)**, Xuahwu District; **Beijing Art Museum**, Wanshousi St, West District; the **National Art Gallery**, Wusi St, East District; the **Natural History Museum**, Tianqiao St (for those into gore, this has pickled humans with their bodies skinned and lots of graphic pictures of experiments on Siamese twins).

## EXCURSIONS

### The Great Wall

There are lots of sections of the Wall open to the public and most make an easy day trip. The majority of tourists head for **Badaling** (Y45), which is an excellent reason for going somewhere else. Our favourites are **Simatai** (Y30), **Mutianyu** (Y35) and **Jinshanling** (Y40).

Wherever you go, allow a full day so you can have a good two- to three-hour wander when you get there (it's a two- to three-hour drive to Mutianyu and a three- to four-hour drive to Simatai). Be prepared for some intensive stair climbing, although there are cable cars at Mutianyu, Badaling and Simatai. If it's hot you'll probably want to use them going up if not down but as the Mutianyu sign says, if you walk the whole way 'You will have greater pleasure and be a true hero'. Quite so.

At Simatai, there is a guard at the tenth tower who won't let you go any further but the views across the surrounding hills with the wall snaking away are fantastic. There is an aerial runway down over the lake (Y30), which is great fun – if you're prepared to trust the Chinese engineering! At Mutianyu there is a toboggan slide down.

While most visitors spend long enough at the Wall to have a walk and take some pictures, there is the scope here for longer excursions. If the weather is fine, more energetic types might opt for a day hike along the Wall between Jinshanling and Simatai – it's three to five hours of hard walking and is not for the faint-hearted. Bring lots of water and good shoes (your tour should agree to drop you at one end and pick you up at the other).

You can get to most parts by public transport but it takes much, much longer than going on a tour; tours run from virtually every hostel/hotel and are not too expensive.

Finally, check the listings guide, *Beijing Scene*, for occasional special events, which can be quite fun ('Jazz on the Wall' and 'Hamlet on the Wall' are two examples). Camping out on the wall, however, is forbidden.

### To Xanadu

If you were inspired to make this trip by reading Coleridge's poem or Marco Polo's travelogue you might want to emulate William Dalrymple and make it all the way to Kublai Khan's summer capital. Looking at a map, it should be quite simple because although it's in Inner Mongolia, it's not that far from Beijing and not much farther than some of the parts of the Great Wall, which you can visit easily. The problem is that the Chinese have no interest in the site – well at least the Han Chinese. We went to see a director of the second largest tour operator in China (CTS) at his head office in Beijing and he couldn't even point to it on a map. As for advice on how to get there: 'Hire a taxi and a driver but it will take you three days'. Another problem is that Xanadu was chosen not just because it was cooler than Beijing but also because its location up in the first wave of Mongolian steppe reminded Kublai and his followers of their roots. This means that it was effectively in the middle of nowhere.

*In Xanadu did Kubla Khan*
*A stately pleasure-dome decree*
From *Kubla Khan*, 1816
**Samuel Taylor Coleridge**

Over the years, most of the remains have been swept away and now there is little to see. It was rediscovered (accidentally) only in 1872 by the physician to the British legation in Peking, Dr S W Bushell, by which time it was already 'overgrown with rank weeds and grass'. The only people we met who had successfully made the visit had joined an expensive two-day tour from Hohhot (see box p354). Otherwise, it does seem possible, *on paper*, to get there by public transport:

Take a train to **Chengde** (which was the summer retreat of the Manchu emperors and is now a World Heritage Site) from Beijing Central. Chengde is pretty well equipped for visitors and there is plenty of accommodation – the CITS office here might be able to help with the next leg of the journey. From there take a bus to Doulon (the closest city to Xanadu), described by one of our readers as 'an industrial nightmare' – you may struggle to find accommodation here. From Doulon you need to hire a taxi but you may well have difficulty finding someone who knows the way out to the ruins.

Finally, although at the time of writing Xanadu was accessible to the public, in the past the site has been deemed a 'closed area' to all but organized tours, so ask around in Beijing or Hohhot to double-check before setting off.'

## PRACTICAL INFORMATION
[☎ code 010]
### Orientation and services

It's worth buying the official colour map of the city (Y5). You will be approached by map sellers both on the train and in the station but make sure you get the one in English. The local listings magazines, *That's Beijing* (🖥 www.thatsbj.com), *City Edition* and *Metro*, are really worth picking up for the latest nightlife information (you can either buy them or nip into a posh hotel and take one from the foyer).

Finding your way in Beijing is made simpler by the fact that streets run either east–west or north–south but it can be difficult to follow the street names because, as is so often the case in China, each street has a number of names. This is best illustrated by the main west–east thoroughfare, Chang'an Avenue, that divides the Forbidden City from Tiananmen Square: it starts off in the west as Fuxing Lu, then becomes Fuxingmenwai Dajie, Fuxingmennei Dajie, Xi Chang'an Jie, Dong Chang'an Jie (see map pp360-1), Jianguomennei Dajie and then Jianguomenwai Dajie – to walk the length of it would take a few hours.

The **Tourism Hotline** (☎ 6513 0828) is open 24 hours (all its staff speak English) but, like the main **CITS** office next to the

Peninsula Palace Hotel, is of little use to independent travellers. If you want to book a tour or a flight you are better off using a private travel agency: a good one is **Monkey Business** (☎ 6591 6519; 🖳 www.monkeyshrine.com), Room 35, Red House Hotel, 10 Chun Xiu Lu, Dongzhimenwai. The **CAAC** office (☎ 6601 7755; open 08.00-20.00) is to the west of the Forbidden City at 15 Fuxingmen Dajie, on the north side of the road.

The **PSB** is immediately to the east of the Forbidden City on Beichizi Dajie and the visa office here is open 08.30-11.30 and 13.00-17.00 (closed Saturday afternoons and Sundays). Beijing, however, is not the best place to **extend your visa** (see p17)

The main **post office** is east of Beijing International Hotel, off Jianguomenbei Dajie. There is an efficient 'poste restante' counter here. There's also a new post office almost directly opposite the Beijing International. **International telephone calls** can be made from China Telecom on Xi Chang'an Jie, which is open 24 hours, but you might prefer to buy a phone card at one of the Internet cafés and phone from there, as it is usually cheaper.

If you need hard currency, **CITIC Industrial Bank** will change travellers' cheques into US$ and also allows US$ withdrawals on major credit/debit cards. They have a branch (open Mon-Fri 09.00-12.00 and 13.00-16.00) next to the Friendship Store on Jianguomenwai Dajie. **Bank of China** branches and **ATMs** are everywhere (particularly in shopping centres) and most accept foreign credit/debit cards.

You should have no problem finding an **Internet café** and will usually be one in your hotel/hostel. If you are struggling there is one in every YHA.

The **Kyrgyz Embassy** is at 2-4-1 Ta Yuan Diplomatic Building, Chaoyang district (☎ 6532 6458). The **Pakistani Embassy** (☎ 6532 2660, open Mon-Fri 08.30-11.00), 1 Dongzhimenwai Dajie, is a Y14 taxi ride from Dongzhimen metro station. The **Kazakh Embassy** is at 9 Sanliturn Dong Liujie. For visa applications, see pp15-18.

## Local transport

**The metro** The metro is by far the best option to get around town, particularly since it has been extended (see map p370). The network covers nearly all the major sites and tickets are Y3 per journey (you can buy a few at a time to avoid queuing). All stations are signposted by a large blue 'D' inside a circle. Five new lines are promised in time for the Olympics.

**Buses** These go everywhere and on the major routes they are duplicated by private minibuses; they are slow in Beijing's heavy traffic, however, crowded and not very user-friendly for non-Chinese speakers. The endless construction works all over the city don't help the congestion and most visitors ignore the buses now there is a metro.

One useful bus is No 1, which runs east–west along Chang'an Avenue from the West Train Station (where trains from Xi'an and Luoyang arrive) to the city centre. You should have no problem spotting this one: it's a double-decker. Bus No 4 also runs all the way along Chang'an.

An excellent bus service to/from **the airport** (Y16) leaves every half-hour from various locations in town (until about 19.30). The most useful stops are outside the CAAC office and behind Beijing International Hotel; from the airport there are three bus services but the most convenient will drop you at Beijing International Hotel or behind the main train station. A light-rail link is due to open in 2007.

**Bikes** You can hire bikes from most hotels/hostels (Y20/day) and they are definitely worth it for a day's touring. Most main roads have cycle lanes but cars use them too, often driving the wrong way!

**Taxis** Taxis charge a minimum fare of Y10 and Y20 should cover most fares around the city centre. Newer taxis charge Y1.60 per click and old ones Y1.20. On the whole they are honest and few away from the main train station will claim to have a 'broken meter'. Even taxis can't beat the rush-hour gridlock though, so plan your day with this in mind.

# Beijing Metro

# Beijing – Practical information

## Where to stay

Like most capital cities, you'll never be short of a hotel room in Beijing and with the arrival of YHAs it's easy to get good cheap accommodation near the centre.

If you have just come the 8000km across Asia and this is the end of your trip, our advice is to treat yourself at least for a couple of nights. This doesn't necessarily mean the Hyatt or the Hilton or the Sheraton or the Shangri-La – although they are all here – but you deserve a bit more than a dorm bed and a shared shower.

**Budget accommodation** There aren't many cheap places in the city centre so most foreign visitors stay in one of the five central *International Youth Hostels* (Y60/ dorm); our favourites are *Saga IYH* (☎ 6527 2773; 💻 www.sagahostel.com), 9 Shijia Hutong, and *Jade IYH* (☎ 6525 9966; 💻 xihua_zhide@126.com), 5 Zhide Beixiang, because of their cleanliness, friendliness and locations though others (eg *The Far East*; 90 Tie Shu Xie Jie, Xuan Wu; ☎ 519 588 11; 💻 www.fareastyh.com) are of a similar standard .

*Jinghua Hotel* (☎ 6722 2211; Y30/ dorm), about 8km south of Tiananmen Square at Nansanhuan Xi Lu, is the old backpacker haunt but it is as legendary for its smell as its parties and now there are more central options it is fast losing its appeal with all but the overland buses.

**Mid-range hotels** *Da Bei Hotel* (☎ 6568 5511), right by Guomao metro station at No 1 Jan Nan Lang Jiayuan, Jian Guo Men Wei St, has good clean rooms (Y280-350/Db). *Hao Yuan Guesthouse* (☎ 6512 5557; 💻 www.haoyuanhotel.com; Y480-680/Db) at 53 Shijia Hutong is a beautifully converted courtyard house dating from the Qing dynasty and a real treat. *Red House Hotel* (☎ 6416 7500; Y250-400/Db) at 10 Chunxiu Lu is an efficient place and has a convenient position near Sanlitun and is also where Monkey Business (see p369) has its office.

**Upmarket hotels** High-rollers should head for *Peninsula Palace Hotel* (☎ 8516 2888; 💻 www.peninsula.com), 8 Goldfish Lane, where the cheapest rooms start at US$260. For tips on booking, see p292.

## Where to eat

If you've been holding out to sample some 100 per cent genuine Peking duck, the choice is endless. Before partaking, however, you might do well to ruminate on some advice from Alexander Hamilton, who recounts *'The abominable Sin of Sodomy is tolerated here, and all over China, and so is Buggery, which they use both with beasts and fowls, in so much that Europeans do not care to eat duck'*. We can only hope that things have changed since 1727.

*Liqun* (☎ 6705 5578), 11 Beixiangfeng, is a hidden treat even if you usually get lost trying to find it (follow the signs painted on the side street walls). Another favourite is *Qianmen Roast Duck Restaurant* (☎ 6701 1379), 32 Qianmen Dajie. The massive 'Super Duck' style restaurants are best avoided despite their impressive size. Scout around the south side of the Qianmen Square area and you should find a whole duck for around Y30.

During the day it's more fun to eat at the snack counters in the side streets. In the evening, however, it is worth being a bit more choosy. One of the swishest places in town is *Green Tea House* (☎ 6552 8310) at 6 Gongtixilu Chaoyang. Vegetarians might like to try the *Red Phoenix* (Chaoyangmen Nanxiaojie). For excellent **contemporary Chinese restaurants** try the area around the bridge separating Houhai Lake from Qianhai Lake; there are dozens of options here and in the summer it's a great spot.

For non-Chinese food restaurants see *That's Beijing* for all the listings.

## Entertainment

Again you're better off consulting your hotel/ hostel or *That's Beijing* for the latest.

**Opera** Forget what the experts tell you about Chinese opera; if you enjoy elaborate costumes and ear-wrenching wailing, this is for you. Most fans head for the **Peking Opera Troupe** at Liuyuan Theatre (☎ 1935 2045) in Qianmen Hotel, 175 Yong'anlu.

**Acrobatics** You are unlikely to see better acrobatic displays than those here: there is a lot of leaping through hoops, throwing small children around, spinning plates on sticks and much, much more.

There are usually shows at 19.15 nightly at **Chaoyang Theatre** (☎ 6507 2421), 36 Dongsanhuan Beilu, Hujialou.

**Bars and clubs** The **Sanlitun** area is packed with bars and for many years was *the* ex-pat hangout. Nowadays, it is looking tired and can be a bit sleazy but it is still popular. Try the side streets off **Sanlitun North**: *Poachers* and *Bar Blue* are probably the best if you want a Big Night Out. **Sanlitun South** is quieter (it's not the street directly south of Sanlitun North but a small dog-leg to the west). *Nashville's* is a good option with its live band and pub grub.

Houhai Lake is the other main area (see p371), and many prefer its more relaxed atmosphere. There is also a branch of *Huxleys* here for those who want to step up the pace.

*Club Football Centre* (in the same building as Red House Hotel) is one of Beijing's true pubs and shows all the major games from around the world on big screens.

Clubs are more difficult to predict but whichever you choose, it is likely to be on the top floor of a shopping complex – an odd Chinese trait. *Club Top* and *Kai Club* in Sanlitun are popular. *That's Beijing* has extensive listings and regularly reviews all the new arrivals on the party scene.

---

### Excursion to the coast (see Shanhaiguan map opposite)

A nice break from the pollution of Beijing can be found at **Shanhaiguan** on the coast. It's not far from the capital and if you started in Istanbul you can claim to have travelled across Asia 'coast to coast', from the Mediterranean to the Pacific. It is also home to one end of the **Great Wall of China**.

**First Pass Under Heaven** (Y42), built in 1381AD, has had a facelift and now dominates the town; you can climb up the walls and visit the small museum but it is not that exciting. The town's **central drum tower** is of architectural interest, too and **The Great Wall Museum** has a worthwhile collection. In the central square you can rent bikes (Y10 a day) and cycle up to the Great Wall at **Jiashan** (entrance Y15) The initial climb here is steep (there is a cable car) but the views over the mountains and out to sea are fantastic (unless there is a sea mist which, unfortunately, is quite common).

You can also cycle down to where the Great Wall meets the ocean at **Dragonhead** (entrance Y35). This can be a bit of a letdown as it is so reconstructed it appears almost like a toy fort, though the museum has some great photographs of how it used to look. If you're cycling, take a left at the last fork before the entrance as this takes you down to the beach and from here you can climb up into the fort, saving yourself the entrance fee – suddenly everything seems more interesting! Unfortunately, the beaches are all dirty as there is a massive oil tanker depot a few kilometres up the coast.

*Jingshuan* (☎ 0335 505 1130; Y160-360/Db), Dong Dajie, has two wings and the cheaper option is good value. North St Hotel has unfortunately closed. The town is compact and there are plenty of **restaurants** on the main streets near the hotels – try the very friendly *Li Da* (Dong Dajie; they have an English menu). The **CITS** office is pretty useless. The **Bank of China** has no credit/debit card facilities.

On your way back to Beijing you can set off early and stop off in **Beidaihe**, where the beaches are cleaner and sandier, for a swim.

The standard train from Beijing to Shanhaiguan takes 5 hours (Y65, via Tianjin) but Beidaihe can be reached in 2½ hours by express train (Y60) and from Beidaihe's train station you can catch a bus to Shanhaiguan (Y5/45mins), although you might have to change at **Qinhuangdao**.

## Shopping

Lazy shoppers make for the large **Friendship Store** on Jianguomenwai Dajie, where shopping is straightforward, numerous Western luxuries are available (including books and newspapers) and prices are high. Still, it's very convenient. A good present from here might be one of the fragile silk or paper kites you'll have seen people flying at the Temple of Heaven.

If you're after books, go to the **Foreign Languages Bookstore** on Wangfujing Dajie, where choices are a bit limited but prices are cheap. Check out the CDs and tapes upstairs.

Browsers often head to the pedestrianized **Wangfujing** area directly east of the Forbidden City, which is Beijing's Oxford St, with lots of designer stores. Bargain hunters and shopping addicts favour the little streets to the south of Tiananmen Square in **Qianmen** District, where almost anything seems to be available from small stalls and shops.

The best place for souvenirs is the **Pearl Market** (Hongqiao), which is in a large multi-storey building opposite the north-east corner of Tian Tan Park. Bargain hard! Another great shopping spot is the **Silk Market** on Jianguomenwai Dajie. Fake Calvin Klein trousers, Ralph Lauren casuals, Northface hiking gear, Gucci shoes and Samsonite suitcases (the list is endless) are all big sellers in this five-storey warehouse. With a bit of nerve, it's possible to haggle most things down to US$10-15. Beware

# Shanhaiguan
# 山海关

> **Going home?**
> For many of you it will now be time to go home. If you are heading back to Europe you could try the scenic route and take the Trans-Siberian, Trans-Mongolian or Trans-Manchurian Express back to Moscow (see Monkey Business, p369, and Bryn Thomas's *Trans-Siberian Handbook* (see p383), also published by Trailblazer, for more information); or you could follow the Southern Silk Road (see box p34) back through India – theoretically, you could almost go all the way back to the start without visiting the same place twice.
>
> If you want to see China's economic boom in the flesh you shouldn't leave the country without experiencing Shanghai and Hong Kong. Or you can head back across China and follow some more of the Silk Road down to Pakistan (see pp243-77).

though: the designer labels are hitting back and a lawsuit was brought against the market in 2006 in an attempt to close it down.

### Moving on

**By air** Numerous airlines offer flights to **Xi'an**, **Dunhuang**, **Kashgar** and various other Silk Road cities. Even more offer international flights to major cities worldwide, although prices are more expensive than flights from Shanghai and Hong Kong.

For information on getting **to/from the airport**, see p369.

**By rail** Beijing has two railway stations but tickets for all routes can be bought at either. You will usually need to do this a couple of days in advance. Trains for **Pingyao** (8-10hrs, try to get an express train) and **Xi'an** (16hrs/Y150) leave from Beijing's West Station (Xi Zhan) – take bus No 1 from anywhere on Chang'an Avenue which drops you at the entrance.

Trains to **Datong** (5-6hrs/Y45) and **Shanhaiguan** (see box pp372-3) leave from the central station, Beijing Zhan.

Note there is a **Foreigners' Ticket Office** in Beijing Zhan where English is spoken (it's through the 'Soft Class' waiting room).

# APPENDIX : USEFUL WORDS AND PHRASES

As noted in the opening chapters, language difficulties will leave you feeling completely frustrated and helpless at least once on your journey, no matter how many phrasebooks you have swatted up on. The phrases below are the ones we found most useful for the three main languages in the territories you visit, although a phrasebook or two will help enormously and win you lots of friends. Try to learn at least some phrases and practise them if only to be polite and show some respect for the countries you are visiting.

## Arabic

Obviously, Turkey, Iran and Pakistan have their own languages (Pakistan has over 300) but Farsi and Urdu are written in a modified Arabic alphabet and quite a few people understand Arabic (Turks, Iranians, and Pakistanis also speak more English than people in these regions).

### USEFUL WORDS AND PHRASES

### General

| | |
|---|---|
| Hello | *ahlan wa sahlan* |
| Goodbye | *ma'a salama* |
| Please/thank you | *min fadlak/shukran* |
| Sorry | *assif* |
| What is your name? | *shu ismak?*(m)/ *shu ismik?*(f) |
| Do you speak English? | *Btah ki inglizi?* |
| Yes/no | *aywa/la* |
| How much? | *qaddaysh?* |
| Good/bad | *kwayyis/mish kwayyis* |

### Directions/travelling

| | |
|---|---|
| Where is ...? | *Wayn ...?* |
| the bus station | *mahattat al-bas* |
| a hotel | *al funduq* |
| Double room | *ghurfa bi sarirayn* |
| Single room | *ghurfa moufrideh* |
| Toilet | *twalet* |
| Mosque | *al jame* |
| Tourist office | *maktab as siyaha* |

### Time/numbers

| | |
|---|---|
| What time is it? | *adaysh as sa'a?* |
| When does the bus go? | *mata yazhab albas* |
| Yesterday/today/ tomorrow | *imbarih/al-yom/ bukra* |
| Monday/Tuesday/ | *al itnin yom/at talata yom* |
| Wednesday/Thursday/ | *al arbi'a yom/al khamis* |
| Friday/Saturday/ Sunday | *al jum'a/as sabt/ al ahad yom* |

### Numbers

| | | | | | | | | |
|---|---|---|---|---|---|---|---|---|
| 1 | ١ | *wahid* | 11 | ١١ | *ihdashr* | 70 | ٧٠ | *saba'i'in* |
| 2 | ٢ | *ithnayn, tnaan* | 12 | ١٢ | *itnaysh* | 80 | ٨٠ | *tamaani'in* |
| 3 | ٣ | *tala'ata, tlaat* | 13 | ١٣ | *tala'atash* | 90 | ٩٠ | *tis'i'in* |
| 4 | ٤ | *arba'a* | 14 | ١٤ | *arba'ata'ash* | 100 | ١٠٠ | *miyya* |
| 5 | ٥ | *khamsa* | 20 | ٢٠ | *ishri'in* | 200 | ٢٠٠ | *mittayn* |
| 6 | ٦ | *sita'a* | 21 | ٢١ | *wahid wa ishri'in* | 1000 | ١٠٠٠ | *elf* |
| 7 | ٧ | *saba'a* | 30 | ٣٠ | *talathi'in* | 2000 | ٢٠٠٠ | *alfayn* |
| 8 | ٨ | *tamanya* | 40 | ٤٠ | *arba'ati'in* | 3000 | ٣٠٠٠ | *tala'athat aalaaf* |
| 9 | ٩ | *tissa'a* | 50 | ٥٠ | *khamsi'in* | | | |
| 10 | ١٠ | *a'ashra* | 60 | ٦٠ | *sitti'in* | | | |

### FARSI

| | |
|---|---|
| Hello/welcome | *salaam aleikoom* |
| Please/thank you | *lotfan/mersi* |
| Do you speak English? | *shoma engelisi baladid?* |
| Where is the bus station? | *Kojast terminal?* |
| Toilet | *dast shu'I* |
| How much is it? | *chand e?* |
| Double room | *otagh e do nafari* |
| Single room | *otaghe yek nafareh* |
| When? | *Chi vaght?* |

# Russian

The Central Asian countries all have their own languages but everyone you meet will have been brought up on Russian at school and despite government action to encourage the use of native languages and drop Russian, it is still the *lingua franca* for many people, especially in the big cities. More and more people are learning English but these numbers started from a very low base. The biggest problem with Russian is usually the Cyrillic alphabet but the Central Asian states have largely converted to the Roman alphabet which makes things a lot easier.

## USEFUL WORDS AND PHRASES
### General
| | |
|---|---|
| Hello | *zdrahstvuyiteh/* |
| Good day | *dobreevanden* |
| Goodbye | *das-vedahneya* |
| Please/thank you | *pozhalsta/spaseeba* |
| OK/good | *harasho* |
| How are you? | *kak dela?* |
| What is your name? | *kak vas zavut?* |
| My name is … | *minya zavut …* |
| I don't speak Russian | *ya ni gavaryu pa ruski* |
| Do you speak English | *vy govoritye po-angliskiy* |
| How much is it? | *skol'ka stoit?* |
| Money exchange | *abmen valyuty* |

### Directions/travelling
| | |
|---|---|
| Where is …? | *gde …?* |
| the bus/train | *aftobus/poyezt* |
| the bus/train station | *autovokzal/vokzal* |
| (Lenin) street | *(Lenin) ulitsa* |
| a toilet | *tualet* |

| | |
|---|---|
| Where is …? | *gde …?* |
| a restaurant | *ristaran* |
| a hotel | *gastinitsa* |

### Time
| | |
|---|---|
| When? | *kagda?* |
| What time is it? | *kato'riy chahs?* |
| Yesterday/today/tomorrow | *vchira/sivodnya/zaftra* |

### Food and drink
| | |
|---|---|
| Menu | *menoo* |
| Water/tea | *vada/chay* |
| Vodka/beer | *wodka/peeva* |
| Cheers! | *zah vasheh zdaro-vyeh!* |
| Caviare | *eek-ry* |
| Chicken/beef | *tsyplonka/beef* |
| Pork/sausage | *sveenooyoo/kalbasoo* |
| Bread/potatoes | *khlee-ep/kar-toshka* |
| Eggs/omelette | *yait-sa/amlet* |
| Butter/cheese | *mah-sla/sir* |

### Numbers
1 *adeen*,
2 *dvah*,
3 *tree*,
4 *chetir*,
5 *p'aht*,
6 *shesh*t,
7 *s'em*,
8 *vosem*,
9 *d'evat*,
10 *d'e'sat*,
20 *dvatsat*,
50 *p'ad-desaht*,
100 *sto*,
1000 *tees-acha*

# Chinese

China is where you will encounter the most language problems. 'Chinese' is actually a misnomer because, just like its economy, China has a 'one country, two systems' policy when it comes to language: there is Mandarin (which dominates the northern half of the country and is the language of government) and Cantonese which everyone in the south and south-east speaks (there are actually nearly another hundred dialects and regional languages, not to mention Uighur and Tibetan). In Xingjiang, most Uighurs you meet are likely to speak Mandarin at least well enough to help you (there are plenty who don't but they tend to be in the small villages of the countryside).

The biggest problem is, of course, the script so try to get someone to write down instructions for anything you might need (eg a train ticket). The other problem is tone but you should pick this up as you go along.

## KEY PHRASES

The following phrases in Chinese characters may be useful to point to if you're having problems communicating:

| | |
|---|---|
| **Please write it down for me** | 请为我写下来 |
| **Help me please** | 请帮帮我 |
| **Please call a doctor** | 请叫个医生来 |

## USEFUL WORDS AND PHRASES
### General

| | | |
|---|---|---|
| Hello | *Ni hao* | 你好 |
| Goodbye | *Zai jian* | 再见 |
| Please | *Qing* | 请 |
| Do you speak English? | *Ni hui shuo ying yu ma?* | 你会说英语吗? |
| Yes/no | *Dui/Bu dui* (literally correct/incorrect) | 对/不对 |
| No/Sorry, but no | *Mei you* | 没有 |
| Thank you | *Xie xie* | 谢谢 |
| Excuse me (sorry) | *Dui bu qi* | 对不起 |
| Excuse me (may I have your attention?) | *Qing wen* | 请问 |
| Good/bad | *Hao/bu hao* | 好/不好 |
| I understand/do not understand | *Wo dong le/wo bu dong* | 我懂了/我不懂 |
| China | *Zhongguo* | 中国 |
| Foreigner | *Wai guo ren/Guilo* | 外国人/鬼佬 |

### Directions

| | | |
|---|---|---|
| Where is...? | *Zai nar...?* | 在哪儿? |
| Toilet (ladies/gents) | *ce suo (nu/nan)* | 厕所 |
| Telephone | *dian hua* | 电话 |
| Airport | *ji chang* | 机场 |
| Bus station | *che zhan* | 长途汽车站 |
| Train | *huoche* | 火车 |
| Railway station | *huo che zhan* | 火车站 |
| Taxi | *chu zu qi che* | 出租汽车 |
| Museum | *bo wu guan* | 博物馆 |
| Hotel/restaurant | *fan dian* | 饭店 |
| Guesthouse | *binguan* | 宾馆 |
| Post office | *you ju* | 邮局 |

# Appendix: Useful words and phrases

| | | |
|---|---|---|
| PSB/CAAC office | Gong an ju/Zhong hang gongsi | 公安局/中航公司 |
| What time will we arrive at...? | Lie che shenme shi jian dao...? | 列车什么时候到? |
| What station is this? | Zhe shi na yi zhan? | 这是哪一站? |
| How much? | Duo shao qian? | 多少钱 |
| That's too expensive | Tai gui le | 太贵了 |

## Time

| | | |
|---|---|---|
| Monday/Tuesday/Wednesday | Xing yi.yi/er/san | 星期一/星期二/星期三 |
| Thursday/Friday/Saturday | Xing qi.si/wu/liu/ri | 星期四/星期五/星期六 |
| Sunday | Xing qi ri | 星期日 |
| Yesterday/tomorrow/today | zuo tian/ming tian/jin tian | 昨天/明天/今天 |

## Transport

| | | |
|---|---|---|
| Ticket | piao | 票 |
| Hard seat/soft seat | Ying Zuo/Luan Zuo | 硬座/软座 |
| Hard sleeper/soft sleeper | Ying Wo/Luan Wo | 硬卧/软卧 |

## Food and drink

| | | |
|---|---|---|
| menu | cai dan | 菜单 |
| Mineral water/tea/beer | kuang quan shui/cha/pi jiu | 矿泉水/茶/啤酒 |
| noodles/noodle soup | mian/tang mian | 面/汤面 |
| bread/egg | mian bao/ji dian | 面包/鸡蛋 |
| pork/beef/lamb | zhu rou/niu rou/yang rou | 猪肉/牛肉/羊肉 |
| chicken/duck/fish | ji/ya/yu | 鸡/鸭/鱼 |
| vegetables | shu cai | 蔬菜 |
| Do you have any vegetarian dishes? | Ni zher you su-cai ma? | 你这儿有蔬菜吗? |
| steamed rice | mi fan | 米饭 |
| Delicious | Hao chi | 好吃 |
| Cheers! | Gang bei! | 干杯! |

## Numbers

| | | | | | |
|---|---|---|---|---|---|
| 1 | 一 | yi | 18 | 十八 | shi ba |
| 2 | 二 | er | 19 | 十九 | shi jiu |
| 3 | 三 | san | 20 | 二十 | er shi |
| 4 | 四 | si | 21 | 二十一 | er shi yi |
| 5 | 五 | wu | 30 | 三十 | san shi |
| 6 | 六 | liu | 40 | 四十 | si shi |
| 7 | 七 | qi | 50 | 五十 | wu shi |
| 8 | 八 | ba | 100 | 一百 | yi bai |
| 9 | 九 | jiu | 101 | 一百零一 | yi bai ling yi |
| 10 | 十 | shi | 110 | 一百一十 | yi bai yi shi |
| 11 | 十一 | shi yi | 150 | 一百五十 | yi bai wu shi |
| 12 | 十二 | shi er | 200 | 二百 | er bai |
| 13 | 十三 | shi san | 500 | 五百 | wu bai |
| 14 | 十四 | shi si | 1000 | 一千 | yi qian |
| 15 | 十五 | shi wu | 10,000 | 一万 | yi wan |
| 16 | 十六 | shi liu | 100,000 | 十万 | shi wan |
| 17 | 十七 | shi qi | 1 million | 一百万 | yi bai wan |

# INDEX

**Abbreviations**: China (**C**); Central Asia (**CA**); Middle East (**ME**); Pakistan (**P**); Iran (**I**); Kyrgyzstan (**Kr**); Syria (**S**); Turkey (**T**); Turkmenistan (**Tm**); Uzbekistan (**Uz**).
Page references in bold type refer to maps

Abyaneh (I) 148
accommodation 72-3 (ME),
  179-80 (CA), 257 (P), 292-3 (C);
  *see also place name*
Afghan wars 246-8
Afghanistan 10
Afrosiab (Uz) 221
air services 13, 75 (ME), 182 (CA), 258 (P),
  297 (C); *see also place name*
Alamut (I) 133
Aleppo (S) 103-7, **107**
Alexander the Great 37-40, 159, 205, 244
Aliabad (P) 270
Ankara (T) 95
Antakya (Hatay) (T) 100-3; **101**
Apamea (S) 110
Arabic vocabulary 375
Aral Sea 178
Ararat, Mount (T) 128
Armenians 67
Ashgabat (Tm) 194, **193**
Assassins 133
Astana Graves (C) 316
Astan-e Ghods-e Razavi, Mashad 155
Astor (P) 270
Atatürk 63
Ayding Kul (C) 318

background reading 24-30
Badaling (C) 367
Bangladesh 250
Banpo neolithic site (C) 346-7
Beidaihe (C) 272
Beijing (C) 354-74, **360-1**, **370**
Besham (P) 274
Bezeklik Caves (C) 316
bicycles 296 (C)
Bingling Si Buddhist Caves (C) 337
Bishkek (Kr) 234-6, **237**
black market 22
bookings 13-14
border crossings
  China/Pakistan 260-1
  Iran/Pakistan 154
  Iran/Turkmenistan 156
  Kyrgyzstan/China 234, 242
  Turkmenistan/Uzbekistan 197
  Turkey/Iran 129
  Turkey/Syria 103
  Uzbekistan/Kyrgyzstan 231

Borit Lake 266
Bosra (S) 122
Buddhism 38-9
budgeting 11
Bukhara (Uz) 205-14, **208**
buses 74 (ME), 181 (CA), 257 (P), 295-6 (C)

camping 73
Cappadocia (T) 95-9
caravanserais 97
carpets 136-7
cars and car hire 74, 75 (ME), 182 (CA)
  257 (P), 295 (C)
Caspian Sea 159
Chalt (P) 270
Charklik (Ruoqiang) (C) 323-4
Chengde (C) 368
Cherchen (Quiemo) (C) 323
China: history 278-86;
  people & religion 287-8;
  practical information 289-301; visas 17
Chinese language 299, 376-8
Chinese medicine 288
Chor Bakr (Uz) 213
Christianity 55, 288
climate 11-12, 71 (ME), 177-8 (CA), 256 (P),
  291 (C)
clothing 19-20, 259-60
Confucianism 288
Connolly, Captain Arthur 207, 209
costs 11
credit cards 21
Crescent Moon Lake (C) 327
Crusades and Crusaders 47, 56-60
Cultural Revolution, China 284
customs declaration forms 71 (ME), 174 (CA),
  291 (C); *see also documentation*
cycling 157

Daheyan (C) 312
Damascus (S) 117-24, **119**
Dashoguz (Tm) 194
Datong (C) 351-4, **353**
Deosai Plains (P) 271
Diyarbakir (T) 126
doctors 23
documentation 15-18; 71 (ME); 174, 177 (CA);
  256 (P); 289, 291 (C)
Doğubeyazit 128-9, **129**
Doulon (C) 368

## Index

dress codes for women 19
drinking water 23-4
drinks 80-1 (ME), 185-6 (CA), 262 (P), 301 (C)
Dunhuang (C) 324-9, **329**

Elborz Mountains (I) 53, 71
electricity 76 (ME), 182 (CA), 258 (P), 297 (C)
embassies *see place name: services*
Enver Pasha 164-5
equipment 19-21
Erzurum (T) 126-7, **127**
Esfahan (I) 142-8

Ferghana Valley (Uz) 158, 230-1
Flaming Mountains (C) 315
flight tickets 13
food 79-80 (ME), 184-5 (CA), 260-2 (P), 300 (C)

Gaochang (C) 313
Genghis Khan 47-50
geographical background 53-4 (ME), 158 (CA), 243 (P), 278 (C)
George, Saint 98
Ghazvin (Qazvin) (I) 132-4, **132**
Gilgit (P) 271-4, **273**
Gobi Desert 330
Golden Road, The 215
Gonur (Tm) 190
Göreme (T) 95-9, **99**
Grape Valley (C) 315
Great Game, The 163, 206, 207
Great Mutiny 247
Great Wall of China 329, 331, 332, 366, 367
Gulmit (P) 267, 270

haggling 260
Hama (S) 108-10, **109**
Hami (C) 317
hammams 105
Harran (T) 126
health problems 23
Herbiye, waterfall (T) 102
Hetian (C) 320-3, **322**
Hindu Kush 243
historical background
  Silk Road 31-5; 54-65 (ME),
historical background *cont'd*
  158-72 (CA), 243-52 (P), 278-86 (C)
hitching 181, 257
Hohhot (C) 354
Homs (S) 110, 117
Hoper (P) 270
hot-air ballooning 96

Huaqing springs and palace 347
Hunza Valley (P) 267-9
Hussaini (P) 266

identity cards 10, 177, 291
Ilhara Valley (T) 97
Imperial Palace, Beijing 359
Incense Road 45
Inner Mongolia 354
inoculations 22-3
International Student Identity Card (ISIC) 11
internet 30; 77-8 (ME), 183 (CA), 259 (P), 298 (C)
Iran: accommodation 73; communications 78; customs & attitudes 79; history 64-5; money 76-7; peoples 68-9; visas 15-16
Iraq 9
Irkeshtam Pass 234
Iskenderun (T) 100
Islam 57, 159-60, 245
Islamabad (P) 274, 275-7
Islamic holidays 12
Ismailis 253
Issyk Kul (Kr) 238-40, **239**
Istanbul (T) 81-94, **85**, **87**; side trips 93-4

Jade Road 321
Jiaohe (C) 313
Jiashan (C) 372
Jiayuguan (C) 329-33, **332**
Jinshanling (C) 367

Kuhta (T) 124-5
Kara Kul (C) 307
Karakol (Kr) 238
Karakorum Highway 9, 254-6, **255**, 274
Karakorum Pass 9
Karakum Desert (Tm) 194, 195
Karez Wells (C) 314
Karghilik (Yecheng) (C) 320
Karimabad (P) 268, 269-70, **269**
Kashan (I) 148
Kashgar (Kashi) (C) 305-9, **308**, 320
Kashmir 248
Kazakhstan 229
Keriya (Yutian) (C) 323
Kerman (I) 154
Khiva (Uz) 199-205, **202**
Khotan (Hetian) (C) 320-3, **322**
Khunjerab Pass 243
Khyber Pass 277
Kizil Thousand Buddha Caves (C) 310
Kokand (Uz) 231
Konye-Urgench (Tm) 194-7
Korla (C) 312

Krak des Chevaliers (S) 111-13, **112**
Kuqa (C) 309-12, **311**
Kurds 66
Kushans 245
Kyrgyzstan: accommodation 180; history 170; money 183; peoples 173-4; visas 18

Lady's Finger (P) 268
Lamaisar (I) 133
Lanzhou (C) 334-9, **336**
Liuyuan (C) 329
Long March 283
Lop Nor (C) 323
luggage 20
Luoyang (C) 348

Maalula (S) 124
Macclesfield 51
Mangnai (C) 324
Malatya (T) 124-5, **125**
Manichaeism 315
Mao Zedong 356, 357
maps 29
Mary (Tm) 186-90, **189**
Mashad (I) 155-7
Mauryans 244
medical supplies 20
Melikawat (C) 321
Merv (Tm) 186-9, **188**
Middle East: accommodation 72-4; climate 71-2; geographical background 53-4; history 54-65; peoples & religion 65-9; practical information 69-81; visas 15
Miran (C) 323
Mirjave (I) 154
Mogao Caves (C) 325-7
Moghuls 245-6
money 21-2; 76 (ME), 182-3 (CA), 258 (P), 297-8 (C)
Mongols 47-51, 160-1, 355
motorbikes *see* cars
Mutianyu (C) 367

Nagar Valley (P) 267, 270
Naltar Valley (P) 270
Naran (P) 274
Naryn (Kr) 235, 241
Nasreddin 213
national holidays 78 (ME), 184 (CA), 259 (P), 298 (C)
Nazaroff, Paul 164-5
Nemrut Daği (T) 125
Nestorians 44-5
Nisa (Tm), 192

Niya (Minfeng) (C) 323
Nukus (Uz) 197-9, **198**

Osh (Kr) 232-4
Ottomans 60
Ozgon (Kr) 234

Pakistan; accommodation 257; climate 256; geographical background 243; history 243-52; peoples & religion 252-3; practical information 257-62; visas 18
Palmyra (S) 114-17, **115**
Pamir Mountains 244
Parthian shot 41
Partition 249
Passu (P) 263-7, 270
peoples & religions 65-9 (ME),172-4 (CA), 252-3 (P), 287-8 (C)
Persepolis (I) 152, **153**
Persian poets 151
photography 22
phrasebooks 30
Pingyao (C) 349-51, **350**
Pir Sar (P) 274
Polo, Marco 32, 49-50, 262

postal services 77-8 (ME), 183 (CA), 259 (P), 298 (C)
Przewalski, NM 238

Qinhuangdao (C) 372
Qiuci City (C) 310
Quetta (P) 154

rail travel 8-9
Rakaposhi, Mount (P) 267
Rawalpindi (P) 274-6, **275**
Rey (I) 135
Richtofen, Baron von 31
route options 8-10; 69, **70**, 71 (ME); 74, **175** (CA); Pakistan/Karakorum Highway 254-6, **255**; 289, **290**, (C)
royal purple 43-4
Ruoqiang (C) 323-4
Russian vocabulary 376
Russians 162

safety, Central Asia 178-9
Samandag (T) 102
Samarkand (Uz) 215-22, **218**
Sanliurfa (T) 126
Sari (I) 138, 157
Seljuks 160
Shahba (S) 122

Shakrisabz (Uz) 221
Shanhaiguan (C) 372, **373**
Shi'ites 68
Shiraz (I) 149-54, **150**
Sikhs 246
silk 35
Simatai (C) 367
Skardu (P) 271
Soganli (T) 98
Solomon, throne of 131
Song Kul (Kr) 240-1
Sost (P) 263
Southern Taklaman route 320-4
spitting 299
Stoddart, Colonel Charles 207
Stone Tower 33
Subashi (C) 311
Suweida (S) 122
Syria: accommodation 72-3;
　　communications 77-8;
　　customs & attitudes 79;
　　history 63-4; money 21, 76;
　　peoples and religions 68; visas 17
Syrian Orthodox Church 106

Tabriz (I) 130-1, **130**
Taer Si Monastery (C) 338
Taftan (P) 154
Tajikistan 176
Taklaman Desert 303
Tamerlane 161, 216
Taoism 288
Tashkent 222-30, **225**, **227**
Taxila (P) 276
taxis 74 (ME), 181 (CA), 258 (P), 296 (C);
　　*see also place name*
Tehran (I) 134-5, 138-42, **139**, **141**
telephones 77-8 (ME),183 (CA),
　　259 (P), 298 (C)
Terracotta Army 346
Thakot (P) 274
Tian Chi (C) 318
Tiananmen massacre 285
Tiananmen Square, Beijing 357
Tianshui (C) 339
Tibet 46
time 76 (ME),182 (CA), 258 (P),297 (C)
tipping 77
Torugart Pass 174, 242
tour groups 13-14
trains 75 (ME), 181 (CA), 258 (P), 294-5 (C)
transport 74 (ME), 180-2 (CA), 257-8 (P),
　　293-7 (C); *see also place name*
travel agencies/tour companies 74 (ME),
　　180 (CA), 257 (P), 293 (C)

travel insurance 24
travellers' cheques 21
travelling companions 18
trekking 266
Turfan (C) 312-20, **319**
Turkestan 158
Turkey: accommodation 72;
　　communications 77;
　　customs & attitudes 78-9; money 76;
　　peoples 66-7; visas 18
Turkmenistan: accommodation 179;
　　history 167-9; money 183; peoples 172-3;
　　visas 16-17

Uighurs 287
Ultar Meadow (P) 268
Urgench (Uz)199
Ürümqi (C) 318
Uzbekistan: accommodation 179;
　　history 169-70; money 183; peoples 173;
　　visas 17
Uzbeks 162

vaccinations 22-3
visas 15-18, 23-4, 289

water 23-4
weather 11-12
women travellers 16, 19, 259-60
words and phrases 375-8
Wuwei (C) 333

Xanadu (C) 368
Xiahe (C) 340
Xi'an (C) 340-9, **343**
Xining (C) 338
Xinjiang province (C) 302-5
Xuan Zang 345

Yakub Beg 303-4
Yarkand (Shache) (C) 320
Yazd (I) 154
Yellow river 335
Yellow Top (P) 267
Yensigar (C) 320
Yungang Caves (C) 351

Zahedan (I) 154
Zhang Qian 40-1
Zhangye (C) 333

## Some other guides from Trailblazer

### Himalaya by Bicycle – a route & planning guide
*Laura Stone* 336pp, 28 colour & 50 B&W photos, 60 maps
ISBN 978 1 905864 04 1, *1st edn*, £14.99, – due Aug 2007
An all-in-one guide for Himalayan cycle-touring. Covers the Himalayan regions of Pakistan, Tibet, India, Nepal and Sikkim with detailed km-by-km guides to main routes including the Karakoram Highway and the Friendship Highway. Plus: town and city guides.

### Adventure Motorcycling Handbook – a route & planning guide
*Chris Scott, 5th edn,* 288pp, 28 colour, 100 B&W photos
ISBN 978 1 873756 80 5, £12.99, Can$29.95, US$19.95
Every red-blooded motor-cyclist dreams of making the Big Trip – this book shows you how. Top ten overland machines, choosing a destination, bike preparation, documentation and shipping, route outlines. Plus – ten first-hand accounts of epic biking adventures worldwide.
'The first thing we did was buy the Adventure Motorcycling Handbook'
**Ewan McGregor,** *The Long Way Round*

### Adventure Cycle-Touring Handbook – a route & planning guide
*Stephen Lord* 320pp, 28 colour & 100 B&W photos
ISBN 978 1 873756 89 8, *1st edition,* £13.99, US$19.95
New guide for anyone planning (or dreaming) about taking their bicycle on a long-distance adventure. This comprehensive manual will make that dream a reality whether it's cycling in Tibet or pedalling from Patagonia to Alaska. Part 1 covers Practicalities; Part 2 includes Route outlines; and Part 3 has Tales from the Saddle.
'The definitive guide to how, where, why and what to do on a cycle expedition' **Adventure Travel**

### Tibet Overland – a route & planning guide *Kym McConnell*
*1st edition,* 224pp, 16pp colour maps
ISBN 978 1 873756 41 6, £12.99, Can$29.95, US$19.95
Featuring 16pp of full colour mapping based on satellite photographs, this is a guide for mountain bikers and other road users in Tibet. Includes detailed information on over 9000km of overland routes across the world's highest and largest plateau. Includes Lhasa–Kathmandu route and the route to Everest North Base Camp. '... a wealth of advice...' **HH The Dalai Lama**

### Trekking in Ladakh *Charlie Loram*
*3rd edition,* 288 pages, 75 maps, 24 colour photos
ISBN 978 1 873756 75 1, £12.99, Can$27.95, US$18.95
Fully revised and extended 3rd edition of Charlie Loram's practical guide to trekking in this spectacular Himalayan region of India. Includes 75 detailed walking maps, guides to Leh, Manali and Delhi plus information on getting to Ladakh.
'Extensive ... and well researched'. **Climber Magazine**

### Trans-Siberian Handbook *Bryn Thomas*
*7th edition,* 448pp, 60 maps, 40 colour photos
ISBN 978 1 873756 94 2, £13.99, Can$29.95 US$19.95
First edition short-listed for the **Thomas Cook Guidebook Awards**. New seventh edition of the most popular guide to the world's longest rail journey. How to arrange a trip, plus a km-by-km guide to the routes. Updated and expanded to include extra information on travelling independently in Russia. New mapping.
'The best guidebook is Bryn Thomas's "Trans-Siberian Handbook"'
**The Independent 28 Jan 2006**

# TRAILBLAZER GUIDES – TITLE LIST

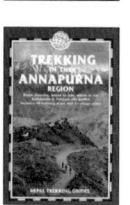

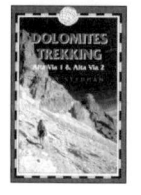

| | |
|---|---|
| Adventure Cycle-Touring Handbook | 1st edn out now |
| Adventure Motorcycling Handbook | 5th edn out now |
| Australia by Rail | 5th edn out now |
| Azerbaijan | 3rd edn out now |
| The Blues Highway – New Orleans to Chicago | 2nd edn out now |
| Coast to Coast (British Walking Guide) | 2nd edn out now |
| Cornwall Coast Path (British Walking Guide) | 2nd edn out now |
| China Rail Handbook | 1st edn Jan 2008 |
| Corsica Trekking – GR20 | 1st edn Apr 2007 |
| Dolomites Trekking – AV1 & AV2 | 2nd edn out now |
| Hadrian's Wall Path (British Walking Guide) | 1st edn out now |
| Himalaya by Bicycle – a route and planning guide | 1st edn Aug 2007 |
| Inca Trail, Cusco & Machu Picchu | 3rd edn out now |
| Indian Rail Handbook | 1st edn mid 2007 |
| Japan by Rail | 2nd edn Apr 2007 |
| Kilimanjaro – the trekking guide (with Mt Meru) | 2nd edn out now |
| Mediterranean Handbook | 1st edn out now |
| Nepal Mountaineering Guide | 1st edn July 2007 |
| New Zealand – The Great Walks | 1st edn out now |
| North Downs Way (British Walking Guide) | 1st edn out now |
| Norway's Arctic Highway | 1st edn out now |
| Offa's Dyke Path (British Walking Guide) | 1st edn out now |
| Pembrokeshire Coast Path (British Walking Guide) | 1st edn out now |
| Pennine Way (British Walking Guide) | 1st edn out now |
| The Ridgeway (British Walking Guide) | 1st edn out now |
| Siberian BAM Guide – rail, rivers & road | 2nd edn out now |
| The Silk Roads – a route and planning guide | 2nd edn out now |
| Sahara Overland – a route and planning guide | 2nd edn out now |
| Sahara Abenteuerhandbuch (German edition) | 1st edn out now |
| Scottish Highlands – The Hillwalking Guide | 1st edn out now |
| South Downs Way (British Walking Guide) | 1st edn out now |
| South-East Asia – The Graphic Guide | 1st edn out now |
| Tibet Overland – mountain biking & jeep touring | 1st edn out now |
| Trans-Canada Rail Guide | 4th edn Apr 2007 |
| Trans-Siberian Handbook | 7th edn Apr 2007 |
| Trekking in the Annapurna Region | 4th edn out now |
| Trekking in the Everest Region | 4th edn out now |
| Trekking in Corsica | 1st edn out now |
| Trekking in Ladakh | 3rd edn out now |
| Trekking in the Pyrenees | 3rd edn out now |
| West Highland Way (British Walking Guide) | 2nd edn out now |

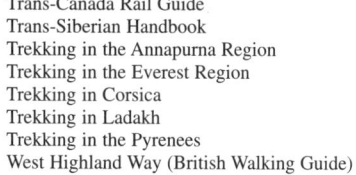

For more information about Trailblazer, for where to find your nearest stockist, for guidebook updates or for credit card mail order sales visit:

**www.trailblazer-guides.com**

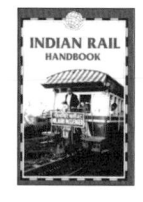

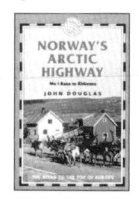

# Route map
## MAP 2

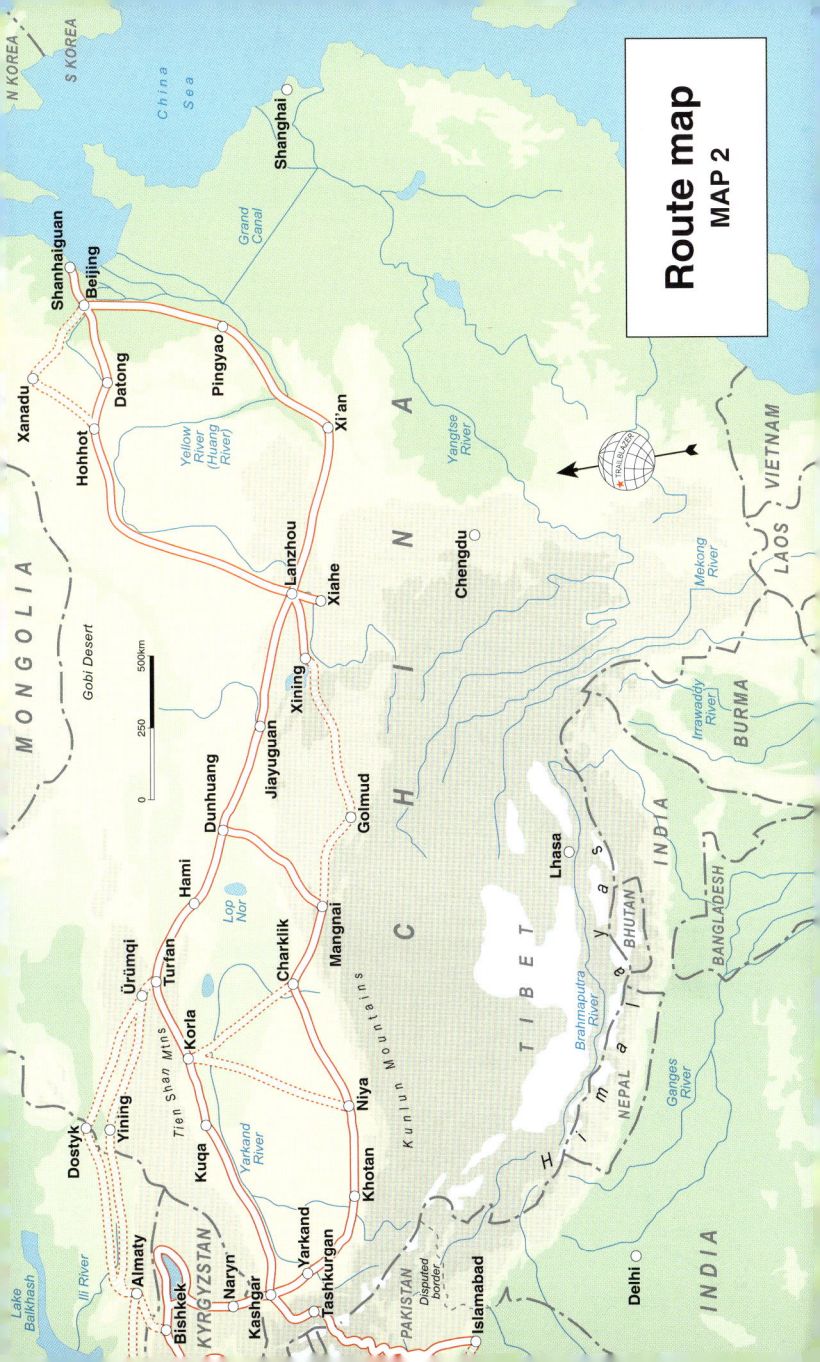

# Route map
## MAP 1

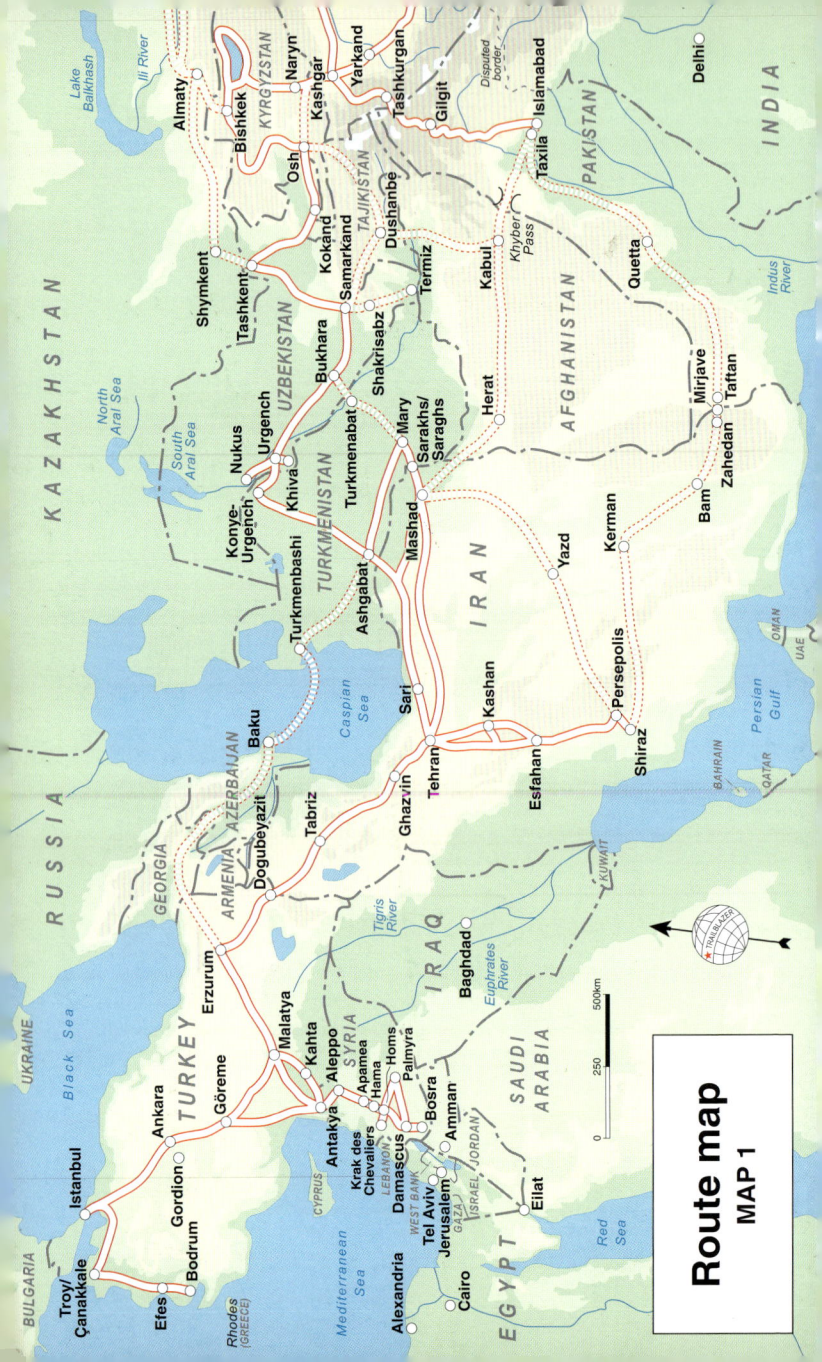